NATIONAL INSECURITY

ALSO BY DAVID J. ROTHKOPF

*Power, Inc.: The Epic Rivalry Between Big Business
and Government and the Reckoning That Lies Ahead*

*Superclass:
The Global Power Elite and the World They Are Making*

*Running the World: The Inside Story of the National Security Council
and the Architects of American Power*

Cuba: The Contours of Change
(coauthor and coeditor with Susan Kaufman Purcell)

*The Price of Peace:
Emergency Economic Intervention and US Foreign Policy*

The Big Emerging Markets
(editor and principal author)

The Common Market
(coauthor with Carol Zeman Rothkopf)

NATIONAL INSECURITY

AMERICAN LEADERSHIP IN AN AGE OF FEAR

David J. Rothkopf

PublicAffairs
New York

Published in the United States by PublicAffairs™,
a Member of the Perseus Books Group

Book Design by Cynthia Young

Library of Congress Cataloging-in-Publication Data
Rothkopf, David J. (David Jochanan), 1955–
    National insecurity : American leadership in an age of fear / David Rothkopf. —
    First edition.
        pages cm
    Includes bibliographical references and index.
    ISBN 978-1-61039-340-9 (hardback)—ISBN 978-1-61039-341-6 (e-book)
        1. United States—Foreign relations—History—21st century.   2. National
    security—United States—History—21st century.   I. Title.
E744.R84 2014
355'.033073—dc23

                                                                2014021345

First Edition

10 9 8 7 6 5 4 3 2 1

For Adrean, the most fearless person I know,

With love

Contents

"America is a great power possessed of tremendous military might and a wide-ranging economy, but all this is built on an unstable foundation which can be targeted with special attention to its obvious weak spots. If America is hit in one hundredth of those weak spots, God willing, it will stumble, wither away and relinquish world leadership."

—OSAMA BIN LADEN

"At what point then is the approach of danger to be expected? I answer, if it ever reach us, it must spring up amongst us. It cannot come from abroad. If destruction be our lot, we must ourselves be its author and finisher. As a nation of freemen, we must live through all time, or die by suicide."

—ABRAHAM LINCOLN

The Enemy in the Mirror

Carrie: I'm just making sure we don't get hit again.
Saul: Well, I'm glad somebody's looking out for the
country, Carrie,
Carrie: I'm serious. I, I missed something once before.
I won't, I can't, let that happen again.
Saul: It was ten years ago. Everybody missed something
that day.
—*HOMELAND*, SEASON 1, 2011

Midway through the second decade of the twenty-first century, America faces a world in turmoil. We are uncertain of our place in that world and of what role we are to play going forward.

For all of our native confidence and fundamental optimism, we have spent much of the past decade shaken and unsteady. Many of the events that created these circumstances have origins far outside America's borders. Some, though, are of our own making. Faced with not one but two major crises and their aftershocks, our leaders responded at times with actions that put us or our interests in greater jeopardy. If we are to fully recover, we have to ask what went wrong. We also must try to understand where we made gains, and why.

Doing so requires a closer look at our leaders. It requires the discipline to set aside politics and the reflexive reactions it breeds. It demands a willingness to see our presidents and their senior advisors in their totality, the good and the bad, to know that those who blunder one day can make

1

major contributions the next. And because so much of what happens in the American system and the world happens within the closely knit, often opaque world immediately around the President of the United States, it requires a concerted effort to pull back the curtain and truly understand what is going on in that rarified environment.

Exploring this vantage point makes it possible to take a story that seems very familiar—that of the past decade, of Presidents Bush and Obama, of Iraq, Afghanistan, terror, financial crisis, and the rise of new powers—and to see it in an entirely new and often unexpected way. We can then come to see how the forces that have over the past few decades led us to concentrate more and more power within the White House may be as responsible for many of the challenges we have faced as any individual or distant event. In the same way, it becomes possible to understand that very often what goes on behind the scenes, from personality struggles to issues of character, from the choices presidents make as managers, as chief *executives*, to the processes by which they reach decisions as commanders-in-chief, can be as important to preserving and advancing America's interests as all the speeches and summit meetings, the high-profile actions of our leaders that we are more accustomed to seeing on the news or reading about on the Internet.

This book is an effort to tell that story, to give the reader a glimpse into what it was like in the innermost circles of American power at a moment of unprecedented challenges, a moment in which America felt more vulnerable and adrift than at any time in modern memory, and to draw concrete lessons from this period for rejuvenating US global leadership in a rapidly changing world.

The war that began for America on the morning of September 11, 2001, was the first in the country's history that began with an image. It was a scene that within hours of taking place was almost universally observed.

In the past, wars were triggered by actions that were reported in dispatches, recounted in newspapers, described in speeches—whether before the Congress, in local meeting halls, or on radio or television. They were presented in prose, couched in arguments that, even when infused with emotion, appealed to citizens through their intellects. Yes, populists and demagogues and newspaper publishers sought to tug at heartstrings and stir anger, but the path to these reactions always traveled through the mind before it reached human hearts.

The gallery of images presented on the morning of al-Qaeda's attacks on the World Trade Center and the Pentagon was something else again. Jetliners piercing the glistening glass skin of towers that had been targeted precisely because they were longstanding symbols of American vibrancy and strength. Another plane smashing into the side of the headquarters of our military. Desperate souls, tiny silhouetted dolls, plunging helplessly, horrifyingly, to their deaths rather than face incineration in the jet-fuel-fed fires that melted the Trade Center from within. And then, ultimately, the indelible, unthinkable sight of the crumbling towers, seemingly consumed by great steel-grey clouds of dust and rubble.

As the crowds ran from the disaster, pursued by those almost demonic clouds snaking through the streets of lower Manhattan, what we saw on their faces we felt in our hearts. There was no need for words. Indeed, commentators were left speechless. We were shaken. We were made afraid. We could hardly believe our eyes.

This moment electrified us, firing neurons that often bypassed the reasoning lobes of our brains and pumped adrenaline to our hearts. This spoke without translation or dilution to our animal selves. September 11 challenged basic feelings that our parents, our society, had worked from our births to nurture in us—the feeling of security in our homes, order in our lives, a sense that this nation was safer than others, beyond the reach of such attacks. Even the palpable fears of the Cold War years—when some of us lay awake in our beds imagining the sound of Russian boots marching down our streets, or sat crouched beneath our school desks with our coats over our heads wondering if they would provide protection from thermonuclear attacks—seemed abstract and remote, diminished by this brutality that played as if on a loop on our televisions and in our minds, by the blackened scars the attacks left on the bedrock of Manhattan, the walls of the Pentagon, and in that field in Pennsylvania.

Few Americans saw images of Pearl Harbor before war was declared and, when they did, what they saw were grainy newsreels of a place far, far away. The torpedoing of the *Lusitania* was just a headline, as was the sinking of the *Maine*. There were no cameras at Fort Sumter, even though the Civil War was to become the first during which Americans far from battlefields got a sense of the losses through the photographs of men like Mathew Brady. News took so long to travel that the Battle of New Orleans was fought weeks after the peace treaty was signed that was supposed to have ended the War of 1812. Pamphleteers tried to stir anger in the wake of battles at Lexington, Concord, and Bunker Hill. In those older instances, slogans and caricatures of our enemies were used to fuel the will to fight in ways that were entirely unnecessary after what Americans saw for themselves that very morning in September 2001.

We had been touched, and we trembled and we boiled. But little did we realize that those images and what they etched on our hearts would usher in an age more defined by emotion than any other in memory. We were entering an era in which emotions—from fear to an appetite for revenge—more than reason, would dictate our actions, invite our errors, and in the end transform how the world would view us and how we would view ourselves.

Consider the contrast that 1945 provides. Fewer than five years after America declared war on Germany and Japan, despite the bloodiest conflict in the history of mankind, despite the Holocaust, despite losses that touched every family in America, we not only signed armistices but we immediately began the process of helping our enemies to rebuild, of forgiving, and, over time, forgetting. Yet for more than a decade after 9/11, the war continued, having morphed to include the furtive arsenal of drones and special operations and cyber-attacks and unprecedented global surveillance—and the almost paranoid search for potential enemies among allies, friends, and even American citizens. This book describes how an age of fear transformed the process of making American foreign and national security policy. It examines, through the words of many who shaped those policies—including many that were enacted behind the scenes and outside the public eye—how our sense of vulnerability drove us and changed us. This is the story of how the best and some of the most obscure among our public servants strove to contain that insecurity, put it into perspective, and set America back on a course guided by our aspirations. And it is the story of others, many also well intentioned, who were too driven by that welter of emotions or who capitalized on them, to create policies that in the end only undermined our safety further or, in key circumstances, even undercut our standing as a nation.

Beyond that, it is also a look at how the character of our leaders is translated into action. The United States government is the largest and most complex organization on the face of the earth. But at its heart it is people. When it works well—as it often has in the past—it enables presidents to sort through the recommendations of professional policymakers, make informed choices, and ensure their effective implementation. When it does not—and in the past decade it sometimes did not—it is because those in power did not take advantage of its inherent strengths and neglected to learn the lessons of the past. This book is also an effort to understand where the National Security Council process worked and where it did not, and why.

On September 11, 2001, in the hours immediately after the attacks on the World Trade Center and the Pentagon, a dreadful silence fell over Washington, DC. Many officials and business people had returned to their homes, gathering up their children from school, unsure of what would happen next. (I left my children in their school near Georgetown, thinking they would be safer there. By the time they were picked up they were almost alone save for a few teachers. They have yet to fully forgive me for this.) The White House complex was pulsing with activity, the nerve center of a national security apparatus that had just been so shocked that, even as it was responding to the day's events, it was beginning a process of reassessment and reinvention that is not yet complete at the time of this writing more than a dozen years later.

At lunchtime that day, I sat at an outdoor table with three colleagues from the small advisory firm at which I worked. We were at Café Milano in Georgetown, a place that itself would later be targeted in a terrorist plot that was foiled by the US anti-terror operations that were born on that crystal clear September morning. As I recall, we too were almost alone. We had been watching reports of the attacks all morning, speculating about their origins and their impact, calling around DC for real-time insights, checking in with our own families.

With me were Anthony Lake, former US national security advisor; John Gannon, former deputy director of the Central Intelligence Agency; and Susan Rice, a former State Department official who would later herself become US national security advisor. Earlier, as we stood in our offices watching on television as the second plane struck the World Trade Center, Tony Lake had turned to John and said simply, "al-Qaeda." They had both been tracking the organization for years, and both were certain no other terrorist organization could have managed such an attack.

The eerie stillness of the city made every distant noise ominous. Flights had been stopped nationwide, so when the occasional rush of a jet engine was heard it was hard not to wonder if another attack was on the way. It was rumored several aircraft were unaccounted for. There were a lot of rumors that day.

Not much, in fact, was clear. Our lunch conversation, like millions of others that day, tried to sort out what had just happened and what might come next. If it was an attack, as it seemed it was, President Bush would have little choice but to move to a war footing. Just where that war would be fought and against whom was an open question, but it seemed very likely that the Middle East would be in the crosshairs of any retaliation. What was not contemplated was the degree to which those attacks would trigger changes that would transform America and the world.

A dozen years later, with Osama bin Laden lying at the bottom of the Indian Ocean, we have learned that it would not be a matter of strike and counterstrike, identification of a threat and its elimination. Losing 3,000 people and watching an iconic symbol of the United States crumble into dust had instilled Americans with an unfamiliar but palpable sense of looming risks, feelings that would in turn lead the country's leaders to take actions that even more than the attacks themselves would weaken us and produce bouts of national introspection and self-doubt that would alter our worldview and our sense of our nation's role in the world. Our strength and our distance from the rest of the world had given us a sense of security that had now been shattered, making it difficult for us to absorb the blow, respond in an appropriately tough but measured way, and simply go on about our business, as governments and peoples more accustomed to such attacks, from Israel to Colombia, typically did.

Not inconsequentially, the actions we would take while decapitating the old al-Qaeda that had launched the 9/11 attacks would indirectly result in new, greater, more diverse terrorist threats. Although at the time of America's invasion of Iraq in 2003 there were essentially no elements of bin Laden's organization in that country, at the time of the writing of this book there are thought to be perhaps more than had belonged to all of al-Qaeda in 2001, and they were threatening the very existence of the country, killing thousands, and controlling large swaths of territory. There are estimated to be as many as 10,000 more extremists in neighboring Syria, according to Director of National Intelligence James Clapper, with at least 7,000 of them having shipped in from Europe. (Estimates by Israeli intelligence and our allies on the Arabian Peninsula suggest the number may be two or three times that.) In fact, a Rand Corporation report published in June 2014 asserted that the number of Salafi-jihadist groups had grown from just 28 in 2007 to 49 in 2013, that the number of Salafi-jihadists, which was between 18,000 and 42,000 in 2007, had grown to between 44,000 and 105,000, and that the number of attacks attributed to these groups had increased more than ninefold in the same period, from 100 to 950. Northern Mali is the largest al-Qaeda controlled territory on earth. In fact, al-Qaeda in North Africa and al-Qaeda in the Arabian Peninsula have grown to be threats on a par with what we once found in Afghanistan and on the rugged mountains of neighboring Pakistan.

None of us that day in Georgetown could possibly have imagined the degree to which the al-Qaeda attacks would achieve their goals of shaking America to its very foundations. Indeed, it hardly seems possible that bin Laden himself could have imagined that the superpower against which he had struck would so consume itself with a desire for revenge and to restore a sense of security that it would spend trillions of dollars it could ill afford, deplete to the point of near inoperability its armed forces, violate the most fundamental principles for which it had long stood, alienate its allies, and ultimately turn inward. Nor could bin Laden have dared hope that the United States and indeed the international system would eventually largely abandon Middle Eastern battlefields, leaving them to descend into a void that Islamic extremists battled to fill. (Although that is the strategy he implied in the quote that appears among those that begin this book.) Further, none of us, nor our attackers, could have imagined the greater costs associated with ill-conceived reactions to the perceived new threat to a degree that made it impossible for us to truly identify, debate, or respond to the greater next-generation threats to American leadership and prosperity.

In 2005, I wrote a book called *Running the World: The Inside Story of the National Security Council and the Architects of American Power*. It was a history of the modern US national security establishment since its creation in the wake of the Second World War. As the title indicated, it was published at a time when President Bush's initial reactions to the events of 9/11 had produced the most massive deployment of American force since the system I was writing about had been created. It was a period in which terms like "shock and awe" and concepts like "us versus them" and brazen unilateralism were not only common but were so widely embraced by the American people that, even with setbacks on the ground in Iraq and Afghanistan, even with scandals in Abu Ghraib and doubts about Guantanamo and the Patriot Act, Bush won a renewed mandate from American voters.

Running the World traced the evolution of a system developed in the wake of a world war that left America as the only major power in the world that was unscathed—the clear victor and principal architect of the new international order. The book followed that post-WWII growth from the remarkable flowering of creativity and institution-building that led to the creation of the UN and the Bretton Woods institutions globally, and to the birth of the Department of Defense, the CIA, and the National Security Council in the United States, through the first term of the administration of President George W. Bush. Throughout that period—through the Cold War and its immediate aftermath and on to the first years after the 9/11 attacks—America may have been threatened from time to time and stumbled not infrequently, but the country's strength and resolve were such that there was a belief at home and abroad that this was a nation in a commanding position, with leaders who regularly demonstrated a willingness, for better or worse, to wield that power.

The men and women at the top from the days of Truman through those of Bush ran the world if not literally then figuratively, dominating their respective eras. American presidents, paramount symbols of that strength, were typically called "the most powerful man in the world."

But in the decade since that book was finished, from the second term of the Bush administration and the Obama years, something has changed. Suffering self-inflicted wounds in Iraq and Afghanistan as a result of unilateralism and violation of international laws, reckless military spending, and fecklessness and political division at home, our perceived power waned, and the wellsprings of real power sputtered. Backlash against those policies produced an era in which America pulled away from her leadership role more strongly than at any time since the aftermath of World War I. The financial crisis, the rise of new powers, and geopolitical shifts for which we were unprepared compounded the problems.

During that same period, the past decade, there have also been changes in the way the national security apparatus of the United States was used. At times, leaders appeared to heed the lessons of the decades since its establishment that I wrote about in *Running the World*—notably that the president's national security team in the White House focused on their role of helping the president to make decisions by bringing together the best views from all the relevant agencies of the US government and then helping to ensure the decisions the president made were implemented by those same agencies. When this happened, the system worked well. But at times, especially recently, the president's White House advisors and an ever more bloated national security staff played a role that history should have warned them would cause problems—they supplanted the agencies they were supposed to lead, attempted to do their jobs for them, micromanaged decisions, and as a result did not have time to do the strategic planning and coordination work that only they could do. This, too, undercut American leadership.

Indeed, for reasons including these, it may well be that Barack Obama is the first American president of the modern era who is not universally perceived to be the most powerful man in the world. Nowhere has the change to America been felt more sharply than among the inner workings of the US national security establishment—it has impacted the president and his advisors, collaborators, and rivals within the political realm of this country, who together shape US policies worldwide. By the second term of the Obama era the National Security Council was ten times the size it had been during the Nixon-Kissinger years; the Directorate of National Intelligence (DNI), Central Intelligence Agency (CIA), National Security Agency (NSA), Defense Intelligence Agency (DIA), and the massive new bureaucracy portentously named Department of Homeland Security, plus the tiers of political operatives and those who influence their thinking, had overwhelmed the other agencies of government. They had become the national psyche, for better or worse.

The world of senior officials, generals, spies, and spin-doctors from the Cabinet Room to the Situation Room, from the warren of offices on the White House grounds to those scattered across Washington and its outposts around the world, is worth viewing up close because it is the stage for every real-life espionage drama, international incident, and war and peace initiative that fills headlines and provides fodder for Hollywood. But it also demands consideration because there is a direct correlation between how it works, how well it works, and how the US government performs, whether Americans and citizens worldwide are secure or not, and which issues are addressed and which are ignored.

Other books may take a more theoretical approach, focusing primarily on policy and process, but I have discovered that you cannot understand either of those aspects of the story without understanding the personalities driving them. They are fascinating characters, in part because so many of them are so ordinary, so much less special and exalted than they are made out to be in dramatic treatments or novels. They are also constantly surprising either in their inspiration or their pettiness, their creativity or their duplicity. Furthermore, in an age that is characterized by an overriding emotion—fear—personalities matter much more than process.

One characteristic of this otherwise widely diverse group of men and women runs contrary to both conventional wisdom and the tenor of the headlines and cable news commentaries that shape that dubious "wisdom." In the course of the many years I have spent studying them, working with them myself both when I was in government and afterward, getting to know a great many as friends and even getting to dislike a few of them (for good reasons, I'd like to think), I have been struck by one thing above all else. For the most part, the people who occupy senior jobs in our government, our military, and our intelligence community, the policymakers who have devoted their lives to grappling with some of the toughest issues on earth, are just the kind of people you would like to see in those jobs. They are, largely, smart and hardworking, exceptionally dedicated, and committed to doing what is in the interests of the American people and the world.

Because they differ on what our best interests are and how to achieve them, there are divisions among them. And because we live in a polarized and dysfunctional political moment, one that is seen through media lenses that focus primarily on conflict and crisis, the divisions between these most senior government officials, and their relative risings and fallings, are what typically dominate the stories we hear about them. Some have made great mistakes, some even catastrophic ones. But very, very few have been evil in their intent, even if the consequences of some of their actions have effectively been so in many other respects.

I've interviewed well over one hundred of them, about half from the Bush administration and half from the Obama administration. And while I will, of course, provide my own perspectives in telling the story of the past decade, I have tried to let as much of the story as possible unfold in their words.

In the same way that the defining event of the first half of the first decade of the twenty-first century—the period during which my last book on this subject concludes—was 9/11, the defining event of the next decade for US foreign policy was the subject of the first chapter of this book, our ill-fated prosecution of the war we chose to wage in Iraq. Our reaction to being attacked was so overheated, so ill-considered, of such scale, and so broad in its unintended consequences that it became more defining, constraining, and damaging than the original event to which it was intended to respond. It was a second-order catastrophe. The desire to get out of it ultimately led Barack Obama, the president who was effectively elected to get out of it, to "double down" in Afghanistan to make the political point he was not "weak on terror." That in turn became a third-order calamity. The desire to move away from conventional means of fighting our enemies, and embrace instead drone warfare, cyber-attacks, and more special forces operations violating the sovereignty of other states than any previous post–World War II president, produced fourth- and fifth-order calamities. Still another set of calamitous consequences is associated with the fear that another big attack might come, particularly one that might employ weapons of mass destruction. That singular concern grew so great that it was used throughout both the Bush and the Obama years to justify the creation of a massive global surveillance apparatus, which in turn triggered a global backlash of cyber-nationalism that is Balkanizing the Internet and undercutting its globalizing, unifying, democratizing capacity. We only truly began to realize the scope of those surveillance operations and their potential risks thanks to the random if utterly predictable set of leaks produced by former intelligence contractor Edward Snowden. Snowden himself was one of a vast army of contractors hired in the wake of 9/11 that, in order to combat the perceived risks associated with a terror threat that was and is grotesquely overstated (as we shall see in the course of this book), grew to encompass more than half a million people with top secret clearance. That is a group so large that it invited a leak more surely than we would have had, had we left open the front doors of the CIA each night after work.

So the NSA scandal and the aftershocks that unfolded during 2013 and into 2014 might itself be seen as a kind of sixth-order disaster—or, regardless of how you might order such knock-on effects, it is one of many cascading consequences of 9/11 that illustrate how creating terror works and is such an effective tactic. Add to them, depending on your view of the damage they may have done to America and its interests, the violations of longstanding principles of American law associated with the use of torture, the abuses in Abu Ghraib prison, Guantanamo, the Patriot Act, kill-lists, and ordering the deaths of Americans and others without due process.

Zbigniew Brzezinski, among the most strategically gifted and intellectually rigorous of all former US national security advisors, famously noted that the so-called war on terror was the first in US history to have been conducted against a tactic rather than an enemy. He was right, of course, to a degree. But as it happens sometimes, the label we gave the war ultimately became a self-fulfilling prophecy. Our greatest enemy—the one capable of doing us the greatest damage—quickly ceased to be the several thousand often poorly armed, poorly trained, cobbled together members of al-Qaeda or any other extremist group that existed in the years immediately after 9/11. It was in fact terror itself. The fears within us drove us to take actions that were so profoundly costly in economic, human, political, and diplomatic terms that only one or two major powers on earth could have inflicted them on us. Indeed, given the circumstances, the damage we did could only have been a self-inflicted wound, much as was prophesied by twenty-eight-year-old Abraham Lincoln in 1838 in his famous Lyceum speech in the quote that also appears in the front of this book.

The main reason to read any history is, of course, not simply to indulge in the blame games so popular in America's dysfunctional capital these days. There is, after all, as this book shows, both plenty of blame to go around, and indeed, a great deal of credit to accrue to public servants who, after all, were typically simply trying to advance US interests as best they could. But the value in following the events of a decade is in finding the lessons and identifying trends that will be important to America and the world going forward. By listening to the words of those who have had their hands on the tiller during this unprecedented era, we may find ways to avoid prolonging it or, worse, going through it again. This is especially important because one of the inescapable conclusions is that we're not very good at anticipating the future. On the one hand, senior policymakers, especially those closest to the President of the United States and the White House political apparatus, are trapped in a bubble that often isolates them from views that might benefit them, and they are also trapped in the present, fighting the news cycle. In fact, during the past decade, that news cycle, cited as a pernicious constraint on strategic thinking in my last book and in the work of many other students of how the national security apparatus works, has actually grown more constrained. Twenty-four hours seems luxuriously extended. Thanks to Twitter, Facebook, Reddit, and other social media, political messaging battles are fought out on a global scale against legions of critics in multiple languages in real time. Minutes are all it takes to turn a slip of 140 characters into a diplomatic incident or a political wound that resists healing. It is surely not a coincidence that the TV drama that was most redolent of this era, launched as it was in November 2001, was the frantic disaster aversion drama, *24*, in which the clock is visibly ticking down throughout every episode. So it was in policy circles.

Given that the business of managing America's international interests has steadily grown more complex over time and the tools by which they and threats to them can be monitored with ever greater detail, the problems associated with the now-now urgency of the bubble world of the White House have been compounded by what are nearly impossible challenges to the bandwidth of those at the top. This is especially true in the early years of any administration when senior officials who have been out of the loop for a long time, many of whom are not practiced managers of complex organizations, are often overwhelmed. Further the pressures of the jobs nearest the president himself are so intense that not only do family lives suffer in a city that often champions "family values," but perspective is lost. Exhaustion is one consequence of never leaving the confines of your workplace; spending all your time talking to few beyond a small, like-minded group of colleagues makes groupthink another.

Condoleezza Rice, in fact, confided to me in her Stanford University office after she ended her tenure as secretary of state that "in the aftermath of 9/11, we were essentially just reacting. It took some time before we could stop, catch our breath, and make a critical reappraisal of what we were doing." Her comment was echoed over the course of my interviews by many on both the Bush and Obama teams.

Beyond being trapped in the present, however, one of the other disturbing lessons of a historical look backward is that it also reveals that the only thing that rivals the attention the Washington policy community gives to "right now" is the degree to which it devotes its attention to what has just happened. If America is a car, those entrusted with driving it tend to focus almost entirely on what the gauges on the dashboard tell them and on the rearview mirror. Far too seldom do they look upward through the windshield to see what's ahead. Just as, famously, generals fight the last war, so do policymakers interpret the next crisis in terms of the last one. Indeed, not only is government policy the ultimate lagging indicator of events but even those parts of the US government tasked with anticipating trends—like the National Intelligence Council, which produces regular outlook documents peering a decade or more into our future—consistently produce work that tells more about what happened in the past year than that which is likely to emerge as important in the years ahead.

I remember reading such reports when I was a senior official in the Clinton administration. At the time, we felt that the end of the Cold War was a watershed, just as for most of the past dozen years, most people you asked would have described 9/11 as such a defining moment. But the broader changes affecting the world, likely changing it fundamentally, are often overlooked: in 1990, for example, there were 11 million cell phones in the world, and at the time of the writing of this book there are 7 billion. Within a couple of years, for the first time ever, virtually every man, woman, and child on earth will be linked in a man-made system via which every aspect of their life will be affected—education and politics, how they shop, and how they pay for goods. What is more, in the past few years, the national security establishment has discovered that many of the most complex issues it faces have to do with the rules of this emerging global digital commons—about how we fight cyberwars and by what rules, about the nature of privacy and surveillance, about taxation and who controls the Internet. None of this depends on the Cold War or 9/11—it is the big canvas against which those events played out.

It is striking that during the Bush and Obama years the government was utterly ill-prepared to anticipate these developments or their implications. The consequences of this lack of consideration have been profound. The same is true with regard to the rise of new powers on the planet or how we deal with environmental challenges that seem a long way off but require very urgent attention today.

The company that I was working with at the time of those 9/11 attacks was a little advisory firm called Intellibridge. Its goal was to use the burgeoning information riches of the Internet to provide open-source insights to companies and governments. The big idea we thought we had was that we could go to any organization and answer whatever questions they might have by mining data from the constantly expanding ocean of web-based information. What we discovered fairly early on, though, was that the problem for most organizations was not that they lacked the answers they needed. They didn't even know the questions they should have been asking.

It is clear that this is a problem in many big organizations today, and in few is it so pronounced as our national security apparatus. (This dearth of understanding is not helped by the fact that our ugly and dysfunctional political process has dissuaded so many who could help frame and answer these questions from ever seeking a career in public service.) For that reason, some of the story that follows contains an effort to identify those questions that recent events should be posing, but which we are not yet grappling with sufficiently. The last chapter of the book focuses on that particularly.

The reason for focusing on these emerging issues is because it is my strong belief that in order for America to return to the kind of growth and leadership that its people expect and deserve, we must bring an end to this Age of Fear—a period in which responding to perceived and often overstated threats, like terrorism, has distracted us from looking to the horizon as we should. The blame for not doing so does not in my mind lie exclusively with the policymakers, generals, and politicians. It also lies with those who seek to influence them in the opinion-leader community, like the media or think tanks, and with their bosses, the American people who have a much greater responsibility to lead than they are currently fulfilling.

In preparation for this book I wanted to see just what the intellectual context has been for the kind of setbacks and mistaken priorities that have marked the last decade. These organizations are supposed to be on the cutting edge of policy issues, and they regularly interface with government officials both to do their research and to present their findings so they can influence outcomes. They also are a kind of landing zone for once-and-future officials, a place that former government executives can reflect on what they have done and prepare for future jobs. I once rather uncharitably joked that in this respect they are rather like giant meat lockers for storing ex-government officials until you need them again. It is the revolving door between these organizations and folks in top jobs that gives them such influence and makes what they are thinking such a useful proxy for how the mind-set of the policy community works.

As Washington has become more polarized and the process of vetting and approving nominees has become just another part of the blood sport of winning points by destroying the reputations of others, the effect on the policy community has been chilling. Potential job seekers in some future administration dare not write or say anything for the public record that might be seen as too extreme or controversial lest an opponent use the statement as reason to hold up or block a nomination, or some potential hirer see it as making the applicant just too risky to be offered a job. That is why so many articles you see by distinguished names who are whispered to be on the short list for the big jobs of tomorrow are so bland and boring, mere exercises in reputation management, in which the main goal is to indicate that one is cleaving to the party line with perhaps a creative flourish of a deviation from past statements by a new heading of three or four degrees to port or starboard.

Similarly, think tanks tend to focus their efforts on those issues most in the news and relevant to the debate of the moment because those are the ones most likely to garner attention and win the institution or its people a "seat at the table." It contributes to the sense that Washington is, as it has often been described, a game of peewee soccer with all the kids on the pitch crowded around the ball. Sometimes this analogy is used to describe the way members of an administration all scramble to get close to the president or his top aides or their immediate agenda. But it also can mean the scramble to be engaged on the issue of the moment.

So you take a fairly conservative town—not politically speaking, but in terms of the instincts of the players, their aversion to risk—add in a political atmosphere that discourages risk-taking, and compound it with an intellectual context in which a narrow focus on a few issues with political traction is rewarded—and the result is an institutionalized aversion to creativity. This is a system that steadfastly resists thinking outside the box and, as we shall see, in some cases is almost incapable of even the most basic analysis or monitoring of developments.

My research assistants at the Carnegie Endowment for International Peace, led by my excellent senior researcher Tara Chandra, compiled an analysis of every single study, paper, and event produced by ten of Washington's leading think tanks between January 2005 and mid-April 2013. The think tanks spanned the political spectrum; the ones we examined were the American Enterprise Institute, the Brookings Institution, the Carnegie Endowment for International Peace (with which I have been associated for about a decade and a half), the Center for American Progress, the Center for Strategic and International Studies, the Council on Foreign Relations (with which I have been associated for over two decades), the Heritage Foundation, the New America Foundation, the Peter G. Peterson Institute for International Economics, and the Woodrow Wilson International Center for Scholars.

I know these organizations well. They perform many valuable services and periodically offer forward-looking insights that are of value to policymakers, legislators, and other active stakeholders in US foreign policy.

We looked at every event, report, and commentary produced by these organizations over the eight-year period in question, one roughly corresponding to the period of time that is the focus of this book. Just a list of every item covered filled a three-inch-thick binder to bursting. The total number of entries is 9,858.

The top individual countries covered included China with 878 items, Russia with 618, Afghanistan with 405, Iran with 334, Iraq with 286, India with 262, Pakistan with 256, Israel-Palestine with 204, Turkey with 194, Brazil with 125, North Korea with 109, and Egypt with 92. Stragglers included Syria with 54 and Libya with 27. The regional foci of events and papers included the Americas with 611, Africa with 590, the Middle East with 547, non-EU Europe and Eurasia with 526, the EU with 484, East Asia with 429, Central Asia with 203, and Southeast Asia with 142. In terms of broader themes you find national security and defense (as a general topic) with 619, the economy (as a general topic) with 611, the war on terror with 341, international organizations with 261, and nuclear non-proliferation with 169.

Although this distribution seems to cover the world, there are some clear biases in what are apparently the subjects of greatest interest to the broader Washington policy community. Some seem to be related to a kind of generational bias among a cadre of academics brought up during the Cold War. This helps to explain, in part, the attention given to Russia or the former Soviet Union (1,340 total events and papers). Clearly, another bias is to the news of the day and during this period of war on terror and related conflicts and unrest in the Middle East we find that there were 2,740 events with regional or general topics in that area and perhaps another 300 that touched upon related themes through lenses like non-proliferation or the impact of extremism on other regions. In short, almost a third of all work was done on these areas. For the sake of comparison, more than five times as many events or reports were done on the EU and the Eurocrisis as were produced on Africa or the Americas.

That said, other anomalies are also worth noting because they underscore the tendency of the policy community to either focus on the news or to follow trends. Between 2005 and 2007 Afghanistan was, literally, the forgotten war, with only a total of 63 events or papers during that period. As the election and then the promises of President Obama to return the national focus there resulted in a renewed interest in that country, the number rose from 28 in 2008 to 70 in 2009. (It was down to 28 again by 2012 when it was clear the United States is leaving and interest again waned.)

More worryingly, however, and of central interest to the overall thrust of this book is the tendency to focus policy through a primarily political and regional lens with economic and scientific issues getting much less attention. Given the economic roots of the Arab Spring, the economic components of peacekeeping, the growing threats driven by inequality worldwide, and, of course, the degree to which technology is remaking global affairs at every level, this lack of attention is both glaring and revealing. Of the 619 events and papers in the broad category of national security, only 32 pertained to cyber issues and of these 19 came from one institution, the Center for Strategic and International Studies (CSIS). Also, during the period we examined, only one such event was specifically on the issue of China and cyber-security. Only six events took place during this period focused on the issues, ethics, and consequences of drone warfare. Only five mentioned science as a headline issue, and only ten were focused on technology and the future of the US national security.

Of 119 economic events that took place in the three years leading up to the financial crisis, precisely none were focused on or raised as a central point the risk of a major financial crisis. (But in the reactive mode of this community, during 2009 and 2010, the financial crisis was the most discussed topic, ceding leadership back to the Middle East only after the events of the Arab Spring took place—with events on Egypt rising from 7 in 2010 to almost five times that in 2011.) Eleven events took place between 2005 and 2009 on the future of the Eurozone and the Euro. Just one such event took place in 2009, though by 2011 and 2012, the number rose to 17 one year and 18 the next. Arguably, of course, the risks posed to the United States and to the world economy were far greater from our financial crisis or from that in Europe than those posed by terrorists or unrest in the Middle East (or by Russia) but, even in the midst of the reactive surge of interest in them, they lagged well behind the focus given to even secondary issues associated with the global war on terror or the big countries of the Greater Middle East. (It should also be noted that we are not helped by a ghettoized system in which economic policymakers and thinkers too seldom interact with their political or national security or science and technology counterparts. This produces discussions within silos that miss critical factors, risks, and opportunities.)

In short, not only have we been driven by our fears for over a decade, we have done so in an atmosphere in which we are trapped either in the present moment or in the past, and we lack the tools and inclination to either consider or creatively analyze possible scenarios for the future. It is no wonder that the single most common lament of the national security advisors with whom I have spoken—and I have spoken with all but one of those from the past half century—is the inability of the national security apparatus of the United States to foster strategic thinking or cultivate useful ideas about the future. The intellectual community surrounding that apparatus—the rest of the US policy ecosystem, if you will—is no better. The result helps explain how we have gone from a brief moment of US triumph as the victor in the Cold War and the world's sole superpower, to a period in which decline seems a real possibility and the United States has had a string of notable, disturbing, and interrelated international policy failures, misfires, and duds.

To consider this trajectory from the perspective of those entrusted with primary responsibility for shaping America's role in the world is the objective of this book. The approach to doing so will be through a structure that is both chronological and topical. The great issues of the day will be organized in the order of where their centers of gravity came, when they dominated the narrative.

This book is not primarily about the process of how the national security apparatus works or has evolved—although I will, of course, touch upon those issues. Instead the focus in each chapter will be on the central decisions that have shaped recent US foreign and national security policy and the influences that shaped those decisions—getting inside the drama of how American foreign policy was shocked into a series of missteps, what it tried to do to recover, and what it must do to emerge from this era that certainly will go down in history as a low-point in the story of America as a leading world power.

Chapters One and Two begin with Iraq, the great carryover issue from the first term of the Bush administration, and the one that was viewed as perhaps the greatest immediate challenge by the president and his team as they began their second term. The next chapter looks at the makeover the Bush administration got in the second term and how it did and did not change the character of its international policymaking. The fourth chapter examines the role national security issues—including a great economic shock to our system—played in the 2008 election, the role the election played in influencing national security policy choices, and ultimately the transition between administrations. The fifth chapter looks at Afghanistan and Pakistan, the first big national security initiative of the Obama team. Chapters Six and Seven deal with the evolving relationship with a great Cold War rival that may be our great rival in the century ahead, China, and the one that is not likely to be but is still a source of regular consternation, Russia. The story of the Arab Awakening and the enormous complexities it and the aftershocks associated with it posed for US policymakers comes next. Following that is a chapter that circles back to look at two big events tied to where this period started and where it may be going—the death of Osama bin Laden and the advent of the cyber-era, including notably the NSA surveillance scandal. Finally, in the conclusion, we look at emerging challenges both for President Obama and for the future of US foreign policy, and we consider whether or not the US national security system is evolving fast enough to address them and what must be done to ensure that we are ready for the next generation of challenges we are likely to face.

One lesson of the era just past is that America has a very special place among nations. As unhappy as many around the world are with what is sometimes seen as American bullying or arrogance, there is an equal hue and cry when America chooses not to lead or fails in its leadership role. Even when we and others think we are in retreat, many in the rest of the world still look to us. Even when the American people are weary of war and the costs and risks of leadership, there is still palpable discomfort when we are seen to be falling behind, losing our unique international standing. As a consequence, there is a presumption of leadership that American presidents and their advisors cannot shirk or shrug off. This perception, and the responsibilities that come with it, creates a special urgency to ensure we have the people, the institutions, the resources, and the strategies we need to play that unique role. The purpose of this book above all is to seek lessons in the recent past that may help us rise to that special challenge.

CHAPTER 1

Iraq: Debacle Accomplished

To him who is in fear, everything rustles.

—SOPHOCLES

Few things so divided the first two American presidents of the twenty-first century as did Iraq. George W. Bush bet his legacy on an invasion of that country and Barack Obama won his presidency by promising to end Bush's war. Yet, few things so link the presidents as the way that distant land, the "cradle of civilization," bedeviled them and their national security teams.

Bush got in too deep. Obama got out too quickly. The cost in both cases was high for the United States, for our national standing, and for the region. The story of the aftershocks of America's invasion of Iraq in 2003 is still unfolding as of the writing of this book. The country is in chaos, ancient enmities fester, and it is now painfully apparent that the dangers Iraq may have posed under Saddam Hussein have been swept aside only to reveal perhaps greater threats. Today it seems likely that history will view this period as one of continuous warfare and upheaval in the Middle East, not of the discreet wars that we talk of, but perhaps as the Gulf Wars, a decades-long struggle between Shias and Sunnis and among moderate and extremists within both groups. America's interventions and withdrawals in that protracted conflict may someday be seen as peripheral—catalysts around which opponents might rally. But they will also provide a telling window into how, even among their innermost teams of advisors, America's leaders grappled with differing visions of this country's role and how it should set its priorities.

In my previous history of the National Security Council, there were clear illustrations of how those advisors work together best, as in the decision by the team of President George H. W. Bush to cease hostilities in Iraq without continuing to Baghdad to topple Saddam Hussein, and how imbalances and presidential inexperience can lead to serious errors, as was the case when President George W. Bush made the decision to invade Iraq. But as we pick up where that book left off, in 2005, and continue ahead, we see that this issue will not go away, both educating and entrapping presidents and their teams, testing them, revealing their strengths and weaknesses, and ultimately having a major impact on how the world views the United States.

The warnings Bush and his team received upon taking office in 2001 that Osama bin Laden and al-Qaeda posed an imminent threat to the United States were not sufficiently appreciated by many, and were prioritized by few, other than the likes of counterterrorism experts like Richard Clarke. Within weeks of the 9/11 attacks, the focus of the country's national security leadership shifted from addressing the original sources of the attacks—al-Qaeda cells based in Afghanistan—to finishing old business in Iraq and doing so under what later proved to be the false pretext that Iraq was developing large stockpiles of weapons of mass destruction (WMD). The national security team around the president was riven almost from the start by rivalries between the State Department and the Department of Defense. The team lacked a cohesive process because the new president didn't demand one. Further, it suited some of his inner circle, notably Vice President Richard ("Dick") Cheney and Secretary of Defense Donald Rumsfeld, to circumvent the decision-making process that first-term National Security Advisor Condoleezza Rice sought to create, and they gave the president bad advice concerning the bad choices they offered him.

As a direct result of the Iraq disaster, a series of cascading calamities also befell the United States, from insufficient prosecution of legitimate national security goals in Afghanistan to abuses perpetrated in the Abu Ghraib and Guantanamo Bay prisons and on the battlefield. Of course, financial and human costs for the United States were enormous. However, perhaps the most damaging fallout of the mismanaged, misconceived wars in Iraq and Afghanistan were their effects on the American people. So deep was the public disaffection with the costs and complexity of international engagement that Bush's successor, Barack Obama, presides over a period of global affairs in which American timidity is as disquieting now as the misuse of America's strength was feared in the early Bush years.

But administrations are neither robotic machines nor the caricatures that emerge in the press or in the context of charged political debates. They are collections of people—typically people committed to doing what is best for the country and eager for approval, just like most of the citizens they represent. And people are changed by their experiences, they grow, and they learn. George Bush, like Bill Clinton before him and Barack Obama after him, entered office with very limited international experience. As is the case for most presidents, little that Bush had experienced in his life had prepared him for running the world's largest and most complicated organization. Further, the blow sustained by the United States on 9/11 had rocked the national psyche as it had not been unsettled since the onset of the Second World War. Not only Bush but his team followed an all-too-familiar Washington pattern in the wake of a crisis. First they had an emotional reaction, then they took action. Only later, in the wake of the consequences of their impulses, did they consider more thoughtfully their options and the processes by which longer-term success might be achieved. In their case, that process really did not begin to show effective results until after Bush's reelection and the beginning of his second term in January 2005.

Stephen ("Steve") Hadley, the man who became President Bush's national security advisor in January 2005, reflected on the policy processes that led him, like most of the Bush team, to believe it was necessary to make the signature error that has defined America's early twenty-first-century foreign policy—the invasion of Iraq. "Thinking back, I now wonder if our mistake may have been in not considering whether the reason Saddam Hussein was so secretive about his weapons of mass destruction capabilities was not because he had the weapons and wanted to conceal them, but because he did not have them and he wanted to hide that."

"From the Iranians," he posited. "From us."

Hadley is a thoughtful man. In many ways, if you were to describe the epitome of the modern US national security professional (at least of the seasoned, Ivy-league educated, white male variety) he would look, sound, and act like Hadley. By virtue of his experience, his cool, and his seriousness of purpose, he is precisely the kind of person you would want making or influencing America's biggest policy decisions. Hadley was once an aide to Henry Kissinger. He served as the general counsel on the Tower Commission that led to the reinvention of the National Security

Council after the Iran-Contra affair. He was a long-time colleague and protégé of the man who is the acknowledged standard by which all US national security advisors are judged, General Brent Scowcroft. However, as deputy to National Security Advisor Rice, Hadley was also a key part of the team that oversaw one of the most troubled periods in US foreign-policy history between 2001 and 2005.

There is a lesson in that seeming contradiction that resonates with key moments in both the Bush and the Obama years and back through Rwanda, Vietnam, the Bay of Pigs, and other US policy calamities of the previous century. The best—and the best intentioned—are subject to forces, circumstances, failures of leadership, process, and team chemistry that can produce devastating outcomes. It is too often forgotten that the title of David Halberstam's book, *The Best and the Brightest*, an account of how America slipped ever deeper into the quicksand of Vietnam, is infused with bitter irony. Robert McNamara and his team of "whiz kids" were brilliant; nonetheless, they made a series of ghastly miscalculations.

Although neither Hadley nor almost any of his other senior colleagues are yet willing to repudiate those first-term decisions completely, it is clear that many of them understand that the several years immediately after 9/11 were marred by misjudgments. Each member of the senior national security team—Bush, Cheney, Rumsfeld, Rice, and Bush's first-term secretary of state, Colin Powell—and supporting players like Hadley, Deputy Secretary of State Richard Armitage, and top military leaders have publicly and privately reflected on what happened. They don't all agree, and there is an inevitable degree of finger-pointing and blame-shifting. Battles among them continue to be fought out in the press, in dueling recollections of big events, in cocktail party conversations in Washington. But the second term of the Bush administration suggests that from the president on down, there was an awareness that mistakes had been made and that midcourse corrections were called for—some quite significant in their consequences. This often happens in second terms. As former national security advisor Sandy Berger once said to me, "experience is really the only way to learn how to be president of the United States. There is nothing that prepares you fully for the job."

One of the most important and least appreciated aspects of the US national security process is that it contains the seeds of its reinvention. Indeed, paradoxically, it is the system's connection to the volatile, overly emotional world of American politics via the mechanisms of democracy that force even those in power to question their decisions and to recognize that their power is related to the degree of popular support for their actions. In other cases, it is simply the desire to serve combined with self-awareness that leads some administrations to seek to change both people and approaches to challenges as time goes by. Gerald Ford, in his continuation of the Nixon years, saw that having one man, Henry Kissinger, as both secretary of state and national security advisor represented too much concentration of power. He emphasized to me during a conversation late in his life that he viewed redistributing that power between Kissinger and a separate national security advisor, Brent Scowcroft, as the single most important contribution he made to the foreign-policymaking process as president. When Ronald Reagan's mismanaged National Security Council produced the Iran-Contra scandal, a reappraisal followed that led Frank Carlucci and Colin Powell to introduce significant and much-needed reforms that got the NSC out of the business of supporting the kind of independent operations without adult supervision that marked the early and mid-Reagan years. Bill Clinton fielded a significantly upgraded national security team during his second term, moving to a national security advisor in Sandy Berger with whom he had a stronger relationship than he had with predecessor, Anthony Lake; a more effective secretary of state in Madeleine Albright than he had in the competent Warren Christopher; and to cite another example, a most effective CIA director, George Tenet. Further Berger introduced key process steps within the NSC and among the national security principals that helped enhance cooperation and comity.

Among the contrasts between the Bush and Obama years is the degree to which the Bush team and its president learned from its first term and was willing to embrace change and personnel adjustments that made a positive difference, and that to which Obama resisted such changes. Unlike Bush, Obama actually saw his national security team substantially decline in effectiveness (despite the tireless efforts of many on that team) during at least the first two years of his second term.

A decade after Bush's reelection it is becoming clear that the response to the failures and missteps of his first term produced a period of turmoil and gradual reinvention at the outset of his second. Central to that process were a series of critical changes to the president's team and a reconsideration of the processes by which Bush's wars in Iraq and Afghanistan and against al-Qaeda were being managed. As a direct result, especially in the last two years of Bush's eight in office, an administration still best known for its early foreign-policy failures nonetheless became home to one of the more high-functioning, successful, national security processes in the past quarter century—one with Hadley in a central and importantly constructive role. But its primary task was to recover from a disaster of its own making.

No Time to Think

Hadley's boss for the first four years of the Bush administration was Condoleezza Rice. She was the national security advisor; he was her deputy. Both are reserved by nature. Both are also tenacious and loyal to a fault. Today, they continue to work together in a consulting firm that includes, as a third partner, their former colleague from both Bush administrations, former CIA director and secretary of defense Robert Gates. Rice is still extremely protective of the president. Nonetheless, in a conversation in her office in Palo Alto—she also continues to teach at Stanford where she served as provost before entering the Bush administration—she admitted that "it was not until some time had passed that we really had a chance to gain any perspective."

One of her top aides at the State Department, who still holds her in the highest regard, echoes his boss's assessment: "she was not very reflective during her tenure. And I don't think that was a personality flaw. I think it was a defense mechanism. I mean—because you know, the pressures of these jobs are enormous, and if you were to spend your time sitting there gazing at your navel you would just drive yourself mad."

He continues, "when you think about it, it *was* dysfunctional. It didn't work. For one brief shining moment at the beginning it came together with our first steps in Afghanistan. And they succeeded. And then the flaws and the divisions and the bad judgment showed [themselves] during Iraq, around the decision to go into Iraq."

One senior member of the Bush national security team put it more bluntly: "the policy process was broken for much of the first term." This insider made it clear that Dick Cheney and Donald Rumsfeld wielded too much influence and worked outside the national security policy process, abetted by others who failed to challenge some of their critical assumptions, like whether to go into Iraq in the first place, what the goals of the invasion should be, or how many troops would be needed to achieve the goals once the decision was made to go.

One former member of the cabinet of Bush's immediate predecessor, Bill Clinton, also laid a portion of the blame for this dysfunctional process at Condoleezza Rice's feet, saying that, as Bush's first-term national security advisor, "she either was incompetent, or culpable for Iraq. She can't have it both ways. And I really think what happened was that she was more interested in being friends with the president and she was incapable of making all those mega-personalities work together and that Cheney had established a separate channel for influencing policy outside of the NSC [National Security Council]. And, as is obvious to anyone who is familiar with the situation, she and Colin Powell do not get along. And she was a little too concerned with fitting in, with finding a role, with what it was like being the first woman national security advisor."

Another regularly recurring critique of the Bush first term was that the president and his team were too willing to accept military plans that were underdeveloped or misguided. One of Bush's top NSC officials with direct responsibility for key dimensions of the wars in the Middle East observed ruefully that "it took three years before we stopped to question whether the generals had a plan for anything beyond the first stages of the invasion." Or, as former National Security Advisor Zbigniew Brzezinski observed, "what arose in Iraq was that the end of the war wasn't the end: it was just the beginning of the next phase—which was counterinsurgency, stabilization, politics, how to cope with fragmentation, how to deal with a huge influx of Americans into Iraq who were really there to enrich themselves. . . . And that became more messy."

Brzezinski continued: "In the initial phases, the military operated well. And they operated well because they were fighting a traditional war against an army. And an army can defeat another army by being intelligently run by generals. The problem arises when you're no longer fighting an army but you're beginning to fight a people. And for that the US Army wasn't all that ready. I'm not even sure that it's ready yet, even in Afghanistan."

This book concerns itself with the period after the first term of the Bush administration and, thus, will largely leave discussions of the earlier stages of American involvement in Iraq to others elsewhere. But in all such conversations a central focus is naturally on the president himself. As Brent Scowcroft, the former national security advisor to both Presidents Gerald Ford and George H. W. Bush, observed to me in his spacious office overlooking Farragut Square in downtown Washington, "in the end, you must look to the president. In our system, he is the one who drives the process, shapes it, determines who has a role and who does not. Others, like Dick Cheney and Don Rumsfeld may have been influential, but responsibility lies in the Oval Office." Or as another senior Bush administration official with decades of top-level national security experience summarized the problems he associated with Rice, "for a while I was quite harsh on Condi Rice's job as national security advisor because I was used to a different type of national security advisor—more like Frank Carlucci or Colin Powell, where everyone had complete trust that they would honestly put their views forth. But," he said, "I've mellowed on that a bit because I finally realized that I didn't get the national security advisor I wanted but there's only one nationally elected president and he got what he wanted."

Bush himself had seemed to give clues about how he might handle the kinds of challenges that he faced during his first term while on the campaign trail. As early as September 1999, in a speech at The Citadel in South Carolina while campaigning for the Republican Party nomination for president, he outlined a focused, reasoned, strong defense argument. He carefully contrasted his policies with a Clinton administration that, he asserted, sent the US military on "endless and aimless deployments" and that wanted to "launch today's new causes with little thought of tomorrow's consequences." He condemned the fact that the United States was overextended worldwide and promised that under a Bush presidency "we will not be permanent peacekeepers dividing warring parties." With a prescience for which he is not often credited, Bush also asserted that "terrorists may try to disrupt finance, communication, transportation, and public health. Our first line of defense is a simple message: every group or nation must know that if they sponsor such attacks our response will be devastating."

But of course, in retrospect, Bush's Citadel speech is as noteworthy for the ways in which he deviated from its focus as for its elements of foresight. In part, this is linked to the critique offered by Brzezinski that the US military was not suited to the missions it was assigned; it was unable to follow early military success with stabilization of the situation on the ground and "winning the peace" as it had "won the war." From within the GOP itself, one critique of the missteps of the early Bush years was linked to the fact that, despite the swipes at the Clinton administration's predisposition to "nation-building," Bush had fallen into the same trap, particularly in Iraq.

Former deputy secretary of state Armitage observed, "I think the vision that the president outlined in his Citadel speech was the correct one. But the Iraq invasion was not only poorly planned, it was improperly resourced. And among the reasons was precisely because we didn't want to do nation-building. . . . I think Rumsfeld was dead on not interested in it but he was caught in the middle after not having resourced the Iraq invasion properly.

"When that statue of Saddam Hussein came down," Armitage continued, "everybody looked at George Bush like he was a freaking genius. And then things turned to hell very quickly. And then we had to decide what to do."

Rumsfeld's antagonism to nation-building conflicted with his desire, as defense secretary, to control whatever went on in Iraq. He wanted the command, but not the mission, or as Armitage put it, he "grabbed it then walked away." The defense secretary and the national security advisor sniped at each other over who was responsible for the fact that US control in Iraq was falling apart: "one day I was coming out of the White House Situation Room and Condi was right in front of me. And Don was right behind me. And she was like on the top step where you head out to go into the West Wing. And she turns back and so I stopped and Rumsfeld stopped. And she said, 'Don, would you call Jerry [Paul "Jerry" Bremer, the head of the Coalition Provisional Authority, the post-invasion entity responsible for running Iraq] and tell him X, Y, and Z?' And he said no. And she looked and said, 'why not?' And Don said, 'he doesn't work for me.' She said, 'for whom does he work?' And Rumsfeld said, 'oh, he must work for the NSC, because I understand you folks have been talking to him.' So part of it was a predisposition against the policies we found ourselves needing to implement, and part of it was the people, the process, and pure bureaucratic pettiness."

"Colin [Powell] said he heard the same thing," said Armitage, "heard the same kind of thing on a different day. If I had been national security advisor, I'd have been in the president's office and said, 'him or me, him or me.'" Others, including Bush cabinet members with whom I spoke, confirmed that the problems involved bureaucratic squabbles and personality differences as well as some "bad policy calls by some of the folks at the top."

By then—with America committed but under-resourced in Iraq and with a burgeoning insurgency breaking out across the country—the die was cast. The administration was stuck with a prolonged commitment it had never planned for, one that would dominate the day-to-day life of the rest of the Bush presidency. So why did the president and his team choose to intervene in Iraq in the first place?

When the Threat Assessment Is More Dangerous
Than the Threat

In his perceptive book, *The Longest War: The Enduring Conflict between America and al-Qaeda,* terrorism expert Peter Bergen asserts that the Bush administration's national security team was unprepared for 9/11 because of "their inability to comprehend that an attack by al-Qaeda on the United States was a real possibility, much more so than attacks by traditional state antagonists such as China or Iraq." As a consequence—and even though their initial impulse was probably correct to treat the danger as more limited than threats posed by traditional nation-state enemies—they soon reverted to doctrines, approaches, and false analogies with which they were more familiar. In fact, rather than treating the attack as a manifestation of a new, different, and more limited type of threat, they reflexively responded with the strategies and traditional warfare approaches that had once been reserved for states. The old maxim is that, when all you have is a hammer, everything looks like a nail: we had an army designed to attack and invade nations, so we transformed a struggle between state and non-state actor into a war between state and state.

Then, in the short span of eighteen months, we committed to what in retrospect might seem like breathtakingly sweeping mission creep—from responding against the non-state actor (al-Qaeda) that had attacked us to invading the state (Afghanistan) that harbored al-Qaeda to occupying another state (Iraq) that had nothing to do with the 9/11 attacks. From the perspective of the Bush national security team at the time, however, each step made sense. In Afghanistan, to destroy the threat posed by al-Qaeda, it was necessary to depose the Taliban government that protected them. Further, as 9/11 had shown that the nation was vulnerable to terrorist attack and it was believed that Saddam Hussein had weapons of mass destruction that might be transferred to terrorist organizations, there was little choice but to act. Additionally, Saddam had flaunted seventeen UN resolutions designed to contain his WMD programs and the US was, in the view of the Bush team, acting to support the will of the international community. Perhaps on another level it was because victories against small bands of terrorists in the mountains could not expiate the pain or trauma of 9/11. Perhaps we needed to enlarge the enemy to be commensurate with the damage done to our national psyche. We needed to gun down a big, recognizable, bad guy. In any event, while the decision to broaden the scope of US actions in the region as rapidly as we did is widely discredited in retrospect, both Pew and Gallup polls from 2003 show almost three-quarters of the American people supporting military action against Iraq and there was substantial Democratic as well as Republican support for the action on Capitol Hill.

We had a ready-made portfolio of theories and plans about the threat Iraq represented. Such well-worn theories and plans concerning Iraq were more conveniently available than were any new conceptions the administration would have needed to create in order to respond against the actual source of the World Trade Center and Pentagon attacks. As Bob Woodward notes in *Bush at War*, before 9/11 "the Pentagon had been working for months on developing a military option for Iraq. Everyone . . . believed Iraq President Saddam Hussein was a menace, a leader bent on acquiring and perhaps using weapons of mass destruction. Any serious, full-scale war against terrorism would have to make Iraq a target—eventually."

So, what was the actual threat posed by the two states that we attacked? At no point since 9/11 has anyone argued that the government of Afghanistan posed any material threat to the United States other than allowing al-Qaeda to operate within its borders. It hardly could. Estimates suggest that the Taliban military organization in the years immediately prior to the 9/11 attacks possessed perhaps 400 tanks, 200 armored personnel carriers, and 15 fighter planes. The country was one of the world's poorest with a GDP of only $2.5 billion (roughly half the cost of one *Nimitz*-class US aircraft carrier) and suffered, as it does today, from significant shortages of jobs, water, electricity, and other necessities.

Although Iraq was seen as a potential threat to its neighbors, no study conducted by any reputable organization has ever suggested that it posed any direct threat to the United States. The United States had constrained Iraqi air strength by creating and maintaining no-fly zones since the First Gulf War. According to a 2001 assessment conducted by Center for Strategic and International Studies (CSIS) regional and military expert Anthony Cordesman, "Iraq's Gross Domestic Product (GDP) has been cut sharply since before the Iraqi invasion of Kuwait with per capita income (around $587 in 1999) and living standards far below pre-war levels. . . . In 1999, inflation was estimated at 135% and unemployment was high as well." In other words, in the moment before we attacked, Iraq was an impoverished country, and not one that could project any protracted threat to anyone.

Of course, a primary justification for the US attack was the possibility that Iraq had WMD and would be capable of delivering a deadly blow in the region or of offering deadly support to terrorists anywhere around the world. However, two years before our invasion, Cordesman wrote with regard to chemical weapons that "the Gulf War and subsequent UN inspection regime may have largely eliminated some stockpiles and reduced production capability." UN inspections and sanctions were also believed at the time to have had a significant impact on whatever capabilities the Iraqis may have had. Furthermore, although the entire Iraqi army was estimated at between 300,000 and 375,000 troops at the time of the US invasion, only approximately 50,000 to 60,000 were elite Republican Guards, and only about half of the army's divisions were appropriately manned and "in a fair state of readiness." Most Iraqi soldiers fled and did not fight when the Americans invaded, and much of their equipment was, in the words of a Council on Foreign Relations assessment from early 2003, "aging and outdated." Perhaps 1,800 of its tanks were considered combat-capable but the CSIS assessment found that "Iraq has no modern tanks by U.S. standards." Also in the words of the CSIS report, its air force had perhaps 300 combat aircraft, "although many have little, if any, sustainability or effective combat capability." Its navy had just nine ships.

Entering a "New World"

One state trapped in the fourteenth century. Another state so devastated and impoverished by a war a decade earlier that it posed no sustainable danger, even to its immediate neighbors. Those were the true nature of the threats the United States faced as it embarked on the longest and most expensive conflicts in its history. Never before in American history, or perhaps not since the genocidal wars against the native peoples whose lands we claimed as the country expanded, has such disproportionate force been applied.

George W. Bush and his administration framed the US response to the attacks of 9/11 as an immense threat analogous to those we faced in the great wars, hot and cold, of the twentieth century. On September 20, 2001, during an address to a joint session of Congress, Bush said:

The terrorists' directive commands them to kill Christians and Jews, to kill all Americans and make no distinctions among military and civilians, including women and children. This group and its leader, a person named Osama bin Laden, are linked to many other organizations in different countries including the Egyptian Islamic Jihad [and] the Islamic Movement of Uzbekistan. There are thousands of these terrorists in more than 60 countries. They are recruited from their own nations and neighborhoods and brought to camps in places like Afghanistan where they are trained in the tactics of terror. They are then sent back to their homes or sent to hide in countries around the world to plot evil and destruction.

"We watched the twin towers collapse before our eyes," said President Bush in a speech five years after the attacks, "and it became instantly clear that we'd entered a new world and a dangerous new war." In Peter Baker's *Days of Fire*, his exceptionally well-reported account of the Bush-Cheney collaboration, he quotes Bush speechwriter David Frum as observing that "until September 11, Bush lacked a big organizing idea," and then concluding that the war on terror became that central concept thereafter. This expansive concept was supported by effectively every member of the president's national security inner circle—whether by the vice president because it conformed to his long-simmering sense that peril was looming for the United States from extremists, or by Defense Secretary Rumsfeld because he felt that only a big response to 9/11 could ensure our self-defense. Even sometimes dissenters within the administration, such as Colin Powell, who had been persuaded of the existence of Saddam's WMD, embraced the idea of a wide-ranging threat when he made the case against Iraq to the UN Security Council.

The power of the images and rhetoric generated in the aftermath of bin Laden's attacks, the visceral nature of the impact of that moment on the country and its people, persists throughout this story. In the Obama presidency, long after America lost its taste for conventional conflicts, its leaders still felt that the threat posed by a band of terrorists roughly the size of an average American high school was sufficiently great to warrant spending billions of dollars and violating the sovereignty of untold millions of people worldwide. At the very least, this suggests a belief that the political cost of *not* waging a vigorous war against the terrorist threat would be too great, should any future attack materialize.

In the early days of the wars against these still mysterious enemies, support for the president and his plan was as widespread and enthusiastic outside the White House as it was within. Bush had an average Gallup poll approval rating of 62 percent during his first four years in office. It peaked at 90 percent in the immediate wake of 9/11 but still exceeded 70 percent as he ordered the invasion of Iraq. A *Wall Street Journal* NBC News poll taken shortly after the beginning of the war showed almost two-thirds of Americans supported the war. By May 2003, after the initial invasion had appeared to be a success, more than eight in ten Americans thought the war was justified (in a CNN/USA Today poll), "with or without conclusive evidence of illegal weapons."

It was not until over a year later, in August of 2004, that the mood began to shift and two-thirds of those responding said they felt the war was based on incorrect assumptions. By 2005, almost six in ten Americans said they didn't think the Iraq war should have been fought. And by April 2006, in a CBS News poll almost two-thirds said they did not approve of the way the president was handling the war, a level of disapproval that dogged the Bush administration for the remainder of its term.

The shift in mood was not due, however, to a recognition by the American people that we had gotten our priorities wrong. Rather, it was linked to a more pragmatic, very "American" perception that something was going wrong on the ground in Iraq. While it may seem a sentiment worthy of the Frank Underwood character in television's *House of Cards*, it is nonetheless an axiom of American politics with over two hundred years of history to back it up: the American people are willing to be lied to, and even misled, if it makes them feel good about themselves. But make them feel like losers, inferior, like our standing in the world is slipping, and no amount of rhetoric—truth or lies—will help. They will demand change.

The First Course Correction

A series of developments during the first term of the Bush Administration sent the American people precisely the message they did not want to hear.

The first discordant rumblings emanated from within the administration and were not resolved by either the president or the policy process. One top NSC official from the period told me that Rumsfeld was "imperious, cavalier, and impossible to deal with." General Norton ("Norty") Schwartz, former Air Force chief of staff, highlighted differences between the top military brass and Rumsfeld, observing that on one issue critical to success in Iraq, "he believed that it was possible to do the mission with far fewer troops than much of the uniformed leadership was comfortable with, and we were never able to overcome that presumption." When asked if he felt Rumsfeld was off base on this point, Schwartz—who would ultimately come to be known as one of the architects of America's drone programs—said, "yeah, he was mistaken. I think he might acknowledge that today."

As Bob Woodward has reported, "Rice found that Rumsfeld at times would not return her phone calls when she had questions about war planning or troop deployment." What's more, the president brushed off her concerns, suggesting that she "try to be playful with Rumsfeld instead." In her own memoirs Rice called the Defense Department's early management of its Office of Reconstruction and Humanitarian Aid "high handed" and "dismissive."

State Department relations began warily with Defense and many in the White House and went downhill rapidly. In part this may have had to do with Powell's standing as a nationally known figure, an independent political entity with his own base and great popularity. Powell's deputy, Richard Armitage, said as much when he asserted that "the fundamental rift between Powell and . . . some in the White House and at Defense had to do with the overwhelming popularity of Powell. In particular for the neocons, I think it bothered them a lot." Part of it had to do with Powell's doubts about some of the fundamental beliefs at the core of the invasion. Rumsfeld's decision to proceed with smaller invasion forces ran counter to Powell's well-known doctrine requiring overwhelming force.

In the view of top officials at State, the neocons too complacently swallowed the blandishments of certain favored advisors, notably the Iraqi exile Ahmed Chalabi. For years, Chalabi had actively and effectively networked among Washington national security policymakers, seeking another intervention against Saddam Hussein, hoping to advance his own role within Iraq. One high-ranking State Department official observed, "one of the things with Ahmed Chalabi was that he used to say that the invasion of Iraq will be—my word—a cakewalk, easy, people will love you, they will throw candies at you, and we will be a beacon of democracy in the Middle East. And once we're established in Iraq, we will be able to use the bases there to pressure the Iranians. And that they would recognize Israel. Now all this sounds good. But in reality—it was absurd, absurd." Armitage in fact, cited the appearance of Chalabi in the president's box at the 2004 State of the Union address as proof of this point. He also was sure that Chalabi occupied that spot for one reason only: "now there was only one person who could have made that happen and his name was Dick Cheney."

Further differences arose over the fundamental policy question of what would happen after the invasion of Iraq had been successfully completed. Rice wrote that "the President wanted the United States to lead in the aftermath of the war." She notes that in one NSC meeting in the Situation Room, the president made it clear he felt America owed the Iraqis a chance to build a democratic future for themselves. But she told me directly that with regard to the post-invasion phase of Iraq operations, "we simply couldn't penetrate the Pentagon." Rumsfeld has argued that the approach was clear: get in and get out. "If the Iraqis wanted to adapt their government to reflect the liberal democratic traditions espoused by Thomas Jefferson and Adam Smith, we could start them on their way and then wish them well," he wrote in his memoir, *Known and Unknown*. He then added "in discussions of postwar Iraq, the toughest challenge was the tension between the two different strategic approaches. The debate between them was legitimate, but it remained just that—a debate. It was never hashed out at the NSC and never finally resolved."

These divisions continue to echo in the books that the principals all published after they departed. Cheney wrote: "a question that came up early and often in our discussion of a government to follow Saddam was whether we were committed to establishing a democracy in Iraq. I believed we had no alternative." Rice recalls: "Don argued we had no such obligation. If a strongman emerged so be it." Rumsfeld's encapsulation of his commander-in-chief's views seems a bit acid in retrospect: "Bush often expressed his belief that freedom was the gift of the Almighty. He seemed to feel almost duty-bound to help expand the frontiers of freedom in the Middle East." These extracts don't suggest a coherent point of view for the simple reason that there wasn't one.

Operational rifts, not surprisingly, followed strategic ones. Former members of the Bush NSC recall principals meetings in which petulant or prideful cabinet members would make presentations and then willfully ignore those of their rivals. In other instances, some, like Rumsfeld, would come to meetings unprepared to advance issues openly, planning instead to deal with them later, via back channels. With antics like these, it is no wonder that disputes arose over controversial decisions such as eliminating Saddam Hussein's Baath party and disbanding the army. Indeed, it is striking to this day that, in speaking to top officials from the period, almost none can trace the origins of these two decisions, many suggesting that Bremer effectively chose to implement them on his own.

Bremer has told me that both initiatives had been approved by both the Department of Defense and the White House prior to his executing them. A good many others assert that the decision was made to take one path (comparatively minor cuts of key players at the top of the Baath party and the military) and that this decision was, in the words of one cabinet official, "lost in translation" on the way to Bremer.

To get a sense of the breadth of the frustrations with the execution of this phase of the Iraq occupation, the Hoover Institution published an assessment by Michael O'Hanlon that called Iraq "the least well-planned American military mission since Somalia in 1993, if not Lebanon in 1983, and its consequences for the nation have been far worse than any set of military mistakes since Vietnam." However the decisions might have been arrived at, it quickly became clear that the disbursal of almost all of those Iraqis with any sense of how to organize or run the institutions of national life was calamitous for the Americans. Disbanding and alienating both the Baath party and the military set the stage for the insurgency that followed and, indeed, for problems that would linger long after American forces ultimately left Iraq. Some members of that disbanded army's leadership ended up working with extremist groups like the Islamic State in Iraq and Syria (ISIS, also known as the Islamic State in Iraq and al-Sham, or the Islamic State in Iraq and the Levant), which would wreak havoc in Iraq during President Obama's second term.

In fact, in the months between June and October 2003, insurgent attacks in Iraq nearly doubled to approximately 1,000 a month. General Stanley McChrystal, a senior Iraq war planner at the Pentagon as vice director of operations and, as of September 2003, commanding general of the Joint Special Operations Command (JSOC), wrote that "the initial post-invasion elation of April and confidence of May had quickly muddied, turning to growing unease by June. By August, nervousness tempered the halls and offices of the Pentagon." While the team in the White House was careful not to refer to the prospect of Iraq falling into a civil war because it was felt that the US public would be reluctant to have American troops caught in the middle of such a fight, it was clear that the situation in Washington was combining with very complex and fast-moving conditions on the ground in Iraq to produce an extremely volatile and dangerous environment.

George Bush may have objected to the use of the word *insurgency* in the White House, but on the ground in Iraq there was no mistaking it as a central and growing concern. (A rule of thumb for future policymakers might be that if an idea seems too dangerous even to be referred to in policy discussions, it really ought to be the first issue addressed.)

The insurgency was complicated by the fact that multiple actors were on the ground. The biggest were al-Qaeda, led by Musab al-Zarqawi, and Muqtada al-Sadr's Jaish al-Mahdi Militia. Zarqawi's group was composed of representatives of Iraq's Sunni Muslim minority; Sadr's supporters were drawn from the country's Shia majority.

The fact that the White House was simultaneously "surprised"—to use the president's term—to discover that Saddam Hussein did not in fact have stockpiles of WMD contributed further to erosion of popular support for the war. After all, the premise that such weapons existed had enabled the administration to build what limited international support it could muster for the invasion. (The administration shopped a wide variety of alternative rationales over several months, lighting on the WMD approach only after that seemed to resonate especially well with the Europeans with whom State and Defense officials were meeting.) One former senior official in both multiple Democratic and Republican administrations recalled international arms inspector Hans Blix rhetorically asking, "How can a country that is so sure that Iraq had stockpiles of weapons of mass destruction be so unsure of where they were?"

Nicholas Burns, an exceptionally well-respected career diplomat, served as US ambassador to NATO during this period. Sitting in his office at the Kennedy School of Government years later, he recalled, "NATO was terribly divided with France and Germany very much opposed to what we were doing. And it really was very harmful to the alliance, that whole episode. And then there was Guantanamo and there was torture. There was Abu Ghraib. It was all of that that really produced growing public opposition from Europe to the United States. There was tremendous public dissatisfaction."

One senior official who served in the White House during the first Bush term and later at the State Department said that "things started falling apart in late 2003. It was a total shock. And we were really ill-equipped to deal with it. . . . I would sit through these briefings about, you know, where we were with pipelines or restoring electricity in Iraq and it was like the movie *Groundhog Day*. You kept hearing the same reports about falling short in the same ways over and over and yet we were failing to respond. There was a problem that was clearly hard-wired into our process." At the time, and even for years afterward, it seemed—like the commercials for vacations in Las Vegas promise—that the mistakes being made in Iraq would stay in Iraq. Only later did it become clear that the toll would be more widespread, with disbanded army members and Sunnis—alienated by the Shia-dominated regime that the United States later put in place—embracing extremism that would fuel civil conflict in Iraq and Syria and actually become a magnet for the kind of terror threat that had only really existed in American rhetoric about Iraq prior to our destabilization of the country.

A Crucible and a Prism Called Fallujah

Sitting in the heart of Iraq's Anbar province, the city of Fallujah has gone by many names since its birth in antiquity. Because the Euphrates River was rechanneled into a canal there, one of its names, Pallgutha, meant "division"—a meaning perhaps sadly emblematic of the rivalries and battles that have brought the city into almost constant focus for the past decade. Once also known as Pumbeditha, the city was the home for a millennium to one of the most important seats of Jewish learning in the world. More recently, it has been known as the "city of mosques," due to the over two hundred places of worship found within its limits and nearby.

Sitting in the midst of what came to be known as the "Sunni Triangle," forty-three miles from Baghdad, Fallujah is known to US policymakers as a vital strategic location as well as a symbol of the virulent insurgency that emerged among radicalized Sunnis in the wake of America's invasion of Iraq. The initial onslaught largely spared the city. But due to the insurgencies, it has since been the site of three, arguably even four major battles, one producing the worst US casualties since the Vietnam War, and several producing claims of atrocities committed by insurgents and US troops alike. In the most recent battle, beginning in late 2013 and continuing into 2014, the city was claimed again by extremist insurgents, suggesting that the three previous conflicts, brutal though they had been from the perspective of the US and the Iraqi governments, may have gone for naught.

On April 28, 2003, two days before President Bush stood before a shipboard banner emblazoned with the words "Mission Accomplished," a defiant crowd in Fallujah protesting the closing of a local high school came under fire from soldiers of the US 82nd Airborne Division. The nearly ninety Iraqi casualties included seventeen deaths. Two days later another protest resulted in two more fatalities.

These incidents would later be seen as warning signs of the volatility that lurked within the streets of the city of 300,000 inhabitants. Roughly a year after the first incident, insurgents attacked a convoy delivering supplies to US troops. Four contractors from the Blackwater firm were captured, brutalized, burned, and hung from a local bridge. This triggered what is today known as the First Battle of Fallujah, called Operation Vigilant Resolve by the military.

McChrystal argues the mission was hampered from the outset. Ill-will against Americans was high in the city. Anti-American rumors were rampant, even fancifully concocted: one suggested that the night vision goggles of US troops enabled American soldiers to see through the clothing of local women. Rumors of American atrocities spread and were hard to contain, given the experiences a year earlier. Marines surrounded the city, but then political pressure from American allies and from the interim Iraqi government, which threatened to disband if the Americans did not withdraw, grew so intense that the president was forced to order the troops to stand down.

Efforts to arm local Iraqi forces were unsuccessful and many members of a hastily assembled "Fallujah Brigade," armed by the United States, had soon melted into the insurgency. Zarqawi saw the situation as an opportunity to make a stand with the strong support of the populace.

Behind-the-scenes efforts to remove political obstacles proved successful enough that by November 2004 Operation Phantom Fury was unleashed. The resulting Second Battle of Fallujah was the most intense fighting of the Iraq War for the United States. Military accounts detail intensive artillery and aerial bombardments that resulted in the deaths of over 1,000 insurgents. The attacks included the use of white phosphorous anti-personnel munitions that melted the skin of victims, another example of the brutality of US troops that stirred further resentment among the people of the city. The battle was won, but at the cost of taking another step toward losing the war. The anger was, of course, further stoked by the damage and destruction wreaked on the vast majority of the homes and buildings of the city. About a third of the two hundred mosques were destroyed. The devastated city was calm for a period, but by 2005 almost daily attacks had resumed.

Sweating and Fretting

During the summer of 2004, after a season of growing unrest, the United States effectively shifted its civilian leadership on the ground in Iraq from an occupation government to a US embassy (the largest in the world) committed to helping the Iraqis establish a self-sufficient state. The leadership transition was from Bremer to John Negroponte, a sophisticated diplomatic veteran who had been trained as a young man in a number of Foreign Service posts, including the US embassy in South Vietnam. Like Bremer, Negroponte had worked beside Henry Kissinger, and he subsequently rose to become US ambassador to the UN immediately prior to his Iraq service. At the same time, George Casey became the US commanding general of the Multinational Force in Iraq. Casey's father was a West Point–educated general who had served in both the Korean and Vietnam wars before dying in a helicopter crash during the latter conflict.

Although Cold War experience may have influenced the way the United States chose to cast the threat from our extremist enemies during the war on terror, it was a fear about repeating the errors of Vietnam and suffering the consequences of its aftermath that has most influenced US military actions and national security policy. Powell's experience in Vietnam led to his adherence to the concept of the use of overwhelming force, and to his strong arguments during the First Gulf War that the United States stop short of an invasion of Baghdad lest it be caught in a Vietnam-like quagmire. The sense that it was vital to counteract America's post-Vietnam humiliation and division influenced Republican national security policy from Reagan onward. Rumsfeld's allergies to nation-building and his advocacy for quick-in, quick-out actions also trace to this period. The fear of "a defeat like we suffered in Vietnam" drove President Bush to push his team to seek new strategies and tactics in Iraq, beginning an improvement in US performance on the ground there. Most of the military's top leadership during America's Gulf Wars were trained during the Vietnam era or in its immediate wake, soaking up, debating, and writing about its lessons. Nonetheless, the failure to understand and apply Vietnam's lessons well enough led to errors in Iraq, Afghanistan, and the war on terror—errors that in turn are likely to influence the next generation of American leaders much as Vietnam has influenced recent leadership. America's hesitation to get involved decisively anywhere during the Obama years is certainly one clear sign of that.

Unlike Bremer, who famously had multiple reporting responsibilities, to Powell at State and to the President, Negroponte went into Iraq solely as a representative of Secretary of State Powell. Many on the NSC staff in the White House were frustrated that the career diplomat Negroponte insisted on reporting up through traditional State Department channels. Negroponte notes that one of those most irked was Bob Blackwill, another career Foreign Service officer. Blackwill had been Bush's ambassador to India earlier in the first term and then joined the White House as deputy assistant to the president and coordinator for strategic planning under Rice. He was known for his rough personnel style, including even a pushing incident with a staffer who worked for him. One person who worked very closely with him commented that "he's a very brilliant guy with zero people skills. Not zero. Subzero."

Negroponte commented on Blackwill's reaction to his and Powell's resort to traditional channels for reporting relationships: "Bob was very frustrated with me. You know, he'd sometimes call me, and he'd just say, well, you know, we wish we'd hear more from you about what's going on. And I'd say, 'Hey, Bob, ask Colin Powell.' Or read my cables. I multiplied by a hundred the number of telegrams that were going from Baghdad to Washington."

Negroponte continues, "the first thing that Colin asked me to do when I went out was to evaluate the quote unquote reconstruction program and come back with recommendations as to how it should all be modified." Negroponte and Bill Taylor, who went on to become ambassador to Ukraine, recommended "reprogramming" certain types of training for the Iraqi army and policy, motivated by Negroponte's belief, based on his Vietnam experience, "that we started Vietnamization in Vietnam too late." In other words, they wanted to get the Iraqis involved as early as possible in ensuring their own security.

From Vietnam Negroponte brought "a civilian military model of cooperation." He had seen how General Creighton Abrams didn't really emphasize Vietnamization "because Westy [General William Westmoreland] wanted the U.S. to do all the fighting." So Negroponte fortified an already good relationship with General Casey—"I mean, we're really best friends"—a collaboration that right from the beginning focused on the integration of civilian and military efforts at the earliest possible stage, from top to bottom. It helped because Jerry Bremer and his military counterpart General Ricardo Sanchez "were barely on speaking terms." Another high-level Bush national security insider was less diplomatic:

"they couldn't stand each other. And I'm not sure either of them really knew what they hell they were doing."

To get a better understanding of the elements that comprised the insurgency, Negroponte and Casey established a "red cell" (also known sometimes in the government vernacular as a "red team," a group convened to challenge and test scenarios, plans, and assumptions)—a team of analysts composed of both military and embassy staff. They reported in September of that year that "the principal danger came from the Sunni tribes who needed to be lured into the political system before they fully bonded with [Zarqawi's] insurgents." The analysts estimated that insurgents numbered between eight and twelve thousand and concluded that "the insurgency is much stronger than it was nine months ago and could deny the Interim Iraqi Government (IIG) legitimacy over the next nine months." The group urged an effort to pursue political reconciliation as a priority.

Negroponte credits the White House and the NSC team led by Blackwill with playing a constructive role in the January 2005 elections. The objective was to convene an assembly to write a new constitution for the country and advance the country toward self-rule. Negroponte and his team in Baghdad noted, however, the frustrations associated with micromanaging the process from Washington. "The elections were carried off rather effectively under difficult circumstances. However, we did have to deal with NSC staffers at the White House working for Meghan O'Sullivan," then a senior director at the NSC, later deputy national security advisor for Iraq and Afghanistan. Said Negroponte, O'Sullivan "would be giving the President questions to ask me on the video teleconferences. Like, you know, why can't they vote by mail? Or why can't they vote by Internet? It was a bit frustrating—they were just sweating and fretting it."

Negroponte also notes that General Casey did a "masterful" job in managing the security side of the elections, although Casey himself recalls that there were "almost 300 attacks on election day." Nonetheless, 58 percent of eligible Iraqi voters showed up at over five thousand polling stations, which gave the election sufficient credibility for the newly elected assembly—even though the vast majority of voters were Shia and Kurds. Sunni turnout was just 2 percent. "The elections," Casey wrote in his memoir, were successful because of "turnout and security efforts." But "the lack of Sunni participation meant that they would have limited influence in the development of the constitution." In his view, however, the fact that al-Qaeda had been unable to "prevent the vote" suggested that there was "little support for the enemy." (The full short-sightedness of ignoring the potential risks associated with Sunni disenfranchisement and alienation was realized with growing impact during the years after the American pullout from Iraq and would fuel unrest and future battles between Sunni extremists and the Baghdad government they distrusted—again in Fallujah and later all across western and northern Iraq.)

Casey's perspective was therefore, to be charitable, rather optimistic. It would be challenged as the insurgency gained steam during 2005 and would ultimately lead to the one major Iraq policy innovation that at least momentarily turned the tide for the Bush initiative in that country, staved off perceived defeat, and created the conditions necessary for US troops to begin their departure from the country. In later years, that initiative—called "the surge"—would be hotly debated and then misapplied in Afghanistan. As a new insurgency emerged during the second term of the Obama administration, it would be seen as a measure that was not sustained (or sustainable) long enough to have lasting results. But it also offers a good example of how a new Bush team learned from the missteps of the first term and laid the foundations for important progress in other areas during the last years of the administration.

CHAPTER 2

A Very Different President

I love the man that can smile in trouble, that can gather strength from distress and grow brave by reflection. 'Tis the business of little minds to shrink, but he whose heart is firm, and whose conscience approves his conduct, will pursue his principles unto death.

—THOMAS PAINE

Given the deteriorating conditions on the ground during 2004 for George Bush's signature endeavor in Iraq and the level of fractiousness within his team, it was inevitable that change would come should the president win reelection. He did so on November 2, 2004, when he edged out his Democratic opponent and a future secretary of state, John Kerry, by just over 3 million popular votes, 50.7 percent to 48.3 percent.

But the groundwork for the process of transition had been laid even earlier. General Colin Powell had begun the process of identifying the flaws in the national security team and envisaging a new lineup. According to a source familiar with the exchange, Powell was straightforward with Bush: the secretary of state conveyed to his boss "on a couple of occasions that the NSC system simply wasn't working right. Personalities and views of personalities were too far apart. [Bush's] response was, 'well, it's just like [Caspar] Weinberger and [George] Schultz,'" secretaries of defense and state, respectively, during the Reagan years. Powell reportedly replied that it was not like Weinberger and Schultz, that he was there with Weinberger and Schultz. In the exchange, Powell is said to have asserted that Weinberger and Schultz "could figure out a way to resolve things. But now it's just not working well and it isn't serving you well. And so you know, you really need to make some changes after the election and I think you really ought to shake up your national security team, bring in new people, and it starts with me. I should go."

Those close to Powell say he affirmed to Bush that he had only ever intended to serve as secretary of state for one term, but that his departure would have been essential anyway. Powell reportedly argued that he had to be the first to go because he was "so philosophically different from the rest of them. And they have the same view of me. And so it's not functional." Bush was reluctant to accept Powell's message, "but he heard it."

The chill between Powell and Rumsfeld had by 2004 grown as dysfunctional as any State-Defense relationship, ever. A top military aide to Rumsfeld told me the SecDef was "counting the days" until Powell left. In his memoirs, Rumsfeld's silence is thunderous. He does not address the issue at all except to say that Powell "departed" his post as secretary of state. Rumsfeld's former protégé and lifelong friend, Vice President Cheney, was more explicit. "Getting a new Secretary of State was a top priority," he wrote, saying that while he had once supported Powell's nomination, a transition was in order because he was "disappointed in the way [Powell] handled policy differences."

Continuing, Cheney wrote, "time and again I heard he was opposed to the war in Iraq. Indeed, I continue to hear it today. But never once in any meeting did I hear him voice objection. It was as though he thought the proper way to express his views was by criticizing administration policy to people outside the government."

Powell had a discussion with Andrew Card, Bush's chief of staff, in the period after Bush's reelection. Card told Powell that the president wanted his resignation, as had been discussed. Powell offered to stay on a couple of months to finish up on some projects and attend several upcoming meetings, including a high-level NATO gathering, but Card stated that Bush wanted the resignation immediately. Powell was told that, subject to her confirmation, his successor would be Condoleezza Rice, whereupon he would depart. Powell reportedly noted that in his prior discussion with Bush he had envisaged a wider reshuffling of the national security team, but Card brushed off the comment and said that he didn't want to get into that. While Powell left, Rumsfeld, who Powell and others saw as a particular impediment to an effective and cohesive process, remained in place. It was clearly galling to the ex-general.

A little later Rumsfeld's deputy, Paul Wolfowitz, would leave and Rumsfeld himself left the administration late in 2006, but those moves were not yet apparent at the time Powell left.

Rice recalls, "when the president was reelected the first conversation we had was . . . we've broken a lot of china in response to the worst attack on the American homeland since the War of 1812, but you know, we've got to leave something in place. We can't just go on breaking china.

"And so, when he asked me to be secretary of state," she recalled, "that's what this was about. We were going to have to reestablish these relationships with allies. That we were going to have to find a way to leave some architecture in place. He wanted to do something major in the Middle East with Palestinians and the Israelis. . . . And he laid out a whole agenda of things that in many ways during the first term never quite got to the surface because we were reacting, reacting, reacting and because 9/11 had had such a huge impact on how we saw the world."

Rice had been exceptionally close to Bush as national security advisor, sometimes spending as many as six or seven hours a day with him. In this respect, she performed, arguably to a fault, one of the two central jobs Brent Scowcroft has said are the top priority of a national security advisor: staffing the president. But she also had, for the same reason, less time for the other job—managing the interagency process—a task made much more difficult both by the divisions within the national security cabinet and the president's first-term unwillingness to enforce the discipline of working within the system.

"There's no doubt," Rice said in a candid and self-aware reflection, "that going to State with the experience of having been national security advisor and having seen some of the problems State had been having, was an advantage. And it helped of course to have Steve Hadley at the NSC, who was a way better national security advisor than I was because he was the right personality for it. And I think I was the right personality to be Secretary of State. I always laughingly say, we finally got into the right positions. And of course, I had the president's confidence."

Condoleezza Rice knew that there was another factor that would shape the new national security team: George Bush himself. He was no longer the neophyte president. In Rice's words, "the president had grown." She saw evidence of this in particular with Bush's newfound ability to corral the Defense Department. He would "demand things from

the Pentagon. He was so much more confident, for instance, in putting together the surge than he was in the questions he would ask of the military
going into Iraq." And as Bush took a firmer hand on the policy in Iraq
he gradually dislodged the iron grip of his vice president (who one senior
Bush NSC official described as wanting to "keep breaking china.") The
official continued, "And the president—he doesn't want to do anything
militarily at that point with North Korea, he doesn't want to do anything
militarily with Iran. He wanted to engage in diplomacy. The president
was in a different place." Rice is clearly protective of the president, but
many top officials who were close to the president also support her viewpoint. So too do the actions of the administration. Other than the surge
within Iraq, there were no new major confrontations during the second
term of the Bush administration, even in the face of provocations like the
deteriorating situation in Afghanistan or Russia's aggression in 2008 into
Georgia. Wherever possible, diplomatic or much more limited and ideally
covert military responses were sought.

Rice's sense is echoed by Hadley's recollection of a discussion of the
differences between the first and second terms he had with Joe Nye, a
distinguished political science professor, former dean at the Kennedy
School, and former chairman of the National Intelligence Council during
the Clinton administration. Nye told Hadley, "I have a theory that when
people contrast the challenges Condi faced at the NSC with the challenges you faced, that your big advantage was that you were dealing with
a second-term president. He knows what he thinks. He has been through
two wars, 9/11, the war on terror, knows every world leader, has met with
them a bazillion times, largely has developed his policies for better for
worse and is confident in himself. That's a very different president."

In recounting the transition, Rice also said she addressed the issue
of the Powell-Rumsfeld dysfunction. "I don't think Colin had full rein
as secretary of state where he could be fully effective. And I remember
telling the president point blank: I do not intend to spend my time at
State debating foreign policy with Don Rumsfeld. I'm not going to do it.
If that's what you want, find another secretary of state.

"And, you know, we had a relationship where I could say that."

Rice was determined that as secretary of state she would be empowered and not "get nitpicked to death." She credited Hadley for his
supportive management of the NSC's core responsibilities such as coordinating the interagency process by which policy options for the president were developed, advising the president directly, and overseeing the

implementation of the policy decisions the president ultimately made. Rice insists Hadley performed much better than she had been able to for Powell: "Steve's role was essential."

Given his decades of experience within and around the NSC apparatus, Hadley came with a clear philosophy of the job. He observed two ways of running an interagency process. "On the domestic side, it always has tended to be very White House staff–focused. The White House staff has some dialogues with the president and comes up with policy initiatives. And then, when policy was essentially cooked or well along, the cabinet secretaries were brought in to get them bought in and to get them involved in the implementation program."

Things were usually different on the national security side, however, where Hadley noted a more "principle-centric process" in which "we developed the policy with the national security principals, the secretary of state, defense, you know, the chairman of the Joint Chiefs, intelligence folks, and then, collectively, we brought our recommendations and choices to the president." In an aside, he observed that in his view, the Obama administration often adopted the traditional White House–driven domestic policy approach for use on a wide range of foreign policy and national security issues.

Hadley also underscored that the approach he described was the one Bush wanted. Especially in the second term, the president realized, with what Hadley characterizes in a complimentary way as a "businessman's" perspective, that he wanted to empower his cabinet members.

Hadley both advocated and implemented changes to a Bush NSC process that was not firing on all cylinders. In fact, he too says that he had gone to Bush and Card and argued for the complete replacement of the national security team because of the dysfunction during the first term. "There was clearly tension between State and Defense. There was clearly a kind of back door in the policy process that was being taken advantage of by key players. There were clearly policy decisions that were mistakes," he recalls. His suggestion was also brushed off at first, and so when he began as national security advisor in 2004 he still had to contend with prospective conflicts of the kinds that had dogged the first term. He saw two ways of dealing with this, both of which were forms of very deft, bureaucratic jiu-jitsu. Rather than trying to muscle through an outcome based on the force of his own personality, Hadley would try to use the clout of others—the president or other cabinet secretaries—to produce a better outcome.

He illustrates these approaches with vignettes. "The president used to have an NSC meeting, think about it overnight, and come in the next morning at 7:10 and say, 'Hadley, I just concluded X, go call Gates' [Bob Gates, who replaced Donald Rumsfeld as secretary of defense in 2006]. . . . And I would say, 'no, no, Mr. President. You've got a phone right on your desk that has a button on it that says 'SecDef.' You push that button and Bob Gates will be there, trust me. And he's in the chain of command that goes from you to the military, and I'm not." Says Hadley, "I really felt that was important as was encouraging regular weekly meetings with the key cabinet secretaries, the president, the vice president, and [new] chief of staff Josh Bolten. So he could communicate his views directly and hear from them directly."

Hadley describes a second situation that offers an excellent insight into his management philosophy and a useful model for future national security advisors who want to be able to serve the president and guide the process but also maintain the trust and support of other senior members of the president's national security team: "assume you arrive at the office at 5:15 a.m. You look at the newspapers. And there's a story based on a leak that comes from the State Department. There's two ways you can handle that. You can go to the president at 7:10 in the morning and say, 'Mr. President, I'm sure you saw the article in the *Post*. It's a leak from the State Department. I've called Condi to say she's got to get a hold on that building. So don't worry about it, I'll get it fixed.' That's always a temptation for the national security advisor because you always want to please the teacher, the boss. The alternative, which is my recommended option, is you call up Condi at 5:30 a.m., when she's on her Stairmaster. And you say, 'Condi, have you looked at the paper yet? There's a front page leak from your building. Take a look at it and call me back.' And she calls back fifteen minutes later and says, 'I've read it. Here's the problem. Here's what I'm going to do about it.' And I would say, 'Great. Why don't you call the president at 7:00, and as soon as he gets into the office, bring it to his attention, tell him how it happened and what you're going to do about it.' She's no fool. She knows she's got to stay close to him. She does it. You walk in at 7:10. The president's on the phone. With his hand over the receiver he says, 'It's Condi. She's talking about that leak in the *Post*.' That's making the system work in national security advisor terms that does not undermine the relationship between the cabinet secretary and the president and makes everyone look good at the same time."

As an aside, the best US national security advisors approached the job with well-developed, well-thought-out management strategies such as this one. Although each was different, they had the common characteristic of seeking to empower staff and, typically, to do so while resisting the temptation, despite their proximity to the president, of upstaging their peers in the process. Brent Scowcroft was a master of this, in part because he entered office during the administration of George H. W. Bush having done the job once before and having confidence in his close relationship with the president. This allowed him to sit with James Baker, the secretary of state, in advance and delineate clearly defined roles. Baker would be the spokesperson for the administration and Scowcroft would defer to him in that respect, but requiring that Baker, who also had an exceptionally close relationship with the president, would work within and not around the national security process. Zbigniew Brzezinski, who had a notably rougher relationship with Secretary of State Cyrus Vance, nonetheless employed several carefully conceived and effective management strategies as well. For example, he would host a weekly meeting of his senior staff, then consisting of about forty people (a little more than a tenth of what the NSC staff would grow to be during the Obama years), at which he would recount his personal exchanges with President Carter because "I knew that gave everyone present a certain kind of currency within Washington, a sense of being valued and having access." He also would receive from each senior staffer a daily summary of their accomplishments and questions for him. He had these assembled in a binder that he would read in the car on the way home from the White House. He would annotate the one-pagers and return them with comments and questions to the staffers. In this way he was able to remain connected with the entire team and manage its activities. But, understanding the sensitivities of Washington insiders who are constantly wondering what their colleagues are up to, he would take the unannotated version of the daily reports and put them in a binder that was available to all on his secretary's desk in the outer office of his suite in the West Wing of the White House. In this way, he created complete transparency and minimized backbiting. During the Clinton years, National Security Advisor Sandy Berger hosted weekly ABC meetings (Albright, Berger, and Cohen) to ensure smooth relations between the secretary of state, himself, and the secretary of defense. Later, Tom Donilon would act similarly during the Obama years.

Hadley describes his first meeting with the national security press as national security advisor. "They were very nice. But the implicit question was, 'If Condi, a powerful personality, the closest person to the president, couldn't knock heads between Colin and Rumsfeld and Cheney, how can a wimp like you do it?'"

"How," he continued, "are you going to deal with these 700-pound gorillas? How are you going to knock heads? My answer was, 'I have no intention of trying.' When 700-pound gorillas disagree, I'm going to walk down the hall about forty feet to the 1,200-pound gorilla who is the best strategist in the administration. And he's going to hear the arguments and he's going to make the decisions. And because all my colleagues are professionals, if I give them the hearing, they will salute whatever the position of the president is."

Hadley added that to help ensure this process he would also meet with the core national security principals, much as many of his predecessors had done, including the secretary of state, secretary of defense, vice president, director of national intelligence, director of central intelligence, and key generals, and they would sit together at the table in the national security advisors office from 4 to 6 or 6:30 p.m. if necessary and "we would discuss all the difficult operational issues. And people could be candid because there was no staff there and there were no risks of leaks."

And he added, with the kind of eye for detail that is essential to anyone who understands that at the end of the day the process is all about the people in it, "I would serve them soft drinks and chile con queso and tortilla chips because you know, people get a little cranky and hungry in the afternoon."

Try as We Might, We Can't Choose Our Allies, Either

So with a president in Washington reshuffling his team and his priorities, following an election in the country on which his legacy would almost certainly turn, 2005 was a year in which transitions could compound the already difficult situation on the ground in Iraq. After the elections, interim prime minister Ayad Allawi lost credibility, and though Negroponte and Casey reportedly liked working with him, the United States began to pressure him to cede authority. On April 7, Ibrahim al-Jaafari succeeded him. Jaafari was a troubling choice to some in the embassy in Baghdad, viewed as being too close to Iran and too insensitive or deliberately inattentive to the growing costs and risks associated with sectarianism.

According to Casey, relations with the Iraqi government deteriorated during this period, with the Americans losing ground with "many ministries." Nonetheless, Casey did not deviate from his strategy of attempting to transfer responsibility to the Iraqis. In late June 2005, another personnel shift was announced atop the US civilian apparatus in Baghdad that had its roots in Washington. Earlier in the year, Negroponte had been named the United States' first director of national intelligence (DNI) as part of a sweeping restructuring of the intelligence community. The creation of the DNI post had come in the wake of post-9/11 concerns about the lack of communications among the fragmented elements of the US intelligence community (IC). The new post would ostensibly be the master coordinator and would wield that influence through overseeing the budget process for the intelligence community. In the words of a senior Bush advisor, "The purpose of creating the DNI was to separate the interagency intelligence responsibilities (e.g., to knit the intel community together—the Director of Central Intelligence function) from running the CIA (e.g., the Director of the Central Intelligence Agency function) since when the two were merged, the DCIs had subsequently focused on running the CIA and largely ignored their responsibilities for integrating the intelligence community."

In the near decade since the establishment of the new post, many, including three former occupants of the job with whom I have spoken, have come to see its creation in large degree as an error. The mandate it had was essentially the reiteration of the coordinating role originally conceived for the director of central intelligence in the National Security Act of 1947. It also sought to promote coordination and better communication essentially by adding another layer of bureaucracy that ultimately would include more than 2,000 people. In both respects, it was a classic Washington response to a problem: say it again, only louder and with more bureaucrats. Nor did the creation of the DNI fully resolve the tensions between the CIA, the FBI, the NSA, the Defense Intelligence Agency, and other elements of the IC. It did not by any measure bring intelligence budgets into better focus or contain them any better, nor did it ultimately result in the creation of an unchallenged top dog in the intelligence process. Almost immediately, CIA directors demanded direct access to the president if they were to take the job, and old habits and bureaucratic infighting gradually restored the CIA post to at least the equal of the DNI in most policy circles. In other words, a complicated situation was just made more complicated.

At its inception though, Negroponte was a widely embraced choice in the job and is considered to have had a successful tenure in it because he helped establish the role, oversaw the first efforts at budget consolidation, and most important, focused heavily and effectively on modernizing the tech side of the IC.

Negroponte's replacement as ambassador in Baghdad was Zalmay Khalilzad, a garrulous, Afghan-born former national security council senior director for Southwest Asia, Near East, and North African affairs who was serving as the US ambassador to Afghanistan at the time he was asked to go to Iraq. His language skills, knowledge of the region, close connections with the president and the key players on the new national security team, as well as his affability, resulted in his quick acceptance in the role at a time when immediate traction was much needed. He arrived in Baghdad on July 24, 2005.

Khalilzad revealed that he was originally supposed to go into Iraq as part of a two-person civilian team to run the place but asserts that Bremer persuaded the president that that plan would be unworkable, and that Bremer should go alone. As a result the president had asked Khalilzad to go to Afghanistan as ambassador.

"The level of violence in Iraq and the losses suffered [were] having a political impact," observed Khalilzad, who later went on to become US ambassador to the United Nations. "There was a belief that kept becoming more pronounced that the president and maybe the country was losing confidence in whether our strategy was working because the level of violence was so high. I think it was therefore natural to take a look at what we were doing and what was and wasn't working. From the questions the president started to ask General Casey, you could tell he was starting to look for new answers and approaches. . . . My task was therefore initially to get political agreements among the various ethnic and sectarian communities in Iraq, because we had diagnosed the country to be increasingly sectarian. And that's what we worked on initially."

Casey welcomed Khalilzad to Baghdad with a briefing called "Securing Strategic Success" that underscored Casey's continued belief that things were at least on a track that could ultimately result in an Iraqi assumption of responsibility for Iraqi security and therefore open the door to a substantial reduction of US troop levels. That said, following in the tradition of the Negroponte-Casey red-cell process, the new leadership produced a report in August 2005 contending that, to achieve the security goals the United States had set, more US troops, not fewer, would be needed. The approach they suggested involved securing areas with more intensive application of force, stabilizing them, and then moving on to the next areas of concerns. These were among the first stirrings of the counterinsurgency (COIN) strategy. Given Casey's clear predispositions against bringing in additional troops, according to the excellent reporting of Michael Gordon and Bernard Trainor in *The Endgame: The Inside Story of the Struggle for Iraq,* the team argued for targeting "specific areas to effect a mini-surge."

The report contradicted a different red-team assessment from nine months earlier and, given Casey's opposition and Khalilzad's predisposition to focus on political healing, did not gain traction. Policy would not change in a fundamental way for a further eighteen months. Casey campaigned in the White House and in Congress to make the case that the mission was "realistic and achievable," but that goals had yet to be met and that it was reasonable to expect that the United States would be in Iraq for some time to come. He was supported by senior officials in the Pentagon who in the first instance were guided by assessments that were often filtered through Casey's perspective. Second, they were predisposed (as most of us might also be) to believe in themselves and the plans they had approved, often for longer than facts on the ground warranted. (Red teams are important for providing assessments from people with less of a stake in a given plan than the authors and managers of that plan.)

Meanwhile, at the State Department, Condoleezza Rice asked her counselor Philip Zelikow, a brilliant and trusted advisor, to undertake his own assessment of the situation. In contrast to the military's take, he felt that the insurgency was growing and adapting, and that US forces were overstretched. He was concerned that the situation was beginning to look much like Vietnam, and started to look for approaches that had worked there. He came up with an idea that echoes the mini-surge approach, which in military parlance would be characterized as "clear and hold." This approach, with the added recommendation that the United States assist Iraqis in building infrastructure and capacity in addition to holding cleared territory, became the centerpiece of an approach Rice argued for in Congress on October 19, 2005.

Not surprisingly, Rumsfeld was not happy to see Rice operating outside State's diplomatic domain. He was also concerned that such an approach would lead to the deployment of more US troops; getting out would become harder to do. Meanwhile, the Iraqis ratified their constitution in October, but again, the process largely bypassed the Sunnis, exacerbating the sectarian problems that Zelikow and others had identified.

Rumsfeld defended Casey's viewpoint with the president and within the NSC and arranged for Casey to brief Hadley. Rumsfeld's memoirs describe an NSC meeting on November 2, 2005, to "discuss the security strategy for the [Iraqi] election and the perennial issue of U.S. troop levels." Bush and others present reportedly asked whether troops in addition to the 160,000 already in the country should be added in preparation for the upcoming elections in mid-December. Casey argued that "none of his commanders" needed additional forces.

Rumsfeld wrote of Casey and his team, "they knew well that having too few troops could result in violence that might have been deterred. But like them I was aware that if we added more troops at the wrong time and in the wrong places, we could weaken Iraqi leadership and stunt the development of a sovereign nation still in its formative stages." Looking back at this debate from the perspective of 2014, with Iraq wracked by unrest again, it might well be possible to argue, in fact, that this view was correct—that the surge of troops only temporarily stabilized the situation in that country and may have created a false perception that stability was taking root.

One of the commanders cited by Casey Air Force general Norton "Norty" Schwartz, then commander of the US Transportation Command and later Air Force chief of staff, said afterward, "I think it was clear—and it should have been clear sooner—that the clear-and-hold strategy was not going to produce the outcome we needed. And so, as a result, the "clear, hold, build" thing evolved. And I would argue that it too was largely unsuccessful, because in my view, remaking societies is a complicated and demanding endeavor which ultimately required an even greater commitment."

Intelligence reports in December 2005 suggested one unexpected way the situation was darkening: coalition detention facilities were effectively becoming recruiting schools for the opposition, as insurgents managed to make connections within the concentrations of detainees. Rather than weakening the insurgency, the facilities were, perversely, strengthening it.

Further, the December 15 parliamentary elections were again having a divisive effect, within an electoral framework that played to the strengths of established Shiite groups and put moderates and Sunnis at a disadvantage. As Gordon and Trainor wrote:

> to level the playing field, Tom Warrick, a State Department official and Arabist, advocated an overt program of financial and material

assistance to Iraq's emerging political groups. The funds would be channeled to those parties that adhered to democratic principles. Despite years of lobbying for the proposal, the idea was never carried out. Resistance on the part of some State Department and even White House officials to intervening in Iraq's electoral process stymied the effort, an inhibition that was not shared by Iran or Iraq's other neighbors.

Concerned about the threat that Iran posed, America had once embraced Saddam Hussein, even going so far as to provide him with the intelligence that enabled him to launch nerve gas attacks against Iran during the 1980s. Leaving Saddam in place at the end of the First Gulf War was in part based on a fear of creating a void that the Iranians could exploit should he be removed. But in the wake of 9/11, the strategy shifted. Removing Saddam became an end in itself. Chalabi and others argued that only in the wake of Saddam's removal could Iraq become a truly dependable American ally, dulling the administration to the risks of what would ultimately happen. Gradually, the United States ended up supporting political and military policies that not only made it highly unlikely that any Iraqi government would ever truly be a supportive American ally, but also strengthened Iran. As a result, the role of Iraq as a counterbalance to the would-be hegemonic power in Tehran was lost, and Iran's position was correspondingly strengthened.

The December 15 elections went off without much violence and with a turnout of 70 percent, largely because Khalilzad and Casey had struck a deal with Sunnis to mark the election period with an American cease-fire in exchange for a similar reduction in attacks by Sunni insurgents. Terrorist violence fell to a third of the level experienced at the beginning of the year, underscoring the direct conduit between the Sunni political leadership and the insurgents that they had once argued were beyond their control. Negroponte notes, "some people may criticize Casey for the way he dealt with sectarian violence but I can tell you that one thing he did—and I questioned its wisdom at the time—was that he decided to ban any vehicular movements in all of Iraq for three days. And it turned out to be really a decisive device that kept lots of improvised explosive devices from going off."

The brief quiet was shattered in a momentous way two months later, when in the early hours of February 22, 2006, one of the holiest Shiite mosques in Iraq, the Al-Askari Mosque in Samarra was destroyed by a bomb. The site, noted for its golden dome, was the holy burial site of two of the twelve imams considered by Shiites to be the heirs to Mohammed's spiritual legacy. It was a totemic symbol, arguably as important to the Shiites of Iraq as the twin towers had been to Americans, but had been inexplicably left unguarded by the Americans. And its destruction was seen as an elevation in the country's violence to something nearing open civil war between the Sunnis believed responsible for the attack and the Shiites.

Khalilzad and Casey reached out to President Jaafari to assist with containing retaliatory attacks, but Jaafari, who in the words of Casey viewed the attack "as a direct attack on Iraq's Shia population," was slow to move. When US intelligence reported that the attack was the work of Zarqawi and al-Qaeda, they realized that it had been a game changer, a deliberate attempt to provoke the kind of escalation of hostilities that could undo all the progress America had made to this point. (As noted earlier, Sunni-Shia tensions would continue to roil the region, spreading into Syria and the Gulf and underscoring that America's intervention in Iraq was roughly akin to dancing atop an earthquake: we were there, we were active. But bigger forces were at work over which we had effectively no control—a rift that dated back some 1400 years to a succession dispute in the year 632 after the death of the Prophet Mohammed. In retrospect, the notion that the brief intervention of the United States would be able to manage, sidestep, or resolve that tension is one of the most colossal examples of foreign-policy hubris in modern memory.)

One senior NSC official from the time said to me, "that attack was a watershed in our thinking at the White House, too. Some of us . . . at a higher level than before . . . began to wonder whether Casey's strategy was simply out of touch, whether he was in denial and as a consequence were we getting the right kind of leadership on the ground and intelligence from that leadership back in Washington." The criticism is echoed by Gordon and Trainor: "even in the middle of the [Samarra] crisis, however, Casey was reluctant to abandon the central tenet of his strategy: shifting responsibility to the nascent Iraqi forces."

Casey's reluctance to switch strategies, which reflected that of his boss at the Pentagon, Rumsfeld, was linked to their core belief that the presence of American forces was an irritant in Iraqi society—that it was not so much an antidote to attacks as it was a potential trigger for those attacks. True or not, their approach was not working. On March 21, 2006, the CIA issued a report asserting that al-Qaeda was not being controlled by US forces but to the contrary was "continuing to grow" and was "undermining security and preventing legitimate political and economic development." Paradoxically, despite such reports—and Zelikow had submitted another to Rice with a similarly unsettling tone—another dimension of the Casey strategy that is open to question in retrospect was the insistence on capping the Iraqi military and police forces at 325,000, a number that numerous subsequent critics have suggested was too small. But just as the Americans saw their own troops as a potential irritant, they saw too big an Iraqi force as both risky and costly. The result was a tactical approach more geared to managing force levels than adequately addressing the underlying security problems throughout the country.

In April 2006, Iraq got its first "permanent" prime minister, Nouri al-Maliki, a Shiite politician who had opposed Saddam Hussein. Khalilzad had, in fact, encouraged Maliki to consider taking the post. Bush was pleased with the selection and contacted him immediately after the news was official. "Congratulations, Mr. Prime Minister," he said. "I want you to know the United States is fully committed to democracy in Iraq. We will work together to defeat the terrorists and support the Iraqi people. Lead with confidence." Both men have subsequently reported that they wanted a close relationship and the fact is that they ultimately developed one that was important to at least temporarily stabilizing Iraq. In fact, the more confident second-term American president that Joe Nye had described to Steve Hadley undertook to be more deeply involved with the week-to-week decisions being made by Maliki and the American team in Iraq. Bush connected to them with regular video conferences in which, according to Khalilzad, "he displayed a remarkable mastery of details and a knowledge of the critical issues. This was clearly a man who had been schooled in Iraq by the experience of the prior three years." In Bush's words, he wanted not to pressure Maliki but to gain "his trust" so that he could "help him make the tough decisions." Maliki subsequently proved to be a very challenging partner at times, but not only has he endured much longer than his predecessors, he is also seen by his American interlocutors as having been much more capable than Allawi or Jaafari.

This last point underscores a vital truth, one that may seem obvious but is often overlooked: when evaluating the performance of US national security policymakers, it is important to remember that they are constrained by the quality of their overseas partners and the choices they make. National security policy is about collaborations—often with counterparts who seek to undermine or undo American policy choices, or with those who are

simply unwilling or incapable to help. As the Bush personnel team changed
for the better in the second term, it was in part due to gains, sometimes
just incremental, made among this group of international partners. Maliki illustrates this point particularly well because, while he was able to
offer an incremental improvement over his immediate predecessors, his
own substantial flaws as a leader would eventually make him so unreliable
and counterproductive a counterpart for President Obama that the United
States would later make Maliki's renunciation of power a condition for
providing aid to a civil-unrest ravaged Iraq. Enduring the sectarian turmoil tearing through the country and pressure from the US and others
to step aside, Maliki resigned on August 14, 2014.

"A Low Point"

As the situation in Iraq deteriorated, Congress mandated the creation of
a commission chaired by former secretary of state James Baker and Congressman Lee Hamilton, one of the most universally respected foreign-
policy leaders on Capitol Hill, to recommend a way forward. This was
"an uncomfortable moment" according to one top Bush White House
aide. Unsurprisingly, it produced a lot of the dirty laundry that insiders
had been aware of for several years.

On May 19, 2006, Colin Powell appeared before the committee, which
came to be known as the Iraq Study Group, and essentially blasted the
administration he had been part of. He criticized the decision to go into
the country with too few troops, saying he had recommended to General Tommy Franks, who oversaw the operation, that more be involved
but was rebuffed. He reiterated the familiar State Department critique
of the administration's overreliance on Ahmed Chalabi and his promises to lead 10,000 men into battle to support the administration's goals.
In the end, said one top State Department official, it "was just Chalabi and 600 thugs." State Department insiders also assert that Powell
"wasn't told about the decision to disband the army until it happened."
He criticized his former colleagues' lack of understanding about the nature of being an occupying force; the selection of General Jay Garner to
lead the occupation, given his background as an air defense officer; and
Bremer for blocking Khalilzad from serving with him, when Khalilzad
could have been a useful conduit to the Iraqi political elites that Bremer
struggled with. Powell also argued that Bremer and Sanchez often were
at cross-purposes because the chain of command was not clear. When

asked directly by study group member Robert Gates, former CIA director and subsequently secretary of defense, whether the Bush team knew what it was doing, Powell responded, "No. The NSC process did not work."

According to one of Condoleezza Rice's closest aides, "things came to a crisis with respect to Iraq with the Baker-Hamilton Commission. . . . There were so many fundamental breakdowns of trust in the government, in the media in the wake of what had happened in Iraq that it was just a real low point. And I remember going to Condi . . . and saying, 'Look, people just want some hope. They want to know that we have a way out of this and that we have a plan.'"

Matters were not helped by a joint trip to Iraq by Rice and Rumsfeld, which Bush had urged to demonstrate team unity. Rice wrote that she "doubted it would stem the tide of 'Don hates Condi' and 'Condi hates Don' stories that had become standard fare in Washington."

While Rice was "skeptical" of the idea of the trip, Rumsfeld was in her view "downright hostile to the idea." Once they arrived, things went from bad to worse. Rice wrote of the trip in her memoir, *No Higher Honor*:

> Every public appearance with Don was a disaster, though. It started when we held our first press availability. During a roundtable with members of both the Pentagon and State Department press corps, Janine Zacharia of Bloomberg asked whether our "secret" arrival said anything about the security situation. Well, of course it did, and what it said was not good about conditions on the ground. But one learns just to answer and not cause a scene. Don shot back, "I guess I don't think it says anything about it. . . . I just don't see anything to your question." I tried to smooth things over by saying something about improvements in Iraqi security forces and then took the next question. In fact, I took several of the next questions while Don doodled conspicuously on a piece of paper. . . . Our performance had solidified the narrative of discord between us, and there wasn't much to do about it.

After her return, Rice asked Zelikow and Jim Jeffrey, her special advisor on Iraq, to assess the chances for strategic success in Iraq. She confirms that by that time—the summer of 2006—the White House had begun to question more seriously whether the policy was on the right track. She encouraged her aides to produce a "no-holds-barred assessment" that questioned assumptions and developed new options. Their response listed three options: "full counterinsurgency," which could require more forces; "selective counterinsurgency," which was really a variant on clear-hold-and-build; and "keep-the-lid on," which was essentially avoiding deterioration but not actively seeking to improve the situation. Not surprisingly, given the way government recommendations tend to work, the aides preferred the middle option.*

Frustrated with what she saw and with the Defense Department's resistance to changing its approach, Rice ultimately conveyed her view in an informal, unvarnished way to the president. "Mr. President," she said, with the confidence of a close aide who had been at his side since his presidential campaign began eight years earlier, "what we're doing is not working—really not working. It's failing." That she felt it was necessary to underscore this in an aside does suggest a flaw in the day-to-day policy process that should have been objectively delivering to the president an unvarnished picture of what was happening in Iraq.

There was, it should be noted, "one bright spot" in 2006. McChrystal and his JSOC (Joint Special Operations Command) troops found and killed Zarqawi. It is telling that when Casey called Rumsfeld with the news, the SecDef was in his own words "uneasy" because he "had been getting reports from Iraq and few of them had been good. Jesus Christ, I was saying to myself, 'What else could have gone wrong in that place?'" But Zarqawi's death contained a darker message that was not entirely appreciated by those in the chain of command. US officials—often egged on by personality-obsessed media—tend to overpersonalize our enemies. This sometimes works, as in national movements in which one leader has built institutions to work only with him at the center. But in decentralized and loosely affiliated organizations such as al-Qaeda, the deaths of top officials do not always reduce the threat. President Obama would later discover that the death of Osama bin Laden was followed by the greatest expansion in the numbers of extremists within al-Qaeda-affiliated groups ever. Even though Zarqawi was gone, the insurgency in Iraq kept growing.

Regarding our tendency to overpersonalize some national security threats, former Obama undersecretary of state Robert Hormats

---

*Henry Kissinger once jokingly told me that his preferred method with Richard Nixon was to offer three options: global thermonuclear war, complete capitulation, or, as the third choice, the approach he wanted the president to take.

insightfully observed that "there is a tendency in presenting foreign policy and national security issues to the public to demonize adversaries. In the case of Bin Laden and Zarqawi, appropriately so, because they were evil in all respects. But the risk is that after they are killed or demonized we often feel a sense of relief and accomplishment that reduces our attentions to the underlying forces that supported them. And even if government policies don't lose focus, public attention often does."

Throughout the summer of 2006, the drumbeat for new approaches kept coming from other sources as well. At Camp David on June 12, Bush met with top aides plus outside experts, including Robert Kaplan, a journalist and influential commentator; Michael Vickers, a former CIA operative; Eliot Cohen, a professor at the Johns Hopkins School of Advanced International Studies; and Fred Kagan of the American Enterprise Institute, who would later team up with General Jack Keane to become perhaps the most influential external advocates of "the surge." The theme—which Cheney later wrote he was open to—was again whether more troops and different approaches might better support successful counterinsurgency efforts. Bush went straight from the meeting to Iraq where he said to Maliki, "I've come to not only look you in the eye, I've also come to tell you that when America gives its word, it will keep its word."

Upon his return, Bush was asked in a press conference about troop levels. He said, "troop levels will be decided upon by General Casey. He will make the recommendations in consultation with an Iraqi government. But whatever decision General Casey makes, the message is going to be 'we'll stand with you.'" But behind the scenes, the president had his doubts about Casey's publicly reiterated message of not needing additional troops, much less Casey's suggestion to the president that it might actually be possible by year's end to reduce troop levels. Casey's position seemed disconcertingly disconnected from the reality of the reports the president was getting. Soon, even Casey realized that the retaliatory attacks following the death of Zarqawi ruled out further consideration of any troop reduction scheme.

Hadley quietly began the NSC's own policy review, careful to keep it secret lest its mere existence belie the public statements of Bush and Casey that everything was under control or improving. Given Hadley's typical method of managing the policy process, he preferred that, in the end, any changes in approach emanate from Casey in Baghdad. He sent a long list of questions to all the principal players, including Rumsfeld,

Casey, and Khalilzad. The latter two agreed to respond to them in detail even though they felt, according to Bob Woodward's reporting, that it was "demeaning."

On Hadley's staff was Meghan O'Sullivan, a former aide to Bremer in Iraq. O'Sullivan had been a supporter of the status quo strategy but now had gradually come to the conclusion that it was "indefensible." She felt only the United States had the capacity to control the sectarian violence, that the Iraqis weren't there yet, and that if there was no new US approach, violence would only intensify. After the review, she advanced "The Way Forward: Four Organizing Constructs," a memo outlining options. The choices were to "adjust at the margins," which meant do little differently; "target our efforts," which meant focusing on al-Qaeda while letting the Iraqis handle sectarian issues; "double down," which meant a significant commitment of more US resources; or to "bet on Maliki," which meant providing the Iraqis with more resources and hoping they could address the evolving problem better as a consequence.

O'Sullivan's report was one of a flurry of other such efforts that came during mid- to late 2006. Earlier, there had been an influential trip report written by another NSC staffer, Brett McGurk, who returned from Iraq concluding that "General Casey still has no serious plan for stabilizing the capital" and urging a "radical course correction." In late August, another NSC staffer, Bill Luti, produced a series of recommendations entitled "Changing the Dynamics in Iraq: Surge and Fight, Create Breathing Space and Then Accelerate the Transition." He, too, concluded Casey was floundering and that there were growing costs at home and in Iraq. A "Council of Colonels" that convened at the Department of Defense was also critical of the strategic drift of their bosses on the Joint Chiefs and recommended six possible options for proceeding in Iraq, all of which addressed the drift. They concluded that "properly characterizing the war was critical" and that to achieve victory in Iraq, American policymakers and military leaders had to "overcome" the "short-war" mentality they currently embraced. It was a clear blow to the quick-in, quick-out philosophy of Rumsfeld.

Hadley himself wrote a memo to Bush after an October trip that echoed many of these concerns. Bush recalled, "Steve's assessment was that Maliki was 'either ignorant of what [was] going on, misrepresenting his intentions, or that his capabilities [were] not yet sufficient to turn his good intentions into action.'" By late November 2006, Bush was communicating to Maliki that he would be willing to commit "tens of thousands of additional troops" if Maliki would give the assurances he needed that he would cooperate and support US efforts. Bush reported in his memoirs that "on every point, Maliki gave me his word that he would follow through."

Again, it is worth emphasizing that Bush was following through on his promise to remain deeply engaged with Maliki, communicating with him with a frequency that aides considered "a clear sign of his commitment." Whatever the merits of the approaches, it is an interesting contrast with the more hands-off approach to interacting with foreign partners that would distinguish the administration of Bush's successor in the White House. Presidents should probably adjust their approaches to the situation and their own personalities. That said, when Bush became more directly involved, he helped lead the policy changes that were needed in Iraq, if only to reverse the deterioration that had made this period in 2006 "the worst" of his presidency.

Maliki was not helping matters, however, behind the scenes. His government institutions that were supposed to be preventing sectarian violence were actually contributing to it. The Iraq National Police conducted mass kidnappings and arrests of Sunni Arabs, often on trumped up charges. Many of these people disappeared, often never to be seen or heard from again. And earlier in the summer, when Casey undertook a new operation—called Together Forward—to demonstrate the viability of giving the Iraqis ever greater responsibility for their security, it instead became evident that the Iraqis were not up to the challenges they faced.

Khalilzad echoed Casey's reluctance to add troops. In mid-November, he wrote a memo asserting that "sending more U.S. forces is not a long-term solution. Additional troops can impact the areas where they are deployed, though the violence can simply shift to another area. Iraqis securing Iraqis is the enduring solution. As we draw down, our forces should focus on specialized roles, such as striking al-Qaeda, disrupting external interference, and reinforcing and monitoring Iraqi forces." On November 22, Casey outlined an almost identical view during an NSC meeting he joined by teleconference. (From the perspective of the process of the NSC, it is worth noting that the expanding use of teleconferencing has also resulted in a broader dialogue and the ability to bring current crises and situations of interest directly to the White House, connecting actors on the ground in a way that adds an important element to policy deliberations.)

In my conversations with Khalilzad, he acknowledged, "the surge was certainly not our idea, neither Casey's nor mine. But I was not opposed to it. I argued that it shouldn't be seen as the thing that was or would be decisive. I thought that a political deal between the different communities . . . would be more important. But we did not oppose it." Khalilzad knew that the political process would take time and that the additional security provided by the surge would be useful.

"A Stunning and Devastating Realization"

The old axiom that "success has many fathers, but failure is an orphan" is no better illustrated than in comparing the two decisions to disband Iraq's army and to initiate the Iraq "surge." In the former case, universally seen as a catastrophic misstep, no one is willing to be associated with the decision, or even with the processes that contributed to the decision. But in the latter, largely considered as at least a temporary success, many have sought and even deserved credit for arguing that a switch in strategy was called for.

Such a disparity is also a comment, of course, on the policy processes involved. In the one case, the processes completely broke down, producing a bad outcome that all involved disavow. In the other case, the processes produced not one but two good outcomes. The lesser of these is arguably the surge itself. More significant is that—despite inertia, internal opposition, and the possibility that a course change would make them look weak—the president and his team could come to a conclusion that a change in course was necessary. Sometimes the best and toughest policy choice is to admit when you have a made a mistake. Indeed, among the most severe criticisms that can be offered of the Bush NSC process with regard to Iraq strategy is that it took them so long to realize their errors. (And some—a minority now—are to this day unwilling to admit that the first of those errors was going into Iraq in the first place.)

But if the surge had many fathers, there is a widespread sense that among the most influential of these was General Jack Keane, former army vice chief of staff. As it became clearer that Casey's approach was failing, Keane became more vocal about the need for a change. In September 2006 he went to see Rumsfeld. Reports of the meeting differ.

Rumsfeld, again with the benefit of hindsight and seeking to burnish his damaged reputation, wrote that Keane's views "largely dovetailed" with his own. Woodward offered an alternative view in which Keane was frank with Rumsfeld and Rumsfeld was aghast by Keane's assessment that "we're edging toward strategic failure."

Echoing critiques of Vietnam, Keane argued that "using conventional tactics against an unconventional enemy" was a formula for disaster. He also attacked the trap created by the "short war strategy" in which, ideally, US forces would hand over responsibility to the Iraqis as soon as possible, but were unable do so until the Americans had assumed the role of "protecting the population," which they had not done. Keane asserted that the answer was to increase the number of troops involved in Iraq and to achieve "the permanent isolation of the insurgent from the population." Although history has shown this to be an impossible goal, substitute the idea of isolating the population from the insurgents long enough to stabilize the situation and give the local government a chance to assume responsibility and you have roughly the formula that was pursued. As it turned out in both Vietnam and Iraq, insurgents seldom face the constraints of the "short war" strategy; they are there for the long-haul, and that gives them their greatest advantage: patience.

Keane's final point was directed at Casey. "We have to have someone in charge," Woodward reports him as telling Rumsfeld, "who knows what he's doing." Keane had someone in mind, his protégé and an expert in counterinsurgency strategy, General David Petraeus, a man who had already established himself as one of the most creative thinkers in the US military. Petraeus had a PhD from Princeton and, perhaps more important, the credential of having helped draft the army's counterinsurgency field manual.

Richard Armitage is one of many to cite Keane's role in helping to tip the scales. "I think the main father [of the surge] is probably Jack Keane. He takes and deserves the most credit for it. I personally think that it's one of the more valiant decisions of George Bush's presidency because it came at about the nadir of his popularity. . . . It wasn't solely successful and other factors were important to it. But the surge combined with the Sunni Awakening is what brought the level of violence temporarily down." Again, the emphasis here needs to be placed on *temporarily*, given what has transpired in the country since. What is more, the failure to assess sufficiently whether the surge's gains would be lasting or not—along with drawing false analogies between two very different situations—helped contribute to the idea that if the surge "worked" in Iraq it should later work in Afghanistan.

Bob Blackwill, the former ambassador and deputy national security advisor, argues that others, including the team at the NSC that included himself and Meghan O'Sullivan, played a formative role in shaping the policy at the White House. Indeed, Blackwill gives special credit to O'Sullivan, now at Harvard, as one of the most important intellectual forces behind the idea. Those at State tout the influence of Zelikow and Jeffrey's review. Some proponents within the Pentagon cite "the Colonels" as playing a decisive role. And of course it is indisputable that events in Iraq, and the growing discordance between the views of Casey and the results he was achieving, made some sort of course correction inescapable.

All these views were shaped into a policy by an active, multilevel NSC process sought by Bush and orchestrated by Hadley. NSC deputies, led by Hadley deputy J. D. Crouch, shaped policy options that were deliberated upon in an on-going series of NSC principals meetings that regularly involved the president. A "wide range" of outside views and information sources were brought into the mix by Hadley and other senior members of the White House team at the request of Bush to help support his decision-making process. In the iterative nature of this process, according to those who participated in it, the elements of the new strategy were developed. In addition, the president was able to bring "dissenting NSC principals" like Rice around to support the surge. The president and Hadley (working with General Peter Pace) were also actively consulting with the military's leadership throughout to ensure that there was no split between the Commander-in-Chief and the Pentagon that the Congress could have used to derail the initiative.

In the end, of course, the final decision lay with President Bush. He wrote that by the fall he had "decided that a change in strategy was needed." In his memoir he then goes on to describe another factor in the equation for realizing successful change—a factor not known to Keane when he met with Rumsfeld. "To be credible to the American people," the president recalled, a strategic change "would have to be accompanied by changes in personnel. Don Rumsfeld had suggested that I might need fresh eyes on Iraq. He was right. I also needed new commanders. Both George Casey and [CENTCOM commander] John Abizaid had served extended tours and were scheduled to return home. It was time for fresh eyes in their posts as well." Rumsfeld himself records that he had been considering making the move since earlier that summer, if the Democrats were to reclaim control of either house of Congress, as it seemed likely they would do. Further, in the eyes of senior Bush advisors, the surge was not seen as an alternative to the Rumsfeld/Casey strategy of gradually handing security responsibility over to the Iraqis. Rather, it was seen as a means of getting the security situation back in control to buy time "for the political process and strengthening of Iraqi security forces that would be required for the 'stand up/stand down' to work."

Bush told Cheney of the move on Halloween. He said he had decided that he would be making the change and that he had asked Bob Gates to be Rumsfeld's successor. It was a clear sign that Cheney's influence was also ebbing. Twice before, he had discouraged Bush from firing Rumsfeld—after the 2004 elections and once again in 2005. But this time, the president announced the fait accompli and left Cheney to mull the implications. "He knew I'd be opposed," the vice president recollected, "and I suspect he didn't want to hear the arguments he knew I'd make." On the weekend after the election, Cheney telephoned his one-time mentor to tell him that the president was making the change. With Rumsfeld's resignation on November 7, 2006, a major source of the tension and division that haunted the Bush interagency process from its beginnings was gone. So too was the man who was, other than the president, Cheney's most important ally, one who played a key role in making him the most influential vice president in American history. But the writing was on the wall on that front as well. Although Cheney continued to play an oversized role in administration deliberations until the end of the Bush tenure, it was clear that he would not be playing the role he had once had and that the president himself was more confidently reclaiming power that he had once invested in his vice president.

In Gates, Bush also got one of the most distinguished career national security professionals the US government had seen over the course of the preceding three decades. Gates had not only been CIA director, he had also been Brent Scowcroft's deputy national security advisor at the moment when the NSC was widely acknowledged to be at the most high-functioning, well-run period in its history. He was decisive and close to the president's father and was seen as a team player. In almost every way he would be perceived as an antidote to the disruption and abrasiveness of the Rumsfeld era.

Three days after Rumsfeld's resignation (he would not leave office until mid-December), Bush met with his core national security team including Hadley, Rice, Cheney, Rumsfeld, Negroponte, General Peter Pace

(chairman of the Joint Chiefs), and J. D. Crouch. He asked that they
undertake a strategy review. Hadley recognized that the president was
moving toward backing the surge and began to work behind the scenes
to support that decision. He addressed the concern that Maliki would not
fully cooperate, despite his promises to the contrary, and of course the
problem that Casey was still opposed to the idea. Ensuing NSC meetings
moved ever closer to embracing the plan.

On December 11, Hadley arranged for five experts to go to the White
House to meet with the president. The group, which included Jack Keane,
Eliot Cohen, and Fred Kagan, largely argued for a shift to a COIN strategy. During an NSC teleconference the next day, Casey finally recognized
the shifting viewpoint in Washington, calling it "a stunning and devastating realization." Rice also opposed the surge option throughout this
period, primarily because she and Zelikow were concerned that adding
troops without having a really new strategy in place would just lead to
"further frustrations and actually greater risks," in her words.

In the Tank

Two more vitally important personnel transitions had taken place during
2006. On April 14, President Bush replaced his first-term chief of staff,
Andrew Card, with Joshua Bolten, a soft-spoken, motorcycle-riding lawyer. Bolten had been director of the Office of Management and Budget during Bush's first term and had served as deputy chief of staff for
policy immediately prior to that. For much of the 1990s he had been a
senior executive at Goldman Sachs. Card's performance as chief of staff
had been solid. He was respected by his colleagues and seen as a shrewd
judge of Washington politics. He had once been chief lobbyist for the US
auto industry and served Bush's father as secretary of transportation.
But clearly, processes within the White House were not functioning like
a Swiss watch during the first term of Bush the Son's administration, and
the switch to Bolten helped remedy that.

In many respects Bolten was much like Hadley: a brilliant man with
exceptional credentials, quiet, lawyerly, and very happy to remain in the
background. He was assiduously fair in representing the views of com-
peting voices within the administration. White House chiefs of staff can
be very much like deputy presidents, the ultimate gatekeepers atop the
world's largest and most powerful organization. But the best of them
keep their own egos in check and become extensions of the president

himself. Bolten would turn out to be among the best at this very difficult job and helped to engineer a turnaround in very challenging circumstances. He also had one big advantage denied his predecessor: a much
more experienced and confident boss.

Speaking of taking on the job, Bolten said, "I did tell [the president]
on my way in that my instinct about some of his national security process was that it would benefit from some ventilation. . . . The instinct was
borne out in the first few months on the job where I felt that from the
Defense Department and the military that the president was getting views
that reflected a heavier dose of aspiration and a smaller dose of reality
than I thought was really warranted." Bolten went on to gently criticize
his boss for having given too much respect to the military during the first
term: "because of what I knew to be the president's just visceral, strong
support, and appreciation for those in uniform, I found him more reluctant to challenge them than he was their counterparts on the domestic
side where I had a lot more experience with him—where he would challenge the assumptions and plans of everybody that came before him."
Bolten urged some other viewpoints and invited a group of retired senior
military officers to meet with the president and tell him how the facts on
the ground in Iraq looked to them.

The second big personnel change is one that Bolten gets much credit
for. After trying and failing three times, he managed to persuade his
friend, the chief executive of his former employer Goldman Sachs, Henry
"Hank" Paulson to join the administration as secretary of the treasury.
On the day Paulson was appointed, I happened to be in the office of former secretary of commerce Pete Peterson, himself the chairman of one
of Wall Street's leading firms, the Blackstone Group. I asked Peterson
why Paulson would leave one of the best jobs in the world for one of the
toughest and potentially most thankless. He said he thought, based on
conversations with Paulson, that the Goldman CEO was concerned that
the world economy might be heading to a crisis and that someone like
him might be needed to help address it.

Bolten confirmed Paulson's prescience, and that it was indeed concern about an imminent financial crisis that finally persuaded Paulson to
accept the job he had passed on for months. Paulson was also given an
important international portfolio in the Bush administration that contributed to his decision—he was made the lead on China matters. He
had an interest in the world's largest economy, and great contacts and
respect there. In taking much of that portfolio to Treasury, he ensured

that it would get high-level attention even when much of the traditional foreign-policy team was tied up in the Middle East, repairing "broken china" of another sort, as Condoleezza Rice had noted.

Bolten, and especially Paulson, would play central roles in the second great crisis that confronted the Bush presidency, one that by almost any metric exceeded in global impact and severity that of 9/11. Wall Street was struck again, but this time it was by a global financial catastrophe that triggered the worst economic collapse since the Great Depression. In the starkest case study of how the Bush administration had grown during its time in office, the handling of the financial crisis would stand in striking counterpoint to 9/11 as exceptionally well-executed disaster management by the president and his team, during which they would show great personal courage and tenacity. But that is a story for a later chapter in this book.

When it comes to Iraq, Bolten also played an important role ensuring that Hadley and his team had the access they needed to support a president who was pushing increasingly deeply for a solution there. "One of the things that people don't realize about President Bush," said Bolten, "is the degree to which he was a team leader, a kind of a coach. He really felt that as things got dark that it was his job to help pick people's spirits up, to keep them engaged and hopeful. It was not easy to do that when I got there but even when he himself was exhausted and full of doubts, I would see him go into cabinet meetings and literally grab people by the shoulders and help lift them up emotionally." It is a comment I heard regularly from members of Bush's second-term team, including Hadley, Rice, members of the military, and top NSC team members like Jim Jeffrey. Even career civil servants who sometimes were not deep believers in policies followed by the Bush team commented on this human dimension to Bush's leadership.

One example of the degree to which Bush felt compelled to motivate his team and to seek the fresh solutions that Bolten urged him to consider was a trip the president made to the Pentagon on December 13, 2006. On that day, Bush and Cheney went to meet with the Joint Chiefs in "the Tank," the facility at the Pentagon where the top brass meet and plan. The purpose of the visit was to get the military brass fully on board with the surge. The chiefs held a position roughly like that of Casey and many Democrats in Washington. They wanted to see more responsibility shifted to the Iraqis—at least to see if the Iraqis would try to assume more responsibility—before committing more US troops.

Bush was going to the Tank to face down his commanders, but as Bolten recalled, "even when he was telling the Joint Chiefs he was basically rejecting their advice and he was doubling down and going for the surge, he managed to do it in a way that he was communicating to them that I am one of you guys. . . . He had basically made his decision to proceed with the surge," Bolten continued, contradicting slightly Bush's own account that he did not make his final decision regarding the surge until he was actually at the Tank meeting, "He was aware that the Chiefs, by and large, were opposed. So he had me call Rumsfeld and say that the president wanted to meet with them. Rumsfeld had already been replaced, but was finishing up in the job. Rumsfeld was by the way, very respectful, but still a stickler for the chain of command so, you know, any communication with the Chiefs was through him.

"So Rumsfeld said, 'OK, sure, I'll bring them over. When do you want us?' And I said. 'No, he wants to come to the Pentagon.' And he said, 'OK, I'll set it up for my office.' And I said, 'No, he wants to go to the Tank, which is the Chiefs' territory, as you know, and he wants to visit with them there.' And Rumsfeld resisted because, you know, he's the secretary of defense and he's in between the Joint Chiefs and the president. And—although the chairman of the Joint Chiefs supposedly has a direct relationship with the president, I think in Rumsfeld's view, not really."

Bolten continued, "we went to the Tank and the president heard them all out. You know, he went up and down the line. And there was a moment when I think it was the chief of staff of the Army, who said, 'Candidly, Mr. President, we're worried that the kind of thing you are talking about will break the Army.' And the president kind of paused and leaned across the table and said, 'let me tell you what I think will break the Army. I think a defeat like we suffered in Vietnam will break the Army for a generation, just like it did after Vietnam.' But he said that in a way that communicated, 'I hear you. I care about the men and women in the Army. In fact, that's the one reason I want to do this. Because we can't afford to let this great institution be broken again.' And I am sure that some of the chiefs came away . . . thinking 'big mistake.' But I'm sure they also felt like, 'Hey, the president came to us, he listened to us and he cares about our people as much as we do.'"

It was a meeting that was telling in several respects. It underscored not only Bush's approach and touch with the military but also the shift in management styles that marked his second term. It overtly raised the very real specter that stalked the halls of the White House for much of

2006, that Iraq could in fact become the Vietnam of this generation. It underscored Bush's recognition of what was at stake: he was in a hole, his army was with him, and he knew that even if his previous decisions were responsible for the situation, his leadership was now needed to get everyone out.

Rice, who had resisted the surge, revealed again the direct nature of her relationship with the president when, in discussing it with him during a meeting at his ranch in Texas she said, "you're going to do it and it's the right thing to do. . . . I'm there and I'll do everything I can to support it. But Mr. President, this is your last card and it had better work." Bush himself wrote that "the decision had been tough but I was confident that I had made it in the right way. I had gathered the facts and opinions from people inside and outside the administration. I had challenged assumptions and weighed all the options. I knew the surge would be unpopular in the short term. But while many in Washington had given up on the prospect of victory in Iraq, I had not."

It was not the first nor would it be the last time that Bush showed a willingness to choose a course he knew would be politically tough. It should also be observed, however, that for all the talk of "victory," the surge was never conceived to be a long-term operation, in place until democracy or enduring stability took root in Iraq. Despite Keane's descriptions of "permanent" defeat of the insurgents, every element of the execution of the plan revealed a focus on stabilizing Iraq long enough to achieve two simultaneous and related goals: handing over responsibility for Iraqi security to the Iraqis, with the country in a condition that could be managed, and enabling the United States to leave with the appearance that it was doing so in good order—that it had not only got Saddam but that it had fixed what it had broken on the path to doing so.

The surge would ultimately achieve those short-to-medium-term goals. By the end of 2008 it had brought comparatively greater stability to Iraq. But violence never completely abated, the insurgents rebuilt, the government continued to play sectarian games behind the scenes, and the Iraqi security forces, thanks in part to the politicization of their leadership, continued to show serious limits to their capabilities. Further, Bush's successor, Barack Obama, who felt one of his core mandate's as president was to get out of Iraq as completely and swiftly as possible, was unable to achieve the necessary agreements with the Iraqis to keep a residual force of US troops in that country. Critics, including some administration insiders who were based in Iraq at the time, argue the

Obama administration did not try as it might have to secure those agreements. Subsequently, also during the Obama years, when Syria began to descend into chaos in 2011, neither the US nor its allies had the appetite to intervene or actively support moderate opposition forces in that country when that crisis was in its early stages and extremist-fomented unrest in that country soon spilled across the porous borders with neighboring Iraq. Within half a dozen years of the surge, therefore, the threat of insurgents was again strong enough to threaten the cohesiveness of the Iraqi state, the stability of the region, and raise new questions about the need for American involvement.

Petraeus and the Surge

One person for whom the surge was not welcome news was General George Casey. Casey says he was notified around Christmas, not only that the president was adding forces, but that the two-brigade surge to which Casey had previously reluctantly agreed was judged to be "too modest." A few days later Marine Corps general Peter Pace told Casey that "the President had decided on the five-brigade surge and that the President intended to nominate LTG Dave Petraeus as Casey's replacement." Casey has written that he was disappointed in Bush's decision to choose "a different course of action," but that he "immediately set out to make it successful."

In his memoirs, Casey wrote:

> I believe that I should have directly offered the President a broader range of options for achieving our objectives in Iraq. I had discussed different options for improving the security situation with the Secretary of Defense and the Chairman: accelerated transition of security responsibility; local (with in-country forces), small, and large coalition reinforcement; coalition withdrawal on a fixed timeline; and maintaining the status quo. In the end, I only presented the President the course of action we selected—accelerated transition—and I believe I should have offered him a wider range of options to meet his policy needs.

This is a deft Washington insider way of critiquing his superiors even while accepting responsibility for his actions. But one of the mistakes Casey made, it seems, was consulting with the wrong generals. Rather than his bosses among the chiefs, perhaps he should have been talking more to Jack Keane. Cheney has written that Keane "brought an important perspective to the matter of what our forces could bear and how far we could push the chiefs," and that the former Army vice chief's advice "carried a good deal of weight." Keane's opinion, in the eyes of the vice president, "went a long way toward giving [Cheney] and other policymakers a sense that a surge was doable."

Bush announced the surge in a televised address on January 10, 2007. One month later, command of the multinational forces in Iraq (MNF-I) was officially transferred from Casey to Petraeus. Improvement was seen almost immediately. In part, the United States adopted a new measure to determine whether conditions in Iraq were improving or not, and this helpfully showed the impact of the announced US change in policy even five months before additional troops were supposed to arrive (in June).

Bush wrote: "General Petraeus drew my attention to an interesting metric of progress: the number of intelligence tips from Iraqi residents. In the past, Iraqis had feared retribution from insurgents or death squads for cooperating with our forces. But as security improved, the number of our tips grew from about 12,500 in February to almost 25,000 in May. Our troops and intelligence operators used the tips to take insurgents and weapons off the streets. The counterinsurgency strategy was working." This revealed a core element of the surge and any successful COIN strategy. The goal was not just to defeat the insurgents to achieve an American military objective. It was to protect the citizens of Iraq and thus not only to make them safer but recast their relationship with the occupying troops from the United States.

Petraeus is seen by some in Washington as the ultimate political general. Not only does he have exceptional military and academic credentials, but he has done well in the capital's environment of shifting alliances and intrigues. He knows how to work a room, charm reporters, and win the confidence of senior policymakers. He is good on camera and good in the back rooms, offering crisp advice, a diplomatic touch, and toughness when warranted. He is the kind of general who can at the same time instill confidence in political leaders and jealousy among some of his rivals in the military who lack his ability to move easily among the overlapping worlds of politics, policy, diplomacy, and the media. However, any such resentment was ultimately undermined by the effectiveness of Petraeus's actions on the ground in Iraq and in the broader Middle East. Political skills are essential for a good commander, especially one commanding an occupying force and executing COIN strategies in a very complex political environment.

Petraeus came to the job with clear ideas of what he was trying to do. He was perhaps the first commander in Iraq since Tommy Franks to have a plan that everyone recognized and was prepared to support. In part this derived from his work on the counterinsurgency manual. He noted how this resonated even during his confirmation hearings for his new post: "When we did the counterinsurgency manual many people advised me not to put ratios in there on the minimum number of counterinsurgents to citizens. And I argued that we needed to be intellectually honest: we needed to acknowledge that there was a rule of thumb based on experience, that for every 20–25 citizens you need one counterinsurgent to be successful. It's a sort of law of physics. And I said, 'I realize that they're going to hang me on it. Anybody who's really astute is going to put that around my neck in a confirmation hearing.' And darned if then-Senator Hillary Clinton didn't come at me with it. She said, 'General, by your own calculations [given the size of the population], you know you would need X number of troops but you will only have this number.' And I said, 'Yes, thank you, Senator, but remember that contractors—those that are actually replacing or augmenting our soldiers in a variety of tasks—should be included in the equation as well.' In truth, I knew I was going to get hoist on my own COIN manual and I was."

Petraeus had another advantage in that one month after he took office: a new US ambassador to Iraq took office as well. That man, Ryan Crocker was one of the most experienced and respected diplomats in the US Foreign Service. A former ambassador to Lebanon, Kuwait, Syria, and Pakistan, he would later go on to serve President Barack Obama as ambassador to Afghanistan. He was also known by administration insiders as the coauthor of a 2002 assessment done for Colin Powell on the potential perils of a US invasion of Iraq. The memo, cowritten with another distinguished diplomat and later deputy secretary of state, William Burns, predicted that such an intervention could result in precisely the kind of sectarian violence and regional upheaval that in fact did occur. It also noted—as some assessments, notably those of Iraq's WMD capacity, did not—that sanctions and the prior Gulf War had left the Iraqi economy a shadow of its former self, and that rebuilding the country would be a complex, costly task.

Keane was sent to Iraq to conduct an informal assessment just weeks after Petraeus had arrived. He reported back that Petraeus had made progress with Maliki in ways Casey could not; for example, receiving the go-ahead to target Shiite militias. Keane also cautioned patience—a not uncommon first recommendation from policymakers and influencers who get their plans approved. When recommending new plans, the pattern in the policy community, as in business, is to push hard for approval and then, as soon as that happens, request as much time as possible to achieve stated goals. Expectations, after all, are everything.

Petraeus, meanwhile, employed the strategies he had been developing throughout his career, since he wrote his doctoral dissertation on "The American Military and the Lessons of Vietnam." As he said to me, again underscoring that political skills and military ones have powerful common elements, "human terrain is the decisive terrain. You have to secure the people. The focus has to be on providing that security, not on handing that job off to Iraqi security forces that can no longer handle the level of violence they are facing. And the only way to secure people is by getting off the big bases on which we have been consolidating forces and getting back out into the neighborhoods with the people—right where the sectarian fault lines are, right where the violence is highest." As an example of the magnitude of the new effort, Petraeus noted that seventy-seven additional locations were established by American and Iraqi forces over the first year of the surge in the Baghdad divisional area alone. "Our troops had to clear areas block by block by block, isolating them with cement barriers as you went through so that suicide bombers couldn't get in and so forth. So that's the biggest of the big ideas: securing the people by living among them, as opposed to consolidating on large bases and living apart from those we are seeking to protect."

The changes went beyond the deployment of American troops to training the Iraqi security forces. "We had to completely reform the Iraqi police divisions, which had been hijacked by sectarian elements, or had been seriously intimidated or corrupted. All the general officers in the police divisions were changed out. All the brigade commanders were replaced (in some brigades more than once) and seventy percent of the battalion commanders were removed, too. And then we went through a formal retraining and reequipping process. We had to do that for a number of Iraqi army units as well.

"The other big idea was that we couldn't kill or capture our way out of an industrial-strength insurgency, so we had to reconcile with as many insurgents as was possible—to try to make as many of them as possible part of the solution in Iraq rather than a continuing part of the problem.

This wasn't serendipity. It didn't fall out of the tree into our laps. We didn't get lucky. We knew what we needed to do. I had done reconciliation when I was commander of the 101st Airborne Division in the north in the first year of the war, the first summer of the war, with the express personal approval of Ambassador Bremer. And we were the only division allowed to do that."

Unsurprisingly, given the history of the war in Iraq, a parade of evaluations was to follow the arrival of the new team. The stakes were high and all parties wanted a sense of what was working and what was not. Petraeus asked H. R. McMaster, a member of the Council of Colonels who had actually implemented an effective COIN effort in Tal Afar earlier in the conflict, to lead an assessment a month after he arrived. Of the report, Gordon and Trainor say that some "of the still classified assessment reads like a miniature version of the Pentagon Papers—a damning account of false assumptions and miscalculations as U.S. involvement in Iraq deepened."

Keane visited again in May, reporting "a significant shift in momentum" back to Cheney. He again cautioned against hoping for quick success and warned that casualties might go up before they went down. But overall, he had praise for his protégé.

In June, Secretary Gates faced the choice of whether or not to recommend that Pete Pace continue as chairman of the Joint Chiefs. After taking the temperature of Capitol Hill, he concluded that renominating him would only result in more debate about Iraq policy. He recommended replacing him, and Bush, who asserts he admired Pace, agreed. Mike Mullen was nominated instead. Pace's tenure was truncated not by his performance so much as it was by the politics of the moment.

Keane returned and saw more progress in July. But he also reported back that he did not feel Washington was being as supportive as it could be of Petraeus. Clearly reporting frustrations that Petraeus himself felt, Keane cited the lack of visible support for the team in Iraq from Rice and implied resistance from others up the military chain of command.

For his part, Petraeus suggests the picture was mixed. "Gates could be tough," he recalled. "There was no question who was in charge with Gates and he reminded people of that periodically and almost reveled, I think, in occasionally demonstrating that he could be tough. But I was very fortunate to have a good relationship with him because I was, you know, I was his guy in Iraq, and he also knew that there were some in my chain of command who were not supportive of me." According to senior sources in the chain of command, one of the first things that happened after Admiral Fallon took command at CentCom was that he sent out Admiral James Alexander "Sandy" Winnefield (who later became vice chairman of the Joint Chiefs) to assess the situation in Iraq and to do a drawdown plan for Fallon. Apparently, he wasn't initially allowed to tell Petraeus what he was doing. And ultimately this led to a confrontation with Petraeus in which the general reportedly said, "either you tell me what you're doing here or I'm going to throw you out. Fallon can fire me but this is my AOR [area of responsibility], and I have a right to know what's going on in it." As a consequence, Winnefield told Petraeus what was going on and eventually showed him the plan, which Petraeus assessed as completely irrelevant, as the surge buildup was only halfway complete. Tensions of this sort continued for a number of months with Fallon although Petraeus was, reportedly, backed up by both Gates and the President on a regular basis.

This illustrates how a "political general" uses the power he gets, as well as how he can alienate his colleagues, including his superiors.

Rice reported that the mood in Washington had shifted. "For the first time in almost two years" there was a sense that the "administration had turned a corner." The surge "was beginning to have an effect on population security both in perception and in reality. Finally, the Iraqis were determined to liberate themselves—it was their fight now, not just ours." In this assessment, of course, she expresses the success of the surge in terms of the metrics by which those who opposed it sought to judge long-term success—not so much the defeat of the insurgents as the transfer of responsibility for security to the Iraqis. Nonetheless, winning over skeptics was certainly a sign of the progress the new strategy was making.

Political progress was slower to come in Iraq. Crocker and Petraeus had agreed to brief Congress in September 2007, which raised the possibility of tough questions for the new team. Petraeus offered a small troop drawdown as a kind of political bone to throw to the Congress, but Bush and Cheney were skeptical. Still, the internal discussion on this was less fractious than it would have been just a couple years earlier. Rice wrote, "there was less friction inside the administration on that point than one might have thought. Now that things were going better in Iraq, we could talk about 'the end in sight' without the implication we were cutting and running."

Crocker and Petraeus appeared in Congress exactly eight months after Petraeus had taken over in Baghdad. The two appeared exceptionally in sync. It was a far cry from the openly hostile relationship between Bremer and Sanchez, and the coordinated but not terribly effective one between Casey and Khalilzad. Crocker argued that a "secure, stable, democratic Iraq" was possible if the United States stayed its current course. The two offered up statistics that supported the assertion, including a fall of civilian deaths by 70 percent in Baghdad and by almost half Iraq-wide. They also underscored steep declines in sectarian violence and meaningful reductions in IED attacks and bombings. Bush called their performance "stoic, resilient and highly credible. . . . The picture was unmistakable. The surge was working." He announced three days after their appearance that over 2,000 Marines would depart Iraq later that month and that another brigade would be gone by Christmas. Two days after that, Keane delivered a personal message from the president to Petraeus that at its heart said, "I want Dave to know that I want him to win. That's the mission. He will have as much force as he needs for as long as he needs it." The fact that it was a back-channel message may have added to its impact on Petraeus, who said, "it meant a great deal to me."

Several theories exist about why the surge was for a time as successful in tamping down the insurgency as it was. Woodward argues that three factors were key: intensified US intelligence that enabled better targeting of insurgents, the effects on the populace of al-Qaeda's "sheer brutality," and "an unexpected source of good luck," the ceasefire ordered by Shiite leader Muqtada al-Sadr, which was important, given the strength of the militia he commanded.

Khalilzad continues to argue the surge was secondary. "We exaggerate," he says. "People think that because we added 30,000 troops, the surge was decisive to changing the equation. Of course it was important. But other things were just as important. First, Maliki was a more effective prime minister. We had Jaafari as prime minister for a long time. He was just a talker and a pontificator, not a decider. Maliki, once he finds his bearing, he wants to fight to move things forward. I remember once Petraeus actually called me to ask my help in getting Maliki not to go into Basra and fight against the Mahdi militia. But that's what made Maliki a national leader. Second, al-Qaeda's excesses alienated many Sunni Arabs who were part of the armed opposition. This led them to switch sides—with the Sunni Awakening—they began to be more constructive, helpful to our common goals. Third, the buildup of the Iraqi security forces reached critical mass. Fourth, in addition to the increase in troops, the Coalition adopted population-security counterinsurgency strategy.

"Now, of course," he added ruefully, "we think the surge in troops is everything, and we want to do it everywhere. And look how it is not working in Afghanistan." This point highlights a corollary to the "success has a thousand fathers" maxim and also to the "generals always want to fight the last war" maxim. It is the Peter Principle applied to policy. Once something succeeds, we keep using it over and over again until it does not. It dovetails with yet another commonly recurring policymaking error: the embrace of false analogies. Going into Iraq, many among the Bush administration's ex–Cold Warriors who had had the greatest success of their lives with the fall of the Soviet Union and the wave of peaceful revolutions that swept across Europe expected Iraqis to respond the same way. But the situations could not have been less analogous. The most common such false analogy is that whenever a country is battered by war or crisis, someone will argue that a "Marshall Plan" should be launched. But in the case of the Marshall Plan, certain conditions existed that almost never exist in the subsequent situations. First, we had achieved total victory in Europe and felt comfortable imposing our will on those we had defeated. Second, the threat of the Soviet Union gave us a huge stake in accelerating the reconstruction of the buffer that Europe would be. And finally, the countries we chose to help rebuild had actually had a history of economic success, something that is seldom the case in many of the countries for which such plans have subsequently been recommended.

Petraeus offers another contributing factor to the greater success the United States was achieving during Bush's second term: the engagement and commitment of the commander-in-chief. "The degree to which the President kept his eye on the ball in Iraq was incredible. I think it is unprecedented for the President of the United States to do a weekly video teleconference with the commander and the ambassador in the field carrying out a policy together. And he did it at 7:30 a.m. each Monday morning for an hour, with the entire national security team there—vice president, all the principals. . . . It was an unbelievable, unprecedented commitment of his personal time."

Rice offered a complementary perspective both about Bush's use of teleconferences to connect to the situation on the ground and his growing skills during the second term in dealing with international issues and leaders: "I'll give you two very good examples—Maliki and Karzai. These guys are no prize. They're difficult. They're prickly. But he decided early on that . . . I'm going to develop a relationship with these guys and we're going to . . . head-of-government to head-of-government work with them as equals. . . . And so he would do these long videoconferences with these guys—which by the way, the Obama administration decided not to keep doing—and Maliki would sort of puff himself up and he'd make better decisions because he knew that the president was there with him."

Rice saw Bush work the same way with Ariel Sharon, "where he gets Ariel Sharon to the two-state solution when I don't think anybody else could have." Bush, said Rice, could work on "the strategic level" but was also "able to put himself in the other guy's shoes and to kind of sketch out a way that you could get there if we did this together. And I watched it time and time again, and I thought, this is a remarkable gift that he's got."

"So," she concluded, "he evolved. He was always pretty strategic. But he became more strategic in a way that he could marry the tactics with the strategy in ways that were very important." This is another way of saying that during the second term, after the wrong moves and bad results of the first, Bush was starting to find ways—from time to time—to score at least some modest victories.

CHAPTER 3

The Other George W. Bush

Fear makes us feel our humanity.

—BENJAMIN DISRAELI

At the end of his presidency, the image of George W. Bush held by many was of an inarticulate, bumbling man who had been duped by his vice president and secretary of defense into pursuing policies overseas and at home that were harsh, unilateral, and damaging to America's standing in the world. However, the gap between perception and reality for the forty-third president may have been greater than that for any president since Ronald Reagan, whose affable warmth on camera was often replaced by remoteness and a chilly demeanor behind the scenes.

In the years since, Bush's standing has slowly rebounded. At the time of this writing, his approval-disapproval ratings now stand at roughly even levels. This is due in part to the fact that the media coverage of ex-presidents is typically less overwrought than that of their successors in office. But it is also simply because perspective highlights aspects of their presidencies that seldom made the contemporary front pages and allows the caricatures to fade while more nuanced views come to light.

Those closest to Bush have been frustrated by the disparities between the man they say they saw in office and the one who was depicted in the media. But in the course of researching this book, I can also say that those who were not his allies, indeed many who might be expected to be unsympathetic to him, articulated a similar view. Of the three dozen or so foreign leaders with whom I spoke in the course of researching this book—heads of state, heads of government, and foreign ministers—not only did the majority of those who met with Bush speak admiringly of his attentive engagement with them, but virtually all also cited the degree to which he was knowledgeable, well-prepared for meetings, a good listener, responsive, and, especially, trustworthy. "At least with George W. Bush," said one Latin American president who was still in office at the time of the writing of this book, "you always knew where you stood. He was always direct and a man of his word. I cannot say the same for Obama." Interestingly, this leader is from the far left and is regularly extremely critical of the United States. But this view of Bush came worldwide, from left and from right, from the emerging world and from traditional allies like Britain and France. A foreign minister from a US ally in the Middle East said to me, "whatever may have happened here that were mistakes by America and by Bush, I can tell you that he is missed today. He was not perfect, but to his friends, he was a true friend."

Even though Barack Obama and his administration later adopted policies that much more closely conformed to what might be characterized as the role for America prescribed by international public opinion, not a single one of those foreign leaders with whom I spoke preferred Obama to Bush. That is not probative of anything, not suggestive of whether the policies of Bush or Obama were superior or better for the United States. It is simply a fact that is discordant with the view that may have prevailed at the time Bush left office. Bush, the unilateralist, the invader, the sometimes buffoon, had left an impression with those with whom he worked that was quite different from that generally offered up in the media and the press.

The Internet is full of sites devoted to Bush's grammatical blunders, his so-called Bushisms. He himself has made poking fun at his oratorical missteps and gaffes a staple of his post-presidency public-speaking engagements. But this easy humor bears little more relationship to the underlying truth of the man than did the *Saturday Night Live* skits lampooning Gerald Ford's clumsiness. Ford, an All-American football player at Michigan, was very likely the most athletically gifted of all US presidents.

Bush's second-term chief of staff, Josh Bolten, shares the frustration that the president he served was not more accurately represented, but he smartly lays some of the blame for that at the president's own door. "Most of my colleagues like to blame the media, but I actually think that Bush himself bears a lot of responsibility for his image, because even though he is extremely bright and strategic, I think he grew up with a resentment of the entitled and privileged class of intellectuals and so never wanted to be considered one of them and almost went out of his way to appear more of a frat boy than an intellectual."

Bolten continued, expressing a view I heard often both from Bush staffers and from career civil servants who worked in the White House, Department of Defense, and State Department: "I wouldn't describe him as an intellectual, actually. But he almost seemed to go out of his way to reinforce the stereotype of the inarticulate regular guy who didn't have much time for books. I don't think he was doing it consciously. But it was a persistent frustration of mine, and I think we ill-served him on the staff in never succeeding in portraying to the public the guy we saw in private."

Bolten argued that Bush was underestimated—or perhaps misunder-estimated, to borrow a celebrated Bushism—not only in his second term but from the moment he took office in 2001 after the bitterly contested Supreme Court adjudication that gave him victory over Al Gore. "While I agree he grew greatly from the first term to the second and learned from his mistakes, I also think he came into office with an unusually good sense of what it is to be president. And here's where I think being a president's son really helps. He was able to see the whole arc of his Dad's presidency. I think it gave him perspective on how you ought to focus your energy as president.

"We also went through a series of briefings," continued Bolten, "from experts on all of the subjects you need to know about when you're president." Bush was well-prepared by temperament and experience to be president, but not particularly by substance. "He knew the issues a governor knows, which is . . . maybe half the issues that a president might confront. And he would come to every one of the briefings having read an often dense set of memoranda, prepared by, for example, our national security team," Deputy Secretary of Defense Paul Wolfowitz, Deputy Secretary of State Robert Zoellick, and chair of the Defense Policy Board Richard Perle, and led by Condi Rice. And, said Bolten, "he would come in with a statement of principle about the issue at hand which he was trying out as an articulation of his own perspective and philosophy. And I saw him do that consistently throughout his presidency. He would always lead with a clear articulation of his view and we might debate that, but more often the meeting was about how to implement it."

This perspective was reiterated by John Negroponte, the lifelong civil servant, who worked closely with Bush as the nation's first director of national intelligence: "he cares more about intelligence in a hands-on way than any president I can think of. He loved his briefings. He would have half an hour every day, at least six days a week. . . . And, of course, by the time I was working for him . . . he knew all the leaders around the world, he knew all the issues. So he was an extremely good customer."

Negroponte's observations do not fully support Bolten's depiction of Bush as a studious reader—a depiction that Bush himself likes to joke about—but they nonetheless support the overall impression of Bush's dedicated preparation for the job. "He preferred not to read the stuff. He would read it if he had to, but he'd rather hear it orally because he loved the interaction. We would do deep dives into different issues. He got very interested in meeting directly with the analysts. He loved to argue with them. . . . He'll often lead with his point of disagreement. He asked lots of very smart questions. And of course, it was very often in those mornings when we briefed him that he'd tell us about the latest books he read . . . and contrary to popular belief, he read heavy duty stuff."

Bolten identified other qualities that made Bush a good leader: "he was inclined to empower people, including his chief of staff. And while he would have views on issues like White House personnel, he would say, 'you're in charge and I'm going to trust you until I don't trust you.' And I think he communicated that effectively to the team with whom he worked."

Bolten also illustrated Bush's leadership skills with another point I heard frequently: "he was a kind of a coach for the entire team, as well. I mean, the specific example that comes to mind is from the financial crisis. . . . There was a fateful meeting in which [then chair of the Federal Reserve Ben] Bernanke and Paulson and [then president of the Federal Reserve Bank of New York Timothy] Geithner came in and said, 'we're now on the verge of a meltdown and we're literally looking over the precipice and at another Great Depression. And unless we get authority from the Congress to spend maybe a trillion dollars bailing out the banks'—a request which Bush, by the way, hated as much as anyone—'then we will touch off a catastrophe. And so he made the decision to go up to the Hill and tell them we want $700 billion, and after he made the decision everyone was kind of in shock, and especially the triad of Paulson and Bernanke and Geithner. And he went over to each of them individually. . . . I don't remember specifically whether he put his arm around each of them, but that is basically what he did, and said, 'don't worry, we're doing the right thing, we'll get through this.'" Geithner confirmed the thrust of the story. Another senior official, who like Geithner went on to serve in a very high national security position in the Obama administration, recounted a story from the same period in which he said, "I saw the President spend literally twenty to thirty minutes talking a cabinet official off the ledge. . . . He was very shaken by events. . . . He was really at wit's end. And the president lifted him up, and I've always thought that if the American people could have seen him for those twenty or thirty minutes at just that moment of crisis, they would have a different view of him, and they would have felt, given the stakes, that they had gotten their money's worth from this man." It is also a view that contrasts dramatically with that of the president and his administration during the first term when in fact the entire administration seemed shaken by the events of 9/11, the beginning of the age of fear. It was another sign of Bush's growth that he did not just appear cool or composed himself but went further by shoring up those around him.

Elliott Abrams, former Bush deputy national security advisor for global democracy strategy, saw the approach as something more than empathy at work. He said, "I think that Bush saw himself as someone who—as a leader of the country and as a leader of the administration—had to avoid pessimism and depression and constantly transmit confidence and energy and optimism. I think he did this not just as a matter of character but I think he did it deliberately as a management style. That is his view of the office of the president."

Former commerce secretary Carlos Gutierrez, himself a former chief executive of Kellogg Corporation, the cereal maker, asserts that part of what made Bush effective, especially in the second term, was the emphasis he placed on management skills. "Look at the team. Management skills were emphasized in a way that they haven't been since. Cheney was a CEO. Rumsfeld was a CEO. Paulson had been a CEO. I had been a CEO. Powell had held top commands. Condi ran the NSC. Hadley had been her deputy. Bolten was from a top bank. There was a recognition that management skills mattered. I mean, under Bush, you better have had your information ready and on time. There was a discipline about it. And it started at the top." This does not scan with the chronic lack of discipline of the policy process of Bush's first term—such as the way that Rumsfeld and Cheney bucked the NSC process by back-dooring it and seeking approval out of the sight and reach of colleagues like Powell or Rice—second-term colleagues describe a ship that was run more tightly with each year that passed after Bush's reelection. For example, Petraeus observed that "the president was always engaged, always prepared, regularly surprised me with his mastery of detail. But he was also a good leader, listened well, supported his team, and at some really difficult moments, such as during the early days of the Battle of Basra, in March 2008, he was unfazed and never wavered."

In such comments, several impulses are at play. One—as in the overstated observations of Gutierrez—is to cheerlead, to be loyal. Another is to seek to contradict the prevailing view of Bush the Bumbler, which became as widespread as it was cartoonish, and to set the record straight about a president who grew to be more effective than contemporaneous media coverage might have suggested. A third is linked to the awareness that has come too late in the last three administrations—Clinton, Bush, and Obama—that of all the skills important to the success of top officials, the one most often undervalued is the ability to manage. One of the most rampant problems in Washington is that the ability to articulate a point of view is so often mistaken for the ability to get things done. It is common to see people nominated for top jobs who come from academia or think tanks or law firms or legislative roles where they have never managed anything. These people are put into roles atop big, complex organizations. Later on, people wonder why they weren't more effective, and mistakes, sometimes very large ones, take place. This syndrome befell Bush as it did his predecessor and successor. Like Clinton, Bush learned as he went and focused especially on having a better team around him to manage his White House and his NSC. Both upgraded their management structures substantially in their second terms.

Condoleezza Rice notes one source of management experience that her boss shared with Clinton but does so to draw a contrast with Obama, still struggling with accusations of management failings well into his second term: "President Bush had been a governor. He knew how to empower people . . . and in the second term even more so. Hank Paulson is a good example. He brings in Hank Paulson, and it's not like somebody is going to run the Treasury Department out of the White House when Hank Paulson is secretary. Bob Gates is another example. Massive experience. He's going to really run the Defense Department." Rice points out that Bush not only delegated to his cabinet secretaries, he truly encouraged them to have high-profile roles: "he really pushed his secretaries to the front lines. And it was good. You felt you were able to do your job."

"That's not what you get out of lawyers," said Hadley, himself a graduate of Yale Law School, without wanting to target the team that succeeded his in office. "Lawyers learn to pull everything in toward themselves. It is a weakness and it is a problem because the truth is, managing a big organization is a real skill. Obama has some talented people on his team who, if unleashed, could do a lot of good for our country and make the president look good too. But, it requires them knowing how to send signals to a workforce, most of whom you never meet face-to-face. Knowing how to lead that kind of organization, particularly how to provoke change, is a real skill."

You need people who have demonstrated success at this," continued Hadley. "It was a criterion in the Bush administration." Hadley's analysis finds support in the Obama second term where there had been some changes, particularly on the economic side. Secretary of Commerce Penny Pritzker was a businessperson. National Economic Council economic director Jeffrey Zients was a businessperson. Michael Froman and Jacob Lew, respectively the United States trade representative and secretary of the treasury, had worked in banking at Citibank. And there were other examples as well.

(On the flip side, one former top State Department diplomat in the Middle East noted that Obama's lawyerly instincts were often used as a tactic to justify inaction. He would assert that elements of domestic or international law, for example, precluded him from taking action. Although, as the former ambassador noted, he was inconsistent in how he used the law—he suggested that it obligated him to seek Congressional approval for intervention in Syria when he knew that it would block an action he didn't want to take, but a year later he argued that a legal technicality allowed him to circumvent consulting Congress regarding the release of five Taliban prisoners from Guantanamo Bay in exchange for captured US soldier Private Bowe Bergdahl.)

Hadley recognized that management skills alone were not enough, and here he offers a defense of Bush that diverges widely from most media assessments: "management skills are important. But policies matter too. What I think many missed about Bush was that he was especially strong as a strategist. I saw an article the other day criticizing Obama for trying to be his own strategist. But the president *is* the strategist. He is the person, after all, that the country elects to make these decisions. And if you've gone through the gauntlet of what it takes to be president, you actually think you're the person who should be making these decisions."

In Hadley's view, Bush was "actually quite a good strategist." And he credits his former boss with having "a way of looking down the road, being able to take decisions that initially people might have objected to, and over the course of time, turned out to be visionary and right." Hadley continued: "sometimes, those decisions were choices that many people might have seen as out of character, inconsistent with his public image. And yet they were dependably consistent with his principles and values." But they were not to be found in the strategic choice made to invade Iraq, which was the absolutely dominant issue of Bush's second term until the financial crisis overwhelmed it. So where are the "visionary and right" episodes that Hadley had in mind?

"Africa Is a Nation . . . "

George W. Bush did not serve his image or his objectives when he clumsily said, "Africa is a nation that suffers from incredible disease." But beyond that gaffe lay the Bush team's actions in Africa and a claim to a genuinely significant legacy. Africa experts and activists alike from both parties and from around the world cite Bush's initiatives in Africa, and particularly those associated with development and AIDS, not only as among the most significant contributions of the Bush presidency, but as the high-water mark in US relations with that part of the world.

Bono, U2's front man and a leading activist, who had been critical of many Bush policies, surprised many when he said in an interview with Jon Stewart on *The Daily Show*, "we're hoping very much that President Obama is going to follow through on what President Bush did. I know that's hard for you to accept. It was amazing. You know, people like John Kerry worked for this, and Hillary Clinton, and eventually President Clinton did some extraordinary stuff negotiating the prices of . . . very expensive drugs down. But George kind of knocked it out of the park." The singer argued that five million Africans were alive because of drug programs started and funded during the Bush years. Another independent perspective from within the government came from Bill Burns, the professional diplomat who rose to career ambassador, the highest rank in the US Foreign Service, and served in the Obama administration as deputy secretary of state. He cites as special achievements the two programs at the core of the Bush administration's Africa policies: the Millennium Challenge Corporation and the President's Emergency Plan for AIDS Relief (PEPFAR). "I think when people write the history of that administration ten, twenty, thirty years from now, those two things will stand out, PEPFAR especially."

"Africa policy," said Condoleezza Rice, "is an example of something that we started with during the first term and focused more intensively on during the second that came from a deep belief that the president and I shared that we needed to do more, to lead in that part of the world." Bush has written that he had decided during a conversation with Condoleezza Rice at the Texas governor's mansion that Africa would be an important focus, even before assuming the presidency. He recalled, "Condi had strong feelings on the subject. She felt Africa had great potential, but had too often been neglected."

The Millennium Challenge Account (MCA) was created in 2002 to oversee the distribution of aid to poor countries. When announcing the program, Bush articulated a goal of doubling US foreign aid. Distinguishing the program from past aid efforts were the criteria that had to be met by recipient countries prior to receiving US aid. In her memoir, Rice writes of the program, "we thought of the MCA not as rewarding good behavior, though it did. The point was that countries would never develop without good governance and a fight against corruption. Foreign assistance on any other basis was worse than wasted: it was creating permanent wards of the international system who could never deliver for their people." The criteria involved included commitments to openness, transparency, necessary reforms, free markets, and democracy. From 2002 through 2008, according to the calculations in Bush's memoir, the MCA invested $6.7 billion of seed money with thirty-five partner countries.

Rice wrote that "the MCC used strict criteria and a process of negotiation to create compacts between aid recipients and the United States. The countries that were selected were certified using quantitative indicators such as governing wisely, fighting corruption, and investing in their people. For countries that did those things well and earned an MCC contract, the sums of money were large: $698 million to Tanzania, $457 million to Ghana, $697 million to Morocco, and $461 million to El Salvador, to name a few."

Bush recounted an encounter with French President Jacques Chirac at a G-8 summit in Canada hosted by Canadian Prime Minister Jean Chrétien shortly after the MCA program was announced:

> I was one of the first to speak. I talked about the results-oriented principles of MCA, a stark departure from the G-8's tradition of measuring generosity by the percentage of GDP a nation spent on foreign aid. When I finished, Jacques Chirac leaned over and patted my arm.

"George, you are so unilateralist," he said. Then he unleashed, "How can America insist on tying aid to anti-corruption? After all, the free world created corruption!" He made it clear he thought I really didn't understand the African culture. . . . When the lecture concluded, I raised my hand. Chrétien shook his head. He wanted to give the other leaders a chance to speak. But I couldn't let Chirac's statement stand. I butted back in: "America did not colonize African nations. America did not create corruption. And America is tired of seeing good money stolen while people continue to suffer. Yes, we are changing our policy, whether you like it or not."

The program gradually gained supporters as the funds flowed out to participating countries. Some, like Bono, were resistant. Rice observed, "he agreed with its principles but I suspect that standing with George W. Bush was not exactly what he had in mind." Bush, for his part, would later salute the rock star's contribution to the program, saying, "my respect for Bono grew over time. He was warm to Laura and the girls. He frequently sent notes of thanks. He is a man of genuine faith. Bono could be edgy, but never in a cynical or political way."

Another promoter of the program—perhaps less surprising except to those aware of the tensions that led to his departure from the Bush team—was one of its architects, Colin Powell. In a 2006 *Foreign Policy* article, "No Country Left Behind," the former secretary of state argued that the program was a key element of Bush's evolving foreign policy. Powell observed that the "symbiosis between political and economic freedom is the basis for the Millennium Challenge Account, which offers a contract modeled on the free market itself—that is its genius." Powell, noting that US foreign assistance doubled between 2000 and 2006, also cited in the same article other companion programs aimed at needy nations, including the Digital Freedom Initiative, which sought to close the digital divide worldwide, the Food for Peace Program, PEPFAR, and the Congo Basis Forest Partnership, which created a "coalition of 13 governments, 3 international organizations and 10 civil society groups united to protect the world's second largest tropical forest."

Powell also argued, correctly, in my estimation, that "development is not a 'soft' policy issue but a core national security issue. . . . Poverty breeds frustration and resentment, which ideological entrepreneurs can turn into support for—or acquiescence to—terrorism, particularly in those countries in which poverty is coupled with a lack of political rights and freedoms." This is a view that has been embraced broadly on both sides of the Washington political divide—at least among those in the executive branch—with prominent cases being made to support the viewpoint by Bush, former Bush US trade representative and deputy secretary of state Robert Zoellick, both Rices—Condoleezza and Susan—and former secretaries of state James Baker and Warren Christopher.

Washington being Washington, it is not surprising that critics emerged. Nor is it surprising that two of those critics were partisans who would later assume top roles in the Obama administration.

A year after the MCA was launched, Gene Sperling, who later would become the head of the Office of Management and Budget and later still of the National Economic Council during the Obama administration, coauthored with Tom Hart an article that suggested that "in its current form, the MCA could be a step backward in the ongoing U.S. effort to reach out to a majority of poor countries in a coordinated and effective way." They argued that it represented "a new layer of bureaucracy for poor countries to navigate" as it "offers no clear process by which other bilateral or multilateral donors would collaborate."

Susan Rice, then a senior fellow at the Brookings Institution, while supportive of active aid for Africa, nonetheless was critical, saying the Bush efforts did not go far enough. She minimized the impact of MCA, saying that while Bush had "pledged to double aid to Africa by 2010 . . . relatively little of that commitment represents new money." She added that "the president also claims to have 'tripled' aid to Africa over the past four years; in fact, total U.S. assistance to Africa has not even doubled. It has increased 56 percent in real dollars from fiscal 2000 to 2004, the last completed fiscal year [as of her writing]. More than half of that increase is emergency food aid—not assistance that alleviates poverty."

Once in office, the Obama team kept the MCA going but requested funding for it at only about a third of the funding level initially requested by Bush. This was no doubt due in part to the economic straits in which the United States found itself at the time of the most recent requests. On one key metric, Obama does outshine Bush—when Bush announced the MCA, there were no provisions requiring improvement in gender equality before a nation could obtain an MCA compact. Under Obama's influence, that has changed, and creating conditions that empower women and reinforce gender equality is now a significant part of determining which states get MCA compacts and how those compacts are implemented.

Thinking Big About AIDS

Early in his presidency, Bush concluded that the United Nations–led approach to addressing the AIDS crisis—the Global Fund to Combat HIV/AIDS, Malaria and Tuberculosis—was "cumbersome, bureaucratic and inefficient." He turned to his deputy chief of staff for policy, Josh Bolten, to look at options for doing better. Bolten pulled together a team from the National Institutes of Health and from within the administration. His deputy, Jay Lefkowitz, described the first meeting of the group:

> Relating the President's desire to focus on the international AIDS crisis, Bolten turned to [senior National Institutes of Health researcher Anthony] Fauci, who had just returned from a trip to Africa with [Health and Human Services] Secretary [Tommy] Thompson and whom we all expected to propose an enormous infusion of funding for his vaccine project. But we were wrong. Putting more money into research, Fauci said, would not necessarily produce a vaccine any more quickly. Instead, he pointed to one of the most acute problems within the AIDS world: transmission of the virus from mother to child. In Africa, more than two million women with HIV were giving birth each year, resulting in at least 700,000 infected during pregnancy, during birth or through breastfeeding. . . . But the good news was that a new drug, Nevirapine, had come on the market that already proved effective in reducing the odds that a pregnant woman infected with HIV would transmit the virus to her baby. If we could purchase enough of the drug and develop a system of delivering it to those in need, we might be able to affect significantly the spread of AIDS.

This idea, later dubbed the Mother and Child Prevention Initiative, became the core of a program that the Bolten-led task force recommended be funded at $500 million. Bush embraced the idea but felt it was too small to make the kind of difference he hoped against the disease, so he ordered the team to go back to the drawing board and come up with something even broader in scope and impact. Lefkowitz later recalled Bolten coming back to the group with the guidance that "the President wants us to think really big about AIDS." He added, "assume money is no object." The result was PEPFAR, which originally had three objectives described by Bush as "treat two million AIDS patients, prevent seven million new infections and care for ten million HIV-affected people."

"The next question," Bush wrote, "was which countries to include. I decided to focus on the poorest and sickest nations, twelve in sub-Saharan Africa and two in the Caribbean. These fourteen countries accounted for 50 percent of the world's HIV infections." Despite the economic hardships the United States was facing when the program was conceived during Bush's first term, the president requested $15 billion in funding for its first five years. Despite facing hurdles on Capitol Hill—including from Democratic senators like John Kerry, who was planning his own presidential run and had his own plan—Congress ultimately approved the initiative.

Controversy followed when the program embraced what was called the ABC method of preventing the spread of the disease. That stood for "abstinence for youth, including the delay of sexual debut and abstinence until marriage, being tested for HIV and being faithful in marriage and monogamous relationships, and correct and consistent use of condoms for those who practice high risk behaviors." This approach led to a number of criticisms, suggesting a view well-summarized in the title of a 2010 report from the left-leaning Center for American Progress, "How Ideology Trumped Science: Why PEPFAR Has Failed to Meet Its Potential." The report argued that under the program, the "C" component, condoms, was de-emphasized by many of the faith-based on the ground distributing the aid, whereas the "A" component became more central despite the fact that it didn't work as well. Although Bush himself was fond of pointing out that abstinence "worked every time," that view was rebutted by researchers who pointed out that the highest-risk group for infections was actually married women for whom the "A" approach would not work. A 2006 Government Accountability Office also raised this flaw in the approach as a problem to be addressed.

Another criticism was that the United States was diverting potential support from the UN Global Fund. This was not only a complaint offered by those simply seeking money for the UN effort, it also was related to the fact that the Global Fund was more oriented to the provision of lower-cost medications for HIV/AIDS sufferers than was the more religiously motivated (as some saw it) ABC approach of PEPFAR. (The Bush Administration did eventually approve the use of generic drugs in 2005, dropping the cost of treating a PEPFAR-funded patient by three-quarters.)

Nonetheless, the achievements of PEPFAR have come to be acknowledged and widely hailed even by critics who took issue with elements of the approach. By 2008, the program had supported, according to Lefkowitz, "care for approximately 6.6 million individuals, including 2.7 million orphans and vulnerable children." Condoleezza Rice drew attention to the fact that the program included counseling to "some 57 million," a population equivalent to every man, woman, and child in France. It was a vast effort. In 2007, Bush sought another five years of funding, which was approved in 2008.

President Obama has maintained roughly similar funding levels for global health, but the funds are now diversified across more programs, which has actually reduced the amount of funding dedicated to PEPFAR and combating AIDS. In a 2010 *New York Times* editorial, South African archbishop Desmond Tutu wrote that "President Obama added only $366 million to the program this year—well below the $1 billion he promised to add when he was on the campaign trail. . . . Most of the countries in Pepfar [sic] will see no increase in aid." He continued: "under the Bush administration, about 400,000 more African patients received treatment every year. President Obama's Pepfar [sic] strategy would reduce the number of new patients receiving treatment to 320,000—resulting in 1.2 million avoidable deaths over the next five years. . . . President Obama has also proposed to cut America's contributions to the Global Fund to Fight AIDS, Tuberculosis and Malaria to $1 billion, down from $1.05 billion this year."

In 2013, a major study by the independent National Academy of Science based on 400 interviews worldwide found PEPFAR to be "'globally transformative,' 'a lifeline,' and credited around the world for 'restoring hope' in the long, difficult struggle against HIV/AIDS, which has taken nearly 30 million lives over three decades." Prior to PEPFAR, fewer than 100,000 people in sub-Saharan Africa had received antiretroviral drugs. By the end of Bush's time in office, that number had increased twentyfold. Bush's malaria initiative, according to the BBC, has resulted in the number of those infected by the disease to be halved in fifteen countries.

By the time of the opening of the Bush Presidential Library in 2013, a growing consensus had emerged that Bush's Africa policy was not only a highlight of his administration's international initiatives but was to that point in history perhaps the most far-reaching and positive such policy of any US administration in history. Referring to the fact that the Bush administration averaged humanitarian assistance of over $5 billion a year to the African continent, more than any administration before or since, former US president Jimmy Carter said, "Mr. President, let me say that I'm filled with admiration for you and deep gratitude for the great contributions you have made to the most needy people on earth." Bill Clinton said that he had "personally seen the faces of some of the millions of people who are alive today," thanks to Bush.

Another rocker-activist, Bob Geldof, traveled with Bush to Africa and afterward said, "the Bush regime has been divisive—but not in Africa. I read it has been incompetent—but not in Africa. It has created bitterness—but not here in Africa. Here his administration has saved millions of lives." Bush, ironically in view of what was said about his successor, perhaps best deserves to be credited with being America's first Africa-focused president.

Obama himself has acknowledged the impact of the Bush anti-AIDS program: "President Bush deserves enormous credit for that. It is really important. And it saved lives of millions of people." Obama entered office with high expectations for his own Africa policy, especially since he was the first American president with strong African connections, a father born in Kenya, and one who made significant campaign promises of commitment to African issues. The expectations and the comparisons to Bush became a burden.

In one *Foreign Policy* article, Sudanese-born entrepreneur Mo Ibrahim wrote, "I don't think President Obama gives much thought to Africa," noting also that, "George Bush is a hero in Africa."

Recognition of the Importance of the Emerging World

By the time George W. Bush was president, it was clear that the United States needed to find a new approach for dealing with the rising economic powers. In 2001, Goldman Sachs economist Jim O'Neill published a paper, "Building Better Global Economic BRICs." *BRIC* was an acronym for Brazil, Russia, India, and China. His paper was a watershed in how the world viewed these engines of economic growth and social and political change.

Just the four countries in question covered a quarter of the world's land mass and were home to 40 percent of the world's population. China was the world's most populous country and its fastest growing major economy, already on a trajectory to become the world's second largest economy in GDP terms. As such, it was a rising economic superpower and seemed likely to become America's most important geopolitical rival within just a few years. However, unlike America's rivalry with the former Soviet Union, US relations with China were not a zero-sum game. The two countries' economies were growing increasingly interdependent. Their growth was good for us, and their problems would rapidly become our problems. And yet we needed to find a way to counterbalance them in Asia to ensure security for our allies, maintain access to resources, and protect other national interests. Russia, although a shadow of its former self, was rapidly gaining a new form of influence as a leader in global energy and mineral resource markets, and it still had the second most important nuclear weapons capability in the world. Brazil was the next most populous country in our own hemisphere, the fifth largest in the world in terms of land, and home to the world's seventh largest economy. India, the fourth of the BRICs, and soon to be the world's most populous nation and currently its largest democracy, is covered at greater length in a section immediately below.

By the time the Bush administration took office, America's post–Cold War geopolitical stance required us to devote much more time to these countries. The events of 9/11 distracted focus from this emerging reality during the first term, but by the second term it was clear to the president, Rice, and the team at the NSC that a rebalancing of diplomatic and national security efforts could wait no longer.

The Bush administration took innovative steps in its focus on some of the developing world's struggling nations, especially with respect to the outreach it made to India and Brazil. At the center of the former effort was a bold diplomatic initiative; in the latter, an unexpected but highly durable personal alliance. (China and Russia are the focus of Chapters 6 and 7.)

The India Deal

The push to strengthen US ties with India started during the Clinton years. First Lady Hillary Clinton made an important trip there, and Deputy Secretary of State Strobe Talbott took the lead in shaping a more engaged policy, even when the Clinton administration had to contend with the twin tests of nuclear weapons by India and Pakistan in 1998.

When Bob Blackwill took over as US ambassador to India in 2001, he actively sought more attention for the relationship. His regular cables back to the State Department and calls to colleagues on the NSC staff urged that more time be devoted to what he saw as a strategically vital relationship. India was, in his view, perhaps the most important partner in counterbalancing the growing power of China as well as helping to offset, monitor, and contain threats that might emerge from Pakistan. As the *Washington Post*'s Glenn Kessler noted in his book, *The Confidante*, Blackwill's "cables were ignored by Powell who detested Blackwill." (We've discussed Blackwill's people skills earlier.)

The 2002 National Security Strategy included text, inserted at the insistence of Condoleezza Rice, that underscored the potential importance of the relationship with India. Kessler wrote that the section was authored by Phil Zelikow on behalf of Rice, who wanted "language that pointed to the possibilities of a broader partnership with India and a willingness to downplay the nuclear issue." This last point is a reference to tensions that had bedeviled the relationship since India's nuclear tests in 1998. The tests elevated tensions between India and Pakistan, significantly raising the specter of nuclear conflict between the subcontinent's geopolitical rivals and exacerbating concerns about the continuing proliferation of nuclear weapons worldwide. In addition, the ability to offer civil technology or shape agreements that might rein in the Indian program was complicated by the fact that India was not a signatory of the nuclear Non-Proliferation Treaty (NPT). In accordance with the treaty, the United States was prohibited from agreeing to any transfer or sale of nuclear energy technology to India.

The section prepared by Zelikow read: "differences remain including the development of India's nuclear and missile programs, and the pace of India's economic reforms. But while in the past these concerns may have dominated our thinking about India, today we start with a view of India as a growing world power with which we have common strategic interests. Through a growing partnership with India, we can best address any differences and shape a dynamic future." During Powell's tenure as secretary of state, the United States made some progress in Indian outreach, at the entreaties of Blackwill to do so. By 2004, a bilateral mechanism called the Next Steps in Strategic Partnership was created, but it produced only modest gains, largely because of Indian bureaucratic reluctance to follow through on the establishment of the export-control regime they had promised to implement at the outset. Such a regime would be essential to limit India's ability to share its nuclear technology with others, thus addressing the proliferation problem.

When Rice took over at State, she sought to ramp up the efforts with New Delhi. In *No Higher Honor*, she wrote that "India needed civil nuclear power and wanted to break out of the constraints on high-technology cooperation that were stunting its growth. . . . But the break-through was not just about nuclear power—it would unlock a wide range of possible areas of cooperation with a country that was an emerging power in the knowledge-based revolution in economic affairs."

She continued, "and for us, even though we were not seeking to 'balance' China, cooperation with another emerging power in Asia, especially a democratic one, was a welcome development." Said one senior State Department official who worked with Bush, "she had to write that. We never say we are 'balancing' China. But the statement comes with a certain wink-and-a-nod. Because of course, that's precisely what we are trying to do on some level."

Rice then actively sought to persuade her boss in the White House that a deal with India on the transfer of nuclear technology was in America's interests, legal obstacles and past history aside. Bush agreed. He also unwittingly accelerated progress on the deal with a parallel decision to sell advanced American fighter aircraft, F-16s, to Pakistan. This move was designed to help foster ties with friendlier elements of the Pakistani leadership, notably the military and President Pervez Musharraf. It was consistent with US policy in that part of the world because Pakistan was seen as an essential if somewhat unreliable partner in the battle against al-Qaeda and other extremists in the region. When Deputy Secretary of State Bob Zoellick heard about the sale, he urged that the Indians—who would not be happy with the strengthening of their adversary—be consulted. The strategy would be for Rice to go to New Delhi in March 2005 to tell the Indians about the sale but also to offer some big ideas about improving the US-Indian relationship at the same time. During these meetings Rice told Indian Prime Minister Manmohan Singh that one of those ideas would be to cultivate cooperation in civil nuclear energy.

Nick Burns, former under secretary of state, recalls, "the idea was really Condi's. It came out of her visit to New Delhi, one of her first as Secretary. She met with the Prime Minister, and had decided before the meeting that we weren't going to be able to move forward with India militarily, politically, unless we got this big elephant in the room, as we called it, taken care of—the fact that we had sanctioned India for 30 years and that India was not in the non-proliferation system and was effectively an outcast but was actually playing by the rules and had not proliferated its nuclear materials the way Pakistan had. And when she came back from that trip, she called me down to her office and said, 'I want you to be the point person on India and on this deal.' I said I had never been to India; I'm not an India expert. She said, 'You're a negotiator. Negotiate the deal.' And so I became immersed in the deal over the next couple of years."

The deal to work together on peaceful uses of nuclear power would be announced during Manmohan Singh's visit to Washington in July 2005. With the Indians in Washington and the White House expecting an announcement, Rice's Indian counterpart, Natwar Singh, informed her of a hitch. Prime Minister Singh was losing confidence that he could sell the deal in India's often fractious parliament. Behind the scenes diplomatic scrambling took place. Rice dispatched Under Secretary Nick Burns to see if a solution was possible, while she prepared the president for the possibility that the deal itself would blow up.

After having gone to bed with the president's "too bad" ringing in her ears, Rice "woke up at 4:30 a.m. and sat straight up in bed. I am not letting this go down, I thought. I called Nick at 5:00 a.m. 'I am not prepared to let this fail. Arrange for me to see the Prime Minister.'" This produced further negotiations and the Indian PM finally agreed to meet with her at his hotel, the venerable Willard on Pennsylvania Avenue, a block from the White House.

During the encounter, Rice recalls saying: "'Mr. Prime Minister, this is the deal of a lifetime. You and President Bush are about to put US-Indian relations on a fundamentally new footing. I know it is hard for you, but it's hard for the president too. I didn't come here to negotiate language, only to ask you to tell your officials to get this done.' Prime Minister Singh, a mild-mannered man who speaks slowly and softly, pushed back but eventually gave his nod to his people to try again." The push worked, and later that day the deal was announced.

Nick Burns, who became the chief negotiator on the deal, working with the NSC's Ashley Tellis, told me, "when we announced on July 18th, 2005, that we were going to try to reach this deal—and it took us two years to reach it—the non-proliferation community, all the think tanks rose up against it. There were a lot of members of Congress very uneasy with it. There were some people in the administration who were uneasy too—those who work on non-proliferation. But it was clear to us that we needed India, not to contain China, but we needed a big relationship, a bigger relationship with India to reinforce our own position in the Indian Ocean and East Asia. And so that was part of the impetus for the deal."

He went on, "I wouldn't say that there was much dissension at the top levels of the administration. Maybe some at mid-levels and at some of the agencies because this was, after all, an abrupt, dramatic change of thirty years of US policy." Burns then pointed out that "this is where an effective NSC process comes into play," adding, "Steve Hadley was a master at managing such issues and resolving differences."

The process of finalizing the deal was massively complex. For the deal to be legal under US law, the Atomic Energy Act of 1954 would have to be amended to allow the sale of nuclear technology to a non-signatory of the Non-Proliferation Treaty. This required extensive negotiations with Congress, and considerable wrangling before a deal on that front was reached in late 2006. In addition, a "Section 123 Agreement had to be negotiated with India which detailed the terms of the transaction and then the deal needed to be approved by the International Atomic Energy Agency's governors and the Nuclear Suppliers Group." And after all that, Congress had to approve. Singh also faced pushback, especially from those in the Indian parliament who held the principles of the non-aligned movement dear and feared being drawn too closely into the orbit of the United States. Indeed, the Indian PM faced down a vote of no-confidence over the issue in 2008.

Rice recalls that when it came to the final Congressional vote, "Jeff Bergner, the assistant secretary for legislative affairs, told me we were short on votes. But a last minute deal satisfied New York Congressman Gary Ackerman and with him came the requisite number of Democratic votes. The House passed the legislation 298 to 117." She then credits Josh Bolten in helping to engineer passage in the Senate, underscoring the vital nature of a kind of "whole-of-administration" approach to getting major deals done. The bigger, more cohesive, and more competent the team, the more likely that complex breakthroughs like this become both diplomatically and politically possible.

Reflecting on the significance of the breakthrough, veteran diplomat Bill Burns said, "I remember when Prime Minister Singh came out and we finished that deal that none of us had been confident we could pull off. But the president really pushed. And that's another case where his leadership had strategic significance. He had a very easy relationship with Singh and, to this day, he is held in very high regard in India. He understood

that you have to use the frame of long-term strategic concerns with countries like India."

"You know," said Nick Burns, "it was really Condi and Steve. And
in the second term they wanted us to focus on not only civilian nuclear
relations but also our military-to-military relationship and our political
relationship. . . . We worked on all sorts of issues with them in a way we
never had before. . . . In my view one of the most important strategic
initiatives President Bush made was this new relationship with India."
Burns also pointed out another aspect of the deal: "the great thing about
it—and this is a rare occurrence in Washington—is that it had bipartisan
support. I remember on the civil nuclear deal I had to meet often with
Senator Biden and I also met with Senator Obama and Senator Clinton
to try to convince them to support it and they all did eventually. And
the beauty is that when Obama came in as president, he had Republican
support to continue the big relationship with India."

Bush and Lula

George W. Bush and Luiz Inácio Lula da Silva were born within a year of
each other. Both grew up to be presidents. But the apparent chasm between
the characters and experience of the two men seemed even greater than the
distance between Caetes, Brazil, where Lula, Brazil's thirty-fifth president,
was born, and Grace–New Haven Hospital, where George W. Bush was
born. Bush, as is well-known, was the son of a president and grandson of
a senator, born of wealth and sent to the best schools in America. Lula was
raised in humble surroundings, did not learn how to read until he was ten,
and quit school in the second grade. Bush worked in the oil industry and
major league baseball. Lula worked in factories much of his life, losing a
finger on a lathe when he was nineteen. Bush became part of the establishment within the establishment, a blue blood of the US Republican Party.
Lula became a union leader and ultimately the head of the Partido dos
Trabalhadores, on the left wing of Brazilian politics.

After Lula was elected president of Brazil in 2003, he approached his
relationship with Bush with what one of Lula's top aides characterized
as "wariness and skepticism." This was not just because Brazil's leaders
have often approached their American counterparts that way. These two
in particular, it seemed, were oil and water.

But Bush, former governor of Texas, geographically close to Mexico, had come into office with a determination to improve US relations

with Latin America. A few weeks after he took office he said, "the best foreign policy starts at home. . . . We've got to have good relations in the hemisphere." In this spirit, Bush met with Mexico's president Vicente Fox on September 10, 2001, discussing plans for future initiatives between the United States and Mexico. However, the plans were put on hold, pushed off the front burner by the attacks that came a day later.

In the wake of Lula's election, given his left-wing credentials, there was also much concern about him in Washington. Would he maintain the reforms and the positive relationship with the United States that his well-respected and well-liked predecessor Fernando Henrique Cardoso had put in place? Some described him as a radical, someone who would be far more comfortable with Fidel Castro of Cuba and Hugo Chávez of Venezuela than with a Republican president of the United States.

"Initially," said one senior career diplomat from Itamaraty, the Brazilian Foreign Ministry, "there was a sense the relationship would be cool. That perhaps it would not be as active as under FHC [Cardoso]. Just prior to the first meeting between Bush and Lula at the end of 2002, we simply didn't know what to expect."

Condoleezza Rice was succinct in her skepticism: "Lula was viewed with suspicion in the global business communities—and in the White House."

"We didn't need or want another Chávez and were wary of a perceived shift throughout Latin America to the left," said a former NSC staffer. All round, Lula looked like a bit of a challenge.

At the first meeting, however, after an awkward start in which Bush, according to Rice, seemed transfixed with a socialist pin that Lula was wearing, something happened. A chemistry between the two men slowly began to surface. Rice characterized Lula as "authentic," an adjective I often heard used by foreign leaders in describing Bush. "Lula," she wrote, "seemed to be someone we could work with."

One of Lula's top advisors said, "Lula appreciated the sense that Bush was listening to him with genuine interest. There was a respect almost immediately between the two of them as men. Both liked to joke, to use humor and to communicate informally. We saw they had more in common than we thought."

The relationship evolved, and a year later the two men met in Brazil, at which time they agreed on high-level consultations on issues from counterterrorism to Africa, which was also a top priority for Lula, whose country had strong African ties. Afterward Lula said, "without any question I believe we can surprise the world in terms of the relationship."

Over the years that followed, the relationship built into something between both men that ultimately benefited the two countries with rapidly expanding trade, reduced tensions over international issues, and cooperation on key areas from energy to counterterrorism. Throughout this time, Lula was also able to maintain strong ties to leaders on the left throughout Latin America. Indeed, his ability to act as an interlocutor in that respect was "very much appreciated by the president and the NSC," in the words of a White House staffer from the period.

Part of the reason for the improvement, of course, goes beyond personal diplomacy. The focus on relations within the hemisphere by Bush, Rice, Hadley, top DoD staff, and the military enhanced relationships and generated appreciation from potential partners who had otherwise felt neglected. It also increased the sense of self-worth among those working in the government on Latin American issues.

Roberta Jacobson is a career Foreign Service officer who was named assistant secretary of state for Western Hemisphere affairs at the beginning of 2012. Prior to that, after a brief stint at the NSC, she had served in a variety of ascending capacities at the State Department, including director of the Office of Mexican Affairs from 2002 to 2007, and deputy assistant secretary of state for Canada, Mexico, and NAFTA issues. As a consequence she has a clear view of what shifting priorities can mean for the teams working on them.

"We do sometimes feel like the Rodney Dangerfield of foreign policy," Jacobson says, speaking from the perspective of Latin America specialists generally. "There is a certain amount of resentment among some of the folks who work on Latin America toward our colleagues from other parts of the world who think there is really not much skill needed to work in our area.

"It's a very interesting phenomenon," she continued. "Every year I find that my PDAS [principal deputy assistant secretary] is absolutely incensed by the number of people who believe that because they've served in Western Europe or Asia—in some cases including the Middle East, i.e., 'real' places . . . where 'real' policy gets done—that of course, they should be entitled to an ambassadorial position in the Western Hemisphere because . . . how hard can that be, right? And so when there is a shift in policy and our issues become more highly prioritized, it helps offset those prejudices."

Rice emphasized the priority she, Bush, and the NSC gave emerging powers. Nick Burns described some of the consequences: "I worked very closely with a guy named Antonio Patriota, who became foreign minister of Brazil and is now their UN Ambassador. . . . We had a very active assistant secretary, Tom Shannon [who later became US ambassador to Brazil and currently serves as counselor to Secretary of State John Kerry]. We had a biofuels agreement with Brazil. We worked on Security Council reform with Brazil. Because we just felt that the world balance of power was changing. We were still on top, but we had—we had to have— better working relations with some of these other countries."

Patriota underscored the point in return: "it may be that the period of the Bush presidency was a high-water mark for US-Brazil relations through that time. And in part that was because they had a multifaceted, multilevel approach. You saw engagement throughout the US bureaucracy from the top down." Shannon reaffirmed the sense of purpose that was created at the top: "I always felt this was a top priority and that Condi, Steve, and the president were responsive to my requests and guidance."

Bush commerce secretary Carlos Gutierrez illustrated another dimension of the impact of personal, presidential level diplomacy. "As you know," he said, "Bush got along famously well with Lula . . . which had the benefit in the region of keeping Lula from criticizing Bush. . . . Remember how [Hugo] Chávez called the president "a devil"? How he said, "it smells like sulfur in here"? And then [Ecuadorian finance minister Rafael] Correa had said, "that's an insult to the devil." But when Correa was elected [president of Ecuador], Bush called him up and congratulated him and it just disarmed him. Correa never publicly criticized Bush after that. He criticized imperialism and some US policy—but he never went after the president. He [Bush] just had a way of doing that."

This approach and the improving understanding with Brazil translated into other aspects of the US relationship with other countries of the hemisphere. A centerpiece of this was Plan Colombia, a joint US-Colombian initiative to help end that country's decades-long civil war. Begun during the Clinton administration, the program demanded president-to-president collaboration from the beginning to ensure that it received the funding and produced the government-to-government cooperation it needed to be effective. A moment from the earliest days of the effort exemplifies the importance of personal contact between presidents. After the American side hammered out its vision for the program (quarterbacked by Under Secretary of State for Political Affairs Thomas Pickering, one of America's most distinguished diplomats of the modern era), the subject of funding came up. The program's authors felt they needed $1.7 billion allocated to the program but they were not getting much support for new monies from Capitol Hill. At one dark moment in the process, it was determined that Clinton would have to call Colombia's president, Andrés Pastrana, and tell him the United States was simply not able to underwrite this project, though it was considered crucial to Colombia's future. Talking points were prepared. When Clinton made the call, the only person in the room with him was NSC senior director for Latin America Arturo Valenzuela, later assistant secretary of state for Western Hemisphere affairs in the Obama administration. Clinton got Pastrana on the line and explained the situation. His team simply couldn't find the money. There was a long silence. Pastrana was devastated. After they hung up, Clinton turned to Valenzuela and said, "that was the worst call I have ever had to do in this job." He had tears in his eyes. And then, so frustrated with the situation, he said, "I'm going to call [Speaker of the House Dennis] Hastert."

Clinton did that and used all his considerable powers of persuasion and the potency of his office to prevail upon the Speaker to find the money. Had he walked away, the program wouldn't have happened; it took the personal chemistry between two leaders to motivate one to make Plan Colombia possible.

One of the strengths of Plan Colombia, which has ultimately proven to be one of the really meaningful success stories in Western Hemisphere relations in the past half century, was that it was a whole-of-government effort involving the effective collaboration of the entire NSC team and constituent departments. It was also an excellent illustration of how successful programs depend on continuity from one US or foreign administration to another—continuity that often must persist despite a change in political party or direction within those countries.

Fortunately for this initiative, as good as Bush's relationship was with Lula, it was even better with Pastrana's successor, Colombian President Álvaro Uribe. Uribe was also very different from Bush. As loose and affable as Bush was, as approachable and garrulous with his friends as the American president could be, Uribe was the opposite—as tightly wound a world leader as there was. Even over dinner, he spoke in intense, bulleted talking points that made observers wonder whether he ever really relaxed. But for all Uribe's sometimes intimidating intensity, he was also dedicated to fighting Colombia's rebel groups who were, in his mind and in Bush's, directly analogous to the terrorists the US president was fighting as his central initiative. Both men had common purpose and it bonded them. It did not hurt that Colombia's ambassador to the United States at the time, American-born Luis Alberto Moreno, who would later become president of the Inter-American Development Bank, was widely viewed as the most effective diplomat in Washington. Moreno maintained very deep ties at the highest levels in the Bush White House, NSC, State Department, and on Capitol Hill. He helped orchestrate the development of the relationship in ways that only the most successful diplomats can do.

Bush, however, came into office skeptical of whether Plan Colombia could work. Pastrana's efforts to negotiate with rebels or rein in drug traffickers had faltered, costing him his job. Uribe was unproven. Bush wanted to reevaluate and redirect the program, to "change its character." In Rice's words: Uribe "made clear that he'd go after the paramilitaries too, even though some of them had been associated with his political party. When he met with President Bush the first time, he described the challenge and his commitment to confronting it. The President was immediately attracted to him and his toughness. 'Do you really mean it?' the President asked. 'Because if you do, you have to be prepared for really tough action. Kill their leadership and they will start to fold.' Uribe assured the president that he intended to do exactly that."

Employing an approach that became a recurring theme throughout the post-9/11 "Age of Fear," Bush maintained support for Plan Colombia by framing it as a new front in the war on terror—even though during another period in our history it might have been seen as a step in shoring up hemispheric relations, or enhancing regime stability, or advancing the war on drugs. This in itself offers a bit of a glimpse into one characteristic of Washington. When politicians find an approach on an issue that resonates with the public, they tend to use it and then beat it to death until it works no longer. When one overarching issue dominates the national media conversation, the entire town can therefore become monomaniacal—it can have a hard time keeping more than one thought in its head. During the years of the global war on terror—the Bush years—no formula was more overused than playing to the fears of the American people of another devastating attack. Fighting terror and security became the rationale for multiple initiatives, some with a highly tenuous relationship to antiterrorism of any kind. Border issues with Mexico became not about immigration but about "securing the border" against potential infiltration. Ports and domestic infrastructure were upgraded to "harden our assets." Health programs grew up to ensure the ability to respond to "biothreats." Police departments got more money in support of "first responders." Even if the primary reason for an action had little to do with terror, if you could find a security angle, it greased the skids toward getting more cash. Politicians played on the country's collective post-traumatic stress disorder to achieve a wide array of non-terror related goals. Plan Colombia was actually more in the grey area on this. Some of the program did help interdict arms shipments and drug shipments that benefited terrorists. But some of it was simply oriented toward fighting drug dealers and stabilizing an important ally in the region—one of the few Latin American countries that was willing to embrace an unabashedly pro-American stance.

Plan Colombia was ultimately successful in helping quash the country's civil conflict and in reducing violence within its borders. However, the drug flow was largely uninterrupted. A 2006 Congressional Research Service report noted, "despite increased eradication of drug crops and interdiction efforts under Plan Colombia, U.S. government agencies responsible for tracking drug trends report that the availability, price, and purity of cocaine and heroin in the United States have remained stable. Colombia produces most of the world supply, with 90 percent of cocaine entering the United States originating or transiting through Colombia."

Critics also note that while Bush and Uribe's collaboration was successful on the security front, it came at a cost in terms of reported human rights abuses. Both men shared an ends-justifies-the-means view on combating their enemies that led to harsh behavior. Only toward the very end of the Bush years—and even more so when the Obama State Department made working within the law and international norms essential to the future of the relationship (and to the passage of the US-Colombia Free Trade agreement)—did Uribe make addressing these concerns something of a priority.

Mexico had never risen to a priority since the symbolic first overseas visit in 2001 was washed out by the effects of 9/11. But with the resetting of perspectives during the second term of the Bush administration, Mexico could again figure more prominently in the team's plans. In addition, a new Mexican leader was elected in 2006 who shared Bush's strong views on fighting drugs and organized crime. Felipe Calderón made it clear that he wanted to work with the United States on these problems, and in October 2007, the Merida Initiative was announced. Bush's team embraced the idea, framing it as a "national security priority." The initiative was different from past efforts because it was conceived around the idea that both the United States and Mexico were contributing to the cross-border drug problem. The United States would have to work on curbing demand as well as helping Mexico defeat the narcotraffickers. The United States pledged $1.5 billion for the first three years of the program. The Congressional Research Service evaluation of the effort suggested it was effective in increasing US-Mexican communication and cooperation.

The scope of US government agency involvement was broad—it might be called a whole-of-NSC effort. Roberta Jacobson ran the State Department Mexico office at the time and helped draft the Merida Initiative. She worked with "fifteen US government agencies in some of the first meetings with the Mexicans when we weren't sure exactly where they were prepared to cooperate. And when we needed policy blessing and to work out tensions we were having with the DoD or DHS [Department of Homeland Security] or occasionally with DOJ, the NSC performed what I see as their classic role as mediator, as broker, as policy coordinator. But then they let us go back to running the programs and adjusting them as needed and doing the nitty-gritty, including negotiating with the host countries."

A sign of the success of the Merida Initiative is that it has been continued under the Obama administration, which, as new governments are wont to do, renamed it "Beyond Merida." This is the policy world's equivalent of stamping "new and improved" on a box of toothpaste and very often such rebranding is of just as much consequence. In the case of the new and improved Merida Initiative, the Obama team has promised to expand the focus on strengthening the Mexican judicial and law enforcement mechanisms on which the program depends. Funding levels for Merida have gone down, however, to about a third of the initial annual commitment level.

Bush's Latin America plans had grander elements that perished in the aftermath of 9/11. One of these, the grandest perhaps, was born during the Clinton era and was a scheme for a Free Trade Area (FTA) of the Americas. In April 2001, Bush had made the case for the initiative at a Summit of the Americas. He envisioned a market that would "include 800 million consumers and a total economy of some $13 trillion." In the wake of 9/11, and because of US policies that alienated many on the Latin left, and as a consequence of tepid reactions to preexisting trade deals from NAFTA to MERCOSUR (the trade agreement for Brazil and the

Southern Cone countries), and frankly because the United States became distracted, discussions petered out and by 2003 had stalled completely. At the fourth Summit of the Americas, while most nations supported restarting the discussions, MERCOSUR objected (even Bush's strong relations with Lula could not overcome the inherent Brazilian distrust of welcoming further US integration into their region). This sent the Bush team looking in other directions in which to make progress.

These were part of a broader Bush trade agenda that was led in the first term by US Trade Representative (USTR) Robert Zoellick and then in the second term by USTR Susan Schwab. With active support in the White House, from Secretary of the Treasury Hank Paulson, Gutierrez at Commerce, and Rice and Zoellick (now at State), Schwab was able to help advance an agenda that has essentially defined the biggest steps taken in US trade during both the Bush and Obama eras. These included deals with the countries of Central America and the Dominican Republic (CAFTA-DR), as well as the aforementioned Colombia FTA, one with Panama, one with Peru, one with Colombia, and, outside the hemisphere, one with South Korea, as well as the broader Trans-Pacific Partnership (TPP) initiative. Of these, it took until the Obama years to bring into force the Colombia, Panama, and South Korea deals, and the future of TPP is uncertain as of this writing, primarily due to Democratic opposition on Capitol Hill (and an apparent unwillingness of the Obama administration, and in particular of the president, to step in and try to turn things around).

Progress on trade should be counted among the foreign-policy achievements of the Bush era that are often overlooked due to the controversy associated with Iraq, Afghanistan, and the war on terror. The fact is that much good work was done during the second Bush administration that was unfairly overlooked or ignored because it didn't affect the mega-narratives of those years—the ongoing grind in Iraq and Afghanistan and, from 2007 onward, the epic catastrophe that was visited on the American financial system. The financial crisis dominated George W. Bush's last days in office, ensured the election of Barack Obama as his successor, and revealed the true character of the American leader and his team after almost a full two terms in office.

CHAPTER 4

Elections Select Presidents, Crises Reveal Them

Keep your fears to yourself,
but share your courage with others.

—ROBERT LOUIS STEVENSON

In a democracy, with rare exceptions, presidents are symptoms of their times to a far greater degree than they are shapers of their times. Yet, there are few roles a human being can hold in which an individual's character can have a greater impact on so many people than that of President of the United States of America. That character is seldom presented intentionally, and seldom is the reality matched with the character advertised in campaign speeches or television commercials. Rather, it is typically revealed in times of crisis, often in private. Indeed, almost all presidents face at least one great crisis that shows them for who they truly are.

George Bush faced two. Each occurred with a ground zero in Lower Manhattan's financial community and each offered shocks that fundamentally shaped the narrative of the Age of Fear by shaking America's confidence in itself and spreading a sense of vulnerability down main streets and into homes across the country.

Unfortunately for Bush, the narrative of his presidency was shaped by only one of them. Perhaps this was because it came first, in September of the first year of his presidency. Perhaps it is because the second crisis came so close to his departure. Whatever the case, Bush's second crisis revealed him in a different light from the first—precisely because some aspect within him both forced and allowed him to change and evolve as a president. He was able to move past the reactive errors of a neophyte president leading a shocked and somewhat disoriented nation during his first term, and to grow.

The complex reality of George W. Bush loomed very large over the presidency of the man who followed him in office. It did so first in inspiring Obama to offer himself as an un-Bush and to run on a campaign that turned largely on a promise to reverse the political, economic, domestic, and international courses on which Bush had led America. But he also did so by leaving a legacy of policies and approaches, many of which were embraced by his successor. Bush was a ghost who walked the halls of the Obama White House and influenced many decisions, sometimes in ways greater than did the current president or members of his inner circle themselves.

Classic Vulnerabilities Accumulating

The first time I met Tim Geithner, he was a young aide in the Treasury Department of Lloyd Bentsen. We were on a mission to China and Japan. Geithner was a relatively junior official at the time. My two main impressions of him were that he was very smart and that he was very young, looking as though he had just wandered straight out of high school and onto the aging Boeing 707 that was ferrying us across the Pacific. He was also polite, businesslike, and—I was grudgingly forced to acknowledge—very impressive, despite his youthful appearance.

During the course of the Clinton administration, I watched him rise meteorically under the sponsorship and tutelage of the next two treasury secretaries, Robert Rubin and Larry Summers. Both appreciated his sharp analyses, uncompromising work ethic, and cool ability to handle complex challenges without much of the drama that is common in Washington. During the last three years of the Clinton administration, Tim was under secretary of the treasury for international affairs. A former Asian studies major at Dartmouth, Geithner—who has a graduate degree from Johns Hopkins and also studied in China—was clearly on a fast track to the stratosphere of the American economic policy establishment. His next major stop, in 2003, at the age of forty-two, was his appointment as president of the Federal Reserve Bank of New York.

During a long conversation in a rather spare office at the New York headquarters of the Council on Foreign Relations where he was decamping after serving as Barack Obama's treasury secretary, Geithner described what he quickly saw as his priorities when he arrived at the Fed. He quickly developed a sense that a crisis might be looming, that the financial system was sending out the kind of signs that come before a big disruption. Geithner started to evaluate these risks. He asked his predecessor in the New York Fed job, Gerald Corrigan, to convene a group of risk managers across the system to look at the state of the art of risk-management practice in major financial firms. They were to examine where they were behind the curve, where things had improved, and what the new challenges were and then prepare a set of recommendations.

Geitner asserts that he sought to modernize what he saw to be an outdated and vulnerable derivative infrastructure and to try to prepare a better foundation for moving toward a more resilient system. He did so through close collaboration with the SEC and with the other major supervisors of the other major global firms, and with the Fed. According to Geithner he had noticed the broad erosion of credit control and the broader leveraging of risk and was trying to anticipate where this might lead. Geithner's basic premise was "that we had a system that had outgrown the set of checks and balances all systems need, outgrown the basic protections that we put in place after the Great Depression, and that we were vulnerable to a storm for all the reasons that ultimately revealed themselves: dubious lending practices, lax risk management, lack of transparency in important areas, the potential that some of our growth was following the classic patterns of a bubble, and so on."

A foreboding of trouble is one thing, of course, and forestalling it quite another. Clearly, a crisis of historic proportions ultimately did befall the markets while Geithner was at the New York Fed. And as it drew closer, he was more acutely aware of the very real constraints on his ability and those of his regulatory colleagues to impede or manage it.

As president of one of the Federal Reserve Banks, albeit the highly influential one in New York, closest in every way to Wall Street, Geithner's capacity to limit financial risk was nonetheless limited. He faced a dilemma: "the Fed's reach in terms of the scope of our authority to constrain risk taking . . . was limited to a fraction of the American financial system. And if you just looked at the mix of the GSEs [government-sponsored enterprises], the investment banks, the big non-bank institutions like GE Capital, like AIG, or even the money market funds or large thrifts that had escaped supervision, most of the risk in the system was outside our scope of influence and was not subject to any meaningful constraints on leverage. And I was deeply troubled by it."

He did not note it at this point in our conversation, but it was implicit that some of that loss of influence and control of the federal government had come during the Clinton administration, with the repeal of key provisions of the Glass-Steagall Act that had ensured the separation of commercial and investment banking activities. With a steady course, the Clinton treasury team had embraced a course that relied on the self-regulation of many emerging financial markets and fed the explosion of risk-laden derivatives markets that later would play a central role in the crisis Geithner found himself anticipating.

Geithner's problem—and the problem for the Fed in general—was that "people viewed us as responsible, as accountable, and as the people responsible for avoiding crises, putting out fires before they spread." But it seemed obvious to Geithner that we were vulnerable, even if he didn't know what form a crisis would take. Geithner liked thinking about the system as having many tools that "had evolved for risk sharing and hedging," and that were good and powerful. "But they were likely to have a paradoxical effect: they would make the modest crises easier to manage, less damaging because they would help spread risk more broadly and people could better hedge in those cases. But in the end they could also make bigger shocks much more damaging and harder to manage."

The financial industry had set itself up so it could manage the bumps in the road but was more likely than ever to drive the car off the cliff. Recognizing the limitations on the formal mechanisms at his disposal at the New York Fed, Geithner talked to Paulson about his concerns and set up a series of regular, informal contacts with him and the other top executives at the dozen or so biggest financial institutions so they could talk in creative and systematic ways. Through such gatherings to discuss risks, best practices, and preparedness, he achieved some measure of progress that might not have been possible otherwise. It was an approach that would be vital to Geithner and Paulson when the storm hit.

The story of the financial crisis of 2008–2009 illustrates a recurring theme for national security planners: the next big risk or shock often does not come from an expected source or direction. It also quickly became evident that it was not merely a challenge localized to the US economy or the welfare of US workers and shareholders. It was intrinsically global and linked to US prestige and authority abroad—that is, to national security. During the years after 9/11, America's security planners scrambled to ensure that another attack like the one that leveled seventeen acres of Manhattan's financial district could not happen again. But the leadership in America's vastly expanded homeland, intelligence, and national security teams did not anticipate that the biggest threat the country faced would come from within precisely the neighborhood that had been targeted by bin Laden. The implications of the brewing risk in the US financial system for America, its economy, and the wellsprings of its national strength were far greater than anything that terrorists or other global rivals could muster. As our eyes were on overseas threats and on threats from terrorists and their sponsors, there was a ticking bomb at the most vulnerable point in the foundations of the US economic system.

Among other problems that this reveals is that the economic sophistication of top national security planners is typically very limited, a fact exacerbated by growing market complexity. The connective tissues linking economic policymakers and national security policymakers in the US government have never been robust, even as joint NEC-NSC appointments and efforts have become more common during the past two decades. This problem is compounded by the biases, old habits, and policy structures of policymaking. Senior economic officials often sit in on foreign policy meetings but foreign policy officials never sit in on domestic policy meetings, even if they have major ramifications for international policy, noted Bob Hormats, the former senior State Department economic official. Echoing others with whom I talked, and conforming with my own experiences in the government, Hormats also observed that on issues involving security, even those with important economic implications, the economic component is sometimes mistakenly seen as peripheral and top officials with important insights into how markets work are often excluded from the conversation.

The biggest national security concerns of the years ahead would all have economic roots. The Arab Spring would be triggered by skyrocketing food prices and fueled by perceived widespread inequality and an absence of jobs for young workers. The rise of China and the other emerging powers was an economic story with profound political and security consequences. From resource conflicts to climate change to the leverage that selling natural gas gave Russia, or might give America, economic concerns are inextricably interwoven with those of politics and security.

As Geithner indicates, the time bomb within the US economy was ticking even as the US leadership was focused elsewhere on Iraq and

Afghanistan, and on the war on terror. The failure to recognize the emerging problem earlier is one for which the Bush economic team certainly must carry considerable responsibility. A classic bubble was forming. Between the late Clinton years and the peak of the US real estate market in 2006, the value of the average home in America had risen over 125 percent. This growth was fed by the availability of mortgages at low interest rates, but by the time Geithner got to the Fed, the overheated system had already more or less exhausted its pool of qualified borrowers and was starting to offer mortgages to subprime customers. The derivatives that Geithner had seen as a risk-management tool were, as he noted, exacerbating the situation. They were helping bankers repackage lousy loans with good ones, and thus pass on bad risks among good ones to investors who were more interested in upside than they were in sound risk management. Bad loans accumulated within big financial institutions that appeared healthy but were increasingly vulnerable to devastating contagion should key nodes within the financial system fail.

The economic crisis was also important because it was a principal driver in shaping the election outcome in 2008. The day before the financial crisis really peaked with the collapse of Lehman Brothers on September 15, 2008, Senator John McCain was seemingly in the lead over Democratic candidate Barack Obama. Within days, due to McCain's missteps and Obama's exceptionally smooth, non-partisan handling of the crisis, the balance tipped the other way.

The Un-Bush

Barack Obama attended college during the Reagan era and law school during the administration of George H. W. Bush. He is the first American president to have spent effectively his entire professional life in the post–Cold War era.

Obama entered politics when he was elected to the Illinois state senate in 1996. He illustrates the speed of his ascendancy in his autobiography, *The Audacity of Hope,* by noting that when he attended the Democratic National Convention in the year 2000 he was practically broke, he had his credit card denied at a Los Angeles rental car office, and could not get a floor pass to the convention. Four years later, Democratic candidate for president Senator John Kerry gave him his big break, selecting him to deliver the Tuesday night keynote address at the Democratic Convention in Boston even though he was still only a state senator, running for a US

Senate seat from Illinois at the time. Nowhere in his seventeen-minute speech that was cheered to the rafters did he make any reference to international policies, not even to the war in Iraq that he had opposed since its outset—seemingly because that would have put him at odds with Senator Kerry, who had voted for the war. His personal story, woven through the speech, revealed a young politician who, for a US presidential candidate, was unusually connected to the world beyond America's shores. Not only was his father's family from Kenya, his mother remarried after divorcing Barack Obama Sr., this time to an Indonesian, Lolo Soetoro. Barack Obama had attended schools in Jakarta and its environs from ages six to ten. His first public speech, at Occidental College (which he attended before transferring to Columbia University in New York), was in protest of apartheid policies in South Africa. At Columbia he focused on international relations as part of his political science major. He traveled during college to Indonesia, Pakistan, and India. His grandmother may have come from Kansas, but Barack's career path wasn't in Kansas anymore.

Obama helped make his name as a state senator when he spoke out at a rally in Chicago against Congress's decision to authorize war against Iraq. He remained active on that issue throughout his candidacy for the US Senate and when he joined the Senate he won a place on the Senate Foreign Relations Committee. The committee chair was Republican Richard Lugar, with whom Obama quickly developed a good working relationship. In 2007, Senator Joseph Biden became the chairman. During his time in the Senate, Obama was active on international issues. Following a trip they made together to the region, including Ukraine, in 2005, he and Lugar sponsored legislation to reduce conventional weapons in the former Soviet Union. He made trips to Europe, the Middle East, Africa, and Central Asia and ultimately became chairman of the subcommittee on European affairs. In actions that would later resonate with key developments during his presidency, he voted to support the FISA Amendments Act of 2008, which protected telecom companies from lawsuits over wiretaps associated with their cooperation with the National Security Agency. He also voted for tighter sanctions on Iran.

Remarkably, again reflecting the special nature of Obama's ascension, from the first moment he became a senator there was speculation he would run for president. In one account, the issue arose as early as the beginning of 2005 when he told his Senate chief of staff Pete Rouse, "I can assure you there's no way I'm running. I have two small kids and I'm not that presumptuous." (So much for his skills as a prognosticator or for his self-awareness.) And his chief campaign advisors, David Axelrod and Robert Gibbs, both suggested a run might be in the cards but certainly not until he had served at least eight years in office. Nonetheless, he and his team were canny enough to recognize that since they had "buzz" they should make the most of it.

The resolve not to seriously consider higher office did not last long. Following his 2005 trip to Russia and Ukraine (again, a trip with considerable implications for the presidency that would follow), he raised his profile further with aggressive and tough criticism for the Bush administration's mishandling of the aftermath of Hurricane Katrina. When television interviews posed the question of a run early in 2006, Obama maintained he would not run, but behind the scenes he was working with experienced campaign pros like Anita Dunn, a prominent consultant and former staffer for Senator Tom Daschle, one-time Senate majority leader whose advice and staff would later be vital to Obama's candidacy. (Daschle himself would be a co-chair of the Obama campaign. Rouse was a former Daschle staffer.)

According to accounts like that of John Heilemann and Mark Halperin, in their lively and insightful campaign book, *Game Change,* Obama was also getting coaxed in the direction of a run by the likes of Senate Majority Leader Harry Reid who told him, "you're not going to go any place here" (meaning, the Senate) and, "I know you don't like doing what you're doing" (meaning, aim higher.) Reid also recounts in his own memoir, *The Good Fight,* that he said to Obama that 2008 might be just the year for him. "If you want to be president," he said, "you can be president now."

Part of the reason for the belief in Obama's prospects had to do with the rest of the Democratic field. Although there were a number of other qualified, well-known prospective candidates (including also future vice president Joe Biden), the heavy favorite was Senator Hillary Clinton. She brought with her high name recognition, a huge and experienced campaign team, enormous funding, and a husband who was one of the greatest politicians in modern American history and who knew a thing or two about becoming president. But she was also seen as vulnerable. The Clintons had a great deal of baggage. Her election would make them into a dynasty akin to the Bushes, a drawback in an environment in which dissatisfaction with the progress of Bush's wars and the economy made a big negative of being perceived as a Washington insider. And the reality was that the Clintons had roughed up plenty of their fellow Democrats during their time in office, leaving hurt feelings and a desire to find an alternative. Reid and Daschle were joined by other senators and leaders of the party establishment, including notably Senator Ted Kennedy, who urged Obama to consider the special conditions that made 2008 especially fortuitous for him.

Among the reasons the timing was so good for Obama was that as Bush's appeal plummeted due to the angry backlash over Iraq, Abu Ghraib, Guantanamo, and other perceived foreign-policy missteps, as well as a cratering economy, Obama appeared to be everything Bush was not—the un-Bush.

Bush came from a patrician American family; Obama came from roots in Africa and a family with a much humbler past. Bush was seen as almost an anti-intellectual even by his closest supporters; Obama was professorial and academic. Bush was a hail-fellow-well-met kind of guy; Obama was cool and above it all. Bush was often inarticulate; Obama was a master of extemporaneous speaking. The two offered the heart versus the head, white versus black, Republican versus Democrat, an older generation's worldview against something strikingly new, the establishment versus the outsider.

A maxim of the wise and knowledgeable in Washington is that presidential elections seldom turn on international issues. Like many such maxims, this one doesn't stand up to much scrutiny. Bush was reelected in 2004 because of a perception he had been and would continue to be tough on terror, the issue that lingered most powerfully in the gut of the American voter in the wake of 9/11. George H. W. Bush had defeated Michael Dukakis in large part because he was seen as so competent on the international front and because it was thought he would build on Ronald Reagan's restoration of the American brand worldwide; Dukakis, forever the funny looking little man in the ill-fitting tank helmet, as a famous photo depicted him during the campaign, was not a convincing commander-in-chief. Reagan promised to restore America's reputation in the world in large part by making the country strong again and ramping up our Cold War confrontation with the Soviets. Nixon had a plan to end the war in Vietnam. Ike was the former supreme allied commander at the center of America's greatest military and foreign policy triumph ever. In other words, foreign policy is often central to the presentation of a presidential campaign, and voters know it, even if they don't credit "foreign policy" as the issue that most matters to them. In personal terms it doesn't, but America's projection of itself abroad clearly does. In 2008, the fact that Barack Obama, even as a little known Illinois state senator, had stood up and said no to the war in Iraq differentiated him from most of his Democratic rivals and above all from the president who was seen as the architect and enabler of that war.

Further, because presidents have more freedom of action in managing foreign policy, thanks to the powers granted them in the Constitution, it is on the international stage that they are least encumbered by the Congress and therefore most reveal themselves. Also, our international conduct translates into America's sense of itself, into national pride or regret. In consequence, even when the specific issues of foreign policy are not familiar to many voters, the general sense of how a president conducts himself as a statesman affects how voters feel about themselves and their country. It impacts an electorate viscerally.

The big Democratic victory in the 2006 midterms gave Obama's party a real sense of the GOP's vulnerability in the upcoming presidential election. The Obama who had spent most of 2006 demurring when it came to questions about running, but planning methodically behind the scenes, finally sat down with his closest advisors and concluded that it was his moment. When Obama met with big-time donors in New York, he found plenty of support. And when he touched base in Washington with the likes of Tom Daschle and even former Bush officials like Colin Powell— now well alienated, of course, from the administration in which he had served as secretary of state—he heard encouragement. Obama advisors suggested Powell might be able to give their candidate some greater perspective on the racial considerations involved in running and, of course, on a range of national security and foreign policy issues. Although Powell had long since decided he did not have the fire in his belly to run for the presidency himself, reportedly he came away from the meeting with Obama certain that the young senator had it and that he could not be put off to wait until 2012 or 2016. Powell would later help Obama enormously on the issue of his national security credibility by endorsing him in 2008 and again in 2012.

Still, there were also signs of how Obama's lawyerly instincts, weighing pros and cons, would translate into a certain perception of ambivalence. In the run-up to the coming new year, he told one of his closest aides, Valerie Jarrett, that he was more or less committed to running, only to tell David Axelrod a few days later that he had new concerns.

Senator Hillary Clinton made a trip to Iraq and Afghanistan in mid-January 2007 to send a message of engagement in these critical issues prior to launching her campaign. Obama followed by launching his presidential exploratory committee. Clinton announced she was running in an email to supporters on January 20. On February 10, 2007, in Springfield, Illinois, evoking that state's greatest native son and former Springfield resident, Abraham Lincoln, Barack Obama formally announced his bid for the White House.

Obama's announcement began much like his convention speech of 2004, with a recitation of his own personal story. It ultimately turned to a few core policy concerns that he felt would resonate throughout the primary season and into the general election campaign against whoever the Republican nominee would be. Several core points touched on national-security themes. He decried the idea that "war can replace diplomacy, and strategy and foresight." He spoke of climate change and the need to reduce dependence on oil. And then he made a core pitch around the foreign-policy themes that would define his campaign and to a large degree his presidency:

> Most of all, let's be the generation that never forgets what happened on that September day and confront the terrorists with everything we've got. Politics doesn't have to divide us on this anymore—we can work together to keep our country safe. I've worked with Republican Senator Dick Lugar to pass a law that will secure and destroy some of the world's deadliest, unguarded weapons. We can work together to track terrorists down with a stronger military, we can tighten the net around their finances, and we can improve our intelligence capabilities. But let us also understand that ultimate victory against our enemies will come only by rebuilding our alliances and exporting those ideals that bring hope and opportunity to millions around the globe.
>
> But all of this cannot come to pass until we bring an end to this war in Iraq. Most of you know I opposed this war from the start. I thought it was a tragic mistake. Today we grieve for the families who have lost loved ones, the hearts that have been broken, and the young lives that could have been. America, it's time to start bringing our troops home. It's time to admit that no amount of American lives can resolve the political disagreement that lies at the heart of someone else's civil war. That's why I have a plan that will bring our troops home by March of 2008. Letting the Iraqis know that we will not be there forever is our last, best hope to pressure the Sunni and Shia to come to the table and find peace.

Here was the core balance he had to strike. America was still trauma-tized by 9/11. America was still in fear of terrorists and terror attacks. No campaign could win in that environment and appear weak on terror. By the same token, though, Obama wanted to separate the question of the war in Iraq from the war on terror. It had become a central contention of opponents of President Bush that the connection between the two wars had been tenuous at best and was more likely just a hawkish concoction designed to justify finishing unfinished business with Saddam Hussein from the First Gulf War. (Even within Bush's own administration, for-mer director of policy planning at the State Department, Richard Haass, famously dubbed the Iraq war a "war of choice.") Obama wanted to lay out alternative ways to fight terror that did not involve such a war. Later, this approach would be expanded to include an emphasis on continuing to fight in Afghanistan (the so-called war of necessity against the rem-nants and allies of al-Qaeda). During the Obama presidency it would be expanded further still to include using drones, cyber-attacks, special op-erations, and warfare by means other than massed deployments of Army and Marine regiments. Obama correctly sensed that the American people welcomed an end to the debacle in Iraq but would continue to define na-tional security in terms of fighting terror in its many forms because the principal political objective of national security policies is to address the nation's greatest insecurities.

A New Inner Circle

One of the great games played by Washington insiders—I've played it myself a couple times, though not very skillfully—is the jockeying for position within emerging political campaigns by members of the policy community. The objective is a job in the next administration. Approaches differ, but for all but the most prominent members of the community, there is a premium on getting involved early. It sends a message of loyalty to eventual victors. It also increases the likelihood of winning a top job and a place in the inner circle, closer to the candidate.

In the early days of the Obama campaign, a number of these indi-viduals formed the core foreign-policy team around the new candidate. At the center were those who knew the senator from his Foreign Rela-tions Committee days, such as his own former Senate staffer and chief foreign policy advisor on the Hill, Mark Lippert, or those who were on other Senate staffs who got to know him, such as former Daschle staffer

Denis McDonough. When Lippert was called into active duty (he was a Navy reserve officer), McDonough was tapped to step into his role in 2007 and stayed in a central role thereafter. Others playing significant roles from the earliest days of the campaign had come from think tanks and other traditional feeder networks for the campaigns. (McDonough had also spent some time at a new progressive think tank, the Center for American Progress.) Among the most important of these for Obama was Susan Rice, a former assistant secretary of state and NSC staffer during the Clinton administration who, like a number of other key Obama team members, was affiliated with the Brookings Institution. Rice, a Stanford-educated Rhodes Scholar, who was the daughter of a former Federal Reserve governor and an education policy specialist, had also been among the policy advisors for the Dukakis and Kerry campaigns and was extremely well-connected at the top levels of Democratic Party policy circles.

Rice left Brookings to join the Obama campaign, alienating many at the top of the Clinton camp, although one said to me, "I don't think Susan would have fit in well here. Some of those closest to Senator Clinton and destined to be key foreign policy advisors like Richard Holbrooke did not get along well with her. The likelihood that she would be edged out was high."

Known for her tenacity and thoroughness, Rice got the key job of building out the rest of the foreign policy and national security advisory team for the new candidate. Like many such advisors on campaigns, during her first two years of work for the campaign, she received no pay. She bonded with the president on issues like Iraq and he was later quoted in the *New York Times* as saying, "I have Susan Rice and she's going to be getting her networks going and making sure I have top-notch foreign policy people." Obama came to rely on her and she quickly took on a central role.

Many of those long close to Rice, like former national security advisor Anthony Lake, former Brookings colleague and NSC specialist Ivo Daalder, former national security staffer Gayle Smith, former NSC spokesperson Tara Sonenshine, and soon, dozens of others, joined the team, dividing into different areas of regional and topical specialization, as is typical of such campaign organizations.

Illustrating the process, Sonenshine, who later went on to become under secretary of state for public diplomacy, said she was contacted by Tony Lake, who had gotten very animated about Obama and asked her to join the small group led by Rice. In it were Tony, Gayle Smith, Brooke Anderson, Greg Craig (later Obama's White House counsel), Mark Lippert, and Denis McDonough. "We would meet periodically to talk about various aspects of the campaign," said Sonenshine. "I ended up working on women, Jews, and veterans issues. We had a Russia subgroup led by Mike McFaul [later ambassador to Russia]. And the way it worked was we would break out subjects, functions, regions, issues, white papers, communications, strategic thinking."

She continued: "in terms of the work of the group it was largely, how do we differentiate ourselves from Bush? And to a lesser extent, how do we differentiate ourselves from other Democratic candidates? I remember us developing an article for *Foreign Affairs* that was sort of the eight or nine core tenets of the Obama foreign policy." Differentiating Obama from Bush, given the forty-third president's battered standing, was a natural strategy for the candidate and would have been a theme for any Democratic candidate in 2008. But, later, when Obama was president, he would find that the concept was double-edged. From one side he would be criticized for policies some saw as merely reflexive counterpoints to Bush's; from the other, he was condemned for sometimes insufficiently distinguishing his approaches from his predecessor's. Veer left or veer right, it was hard after the rhetoric and success of 2008 to drive out from under the shadow of the Bush years.

Other top Democrats were also drawn into the campaign in influential and significant roles, even if not as members of the core group. One was former Carter national security advisor, Zbigniew Brzezinski: "in 2007 in early summer . . . he was beginning to develop speeches and he was going to give a major speech on Iraq and he contacted me. I was a critic of the Iraq War. . . . And that became known and it was Denis McDonough, I think, that actually suggested that when Obama was to give this major speech on Iraq that I introduce him."

Recalls Brzezinski, "Obama asked me to lunch and we had a discussion. He liked very much my book *Second Chance,* which was very critical of the Bush administration. And so he asked if I would introduce him in Iowa, and I agreed and so I became involved in the campaign." Brzezinski's involvement with the campaign remained unofficial. "I told him, look, I am going to be attacked by the right-wing Jewish press or leaders because I am strongly of the view that it's in the American interest that there be a peace settlement between Israel and Palestine. It is actually in my view essential for Israel's long term survival. But I'll take shit for it. And therefore

I don't want to officially be part of your team." Even without a formal connection, however, Obama and Brzezinski continued email contact throughout and even after the campaign. Brzezinski was "immensely impressed" with candidate Obama's "understanding of how the world had changed and how America had to play the game differently. Later I would develop some concerns—for example he has this personal characteristic somewhere in his mind that articulating something and defining it is the equivalent of action, whereas to me it's only the beginning of action because it has to be followed by strategy and implementation. It's not a self-fulfilling process. But from the beginning in many ways he was truly impressive."

Other senior advisors played a more informal role. Michèle Flournoy, for example, who later became under secretary of defense, said, "I didn't affiliate with one campaign versus another. Because I was in a leadership role [at the Center for New American Security], I said I will just help anyone who asks. The only people who asked were Clinton and Obama and I had sessions with both of them." Similarly, John Brennan, who later would head counterterrorism in the White House and ultimately become CIA director, described a similar, intermittent involvement until, like Flournoy, he was invited after Obama's election to become part of the transition process to the new administration.

Bear Market

During the summer of 2007, while the candidates were raising money and building networks and teams, the first tremors of another great shock were felt. The housing market saw prices start to fall after their unprecedented climb, and inventories of housing stock and foreclosures on mortgages started to rise. In June 2007, two Bear Stearns hedge funds were forced into bankruptcy because the AAA mortgage-backed securities in which they had invested were suddenly revealed not to have been AAA in character after all, and their values plunged. By August, Geithner learned that mortgage provider Countrywide was no longer able to finance its repo book. By January 2008, the World Bank warned that a credit crunch would likely squeeze the world's real economy and slow growth. President Bush and Paulson responded with a $168 billion stimulus package on February 13, but by mid-March the first really big, nearly unthinkable collapse of the financial crisis took place. Bear Stearns, one of the great, rock-solid, eminent investment banks on Wall Street found itself embroiled in a crisis.

The eighty-five-year-old firm was discovering that as the market punished its mortgage-backed security positions, its cash reserves were quickly running out. With rumors of problems leaking out, the company's stock began to fall precipitously. Assertions that the rumors were "ridiculous" by the company's widely respected former CEO, Alan "Ace" Greenberg, didn't help. The next day the current CEO, Alan Schwartz, also appeared on television but was hit with questions as to whether the company would be unable to raise additional funds as soon as the next day. By the evening of March 13, the company's executives discovered that they had less than $3 billion in cash available—not enough to begin work the next day. While seeking new money from J.P. Morgan, Schwartz also called Geithner to warn him that if the money did not come in, bankruptcy might well be the only option. Schwartz pushed J.P. Morgan CEO Jamie Dimon, seeking a deal, even as he celebrated his birthday with his family. He sought a $25 billion line of credit. Dimon said he would consider the option.

At 4:45 the next morning, Geithner, Paulson, and Fed Chairman Ben Bernanke held a tense conference call. Bear was on a precipice. If they didn't authorize a loan, the contagion effect in markets could be calamitous. They agreed to put a package together to be financed through Bear. It took a couple of hours for the terms of the deal and the wording of the announcement of it to be worked out. The goal was an announcement prior to the opening of the markets that might stem the panic. After a small blip upward in pre-opening trading, the first wave of activity on the market was more frenzied selling. Paulson initiated a call with top financial industry executives to urge them not to press Bear. But the market continued to plummet, falling over 300 points.

The only thing that would save Bear was for it to be purchased, but J.P. Morgan's look at Bear's books suggested a stock purchase price of $2 a share—a mere fraction of a fraction of what the company had been worth just a few days earlier. Bear's directors had no choice. By Sunday afternoon, March 16, the deal was set. Later that night the Fed revealed plans to allow investment banks to borrow directly from the government—something that had never happened before. (Investment banks had always been treated differently from the more heavily regulated and insured commercial banks. They had more freedom. And until 2008 they had no reason to expect that the government would help them out in a crunch. But they had grown so big and important to the financial system that the government had little choice. Not to assist them would have invited further problems. As it turns out, helping them out only invited later demands for even more extreme support.) But the risk that the Bear Stearns disaster would be followed by another collapse triggered images of a depression-inducing financial domino effect. "We felt," said Geithner, "that we had contained the crisis. But what we were really doing was preparing ourselves for the kind of deliberations and interventions that were to come in just months."

Paulson would say in the wake of the crisis that the Bear "solution" had to be seen as an exception, that market-based solutions should prevail. It was a position that would be challenged again by mid-September.

Against the background of quaking financial markets, Obama was running a successful campaign against the once seemingly invincible Hillary Clinton. He had beaten her handily in the Iowa caucuses and, although she staged a comeback in New Hampshire, by mid-March her campaign was seriously considering that the impossible might happen and the upstart Obama could win. With turmoil at home and abroad, the cry seemed to be going out for "a new broom."

It was at precisely this moment that Obama offered up one of his finest hours, a defining speech on race relations in America that addressed head-on the one thing that made his campaign unlike any other before it. The speech did something else. It changed the subject of the political debate in America away from an age dominated by insecurity and fear and focused instead on something that was deeply resonant and contained the seeds of hope. With the speech Obama sent a message that, should he be elected, it would be a historic watershed for America and as such would be an act infused with promise in the midst of an era of doubts. He sounded strong but he also suggested that politics could make a difference in a way that seem to transcend the day-to-day rancor of Washington.

As a consequence, in this span of just a few hours in mid-March 2008, the crisis of American markets, which would become the greatest national security challenge facing the United States, and Obama's defining speech on the racial politics, which would set his presidency apart from the very first instant he took office, together became a pivot point in American history.

One Presidency Redefined, One Presidency Defined

By the time the primaries and the conventions had come and gone in 2008 and Barack Obama had become the Democratic nominee and John McCain had become the Republican standard-bearer, Obama's once nimble team of foreign policy and national security advisors had grown to corporate dimensions. With over 300 members it was larger by 50 percent than Bush's national security staff (and would be a harbinger of things to come). The Obama foreign-policy team was roughly four times the size of that of the McCain-Palin campaign organization.

Denis McDonough was quoted in the *New York Times* as saying, "it's unwieldy, no question. But an administration is unwieldy too. We also know that it's messier when you don't get as much information as you can." Thanks to the efforts of Susan Rice, the group was organized into "20 teams based on regions and issues" and, after the end of Hillary Clinton's campaign, had taken in members of her team as well. McDonough and Lippert handled the staff policy functions and were based in the Chicago campaign headquarters for Obama and paid by the campaign. In addition a "senior working group on national security" had been named, highlighting thirteen people atop the massive campaign policy hierarchy. They included former secretary of state Madeleine Albright, former secretary of state Warren Christopher, former national security advisor Tony Lake, former Senate Armed Services Committee chairman Sam Nunn, former Clinton defense secretary William Perry, and Susan Rice. Nine of the thirteen were Clinton administration veterans. Notably, Albright had been a Hillary Clinton advisor, but the bulk of the crowd were early Obama adopters.

The Obama approach to organizing this advisory team represents, as did many other aspects of the Chicago-based campaign, the state of the art in convening and managing such policy apparatuses. That is not a comment on the quality or content of the policy recommendations they produced. Rather it is simply to say that it was the natural successor to the very similar and also very large structure created during John Kerry's campaign for president in 2004. Such large groups serve several purposes beyond simply collecting and harnessing experienced advisors. They bring into the "tent" of the campaign prominent commentators and validators, a broad cross section of the women and men who will write op-eds and journal articles, conduct interviews, and serve as surrogates in forums around the country. Increasingly such groups also have a presence as advocates in social media, blogs, podcasts, and other new media mechanisms for reaching potential voters. Participants given a voice in the campaign also gain pride of authorship and are more likely to present a united front. Disharmony typically doesn't really manifest itself until after the jobs are handed out, the game of musical chairs ends, and some people are left standing. Even then, the original campaign team often see themselves as having the inside track for jobs later in an administration and so they keep their heads down, maintain the group discipline, and reduce the likelihood of internecine criticisms within a party. At least, that's the theory.

On Saturday, August 23, 2008, Barack Obama announced one more vital link in his foreign-policy team. He named as his vice president six-term Delaware senator Joe Biden, chairman of the Senate Foreign Relations Committee.

Biden had been a tough critic of Obama's during the primary campaign, even at one point asserting the young Illinois senator was not ready for the presidency. He said, on ABC's *This Week*, "I think he can be ready, but right now, I don't think he is. The presidency is not something that lends itself to on-the-job training." Obama, however, knew Biden from the Senate Foreign Relations Committee (on which also served future Obama secretary of state John Kerry and future Obama defense secretary Chuck Hagel). They had a good working relationship. Also, as Biden liked to point out, he had long experience in Washington, having served with seven presidents. He provided a counterbalance to Obama's youth and a way to offset charges of inexperience. He was also well-known, "a name brand" in the words of one Obama staffer who pointed out that they felt the relative newcomer to Washington was extremely sensitive to the perceptions that he was "too green."

As in all such appointments, immediate context plays an important role. During the final weeks of Obama's vetting process, major international stories loomed large in the headlines. The Iraqi parliament failed to pass a key election law. A judgment came down in the first trial associated with the US prison at Guantanamo Bay. Pakistan's political situation was in turmoil. The Taliban was on the move in Afghanistan—more than a dozen suicide bombers supported by armed militants attacked a US military base in Khost Province—and also in Pakistan, where more than sixty people were killed in a bombing at an arms factory. Perhaps one of the most complex international challenges that made headlines throughout the month had to do with the bold decision by Russian president

Vladimir Putin to send troops in the "breakaway" territories of South Ossetia and Abkhazia, parts of the Republic of Georgia. Although the United States and NATO called for the Russians to pull out, the Russians consolidated their gains and tensions rose. Condoleezza Rice announced a deal in Warsaw three days before the Biden announcement in which the United States agreed to provide missile defense systems "aimed at no one" to the Poles. It was a clear and forceful signal to the Russians to beware escalating the crisis, which soon stabilized—although in the end Russians and Russian supporters remained in control of the two "independent regions."

Later during the campaign, vice presidential nominee Biden would assert that, as president, Obama would soon be tested by foreign leaders. ("Remember I said it standing here," he said at a Democratic fund-raiser in Seattle in October. "Watch, we're going to have an international crisis, a generated crisis to test the mettle of this guy.") Ultimately, Biden was right, although Obama would be tested not once but many times. One of those who sought repeatedly to take the measure of the incoming American leaders would in fact be Putin, who would by 2014 replay almost precisely the gambit in Georgia, but this time in Ukraine. As we shall see, the Obama-Biden response was quite different from that of Bush and Rice, and arguably much less swift or forceful.

Neither the size nor the quality nor the skill with which an organization is put together is any guarantee that it can prepare a leader for the crises that will most challenge him. Much is written about so-called black swans—unexpected game-changing events. It is often stated that precisely because they are black swans they are by definition un-anticipatable. But the reality is that virtually all the most famous international black swans of the past several decades—from the fall of the Soviet Union to 9/11 to the advent of the Internet to the bursting of stock market bubbles—have been predicted. What is unexpected about them is when they happen, how they unfold, the reaction to them, the constraints placed on leaders at the time they occur, the cast of characters who have to deal with them—that is, the context in which events play out. It is coping with that context that is the test, even for those who stood waiting.

Like all candidates, Obama wanted to be prepared. But the event that ultimately convinced many Americans of his suitability to be president, the one that tipped the scales so that he would take the lead from his experienced, media-favorite Republican opponent, the one that suggested

Obama could handle the complexities of global leadership, came not from overseas but from Wall Street.

.The financial crisis continued to unfold in the wake of the resolution of the events that effectively ended the long and distinguished history of Bear in a matter of days. Jobs bled out of the US economy, and over a million were lost in the months following the Bear crisis through the end of the summer. The continuing fall in the value of mortgage-backed securities put the government's big mortgage providers, Fannie Mae and Freddie Mac, into such distress that in early September they ended up going into conservatorship. Big financial institutions on Wall Street that had invested heavily in mortgage-backed securities were hit by a liquidity crisis that few had prepared for. A systemic risk loomed not just for the United States but worldwide. The United States, as the world's largest economy, was crucial to world growth and investor confidence. But the real origins of the crisis can be traced to large inflows of cash, largely from Asia, that had helped fuel the bubble in the American housing market. When that bubble burst, those investors were also hit. The financial and economic consequences therefore reached in every direction.

Within the White House and the Treasury Department, a frenetic pace was kept up. Regular meetings took place within the National Economic Council, the counterpart to the NSC that had struggled to maintain relevance since its first leader, Robert Rubin, left during the first term of the Clinton administration, taking most of the influence with him as he became secretary of the treasury. And in the Bush administration, not only did the towering personality of Hank Paulson as well as his experience at the helm of arguably the most prestigious and influential investment house in the world make him the natural center of gravity, but President Bush, in the words of one of his top White House aides, "saw that Paulson was in command and treated him like a battlefield commander, trying to offer him support. Bush was engaged throughout as were all his top advisors, but Hank was the quarterback."

Bolten put the crisis in perspective: "we were bookended by crises—remarkably bookended. I mean, 9/11 didn't happen until we were eight months into office but the financial crisis took us through our final days in the White House. And from my seat, the financial crisis was actually scarier—not as horrifying obviously—but scarier than 9/11." Bolten admitted that the Bush team was staring into an unknown abyss: "with 9/11 we kind of knew what we were dealing with, with what we ought to do, knew who the enemy was and basically what the response had to be. Destroy the enemy. Secure the country." But the financial crisis was different. "We didn't know what the right steps were from week to week. There was no playbook. And we probably did make a number of mistakes. But it was well-managed. I give a lot of credit to Paulson, Bernanke, and Geithner who operated very closely in a way that was, my sense is, not the case with the National Security team during the run-up to the initial prosecution of the Iraq War."

The triumvirate of Paulson, Geithner, and Fed Chairman Bernanke formed the core of the crisis management team. "We were in constant touch," said Geithner, "and we trusted and respected each other." The calls and meetings increased in frequency during early to mid-September, with tensions rising almost in direct parallel to the increasing pitch and prominence of the presidential campaign, which had the effect of making every move more visible, more politically loaded, and therefore more challenging. This juxtaposition ended up bringing political leaders into the fray more than they might otherwise have been—both President Bush as well as candidates Obama and McCain.

For the public perhaps and also in a public policy sense, the crisis kicked up to another level of gravity and complexity when Lehman Brothers, one of the world's most prominent and respected financial institutions, found itself unable to meet its obligations. When Merrill Lynch simultaneously faced a similar liquidity crisis, it found an acquirer, Bank of America. There was no such white knight for Lehman. It went to the US government seeking a bailout, but after consultation with Geithner and Bernanke as well as Bush, Bolten, and the team at the White House, Paulson let Lehman CEO Richard Fuld know that, as a matter of policy, the administration felt the market should be allowed to prevail, that there would be no bailout, and that Lehman would have to go under. Within days, AIG, the insurance giant, was on the ropes, a run had begun on money market funds, and over $140 billion was withdrawn in the week after the Lehman meltdown—twenty times the level of withdrawals from the week before.

The market was in free fall. The prospect of a global depression loomed. From one day to the next the shifting landscape demanded new approaches. Lehman was allowed to go bankrupt on September 15. Just two days later the Fed lent $85 billion to AIG to prop it up because of stated concerns that failing to do so could bring down the system. Some have posited that pure policy evaluations did not drive these decisions. Former AIG CEO Hank Greenberg noted to me emphatically that

Lehman had always been Goldman's biggest rival and so Paulson's decision to let it go was driven by old animus, whereas AIG's biggest creditor was Goldman, and billions of the Fed's bailout funds flowed straight through to help save Paulson's old firm.

Simultaneously, with the express support of the president, despite the potential for enormous political blowback, Paulson and Bernanke met with leaders on Capitol Hill to help structure a $700 billion fund to purchase damaged assets for which there were no buyers, and that were therefore pulling world markets and the world economy down with them. Decisions came fast and furious thereafter. In every case, the team at the White House strove to stay ahead of the meltdown and stem the worldwide market panic. Two more big financial institutions, Washington Mutual and Wachovia, sought and found new buyers. The bailout was rejected by Congress before market tremors forced the legislators to reconsider. The crisis spread overseas. By October 3, Bush signed the bill creating the $700 billion Troubled Assets Relief Program (TARP). The stock market continued to fall, having its worst week in seventy-five years the week after TARP came into law. The Fed announced major new infusions of capital into banks and companies outside the financial sector. Tax laws were relaxed to make it easier for banks to buy troubled financial institutions and to help companies repatriate funds that would enhance their liquidity. The Fed led a coordinated effort by central banks worldwide to cut rates and thus inject more liquidity into the world economy. The United States convened the G-7 and then, in an unprecedented move representing a major shift in US policy, sought a meeting in mid-November of the G-20, acknowledging the new economic reality that meant that the old industrial powerhouses of the G-7 were no longer enough to manage the world economy, that big new powers like China were now central players. Paulson took another vital step in the midst of this frenzy of activity by convening the heads of the nine biggest financial institutions and pressuring each of them to accept bailout funds. That was an important effort to reduce the stigma of any bank's participation in the program and to send a message that the solution was system wide.

All this happened while the presidential campaign went on. McCain's slight edge in the polls disappeared after his missteps in responding to the crisis. He first minimized it with a tired, reflexive formulation that the fundamentals of the US economy were strong and then overreacted with a misguided offer to shut down his campaign in order to enter into the center of the political deliberations in Washington, thus appearing to attempt to make political capital on the back of a crisis. Contributing to that shift was Obama's cool, seemingly apolitical style. He was briefed by an extremely competent and respected team, including Larry Summers and Bob Rubin. They helped prepare him for the meeting convened by President Bush at the White House on September 25, 2008, to show that both candidates and the president were in coordination during the crisis and were seeking to elevate management of the issues at hand above day-to-day politics—a move for which the Bush team deserves credit. Obama offered a generally conciliatory tone during the conversation whereas McCain reverted to senator-mode, detailing GOP talking points and admitting he had not actually read the plan proposed by Paulson.

According to Jonathan Alter's account, Obama could not help but view the meeting through the lens of the ongoing campaign. He came out of the meeting saying, "that was surreal. Guys, what I just saw in there made me realize, we have got to win. We can't lose this election because these guys can't run the country." Harry Reid later wrote, "I believe it was the stark contrast between the behavior of the two men during this crucial test that sealed the election for Barack Obama."

Since the crisis, there has, not surprisingly, been a debate about the effectiveness of the steps taken by the Bush team. But increasingly there has been a recognition that, whether they made errors or not, the swiftness with which Paulson, Bernanke, and Geithner acted and the support given to them at considerable personal political risk by President Bush and his White House team did begin to stem the tide of the crisis, even though its aftershocks continued to be felt over five years later. One compelling bit of evidence to that effect is that the much less decisive response by Europe's leaders led their countries to suffer—and suffer far more grievously than did the United States—yet another crisis in the years after the initial recession. (Admittedly, some of this has to do with problems in the structure of the European Union system.) I tend to agree with the assessment of two members of the Bush White House economic team—Keith Hennessey, former director of the National Economic Council, and Edward Lazear, former chairman of the Council of Economic Advisors—who made the case that Bush had effectively cauterized the wounds of the crisis before Obama even took office. (However, I do not believe that viewpoint minimizes either the challenges faced by Obama's economic advisors and the president himself or the considerable magnitude of their contributions to managing the recession that should redound to their credit.) Hennessey and Lazear wrote in *Politico* five years after the crisis: "the financial crisis had ended by the time Obama took office in January 2009, a fact largely obscured by the Obama team's rhetorical blurring of the late-2008 financial shock and the ensuing macroeconomic recession. Almost all policies enacted to stem the financial crisis occurred during the autumn of 2008, while Bush was still president. It is possible to criticize the actions the Bush administration and the Fed took to deal with the crisis, and many do. But it is not possible to question that these actions were taken before Obama became president."

Even top Obama campaign advisor and later Obama administration official, Larry Summers, agrees with the premise that the handling of the crisis by Bush and his team was in many ways constructive and stood in contrast with the handling of the crisis that began on September 11, 2001: "I think the Bush administration made two highly important judgments. . . . One, they made a judgment not to bail out Lehman. And you know they have decided now that would have absolutely been illegal and there was no possible legal way to do it. . . . And the second judgment that they made that was in some ways more consequential was that they were going to . . . pursue a capital infusion program where all the banks, all the financial institutions would get capital in order to avoid stigmatizing the ones that took capital. And once you made a judgment that you were going to have a universal program, the capital had to be provided on terms where the institutions that didn't need it would nonetheless take it, which meant that the terms couldn't be very punitive at all, and that enhanced the effectiveness of the effort."

Geithner emphasized the historic dimension of the crisis, noting that both Bernanke and former Fed chair Alan Greenspan have said that the 2008 crisis was caused by a shock greater than that which caused the Great Depression: "I'll give you two reasons why that's the case. If you compare the loss of wealth at the early stage of the Great Depression to the fall of '08 . . . it was five times as bad. Another measure of the risk of financial collapse was the risk in lending to banks. And that was about twice as high in '08 as it had been during the Great Depression.

"If you're in a situation with that kind of risk," Geithner continued, "and you have a lot of dry tinder and a risk of a full collapse, the only way out is to provide a huge amount of financial stimulus to offset the contraction of private demand. And you have to get interest rates very, very low, keep them there a long period of time so you can also help offset and cushion that. But those two things aren't powerful enough and don't work if your financial system is broken."

Geithner explained how they made sure the financial system wasn't broken. With Paulson's authority with the GSEs and the TARP, they "put a huge amount of additional financial force into the system and did a forcible recapitalization of the financial system. It was the combination of those three things that ultimately made growth turn: growth turned positive in six months. It was shrinking at an accelerated rate and then it was growing at 3 percent in six months. That's an incredibly rapid turnaround by any measure." Concluded Geithner, "none of the stuff we did subsequently in the Obama administration to help address the recession would have been possible without those initial choices, particularly those to break the panic in the fall of '08. Our subsequent initiatives during the first years of the Obama administration were also essential—vital—but if we hadn't acted quickly in the fall of '08 it would have been much worse."

One former cabinet secretary called Bush's oversight of the response "his finest hour," and another career civil servant commented that watching him actively lift up the spirits of his team and keep them forging ahead would have changed the public's view of the chief executive who, as also noted earlier, was in the sloughs of very low popularity. Carlos Gutierrez, then secretary of commerce and former CEO of Kellogg, remarked that "it was something to watch. He was a CEO in action, leading exactly as you would hope. Empowering the team and stepping up when necessary to make the big decisions even if they were very unpopular."

Bolten pointed out that there was no political win to be had for the president, and he knew it. "It was a president who knew he was already unpopular and was about to make himself more unpopular and didn't particularly care. . . . You'd be hard pressed to find many people that say they supported it or support it now. Democrats against it because it was a bailout of banks. Republicans against it because it was a bailout. And I've heard Hank [Paulson] riff on this and he said that he was shown some polling results that found that actually torture had a higher approval rating among the American people than the TARP. And Bush knew that. And he said, you know, hell, if it's the right thing to do, let's go." Not taking this action, however, would likely have resulted in a much deeper financial crash and, therefore, as unpopular and courageous as the Bush decision was, it did have the advantage of almost certainly being a better course of action than the alternative.

"And if you talk to Hank or any of the others about it," continued the former chief of staff, himself a former Goldman executive, "Bush was actually very sophisticated about the financial crisis. I found he often grasped the stuff better than I did. Maybe not as well as Hank or Ben but he had a really good sense of what was going on and understanding it. He . . . didn't try to micromanage what Bernanke and Paulson were doing. He insisted on talking to them. He was always available to discuss it. And so like on Friday afternoon we'd be on the phone with a warning from Hank that such and such an institution is in trouble but we think it'll be OK. And then on Sunday, we'd be on the phone with the president and Bernanke with them describing these desperate situations that would unfold first thing Monday or even Sunday night when the Asian markets were opening. And he understood everything that was going on, he kept himself well briefed, asked challenging questions, and I think that was the right instinct and the right way to handle it."

Steve Hadley tried to commiserate with the president, lamenting that Bush had been thrown a genuine catastrophe during the last three months of his presidency. He received a revealing response, which Hadley characterizes as "typical of the man and also true." Bush replied to Hadley that "I'm glad it happened on our watch. We've been at this for seven and a half years; we've got a team; we've weathered a lot of crises. We're in a position to handle this for the country in a way a new president, no matter who he or she is, will be unable to do in their first term." Hadley saw that "even though it's going to be 'Bush's recession' because it happened on his watch, his view was it's good that it happened now because there couldn't be a better team to handle it. We're seasoned. We're experienced. And I think history's going to show that's right."

Lost in Transition

On November 4, 2008, fewer than two out of three of American voters turned out to vote. But those 130 million who did made history by casting 52.9 percent of their ballots for America's first African American president. The country was largely divided geographically, with the Northeast, the industrial Midwest, and the far West providing the bulk of Obama's support, and the South and the Plains states staying solidly Republican and voting for McCain.

Obama's election represented not one but several watersheds. It is easy, years after it took place, to simply accept the presence of an African American in the Oval Office. But it was a massive and profound shift for America. Further, the fact that American voters elected a man with a Muslim name and a father who was raised in a Muslim family just seven years after 9/11 speaks volumes about a level of tolerance and openness to change in America that is often minimized or discounted. These facts about Obama also speak to another watershed of a more traditional political kind. Bush was elected by saying he would help restore traditional American values. Obama was elected by promising change. After two terms of George Bush, the complex, unwieldy, often Byzantine, and not a little corrupt processes of American democracy actually seemed to have produced the kind of breathtaking shift in leadership that a nation shaken by terror and its aftershocks seemed to call for.

Even before the election, Obama had resolved that, should he win, he wanted a smooth transition, one modeled more on the transitions that Republicans were better known for, with a well-managed operation, clearly delineated roles, and crisp appointment of people in the top jobs. To manage the process, Obama picked a team that included close Chicago confidant Peter Rouse, Valerie Jarrett, and former Clinton White House chief of staff John Podesta, known more recently for having been the founding president of the progressive Center for American Progress. Podesta knew how a White House should work and was the kind of guy Obama could trust to manage things in the cool, deliberate, "no drama" style that was already noted as a hallmark of his management style during the presidential campaign.

The effort, dubbed the Obama-Biden transition project, ultimately employed over 400 individuals working out of offices in Washington and the federal building in Chicago. Bush pledged to cooperate completely with the group and Bolten and Hadley both immediately set in motion processes to ensure a hand-off much smoother than that enjoyed by the Bush team when they took over from the Clinton administration—a transition made famous by prankish Clinton staffers who pried the letter "W" off White House keyboards, a reference to Bush's middle initial.

Obama had been advised to "leave his friends" at home as he considered the process. This was an acknowledgment of the fact that so-called Friends of Bill from Arkansas were not seen as great assets in the early Clinton years, and that Jimmy Carter's buddies from Georgia were similarly seen as a liability when given top government posts. Obama had also pledged to keep lobbyists out of his administration as a sign that he didn't want it to be corrupted by DC's money culture. In retrospect, it can be objectively stated that neither of these guidelines were followed nor were the objectives met. The very first appointment made by Obama, on November 6, 2008, was a contact from Chicago, Congressman Rahm

Emanuel, who was asked to assume the role of chief of staff. Within days Rouse, Axelrod, and Jarrett would also be announced in top roles. The inner circle—largely from Chicago and later criticized by many administration insiders as insulating the president from the rest of his team—began to coalesce almost immediately.

With regard to the chief of staff appointment specifically, Emanuel's immediate predecessor Bolten observed, "there are probably two instincts with presidential chiefs of staff that aren't necessarily good—one being to take a buddy who's not experienced as in the Mack McLarty situation [with Clinton]. And by the way I have very high regard for Mack, but I think even he would probably say, not a smart thing to take somebody with no Washington experience and stick them in as chief of staff. And then there's the celebrity mistake where you take somebody who's accustomed to being a principal and a big cheese on their own and stick them into a role where the "of staff" is more important than the "chief" part of the title. A third error is when you bring in someone who is not well integrated into the presidential team—as happened with Bill Daley [Rahm Emanuel's successor] later in the Obama term." In Bolten's view, Emanuel, a former White House staffer who knew the president and his team well but also had served in Congress and thus knew how Washington worked, fell into none of these traps. What would remain to be seen was whether his famously volatile personality would help or hinder him in a job that can sometimes be the second most powerful in the US government and has at times been likened to that of being a deputy president.

Obama surprised his inner circle, however, when he raised the idea that Hillary Clinton become his secretary of state. It was a pick that came as a surprise to Clinton when, nine days after the election, Obama invited her to his office to offer her the job. Podesta, the former Clinton administration official, had been pushing the idea for months and Obama had also been considering it. In his book, *Renegade: The Making of a President*, Richard Wolffe quotes Obama as saying, "we actually thought during the primary, when we were pretty sure we were going to win, that she could end up being a very effective secretary of state. I felt that she was disciplined, that she was precise, that she was smart as a whip, and that she would present a really strong image to the world." It is telling that Obama's description of Clinton could just as easily apply to the president-elect himself. It is also revealing, though perhaps not surprising, that according to senior campaign staffers, "some folks just couldn't bring themselves to get comfortable with the idea. Clinton had been the enemy, the person they focused most at beating." The campaign had been bitter and tensions simmered.

Clinton was, by all accounts, taken aback by Obama's request that she become secretary of state. In her memoir, *Hard Choices*, she describes how the lingering tensions from the campaign infused their first meeting afterward and the awkwardness that resulted. When presented with the secretary of state option, she offered alternative candidates, including former UN ambassador Richard Holbrooke, who likely would have been her choice as secretary of state had she won the presidency. Obama pursued the idea tenaciously however, encouraging Biden, Emanuel, Podesta, and others to coax her into accepting. The pressure did not initially work and she turned him down again on November 19. Obama pressed on, arguing that the country needed her—applying effectively what is one of the greatest powers of any president, the ability to claim that he is not asking on his own behalf but on that of the entire country. Clinton mulled the issue overnight, discussing it with her husband and with close friends. The next morning Obama received the news from Jarrett that she had changed her mind.

An insight into how the transition process worked at the team level is given by Wendy Sherman, who co-chaired the State Department transition with Tom Donilon (Donilon also helped lead the NSC transition). She recalls, "we didn't spend a lot of time talking about how the State Department would interface with the White House. The focus of the transition was how the Department of State should be organized, how it should reflect the president's priorities—so issues like the role of AID [Agency for International Development], for instance, were prominent. We wanted in that case to make sure that there was a role for development along with diplomacy and defense . . . and then that later developed a particular Clinton stamp on it when she became secretary."

Given the swirling economic crisis, Obama named Geithner as his pick for Treasury on November 24, at the same time announcing that Summers would become his top White House economic advisor as director of the National Economic Council, and Christina Romer would become the administration top economist as director of the Council of Economic Advisors. Obama, according to Geithner, first talked to him in October before the election, and at the time had said, "you know I might need to ask you to come do this," meaning work on the recovery and crisis management issues they were discussing.

Geithner demurred: "I didn't want to do it and I was trying to talk him out of it. And one argument I made to him which I think was the right argument was that . . . I've been up to my neck in this and you're going to want to separate yourself from some of it and your capacity to do that is going to be very much diminished if you ask me to do this. You'll be tied much more to those choices and that will be very constraining for you. But in the end he made a choice . . . even though it would come at the risk that he would be more closely tied to the past."

Geithner and Summers report that the first meetings of the team on substantive issues began immediately. An initial call among them in early December, which included the president, Emanuel, and the rest of the core team, began laying out the immediate agenda, even given that, in the words of one of those on that call, "the crisis did not simply stop to give us time for the election and the transition." Both acknowledge the Bush team was extremely focused on ensuring a smooth hand-off for just that reason.

"My recollection was the agenda was the first-term economic agenda," recalled Geithner, indicating that the substance of the conversation suggested that no matter what he, Paulson, and Bernanke may have been able to achieve in the last months of the Bush administration, much work remained to be done. "We were talking," he said, "about how your first priority is going to be how to prevent the next Great Depression. And if you don't do that, that nothing else will be possible, so why don't we start with that? And the president got irritated with me and said, 'that's not enough for me. I'm not going to define my presidency by what I've prevented.' . . . He was also saying, you know, I care about health care, I care about energy, there's a bunch of things we have to do and I'm not just going to talk about how we fix the financial crisis."

On the process front within the White House economic team, there were fewer discussions. Summers reportedly did not have any significant process discussions with the president on these issues and had only one with Rahm Emanuel. During that meeting Summers proposed that the NEC work, much as was intended by its first director, Robert Rubin, during the Clinton years, as a parallel structure to the NSC. Neither Emanuel nor Summers, like their predecessors, managed to fulfill that vision. Rubin brought a clout to the top job at the NEC that had given the entity some initial gravitas, but in the years afterward with its much smaller staff, lack of historical connections with other agencies, the overly dominant role Treasury played among those agencies, and other factors, it always remained a second-class citizen within the hierarchy of White House internal organizations. In fact, it was only able to gain traction on international issues when its deliberations were seen as joint NSC-NEC efforts. Even when, as during the Obama years, the top international economic advisor was someone very close to the president, as was Michael Froman, a former law school friend of Obama's who was also, like Geithner and Summers, a member of Bob Rubin's inner circle during the Clinton years, the NEC's influence remained minimal.

The Obama choice of Geithner spoke to another sound impulse of the president—he wanted to ensure continuity in circumstances in which crises and instability and the complexity of challenges being faced suggested it was necessary. Treasury was certainly one such place. Another was at the helm of the US Department of Defense, given the state of America's involvement in Iraq and Afghanistan. Accordingly, Obama asked Robert Gates to stay on as secretary. Similarly, Obama wanted to send a strong signal that he would not only be getting sound national security advice but that he could work with the military. For these reasons he settled on James Jones, a sixty-four-year-old Marine general and former supreme allied commander of NATO, to be national security advisor. Jones was initially hesitant about moving into what was essentially a staff job, but Obama promised he would dependably seek his national security advisor's guidance before making any major decisions, and the tall, reserved Marine accepted the post. Ultimately, Thomas Donilon, the head of Obama's transition team for the State Department and a former chief of staff to Secretary of State Warren Christopher, was named Jones's deputy. Denis McDonough and Mark Lippert joined the NSC in important supporting roles, with McDonough serving as head of strategic communication and Lippert, who had returned from Iraq having won a Bronze Star, as chief of staff.

Obama announced the Clinton, Gates, and Jones appointments at a December 1 news conference. Joining them alongside Obama were Janet Napolitano, the nominee to be secretary of homeland security; Eric Holder, the nominee for attorney general; and Susan Rice, who was rewarded for her successful leadership of the Obama national security campaign team with a nomination to be the US Ambassador to the United Nations. Rice's job would hold cabinet rank, thus ensuring she would still be a key advisor to the president, who had come to depend on her views. At the event, Obama made the case that having a diverse group of strong personalities was important because "one of the dangers in the White House, based on my reading of history, is that you get wrapped up in groupthink and everybody agrees with everything and there's no discussion and there are no dissenting views." He suggested he would welcome "vigorous debate in the White House."

Michèle Flournoy and former deputy defense secretary John White were asked to chair the transition effort at the Department of Defense. To round out the national security team, Obama had wanted to appoint John Brennan as CIA director. However, Brennan had become a lightning rod for controversy due to his role as a top advisor to former Bush CIA director George Tenet at a time when the CIA was involved in contentious policies such as the use of "advanced interrogation techniques" and the establishment of Guantanamo Bay. He therefore withdrew his name for consideration for that post. In his place, also at the suggestion of John Podesta, Leon Panetta, the former Clinton chief of staff, OMB director, and one-time chairman of the House Budget Committee, was picked for the job. Though he had limited prior direct national security experience, he was seen as a superb manager with a light political touch and he had a reputation for candor. Furthermore, he had recently been immersed in a range of critical issues as a member of the Iraq Study Group.

Panetta chuckled while describing the situation: "this came out of right field because I had obviously spent a lot of my life working on, like, budget issues and other policy areas. Although you know, both as chairman of the Budget Committee and as chief of staff and OMB director, I'd had a lot of relationships with agents and with what they did. So you know I was certainly familiar with it. But you know, when the president asked, I basically said, 'What are you looking for here?' And he said that the main purpose was trying to restore credibility to the CIA. It had been under a lot of attacks, a lot of criticism about what had gone on there and had a lot of issues related to morale. And I said, 'you know if that's what you want, you have to know that I'm not one who pulls punches. I'm going to tell you exactly . . . what's happening with intelligence. And if that's what you want, fine. And if that's not what you want then you probably ought to say it now.' And he said, 'no, that's exactly what I want.'"

Since Panetta's last stint in government, the director of national intelligence (DNI) post had been created. So an early issue was defining the DNI role vis-à-vis the hitherto fiercely independent role of CIA director. Panetta observed that it worked out ultimately because the DNI role is not very well defined. "Almost instinctively people went into that job and . . . when they recognized that there wasn't a hell of a lot of inherent power within the DNI other than this effort to coordinate the intelligence side, then they began to . . . strike out to seek more power over the agencies, and that creates an internal friction that before I had gotten there had broken out into the open in several ways."

Brennan was not forgotten, however. He was named deputy national security advisor and special advisor for counterterrorism. As such, as the president's top aide in the war on terror, based in an office in the basement of the West Wing, he soon became one of Obama's most trusted and relied-upon national security team members.

When asked to what extent the process was focused on righting perceived missteps of the Bush team, Brennan replied that "there was a bit of that" but his interest as a professional intelligence officer lay in preserving as much continuity of effort as possible on the counterterrorism front—at the working level, overseas, and in terms of the cooperation within the counterterrorism community. Greg Craig, as the incoming White House counsel, addressed the decisions to issue some executive orders—ban certain practices, take some steps that were a fulfillment of campaign promises—and Brennan was involved in those discussions: "I tried to . . . make sure that people took into account what some of the implications of those types of actions were."

Within bureaucracies, there was also discomfort associated with questions of restructuring. Said Derek Chollet, who participated in the NSC transition and later became deputy director of policy planning at State before serving at both the White House and DoD: "we would show up on the doorsteps of people in the NSC and people would be a little nervous, you know, worried. The political guys were easy because they all knew they were leaving. It was the career guys who weren't quite sure what we were all about and worried that they were going to lose their job and there'd be some taint because they served in the Bush administration."

Chollet noted that a fundamental reason for such job insecurity is that "the only position in the NSC that exists by statute is the executive secretary, so . . . there's a considerable degree of latitude for the new team to change things up. And obviously things had changed significantly since the Democrats had been in office—with the Homeland Security Council having been created, with the CT [counterterrorism] infrastructure, which was more of a niche outfit at the end of the Clinton administration and was now a major center of gravity. And the whole Iraq-Afghanistan office was entirely new. So there were a lot of process things we set about figuring out."

Chollet observed that the instinct of many within the team—which also included Ivo Daalder, later ambassador to NATO, but also a highly regarded expert on the history and evolution of the NSC—was to create a smaller, more streamlined structure. But the realities of the new roles and responsibilities that had to be incorporated ultimately drove the Obama administration to assemble the largest NSC staff in history, by a wide margin. The size of the national security staff in the White House continued a trend that had seen constant growth from the establishment of the NSC in 1947 through the present, but the really significant aspect of the new Obama team was the message it sent about the president and his intentions for his presidency.

It is dangerous to oversimplify, but one way to look at the team was as two groups. One set consisted of old hands who could help a young president with limited foreign-policy experience navigate both the wide world and the mazes of the government bureaucracy. The other set was younger staffers, many close to the president's campaign, who were seen as both loyal to Obama and as strong advocates for his campaign's core messages about getting out of Iraq, shifting focus to Afghanistan, restoring relations worldwide, engaging with those we might have seen as enemies, and dialing back the overreactions to 9/11 that had been such a signature of the early Bush years. In the first group were Biden, Gates, Donilon, Clinton, Jones, and Panetta. In the second were people like Rice and NSC staffers such as McDonough, Lippert, Rhodes, and Powers. Over the course of the Obama administration, the diversity of views between the two groups would produce tension, and the resolution of those tensions would ultimately reveal the new president's character and aspirations as a leader.

CHAPTER 5

Hello, I Must Be Going

One need not be a chamber to be haunted;
One need not be a house;
The brain has corridors surpassing
Material place.

—EMILY DICKINSON

Afghanistan has been called the graveyard of empires. For Barack Obama and George W. Bush, it was the classroom in which they first learned about the harsh and confounding realities of war. While going to war in Iraq was a source of great political controversy, even the voices of the extreme left in the United States shared the view that we had a legitimate interest in going hard after those terrorists responsible for the attacks on Wall Street and the Pentagon. As activist filmmaker Michael Moore observed, "most liberals I know were for invading Afghanistan right after 9/11."

But as history has shown, few classrooms have offered harsher lessons than the raw terrain of Afghanistan and the Hindu Kush as it rises into the inhospitable mountains of neighboring Pakistan. Writing in the first post-9/11 edition of *Foreign Affairs,* former CIA Pakistan station chief Milt Bearden both offered a warning and captured the despair that fighting in the region had caused for generations by citing the words of Rudyard Kipling:

When you're wounded and left on Afghanistan's plains
And the women come out to cut up what remains
Jest roll to your rifle an' blow out your brains
An' go to your Gawd like a soldier.

In the late 1980s Bearden oversaw the covert efforts to support Afghan insurgents (and jihadist supporters that ultimately included Osama bin Laden) in the efforts to expel the Soviets from that country. He had seen the challenges of waging a war there close up. The initial US effort in Afghanistan was called Operation Enduring Freedom. Just about five weeks after it began, the Afghan capital Kabul had fallen and the Taliban leadership had slunk from the city in the middle of the night.

Two months later, the UN Security Council joined the effort. It created the International Security Assistance Force (ISAF) to provide both a multinational security umbrella for the country and to help train Afghan troops. The same month, at an international conference in Bonn, Germany, an interim government was established with the support of international powers. The new president was Hamid Karzai, an articulate, sophisticated, ethnic Pashtun from a politically prominent Afghan family.

Over the next year, according to the Congressional Research Service, America's presence in the country ballooned, with the average monthly total of boots on the ground growing from 5,200 in fiscal year 2002 to 10,400 in fiscal year 2003. It doubled again by fiscal year 2006 and grew by 10,000 more to 30,100 by the election year of 2008. But as that happened, America's focus shifted to Iraq. In that country, the total average monthly troop strength grew from almost 70,000 in fiscal year 2007 to 157,800 in fiscal year 2008. In the words of one of the Bush administration's White House inner circle, "almost before we got started in Afghanistan, Iraq began to suck all the oxygen out of the room. It just never got the attention it deserved . . . or required."

Afghanistan would also suffer from another affliction—ghosts. Not just the ghosts of Alexander and the others who stalked the graveyard of empires but also those haunting American planners—the ghosts of Vietnam and later, for Obama, the ghosts of 9/11 and Iraq. In the first case, the Vietnam ghosts and Afghan history combined to lead Pentagon planners, including Donald Rumsfeld, to want to go in with as few troops as possible for as limited a mission as possible. They saw the potential for the country to become a quagmire. Obama feared that should he leave too soon and another 9/11 take place, he would be vulnerable to the bitterest form of second guessing, the assertion that he had weakened America at a time when strength was needed. But he, too, feared the costs of an Iraq-like drain on resources and prestige because, of course, Iraq was his generation's Vietnam. The result was one administration that did too little for too long and another that could not decide what it wanted to do.

The Front Porch

Complicating matters further was that Afghanistan was not a problem unto itself. The invasion of that country represented the first time in the modern era in which America violated the sovereignty of another power while primarily in pursuit of a non-state actor, al-Qaeda. From the very start, we knew that al-Qaeda slipped easily from safe havens in Afghanistan to others across the border in Pakistan. We knew it because the CIA itself had used Pakistan as its base of operations when we were supporting the *mujahideen* in their war against the Soviets. Indeed, we also knew that the elements of the Pakistani security establishment, notably its intelligence service, the ISI, had been actively collaborating with al-Qaeda for years. And whereas Afghanistan was a desperately poor, chronically underdeveloped nation of little geopolitical significance beyond its trade in opium and its harboring of terrorists, Pakistan was the world's sixth most populous nation, locked in a dangerous stand-off with the world's second most populous nation, India—a conflict that had led both to develop nuclear capabilities. At the beginning of American operations in Afghanistan, it was estimated that Pakistan might possess nearly 100 nuclear weapons in its arsenal. The prospect that extremists, who were found everywhere, including in the Pakistani government, might gain control of even one of those weapons was so daunting that it made the threats posed by Afghanistan pale by comparison. As a general once told me, "Afghanistan is really just the front porch of Pakistan. That's where the real problems and the real threats are to be found."

Additionally the Pentagon and State Department were deceived into optimism by the speed of their initial success. As Condoleezza Rice noted, "it's hard to remember that in 2005 we thought that the Afghan project was in relatively good shape." Until then the invasion had gone well: the Taliban were routed, al-Qaeda had been damaged and taken to the hills,

and the Afghan countryside the Americans patrolled was relatively violence free, at least compared to what was about to be unleashed. Indeed,
it had been May 2003 when Secretary of Defense Donald Rumsfeld had
declared "the end of combat operations" in Afghanistan.

Bush, of course, as president, must bear responsibility for both the
under-investment in Afghanistan and the over-investment in Iraq. But,
as Rice also observed with regard to the outlook in 2005, "we did not yet
know that [Pakistan's president Pervez] Musharraf was contemplating a
new peace accord with tribal leaders in North Waziristan, cutting a deal
to live and let live in exchange for staging the passing of militants across
the Afghan border. The policy would ultimately lead to a new safe haven
for the Taliban and a downward spiral in Afghanistan, one that we were
unable to halt before the end of our term."

Further, in the view of senior Bush advisors, there was a strong belief
that not only could the Taliban be dislodged and al-Qaeda pursued and
destroyed by a fairly compact contingent of several thousand military
and CIA operatives, but that such an approach was dictated by the lessons of past failed invasions of the country, notably those of the Soviets
and the British. Bush officials sought to be seen "as liberators not as
occupiers" and, notes one looking back on the period, "That is one of
the reasons why even today there is still support in the country for a continued U.S. military presence."

By 2006, there was rapidly growing unease. The Taliban were regrouping in Pakistan and southern Afghanistan. Not only had US financial aid
dropped for the country after the 2004 election, the country continued
to lack the absorptive capacity—the people and institutions—to ensure
that the money we were sending was used as intended. The Afghan government could only spend about 44 percent of the development money it
received. Further, reports of waste and corruption from US and independent auditors were rampant. So the benefits of the Western intervention
were not widely disseminated, which made it easier for the Taliban and
other extremists to promote their agenda across the Afghan countryside. Meanwhile, throughout 2005 and 2006 Rumsfeld had pushed to get
the United States out, consistent with his view that we had very narrow
interests in Afghanistan—limited almost exclusively to counterterrorism—and that any prolongation of our involvement risked the Vietnam
scenario.

Rumsfeld's impulses, combined with the demands of the war in Iraq,
its growing unpopularity, and the domestic challenges faced by President

Bush associated with those issues—the bungled, insensitive Hurricane Katrina response, and economic problems at home—helped shape a perverse conclusion among the Bush national security team and their president. In order to give the appearance of a "victory" in Afghanistan, they embraced a troop drawdown in early 2006 that actually made eventual achievement of even our most limited goals in Afghanistan—degrading al-Qaeda and the Taliban—much less likely. (The troop reduction also involved shifting resources to Iraq, which proved a debilitating and unproductive distraction. Especially egregious was relocating special operations troops, who were critical players in Afghanistan, given the conditions, terrain, and enemy we were fighting there.) We needed a win so badly we invited a more rapid defeat. When Rumsfeld and CENTCOM chief General John Abizaid announced a drawdown of 3,000 to 4,000 troops in early 2006, it sent a terrible message in Afghanistan—where the people were growing more aware of a rebound by the Taliban—and in Pakistan: the United States was cutting and running. Shifting responsibility to NATO, as Rumsfeld also sought to do, had the added effect of making those troops left behind less effective because most of the components of the NATO-ISAF operation had rules of engagement designed to minimize risk and avoid the likelihood of engagement with the enemy, thus blunting their effectiveness.

Rumsfeld acknowledged that "by early 2006, a reorganized Taliban insurgency had emerged in Afghanistan's east and south. Increasing numbers of Taliban fighters traveled into Afghanistan from Pakistan and retreated back across the border whenever coalition forces tried to engage them." What he didn't admit was that the United States had for years been ineffective in tracking the activities of the Taliban in southern Afghanistan or in neighboring regions of Pakistan. It was possible for the Taliban leadership to recoup their strength undetected, waiting for the right time to strike back out at the occupiers. Worrying about a resurgence, Rumsfeld requested a report on the situation on the ground to be overseen by a Khalilzad advisor, Martin Strmecki, a longtime foreign-policy aide to Richard Nixon. Strmecki's report to Rumsfeld was blunt, as Rumsfeld recounts: "Strmecki didn't sugarcoat anything. The bottom-line, he told me, was we faced a 'deteriorating security situation' caused by a Taliban escalation and weak or bad governance in southern Afghanistan that created a vacuum of power into which the enemy moved. The Taliban had in fact created a shadow government in the towns across southern Afghanistan. If we did nothing, it was possible that the southern city of

Kandahar could return to Taliban control." Rumsfeld characterizes his efforts thereafter as though he were rallying the administration to action in response to a seemingly sudden awakening of the previously "dormant" Taliban, without taking any responsibility for setting unreasonably low troop levels and not carefully monitoring the regions in which the Taliban was regrouping.

Bush, too, was also increasingly awakening to the problem in the region. Not coincidentally, he was awakening at the same time to the realization that it was time for Rumsfeld to go. He recalled in his memoirs receiving a briefing in November 2006 that tracked the "increasingly dire reports about Taliban influence." It noted that in the past year "the number of remotely detonated bombs had doubled. The number of armed attacks had tripled. The number of suicide bombings had more than quadrupled." Bush determined it was time to "adjust our strategy." Like Rumsfeld, he blamed the problem on others elsewhere, notably a failure of "the multilateral approach to rebuilding." He also noted what he and his successors would argue for years to come: that Karzai, his corruption, and the incompetence of his government were core parts of the problem. In keeping with another Washington pattern that is also common in Hollywood—that imitation is the sincerest form of the lack of creativity, or "sequel mentality"—he called the 10,000-person increase in troop strength he ordered in response to the new reports a "silent surge." This was accompanied by a very sharp uptick from NATO in the one kind of attack they felt most comfortable with: those from the air. In the last six months of 2005, there were fewer than 100 such attacks. The number increased over twentyfold for the same period a year later.

In his book, *Descent into Chaos,* described by the *New York Times* as a "blistering critique" of the Bush administration, regional and Taliban expert Ahmed Rashid argued that:

> with all its wealth, resources, and expertise, the United States seemed to have a distinguished record of repeating the same mistakes again and again. The failure in Afghanistan would be spectacularly repeated in Iraq, which was conceived on a mammoth scale by Washington as compared with Afghanistan. Without adequate security and law and order, reconstruction was crippled from the start. Condi Rice admitted in 2005 that in Iraq "we didn't have the right skills, the right capacity to deal with a reconstruction effort of this kind." Her confession came after four years of U.S. government experience in Afghanistan

and two in Iraq. In both countries the failure to reconstruct led to intensified insurgencies and the spread of Al Qaeda. In 2006, with the Taliban on the offensive, Washington increased aid to Afghanistan to $3.3 billion—double the sum given in 2003 for "accelerated success." The following year, in 2007, aid was doubled once again as the insurgency got worse.

Rashid put his finger on a problem that has dogged the US national security establishment for years—that while most of the activities of the US military overseas during the past half century have had a major post-conflict reconstruction or peace-keeping function (both closely linked to winning hearts and minds as necessary in counterinsurgency), there is no agency in the United States that owns the special skills or capacity required by such efforts. Because these activities are economic and political, they are seldom seen as an essential component of the military/national security mission, when nothing could be further from the truth. This is an institutional gap that has dogged the United States throughout the post–World War II era and despite potent evidence that it should be reversed in the wake of our more recent involvements in Afghanistan and Iraq, remains unaddressed and an impediment to the ability of the United States to achieve many of its most important international goals.

Bush NSC officials note that it was not a shortage of resources due to commitments in Iraq that was limiting funding to programs in Afghanistan. Rather, there was a concerted effort to "balance needs on the ground against limited absorptive capacity so as to avoid the pattern of inflation and corruption that regrettably we saw later." They provided, in their eyes, "what we thought the situation required and what the political context in the country could accept and sustain. You know that if the military had asked for more troops for Afghanistan, Bush would have given them. Whenever they did, he did."

Still, to rebuild or stabilize, enemies must be fully defeated or at least sufficiently degraded that the threat they pose can be managed. Places like Afghanistan, then, where the enemy is local and patient enough to wait for invaders to tire of the crisis du jour and head home, raise the question, are such goals accomplishable? In Afghanistan, throughout the Bush administration and indeed throughout the entire term of American involvement in that country, we may have faced the perfect storm of challenges: an enemy that was elusive, patient, and resilient; a reluctance to be drawn into a Vietnam-like quagmire; local allies who were incompetent to support us, or who were actually working both sides of the conflict; and the lack of capacity to effectively absorb more than limited amounts of aid thus constraining our ability to effectively use soft power to achieve greater internal progress or build more good will for the United States and our allies throughout the country. But we were there, and neither major reversals nor the appearance of defeat were acceptable options. So both administrations fought on, violating the first law of holes: "when you find yourself in a hole, stop digging."

What's Bad Gets Worse

With Afghanistan's and Pakistan's porous border and closely intertwined history, it was impossible to separate the issues in one country from those in the other. Not only did significant portions of the Pakistani govern-ment vacillate between benignly tolerating and actively supporting the Taliban and al-Qaeda, they did so for reasons that went right to the core of the Pakistani national identity. These are linked in part to the fact that, as one US diplomat stationed there for years suggested to me, "Pakistanis relate more to their Islamic identity than to their national identity. It is after all why the country was born in the first place, why it broke off from India." For many in Pakistan, including military leaders like Musharraf who were trained since entering the army, India was their one great exis-tential foe. The fear that a new government in Kabul might drift toward or be sympathetic to India was overwhelming and had to be prevented at all costs. Therefore Pakistan saw that it was in its direct national interest to meddle in the affairs of Afghanistan; the Afghan regime of Hamid Karzai was incensed by their attitude and their actions.

Few events so dramatically captured the nature of the ill-will as a din-ner Bush brokered to try to ease the tensions in September 2006. Karzai and Musharraf were invited to the White House for a very small, off-the-record, face-to-face encounter. Bush, Cheney, Hadley, Rice, and the re-spective national ambassadors were present. The mood started out chilly and deteriorated from there. According to Bush, "at one point Karzai accused Musharraf of harboring the Taliban. 'Tell me where they are,' Musharraf responded testily. 'You know where they are!' Karzai fired back. 'If I did, I would get them,' said Musharraf. 'Go do it!' Karzai persisted." Rice recounted that Karzai had come prepared for a debate. After listening for an extended monologue from his Pakistani counter-part in which, in Rice's words, he was guilty of "sugarcoating the facts,"

Karzai pulled a document out of his "flowing cape" that supported his assertion that the Pakistanis would not disturb the Taliban. Rice, the former competitive figure skater who was a noted sports fan, recounted, "it was as if we were watching a heavyweight bout. . . . Karzai was proving to be a brilliant prosecutor and Musharraf had few answers."

Within months, the United States was intently turning up the heat on Pakistan. The new secretary of defense, Gates, was eager to get a more accurate take on the complicity of the Islamabad government, and in particular the ISI, in supporting America's enemies. Doubts grew about Musharraf, alternatively because he was viewed as dissembling to American officials or because he was seen as incapable of persuading his government to follow his instructions. The problem was that neither diplomacy nor traditional military means of confronting those aiding the extremists were working terribly well.

In his memoirs Bush recounted the watershed moment in American strategy brought on by the public opprobrium the United States received when its forces were drawn into firefights in Afghanistan, when they would make international news of the wrong kind: "Islamabad exploded in outrage. . . . I looked for other ways to reach into the tribal areas. The Predator, an unmanned aerial vehicle, was capable of conducting video surveillance and firing laser-guided bombs. I authorized the intelligence community to turn up the pressure on the extremists."

David Sanger, one of the foremost analysts of the birth of the next generation of conflict, known as "light footprint" tactics, including drones, cyber-attacks, and special operations, offered a penetrating analysis of this turning point in his book, *The Inheritance*:

> while we dealt with Afghanistan and Pakistan as separate problems . . . the Taliban and al Qaeda acted as if the territory were a single tribal land. . . . Until Bush's last full year in office, when he issued a series of secret "permissions" that finally gave the CIA—and some American Special Forces—greater leeway to attack inside Pakistan, the White House did not treat the area as a single battlefield. . . . It was yet another example of the inability of the administration to change course when circumstances changed. Inside Bush's insular White House, a strategic change was often equated as weakness or viewed as an admission of error.
>
> Instead, the administration mounted a public relations effort. . . . As in Vietnam, the statistics were designed to hide the larger truth

and to distract attention from warnings being circulated inside the administration that laid out the very real possibility of failure in coming years.

One top Bush advisor with whom I spoke strongly objected to Sanger's characterization of the situation, arguing that in fact, "We did see Afghanistan and Pakistan as a single battlefield. And we did adapt and change course." On this latter point, the administration deserves considerable credit as does the US military. Indeed, whatever the flaws in their collective approach to responding to the perceived post-9/11 terror threat, they did ultimately adapt, eschewing traditional approaches to war fighting when confronting unconventional enemies, and pioneered the approaches later embraced by the Obama team. Many of the "light footprint techniques" the Obama administration employed were, in fact, developed and actively implemented during the final years of Bush's term of office by his team, including Rice, Gates, Hadley, and the new top military commanders, and thanks to their willingness to learn and embrace new ideas over their course of their time in office.

Obama's Good War and His New Team

During the 2008 presidential campaign, Barack Obama repeatedly called the war in Iraq a distraction. In mid-July of that year, in a speech in Washington, he expressed the core of his argument saying, "if another attack on our homeland comes, it will likely come from the same region where 9/11 was planned. And yet, today we have five times more troops in Iraq than in Afghanistan." He went on to say that "as President, I will pursue a tough, smart, and principled national security strategy—one that recognizes that we have interests not just in Baghdad, but in Kandahar and Karachi, in Tokyo and London, in Beijing and Berlin. I will focus this strategy on five goals essential to making America safer: ending the war in Iraq responsibly; finishing the fight against al Qaeda and the Taliban; securing all nuclear weapons and materials from terrorists and rogue states; achieving true energy security; and rebuilding our alliances to meet the challenges of the 21st century."

Behind the logic of these ideas was another set of political goals. Iraq was deeply unpopular, and the American people had grown tired of seven years of costly conflicts. Obama's assertions that he wanted to get out of

Iraq, reduce dependence on foreign energy (read: energy from the Middle East), and rebuild our alliances (read: have other nations put themselves at risk so the United States doesn't have to be the world's policeman) addressed this. But running against a war hero like John McCain and the traditional tough national security stance of the Republican Party, he could not appear to be calling purely for winding down US involvement. That would be seen as a sign of weakness and an invitation to future 9/11s—an intolerable risk even to the war-weary. Hence, his decision to refocus efforts on bin Laden and the so-called "good war" in Afghanistan, and to acknowledge the links between that conflict and the growing awareness of the instability in Pakistan. This allowed Obama to appear resolutely tough and simultaneously more strategic than the outgoing Bush team.

It was, however, a trap, given the extreme difficulties associated with making progress on the ground in Afghanistan and with Pakistan. It made for a good balance in a speech, but going from an unnecessary war to an unwinnable one was not necessarily the right formula for achieving long-term national-security policy success.

The process of preparing the president-elect for the business of addressing this challenge began during the last months of the Bush administration when Hadley asked Doug Lute to conduct a strategy review. Bush had wanted a no-holds-barred assessment of where seven years of US efforts had brought the country and the region. So Lute took an interagency team with him to visit the region, only to find that enemy attacks had increased dramatically and were now occurring at a rate of about 200 a month. Back in Washington, he began to prepare the effort, with clear guidance from Hadley not to pull any punches. They might not be able to follow through on his findings, but they would be able to pass on a better road map to whoever was going to follow them into the White House.

The report itself was presented at an NSC meeting late in November. Hadley's admonitions aside, the report was somewhat gentler than a clear-eyed view might have warranted. It argued that the United States wasn't losing in the Afghan theater of operations, but neither was it making progress. The report flagged three problems that had to be resolved: Afghan corruption, the pervasiveness of the Afghan drug trade, and the ability of insurgents to hide out in Pakistani safe havens. What it did not do was clarify what the long-term American goals should be in either country or candidly assess why US military strategies had been, in the words of one Obama NSC staffer with whom I discussed the report, "so wrong for so long in so many ways."

My conversations with a broad cross section of the top national security officials on the Bush team included an acknowledgment that, after initial successes, the effort got shifted to a back burner because of Iraq and suffered as a result. Said one insider, "This was an error that haunts me still. But I do wonder, having watched what happened since, if whatever we had done would have been enough." Rice, in both her memoirs and in private conversation, blamed much of the problem on Musharraf's deal with the Taliban and the corruption and incompetence of the Karzai government. Bush wrote, "our rapid success with low troop levels created false comfort and our desire to maintain a light footprint left us short of the resources we needed. It would take several years for these shortcomings to be clear." Strikingly, Rumsfeld suggested that he—who had been the principal advocate for the low-troop-level approach and who had consistently downplayed the evolving risks even as they worsened—had been the whistle-blower, writing in his memoirs, "my efforts to turn the NSC's attention to Afghanistan in 2006 were only marginally successful." No one version accounted for why the venture in Afghanistan had gone wrong, but there was conspicuous agreement that it had.

One particularly resonant comment came from an insider, a career civil servant who worked for both administrations: "whatever the Bush administration did or did not do in Afghanistan, they will likely be remembered most for Iraq." And so it has proved. The civil servant prophetically ventured that "Afghanistan would become Obama's war."

That war began for Obama just two days after his election, when he received his first intelligence briefing as president-elect from Mike McConnell, the DNI, and Deputy CIA Director Mike Morrell. Bush had ordered that key elements of the briefing be for the president-elect's ears only, and so Obama's aides, who hoped to join the meeting, including top transition team officials John Podesta and Jim Steinberg, were left cooling their heels. One key element of the briefing, according to Bob Woodward's book, *Obama's Wars,* centered on the difficulties in dealing with the Pakistanis and the growing importance of drone activity. It highlighted the American perception that when the Pakistanis were given advanced word of attacks, they would tip off the intended targets and that Bush, infuriated by this, shifted to letting the Pakistanis know about attacks slightly after the attacks took place. Important cyber and special ops initiatives were also detailed. According to Woodward, Obama left the meeting and said to an aide, "I'm inheriting a world that could blow up any minute in half a dozen ways, and I will have some powerful but limited and perhaps even dubious tools to keep it from happening."

A subsequent meeting, about two weeks later, with Joint Chiefs chairman Mullen produced a similarly dispiriting analysis. Mullen asserted that Afghanistan had not received enough attention or support and that there was no strategy guiding US efforts there. It was a critique he would later make behind closed doors of Obama's strategies in Iran and elsewhere in the Middle East.

As a consequence of Obama's intention to make Afghanistan a priority and to recast it in the consequence of AfPak, his transition began to explore ways to reorganize the efforts of key national security agencies to reflect this focus. Pakistan had a new president, Asif Ali Zardari, the husband of slain former prime minister Benazir Bhutto. Vice President–elect Biden and Republican Senator Lindsay Graham undertook an early initiative to reach out to Zardari's administration two weeks before the inauguration in Washington. Biden was blunt about the need for Pakistani cooperation, offering better relations if there was better cooperation, and worse if Pakistan continued to undermine American efforts. Zardari was more conciliatory than Musharraf. However, Biden and Graham's meetings with Zardari stood in stark contrast to the US delegation's meetings with Karzai, which were extremely contentious. During the discussion with Karzai they also put down a marker that Obama would not be handling these issues as Bush had done. Woodward quotes Biden as saying, "President-elect Obama wants to be helpful, but this idea of picking up the phone, calling Obama like you did President Bush is not going to happen." The intent, according to staffers, was to send a message that Karzai could not play the White House as he did before, and that the president was not going to expose himself to the risks posed by Karzai's histrionics, which had hurt Bush from time to time. The message also revealed what would be a distinct difference in how Obama and Bush handled virtually all international interactions—Obama was much less inclined to conduct personal diplomacy unless there was a clearly defined benefit to doing so.

On this trip Biden also indicated to the commanding general of US forces in Afghanistan that the new administration's internal reviews and transition plans called for increasing the number of troops in his theater of operation.

One of the most notable early reorganizational moves of the new team was the creation of the office of special representative for Afghanistan and Pakistan (SRAP) in the State Department. Hillary Clinton fought hard for her friend and ally Richard Holbrooke to get this post. Holbrooke was a brilliant diplomat who, as a young man, initially served in Vietnam and subsequently as an aide to Henry Kissinger. He served with Kissinger during the Paris peace talks with two other young aides, future director of national intelligence John Negroponte and future SRAP James Dobbins, who would serve under Secretary Kerry. Later, in the Carter administration, Holbrooke was assistant secretary of state for East Asian and Pacific affairs. During the Clinton years, he became ambassador to Germany, assistant secretary of state for European and Eurasian affairs, Balkan envoy, and ambassador to the United Nations.

Holbrooke had also been Hillary Clinton's chief foreign-policy advisor during her campaign. And during his Clinton years he had run bitterly afoul of several members of the inner circle of the Obama team, notably Anthony Lake and Susan Rice. Lake and Holbrooke had once been very close but had a nasty falling out over both personal and policy differences. During the Clinton years, there was a widely acknowledged rivalry between the two.

One member of the Lake camp with whom Holbrooke had especially bad relations was Susan Rice. This manifested itself most colorfully in an incident in which the two faced off with one another in a State Department conference room when Rice was assistant secretary of state for Africa. Rice was defensive and abrasive, and Holbrooke looked across the table at her and said, "Susan, I understand. I was the youngest assistant secretary here once myself." The future successor to Holbrooke as America's top diplomat at the United Nations flipped Holbrooke the bird and walked out of the room.

"They thought I was crashing their party," Holbrooke said to me. "But in the end, the issues were too big to let the background noise get in the way." Holbrooke described that his first objective was to put together what he described as "a prototype for government the way it ought to be done." He meant that he felt he couldn't achieve his goals unless he had a genuinely interagency, whole-of-government team that would bring together in one office professionals from State, Defense, USAID, the CIA, Justice, and other agencies, working seamlessly and without regard for departmental rivalries. Clinton embraced the process, and the office of the SRAP, located on the ground floor of the State Department, became a kind of intergovernmental melting pot. Holbrooke also used his extensive Washington contacts to help manage his own transition with the

Bush team. One example, among the many cited by members of his team, was Holbrooke's invitation to his old friend Negroponte to meet with key members of Holbrooke's new team and give them the benefit of his experience at the center of the Bush administration's efforts in the region.

As a senior advisor, Holbrooke appointed Dr. Vali Nasr, an Iranian-born academic with a PhD in political science from MIT and a deep knowledge of the issues associated with the greater Middle East. Nasr, after his tenure with Holbrooke, would write *The Dispensable Nation: American Foreign Policy in Retreat*, one of the first critiques of the Obama administration to come from one of its officials.

"One of the big things that Holbrooke was very focused on was that Pakistan and Afghanistan should be managed out of one office," Nasr recalled. "Under the Bush administration, Iraq and Afghanistan were managed in one office, while Pakistan and Afghanistan were managed in separate offices. And Holbrooke was very clear that Pakistan and Afghanistan constituted a single theater of war."

He continued, "I would say that the transition year of the election, 2008, was where the happy story of the Bush administration fell apart. So yes, there was a smooth handover between teams and yes, General McKiernan carried on for a bit longer. But very quickly, the Obama administration changed the entire national security operation in Afghanistan and Pakistan." Nasr pointed out that all the ambassadors were changed, with the exception of Anne Patterson in Pakistan. "Yes, Doug Lute stayed on and continued to handle these issues at the White House but in part that was because he was a military insider, which was viewed as a plus by the team at the White House."

As the team changed, so did the policy, of course. "We became much tougher with Karzai," Nasr said. "We became much tougher with the Pakistani military. The CIA got a much more overt role, although behind the scenes, in helping to define policy with Pakistan. And so the policy changed abruptly and with it was, with both Karzai and the Pakistanis, a rough landing."

Husain Haqqani was appointed by Zardari as the new Pakistani ambassador to the United States in April 2008. He too remembers the transition from Bush to Obama and to Holbrooke's new team as a tough one: "Holbrooke became the main person, the main point of contact. Holbrooke was another one scarred by Vietnam. He was into the idea of finding a grand bargain—so that the US could get its troops out of Afghanistan but that somehow was also a deal in which Pakistan could sign on and help guarantee the security of the region. He was constantly working on that deal."

Another footnote to Holbrooke's start in the job was that he initially pushed hard for it to include working with the other country he felt was essential to the equation on the ground in the AfPak region—India. But as soon as the Indian government got wind of this they pushed back hard against it. They did not want to be lumped in with the AfPak problem region nor did they want to get involved in efforts by Holbrooke to try to broker deals between them and Pakistan as part of any "grand bargain." The United States took the Indian complaints into consideration and kept the SRAP's work narrowly focused on the already very large problems associated with AfPak.

Holbrooke's reputation for being difficult to work with was not an issue for at least some of his colleagues at the State Department. It certainly was not for Clinton and her inner circle, such as Anne-Marie Slaughter, the former dean of the Woodrow Wilson School at Princeton who became Clinton's director of policy planning: "maybe it's because I'm an academic. We're used to taking intelligent ideas from people who were capable of being difficult. It's part of the game. You judge on the ideas, not the personalities. And you know, he was one of the few people who was an effective bureaucratic player and understood power and really had big ideas."

"Roll Up Your Sleeves"

Members of Obama's transition team and, as they were picked, the new principals of his administration, met not only with Bush administration transition briefers, but they also reached out to former occupants of their offices. Obama, as was typical, read White House histories and sat with former occupants of the office including, notably, Bill Clinton as well as Bush. Jones at the NSC also spoke with predecessors in the job and read histories of the organization.

Tom Donilon, who started out as Jones's deputy, had a very extensive network of contacts of his own within the White House inner circle, at State, and elsewhere in the government, particularly the vice president's staff. He had developed a close relationship with Obama during the 2008 debates when he spent "dozens of hours" working with the president helping him to prepare. Further, Donilon was the closest senior staffer in the White House to Vice President Biden, with a relationship dating back over three decades. (Donilon's brother Mike was counselor to Vice President Biden, and his wife, Catherine Russell, was chief of staff to Biden's wife, Jill, before assuming her subsequent role as the US ambassador-at-large for global women's issues.) Because he helped oversee the transition at the State Department, Donilon was also involved closely in the structural discussions that occupied the new administration as it began allocating to its new priorities.

During one of our conversations, Donilon laid out a lengthy but thoughtful overview of the Obama NSC structure and how it was initially conceived. He began with a central and important concept: "every National Security Council system has to reflect the president. And our system did and does reflect [Obama], who has a penchant towards methodical, extensive analysis and deliberation. And, as he has often said, he likes things 'tight.' And we set up a system to provide him with that." Donilon observed that such a system reflects the fact that national issues need to be carefully coordinated by the White House. "This is because of the multidimensional nature of the problems we face. Currently, you can't really look at a problem from the perspective of a single institution or just decide a problem via sitting down with the State Department or the Defense Department. There's a necessity for an overarching strategy to be applied to the activities. Also, there are institutional biases which, by the way, during a time of war become exacerbated to some extent."

Donilon, who, like Jones, immersed himself in the literature of the national security process, revealed in his comments elements of what was no doubt the intent of the president and his team. Guided by the assertion that a White House–centric system was necessary and a view of the where-you-sit-is-where-you-stand reality of Washington, his expressed perspective was certainly somewhat different from that he held during the Clinton years when he was a top aide to Secretary of State Warren Christopher. It was also different from the original intent for the NSC to serve as a coordinating mechanism for the interagency policy development and implementation process. The bigger it became and the more hands-on its role in the management and even in the execution of US foreign policy, the greater the risk that it would fall into the trap that later befell it during the Obama years after Donilon left—of setting itself up as a kind of rival State Department, that was too operational, too big, while lacking the bandwidth to do those things and effectively fulfill its coordinating or strategic planning duties. Becoming more White House–centric was perhaps inevitable given the long-term trends like a compressed news cycle and around-the-clock Internet coverage of virtually everything, making many more developments large and small politically relevant to the president and his team. Concentrating policy in the White House too heavily was, however, a formula for alienating cabinet members and agencies, for not taking full advantage of their resources, and for distracting the NSC team from its essential core missions. Donilon, aware of this risk, sought to counteract it where he could. In particular he supported a much lower-profile role for the national security advisor, during both Jones's tenure and his own, than would later be taken by Obama's third national security advisor, Susan Rice. But in accepting the premise of the growing centrality of the White House, Obama's NSC was on a dangerously slippery slope. Meetings with the president may have been run on a tight basis, but right from the outset the bloated Obama national security apparatus was seen by many of its participants as conducting too many meetings. There were concerns that many of those meetings did not actually reach conclusions but only led to more meetings—a shortcoming, which reportedly became more pronounced after Donilon's departure from the NSC.

"So the system we set up," continued Donilon, describing the structure of the Obama NSC, at least as it was intended to operate, "was modeled on the Brent Scowcroft–Bob Gates system," that is, from the administration of George H. W. Bush, in which Scowcroft was NSC advisor and Gates was his deputy—regarded by every administration since as the prototype for the modern NSC. "This included as a central component interagency policy committees, a very active deputies committee, which becomes essentially the operating committee of the government." While recounting this in mid-2013, he observed that in the first four years of the government the deputies committee, incorporating deputies from all the NSC member departments and agencies, had met more than 1,000 times. He then noted that above the deputies committee was an active principal's committee (the cabinet secretaries and other named members of the NSC), and above that was the National Security Council, whose meetings involved not only the agency principals but also the President of the United States.

"We also sought and received agreement from the principals at the outset of the administration that this will be the exclusive system for deciding foreign-policy priorities," said Donilon. "It is just inconceivable that you would have in this system, as you did in the prior administration, where a cabinet officer would come in to the president with a very big decision and ask him to just sign on to it. This president would literally look at this person and say, 'What are you doing? Have you talked to Jim or have you talked to Tom? Has this been through the process? Don't ever do that again.' And that would be his reaction. So we have an exclusive system. But of course, for it to be an exclusive system it has to be a competent system, and it needs to give people a sense that in reality decisions can be made in a timely and effective way and that it's on the level, that it can work for them."

Donilon was clearly trying to distinguish his NSC from Donald Rumsfeld's practice during the first term of the Bush administration of coming unprepared to principals meetings, which would then enable him to backdoor the process and go, once he had his position prepared, directly to the president. Having said that, although cabinet secretaries may not have had back doors into the Oval Office, from the very outset it emerged that the process was not quite as exclusive as intended. Whereas it was the vice president and the secretary of defense with the back channel under Bush, it was Obama's closest political advisors and former campaign aides who enjoyed an inside track that some of their cabinet colleagues (and even their national security advisor) did not. A hint as to how that emerged is suggested by Donilon's comments about the regular internal White House meetings, which ultimately were more influential in driving the policy process than were the formal NSC structures: "perhaps most importantly we have had a daily discussion each morning around the president's daily briefing. Again we've done this quite consciously. It's thirty to forty minutes. We have the intelligence briefing at the top of the meeting. And then, every morning since January 20, 2009, we have made a presentation either commenting on the stuff that's in the intelligence or moving around the world to key things that are happening or saying 'we have a couple decisions we have to make today' or 'Hillary Clinton really needs a decision on this and she has asked me to bring this to you today' or 'we have a personnel issue that we really need to work through.' Alternatively, he might say, 'I read X, Y, or Z overnight and I want to have a conversation about that now.' And you know, these conversations have built upon one another. We also would try to take, every Thursday afternoon, ninety minutes or two hours with the president for something we would call 'national security staff time.' And in those sessions we would concentrate on one or two issues where he can have a detailed discussion."

Although Donilon argues that this approach has resulted in a great deal of comity among the principals in the administration, others, including even senior officials, very early on began to sense that the daily inner circle meetings with the president left some NSC principals out of the loop. Attending these daily meetings from the outset were the president, Jones, Donilon, Brennan, Emanuel, and, depending on their role in the administration at the time, Denis McDonough and others. Donilon asserts that political advisors like Axelrod and Jarrett never participated in these meetings, although administration insiders with whom I spoke felt they regularly influenced outcomes via the parallel formal and informal political advisory process that took place.

Bill Burns thought the Obama team had started well but he recognized an early sign of a flaw that would grow: "I think part of a bigger structural problem that I've seen over the past thirty years is that too much gets pushed up too high in the system. . . . Much of what gets talked about in deputies and principals meetings now, compared to what I remember as a note-taker on the NSC staff in the late '80s, can or should be handled at the assistant secretary level. This is a challenge that has been building for a number of years, and it's not unique to the current administration. But what it does, I think, is squeeze time and attention out of some of the bigger strategic issues that ought to be discussed."

One other senior Obama official said of the inner-circle-dominated process: "the trouble with this is that it excluded a lot of people and ideas that should have been at the table. And it was terrible for morale in the agencies. Policymaking by small groups is sometimes needed, but the key is to have the right people in these groups and those in the Obama inner circle were not always the right ones. And often it took a long time for those in these small meetings to communicate with others in the administration, so much time was wasted in people doing work that they need not have done because they were going in a different direction from the president. Few people in the administration felt they were on the Obama Team."

Others from the beginning had concerns about Jones, who had been widely admired and liked by those who had worked with him during his long and distinguished military career. One was Doug Lute, who had worked with him and become friendly with him at NATO. Contrasting him with Hadley, who had in Lute's view been a maestro of the NSC policy process, Lute observed that Jones came to the role after having "been a four star for seven years. He had been commandant of the Marine Corps and then did three years as supreme allied commander in Europe. Those are big, powerful positions with large staffs that accommodate your desires before you desire them. Well that's not the NSC. The NSC is a roll-your-sleeves-up, twelve- to fifteen-hour day, six days a week. You know, it requires rigorous preparation for every engagement with the president and every international leader. But as highly as I regard Jim, I think it was a tough adjustment for him, perhaps as it would be for anyone, because in the end, the national security advisor is a senior staff officer." Almost from his first days in office, other White House staffers were concerned that although Obama respected Jones, he just did not seem to connect with him as he did with other senior staff with whom he had a longer-standing relationship.

The First AfPak Review

Obama's first national security meeting the day after his inauguration addressed Iraq; his second, two days later, turned the discussion to Af-Pak. Obama asserted that he felt that a first step was developing a clear, focused strategy. It needed to blend the views that had been developed in Lute's review as well as those conducted by the military. It was clear that more troops were going to be added, but the president wanted a rationale for adding them, and a long-term plan for achieving American goals. Also, according to one senior insider, there was a view, present from the transition onward, that back-channel connections to the Taliban might be necessary to achieve the lasting political stability the adminis-tration sought. This began a long, often frustrating search for the right back-channel, the so-called elusive "good Taliban" and an openness to dealing with the group in more flexible ways. That effort later manifested itself, for example, in the aforementioned trade earlier that swapped Bowe Bergdahl for five captured Taliban leaders.

Lute himself said, "I credit the administration, the president in par-ticular, with accepting the point of hyphenating AfPak, as much as the Pakistanis didn't like it. I thought that was a substantial move forward conceptually in terms of understanding the problem not as isolated to Afghanistan proper, but (a) centered on al-Qaeda, and (b) therefore the need to geographically approach this in both Afghanistan and Pakistan."

The president also asked Bruce Riedel, the former intelligence an-alyst who handled some of these issues for the Obama campaign, to oversee his own review of US AfPak strategy. Obama had reportedly initially wanted Riedel to join the NSC staff, but he demurred. None-theless, he was able to persuade the thirty-year CIA veteran to lead the review on what the president asserted at the time was one of his top two foreign-policy priorities, along with getting out of Iraq. It would be an interagency process co-chaired by Holbrooke and new Under Secretary of Defense for Policy Michèle Flournoy. The president wanted the review fast-tracked. He gave it two months to be completed. He wanted it done prior to his first NATO summit so he could provide America's European partners with answers to the questions about his plans for Afghanistan.

Obama's primary interest was having a clear goal. Riedel's recommendation would become a mantra for the administration's policy thereafter. It was to "disrupt, dismantle, and defeat" al-Qaeda and its allies, and do everything possible to ensure they didn't return to the regions from which American troops had fought to rid them for over seven years. During early discussions with Jones and top defense officials in the first month, the plan focused on some of the core ideas that had evolved during the last year of the Bush administration: a properly funded and supported COIN plan, more resources for the Afghan army, and more aid to Pakistan if they would deliver the coordinated support the United States sought. "Very early on," however, noted one of the participants in the process, "it became pretty clear that there were two camps emerging on this issue. There was the Riedel school, which was more or less supported by the military. And then there was the vice president and those close to him. Biden just didn't believe in his heart that we were going to be able to succeed in Afghanistan. History was against us."

Biden's answer was to narrow the focus from counterinsurgency—which implied building broad public support against extremists, in essence changing the political culture of the country—to counterterrorism. His idea was that we had gone in to seek revenge on al-Qaeda and ensure they couldn't attack again. We should beat them, beat back the Taliban, and leave it at that. In short, he was echoing Rumsfeld's perspective, although it is unlikely for reasons of both politics and personality that either man would admit they were on the same "go small and get out" page on this issue. Clinton and Gates supported the broader counterinsurgency option.

Obama took into consideration the vice president's arguments and in particular his assertion that a prolonged expansion of activity in Afghanistan was not politically viable, but he was also boxed in by his campaign stance. He had to increase the resources devoted to AfPak and he felt he had to do it quickly. He wanted to ensure it emphasized more focus on Pakistan and explained his decision to increase the number of troops that he was deploying to this distant war. Once he felt that the Riedel process provided what he needed, he announced the new strategy. His speech, from the White House, on March 27, 2009, emphasized how critical it was to succeed: "for the Afghan people, the return to Taliban rule would condemn their country to brutal governance, international isolation, a paralyzed economy, and the denial of basic human rights to the Afghan people, especially women and girls."

It was a powerful moment and a compelling argument. Yet within just four and a half years the White House would be seriously considering plans to get out of Afghanistan at any cost, even though the president's own intelligence agencies warned that to do so would be to invite precisely what the president warned against in his first major policy address on that early spring day in 2009.

The review did not achieve its goal of ending the cycle of constant reviews and second-guessing that had gone on for years. Indeed, it had effectively laid out the battle lines for an ongoing debate about the extent of US involvement in the region, our expectations from our allies, the amount of money we were to spend, and the kinds of metrics by which we should evaluate our progress. Further, while the review was supposed to cast a more realistic eye on the situation on the ground, in order to give us a better reading on outcomes than was possible during the Bush era, one of the greatest concerns was papered over. That was the sense that Pakistan was the place where risk was greatest—largely due to the size and precariousness of its nuclear arsenal and its overt and covert collaboration with extremists. "I personally found the risks in Pakistan to make Afghanistan seem trivial by comparison, but we didn't dare flag them because some were classified and any sign that we were further targeting Pakistan would create a political shitstorm in Islamabad," said one senior Defense Department official familiar with the Riedel process.

Looking back on the process, co-chair Flournoy says, "I think Bruce did a great job of really trying to be an honest broker and bring the players together with a common strategy. I think there were some mismatches between goals even within the team. We kept trying to narrow the objectives and be more specific about what's realistic to achieve in the context of Afghanistan and what's essential to our interests versus just what's nice to have. Some in the State Department gravitated to the more lofty, more ambitious—we have to have free and fair elections, democracy, development, nation-building—you know this sort of thing. And we tried to stay more practical."

Another perspective, described by a top Pentagon official, echoed this view: "the DoD view came to be known as 'Afghan-good-enough,' which was to say, accept that this country would be at the bottom of development list for a long time to come. But Holbrooke was always drawn to the high politics in a place where high politics weren't exactly irrelevant but weren't likely to determine success or failure. Meanwhile people like Doug Lute at the NSC were far more interested in micromanaging the military campaign than they were making sure there was a political strategy to take advantage of any gains we had on the battlefield."

One immediate casualty of the Riedel process and shift in strategy was General McKiernan, who had lost the confidence of Admiral Mullen and the chiefs. On May 11, Secretary of Defense Gates announced that the new commander on the ground would be Stanley McChrystal.

In his remarks announcing the McChrystal appointment, Gates said that he had asked the new commander to rethink Afghanistan, looking for better ways to succeed. According to senior White House staffers, this was a decision reached by the president and with which Gates concurred. Woodward recounts Riedel listening and wondering "what the hell was going on. Just six weeks earlier he had completed the strategy review, the president had given his speech and Gates had embraced it fully. Were they starting over again?" Of course, as Woodward wrote those words, he knew they were rhetorical. Because, indeed, within the military, there was already an emerging push for more troops than Obama had committed. At McChrystal's confirmation hearing in June he brought this view more into the open by stating he did not know if the total number of troops planned for deployment would be sufficient.

McChrystal recounts in his memoirs that Gates had assigned him four tasks. These included undertaking "a strategic assessment of the war" and determining "any necessary changes to the mission, strategy or how our forces were organized." As Obama had done with Riedel before, Gates gave McChrystal sixty days to conduct the second big strategic review within six months. Two weeks after arriving in the country, Jim Jones, who thanks to his military connections had heard the buzz about this new effort to rethink the approach to Afghanistan, surprised McChrystal by asserting that the White House would not consider any new requests for troops until those already promised had been deployed and could be evaluated. The general concluded that meant that no new requests would be weighed until the end of the year. "I was working on what I thought was different guidance from Secretary Gates, to conduct a detailed assessment and an analysis of required resources, which I would submit in the middle of August," he wrote in his memoirs, adding that "the delayed time line National Security Advisor Jones articulated worried me."

It should have. It was a sign that the carefully thought-out national-security policy process that Donilon described was not working. In fact, it had multiple problems. Not only were there splits among the national security principals but some in the Defense Department were apparently on a different page from the White House, and neither Jones nor anybody in the White House was able to effectively keep those differences from growing worse or more distracting.

By the summer of 2009, in fact, problems were beginning to emerge around Jones. Not only was he ill-suited to the staff work, but a whispering campaign was starting to emerge from insiders who had opposed his appointment in the first place. Phone calls from people in the administration or conversations over meals suggested that the national security advisor "didn't understand the nature of the job," had "never really shown an aptitude for foreign policy when he was Supreme Allied Commander in Europe," would leave the office to go home for lunch, would leave promptly at the end of each day regardless of the workload borne by the staff or the need for his active engagement, was disinclined to work weekends, and so on. He was seen as stiff and not receptive to the views of many who had worked hard on the campaign. There were emerging tensions between him and the president's inner political circle—the likes of Emanuel, Axelrod, Gibbs, and particularly McDonough and Lippert, who ostensibly worked for Jones but were granted easier access to the president and the rest of the inner circle of advisors than was the former four-star general. Significant generational and cultural gaps were exacerbated by the fact that Obama and Jones simply didn't have the kind of history or close relationship that had been so important to past successful president-NSA collaborations such as Eisenhower and Andrew Goodpaster, Nixon and Henry Kissinger, Carter and Zbigniew Brzezinski, Bush and Brent Scowcroft, or Clinton and Sandy Berger. Familiarity didn't guarantee success, as the Reagan–William Clark or George W. Bush–Condoleezza Rice experiences showed, but for a president with a great deal on his plate, unfamiliarity with his national security advisor is an unnecessary obstacle to early success. One *New York Times* story by Helene Cooper illustrated the problem when it cited an incident in which McDonough undermined Jones's authority by interrupting his superior during a meeting to correct him about what the president was really thinking.

It is undeniably true that some of the whispers emanated from players who had something to gain from undercutting Jones, but there were other factors as well. One of these was that Jones was military, and the inner circle at the White House had few military ties. One senior civilian at Defense itemized the problems: Jones was "not an inside player"; the people who were closest to the president "didn't understand how to work with the military, how to know whether the military was trying to game them"; Chairman of the Joint Chiefs Mike Mullen and his vice chairman, James E. "Hoss" Cartwright, "barely spoke to each other" because "the chairman has the formal responsibility of being the adviser to the president, but you had a White House that was more comfortable with Hoss and were consistently calling him over to have one-on-ones with the staff and time with the president that the chairman didn't have." All told, the national security team was, in key places, at odds with itself.

The long-time Obama supporter went on to say, "it got to the point where you know the vice president's staff asked Hoss to come over to the White House . . . to counter requests from McChrystal. . . . It ended up that Mullen had many conversations with Hoss saying 'you should resign, this is unacceptable and you've crossed the line.' And Hoss had the president's support. And the president wanted to hear from Hoss. He was a smart, creative innovative guy and he wanted to hear both perspectives." Cartwright, his undeniable qualities as a leader and as an advisor aside, would later become a political target because he was known as "Obama's general."

Against this background of bickering, McChrystal conducted his review. He told his team to be as objective as possible and to set aside preconceptions of what higher-ups might want to hear. His draft document was sixty pages long plus a thirty-page appendix. While it didn't seek additional troop deployments, the core message was unmistakable. It specifically stated that "continued underresourcing will likely cause failure."

Gates, sensing the pushback from the White House, instructed McChrystal to hold on to the assessment until after the Afghan elections scheduled for August 20. Meanwhile, at the White House, the president, vice president, and the inner circle were beginning to focus on a different issue—how to get out. As Sanger writes in *Confront and Conceal*, "returning to the White House one day after visiting wounded soldiers at

Washington's army hospital, he [Biden] told his aides, 'I don't want to be going to Walter Reed for another eight years.'"

Matters were complicated by the fact that the August 20 election in Afghanistan underscored everything that had worried skeptics of a more robust involvement in that country. There were widespread Taliban attacks. Turnout was weak. And Karzai, increasingly difficult for Holbrooke and the military to work with, crudely attempted to tip the scales in his own favor through unmistakable electoral fraud.

"The election fueled the doubters," said one State Department official. "From there on a policy that was marked by real fissures started to come apart much more rapidly. The behind-the-scenes discussions grew much tenser."

On the one hand, McChrystal's still-secret report made a case for another four brigades, 40,000 troops. The bureaucratically savvy Gates, understanding the divides within the policy team and the president's apprehensions, tried to be supportive, but was noncommittal regarding just how many people he could get approved. Biden's reaction was to hammer out an alternative that was heavily focused on counterterrorism— the project on which he had enlisted the input of Cartwright via a back channel. On Sunday morning September 13, a senior group of principals, deputies, and the president convened in the White House Situation Room to discuss this latest strategy review from the new US and NATO commander in Afghanistan. Obama was respectful of McChrystal's warning that, without proper support, failure was in the offing in the year ahead. Peter Lavoy, then a deputy director of national intelligence who would subsequently shift over to a deputy assistant secretary role at the Defense Department, outlined the situation on the ground from the intelligence community's perspective. While the number of core al-Qaeda present in Afghanistan was between merely 20 and 100, according to Woodward, the Taliban was rebounding and patient. Lavoy was one of those who long felt that strategic reviews, including Riedel's, had tiptoed around the problem of Pakistan. He and his boss, Admiral Dennis Blair, a Rhodes Scholar and an exceptionally thoughtful analyst, both suggested that the Pakistani embrace of terrorists and harboring of groups like al-Qaeda and the Taliban could well tip the outcome against US interests.

Clinton recounted the diplomatic lay of the land and Gates highlighted what he thought was important from McChrystal's review, but Biden made the strongest case at the meeting. He argued for his counterterrorism-focused approach and was, in the words of one participant, "passionate and impressive." In fact, ironically, after all the campaign trail grousing about the oversized role of Bush's vice president, it was clear that on foreign policy, Barack Obama's number two would play at least as influential a role.

Obama chaired the discussion by repeatedly laying out the questions he wanted answered, as if no prior review had already taken place. He made the case that what they were doing was constantly updating their views. But he was essentially allowing Biden to pick up his dissent from March and effectively reopen the entire discussion for what might be seen as the fourth time in the Obama administration's first eight months in office—the Lute review, the Riedel review, the McChrystal review, and now the post-McChrystal-review review.

That parade of perspectives does not fully do justice to the fragmented, confused, indecisive policy process that had taken root during the first year of the Obama administration with regard to what had once been called "the good war." The president failed to create a strategy to address what the presidential candidate had identified as a priority. One of the most tortured policy processes in modern NSC history took place during the three months between the McChrystal review's arrival on the desk of the president and Obama's West Point speech on December 1 announcing his "new" Afghan policy.

Having lengthy deliberations about complex issues is hardly a failure of process, of course. Nor is continually reassessing a fluid situation. Nor is encouraging members of any team of senior advisors to offer differing views. Indeed, all of these are components of many successful policy processes. Furthermore, the problems that the United States had undertaken to solve ranged from difficult to impossible. Indeed that was one of the points central to the arguments of Biden and his supporters: we couldn't achieve what we wanted to because we never intended to stay for the long haul nor did we have the means or the know-how (or one might argue even a chance) of transforming these societies to the point that they themselves would come to be effective advocates for and insurers of the conditions we saw to be in our interest. So, as with many unsuccessful undertakings of senior national-security policy teams from both parties, this was a process undertaken by worthy people acting in a worthy way seeking to achieve an outcome that they believed would be in the best interests of the American people. Never mind that it might not be possible.

All such processes need to be managed, and the president is the only person in the ultimate position to manage them. Barack Obama was simply unclear as to the goals and approaches he wanted to embrace. Whereas Bush may have been too impulsive and too accepting of some of the dubious strategies offered up by his advisors during his first term, Obama took a long, long time to decide which way he wanted to go. And he did not yet have a truly tightly run policy process nor had he empowered anyone—such as Jones—to truly drive that process on his behalf.

So from September to December, through dozens of NSC meetings, principals meetings, deputies meetings, informal smaller group gatherings of principals and key White House staffers, the process ping-ponged back and forth. A central debate was framed in the McChrystal paper—whether additional troop strength should be upped by 85,000 to enable a fully supported counterinsurgency, or by 10,000 to put the focus on training Afghan forces, or somewhere in the middle, such as 30,000 or 40,000, to support in a reasonable way the kind of counterinsurgency that McChrystal, McMullen, and Petraeus felt was required to forestall American failure in Afghanistan. Another debate turned on the question of whether the COIN or the CT focus was the right one. Yet another turned on how tough to be on the governments in Kabul and Islamabad to get them to become more cooperative. Other issues focused on how big to make the Afghan armies and police force and how much aid would be necessary to buy Pakistani cooperation.

Brennan recalls that "the process certainly was a very rigorous one, with extensive, extensive meetings. And one of the things I think the president wanted to make sure of was that all views were taken into account. And clearly there were differences of view on the idea of 'doubling down.' . . . And there was the debate on the issue of counterterrorism versus counterinsurgency. . . . And the concept of defeating the Taliban or defeating al-Qaeda is a difficult one. And I think the sense was always that we wanted to be able to get the Afghan government to a point where it could stand on its own after being weaned off of the support from the outside, recognizing that the Taliban was never going to be eliminated from the landscape of Afghanistan."

Most telling, even as the debate over troop strength predictably tossed out the high and low options and turned into one about whether to go for 40,000 or perhaps 30,000 or 35,000, the president brought the question back to the mission in early October and again as late as mid-November. He didn't feel he was getting a clear enough explanation for why the United States was going to commit more troops, money, and time to this conflict. At the core of this was a question about whether the objective was to "defeat" the Taliban or just to "disrupt" them. (Al-Qaeda was much smaller than the Taliban, and it seemed that declaring its defeat was more achievable, although five years later, as it turned out, the spread of al-Qaeda affiliates across the region had led to a sharp reversal in thinking on that front.) Biden, Donilon, and others on the Obama team at the White House argued that the mission in Afghanistan should be as narrowly defined as possible. They thought the focus should be, in the words of one insider, on "defeating core al-Qaeda and preventing the re-emergence of a safe haven for terrorists."

Obama finally took command of this central debate at a meeting on Veteran's Day in 2009. After the old debate started again, he stated that for him the answer was that the goal was to "disrupt" the Taliban and to "degrade capacity to such an extent that security could be manageable by" the Afghan Army. But even after this clarification, the arguments over troop strength and focus carried on. Biden supporters, like Donilon, had reached out to the US ambassador in Kabul to make an "independent" assessment regarding whether the 40,000 troop hike in forces would work. That ambassador, former general Karl Eikenberry, was already known to be skeptical of the force hike and actually proposed that yet another expert group be convened and a new study undertaken. Needless to say, for some, especially those in the military, this was "too much to be believed. We were spinning our wheels."

Although the high and low options for troop increases had been thrown out, a new set of three was in play: 40,000, 30,000, or 20,000. The military insisted that 20,000 was not a viable choice. Biden and his allies pushed back, arguing that it was the higher options that were not politically viable. Obama tipped his hand by saying that in addition to making this decision they also ought to think about starting to draw down these troops in eighteen to twenty-four months—a timeframe one senior NSC staffer said came from Gates. There was also an open and continuing debate about how to get the vacillating government in Pakistan to start cooperating in squeezing the Taliban and al-Qaeda.

This meeting, like the others, ended with no conclusion.

Although answers about policy were not coming, some about people were coalescing. It was clear from these interactions that Jones was not in control of the process. Biden was conducting his own conversations with the military through his allies in other parts of the administration, outside the formal interagency process. Woodward wrote, making apparent reference to a conversation with DNI Blair, that it seemed, given this kind of access, that the president did not have one NSA but instead had Jones, Donilon, Brennan, McDonough, and sometimes Emanuel—for a total of five. And this did not even count the oversized role played by Biden.

"And then there were the president's kitchen cabinet," added Nasr, "who really were like national security advisors. Like Denis Mc-Donough, like Valerie Jarrett, like Axelrod. . . . Seen through a political eye they wielded an enormous amount of influence to the point that they often dominated the process." Every president has advisors whose job it is to offer views on the domestic political consequences of all presidential actions, including those on foreign policy. Problems arise when national security decisions that should be made on the basis of advancing and defending national interests and divorced as much as possible from political factors are instead seen to be overly driven by these advisors. That sometimes happened for both Bush, with Karl Rove being known as "Bush's brain," and with the team led by Axelrod and Jarrett around Obama.

The process also revealed that there were divisions between elements within the military—between those like Mullen, Petraeus, and McChrystal who supported a full COIN approach, and those like Army Chief of Staff Allen and Hoss Cartwright who were more skeptical of it. It was also clear that Obama had very little patience for the style of Holbrooke, who was dressed down periodically. And finally, as a kind of footnote to history, as one of those frequently in the room put it, "if someone who had watched the presidential candidates debates in 2008 had been able to view this, they would have come away very impressed with the clarity, resolve, focus, and effectiveness of Clinton and Biden in advancing their positions. Say what you will, they knew what they wanted from the outset and stuck by it. They had a worldview."

Finally, there was one more opportunity for the parties to make their case during a November 23 meeting with the president. Two days later, a meeting took place in the Oval Office attended by the inner circle, this time including Jones and a young, but very influential NSC speechwriter, Ben Rhodes. They discussed the speech in which the president would make his case to the American people. But even with this kind of progress apparently being made, Obama then spent another week hammering out a detailed "term sheet" with his team to ensure that everybody was on board with the decision—and thus revealing as clearly as anything he did that he was deeply concerned that if the decision were later second-guessed it would not be from anyone on the inside. Donilon said he got the idea for the document from reading *Lessons in Disaster* by Gordon Goldstein, which made the case that a contributing problem to the American conduct of the Vietnam War was that the military often did not clearly understand the decisions and guidance they were getting from the White House. Donilon felt that the process helped ensure that the military would have clear guidelines and that it was also clear that there had been a meeting of the minds between the White House and the commanders on these critical issues. Again, it suggests the president especially feared someday being challenged by military leaders, given the high approval rating they enjoyed with the American people. Finally it was determined that the United States would commit an additional 30,000 troops to Afghanistan with the goals the president outlined on November 11. (Donilon's reading of history was so constant in the job that when he was stepping down as national security advisor he got a call from the White House library asking if he could stop by to have his picture taken with the librarians because he had been "their biggest customer." The search for historical perspective was certainly one that set him apart for the better in reactive, news-cycle-driven Washington.)

However, yet again reflecting the president's ambivalence about his own policy, he asserted to members of the team that he was actually having two speeches drafted. And when the final speech was delivered—in which there was seen to be a much greater emphasis on the beginning of the withdrawal in eighteen months than many in the Pentagon had expected—there was a sense that the system had been "gamed from within." One senior military officer said, "a bunch of it was stuff put in at the eleventh hour. And of course we heard it—the stuff about pulling out and when—and we said, 'I'll fully support it. I'll be your soldier.' But it was still something of shock."

Said one intimate participant of the entire process as well as the speech, "we kept going back to first principles of why we were there, what our interests were, what were our objectives, all that. The process was prolonged. But people also felt there was a gap or a disconnect. It was between the formal process and the decisions made there and the speechwriting. It was in the writing of the speech that I think some people felt that things were said in ways that were different than some of the principals would have said them. It was all a matter of tone and emphasis. And I'm not sure that everybody got to see the speech before the president gave it and I think there was some wording that tilted more towards one side of the argument as opposed to reflecting what everyone thought."

One problem cited was that "people who had the most contact with the president and had the most ability to shape what he actually said about the conflict and about the commitment were all people who were skeptics of the whole enterprise. . . . He had parts of his staff including his vice president constantly telling him that he was wrong and it was going to fail."

When I first heard the speech, I thought of Groucho Marx's famous theme-song, "Hello, I Must Be Going." That's because after all these policy deliberations and the president's reputed demand for rigor and clarity, this convoluted process had produced the only speech I could remember in which a president simultaneously announced the escalation of a military effort and in the next breath announced a planned withdrawal. After thirteen paragraphs outlining the history of our involvement in Afghanistan, the president said: "this review is now complete. And as commander-in-chief, I have determined that it is in our vital national interest to send an additional 30,000 US troops to Afghanistan. After eighteen months, our troops will begin to come home. These are the resources we need to seize the initiative, while building the Afghan capacity that can allow for a responsible transition of our forces out of Afghanistan."

He then said, in an understatement that could be fully understood only by a few dozen administration insiders at the time, "I do not make this decision lightly." And then he outlined goals, which were at their core the same as the Riedel review—"to disrupt, dismantle, and defeat al-Qaeda in Afghanistan and Pakistan." He also soft-pedaled the language even more with regard to the Taliban, saying the objective was "to reverse the Taliban's momentum and deny it the ability to overthrow the government."

The rest of the speech was an explication of the decision and then a shift to a different focus, one the president seemed to feel more at ease with—a discussion of why the United States needed to shift from costly conflicts like Iraq and Afghanistan and toward domestic priorities, arguing that, "in the end, our security and leadership does not come solely from the strength of our arms. It derives from our people—from the workers and businesses who will rebuild our economy."

He concluded by offering a message that "we are passing through a time of great trial. And the message we send in the midst of these storms must be clear: that our cause is just, our resolve unwavering."

The process that lay behind the speech suggested, in fact, that was not the case. The contradictory message confirmed many of the doubts of our allies in the region and, in the view of critics, gave our enemies a timetable by which to plan, thus undercutting the effectiveness of the increases that were being approved. The *New York Times* headline echoed the confused message: "Obama Adds Troops, But Maps Exit Plan."

The Afghan policy process was a mess. It showed a conflicted president learning on the job. It revealed real structural defects in his National Security Council. It virtually ensured that the increased resources it approved would be squandered. And it suggested that the president's principal national security advisor would face an uphill struggle to be successful with the odds being stacked against him by the very president who selected him for the job.

And nothing would confirm these facts more than the reality that within a year the White House would be conducting yet another Afghanistan strategy review, this one focused on dialing back expectations and narrowing goals further, and that it would be conducted under the leadership of Barack Obama's second national security advisor, Tom Donilon. Jim Jones would leave his office—underappreciated, underutilized, with the bureaucratic deck stacked against him—on October 8, 2010.

Still more reviews and course corrections would follow. In 2014, as unrest in Iraq boiled up and debate was triggered about whether America's failure to leave a residual force in that country was a contributing factor to the problem, yet another Afghan assessment resulted in the decision to leave a residual force in that country through 2016. This was colored in part by increasing unrest in Iraq that continued to be linked to Afghanistan in the public consciousness. The decision was also affected by increasing worries as to whether the Afghan government, currently led by the quixotic and corruption-prone President Hamid Karzai and in the throes of turmoil as electoral fraud threatens the democratic contest to find his replacement, alone would be able to manage the challenges posed by the large community of violent extremists that were active in the country despite over a decade of US warfare. After Secretary of State John Kerry and others on the US team performed diplomatic acrobatics to negotiate an agreement to maintain a troop presence in the country (later clarified by President Obama to mean 9,800 US forces in 2015, half that figure in 2016, and a basic embassy security presence thereafter), Karzai refused to sign. As of this writing, it is expected that his successor will sign the agreement. Further, given the unrest in Iraq that was seen by many to be associated with the failure to negotiate a deal to leave a residual US military force in Iraq, the likelihood that a force remains in

Afghanistan through the end of the Obama administration remains high, absent a major deterioration in relations with the Afghan government.

Circumstances change, of course, and that is why on-going reviews are an essential part of the national security policy process. The problems arise when policy processes and adjustments reveal or exacerbate the uncertainty of leaders and the internal divisions with national security teams. These are compounded and overshadowed when the policies themselves produce negligible outcomes or, as in the case of both Afghanistan and Iraq, require massive investments of precious national resources but still have done little to change circumstances on the ground or, indeed, may have made them worse in important ways.

CHAPTER 6

The Most Powerful Man
in the World

Power does not corrupt. Fear corrupts . . .
perhaps the fear of a loss of power.

—JOHN STEINBECK

George W. Bush's second inaugural address read like a manifesto for an interventionist America. It was as infused with the language of divine missions as any fatwa of America's jihadist enemies: "America's vital interests and our deepest beliefs are now one. From the day of our Founding we have proclaimed that every man and woman on this earth has rights, and dignity, and matchless value, because they bear the image of the Maker of Heaven and earth. Across the generations we have proclaimed the imperative of self-government, because no one is fit to be a master, and no one deserves to be a slave. Advancing these ideals is the mission that created our Nation. It is the honorable achievement of our fathers. Now it is the urgent requirement of our nation's security, and the calling of our time."

To a non-American ear, Bush was not merely celebrating our values. The President of the United States was saying that it is America's urgent—even divinely approved—mission to spread those values worldwide. The speech went on to say it is the "policy of the United States to seek and support the growth of democratic movements and institutions in *every nation and culture*" (emphasis added). He continued, "we will persistently clarify the choice before every ruler and every nation: The moral choice between oppression, which is always wrong, and freedom, which is eternally right. America will not pretend that jailed dissidents prefer their chains or that women welcome humiliation and servitude or that any human being aspires to live at the mercy of bullies."

The authors of the speech no doubt had noble intentions—certainly my conversations with many of those in the White House who saw the speech beforehand suggest that was the view. But they were all, in the words of a former colleague, "hearing it through their ears." They were also guilty of succumbing to a classic American misconception, one Henry Kissinger described as "the mistaken belief that any country any-where if given the opportunity would choose to be more like America."

Heng Chee Chan, Singapore's ambassador to the United States, said with the telling sensitivities of anyone from Asia in the first years of the twenty-first century, "imagine how that sounded to the Chinese." I had a chance to speak to a Chinese diplomat shortly thereafter, whose response was terser: "more lectures."

The irony was that amid the carnage and gross missteps of the first four years of the Bush presidency, there was a broad view that during that period US relations with China had hit a modern high point. There were few overt conflicts. Exchanges were generally positive. And truth be told, the Chinese were perfectly happy that America's attentions were directed elsewhere, that we were expending our resources in the Middle East, assuring their supplies of energy at no cost to them, and not med-dling in their affairs.

On her first trip to Asia as secretary of state, Condoleezza Rice of-fered a similarly cautionary and prescriptive tone in a Tokyo speech, saying that Washington's goal was to "push, prod, and persuade China toward a more positive course." Nicholas Burns, who assumed the role of under secretary of state for political affairs in March 2005, said Rice made it very clear that her priority was "repairing the damage from 2002 and 2003," and that Russia and China were top priorities, which helps explain why her meetings with Chinese leaders on that trip were more positive and less contentious.

In an August 2005 interview with the *New York Times*, Rice described the relationship consequently as "big and complicated," with "good parts" and "not so good parts." Among the good parts, she noted, were Chinese cooperation on North Korea and in the war on terror. Looking back today, she says she saw the objective of finding a new footing as "vitally important" because of China's rising influence and power. It's a sentiment reiterated by Bush during a visit from President Hu Jintao in the fall of 2005, when he characterized the US-China relationship as "very important for the United States and the world."

Deputy Secretary of State Robert Zoellick acknowledged the obvious—that China had already integrated itself into the international system—and suggested that our goals should be to help take the relationship to the next level through a multi-tier approach he called "comprehensive engagement."

At the Defense Department, China's growing military was reflected in public expressions of worry in the Quadrennial Defense Review, which asserted that the "pace and scope" of China's expansion were "already [putting] regional military balances at risk." The trade deficit continued to grow, and on Capitol Hill concerns about Chinese currency manipulation—to make their exports artificially cheaper and more attractive, and to deepen the deficit—were burgeoning. So were tensions associated with lax Chinese protection of intellectual property rights. The efforts to improve relations were also bedeviled by unintended problems, as when, during a visit by China's President Hu Jintao to the White House that had the ostensible goal of improving US-China relations, the US interpreter announced that the anthem to be played was for the Republic of China, the official name of Taiwan. And shortly later, a representative of the suppressed Chinese religious sect Falun Gong started heckling the Chinese leader. Some rough spots were created, however, by conflicting White House impulses about how to treat the Chinese leadership. For example, the White House failed to offer Hu a full state dinner, souring the relationship. Secretary Rice argued that such occasions were reserved for "leaders with whom we wanted to highlight our extraordinarily close relationship." Her point at the time was that however important China may be, it was not included on that list.

It was at this moment, when the relationship was threatening to teeter into a period of new tensions, that the administration took advantage of one of its secret weapons. Of all the would-be China experts on the Bush team, perhaps none had been to the country so often or had such high level contacts as Treasury Secretary Henry Paulson. When he was recruited into the administration, it was stipulated that he would have a large role in shaping China policy. This took almost two years to assume a concrete form. However, in conversations with his senior staff and top officials at the White House, it became clear that not only would the relationship benefit from having a clear quarterback within the administration's ranks but that complex bilateral relationships really need their own mechanisms that—much like the NSC—would help coordinate policy among the multiple agencies involved in the relationship.

Against this background, the US-China Strategic Economic Dialogue (SED), a new high-level dialogue with the Chinese leadership, was announced on September 20, 2006. The undertaking would involve multiple US departments, including State, Commerce, USTR, HHS, and the EPA. In this respect it emphasized that much at the heart of the emerging US-China relationship was economic, that it was in this area that shared interests were clearest, and that it was therefore via such a vehicle that we would be most likely able to conduct constructive exchanges.

Carlos Gutierrez, who as commerce secretary was actively involved in the process, observed, "Hank had the expertise. He had been to China like seventy times at Goldman Sachs. So there was no question he was a China guy. And he had very good connections. And so he got approval from the president to form the SED. And you know, while it wasn't entirely smooth, bulldog that he is, Hank bulldogged it through the interagency process."

With the election of a Democratic majority in the House of Representatives in November 2006, one of Beijing's toughest critics in Washington became the senior Democrat in town, Nancy Pelosi. Concern rose in China that, with Pelosi as Speaker of the House, the US Congress would soon turn up the heat on human rights issues and more actively seek to confront China, much as the San Francisco Democrat had advocated throughout her career. Any foreboding that the Chinese may have felt on the eve of the first SED meeting on December 14–15 was compounded by the release just days before of a report from USTR Ambassador Susan Schwab, which called out the Chinese for trade practices in violation of WTO rules. As a consequence, the initial meeting of the SED was more of a throat-clearing exercise for both nations, with a balance of sparring and expressions of hope for better ties. But it laid a foundation for a dialogue that has grown to become a centerpiece of the US-China relationship. It also underscored an important trend. As had been the case under Robert Rubin and Larry Summers during the Clinton administration (and as would be the case under Tim Geithner), the US treasury secretary was to have a central role on a vital foreign policy front that even in the recent past might have been unimaginable.

Even as relations between the two giant countries went through more challenges during the remaining two years of the Bush administration, with more trade, currency, and defense problems—including those surrounding China's expansion of its capabilities to include anti-satellite weapons—the SED began to achieve the goal of offering a trusted and more positive venue for exchanges. During a May 2007 meeting, Vice Premier Wu Yi, the former commerce minister, who was the highest ranking woman in Chinese government history, argued that tensions should be addressed "calmly" and that, given "ever-deepening globalization today, confrontation is not good at all for problem-solving and pressure and posturing can only make the situation more complex." And again speaking the language of commerce, the Chinese signed more deals with Americans, this time for $20 billion. Paulson did not shy away from noting the growing concerns centering on Chinese currency manipulation, and leaders on Capitol Hill confirmed his assertions with threatening language. But enough progress was being made via dialogue that Paulson's Treasury Department the next month declined to name China a currency manipulator. Perhaps that was just as well, as within eighteen months the United States would be pumping money into its economy to stave off a depression, exerting much the same effect on US dollars that the Americans were complaining the Chinese were doing to their own currency.

The positive trajectory in the relationship was highlighted by the fact that even when Congressional leaders presented the Dalai Lama with their highest honor, the Congressional Gold Medal, Chinese anger was not matched by actions. They condemned the action but within three weeks were hosting Defense Secretary Gates in Beijing, at which time another sign of the growing maturation of the relationship was put in place: to help minimize the risk of accidental confrontation between the two countries, both sides agreed to establish a military hotline, similar in purpose to the one the United States had maintained with the Soviet Union. Further new military exchanges were also created "at all levels," reflecting the fact that, other than the Treasury, no department had a more acute awareness of the growing influence of China on a daily basis than did Defense. For example, the leadership of the US Pacific Command, the world's largest military command, is home to some of the most attentive and sophisticated students of Chinese behavior anywhere in the US government. In addition, Bush had won considerable appreciation from the Chinese for very early on signaling his intention of attending the 2008 Beijing Olympics, a gesture that he accurately perceived as being very important to the Chinese leadership. Bush told Hu personally of his intention and then later followed up with a public announcement that not only would he go but that he would bring his family. This was seen by the Chinese as helping to nip in the bud an incipient movement among European leaders to boycott the Olympic opening ceremonies or the games themselves and as a sign of meaningful support from the US president.

The United States may have had some hopes of using the president's trip to the Beijing Olympics in 2008 as a chance to send a message promoting further reforms, but by the time the August sports spectacular arrived, two powerful narratives had emerged that would dominate the attention of all. In the immediate foreground were games that showed off the extraordinary advances that China had made. The games were exceptionally well run, the facilities were beautiful, the headlines were about sports and collegiality, and the entire event was a smashing success for China, sending the message—as if it had to be emphasized yet again—that China had arrived.

In the background, however, was the turbulence of America's growing financial crisis. The Chinese had regularly been in touch with both Paulson and other top Treasury officials as the mortgage problems of the United States grew, flexing their muscles as one of America's leading creditors, and complaining of the losses their leading government investment agencies were suffering. The nature and degree of the pressure has gradually become clearer during the past several years. Particularly striking were revelations in Paulson's 2010 memoir, *On the Brink,* that while the treasury secretary was attending the Beijing Olympics, Russia sought to work with the Chinese to pull the rug out from under US markets.

During the opening ceremonies of the games, Ambassador Jim Jeffrey quietly informed President Bush that the Russian invasion of the Republic of Georgia had begun. Meanwhile, Paulson learned that the Russians had proposed to leaders in Beijing that "together they might sell big chunks of their [holdings in Fannie Mae and Freddie Mac] to force the U.S. to use its emergency authorities to prop up these companies."

"The report," Paulson wrote, "was deeply troubling—heavy selling could create a sudden loss of confidence in the GSEs and shake the capital markets. I waited till I was back home and in a secure environment to inform the president." Fortunately, the Chinese, who had significantly larger exposure to US markets than did the Russians, and who were already stinging from billions in losses, did not take the Russians up on the idea of launching an economic assault on the US Treasury. They did not abuse their newfound leverage, but they did seek to use it during the

American financial crisis to an extent that few on Main Street might have imagined.

Wikileak cables showed that throughout the crisis, the United States was obligated to work tirelessly to address Chinese concerns. Given that the Chinese held hundreds of billions in US securities, it was clear that were they to cease behaving constructively they could have compounded the downturn's negative consequences to a degree impossible for the Treasury to manage.

The Chinese State Administration for Foreign Exchange (SAFE) was one of several agencies with major exposure. Another was China's giant sovereign wealth fund, the China Investment Corporation (CIC). Mid-crisis estimates of CIC losses, according to the *Financial Times*, exceeded $80 billion. When Fannie Mae and Freddie Mac went into conservatorship, there was widespread concern among China's leaders that bigger losses were in the offing. "Several interlocutors have told us that Lehman was a counterparty to SAFE in financial transactions and as a result SAFE suffered large losses when Lehman collapsed," it was confirmed in cables months later from the US embassy in Beijing.

Because of Paulson's relationships with the Chinese leaders, however, he and his colleagues at the Treasury and in the Fed were able to keep open channels with the Chinese that avoided a deepening of the crisis. Indeed, as a sign of respect, Under Secretary of the Treasury for International Affairs David McCormick was dispatched to Beijing at the height of the crisis in October 2008 to consult with Chinese financial leaders. A Wikileaks cable reported, "all of Undersecretary McCormick's counterparts appeared to appreciate his willingness to come to Beijing." The Chinese did say that unless concerns about Fannie and Freddie were handled satisfactorily, the Chinese might no longer be able to assume "greater counter-party risks" or invest further. McCormick, for his part, delivered a message similar to that which Paulson had been relaying directly—the United States didn't actually guarantee investments in government-sponsored enterprises like the two mortgage agencies. Nonetheless, it was "committing to inject up to $100 billion of equity in each institution to avoid insolvency, and that this contractual commitment would remain for the life of these institutions." It was as good as a guarantee, and it was made to satisfy the Chinese.

In taking this trip and in sending this kind of message, the Bush administration was admitting the new dependency the United States had on the deep pockets in Beijing. At the same time, Beijing's huge investment exposure in the United States, unique among world markets in the degree to which it could both absorb and protect China's capital, illustrated a parallel Chinese dependency on the United States. Herein lay the primary difference in the relationship between America and China, its emerging rival of the twenty-first century, and the relationship America had with Russia late in the past century. It is a difference that also illustrates why, when Russia proposed blowing up America's markets at a time of great vulnerability, China took a different path. The Cold War was a zero-sum game. Two more or less independent systems were in competition with one another. A gain for one was a loss for the other. But the United States and China were economically conjoined twins. Thus, the challenge for the new era was going to be developing doctrines, policies, and mechanisms that acknowledged the reality of that interdependence.

Robert Hormats, who served in both Republican and Democratic administrations and was a colleague of Paulson's at Goldman Sachs while vice chairman of Goldman Sachs International, emphasized yet another dimension of the US-China relationship when he said it was also important to recognize that no two countries had a greater stake in the stability and proper functioning of the international system because they were such major players in the global economy. So understandings and modes of cooperation were needed in order that both could share responsibilities for that system commensurate with their influence over it and the benefits they derived from it. The system would not work unless both agreed to a substantial degree, if not fully, on common rules or harmonious practices, and they would both suffer if the system broke down or deteriorated.

"So, over time," he continued, "agreeing that there had to be a rules-based system and what the principles and practices of that system ought to be is a major and ongoing challenge for both countries and for other major players—traditional and emerging ones. For the US the goal remains to demonstrate at home and internationally that a free-market system rather than a government-driven one can deliver real benefits to our peoples, which requires that it be successful at home in the period ahead, especially in light of the financial crisis, and can be effective around the world as well."

One final way that the Bush administration was able to show its understanding of this major shift in global affairs and to institutionalize it was its support for an idea initially promoted by French president Nicolas Sarkozy and British prime minister Gordon Brown to address the international dimensions of the financial crisis by convening not only the G-8, the club of the traditional big economies of the late twentieth century, including Russia, but the G-20, a larger group including China and the world's emerging powers. That meeting, which took place on November 14, 2008, in Washington, was a genuine watershed in the history of the international system, a changing of the guard, as it were, or a resetting of the head table of the international community. The result not only reflected the rising clout of China and other big emerging markets, it was also considerably more equitable, bringing almost another half of the world's population into conversations that would affect the future of all.

In a footnote to that meeting, which had as its most significant official outcome an agreement to continue consultations among the group regularly, the Bush team had also done something rather extraordinary. They invited a representative of the incoming administration to participate. In fact, they invited Obama, but he chose not to attend, sending in his place senior advisor and former secretary of state Madeleine Albright and former US congressman Jim Leach, a Republican from Arizona. This unprecedented arrangement ensured the continuity that both teams sought at a moment of national crisis.

Rebalancing

"One of the narratives that animated the Obama foreign policy coming in was this sense that we had spent the better part of a decade as a country preoccupied by Iraq and Afghanistan, and that as a result, we were out of balance," recounted Derek Chollet, the former top Obama transition official who began in the administration as the number two official in State's Policy Planning Office. "We were overweighted in that part of the world, and meanwhile, things had been happening that would be more defining over the next twenty to thirty to forty years elsewhere in the world where the perception—fair or not—was that we had been absent and that certainly included Asia."

Chollet remembers vividly that immediately after the inauguration Secretary Clinton held a dinner at the State Department, the first dinner in which she brought in outside persons. Clinton was about to travel to Asia for her first trip as secretary "and so this was an effort to bring in outsiders, to sit around the table, to talk to the secretary and other senior folks. This became a model—we did this probably every six weeks or so, usually pegged to a trip—and . . . she would have a kind of salon meal, a good discussion on the topic. . . . The whole point of the event was to get our heads into the game about what's going on in Asia and to send a signal—as we would through her trip—that we were going to place a high priority on the Asia Pacific region."

Jake Sullivan, a close Clinton confidant who later succeeded Anne-Marie Slaughter as head of policy planning, also confirmed that shifting the focus to Asia was atop the new secretary's early list of priorities. He said, "before she even came in, she was in a running conversation with Kurt Campbell, who she had selected to be the East Asia assistant secretary, and with Jim Steinberg, who was going to be her deputy, about placing a heavy emphasis on Asia. And she gave her first substantive policy speech on the Asia-Pacific and took her first trip to both Northeast Asia and Southeast Asia with the conscious intention of sending a signal that this was going to take a new and more elevated place in US foreign policy."

Similar conversations were taking place during the first weeks of the Obama administration at Treasury, at the Commerce Department, in other economic agencies, in the policy shop at the Defense Department, and most important, in the Obama White House. Donilon noted that during the transition, the president started planning his initial Asia trip, and that around the same time Donilon himself began using *rebalancing* as one of the terms branding the administration's efforts to add more focus to the fastest growing region in the world. It was clear that Asia, particularly China, would top the list of the new Administration's priorities.

Any administration coming into office in January 2009 would have sought to give more attention to the US-China and US-Asia relationships. But there was another contributing factor—the people. The Obama team, like Bush's second administration team, had a number of players who sought to play significant roles in shaping China and Asia policy. Not only was the incoming secretary of state, Hillary Clinton, committed to sending an early message that we were prioritizing the region, but so too was Mandarin-speaking Secretary of the Treasury Tim Geithner, NEC Director Larry Summers, Deputy National Security Advisor Tom Donilon, NSC senior aide Denis McDonough, top NSC/NEC international economics advisor Michael Froman, and Deputy Secretary of State James Steinberg. In addition, there were not one but two other cabinet members with Chinese roots and interests—Secretary of Commerce Gary Locke, who in his home state of Washington had become the first

Chinese-American governor in US history, and the Nobel Prize–winning Secretary of Energy, Stephen Chu.

At the under secretary level in agency after agency were key players who came in with significant Asia experience and a desire to play a bigger role in US-China policy initiatives. These included Under Secretary of State for Economic Affairs Bob Hormats, another old China hand from Goldman Sachs; Under Secretary of Treasury for International Affairs Lael Brainard; Under Secretary of Commerce Francisco Sanchez; and Assistant Secretary of Energy for International Affairs David Sandalow. Especially important, in two key supporting positions that would drive much of the day-to-day policy through the Obama first term, the team also had smart, experienced, strong-willed actors in Assistant Secretary of State Kurt Campbell (who is married to Brainard) and NSC Senior Director for Asia Jeffrey Bader.

Of those formative early days, Bader has written, "it was clear to the Obama team that a unidimensional approach to China would yield unsatisfactory results. U.S. policy toward a rising China could not rely solely on military muscle, economic blandishments, and pressure and sanctions on human rights, an overall strategy that had not been notably successful in altering unwelcome Chinese actions when China was weaker." He added, "at the same time, a policy of indulgence and accommodation of assertive Chinese conduct, or indifference to its internal evolution, could embolden bad behavior and frighten U.S. allies and partners."

At the center of this team was a new president who was born in the middle of the Pacific Ocean, in Hawaii, and who spent his formative years in Indonesia. He was, as he characterized it, "America's first Pacific president," and so he encouraged the shifting priorities. As in any such group of strong personalities—and this group had more than its share of sharp-elbowed, willing bureaucratic infighters—rivalries and differences emerged. The result can be division or it can be creativity, a process by which rivalries drive action, differences fuel creativity, and the general alignment of views ensures a common overall direction. During the first term of the Obama administration, thanks to a commitment to a new focus on Asia that began with the president and his team during the transition, and the presence of a strong team of Asia-hands throughout the administration, the result was most often an example of constructive interagency rivalry.

"We had to rebalance our efforts and restore our strengths," said Donilon. "We had just had a period of tremendous exertion—depleted our authority, power, and prestige around the world and depleted our

economy—through the effort in Iraq and the financial crisis, two substantial hits to US authority." As a consequence, he continued, one of
the most important things the administration sought to accomplish was
"a multidimensional rebalancing to Asia that's absolutely critical to our
interest. It's an area where we were underweighted and in which there was
a huge demand signal for US leadership. And getting the relationship
with China right is probably the most important relationship issue we
have in the world."

With Clinton's first trip to the region planned for late February 2009,
as Chollet noted, policy discussions on related issues heated up early,
as did the debate about who would take the lead on them and about
the form the central dialogue associated with the US-China relationship would take. There were initially three different approaches. Clinton and her colleagues felt State should have the lead. Geithner sought
to continue the dominant role Treasury had via the Strategic Economic
Dialogue. And there was even a move to keep the central locus of the
conversation in the White House, with a proposal floated by those close
to the vice president for a Biden-led initiative much like those Al Gore
once co-chaired under President Bill Clinton. Hillary Clinton asserted
that, although economic issues were very important, they were not the
totality of the relationship and that she wanted a "more comprehensive"
approach. She also argued that during the Bush years, especially early on,
there had not been enough focus on political and security issues.

Geithner's response turned on the sensitivity of the issues involved
in the economic recovery and the necessity that the dialogue with the
Chinese be managed carefully due to their role. In fact, even in the earliest days of the Obama administration, it was an absolute priority to
continue the kind of conversations started by Paulson to reassure Chinese investors. Within the NSC, Donilon and Bader also supported the
move to a joint dialogue, which they proposed be held once a year. There
were questions as to whether the Chinese would accept such a bifurcated
structure and how important priority questions like energy and climate
would be handled. However, those would be worked out in conversations
with the Chinese in the run-up to the expected Obama–Hu Jintao conversation, which would take place on the edges of the G-20 summit in
April 2009.

This kind of jostling for place and roles within the administration is
always present and is especially prevalent in the earliest days of any new
government. Out of it this time came what former Bush Deputy Treasury

Secretary Robert Kimmitt light heartedly referred to as "the Obama administration's big contribution to the dialogue we started—an ampersand." The process was to be rechristened the Strategic and Economic Dialogue (S&ED), thus indicating that its scope had been broadened as Clinton wanted and that a two-headed leadership structure had been agreed to.

In her first major address on her first major trip as secretary of state, Hillary Clinton said that "some believe China on the rise is by definition an adversary. To the contrary, we believe the United States and China benefit from and contribute to each other's successes." Her message to the media was that if America was going to focus on its future, it also had to focus on building and deepening ties to Asia. This involved not just a focus on China but an acknowledgment of the desire for American allies in Asia for more attention. For that strategic reason she also stated that her trip sought to develop a "network of partners." She characterized the approach as "rigorous and persistent engagement"—the latest illustration of exercises in semantic shading that command the attention of speechwriters and policy wonks but few others.

During her stop in China, Clinton—who had once stung the Chinese in a sharply critical speech during a women's rights conference in Beijing while she was First Lady—embraced a constructive tone. Deftly communicating both elements of the new interdependency she said, "it would not be in China's interest if we were unable to get our economy moving." On the topic of human rights, she noted that, although she would continue to raise such issues, "our pressing on those issues can't interfere with the global economic crisis, the global climate change crisis, and the security crisis." Many on the American left and the American right—strangely aligned with regard to many of their anti-China views—hoped that she would be more vocally critical of the Chinese, but the balance and pragmatism of her remarks was appreciated in Beijing and throughout the region. "It was a very mature and self-assured performance," said a cabinet-level official in one nation closely allied with the United States.

The G-20 summit took place in London on April 2. Obama underscored the American commitment to getting its economic house in order with a pledge to cut the budget deficit in half once the economy was stabilized. This focus on his part underscored that the United States, which had for decades offered itself up as the example other nations should follow economically, was now in a much more defensive posture. On the other hand, Hu, highlighting how important China's economy had become, sought to assure leaders that China would "ensure sustainable growth and ensure steady and relatively fast economic development." And although both committed to boosting the resources of the International Monetary Fund (IMF), they also called for IMF reforms that would permanently enshrine a more important role within it for the Chinese. Finally, Hu and Obama agreed to proceed with the newly reconstituted S&ED and also announced that Obama would visit China in November. This was followed again by a bit of back and forth within the administration. Clinton and State argued that such a trip should be used as a carrot to incentivize the Chinese to achieve progress on a range of issues, whereas the NSC, and Bader in particular, felt this approach had been ineffective in the past. But, there was an intensity and methodical nature to this early approach to China that was noticed in Beijing and across Asia. The new president seemed serious about making the relationship a centerpiece of his new foreign policy and his cabinet and subcabinet were working the issue energetically. There was some hope—expressed to me several times by diplomats in the region—that the momentum of the Bush and Paulson era in the relationship would be maintained or even built upon.

Geithner followed with his own trip to China in June and then Clinton in a major address spoke of putting a "special emphasis on encouraging major and emerging global powers—China, India, Russia, Brazil as well as Turkey, Indonesia, and South Africa—to be full partners in tackling the global agenda." This followed on the Bush move to elevate the G-20 and echoed the earlier Clinton administration initiative on the Big Emerging Markets (BEMs). It also underscored the general acceptance of this approach not as a new policy but as reflecting a new global economic reality and shifting geopolitical landscape. A week later at the ASEAN summit in Thailand, Clinton further accentuated the emerging theme that "the United States is back" in Asian affairs.

The first meeting of the S&ED took place in July. Clinton and Geithner kicked it off with a joint op-ed in the *Wall Street Journal* that laid out three priorities: "assuring recovery from the most serious global economic crisis in generations and ensuring balanced and sustainable global growth once recovery had taken hold," "making progress on the interconnected issues of climate change, energy, and the environment," and "finding complementary approaches to security and development challenges in the region and across the globe." Obama himself opened the meetings. If there were few concrete deliverables by its conclusion, one senior US official nonetheless characterized it afterward to me as having "sent an important message about our commitment to the issues and setting up the channels of communication we would need to have." He added, "you could tell the Chinese were taking this all very seriously and also that their team was increasingly sophisticated about the US and how to deal with us. It will mean we are going to have to work even harder going forward."

Two months later, Deputy Secretary of State Steinberg offered yet another formulation by which to characterize the relationship. He said that the two sides should pursue "strategic reassurance." He said it "rests on a core, if tacit, bargain. Just as we and our allies must make clear that we are prepared to welcome China's arrival as a prosperous and successful power, China must reassure the rest of the world that its development and growing global role will not come at the expense of security and well-being of others." He specifically cited several areas in which mistrust was a potential outcome, saying the risks were "especially acute in the arena of strategic nuclear weapons, space, and increasingly in the cyber realm." Although the strategic reassurance concept was another flat attempt at coining a buzz phrase, in citing cyber he began a process of raising a set of issues that would be increasingly central to the Obama administration.

If the outward-facing message of the administration was coherent, behind the scenes, tensions existed. Steinberg, frustrated by his near-miss with becoming national security advisor, was seen by some in the White House as difficult to deal with. Derogatory nicknames for him were bandied about in private conversations in the White House and he became frustrated in ways that were readily apparent to those around him, even though within State his expertise on China was broadly respected. At the same time, there were other tensions, derived from the vestiges of the campaign, the Team Hillary versus Team Obama bickering, and the culture of Washington.

One of Clinton's closest aides recounted, "the secretary recognized early on that if you wanted to make progress with the White House you had to have guys who were part of their club. And she didn't like it. But," the aide said, "those of us who wanted her to succeed accepted that that was the way it was. And so we set up parallel networks, but always on the less urgent issues. But on the key stuff, on China, on Iran, on the Middle East, it was always this very, very tight club. And it was all male and very clubby, right? It wasn't helped by the fact that they were not the people who knew the most about the issues."

A "deal" that Clinton struck with Obama, whereby she would be more responsible for appointments within the State Department building per se and the White House would have more influence over ambassadorial posts, turned into a regular source of friction. Plus, White House aides felt some of Hillary's close staff, notably Chief of Staff Cheryl Mills, were too devoted to the long-term career interests of Clinton rather than the president's goals. Old habits die hard. And so there was also an effort by those closest to the president to control which issues and messages were associated with him and to keep the limelight on the man in the Oval Office.

I had some personal experience with this when I wrote an article for the *Washington Post*'s Sunday Outlook section on August 23, 2009. It was called "It's 3 a.m. Do You Know Where Hillary Clinton Is?" and it argued that the new secretary was revolutionizing the way her department operated. Citing some lingering tensions over the definition of her role, I noted that she was blazing a trail where the opportunity existed. "Given the challenges involved, it was perhaps natural that the White House would have a bigger day-to-day hand in some of the nation's most urgent foreign policy issues. But with Obama, National Security Advisor Jim Jones, Vice President Joe Biden, and Secretary of Defense Robert Gates absorbed by Iraq, Afghanistan, and other inherited problems of the recent past, Clinton's State Department can take on a bigger role in tackling the problems of the future—in particular how America will lead the world in the century ahead."

When the piece, which could only be seen as generally positive about the administration's progress to date, came out, the first email message I received early that Sunday morning was from Denis McDonough at the White House. McDonough, loyal to a fault and known in the early days of the administration as something of an enforcer with the media, willing to call out reporters who offered a message the White House didn't like, didn't comment on the piece directly, but rather chose to note that it was interesting that I had focused on Secretary Clinton—as opposed to, it was implied, on the president. It was not a rebuke, exactly, but a seeming message that the White House was keeping score, and, it seemed, that they did not necessarily see a win for Clinton as a win for the president.

A New Swagger

As the Obama team made a concerted push to elevate the focus on China and Asia more broadly, they repeatedly encountered the reality that China's increasing clout internationally also could have the effect of making the United States look weaker. At the November 2009 G-20 summit in Pittsburgh, one attending official from a Latin nation said, "the US did not seem to know what it wanted. At one point, as we were trying to finalize the communiqué, the Americans dithered and it took the Chinese to seize control of the discussion and move us toward our final agreement. They were strong. The US was not."

Even a top US State Department official told me after other meetings with Chinese diplomats that year that "they were running rings around us. They have gotten so good on these issues and we have been so distracted and we don't have the bench depth."

Matters weren't helped when the administration started to distance itself from Steinberg's "strategic reassurance." Leaks from the White House—an essential tool in bureaucratic in-fighting—suggested that Steinberg had gotten out ahead of the administration. With an upcoming Obama trip to the region, the clear message was that if anyone was going to articulate a new stance for the United States in the region, it would be the president.

On the trip, Obama began with a speech in Tokyo in which he said, "the United States does not seek to contain China, nor does a deeper relationship with China mean a weakening of our bilateral alliances." Obama's trip to Beijing carried forward these themes. Although it began with the president flagging the usual issues, such as human rights, Tibet, and Taiwan, and the traditional posturing of both sides, there were also substantive talks, perhaps most of which involved both the president and Larry Summers trying to persuade China to adjust its currency regime. China was singularly unmoved. The Chinese also limited Obama's access to China's people outside the official venues, even going so far as to carefully orchestrate a town hall with a not very representative cross section of the Chinese public. The joint statement at the end of the trip cited progress on key areas of cooperation such as North Korea, Iran, and preparations for the Copenhagen climate summit but also showed that the United States had granted considerable leeway to the Chinese on sensitive language like that pertaining to Taiwan. This not only produced pushback in Washington, it also contributed to a general feeling from the press that the United States was in a new position at these meetings, a weaker if not quite a supplicant power. An assessment in the *New York Times* stated, "this is no longer the United States–China relationship of old but an encounter with a weakened giant and a comer with a bit of its own swagger. Washington's comparative advantage in past meetings is now diminished, a fact clearly not lost on the Chinese."

The bureaucratic dramas in the background didn't help. Not only was State periodically frustrated by being "bigfooted" by the White House, but so too were the press. In one instance, a senior reporter for one of the world's leading newspapers told me of the reaction when the White House offered the president's counselor Valerie Jarrett to provide a background briefing during the China trip "despite the fact that, as far as we could tell, she knew absolutely not the first thing about China. But I guess she was close to the president and to this crew, that's what mattered." The involvement of Jarrett and political aides to the president, like David Axelrod, was increasingly to become a source of criticism from both the press and the policy pros on the inside who felt that the political pollsters and campaign advisors were overstepping their bounds and operating beyond the areas of their expertise.

The perception of a US in decline was not helped by the Copenhagen climate summit. It was there that a plan led by the Atlantic powers to set numerical targets for reducing emissions by a certain date ran aground because China helped lead an effort among emerging powers to resist. The Chinese, Indians, and others knew that the process could go only as fast as they chose to go and they were adamant that they should not be forced to slow their development and be burdened by unfair regulatory limits that had not constrained the growth of developed powers. At that meeting, thanks to their unity on that point, the entire balance of power in global climate talks shifted to the rising powers—who would increasingly be responsible for the fastest growing share of global energy use—and away from America and the Europeans. Symbolizing the shift, the Chinese repeatedly slighted Obama and his team. On one occasion, they sent a mid-level foreign ministry official to represent them at a meeting attended by Obama and other leaders—a problem compounded by the fact that the assembled heads of state and government had to wait for this bureaucrat to receive instructions from China's premier before they could proceed. Later, at an evening session for emerging powers, Obama found the meeting had begun without him. He then crashed the conversation only to be bluntly lectured by China's leading climate negotiator. Overall the meeting was a fiasco. Clinton herself, who witnessed this, was flabbergasted at how badly planned and managed the US effort was (even though her climate team, along with White House and Department of Energy officials, had planned the US involvement there), particularly given that the behavior of all those present was so predictable.

For most of 2010, the course of relations was consistently inconsistent. It maintained a roughly even keel, thanks to the fact that periodic irritants were offset by the ongoing efforts of both sides to work on the relationship, and the underlying reality that the two economies were growing ever more "intertwined," to use a word Clinton often chose. This latter point meant that history—always more powerful than policy or even the most obstructive bureaucrat—was pushing the two sides forward into a deeper, if not always a more comfortable, relationship. Meanwhile, the advantage of having so many senior people in the administration interested in playing a role in the relationship meant that there were perhaps the most extensive set of parallel, multilayered conversations being conducted between the United States and China that had ever taken place. At State, Treasury, Commerce, USTR, Defense, Energy, HHS, and a host of other agencies principal-to-principal conversations were proliferating, as were contacts between deputies and at the working level. (There was no area where the relationship was not central. Sandalow of the Energy Department made more than a dozen trips to China in his four years as assistant secretary and later as acting under secretary of energy. Peggy Hamburg, the head of the Food and Drug Administration, once explained to me at a dinner party that upwards of 70 percent of the active pharmacological ingredients in all US drugs were actually imported from China, an unsettling dependence of an unanticipated kind.)

White House sources emphasized that this interdisciplinary approach was all part of a plan. Said one, "the China and Asia rebalance was part of a government-wide strategy that involved everything from diplomacy to the redistribution of military assets that was enabled by withdrawal from Iraq. It also involved significant economic initiatives. These included pushing for the Trans-Pacific Partnership [TPP], a trade deal [originally put on the US agenda during the Bush administration]."

Sometimes some on the team would push back on these initiatives. The TPP was one such example, with senior members of the economic team pooh-poohing it as "too small." But Donilon and the NSC insisted it be emphasized because of its symbolic importance.

In January 2010, the administration—perhaps reacting to the stings of late 2009—announced a sale of advanced Patriot missiles to Taiwan. China reacted. It announced a week later the test of its own land-based missile defense system. And it offered the usual boilerplate that the test "is not targeted at any country." Clinton responded by making a strong statement (later echoed by President Obama's wife Michelle during her own very successful trip to China in 2014), in which she asserted that Internet freedom was and should be a tenet of US foreign policy. She also singled out cyber-attacks as an area of special concern, stating that "those who disrupt the free flow of information in our society or any other pose a threat to our economy, our government, and our civil society. Countries or individuals that engage in cyber-attacks should face consequences and international condemnation." Had she followed that with language that the statement was "not targeted at any country," no one would have believed it.

In February, a meeting in the White House map room with the Dalai Lama was actively supported by some of those political advisors close to the president, including Valerie Jarrett. In March, Steinberg and Bader were invited to Beijing largely to be redressed for inflaming the relationship around Taiwan. Steinberg used this occasion to press for an initiative he hoped would complement the S&ED and create a permanent dialogue around strategic security issues such as cyber, nuclear force modernization, missile defense, and space defense. In April the mood swung positive, with Hu promising to attend a nuclear security summit shortly after Geithner had demurred naming China a currency manipulator. By May, the goals for the S&ED were modest, "solid singles, not home runs," and that was what was achieved, with modest progress on energy and commercial issues like supply-chain security.

Obama did push China on its focus on propping up exports sales at the next G-20 meeting in late June 2010, and later took a swipe at them for not being tough enough on North Korea. At the same time, moves were afoot that would make the Chinese even more uncomfortable. Donilon and Bader pushed Obama to have the United States join the East Asia Summit (EAS) to give it more of a presence in regional affairs. Behind the scenes, Campbell worked tirelessly at the important work of establishing bilateral dialogues with the countries of the region, one by one. These were not high-profile interactions but instead provided the kind of recognition these countries had long sought from the United States. They gradually served to help the United States develop a broader base of relationships in the region through which it could provide a counterbalance to China's growing clout. Here the administration did some of its very best and most important rebalancing work. "This is the blocking and tackling of foreign policy," Campbell said to me at the time. "It's not glamorous but it ensures that when something happens and you need someone on the other end of the phone, they answer." Clinton put an emphatic punctuation mark on the process in July when she directly and bluntly commented on the disputes between China and its neighbors regarding the South China Sea. She insisted that for the United States it was essential that these claims be resolved consistent with international law, and she offered American resources to help facilitate negotiation of a code of conduct for the area. China's foreign minister was livid (as the US secretary of state admittedly might be if China began inserting itself into issues in the Caribbean) and he warned ASEAN countries not to get involved in an enterprise organized by an outside power. He stated forcefully, "China is a big country. Bigger than any country here."

Later that month, China asserted its "indisputable sovereignty" over the South China Sea. The paradox in this was, of course, that because it did not yet have a blue water navy of real capacity, China depended on others, notably the United States, to protect the sea lanes through which its vital supplies of energy and resources made their way to China. So, just as on the economic front, for all the bluster and posturing, the two nations were, again, mutually dependent and therefore were constrained in how they might pressure each other. (China has embarked on a program to significantly enhance its naval capacity in recent years, however, suggesting they themselves are uncomfortable with this dependency.)

Recognizing the importance of deepening the dialogue between the countries, Obama accepted a proposal conceived by Donilon that he and Larry Summers go to China to have a meeting with the leadership. This was a very unusual arrangement on several levels. It was effectively foreign-policy outreach between top White House advisors and the leadership in Beijing. It created interesting questions of protocol—very important to the Chinese—because Donilon, whose star was in its ascendancy, was still the deputy at the NSC, although Jim Jones was already rumored to be on his last legs as national security advisor. The Chinese, however, recognizing the way power was really being managed in the White House, pulled out the stops, and meetings with all the top Beijing leadership were arranged with both Summers and Donilon being treated equally and with the utmost respect. One person intimately involved with the planning of the trip said that it was, in fact, personally okayed by China's president Hu Jintao.

According to both Summers and Donilon, the trip provided a forum for unusually open and constructive dialogue. Donilon made it clear that, for the president, there were few major international initiatives in which cooperation with the Chinese was not vitally important. Summers made the case that China needed to focus on allowing its currency to appreciate or risk inviting both inflation and political retribution in the United States that would be hard for the White House to contain.

The tenor of the discussions was positive, and the trip was seen as something of a watershed in the relationship—even though it created a kind of parallel White House track to the S&ED. Ever pragmatic, the Chinese wanted to make sure they were interacting with the people who really could get things done. As for the American side, though the effort may have involved a more operational role than was typical for senior White House staff, it reflected the reality of how the Obama administration operated. Furthermore, it demonstrated that even when there are rival initiatives within an administration, the result can be net positive if both are pointed in generally the same direction, Then, in October 2010 Donilon ascended to become national security advisor.

An aspect of this White House–centric approach to governance was well-captured in a February 2010 *Financial Times* article by Edward Luce. Given the retributive mentality of many in the Obama inner circle, Luce showed a great deal of courage by writing "A Fearsome Foursome," describing the reality of the world created by those closest to Obama, notably Axelrod, Jarrett, Gibbs, and Emanuel. It noted that these four were crucially involved in virtually every major decision and had a kind of access and control over who else had access to the president that essentially made it impossible for others to do their jobs. "Perhaps the biggest losers are the cabinet members," said Luce. He cited Kathleen Sebelius, Obama's secretary of health and human services; Janet Napolitano, secretary of the department of homeland security; and Ken Salazar, secretary of the interior as three who seldom interacted with the president. He noted Rahm Emanuel's famed coarseness as a further obstacle to effective communication, recalling a time Emanuel described liberals who wanted to mobilize resources on healthcare reforms as "fucking retards." Said one big Obama supporter, "we are treated as though we are children. Our advice is never sought." Describing the Obama China visit, Luce wrote, "the same can be observed in foreign policy. On Mr. Obama's November trip to China, members of the cabinet such as Nobel Prize–winning Stephen Chu, energy secretary, were left cooling their heels while Mr. Gibbs, Mr. Axelrod, and Ms. Jarrett were constantly at the president's side."

The piece created a firestorm and made life rather tough for Luce in getting access in the White House for some time thereafter. But its thesis was also confirmed and reconfirmed in the years afterward in literally dozens of conversations that I had with Obama cabinet secretaries, their deputies, big donors, current and former senators, and members of Congress.

Steve Clemons, a thoughtful, well-known, and dependably impartial Washington commentator wrote: "this Luce piece is unavoidably, accurately hard-hitting and while many of the nation's top news anchors and editors are sending emails back and forth (I have been sent three such emails in confidence) on what a spot-on piece Luce wrote on the administration, they fear that the 'four horsepersons of the Obama White House' will shut down and cut off access to those who give the essay 'legs.'"

Supporting and adding nuance to the Luce argument, one former Obama cabinet secretary said to me, "the way President Obama operates is that he is not somebody who in fact delegates a lot of power to others. He is somebody who wants to have control and when you want to have control, you tend to rely on people that are close to you to be able to talk with them and work with them and make sure that what you want is being implemented. And I think that's a very fundamental principle with this president." This official, a former top player on the national security side, said that "during the Clinton years, the NSC basically got issues, scrubbed a lot of various options, and then formally presented those options to the president, who then made a decision regarding what he would implement. The Obama White House generally operated differently in the sense that we talked through the options but it was not a very formalized process that would make a formal presentation to the president. It was basically focused on trying to get a kind of instinct as to where the president would like to go and then working to support that. In other words, it began more from the president than the normal national security procedure you might have seen with past presidents." This official, in a critical job, said he saw the president once every two or three weeks one-on-one and more often in a group setting. But underscoring Luce's analysis he added, "it's fair to say that a staff, particularly a staff that had a close relationship with the president, played a large role in pushing issues through and putting a certain emphasis on what direction things should take based on "what the president told me" kind of thing. . . . And so staff members close to the president oftentimes spoke for the president and tended to influence what was taking place. And [other cabinet secretaries] and myself, just by virtue of our backgrounds, said, wait a minute.

If there's any question of precooking a product here, we've got to look at all of the different options and then decide what makes the most sense, not be driven by some quote the president may or may not have given to some staffer."

Vali Nasr, who worked at State, put it more bluntly with regard to the White House insiders, "I think they wanted to run the policy, and that's when it broke down, rather than letting competent and experienced people at State and Defense run with it. Also, the White House had an inclination to run things like a campaign. They wanted total control on things. And it went on a kind of headline-to-headline basis and there's no way a State Department or a Hillary Clinton or a Gates are going to be able to work that way because their agencies have not been built to run that way." Furthermore, continued Nasr, "when we came in they also basically said no one can go on television without approval from Denis McDonough, who (at the time) ran strategic communications at the White House. That included Hillary. So you know, Sunday shows, *NewsHour*—it was tight control not because they didn't trust people [but] because that's a way you run a campaign." Other senior officials in multiple other cabinet departments—on the economic and domestic policy sides in addition to those involved in national security—reported that tight controls of media appearances of this sort were standard operating procedure throughout Obama's time in office.

Steve Hadley observed: "rather than empowering and enabling your cabinet secretaries so you get the leverage of the full federal government, they were disempowering people and pulling it all into the White House. And that becomes a particular problem when you have a series of crises and . . . all you end up doing is crisis management. And if that's all you do then all you're going to get is more crises because you're not going to be shaping events and shaping the future direction of our interests. And I worry that's where they got."

Centralization took a toll. "Nobody would do anything unless the right person in the White House said something to OK the process," said one top State Department official, "otherwise you can't get anyone to do anything. And you know you were constantly fighting where, for example, USAID couldn't get anything done without constantly fighting a back channel in the White House from [former campaign policy insider] Gayle Smith. That was a classic example. And she worked for [Michael] Froman, and Froman [who went to law school with the president] was part of the inside crowd."

Another deficiency fed by the concentration of too much power within the White House was cited by an Obama subcabinet member: "few people are involved in the decisions, so they do not hear all the options and differing points of view. And most of those people are highly operational—so they flip from meeting to meeting. So long-term thinking and fresh perspectives frequently don't make their way to the table. And they don't do their best work because they feel that they are out of the circle. The NSC staff also tends to treat agency people at lower levels as their staff, which causes a considerable amount of friction."

Additionally, most functional responsibilities within the NSC were managed at the senior director level, which caused other problems. A senior Obama advisor on national security issues and a veteran of past NSCs observed to me that when the NSC was smaller (which meant in any other administration), NSC senior staff jobs were seen as more important and you might have, as you did in the Clinton years, former assistant secretaries and others with many years of experience in a number of them. But, "during the Obama years many of these NSC roles were seen as a kind of on-the-job training program for younger policy types." The NSC veteran noted that this not only had a cost in terms of inexperience, but it also made it harder for the NSC to effectively convene high-level interagency meetings because under secretaries, who saw themselves as peers of deputy national security advisors, resisted being managed by what they perceived as more junior staffers. This was another, albeit inadvertent, way in which the structure as well as the approach had the effect of diluting the impact of the agencies in the policymaking process.

So there were circles within circles. The activist NSC and the heavily staffed White House drove much policy. But within the White House, it was the insiders who dictated how priorities were set, which approaches would be adopted, and how. Said a top White House lawyer, "the rest of the White House resents the NSC because they think they know everything. And the NSC resents the political people because they don't know the substance." In his twenty months as national security advisor, Jim Jones never seemed to truly make it into that circle nor did he get a chance to get his legs under him in the role.

Meanwhile, the management task associated with the NSC kept growing. By the end of Jones's tenure, the NSC staff had grown to over 370 people, over ten times as large as the staff under Henry Kissinger in the 1970s, which reflected the long-term trend of consolidation of decision-making power within the White House that accelerated during the Obama years. A problem with this approach is that it makes other parts of the government redundant, or at least, makes them feel that way. As one former NSC principal put it, "when you put 300 people on an NSC staff, they're a cabinet. They've all got to do something. They all have to meddle."

Brent Scowcroft, who describes Jones as a "good friend," called the selection of Jones for the job, "a strange choice. They [Jones and the president] didn't know each other. I think they had met twice before. He was not an inner circle choice." Brzezinski observed, "I think he was older than the president and was a former NATO commander and yet he had to defer to this very brilliant and opinionated civilian who was probably at the same time discounting a large amount of what he said because he preferred to talk to Tom or to Denis."

Larry Summers and Leon Panetta both thought that Donilon's promotion to NSC advisor represented a step forward. "I have a lot of admiration for Tom, I must say," said Summers, "I think he has been very thoughtful, serious, careful. Very free of a personal agenda for national security. He is a national security advisor who put everything into the job." In addition, "one substantial strength that he had relative to many other people in the administration is maintaining a very active connection to the world of thought, with the world of experts on the outside, with the world of what's being written about a wide range of national security problems. And I think to be able to do that while at the same time maintaining a quite tight ship with quite a bit of harmony as these things go is quite impressive. I think the president is very lucky to have had Tom for those years and it would have been much, much more difficult without him."

You Say Pivot and I Say Rebalancing

Because Donilon was one of the principal advocates for shifting America's focus to the Pacific, his promotion helped with giving that policy even more importance within the White House. He had won, during the first two years of the administration, very considerable trust from Obama and those around him and thus was seen, unlike Jones, as one of the insiders and as a loyalist. At the same time, his counterparts in the administration largely saw him as committed to process, thanks to his work in overseeing the deputies process that was the most high-function element of the NSC's roles during those first two years.

Clinton further articulated the policy a month after the power shift with a speech in Honolulu en route to the East Asia Summit in Hanoi. She spoke of the American commitment to Asia as "forward-deployed democracy" and emphasized that it was the administration's objective to bring diplomacy into "every corner" of the region. At the summit, she sought to defuse growing tensions between China and Japan over the small, barren island chain known to the Chinese as the Diaoyu and to the Japanese as the Senkaku. The dispute over control of the islands was more intense than any intrinsic value of the chain might have warranted. Both sides invested the islands with the history of bad feeling that had strained relations between the two countries since before the Second World War. In private meetings, Clinton offered US assistance in mediating the dispute, but to little avail. The tensions would grow well into the second term of the Obama administration, becoming, by 2014, a flash point that produced military near-misses, deep animosity among the Chinese and Japanese publics, and concerns the dispute might accidentally trigger a more violent form of conflict.

Consistent with the overall strategy of reengaging the region more broadly and following up on legwork done by Clinton and her team, Obama took a trip to the region that included stops in India, Indonesia, and South Korea. In India, in a decision that insiders characterized as "nearly improvised," Obama sought to communicate the importance he placed on the US-India relationship by offering to support India's candidacy for permanent UN Security Council membership. This had long been a desire of India, seeking to have status equivalent to the other major powers in the UN's "permanent five." The offer, even though it came with little likelihood of near-term translation into action, was met with great pleasure in New Delhi, though with less in Beijing, where diplomats saw it as the latest clear effort to build alliances intended to offset Chinese influence.

Despite this and tensions over issues in Korea, on currency, and China's own internal debates over the role it should play in the world, President Hu determined that he should accept Obama's offer for a full state visit to Washington in late January 2011. During Hu's visit, Steinberg's idea of a Strategic Security Dialogue (SSD) was accepted by the Chinese, and the Chinese announced an order for a further 200 Boeing aircraft as part of an overall commitment to purchase $45 billion in US goods. The trip set the stage for a year that was all in all a positive one in the relationship, with all departments in the now more closely coordinated NSC process working to deepen communication.

By the fall of 2011 the China policy had coalesced from what were once multiple parallel initiatives and become a better-coordinated effort quarterbacked by Donilon in the White House and spearheaded by Clinton in the field. Seeking to define the policy, Clinton prepared "America's Pacific Century," an article for *Foreign Policy*. She began:

> As the war in Iraq winds down and America begins to withdraw its forces from Afghanistan, the United States stands at a pivot point. Over the last 10 years, we have allocated immense resources to those two theaters. In the next 10 years, we need to be smart and systematic about where we invest time and energy, so that we put ourselves in the best position to sustain our leadership, secure our interests, and advance our values. One of the most important tasks of American statecraft over the next decade will therefore be to lock in a substantially increased investment—diplomatic, economic, strategic, and otherwise—in the Asia Pacific region.

This effort—which would become known, not entirely to the pleasure of all involved, as "the pivot," was the manifestation of the strategy she had earlier referred to as "forward-deployed diplomacy." It had six lines of action: strengthening bilateral alliances; deepening America's relationships with rising powers, including especially China; engaging with multilateral institutions; expanding trade and investment; forging a broad-based military presence; and advancing democracy and human rights. She went on: "in the last decade, our foreign policy has transitioned from dealing with the post–Cold War peace dividend to demanding commitments in Iraq and Afghanistan. As those wars wind down we will need to accelerate efforts to pivot to new realities."

Leon Panetta, who replaced Gates as secretary of defense around the same time, supported the view on his first trip to the region in late 2011 with a statement that "I've made clear that even with the budget constraints we are facing in the United States," there is "no question that in discussions within the Pentagon and discussions in the White House, that the Pacific will be a priority for the United States of America."

Obama then capped the effort with a major speech on Asia policy at the Asia-Pacific Economic Community (APEC) summit in Honolulu in November 2011. He called the Asia-Pacific region "absolutely critical to US growth" and later said, "no region will do more to shape our long-term future." Four days later, he illustrated his commitment to this policy by announcing plans to base 2,500 Marines in Australia "to more effectively strengthen the security of both our nations and this region." He, like Panetta before him, argued that defense cuts would not impede this priority effort. Donilon also followed with a reinforcing op-ed in the *Financial Times*.

The process of coalescing and rolling out the strategy and message was well-coordinated by the new team at the White House, but no good deed goes unpunished in Washington. The term *pivot* was attacked by allies in the Middle East and Mideast specialists in DC who suggested that it meant the United States was turning away from them. The Chinese, of course, were angered that the whole approach smacked of "containment" and a new Cold War. And the elevation of the policy to the status it gained in the White House fueled rivalries with the State Department, which felt a special sense of ownership given, as Chollet noted, their focus on it since literally the first hours of the administration. Campbell and Donilon, in particular, who had begun in the administration as close friends who used to go fishing together, saw their relationship grow more strained as a result. Campbell, who had truly done the heavy lifting behind the venture, working tirelessly in capitals across Asia, building an unparalleled set of deep relationships, and Clinton, who had effectively turned to Asia when the Middle East and other critical issues were controlled from within the White House, had reason to be frustrated.

Donilon preferred the term *strategic rebalancing* in place of *pivot*, largely because it did not imply leaving one part of the world behind, but the lawyerly national security advisor kept his public views to a minimum. He adopted the tactic, perfected by Scowcroft, of staying in the background and of making significant public statements only after close consultation with others, like Clinton, Panetta, and new CIA director David Petraeus. This kind of camera shyness is a virtue found in the best national security advisors, given that it is a role best performed behind the scenes. Any foray into the limelight by the national security advisor risks bringing political damage to the president as well as alienating the secretary of state and other senior officials who see it as their prerogative to be the international spokespeople for the US government.

By announcing the policy as a major change, the administration boxed itself in. Any shift in priorities that might distract attention away from the region—as would happen later because of flaring problems in the Middle East and Ukraine, for example—might be seen as a reconsideration or retreat. The same effect could result if succeeding senior officials have different priorities than their predecessors. That's what happened to the goals so actively pursued with regard to China by the likes of Clinton, Geithner, and Donilon. John Kerry would focus more intently on the Middle East, and Susan Rice, with little Asia experience, would largely direct her attentions to crisis management from the White House. Sometimes, making a big show of announcing a doctrine or policy shift carries with it risks of blowback if the follow-through flags. The same policy, announced with less brouhaha, might make a smaller splash but also represent a lower risk.

A New Fault Line Emerges

With domestic needs of a reelection campaign in 2012 approaching, it was inevitable that the relationship with China would again become a bit more contentious. The year began with the president characterizing China as a threat on trade issues due to unfair trading practices. He boasted of bringing WTO cases against the Chinese at twice the rate of the Bush team. He insisted that the United States would "not cede solar, wind, or battery industries to China or Germany." Then, over the next nine months, the administration kept after China on these issues, announcing anti-dumping sanctions, filing new WTO complaints, and issuing a rare presidential order demanding that a Chinese company divest itself of wind farms near a military base.

Then in late April, shortly before a trip to China by Clinton, a blind Chinese dissident named Chen Guangchen escaped from his Chinese captors and sought help from the United States. After a six-hour, late night consultation with her team, Clinton determined that the United States should pick up Chen and bring him into the US embassy in Beijing. This was done with the White House's knowledge but, according to State Department sources, without their enthusiastic support. Donilon was reportedly uneasy about the undertaking, and Clinton had to push to pursue the approach as conceived by Campbell and the team. Campbell informed the Chinese ambassador in Washington on April 27 that the human rights activist was inside the embassy. Along with US Ambassador to China Gary Locke and State Department Counsel Harold Koh, Campbell undertook negotiations seeking Chinese permission to let Chen come to the United States. China's opening position was that they would cancel the upcoming S&ED meeting, which was scheduled to start in four days. Intense back-and-forth exchanges produced little progress until shortly after Clinton herself arrived in Beijing on May 2. She then personally intervened with State Councilor Dai Bingguo to seal the deal. Chen was freed to seek medical treatment, but when it became apparent that the Chinese did not intend to follow through on promises to treat him and his family well, Clinton again had to intervene directly with Dai to arrive at a deal to allow Chen to come to the United States. What had been a near-fiasco had, thanks to intensive efforts by the State Department team and Clinton, become a success, especially since the subsequent S&ED went off without a hitch and actually produced some good progress with regard to opening Chinese markets to US investment.

"Mature relationships," said Campbell to me shortly after, "between big complicated countries are not simple. It is a sign of maturity that they can withstand the occasional problem."

"One of the Few Things That Keeps Me Up at Night"

In the middle of the year Leon Panetta spoke on "Rebalance Toward the Asia-Pacific" at the Shangri-La Dialogue held annually by the International Institute for Strategic Studies. Almost simultaneously, working the less-glamorous issues associated with that rebalance, Hillary Clinton signed a $50 million initiative to help with funding in the Lower Mekong River, a sign to smaller countries in the region that the rebalancing was more than just rhetoric. Later that year, Obama took a trip to Thailand, Myanmar (where the United States was restoring relations), and Cambodia. This was Clinton's last trip with the president before she stepped down and it was symbolic that it was to the region where much of her most constructive work had been done.

However, while progress was being made on many levels of US relations across Southeast Asia, there was a worm in the apple—the worm of cybersecurity. China was considered by the US intelligence community to be the leading source of hacking into US commercial and government systems, creating rapidly growing economic costs and strategic risks. "Cyber," said former counterterrorism chief John Brennan, "is one of the few things that keeps me up at night."

In February 2013, a National Intelligence Estimate (NIE) revealed that the United States had become the target of massive, sustained cyber-espionage efforts. Although Russia, Israel, and France were mentioned with regard to the theft of economic intelligence and intellectual property, the conclusion of the report was that none of these countries could hold a candle to the comprehensive nature or impact of Chinese efforts. Cyber rose in profile to such a degree that the president singled it out in his State of the Union address for more attention. A week after that speech, computer security firm Mandiant released a sixty-page report documenting attacks led by the People's Liberation Army and a secretive operation based in Shanghai called Unit 61398. It had apparently targeted 141 organizations in the United States and other English-speaking countries and stolen terabytes of data. Almost all of these thefts could be traced to Unit 61398.

Working closely with Brennan and the intelligence community, Donilon had come to view cyber issues as a new top national-security priority. He made a speech addressing this in March 2013, stating, "increasingly US businesses are speaking out about their serious concerns about sophisticated targeted theft of confidential business information and proprietary technologies through cyber-intrusions emanating from China on an unprecedented scale. The international community cannot tolerate such activity from any country." The issue was seen as so important that when Obama made his first call to congratulate China's new leader Xi Jinping days after the Donilon address, he raised the issue of cybersecurity as a "shared" concern. Within the first six weeks of the Xi presidency, three top-level US officials, Jack Lew, Lael Brainard, and Evan Medeiros, came to Bejing to address cybersecurity. Two months later, a Pentagon report on China's military capabilities devoted substantial attention to Chinese cyber-attacks and argued that China had systematically developed state-of-the-art offensive cyber capabilities. It was a topic that would dominate Obama's next scheduled meeting with Xi, in June.

But before that, another watershed development occurred. On May 20, 2013, Edward Snowden, a former US government contractor, arrived in Hong Kong. He was, as the world would soon learn, fleeing from the United States because he had systematically stolen massive files from the super-secret National Security Agency, America's own cyber spies, and was preparing them for release to the media. He sought Chinese asylum. Although China did not grant it, it allowed Snowden to leave via a commercial flight to Moscow. Snowden had planned to use Moscow as a transit point, a temporary stop, but he became stranded there when US pressure made it impossible for him to find a feasible way to get to any of the few countries offering him asylum. Russia ultimately allowed Snowden to take up residence there, infuriating the Obama administration. Just as happened over the financial shakedown proposal floated at the time of the Beijing Olympics, China, the rising power that had gained so much ground during the Bush and Obama years, showed that it was inclined to play its hand more deftly than Russia on this very twenty-first-century spy story.

Even as the US-China relationship inevitably remains a vitally important one, regularly called to the headlines when disputes such as those in the China Sea or cyber-skirmishing flair up, or when the economic interdependence of the two nations is made apparent by currency issues or business deals, the coda to Obama's first-term efforts to restore Asia to a more central role in US foreign policy may well have been one of those developments that doesn't stimulate much public debate because it is so hard to point a camera at. Clinton, Donilon, and Geithner left the administration, along with virtually all the supporting players who were so central to the rebalancing. Although the president, the vice president, and senior cabinet members continued to make trips to the region, the day-to-day engines of the rebalancing, its architects and true-believers, were gone. So too in the eyes of many senior Asian government officials were the people they had come to know, and with whom they had developed the kind of relationships that were so crucial in the context of their culture. (Although this point can be overstated. Good long-term personal relationships are vital in any area of diplomacy as in all businesses.) When traveling to the region after leaving the government, the ex-officials would often hear what one told me was something of a refrain, "Who do we call? Who is in charge? We knew that we could turn to Secretary Clinton or Donilon or Kurt Campbell or Bob Hormats. We don't feel that Secretary Kerry or Susan Rice care about these issues in the same way."

The result is a cautionary tale. Efforts to refocus on new priorities are necessary as the US government adapts to a changing world. But once launched, such efforts need to be carefully maintained or simple neglect or slippage will be taken as a decision to pull back. It is possible through passivity or inattention to make counterparts overseas feel as though something were being actively withdrawn. The blowback from such modulations can damage relationships, as the administration found when it felt compelled to send both the president and vice president to Asia to reassure allies of America's commitment to leadership in the region during the first years of Obama's second term in office.

CHAPTER 7

Eyeball to Eyeball Again

**Above all, avoid lies, all lies, especially the lie to
yourself. . . . And avoid contempt, both of others and
yourself. . . . And avoid fear, though fear is simply
the consequence of every lie.**

—FYODOR DOSTOYEVSKY,
THE BROTHERS KARAMAZOV

If the focus on China during both the Bush and the Obama administrations was on dealing with its ascent and the consequences of that ascent, the situation was roughly the opposite with Russia. As part of the former Soviet Union (FSU), Russia had been in precipitous decline even prior to the end of the Cold War, a victim of its own failed system. That decline had accelerated as the FSU broke up and many of its satellites spun into more Western orbits. The decline was exacerbated within Russia itself by the demographic crisis of a rapidly shrinking population.

Russia's economic system after 1991 was soon rife with corruption, dominated by a handful of oligarchs, major extractive industries, and the well-connected who had won the favor of the government—or who were its leaders. Democracy did not fare as well. Since 1999, the political landscape had been dominated by Vladimir Putin.

Putin personally took it upon himself to use whatever tools were available to him—democratic, economic, military, or otherwise—to engineer a rebound in Russia. He oversaw a major push to tap into Russian reserves of oil, gas, and minerals to build foreign-exchange reserves and to use exports as a source of leverage over importers, particularly in Europe. He granted favors to oligarchs to help promote growth, reportedly often seeking a fee in exchange, and by the time of this writing, rumors swirled that he was one of the world's richest men. One estimate said his net worth was $60–70 billion or more. He also put down potential opponents—from rival oligarchs like Mikhail Khodorkovsky to critical pop singers like the group Pussy Riot—using the old tool kit of the Russian police state. He could resort to rough techniques and he projected a sometimes rather comical public persona—the photos of a bare-chested Putin riding on horseback, practicing judo, and hunting bears, and later of his young athletic girlfriend, evoked a mid-life crisis more than they did his commanding virility. But he promoted nationalism and Russian identity at a time when it was under siege, and won popular support.

One technique for winning that support was his ruthlessness in confronting and challenging what he characterized as foreign enemies that threatened Russia's future, or who had been complicit in bringing it down and were trying to keep it down. This ranged from Islamic extremist groups within Russia and on its southern borders to regular, insistent, and often brash confrontations with the United States and the West.

For the country's citizens, who recalled the stature on the world stage that Russia had enjoyed during the Cold War, this last technique had proven to be especially popular—much to the frustration of both George W. Bush and Barack Obama. Indeed, both presidents seemed continually surprised by behavior from Putin that should have been unsurprising. From his very first days in office, when Russia directly challenged the United States on the ground in Kosovo, racing to the airport to ensure that NATO troops did not seize it, Putin consistently chose to inflame the West whenever he thought he could do so without bearing too high a cost. He was cool and calculated, and he understood that the proud Russian people would put up with much if they felt they were recovering some of their global status. Such renascent nationalism is common in defeated nations and should have been a warning to many in the Western policy elite. Failing to manage it properly in the past had led to world wars, and it was specifically the desire to defuse such situations in the future that led the United States to invest so much in the rebuilding of Germany and Japan after World War II—that, and, of course, the need to contain the Soviet Union.

Instead the relationship was "immature," in the words of Sergey Kislyak, Russia's likeable, capable, and often tough-talking emissary to the

United States from 2008 onward. It was too heavily weighted toward a few issues and not sufficiently counterbalanced by commercial and cultural exchanges. It was dominated by the relationship between a handful of personalities, most notably Putin. In fact, in a number of key respects, the relationship with Russia was the inverse of that with China.

Early in his tenure as president, George W. Bush said of Putin, "I looked the man in the eye. I found him to be very straightforward and trustworthy. We had a very good dialogue. I was able to get a sense of his soul; a man deeply committed to his country and the best interests of his country." If the connection existed at all, it was short-lived. Putin ultimately frustrated and infuriated Bush much as he had done Clinton and as he would Barack Obama.

By the time Bush's second-term administration took office, even as it sought to mend relations with key countries worldwide, there was skepticism among Bush's top officials as to whether real progress could be made with Putin's Russia. Like his boss, Sergey Lavrov, Russia's brilliant foreign minister, regularly inflamed American officials with his bluntness. In her first meeting with her counterpart, Condoleezza Rice explained that going forward the relationship would be predicated on Russia's commitment to democracy. It was clear, given Russia's recent actions, like shutting independent television stations and seizing the assets of private companies, that this was not going to be easy—if it were even possible.

"Condi and Lavrov could get into it," said one of her closest State Department advisors, "part of it was he could be an asshole. He speaks English very well and he would get into these semantic arguments. I remember one time we were at an event—a gathering of the UN P5+1 [the Security Council, plus Germany] group meetings—and they were just going off on each other and you could look at the other ministers and think, boy, this is uncomfortable. And so then the Russians, quote, 'accidentally' turned on the mics in the meeting, so it got broadcast back into the press filing center and the press could hear some of it. Nick Burns was supposed to go to the press and give a read out of the meeting. So he walked into the meeting and started to give a summary that said the meeting went very well . . . he walked right into it. But Condi didn't let that sort of thing get to her. With them it was par for the course."

On point during this period in Moscow was Bill Burns, the US ambassador, and Hadley and his NSC team had a great deal of experience with the Russians. But the relationship remained strained from almost start to finish. At a face-to-face meerting in Slovakia early in the second term, Bush and Putin reiterated their core messages. Bush insisted on democratic reforms and Putin responded that democracy "should not be accompanied by the collapse of the state and the impoverishment of the people." The two did agree to further dismantling of Russian nuclear weapons but the overall tone was, according to a participant, "chilly."

Bush touched a very raw nerve with Putin and the Russians in May 2005 when he announced he would add stops to the former Soviet republics of Latvia and Georgia during his trip to Moscow to commemorate the sixtieth anniversary of the Allied victory over Germany. In the eyes of some sensitive Russians, the trip seemed as much about defeating them in the Cold War as it was about remembering the vital role they played in defeating the Nazis. Bush fanned the flames during the trip by recalling the tragedies associated with the communist takeover of the Baltics and warning Putin that "no good purpose is served by stirring up fears and exploiting old rivalries." He might just as well have been talking about himself, as far as Russian listeners were concerned.

Putin took off the gloves in responding to Bush's further calls for democratic reform by saying, "four years ago, your presidential election was decided by a court. But we're not going to poke our noses into your democratic system, because that's up to the American people."

Hadley and Rice publicly described the meetings between Bush and Putin that took place thereafter in Moscow with the buzzwords of the trade, like *open*, *constructive*, and *straightforward*. But in the words of one of those present, "it was strained from start to finish. You know the Russians. They never make these things easy."

Of greater consequence for the US-Russia narrative was the stop that Bush made in Georgia twenty-four hours after his Moscow meeting with Putin. There the president hailed the peaceful Rose Revolution that had brought reforms and West-leaning aspirations to that country in 2003. He also portentously stated that Georgia's sovereignty "must be respected by all nations."

"I Haven't Given Up on Russia"

Condaleezza Rice, of course, was in the business of trying to improve relationships the world over in the wake of the damage done during the first term. If the behind-the-scenes dynamic was sometimes tough, she made every effort to put a good face on it. A year into her term as secretary she publicly asserted that "in general, I think we have very good relations with Russia, probably the best relations that have been there for some time." This was patently not true. Diplomats are often paid to describe the world as they wish it were.

Bush, too, even as he prepared to confront Putin on recent crackdowns against opponents and his recent moves to suppress western NGOs at the St. Petersburg G-8 summit in 2006 said, "I haven't given up on Russia." Backstage, though, there was still the same formula: Bush pushed reform, and Putin punctured Bush's arguments by pointing out America's hypocrisy and contradictions. Over dinner, Bush told Putin of his desire to promote real freedoms of religion and the press in places like Iraq, to which Putin acidly responded, "we certainly would not want to have the same kind of democracy they have in Iraq, I will tell you quite honestly." If he had been a rapper, at that point he might have performed a mic drop and walked off the stage.

In the penultimate year of Bush's term in office, the relationship hit the shoals of a new debate—this time over the American plan to install a new antimissile system in Eastern Europe. Despite American arguments that the systems were not aimed at any one nation—and behind-the-scenes assurances that they really meant the systems to protect against the possibility of launches from rogue states like Iran—the Russians saw them as targeting Moscow and reopening old Cold War wounds.

Putin responded vehemently, using the 2007 Munich Security Conference as a platform. He accused the United States of provoking a new nuclear arms race and asserted that the "United States has overstepped its national boundaries," which, essentially, it had. He attacked "unilateral" and "illegitimate" American military actions, claiming they regularly "bring us to the abyss of one conflict after another." Robert Gates followed the next day with remarks designed to defuse the tension stating, "one Cold War was quite enough." But Rice and Hadley, and, behind the scenes, Bill Burns, Nick Burns, and others, went into overdrive to send a message that they did not want the relationship to deteriorate further, that they were making an effort. Rice pulled Lavrov aside during a meeting in Berlin to seek collaboration on Iran. Hadley went to Moscow to brief the Russians on the details of US military plans, including the missile defense objectives. Subsequently, the administration offered a proposal to cooperate on defense technology and to integrate US and Russian systems so that "the Russians would not see the missile defense initiative as such a threat." Gates flew to Moscow to continue this effort and said he made considerable "headway in clearing up some misunder-standings about the technical characteristics of the system."

But Putin, raw over the missile defense initiative and the gradual en-croachment on Russian borders that he associated with NATO expan-sion, then counterpunched by announcing the suspension of Russia's compliance with the Treaty on Conventional Forces in Europe. Rice sought to offset this move by continuing the administration's "demys-tification" campaign around the missile defense. At a NATO conclave she said, "the idea that somehow ten interceptors and a few radars in Eastern Europe are going to threaten the Soviet strategic deterrent is purely ludicrous and everybody knows it." Lavrov responded with an-other of those statements that could be referring to the United States or his own country—the diplomatic equivalent of what psychologists call *projection*—by saying that the United States is "still looking for an en-emy." Punch followed counterpunch, and by midyear, Putin was saying that if the United States went ahead with the missile defense he would respond by targeting European cities with his missiles. As for a new Cold War he said, "of course, we are returning to those times. It is clear that if a part of the US nuclear capability turns up in Europe and in the opin-ion of our military specialists will threaten us, then we are forced to take corresponding steps in response. What will those steps be? Naturally, we will have to have new targets in Europe."

This was classic Putin, as he would show regularly in the years to come. On the one hand, he, like many in Russia, were stung more deeply by the aftermath of Russia's Cold War defeat than many in the West cared to consider. NATO expansion seemed to be rubbing Russia's nose in that humiliation. However, as in the case of Germany's collapse after World War I, European history acutely reveals the dangers of humiliating vanquished adversaries. Such humiliation inevitably produces backlash, and nationalist leaders sense and take advantage of popular dissatisfac-tion and anger. That is precisely what Putin has always done.

Further, he was also seeking to divide the bolder United States from its less bellicose European allies. If he could do this through military intimidation, he would. If he could do it later by threatening interrup-tion of vital supplies of Russian natural gas to Europe, he would. He knew many in Europe lacked America's stomach for confrontation, and he knew that in the absence of strong European support, especially in the wake of America's depleting wars in the Middle East, it would be much harder for America to act. Indeed, even as he decried American unilateralism, he knew that, thanks to Iraq and Afghanistan, it was less of an option for the United States than at any time in recent memory.

As relations worsened—despite a visit from Putin to Bush's family home in Maine—threatening rhetoric continued to emanate from Moscow. Again seeking to defuse this, Rice and Gates presented a proposed Joint Regional Missile Defense architecture in Moscow in October 2007. Putin showed up forty minutes late for the meeting and sarcastically discounted the plan by saying, "of course, we can sometime in the future decide that some antimissile defense should be established somewhere on the moon." Then, on December 17, Russia delivered nuclear fuel to an Iranian power plant that was at the center of the international dispute over Iran's conventional nuclear program.

Putin was prevented by constitutional term limits from running for a third term in 2008. Instead, Dmitri Medvedev was elected Russia's president and took office at midyear. However, Putin remained a constant. He became prime minister and continued pulling the strings of Russia's political system. Although Medvedev presented a more muted, amiable front, he was never during his term able to shake the belief that he was just a placeholder for Putin's eventual return to power.

A pivotal moment came in April 2008, when Bush pushed hard to extend membership to Ukraine and Georgia at his final NATO summit. Welcoming applications from Ukraine and Georgia to join NATO, said Bush, "would send a signal to their citizens that if they continue on the path to democracy and reform they will be welcomed into the institutions of Europe. It would send a signal throughout the region that these two nations are, and will remain, sovereign and independent states." One German diplomat who was in attendance later said to me that "we warned the Americans that this was a mistake and could very well produce precisely the opposite effect from that Bush wanted. It would make those countries targets, more at risk." US officials admit Bush was acting against the advice of several of America's NATO allies.

The effort foundered because Germany and France opposed it. Putin showed his contempt for the idea and tipped his hand about how sensitive the issue was by threatening to cancel what would have been his first ever visit to such a summit if Ukraine and Georgia were granted such a path to NATO membership.

In a portent of things to come, Bush and Putin went from the summit to a meeting on the shores of the Black Sea in the little-known resort community of Sochi. Near both Georgia and Ukraine, the spot was rich with symbolism for Putin and the objective was to help defuse the tension regarding missile defense. Rice called the meeting, the last between Bush and Putin, a "high point." It featured an apparent agreement to collaborate on the development of a missile defense system in which Russia, the European Union, and the United States would be partners. In addition, a framework agreement was signed regarding future collaboration on combating terror and fighting the spread of nuclear weapons. However, Bush called the agreements "a significant breakthrough" and Putin said it did "not provide any breakthrough," an ominous contradiction, although for whom remained unclear.

Those doubts were soon removed. In August 2008—as Beijing's Olympic opening ceremonies dazzled an audience of billions worldwide, and just four months after Bush and Putin had their "high point" in Sochi, itself the site of another Olympics that would also take place on the eve of another Russian invasion, in 2014—Russia began its military intervention in Georgia. We can only imagine what the US response might have been had the Russians succeeded in persuading the Chinese to undertake a coordinated financial attack on vulnerable US markets at the same time. The response of the Bush administration was very similar to what would later be seen when Russia invaded Crimea during the second term of the Obama administration. The United States decried the violation of Georgian sovereignty, urged Russia to stop its bombings, and expressed solidarity with the Georgians. Just as Vice President Biden would be at the forefront of that communication, Vice President Cheney called Georgia's president Saakashvilli to offer America's support and to say "Russian aggression must not go unanswered."

Bush, who later wrote that he feared Russia would continue their conquest all the way to Georgia's capital, just as Obama feared the Russians would continue beyond Crimea deep into Ukraine, also responded just as Obama did. He was firm with Putin. He called the action "unacceptable in the twenty-first century." And he then indicated that neither the United States nor NATO was considering a military response—which was not exactly true. The Bush NSC had actively discussed what military options might look like, but in the end "the costs were deemed too high and unjustified by US interests." Instead, as under Obama later, the goal was to contain the damage, push for a ceasefire, and hope the Russians would be happy with gaining only South Ossetia and Abkhazia. And Putin, just as he would after the incursion into Crimea, would argue that the United

States, as a country that had invaded Iraq, lacked the right to criticize any other nation for such a military intervention.

A telling analysis with long-term consequences came from the man who would serve both Bush and Obama as defense secretary, Robert Gates. He said in a press interview at the time, "my view is that the Russians—and I would say principally Prime Minister Putin—is interested in reasserting . . . not only Russia's great power or superpower status, but . . . Russia's traditional spheres of influence. My guess is that everyone is going to be looking at Russia through a different set of lenses as we look ahead."

Lessons Unlearned

Although he was right about that, Gates, who as a CIA analyst was a specialist in the Soviet Union, might also be surprised that he would soon be part of an another administration that within a couple of years would seem to forget everything that the Bush and Clinton years had taught them about Putin's Russia. For while the Bush team did respond to the Georgia incursion by signing two weeks later a missile defense agreement with Poland—a somewhat more forceful action than the very limited economic sanctions launched by Obama in the wake of the subsequent Crimea invasion—within months the incoming Obama team would be hard at work undoing that deal and seeking a "reset" with the Russians that would not address the underlying issues that led Putin to act as he did in Georgia and later Ukraine.

The Obama team would work hard to differentiate itself from the Bush administration that preceded them, but Putin saw what made them similar. Putin calculated that America would not respond against him with force. On the one hand, this was based on the facts surrounding both situations. A senior Bush advisor explained that their decision was based on "a cold calculation based on geography, the 'correlation of forces' and the likely reaction of friends and allies." What this meant was military action would be difficult, costly, and likely unsupported by most of America's NATO allies for whom Russia was a neighbor, a source of vital resources (notably natural gas), and a trading partner. This calculus was as true for Obama as for Bush. Further, an additional factor was that a United States with serious domestic and international problems and the fatigue stemming from two conflicts in the Middle East was unlikely to be able to summon the political will at home to take any sort of significant military action to resist Putin's advances. Further, while unlike the Chinese in many respects, he, too, sought to take advantage of an American and Western alliance that, if not in decline, was no longer the robust and resolute adversary it once was.

Bush essentially failed to move Putin in ways helpful to America, and he knew it. Characterizing his counterpart as "wily," Bush went on to offer a view framed awkwardly in canned Bush-era rhetoric every bit as stilted as old Soviet propaganda chestnuts: "given what I had hoped Putin and I could accomplish in moving past the Cold War, Russia stands out as a disappointment in the freedom agenda." Dick Cheney suggested he had never believed there was much prospect of a Westernized Russia anyway. "I always felt in my dealings with Putin," he said, "that it was important to remember his background was part of the Soviet KGB and in many ways his actions as the leader of Russia reflected that." And Condoleezza Rice signed off on the whole adventure by hinting that she knew she'd not be missed: "I'm sure Lavrov looked forward to the arrival of another team in Washington."

Russia welcomed Barack Obama into the Oval Office by announcing that it would place short-range missiles on its western border. But the first impulse of the Obama team was, as in so many things, to differentiate itself from its Bush predecessors. In so doing, they made the common and somewhat narcissistic error of assuming that a change on the part of the United States alone was enough to redirect a relationship that was largely being guided by someone else.

The absurdity of Medvedev's explanation for his taunting move welcoming Obama into office with the missile defense announcement—"with all my respect for the United States, I absolutely forgot about the important political event that had to take place that day"—should have put into focus the tenor of the US-Russian relationship Obama was likely to face, especially in light of the recent history. But the course to "repair and restore the relationship through active engagement and a repudiation of the Bush administration's Cold War impulses," in the words of one transition official involved in Russia issues, was determined even before the Obama team had settled into their desks at the White House. In fact, in his first major foreign policy address as vice president, Joe Biden told the Munich Security Conference that "it's time to press the reset button and to revisit the many areas in which we can and should be working together with Russia."

David Lipton, at the time a deputy to Summers and perhaps the White House economic official with the greatest experience in the region, said of Biden, "he was great in Russia. The thinking through how we should interact with Russia. I went with him to Russia, went with him to Ukraine on a couple trips. I found him well prepared, insightful, and incredibly crafty in his actual interactions with government officials. A very impressive fellow." But Biden would have no more influence over Putin than the preceding administration had.

The Obama administration began a rapid and systematic undoing of much of what the Bush team had put in place in the wake of the Russian invasion of South Ossetia and Abkhazia five months earlier. This included not only undoing sanctions but gradually repudiating the missile defense program the Bush team had been advocating.

The first concrete sign of the reset sought by the new US administration was a letter to Medvedev drafted by the Obama NSC Russia team led by Michael McFaul. It said the United States would not proceed with the missile defense system if Iran halted its program to build nuclear warheads and ballistic missiles. In this, the Obama team also revealed another element that would guide their Russia policy going forward; their desire to work with Russia in resolving priority issues in the Middle East, the most important of which at the time seemed to be stopping the Iranian nuclear program. Perhaps unsurprisingly, Medvedev responded with cautious enthusiasm to the Obama proposal, focusing less on the Iran issue and more on the fact that the United States was open to reconsidering what had been a central element of Bush policy in the region.

Meeting for the first time on April 1 on the perimeter of the G-20 summit, Medvedev and Obama both sought to widen the opening to better relations by expressing a desire to cooperate on a wide variety of issues, the most significant of which was a new arms control treaty. It was, after all, in the interest of neither side to maintain the massively overlarge and in many respects significantly outmoded nuclear arsenals that had been the foundations of their Cold War security postures. Maintaining and protecting antiquated weapons perpetuated burdensome costs and risks for each nation. Furthermore, it was during their discussions, which were characterized as "extremely wide-ranging" by a top Obama advisor, that the two discussed working together on issues like Iran and Afghanistan, and Medvedev accepted the idea of working with the United States to reopen northern supply routes into Afghanistan that were important to supporting local allies and initatives in the fight against al-Qaeda and

Taliban extremists. This was a positive step although one that would require a great deal of supporting, creative diplomacy from Hillary Clinton and her senior team to take full advantage of.

Obama not only agreed to pursue Senate ratification of the Comprehensive Nuclear Test Ban Treaty (CTBT) but also enacted an agreement of cooperation on peaceful uses of nuclear energy. This second agreement was one of the initiatives that Bush had set aside in the wake of the invasion of Georgia. So, inadvertently, the Obama team sent a message to the Russians that even the fairly limited consequences levied on the Russians in the wake of their incursion into Georgia would be curtailed. It was, in fact, a one-two punch of bad policy. To punish the Russians for their incursion into Georgia, the Bush team suspended some quality initiatives (the CTBT and the peaceful use of nuclear technology initiative) that would have reduced the threat from Russia. So the "sanctions" actually set back American interests as much as Russian. Then, in the hopes of reenergizing the US-Russian relationship, the Obama team undid the Bush sanctions, thereby sending a message to the Russians that there would be no lingering consequences for the aggression in South Ossetia and Abkhazia. As time would illustrate, this was hardly the right approach with Putin.

Obama declared the first meeting a success saying, "what we're seeing today is the beginning of new progress in US-Russia relations. And I think President Medvedev's leadership is and has been critical to allow that progress to take place." However, in several key respects the progress would prove as illusory as Medvedev's role as Russia's "leader."

During Obama's July 2009 trip to Moscow, the US and Russian teams agreed to the terms of a significant treaty to cut both country's nuclear arsenals by a quarter and committed themselves to memorializing the gains in a new Strategic Arms Reduction Treaty (START) by the time the old one expired at the end of the year. The two sides also agreed to undo yet another of the post-Georgia invasion moves of the Bush team by resuming military contacts. Finally, they also established a bilateral commission to strengthen dialogue that was conceived as a kind of starter version of the rapidly expanding S&ED with China.

For all the encouraging progress, though, remaining disagreements were not hard to find. Obama had his first lengthy, and more frosty, exchange with the man really pulling the strings in Russia, Vladimir Putin. The two tried to paper over the clearly awkward back and forth of the meeting with the usual post-dialogue press statements about hope and progress. Later, however, the president was quoted as saying, "I found him to be tough, smart, shrewd, very unsentimental, very pragmatic. And on areas where we disagree, like Georgia, I don't anticipate any meeting of the minds soon." In this respect, Obama's comment reflected a difference between his approach and Putin's. Putin never expected or sought a meeting of the minds. He would be quite content with holding opposing views, provided that the Americans' actions were toothless. Obama could say what he wanted about Georgia but the fact that he was unwinding the penalties Bush had put in place was what really mattered.

Secretary of State John Kerry would later tell me that among President Obama's relations with world leaders, that between Obama and Putin was among the most challenging. He called it "very difficult" and said that the two clearly had a tough time understanding or connecting with one another. Donilon referred to Putin as "one of the more challenging figures for us as an administration," diplomatic speak for "a hard bastard."

In an address during his Moscow visit, Obama made a strong pitch for democratic values and respect for the rule of law. But he also sent an important message—with both positive and negative consequences— when he said, "I come before you with some humility. I think in the past there's been a tendency for the United States to lecture rather than to listen. And we obviously have much work to do with our own democracy in the United States. But nevertheless, I think we share some common values and interest in building a strong, democratic culture in Russia as well as the United States." Obama recognized that Russians were tired of two decades of watching an American post–Cold War victory dance while their own society struggled as a shadow of its former self on the world stage. On the other hand, Obama's apology for America's stance was an opening that hard-liners around Putin would seek to exploit.

On September 17, Obama officially cancelled the Bush missile defense plan for Eastern Europe, opting instead for a ship-based approach that could be located closer to Iran. The move placated the Russians and made greater sense with regard to the Iranian threat. But it also seemed that the president had accepted the argument made in American press releases that the missile defense system was not in fact intended to blunt potential Russian aggression—which it clearly was. The distinction was not lost on the Poles and Czechs, who required serious reassurance that they had not been forsaken by Washington. They, at least, recognized that Russia still posed a threat in their part of the world.

Hillary Clinton, who had been relegated to the sidelines of US-Russian interaction during the first formative period of the "reset" with Russia, made her first trip to Moscow in October 2009. She underscored the themes established by Obama and Biden, saying, "it feels very good to be resetting relations." The trip made further progress on the new arms deal but was in some respects upstaged by press reports that the White House would dial back criticism of Russia over democracy. This revealed differences on this issue between players within the foreign policy team and some within the White House. Mike McFaul, the highly respected former Stanford professor who was the NSC senior director on Russia issues, advocated a robust effort to promote political reform in Russia, and he had the support of top officials at the State Department on this point. A group in the White House inner circle, on the other hand, argued that the criticisms should be soft-pedaled in order to give the administration a chance to make progress on some of its top priorities, from arms control to Iran. Obama sided with this latter group. Said one top State Department official, "this was a prime example of regional experts losing out to a group that was largely political in its background and instincts." It should be noted that such divisions existed in the White House as well. Donilon, for example, has said that he doesn't recall ever being on the other side of an argument with McFaul.

Bill Burns, perhaps the foremost Russia policy expert within the State Department during the Obama years, nonetheless said, "Hillary Clinton, like the president, was conscious of the value of a relationship that had hit rock bottom over Georgia by the end of '08. It was really heading in the wrong direction at that time. And while she remained understandably skeptical about how far we could get, she saw there was virtue in testing relations because if you wanted to get the Russians to do what we needed them to do on Iran—which wasn't necessarily their natural instinct—then we had to invest in the relationship." That investment, then, was "a conscious strategy the administration tried to work out methodically" in the lead-up to the UN Security Council resolution "that stated Iran had failed to comply with prior UN efforts regarding its nuclear program. That Council resolution may have looked inevitable by the time it was voted but it sure didn't look that way early in 2009."

In the near term, the approach of the pragmatists in the White House seemed to be bearing fruit. On the edges of the otherwise frustrating Copenhagen climate conference, Obama and Medvedev agreed to cut nuclear stockpiles from the previous limit of 2,200 to 1,500 a side. They didn't formally conclude the new agreement by the time its predecessor expired, but they did resolve the core issues and in so doing achieved a major step forward on an issue that had haunted the world for decades. But it wasn't much, and it didn't anticipate newer, smaller scale but more deliverable threats.

The new deal seemed only a few short pen strokes away when the Russians sought further formal limitations on missile defenses. They had sensed that they could make further ground on this issue. Obama personally intervened to say he could go no further and that Medvedev and his team should back off or the deal would come undone. The impasse was short-lived, and by April the New START accord was formally signed in Prague.

The Prague visit also gave Obama an opportunity to outline his broader vision for a nuclear-arms-free world in one of the two most important and powerful addresses of his first term in office—along with his 2009 Cairo remarks on repairing and deepening US relations with the Muslim world. It was truly an "audacity of hope" moment and it raised expectations that further progress in the vein of the START deal was to come. But the words in the speech were as good as it got until the Japanese, an American ally, agreed to hand over their militarized plutonium in 2014.

This moment and the months that followed really produced the high-water mark of the "reset" initiative, and indeed of the US-Russia relationship during the entire span of the Bush and Obama years. The United States pushed efforts to help Russia join the World Trade Organization (WTO). Russia removed trade barriers. The two sides announced new initiatives in the area of energy cooperation. By midyear, Obama and Medvedev were grabbing a burger together at Ray's Hell Burgers, a favored fast food joint near DC, and Obama was proclaiming, "excellent discussions, discussions that would have been unlikely just seventeen months ago." Although that was true, it was equally true that such discussions would again be unlikely a couple of years ahead.

Things started to get rocky in 2010 when, contravening promises on the missile defense front, the United States agreed to deploy antimissile defenses in southern Romania. Medvedev declared that Russia would have to respond by accelerating development of its nuclear strike capabilities. This was especially frustrating to Obama national security senior staffers who actively sought to explain to the Russians that the missile defense decision—the result of a review conducted by a team including the

Pentagon's Jim Miller, Michèle Flournoy, and General Cartwright—was not aimed at Russia but at threats emanating from countries like Iran. They argued that the announced installation did not even have "the capability to impact strategic assets." (The Russians surely knew this, which raises the point that their objections were not based so much on the facts as on appearances. They could use the American announcement to shape the image of the United States as the belligerent power and reinforce their message at home and internationally. Sometimes the facts are an ineffective way to rebut an argument when the argument never had any basis in fact in the first place.)

Matters worsened in July when the State Department quietly banned dozens of top officials from Russia and froze their assets because of their involvement in the detention and death of an anti-corruption activist Russian lawyer. (It should be noted in retrospect that more Russians were banned from entry to the United States in this instance than would later face similar bans after the invasion of the Crimean Peninsula.) Relations took a further turn for the worse when the administration submitted a report to Congress that revealed that Russia was "conducting a range of activities to collect economic information and technology from U.S. targets." As with China, cyberspying and cybertheft were becoming greater irritants to the relationship and ever more important American security concerns.

Russia then threatened to withdraw from the New START agreement and to place new high-tech missile systems near the Polish border if the United States and NATO did not back away from the re-emergent plans to develop missile defenses in the region. The US NATO ambassador, Ivo Daalder, an early member of the Obama foreign-policy team during the campaign, said that NATO would proceed with plans "whether Russia likes it or not."

Hillary Clinton's efforts again to push democratic reforms produced a sharp personal response from Putin who said, "the first thing that the Secretary of State did, was say that [the 2011 parliamentary elections] were not honest and not fair, but she had not even yet received the material from the observers. She set the tone for some actors in our country and gave them a signal . . . and with the support of the US State Department they began active work." Effectively reversing the earlier policy to go easy on the Russians, Clinton asserted that the United States would continue to push for reform and democracy because "it's part of who we are." (Later, American political critics on the right would label Clinton as the author of go-soft policies toward Russia, when that was far from the case. In fact, she and Gates, often joined by Panetta, repeatedly provided the strong backbone of the first-term administration's tough stances on Russia and in the Middle East. Indeed, precisely because of her toughness with him, Clinton became a particular target of Putin's invective, sometimes of a sexist variety.)

By late 2011, however, a new issue would emerge that became perhaps the most contentious point of contact in the relationship for Obama's first term. The United States and its allies sought to impose sanctions on the Assad regime in Syria for its increasingly brutal suppression of opposition groups. Lavrov emerged as the principal international diplomatic champion of the dictator in Damascus. He said at the UN, "it is not in the interest of anyone to send messages to the opposition in Syria or elsewhere that if you reject all reasonable offers we will come and help you." Russia's client in Damascus was important because it gave Russia a continuing role in the Middle East and a buyer for its arms but also because Russians saw the Alawite regime of Assad as a barrier against the expansion of fundamentalist groups from the region into easily inflamed Russian regions like Chechnya. One senior Russian diplomat said to me, "Americans fail to understand that Syria is an important regional national security issue to us. The fundamentalists talk of establishing a caliphate in Chechnya. The defeat of the government in Damascus would open the door to that."

Mike McFaul was known to share Clinton's views on promoting reform in Russia. Assigning him to Moscow in 2012 as the US ambassador provoked a Russia media attack on him, saying he was being sent to stir up trouble in the run up to Russian presidential elections later that year. McFaul responded, as he would often throughout his tenure, via tweets in both Russian and in English noting that he was actually there to destroy Cold War stereotypes.

Donilon arrived in Moscow in his capacity as national security advisor on May 4 with a similarly positive message of seeking further cooperation. But newly reelected president Putin was not in a conciliatory mood. During the course of their three-and-a-half-hour meeting, he was sometimes confrontational, asserting he didn't trust America's motives internationally and bluntly asking, "when are you going to start bombing Syria?" Ironically—or perhaps characteristically—he stated his displeasure with America's meddling in the affairs of sovereign nations. The Russians followed this up by undercutting efforts in the UN to call for a political transition to a democratic government in Syria. They allied with the Chinese to veto the move.

As Assad's brutality continued, the United States amped up its criticism of the regime. Clinton rejected Russian assertions that they were mitigating the crisis in that country and said that their continued support of Assad would "contribute to a civil war." Russia's entry into the WTO provided some cause for celebration, but Syria continued to grow as a source of tension. By July, it had gotten to the point of sharp name calling at the UN. UN ambassador Susan Rice called "paranoid and disingenuous" Russia's claims that certain proposed UN resolutions would lead to military interventions by foreign powers in Syria. Rice was known at the UN, as she had been elsewhere, for her sharp tongue. One Latin diplomat asked me, "why does she feel it is necessary to use the language of a sailor to make her points? Doesn't she understand it makes her seem weak?" (Setting aside the sexism in the comment—one seldom hears men condemned for their salty language—the issue he was really addressing was one of brusqueness and confrontation. That said, many of Rice's admirers including, reportedly, her boss, admire her especially because of her directness and fearlessness.) During this period her relations with the Russians grew particularly testy.

Deterioration in the relationship continued. In late 2012, Russia demanded the end of USAID pro-democracy and other programs in Russia and then said it would not renew the Nunn-Lugar program that had successfully assisted in safeguarding and dismantling nuclear weapons systems. Then the US Senate passed legislation building on the earlier State Department sanctions linked to the death of anti-corruption lawyer Sergei Magnitsky in police custody. Obama signed the bill into law and Russia retaliated with a law banning American adoption of Russian children. The tit-for-tat was petty and nasty and it did not promise an easy future.

Bill Burns reflected on the whole idea of the "reset." He thought the term should have been shelved early on, "not because it wasn't worth investing in the relationship, but because it was always meant to be a temporary phenomenon, to put the relationship back on a better footing. And I think that we needed to quite consciously widen the arc, especially on the economic side, which is the most underdeveloped part of the relationship." Stronger economic relations with the Russians might have had a limited effect: "it's not as if it would have changed the Russian calculus on Syria. It probably still would have been pretty rough water with them." But there wouldn't have been much to lose. "We didn't have much leverage left in the relationship by the time of the Syria crisis or over the ensuing eighteen months."

A New Term and Deepening Complexity in a Troubled Relationship

John Kerry had his first meeting as secretary of state with a man who was to become one of the international leaders with whom he worked most closely, Sergei Lavrov. Both sides dutifully reported the discussions were constructive, and by March 15, 2013, in the latest twist in the schizophrenic US approach to its missile defense plans, the Obama administration effectively cancelled the final phase of the European-based defense system. According to a senior NSC staffer, this was "due largely to the fact that it had become an impediment to every area of important cooperation we had going or might need, including both Iran and Syria."

Donilon continued his own diplomacy in Moscow in April. Once again, he sought areas of potential agreement on reducing nuclear weapons stockpiles, strengthening economic ties, and building collaboration with the Russians on North Korea, Iran, and Syria. He also tried to defuse the tensions caused by the US sanctions on Russia following Magnitsky's death.

By the time he left office in June of 2013, Donilon's views had shifted. He agreed with the idea a questioner raised with him that perhaps Russia was one of those powers that actually benefitted from disrupting the status quo. He said, during one of his last days in the spacious West Wing office of the national security advisor, "I think the president would agree with you very strongly that the United States, Europe, China, really form the core of the engine of economic growth in the world. They have a deep interest in integrative work, a deep interest in order and in a world of rules. And ultimately I think it's probably in Russia's interest to have such a view but they don't always act in that way.

"I think that their policy in Syria," he continued, "has been short-sighted and it's been driven by a kind of historical analysis of the recent history of Western activity through the UN and via other means to topple countries . . . they see a trendline from Kosovo through Libya. And so I think they see it as in their interest . . . for political reasons to some extent, to try to articulate an independent path for Russia and to see it as a resister to the West and to the United States and as a counterbalance. In fact, of course, Russia's future is in integration with the United States and with China and Europe."

Donilon concluded, however, by reaffirming the core view he and Biden and others brought to the issue when they entered office. Although they captured to some degree the frustrations that arose over the years, they also remained firm that the differences between the United States and Russia were not inevitable. It is Donilon's firm belief that "in terms of geostrategic issues, there's no sense of inevitable conflict between the United States and Russia."

Lavrov and Putin made Russia a vital counterpart for the United States, though clearly not a like-minded partner, on key issues like Syria and Iran. This could have been the basis for expanding the collaboration Obama and his team had originally envisioned with Biden's promise of a reset. It could have been, had it not been for Russia's decision a few months later, within days of the end of the winter Olympics Putin hosted in Sochi, to invade Ukraine, claim the Crimean peninsula, begin to destabilize eastern Ukraine, and set Russia's relations with the West back to levels grimmer than any seen since the Cold War.

Blindsided by the Russian move despite its uncanny similarity to the offensive in Georgia six years earlier, US officials in retrospect blamed the ramping up of the crisis on their European counterparts. Preceding the invasion had been an EU offer of associate membership to Ukraine. Unfortunately, the Europeans sold the move as an "us versus them" approach, unnecessarily pitting East against West. Pro-EU Ukrainians protested the Ukrainian president's rejection of a Ukraine-EU association agreement, forcing him into exile. This inflamed pro-Russian Ukrainians as well as Putin in Moscow. The United States and the West embraced the pro-EU upheaval, calling it the will of the people. Russia decried it as unconstitutional and portrayed it as a threat to pro-Russian and Russian-speaking citizens in Ukraine, which provided them a pretext for invasion.

Putin calculated that the West would not respond with force, and, again, he was right. Much like Bush, Obama quickly announced he would not take military action but instead would levy sweeping sanctions on Russia. Unfortunately, the Obama team had not worked out, prior to the announcement of sanctions, a plan that all its allies could stand behind. Germany and other European countries were far too dependent on Russian gas and commerce to withstand a large-scale economic confrontation. The sanctions had to be walked back.

"We also kept getting blindsided by the White House," said one State Department official who was involved in trying to work on putting together a unified plan with the Europeans. "Susan Rice and her team at the NSC would be announcing initiatives that we were finding out about on Twitter or from people in the press corps. I don't doubt Secretary Kerry was having good communications, but at the working level the system was not performing at a very high level."

Although the rhetoric was heated and many analysts were predicting the beginning of a new Cold War, in fact the United States and its allies responded to Russia's aggression with a series of tepid sanctions. In the first wave of those sanctions, Washington began by banning travel by a handful of Russian and Ukrainian officials and sanctioning Russia's seventeenth largest bank. It was not an intimidating countermove. Meanwhile, Russia took hold of Crimea without opposition. In the immediate aftermath of recognizing the Russian fait accompli, the United States, in the words of one top official, turned its attention to "cauterizing the wound"—making sure Russia did not go beyond Crimea, so that the worsening of tensions would not derail the legacy issues in Syria and especially in Iran.

Russia did not, however, stop there. It sent GRU intelligence units and troops who had been stripped of their uniform insignia into eastern Ukraine to support pro-Russian activists in their push for more autonomy for those regions. A second wave of sanctions followed from the United States and its allies, banning travel to the United States for a handful of additional members of Putin's inner circle. Another smattering of financial and trade-related sanctions were also launched. But at this writing the sanctions were having little apparent impact on Putin. His support among his people at home remained strong even as the overall economy seemed to show some effects of the stand-off with the West.

One top Obama national security official, speaking to me in the midst of the crisis, said, "I think Putin has succeeded in pushing all of Ukraine into the West but I don't want to think of it in those terms. And I don't want to start driving this East–West narrative, which I think is very harmful." He went on to say, "the Europeans made some mistakes in the way they went after that association agreement and it became a zero-sum game and it didn't have to be." This frustration with America's European allies deepened during the crisis when it was their reluctance—especially that of the Germans—to impose strong sanctions due to fears of negative economic consequences that blunted the United States's ability to orchestrate as strong a counter-response as it had hoped for from the once robust but now rather rudderless Atlantic Alliance.

As of late March 2014, the primary concern was that Putin, undeterred by the weak ability or will of the West to create effective deterrents to his aggression, would take more of Ukraine. Secretary Kerry told me, "if he goes in, he has created a very different dynamic. Then we're back to the very difficult place, very ugly. If he goes into the east [Ukraine] even. If he goes further than he's gone now, it could signal a very ugly period, a very difficult period."

Kerry underscored that he spent much of the crisis working to persuade the Russians to stop their agitation in east Ukraine and Crimea while also trying to maintain a strong collaborative relationship with Russia on Syria and Iran. He spoke to Lavrov daily during the height of the crisis and Lavrov likewise expressed the desire that the Crimea crisis would not derail their other joint initiatives. The two had a working relationship stronger than any Lavrov had with Kerry's recent predecessors.

Illustrating the centrality of Russia to the Kerry and Obama agenda in the Middle East, the secretary of state said, "the key really is for Russia and Iran to decide enough is enough and put enough pressure on Assad to get a political solution. But we have to change the calculation of Russia and Iran and Assad, and that's proven slightly elusive—not because we've not been trying to do that but because the opposition was sidetracked fighting extremists." Assad, said Kerry, cleverly drew on the Russian concerns about an al-Qaeda and violent Salafi-jihadist tide in Syria to portray himself as the best alternative to the extremists. But "there's no way anyone can restore Assad's legitimacy. He could never run the country. Ever. The Russians seem to know it but they don't know yet who could take his place, how you do the transition, and where he would go."

International efforts to deescalate the crisis were dealt a severe setback when Malaysian Airlines Flight 17 was shot down by Russian separatists on July 17, 2014. All 298 passengers aboard the flight were killed when the separatists downed the plane using a surface-to-air missile provided by Moscow. President Obama declared the tragedy "an outrage of unspeakable proportions." The action both finally shocked Europeans into a willingness to impose more severe sanctions on the Russians than they had been willing to previously, and it consequently deepened tensions between Moscow and the west. What it did not do is help to accelerate the crisis toward a close, allowing it to fester on even as this edition of the book goes to press.

It is too early to know the full significance of the seizure of the Crimea and the stirring up of unrest in eastern Urkaine, but several things are clear. The "reset" never really happened. If Putin was encouraged to take action by American weakness, it was not just the weakness or confusion Obama showed in Syria or elsewhere in the Middle East. Nor did any personal irresolution of Obama create an opportunity for Putin to exploit in the Crimea and east Ukraine; precisely the same thing had happened to Bush when Putin invaded South Ossetia and Abkhazia. The weakness that Putin saw was an American lack of will to undertake military action in the immediate aftermath of the depletions of Iraq and Afghanistan. It was a sign of the times for Putin, not a symptom of particular leaders.

Obama's dithering in Syria did not help advance American interests with Russia. Nor did his too-quick revocation of US sanctions— prompted by Russia's incursion into Georgia—bear any fruit for his naïve hope of winning Russian favor. However, the main actor driving events here was not an American president but a Russian one, responding not to the will of the American people but to the needs and desires of his own people. Putin saw an opportunity to satisfy those yearnings with a boldness for which a war-weary America and its risk-averse allies in Europe had no ready answer.

CHAPTER 8

The Place Where
Good Intentions Go to Die

I will show you fear in a handful of dust.

—T. S. ELIOT

Paradoxically, the use of force—the bluntest of diplomatic instruments—
requires the most delicate hand. As America's experience in the Middle
East since 2001 shows, bitter consequences result from using too much
force, or too little, or applying it in the wrong way against the wrong
target. With great power at its disposal, a nation can easily be deluded
into thinking it necessarily has the ability to exert great influence. These
lessons are so clear after the past decade that all it takes is the shorthand
of country names to illustrate these points: Iraq is now a synonym for
the misapplication of American power; Syria, for America's hesitancy to
act when its leadership was needed. All you need to say to the average
American to evoke the most futile exercise of applied, deep American involvement in the world is to say the words *Middle East*, much as the term
Vietnam has come to mean being stuck in a foreign-policy and military
quagmire.

The Way It's Got to Be?

Typically, we measure the success or failure of our leaders by things they
actually have very little control over—the ebb and flow of economic cycles, the state of the world in their respective eras, and so on. They play

at the margins of such events, and we often attribute to their actions a causality that either does not exist or that we little understand. How they respond to big events, of course, does define them in a legitimate way. We just must be careful to keep their roles and options and possible influence in perspective. George Bush was not responsible for the fact that 9/11 happened on his watch. He is responsible for the actions taken in Iraq and Afghanistan. Whether those actions triggered some of the upheaval that followed in the Middle East, or whether that was inevitable for other reasons entirely, is a fine debate, but not a matter of firm fact. Barack Obama is not responsible for the world he inherited. But he does bear responsibility for the consequences of the way in which he extricated US troops from the region and the choices he made in response to the events that stirred the region during his time in office.

"I'm not so sure the role of the United States is to go around the world and say this is the way it's got to be. I just don't think it's the role of the United States to walk into a country and say, we do it this way, so should you." So said George W. Bush during a 2000 presidential campaign debate. In this we find yet another view he might find he had in common with Barack Obama. And like some of Obama's campaign rhetoric, it was another view honored more in its breach than its observance.

By the time Bush reached his second inaugural, he had a different vision. "He wanted," in the words of Condi Rice, "to do something major in the Middle East with the Palestinians and the Israelis."

Rice later wrote that "U.S. policy for sixty years had pursued something very different in the Middle East: stability at the expense of democracy. We have gotten neither." She went on to assess that they had come to be cognizant of the "toxic effect of the 'freedom' gap in the Middle East and the unforgivable association of the United States with the authoritarian status quo" created by the "stability over democracy" policy.

This was not a view held by all in top positions in the administration. Rumsfeld offered a stinging critique of Rice in his memoir, stating that "the State Department's interpretation of the President's conviction about the benefits of democracy led to complications with nations needed as friends and partners. . . . Sometimes the rhetoric came across as lecturing. . . . Sometimes berating countries feels good to the beraters and wins domestic political points, but scolding them can often come at the expense of losing critical cooperation and alienating foreigners who see the United States as a bully." He cites as a particular example a disagreement he had with Rice over whether and how to deal with the regime in Uzbekistan after an incident in which it had killed a number of protestors. "At an NSC meeting," he wrote, "Condi Rice responded to me by declaring, 'human rights trump security.' I wondered if she had really thought that through. She seemed to be saying that if a country didn't behave as we did or as we expected, it would be shunned, even if turning away from us took a toll on our nation's security."

An ironic twist in this division can best be seen in the light of later events. Bush, widely seen as the author of tough, interventionist policies that sidestepped international law and norms, is clearly more of an idealist than Rumsfeld, who is thought of as hawkish but actually played the role of the uber-pragmatist in the Bush years. It was Rumsfeld who said, go in quick and get out fast. He argued for different policies for different situations. In fact, and here's where the irony gets richer, it is Rumsfeld who is in many ways the precursor of the policies that Obama, known for speeches that soared to oratorical heights with idealism, would actually apply. Bush and Rice were idealists. Rumsfeld and Obama, for different reasons, no doubt, were largely realists—although Obama would, on occasion waver, torn between his inner idealist (and some in his inner circle) and his inner pragmatist.

An Epiphany About the Holy Land

During his first term, Bush had taken flack for articulating what many close to the situation in Israel and Palestine already knew. As Hadley put it, "he had taken a lot of tough positions diplomatically, notably like recognizing that [PLO chairman Yasser] Arafat was a failed leader who could not deliver." As the president reflected on his first-term experience he "concluded that the fundamental problem was lack of freedom in the Palestinian Territories. With no state, Palestinians lacked their rightful place in the world. With no voice in their future, Palestinians were ripe for recruiting by extremists. . . . And with no legitimately elected Palestinian leader committed to fighting terror, the Israelis had no reliable partner for peace. I believed the solution was a democratic Palestinian state, led by elected officials who would come to answer to their people, reject terror and pursue peace with Israel."

Although this is a view that one senior Israeli official would later describe to me as "naïve," it reflected the belief that it was no longer a question of if the Palestinians deserved their own state, but of how statehood would be achieved.

Part of the reason Bush was so closely associated with Israel was because prominent positions in his administration were filled by so-called
neocons, who were seen as holding views shaped by ideological and personal closeness to the leaders of Israel's right wing. The word *neocon*
gradually became a political codeword referring to hawkish support for
wars like the one in Iraq. Used to describe a pro-Israeli faction in the
government that was often seen as a cabal, it also took on much of the
tone of traditional anti-Semitic tropes. The fact that many of those in
the group, including Deputy Defense Secretary Paul Wolfowitz, Under
Secretary of Defense Douglas Feith, and Deputy National Security Advisor Elliott Abrams, are Jewish, fed this perception. The unpopularity
of the Iraq War and the desire to blame it on a group helped feed public
interest in the idea that US policies that led to the war and to America's
long-term alliance with Israel (the region's only functioning democracy
and a dependable US supporter for decades) were being driven by this
clique. John Mearsheimer and Stephen Walt, two scholars from leading American universities, argued, for example, that the neocons were
in league with a super-potent "Israel Lobby" that pulled policy strings,
leading the country in the direction not of its own interests but of the tiny
Jewish state in the Middle East. However, the group's core thesis regarding the power of the lobby is undercut by Bush's actions in office. The
president most closely associated with the neocons was so committed to
the establishment of a Palestinian state that he made working toward it a
top priority of his secretary of state. Indeed, several of his second-term
policies, including pulling out of Iraq and seeking to negotiate with Iran,
might be seen as contrary to the views of the Israeli right. (Although his
approach to these two issues tilted more toward the neocon views than
did that of his successor.)

As for a bias within the administration, although no one with whom
I spoke denied prioritizing support for Israel as a vital US ally, Elliott
Abrams, in his book, *Tested by Zion,* addressed the question of whether
there was a "tilt" to Israel in a more expansive way: "I am inclined to
plead guilty, but it depends of course on what is meant by 'tilt.' . . .
[President Bush] did not believe that endless pressure on Israel for concessions would yield as much as a partnership with its leaders, so he
built one. He "tilted" to Israel but to the Palestinians as well, confident
that he could do both and help both sides move toward peace and security in the process." Abrams goes on to say, "President Bush inherited

a collapsed peace process. . . . He left behind a far deeper relationship with Israel and the beginnings of state-building in Palestine." He offered another important insight into the approach that guided the Bush team both with respect to Israel and Palestine and to the region whose affairs he oversaw at the NSC:

> Too often bilateral relations with everyone take a back seat once the goal of comprehensive peace is put on the table. The only important thing about a nation's policies becomes whether it appears to play ball with the big peace effort. . . . Once you commit to a major effort at an international peace conference or attempt to broker a comprehensive Middle East peace, then those goals overwhelm all others. The net result of such an approach is to obscure reality, to ignore the immense complexities Arab countries face, and to concentrate instead on what their foreign ministers say about Israel and Palestine.

The contrast in his view and that of the Obama administration—particularly the State Department under the stewardship of John Kerry—is striking.

It was a view that Rice did not share, and Abrams in his book and in conversations subsequently, clearly bridles at the fact that she took the lead and sought to make progress on a bigger deal. He said, "Remember 2006 was the worst year of the administration, right? With off-year elections, the post-Katrina controversy, and you're pretty sure you're losing the war in Iraq. And it's just an unbelievable disaster. And the Israelis did not do very well in the war with Lebanon, which was that summer and was, to use Richard Haass's phrase, a war of choice. . . . And I think that Condi at that point decides that for her sake, for the president's sake, for the party's sake, for the country's sake—because everything was going wrong in 2006—'I'm going to make something go right.' We're going to get a deal here, the elusive Middle East comprehensive peace deal. I think she makes that decision in the summer of 2006 and that is what she spends her time doing for two and a half years, pretty much independently of the White House. . . . I am not suggesting . . . that [Bush] was not fully informed at all times. But she made this one of her critical activities."

Was such a deal possible? None was reached, of course. Abrams says, "you have to reach a conclusion in your own mind whether [Palestinian leader Mahmoud] Abbas is actually capable of signing a peace deal. I did not think so." Abrams believed Abbas didn't have the character to come through with a deal: "He's not a hero. He's not a charismatic leader. He's not going to do it. Arafat wouldn't do it—even [former Mideast negotiator and later key Mideast advisor to Obama] Dennis Ross notes that in the past the Palestinian people were not prepared for the sacrifices." In Abrams's view, "Condi had a too optimistic view of the possibilities here. And I think she made the big mistake of going for that handshake on the White House lawn, which leads you not to pay attention to other critical issues. . . . [Palestinian prime minister] Salam Fayyad said, "you're not helping me. I'm trying to build the basis of a state here and you're going for the handshake on the White House lawn."

Both Rice and Hadley are of the opinion that much more progress was made than is reflected in the final outcome. There never was a deal, but Hadley insists it was closer than people knew: "by the end, Sharon had withdrawn from Gaza and was willing to make peace with the Palestinians. I saw his maps. I saw it with my own eyes in his office. And if he had not had a stroke, he would have negotiated." After Sharon, his successor Ehud Olmert also engaged in an effort to move the peace process forward that led to discussions in Annapolis, Maryland, that included a comprehensive proposal by Olmert to Palestinian leader Mahmoud Abbas. But then Olmert got into legal and political trouble causing Abbas to withdraw from the negotiations.

And so, as often happens in the Middle East, the sands shifted—partners came and went, conditions deteriorated, and by the end, the intensive efforts of Rice on Bush's behalf came up short. She called it "one of the big disappointments of my time as Secretary."

It's Not Going to Be the Same

Shortly before Barack Obama's inauguration, my wife and I went to dinner in Washington with two other couples, Michael Oren, a visiting professor at Georgetown, and his wife Sally, and Jeffrey Goldberg, a journalist for the *Atlantic*, and his wife Pamela Reeves.

It was a lively and entertaining discussion, as any discussion would be with any of the members of this group, and it covered a wide swath of ground from the backstory of Goldberg's web-based Jewish Rock and

Roll Hall of Fame to the inevitable stories dating back to when Oren and I were graduate school roommates at Columbia University.

At one point the conversation turned to US policy toward Israel and the likelihood that it might shift under Obama. Both Goldberg and I, referring to Obama's past, the views of some of those on his campaign team, and general trends within the liberal wing of the Democratic Party, suggested that a shift was coming, saying that the first time an opportunity presented itself, Obama would seek to demonstrate that he did not cleave to the traditional pro-Israeli "tilt" in US foreign policy. Oren, a well-known historian of US-Israeli relations, was pretty dismissive, suggesting that such a shift made no sense, there was no reason for it. Little did he know that within months, he would become Israel's new ambassador to the United States for the government of Israeli prime minister Benjamin Netanyahu, and he would see up close what the new administration in Washington was like.

Evidence had been accumulating throughout the campaign that Obama—although still supportive of Israel—brought a different perspective. Obama had also been closely associated throughout his career with individuals who held strongly critical views of the traditional US stance toward Israel—like Columbia professor Rashid Khalidi. When it was asserted during the campaign that this relationship might color his views, Obama denied that he consulted Khalidi on policy matters and reiterated his commitment to Israel. But one senior Democratic insider pointed out that, "this was a family friend and if he was not advising Obama, the relationship is at least indicative of the kind of thinking to which Obama was exposed in his formative years." Further, many of his campaign advisors were of the stated view in private settings that the United States needed to show a much more "even-handed" policy toward the Palestinians if progress were to be achieved. Most important, perhaps, the attitudes of many Americans had shifted, following what was perceived as heavy-handed behavior on the part of Israeli governments from the days of the massacres at the Shatila and Sabra camps in 1982 through the intifada and the establishment of extensive settlements on Palestinian land much more recently. It is telling that in April 2008, just as Obama was gaining the upper hand in the Democratic primaries, a new organization, J-Street, was founded in Washington specifically to counterbalance the views of the American Israel Public Affairs Committee (AIPAC), seen as the stronghold of "Jewish lobby" views. The

Mearsheimer-Walt book, *The Israel Lobby and U.S. Foreign Policy*, also came out in 2008.

Early that year, candidate Obama was recorded on tape at a campaign meeting with Jewish-American leaders saying, "this is where I get to be honest, and I hope I'm not out of school here. I think there is a strain within the pro-Israel community that says unless you adopt an unwavering pro-Likud approach to Israel that you're anti-Israel, and that can't be the measure of our friendship with Israel." Later at the annual convention of AIPAC, Obama called for Israel to stop building new settlements and criticized Bush for being too close to Israel. He said Bush's policies caused the United States to be "more isolated in the region, reducing our strength, and jeopardizing Israel's safety."

At the same time, Obama actively sought to convey that he was still staunchly committed to the future of the US-Israel relationship, although he had a different view about how to best advance it. He met actively with Jewish leaders, successfully raised substantial amounts from Jewish donors, traveled to Israel during the campaign, and sought to clarify at every turn that he was talking about a shift in tactics, not long-term policy priorities.

Once in office, Obama began to make subtle shifts. On his first day as president he called both Palestinian president Mahmoud Abbas and Israel's prime minister Ehud Ohlmert (who only served through the first two months of Obama's term, leaving office on March 31, 2009). He affirmed that the region would be a top priority for him and urged the Israelis to stop building settlements, an idea pushed on him by several of his closest advisors, including chief of staff Rahm Emanuel, a former civilian volunteer with the Israeli Defense Forces (IDF). Obama also urged Israel to finish its withdrawal from Gaza and enjoined Hamas to end rocket attacks against Israel. In his midsummer address in Cairo he called publicly on Israel to stop expansion of its settlements. Behind closed doors at a meeting with Jewish leaders in July, he criticized the Bush years: "during those eight years there was no space between us and Israel. When there is no daylight, Israel just sits on the sidelines and that erodes our credibility with Arab states." He also granted his first foreign interview as president to al-Arabiya, the American-owned Arab cable television network and would not grant his first to an Israeli television interviewer until eighteen months into his presidency. During the al-Arabiya interview he said, "my job to the Muslim world is to communicate that the Americans are not your enemy." It was a point that echoed his inaugural remarks in which he said he sought "a new way forward" and "would extend a hand" to regional leaders if they would be willing to "unclench their fists."

Abrams believed that "the president genuinely felt that it was a mistake for the United States to have appeared so close to Israel, to have had a 'no daylight' policy. I think he genuinely thought that was not a smart policy. Later I think he abandoned that view because he came to realize, as Clinton did and as Bush understood, you get more out of the Israelis by hugging them than by distancing yourself from them. . . . The creation of so-called daylight scares the Israelis and makes them less flexible."

Martin Indyk, Ken Lieberthal, and Michael O'Hanlon, in their history of the Obama first term, agreed with Abrams:

> In Obama's mind, the way to handle Israel was not to embrace it warmly like Bill Clinton and George W. Bush had done, but rather to meet all of its security requirements. He would state repeatedly that the U.S. commitment to Israel's security was "steadfast" and he meant it. Under his instructions, the Pentagon, CIA and State Department took security cooperation with their Israeli counterparts to new highs. . . . No matter the level of tension on the political level, there was never any hint from the Obama Administration of withholding security assistance to Israel. . . . On the other hand, Obama was intent on pursuing the "other woman" in the U.S.-Israeli relationship.

On his second day in office, President Obama announced the appointment of former Senate majority leader George Mitchell of Maine as his special envoy for Middle East peace. The move underscored the importance of the Arab-Israeli mission to Obama, which in turn sent the message that this White House, unlike some of its predecessors, would not relegate Palestinian-Israeli peace to an afterthought. Mitchell was a no-nonsense, canny lawyer who had achieved considerable success helping broker the peace in Northern Ireland. Like Richard Holbrooke, Obama's special envoy for Afghanistan and Pakistan, Mitchell was one of a soon to be burgeoning cadre of so-called policy czars who marked the early years of the Obama tenure. The "czars" were top appointments with special missions intended to signal that the president was deeply invested in particular issues ranging from diplomacy to technology.* Almost inevitably such special positions, although helpful in small doses, created tensions with existing bureaucracies.

The overlap in responsibilities and interests between Mitchell and Dennis Ross, who was perhaps the most experienced Arab-Israeli peace negotiator in modern US history and who was a senior player within the NSC hierarchy, would create friction and dysfunction.

Mitchell's first trip to the region came in the week after the inauguration when the Gaza conflict had ended. There was no criticism of the Bush administration's policies or approaches in any of these early meetings. The main thrust was to "create a context in which the peace process could be restarted because we knew that many of the players' attitudes had hardened. And that there was a great deal of emotion and publicity in connection with the conflict."

Mitchell then met with the president's staff that had been assigned to cover the conflict: Dan Shapiro, the NSC staffer assigned to this beat who would later become the US ambassador to Israel; the director of the Near East bureau at State, Jeffrey Feltman, who later would serve as

---

*In a piece I published in *Foreign Policy*, I somewhat mischievously noted that by April the number had grown so high that I could write, "it has finally happened. With yesterday's naming of Border Czar Alan Bersin, the Obama administration has by any reasonable reckoning passed the Romanov Dynasty in the production of czars. The Romanovs ruled Russia from 1613 with the ascension of Michael I through the abdication of Czar Nicholas II in 1917. During that time they produced 18 czars. While it is harder to exactly count the number of Obama administration czars, with yesterday's appointment it seems fair to say it is now certainly in excess of 18." I then listed the 18, which included Bersin, energy czar Carol Browner, urban czar Adolfo Carrion Jr., infotech czar Vivek Kundra, faith-based czar Joshua DuBois, health reform czar Nancy-Ann Deparle, new TARP czar Herb Allions, stimulus accountability czar Earl Devaney, non-proliferation czar Gary Samore, terrorism czar John Brennan, regulatory czar Cass Sunstein (husband of Samantha Power), drug czar Gil Kerlikowske, Guantanamo closure czar Daniel Fried, plus special envoys Holbrooke and Mitchell, Sudan special envoy J. Scott Gration, climate special envoy Todd Stern, and special advisor for the Persian Gulf and Southwest Asia Dennis Ross.

assistant secretary of state for Near Eastern affairs from 2009 to 2012; and Feltman's deputy, career diplomat David Hale, who Mitchell later recruited as his deputy.

In consultation with Clinton, Mitchell crafted an approach to his mission that was deliberately different from that of other czars, notably Holbrooke: "first, when I served in Northern Ireland, where I had been coming and going for a total of about five years, during which I chaired three separate sets of discussions, I found it useful to have a relatively small staff and to rely upon the existing structures of the British and Irish governments for logistical and administrative support as necessary. [Mitchell was not at the time a representative of the US government.] People that I wanted to hire mostly were not administrative people, but rather were professionals who had knowledge in the subject who I thought could help me there. And I felt it would be better to try to do that again here than to build from the ground up a large operation. I was aware of what Dick was doing. We talked about it from time to time. I also received calls from the chairman of the Joint Chiefs offering me a number of military personnel and officials, almost all of which I declined."*

During his first months in office, Mitchell's focus was on building trust with both sides and trying to understand the perspective of other leaders in the region. However, the process was complicated by the Israeli elections, during which Benjamin Netanyahu was elected. Netanyahu had served previously as prime minister during the Clinton years, when he was seen by officials in the White House as difficult, sometimes arrogant, and sometimes an unreliable partner. He made his first official visit to Washington for a meeting with Obama on May 18, 2009. Standing beside Netanyahu, before reporters in the Oval Office, Obama delivered again the message that it would not be business as usual, stating directly that "settlements have to be stopped in order for us to move forward." Privately, Netanyahu was shocked by the lack of deftness in the move. A theme emerged that would mark relations between the two sides for much of the first term, which was that the White House had insufficiently prepared their Israeli partners for what they should expect. This was, in fact,

---

*Such offers are not always extended purely out of team spirit in the government. Commonly the military, intelligence community, and State Department will offer career officials to a new operation to help keep tabs on it.

a common complaint heard also from the administration's other allies in the region who felt that, while meetings and communications occurred often, real sharing and many preparatory consultations that they had come to expect in prior terms did not take place.

At around the same time as the Netanyahu meeting, Obama met with Assistant to the President Ben Rhodes and Chief of Staff Denis McDonough. He expressed his desire to deliver a major address to the Arab world in which he would draw on his personal experience to emphasize the common interests linking the West and the world of Islam and to address some of the historical roots of the tensions that exist. Rhodes and McDonough again assumed an inner-circle role that set them apart from some of their direct supervisors, but the interaction showed the degree to which they had the trust and confidence of the president. Rhodes in particular, as both an advisor and a speechwriter, had a special gift for being able, in the words of a close White House colleague "to channel the president's thoughts and feelings. He was kind of his alter ego when it came to putting together speeches or talking points."

Of all the Obama administration's Middle East initiatives during its first year in office—a year, it must be remembered, that made extraordinarily heavy demands in terms of the domestic economic agenda—perhaps the most resonant was "A New Beginning," a six-thousand-word address that derived from the initial conversations with Rhodes and McDonough. Obama delivered the speech on June 4, 2009, at Cairo University in Egypt.

"A New Beginning" departed from past addresses by American presidents in many ways, though one of its core messages was consonant with a remark made long ago by candidate Bush in the year 2000: "America does not presume to know what is best for everyone." Its rhetoric about the rule of law and justice could also have been drawn directly from the Bush Freedom Agenda. Nonetheless, there was no mistaking the impact of an American president named Barack Hussein Obama, standing in the heart of the Arab World six years after the invasion of Iraq, opening his remarks with a quotation from the Quran—"be conscious of God and always speak the truth"—and hailing the accomplishments of Muslim civilization. Obama described his own extensive personal experiences with Islam, saying, "I am a Christian, but my father came from a Kenyan family that includes generations of Muslims. As a boy I spent several years in Indonesia and heard the call of the *azaan* at the break of dawn and the fall of dusk. As a young man, I worked in Chicago communities where many found dignity and peace in their Muslim faith."

He said, "there must be a sustained effort to listen to each other, to learn from each other, to respect one another and to seek common ground." He drew on remarks from John F. Kennedy to say that "the interests we share as human beings are far more powerful than the forces that drive us apart."

When he turned to the issue of Israel and Palestine, Obama reiterated America's "unbreakable" ties to Israel but then added that the United States would not "turn our backs on the legitimate Palestinian aspiration for dignity, opportunity, and a state of their own. . . . Just as Israel's right to exist cannot be denied, neither can Palestine's." He also argued again for the end to Israel's settlements, called on Hamas to stop its violence, and urged regional governments to stop using the conflict as a distraction from addressing other important priorities.

Obama also connected to the crowd—which was responsive and enthusiastic—by drawing further parallels between his own experiences and those of his audience. "For centuries," he said, "black people in America suffered the lash of the whip as slaves and the humiliation of segregation. But it was not violence that won full and equal rights. It was a peaceful and determined insistence upon the ideals at the center of America's founding." (This rosy view of American history ignores the fact that it took one of the bloodiest wars in human history to bring an end to slavery.)

The speech also had an element of apology to it. Although justifying the conflict in Afghanistan as one of "necessity," he described the war in Iraq differently, saying it was "a war of choice that provoked strong differences in my country and around the world." He added, "although I believe that the Iraqi people are ultimately better off without the tyranny of Saddam Hussein, I also believe that events in Iraq have reminded America of the need to use diplomacy and build international consensus to resolve our problems whenever possible." To underscore his awareness of our history of abuses in the region, he became the first president to acknowledge the US role in overthrowing the Iranian government in the 1950s.

Mahmoud Abbas called the speech "clear and frank . . . an innovative political step." Israel's president echoed the sentiment. But others on both sides were more critical, with one Israeli noting to me, "think about it. This was a speech by an American president to a religion—to the world of Islam. When has that happened? What is that about?" More extreme factions in the region from Osama bin Laden to Ayatollah Ali Khamenei, the supreme leader of Iran, and the American right wing, condemned the speech—one group saying it didn't need more lectures, the other calling it apologist. Later analysis would suggest it may have helped spur reform movements from Iran to Egypt, with local citizens hoping for active, visible support from this American president who seemed to understand their problems so well.

The speech is cited as an Obama high-water mark and a shining example of his ability to use oratory to make an impact, but, like other such speeches, it was not followed with meaninful action. As one former top Obama foreign policy official said to me late in 2013, "sometimes I feel the president and those around him believe that once a strong speech has been made, they have done their work. The speech and the president are the deliverable. And as a result they do not focus as they should do on the follow-up—that is left to others, and it is where initiatives often fall flat."

By the end of 2009, Obama had to acknowledge that his team was struggling to restart peace talks because they had "overestimated our ability to persuade them [the Israelis and Palestinians] to do so when their politics ran contrary to that." The efforts continued, and, by March 2010, Mitchell was pushing for four months of what he called "proximity talks" to help create an interim step toward getting Netanyahu and Abbas get together for more formal discussions. Vice President Biden went to Israel as a sign of the administration's commitment to this new approach— underscoring yet again that Biden, the former Senate Foreign Relations Committee chairman, was undoubtedly the most active US vice president on foreign-policy issues, wielding far more than even the vaunted influence of Dick Cheney on national security issues. In effect, given his stature and political acumen, Biden was used as a kind of second secretary of state, especially on Middle East issues. This was especially the case during the first term of the Obama administration, when the actual secretary of state played more of a supporting role to the White House lead.

The planned impact of the Biden trip was undermined, however, when the Israeli Interior Ministry took the occasion to announce the approval of 1,600 new housing units—settlements—in East Jerusalem. Although Netanyahu insisted that he was blindsided by the initiative, Biden was furious and expressed his anger in a no-holds barred exchange with Netanyahu.

Obama was finding it hard to balance his views with realities on the ground, especially during a first term in which the US-Israeli relationship deteriorated to a level that new Israeli ambassador Oren called the worst in three and a half decades. Obama, especially sensitive to appearances, considered the unexpected settlement announcement a "slap in the face." It was also, in fact, a direct break with an Israeli promise to hold off for the moment on the settlement program. The Palestinians simply suspended involvement in the "proximity talks initiatives." Mitchell and Clinton postponed planned trips and P. J. Crowley, Clinton's spokesperson, said, "the United States considered the announcement to be a deeply negative signal about Israel's approach to the bilateral relationship."

In this moment of frustration, faith began to fade in the White House that Mitchell could make meaningful progress. Worse, separate emissaries representing the White House began to fan out into the region. Reports emerged that Mitchell staffers would say to Arab leaders in the region, "you'd better deal with us or else you're going to have to deal with Dennis Ross and his team at the White House." Further, the Israelis and the Palestinians were all concluding that the State Department just didn't have the juice to get things done, and that they would have to go directly to the NSC, and if possible to those closest to the president—after Jones and Emanuel left in October 2010, this meant Donilon, McDonough, Rhodes, Ross, and others in the West Wing.

In the aftermath of Donilon's appointment as national security advisor, the search began for another approach, specifically one that did not so heavily demand cessation of Israeli settlement construction. Secretary Clinton also began a push to get the president to lay out his own guidelines—"Obama parameters"—by which a path to peace might be achieved. The president agreed in principle to the idea "at the right time," and planning for another speech began. Donilon and Ross were uncomfortable with the idea, feeling that efforts to date had left the relationship on precarious footing and fearing that a misstep would result in further deterioration.

When word got out that the president was planning a big address on Mideast peace, Netanyahu's team jumped into action, arranging for him to give an address to a joint session of Congress during his planned visit for the next AIPAC conference. The White House then determined their speech should come first and set it for two days before the Israeli PM's arrival. Donilon and Ross argued for a speech that was more temperate. Clinton felt it was important to continue with some emphasis on settlements lest it appear that the White House had completely given up on the issue.

For all this debate, when Obama ultimately gave the address on May 19 at the State Department, the phrase that set off fireworks in Jerusalem was the president's assertion that "the borders of Israel and Palestine should be based on the 1967 lines with mutually agreed swaps." This was a departure from past language and got the United States directly into the business of dictating terms in a way that Netanyahu could not stomach. He was outraged and thought the position was now tilted heavily toward the Palestinians. In his address to Congress, Netanyahu made it plain that he totally disagreed with the president: "Israel will not return to the indefensible boundaries of 1967." Netanyahu received enthusiastic support from his Congressional audience. Days later at the AIPAC event, both sides restated their positions. The response to Obama was especially cool and it was clear the relationship had reached a new low, at which point the president's political advisors hit the hold button, urging him to drop further activity in this area until after the reelection campaign the following year.

Unsurprisingly, given that stance and the level of frustration and dysfunction, Mitchell stepped down a few days before Obama's address. "Both the government of Israel and the Palestinian authority had long experience in dealing with American officials. And they'd both reached the same conclusion: that they could best serve their interest by having direct contacts with the White House, up to and including the president, the vice president, the national security advisor—everybody they could. And so they both tried hard to do that. As in most of the dealings, the Israelis are better at it than the Palestinians."

The battle with Netanyahu also diminished American influence with the Palestinians, who were quietly adopting a new tactic. As global public opinion shifted in their favor—in much the same way it was shifting somewhat within key groups in the United States—Mahmoud Abbas boldly and shrewdly decided to seek validation for an independent Palestine via the United Nations. This gambit gradually gained ground despite fierce opposition from Israel and determined resistance from the United States.

At the end of the first term of the Obama administration, Indyk (later recruited to serve by John Kerry as his chief negotiator during his ambitious yet failed effort to resolve Israeli and Palestinian enmities) and his Brookings colleagues would conclude that by focusing on an unrealistic demand for a full settlement freeze, Obama ended up wasting a good deal of time and energy and failed to achieve it. Thus, "Obama damaged U.S. credibility as a mediator in the conflict." It is a sign of the degree to which the administration and incoming secretary of state John Kerry were actively seeking new perspectives on the situation that early in the second term, Indyk, a former US ambassador to Israel, was appointed as special Middle East envoy. This time the structure was much different, however. The Arab-Israeli initiative was being resumed under the leadership of Secretary of State John Kerry and he would not be referring matters back to the White House, nor was he shut out like Clinton. The initiative would be a centerpiece of his early tenure as chief diplomat and, in conversations with him, it was clear he was given broad latitude to pursue a peace initiative by an Obama seeking to reenergize the process.

When asked about his marching orders from Obama, Kerry recalled, "I think we talked more about process, because the president and I served on the Foreign Relations Committee together and later worked very closely together for four years when I was chairman of the committee and I think he knew my positions. It wasn't an interview, but more of a search for common ground."

Though Kerry dutifully pointed out that no secretary of state operates with his or her own vision—"I represent the president of the US. I work for him"—Obama had given him a lot of room to maneuver and one of the most generous political gifts at his disposal, the right to take advantage of ambitious, if risky, circumstances: "I think he's willing to let me go out and take some risks, no question about it, because they are things he believes in. . . . I admire him for the way in which he's been willing to give someone the ability to go out and make a mistake or fail at an effort—it is difficult. And he's unusual in that regard." It works only because, as Kerry noted, "it's also more closely coordinated than it appears to a lot of people. I don't go out and freelance." But Obama has trusted his secretary of state to be "creative in the field and try to make some things happen here and there."

Part of the reason Kerry has been given so much latitude is his unique history with the president. As those close to Kerry note, the Massachusetts Democrat picked Obama to be a keynote speaker at the nominating convention when, in 2004, he himself was the party's candidate for president. They worked together closely in the Senate. Kerry endorsed Obama for president in January 2008—early in the game, especially considering that at the time, Hillary Clinton was widely viewed as the Democratic front-runner. Kerry helped Obama with debate prep during Obama's re-election campaign. In other words, Kerry has with Obama a level of trust that few in his cabinet have enjoyed. He meets many of the criteria of those in Obama's inner circle that the president historically has been most at ease with. While this may have made things slightly more complex in the relationship between the NSC and the Kerry team, it also enabled Kerry to engage creatively in the peace process talks as only a truly empowered representative can.

As a result, the process, which flailed and suffered during the Obama first term, regained some life during the first two years of his second term. It was still widely considered a long-shot, but Kerry's indefatigable work ethic and his commitment to making it one of his very top priorities briefly raised hopes that negotiated progress toward peace was possible and even after those talks too, faltered, that at least the US was engaged and trying to play a constructive role resolving the chronic dispute. One reason for the progress that Kerry did make and the respect he earned among the parties was cited by Jordan's king Abdullah during a private meeting in New York, when he said, "the effort of John Kerry is the most extraordinary in the peace process I have seen during my adult life. He has been absolutely tenacious. I recall one incident during which he was meeting with Abbas in Amman and Abbas said he had to go back to the West Bank for consultations. This is an old technique to stall. But Kerry said he would wait. And he did. And two days later, he called up Abbas and said, 'I'm still here.' That makes a difference."

Even Israelis who are distrustful of the process—including Netanyahu—have credited Kerry with bringing discussions to a level unimaginable just two years earlier. Still, spats have continued to occur. The Israeli defense minister attacked Kerry's efforts as "naïve and messianic" in January 2014, adding that, "the American plan for security arrangements that was shown to us isn't worth the paper it was written on. It provides neither security nor peace." The United States was again furious, and Kerry directly complained to Netanyahu. Weeks later, in early March, Prime Minister Netanyahu responded with a strong defense of Kerry. Speaking again at an AIPAC event, he said, "we could better the lives of hundreds of millions. That's why I want to thank the indomitable John Kerry."

Kerry is modest about what he brings to the task, but he's certain of one thing: "personal relationships matter a lot in this business of diplomacy, there's no question about it. They're very, very important. I think part of the reason I've been able to move on [the peace process] and advance it is that for many years I've gone out to these conferences, I've built relationships with these guys. King Abdullah would have these meetings in Aqaba these last couple of years, which Tony Blair was at, Khalid Khalifa from Bahrain, Abdul Aziz from Saudi, and Sheikh Abdullah from bin Zayed from the Emirates, and his brother Mohammed." Kerry continued, "you kind of know these guys, you listen to them. I love listening to them, to their stories, of the growth of their countries, of their childhoods, of their culture, of the desert, of all this stuff, it's fascinating to me. And I think they, hopefully, sense sincerity in my interest in my relationship with them."

After months of talks with minimal leaks, the peace process reached an impasse in the spring of 2014. Frustrated by their progress at the negotiating table, both sides began to take counterproductive measures. Without a commitment from the Palestinians to continue talks, the Israelis refused to hand over their fourth and final batch of Palestinian prisoners. In response, the Palestinian leadership, led by Abbas, returned to their strategy of gaining further recognition as an independent state within the United Nations. Abbas put the nail in the coffin when he engineered a unity agreement with his Hamas rivals that angered the Israelis, who, like the Americans, view Hamas as a terrorist group. Frustrated, senior officials in the Netanyahu government lashed out not only at the Palestinians but, in some cases, at Kerry as well.

Matters were complicated further by the fact that the White House and in particular the president had grown so frustrated with the process that they decided to walk away from it. This was a source of tension with State Department officials who felt inclined to continue to work the issue but as frustrations with both the Israelis and the Palestinians grew Obama pulled the plug and the talks came to an end.

The breakdown in talks was itself only a harbinger of a deeper decline into a new war between Israel and the Hamas in Gaza, the third such conflict in a decade. Missile fire from Hamas led to Israeli retaliation including air strikes, artillery, and ground operations. The Israeli assault not only led to the death of over 2,000 Palestinians, many of whom were civilians, but it also fed the further deterioration in US-Israeli relations. As a consequence, by late summer 2014, one senior State Department official speculated that the peace process was "unlikely to be resumed during this administration."

Secret Outreach to Iran

Iran was the first country Obama had mentioned during the presidential campaign when asked where he felt his proposed policy of engaging with our enemies might bear fruit. He specifically mentioned Iran as a country from whom he sought an unclenched fist so that we might extend an open hand to it. He reached out to the supreme leader via a series of private letters soon after taking office to underscore his willingness to engage and to offer specific proposals, such as seeing if collaborating in an Afghanistan security summit might open a path to greater dialogue.

Meanwhile, Israelis saw the Iranian nuclear program as "an existential threat," citing the small size of their country, its proximity to Iran, and the repeated rhetoric from Iranian leaders that Israel ought to be destroyed. They let Dennis Ross know that if the United States failed to stop the Iranians they would not hesitate to take military action on their own. In fact, managing the Israelis became a major part of the Iran challenge. The president ordered the entire national security team into a kind of tag-team relationship to ensure the Israelis did not act rashly and trigger a catastrophe that would make it very difficult for the United States to avoid being drawn into another major conflict in the region. Meanwhile, regional allies in the Gulf also pressured the administration to remain tough with the Iranians to try to contain their seemingly growing regional influence. King Abdullah of Saudi Arabia repeatedly called on the United States to "cut off the head of the snake."

Iranian elections took place in June 2009, during which the proponents of a grassroots "Green Revolution" in that country were crushed by the ruling regime. The Obama administration was slow to side with the protestors, in part because Obama did not want to be seen as meddling in Iran's internal politics and thus shut the door to future engagement. The violence against protestors, however, was too much to bear. Finally, on June 23, the president expressed outrage, some ten days after the protests and backlash had begun. The supreme leader subsequently denounced Obama, and the prospects for a bilateral dialogue faded.

The Iran situation—like that with China and Russia—also revealed on several levels the degree to which new technologies were playing an increasingly central role in national security affairs. During the Green Revolution, Clinton's small team, exploring what they called "21st Century Statecraft," began using social media and similar tools to communicate with and show support for the Green Revolutionaries. Later, another initiative of the administration sought to make it easier for US companies to sell software and services into Iran to help the Iranian people use the Internet, a clear effort to offset the draconian approaches employed by Tehran to create a walled-off Iranian Internet that they could better control and censor.

The United States and the Israelis, with European and private sector partners, put together a major cyber-attack on Iranian nuclear facilities. The operation, known within the US government as "Olympic Games," involved placing Stuxnet, a computer worm, into Iranian nuclear testing facilities, thus reportedly disabling roughly 20 percent of Iran's centrifuges. The effort, which targeted the Siemens software managing the centrifuges, was considered a great success within US and Israeli national security circles, although it also motivated the Iranians to step up their own hostile cyber-activity to the point that Iran ultimately became a leader among developing nations (after China and Russia) in the development of malware and other cyber-tools aimed at US and other Western targets. It also revealed one of the complications associated with cyber-attacks. When you drop a bomb on someone, it blows up along with the target. But worms and viruses, even if they succeed in shutting down targeted facilities, leave behind code that can be repurposed by the intended target, which is what reportedly happened with Stuxnet.

Continuing what was one of the best-coordinated multilevel, multilateral diplomatic initiatives of the Obama first term, Obama had Gates and Petraeus reach out regularly to Gulf partners and work to ensure that they had the military hardware they needed to feel secure in the face of the perceived Iranian threat. And the administration scored its biggest victory when the Russians supported UN Security Council Resolution 1929, which cleared the way to a much more comprehensive and intensive program of sanctions on the Iranians. Donilon, Bader, Steinberg, and Ross also supported this effort, working to build and maintain Chinese support. The United States and the EU worked together on sanctions programs that went beyond those called for by the UN and, in some respects, beyond the sophistication achieved by financial-sanctions programs in the past. The US Treasury, for example, put pressure on overseas banks not to do business with the Iranians, and Obama signed into law provisions penalizing companies for doing business with the Iranian oil sector.

For some, the complexity and subtlety of sanctions was not a robust enough response to a nuclear weapon in the offing. One uneasy top general said, "we don't swear allegiance to sovereigns, we don't swear allegiance to kings, and we don't really swear allegiance to presidents. Our oath is the Constitution. And that doesn't give us license to just run amok, but in something as consequential as Iran policy, you know, if it's not getting the attention it needs, a gentle nudge is, you know, not an act of disloyalty."

Israeli officials would regularly report to their US counterparts their concerns that the progress of the Iranian nuclear program toward critical levels was "six months or a year away," after which it would be "too late" and military action would be the only remaining option. "What we just don't know is whether the president means it when he says that all options are on the table," said one Israeli official. Michael Oren was always among those who felt confident that the president meant it when he said he would act if need be. In an interview with Jeff Goldberg in March 2012, Obama reiterated that "all options are on the table" and that included a "military component." Adding an exclamation point to this was his assertion that "I don't bluff." Speaking later to an AIPAC event, Biden said, "let me make clear what the [strategic] commitment is: it is to prevent Iran from acquiring a nuclear weapon. Period. End of discussion. *Prevent*—not contain—prevent. The president had flatly stated that . . . he is not bluffing." This was especially relevant because some of the elements of any effective military strike would require capabilities that only the United States had. For example, certain of Iran's nuclear facilities are covered in concrete, or even dug into a mountain. Delivering the deep-penetrating munitions that could strike such hard targets could be accomplished only by heavy bombers like America's B-52s or B-2s.

Still, by late in the first term Obama was frustrated with his progress with the Iranians. Donilon and Rhodes spoke to me of being graded by the president on a variety of issues, in a regular report card–style assessment. The area in which the president gave his teams' efforts the lowest grade was Iran—not because he was unhappy with the direction or management of his teams' approach to the nuclear issue but because of his concerns about the threat itself and the slow pace of progress to resolve it. Said one NSC official, "what he meant by that was he wanted the team to up its game."

A Second-Term Surprise in Tehran

Given the absolute authority of its supreme leader, Iran is hardly a democracy. It nonetheless went through a substantial shift with the end of President Mahmoud Ahmadinejad's term in office and the election of Hassan Rouhani in June 2013. Rouhani was by no means a reformer but he was a more moderate voice than Ahmadinejad. Within a very short time of taking office, he was sending a message that his views toward the West and the United States might be less hostile and more open to change.

A former head of Iran's Supreme National Security Council for over a decade and a half, Rouhani gained international exposure as a skilled and cagey negotiator for Iran's nuclear program. One of Rouhani's campaign pledges was to work to repair the country's international standing. A more specific objective was to relax the international sanctions regime orchestrated by the Obama team led by Clinton and Donilon and their respective staffs. Speaking to a small group of journalists at the UN General Assembly meeting in New York in September 2013, Rouhani and his foreign minister, the extremely capable Mohammad Javad Zarif, communicated that change was possible, and that their ultimate focus was much as it had been for Bill Clinton—"the economy, stupid." They even went to the lengths of rolling out a member of the Iranian parliament who represented the country's small remaining Jewish community. This was meant to show that they were a tolerant regime, for the benefit of what they perceived as the large Jewish constituency in New York and among the media present. (When asked to speak, the allegedly Jewish parliamentarian offered up a canned speech about why no country—read: Israel—should be allowed to speak for the world's Jews.)

Also at the UN, there was buzz that Obama and Rouhani might have a photo op—a historic handshake perhaps. According to the Iranians, that did not happen because they wanted something more. Just what they wanted became clearer after Kerry and Zarif met during the scheduled P5+1 consultations that followed. Two days after the photo-op near-miss, Obama finally had the high-level engagement with the Iranians he had long spoken of during a phone call with Rouhani. It was the highest-level discussion between the two countries since Iran's 1979 revolution.

Immediately, Netanyahu and leaders in the Gulf denounced Rouhani and urged caution from the United States. Netanyahu called Rouhani "a wolf in sheep's clothing," and privately the Israelis felt that the United States was being gullible. These assertions were unable to stop the apparent momentum triggered by the latest overture, and within just six weeks a deal was reached in Geneva to begin multilateral talks with the Iranians aimed at addressing the Iranian nuclear threat.

Soon, however, it was clear that something more was afoot. As it turned out, the Obama team had actually also been working secret channels to engineer a change in the relationship. According to an Associated Press account, the United States and Iran secretly engaged in a series of high-level face-to-face talks for months before the Obama-Rouhani call and the subsequent deal. With the approval of the president, Bill Burns and Jake Sullivan had been conducting the meetings on behalf of the United States. They met Iranian officials "at least five times" in various locations, including Oman. The Oman meeting was orchestrated even before the June elections to determine if a productive back channel could be established. After the meeting, Kerry went to Oman to ensure the support of the Iranians should the conversation be continued. Following Rouhani's election, Obama sent him a congratulatory letter, and Rouhani's response was considered encouraging—especially since the sequence of events clearly seemed to suggest that Iran's supreme leader had blessed the undertaking. More secret talks involving Burns and Sullivan followed, and a later one also involved Under Secretary of State for Political Affairs Wendy Sherman.

Fits and starts marked the move to the final agreement, involving largely a French snit over feeling underconsulted during the last phase of the negotiations. By mid-November, however, it was clear to all involved that the talks were a high priority, not only for the United States and the Iranians, but also for Russia and the Europeans. The initial deal was for interim discussions to outline the steps needed to reach a final deal, and to provide the Iranians with limited sanctions relief. "We needed," said one senior State Department official, "to give Rouhani a victory, proof that there were good reasons to open up to the West and to move forward with the negotiations. That meant relief. The sanctions had apparently worked just as hoped."

As of this writing, the focus is on achieving a final deal to impose firm guidelines on Iran's nuclear programs so that it cannot be weaponized and, short of that, on keeping talks going and the prospects for a deal alive. Opposition in the US Congress to such a deal—orchestrated in part by the Israelis and a number of America's Gulf allies working side-by-side to urge rejection of any deal and push for more sanctions—is a major potential obstacle. Indeed, a top Israeli predicted to me early in 2014 that no such deal could ever receive the votes needed to clear the US Senate, and for that reason his government felt the Obama administration was considering other paths to keep the discussions on track—multiple successive interim agreements, for example, or perhaps progress via executive order.

One senior former Israeli national security official noted, however, that such an approach poses other risks. As he observed, many discuss how such a protracted process might help the Iranians buy time, but it would have the same effect for the Israelis. They are certainly working hard to ensure that, if a strike must take place, they will no longer depend on the support of any government, including the United States.

Doubts about America's continuing resolve to confront Iran's regional interference in other countries and support for terrorism is not limited to Israel. Gulf allies worried that a possible nuclear deal and the resultant sanctions relief might precipitate a modest thaw in US-Iran relations, and they grew more unsettled as it seemed other common interests might result in greater US-Iran collaboration. Notably, the spreading unrest in Iraq led by the al-Qaeda splinter group ISIS and the threat it posed to the Maliki regime, in which America and Iran had both invested much, led to talks between the two on the edge of nuclear negotiations in Geneva about how they might cooperate in combating that threat. Given that Iran has effectively been America's number one enemy in the region since the late 1970s and that Israel and the Gulf allies have historically been among America's most dependable partners in the region, the potential consequences of even such a modest shift in the US-Iran relationship could have far-reaching ramifications. Such a shift could be positive, especially if it lifts the prospects of those in Tehran who might foster or support reforms. It would also be beneficial if it ultimately led to the reduction of Iranian support for terror groups and bad actors like Assad. Alternatively, should Iran gain influence, financial benefit, and consequent strength from lifted sanctions without having changed its more noxious and threatening behavior, it could be seen as a negative development. This latter concern is common among virtually all moderate Arab and Israeli leaders with whom I spoke. But whatever the outcomes might be, at the moment the shift has produced uneasiness and uncertainty in important US relationships in a Mideast already shaken by unprecedented upheaval.

There's No Such Thing as a Black Swan

The most common complaint that I hear from senior officials who have served on the national security side of the US government is that, in general, despite enormous resources, it doesn't do foresight very well. From Scowcroft through Donilon, there have been efforts to beef up the planning capability within the National Security Council staff, efforts that typically end up, in the words of former National Security Advisor Sandy Berger, giving in to Washington's predisposition to let "the urgent overtake the important." America may be a democracy, but the news cycle is a ruthless dictator that imbues small daily events with political consequences to which White Houses and Congresses feel compelled to respond.

The intelligence community has forward-looking planning units, like the National Intelligence Council, that do long-term assessments, called trend reports. From the first of these reports in 1997 onward through the most recent, "Global Trends 2030: Alternative Worlds," these reports, according to the DNI website, involve intensive labor, drawing on "experts in nearly 20 countries," featuring "in-depth research, detailed modeling and a variety of analytical tools drawn from public, private and academic sources." But read them more closely and you find that they have fallen into the greatest of all heuristic traps: they let our current experience restrict too greatly our vision for the future. In other words, they let the recent past color too greatly our views on what might come next. The headlines in the "Game-Changers" section of the website alone tell a grim story: the Crisis-Prone Global Economy, the Governance Gap, the Potential for Increased Conflict, the Wider Scope of Regional Instability, the Impact of New Technologies, and the Role of the United States. It is a rehash of Davos meetings and McKinsey studies, the dross of popular futurism.

That said, it's better to have flawed reports than not conduct the exercises. They do force us to think in more systematic ways outside the news cycle. Elsewhere in the government, that happens with alarming infrequency. But there are pockets of extraordinary expertise out there. For those looking to discover real insights into the future, it's available. For a long time, the military did it better than anyone else, through war-gaming and scenario planning—which do not lead to the prediction of the future, but rather to being better prepared for what might happen. One of the best small pockets of insight in the US government, also courtesy of the military, is Andrew Marshall's Office of Net Assessment. Marshall, ninety-three, still runs the operation that has forced the Pentagon to consider the impact of new technologies on the development of new threats and strategies. The fact that he is still active at his age is a sign that Pentagon thinkers don't want to be boxed in by traditional standards and are committed to maintaining access to good brains regardless of age. But it also suggests, worryingly, that the skills he brings have not been produced in great supply.

My own experience with my former company, Intellibridge, and in business and government more generally, is that the great struggle lies not so much in finding the right answers as in asking the right questions. In the current era there are essentially limitless information resources within the government or at its disposal. The challenge becomes knowing where to look and how to view what you have found. Contemplating the same kind of issue before meetings he would chair, Hormats said, "I would repeat to myself a quote that I remembered from Einstein: 'if I had an hour to solve a problem I'd spend 55 minutes thinking about the problem and 5 minutes thinking about the solutions.'"

Jake Sullivan has the dual perspective of having led a State Department entity that has had from time to time a foresight role—Policy Planning—and of working as the vice president's top national security advisor. He says, "I've gone back and forth on this question. Foresight is a complicated concept, somewhat abstract, and I'm not sure that you could really have a whole separate [foresight] unit or process disconnected from the policy process for any given issue—disembodied and sitting out there without real connectivity to the day-to-day work of the decision-makers. So I have never been sold on the kind of concept that you have got to set up this whole anticipatory governance system. But we do have to get better at integrating this into our policy processes."

Nonetheless, many shocking events have actually been anticipated within the government, and yet leaders have been caught flat-footed because the insights did not make their way to them or they were not assessed properly. Dennis Ross told me of his work as a young Soviet analyst in the 1980s contemplating how America's Cold War adversary might fall. The rise of China was repeatedly predicted and either dismissed or tabled for future discussion. The 9/11 attack wasn't just predictable, it was actually the second attack on the World Trade Center by the same group in eight years. A couple of years before the building was destroyed, Tony Lake and I actually participated in a scenario exercise on the top floor of the World Trade Center to discuss the consequences of such attacks. The event was sponsored by Cantor Fitzgerald, the Wall Street firm that lost the most employees—over two-thirds of its workforce—in the 9/11 tragedy. Other big shocks were tipped in local media. A paper serving Pakistani Canadians gave early clues of the Pakistani nuclear program before it was publicly revealed. Papers in China provided warning signals of the SARS outbreak months before the World Health Organization announced the crisis. Machete sales in Rwanda spiked before the advent of the genocide there, much as they started to do in early 2014 in the Central African Republic. Even so, many in the intelligence community were caught unawares.

The same could be said of the Arab Spring. "I believe," observed Condi Rice, "that you've got the big arc of history to watch here and that could have told you that these authoritarian regimes were not staying in the long run. They weren't staying. You could see the kindling underneath the Mubarak regime when you've got an authoritarian who doesn't allow any political space, who can't feed its people, who has large numbers of unemployed men, and is corrupt to the core." She recalled going to see Mubarak and being told, "'say what you will. You don't understand my people.' . . . It turns out he didn't understand his people."

This outlook could be seen as Monday morning quarterbacking, yet considerable evidence supports the view that many within the government had anticipated something like the upheaval that became the Arab Spring and its aftershocks. (Dennis Ross prefers to refer to it as the "Arab Awakening" because that underscores its open-ended nature and the possibility that it could take a generation to play out.)

Former NSC Middle East staffer Michael Singh argued, "people say nobody really saw the Arab Spring coming. I think that's actually false. I participated in a roundtable discussion with administration officials in December of 2010 where the possibility was raised that, when it came to succession in Egypt, that the people on the street were going to have a role or a point of view, and the notion was just dismissed. There was a lot of conversation . . . with nobody really taking into account it could be chaos and revolution. We in the Bush administration had been privately warning for a long time—and this is one of the reasons we had the policy we did toward Egypt—that Mubarak looked like he was going to go the way of the Shah and if we didn't figure out a way to head that off there was the risk he would fall."

When asked when these views started to be actively discussed, he says, "certainly when I was director for Egypt in 2005 the view was that we really needed to push Mubarak . . . to allow space for secular opposition . . . because what he has done is set himself and the Muslim Brotherhood as the only two options, using the Muslim Brotherhood to kind of scare us into supporting him. All of us were cognizant that wasn't sustainable, in part because Mubarak himself—having not designated a vice president—was getting old, was losing his edge, and there was nobody else in Egypt who could make decisions."

The Obama NSC was sensitive to the possibilities of unrest across the region as well. Under Jim Jones, a five-page memo, "Political Reform in the Middle East and North Africa," circulated to the principals. It warned that reform in the region had stalled and that unrest was on the rise. Worried that allies like Mubarak would use force to maintain their power, there was concern that the situation could grow very delicate. The objective of the memo was to identify strategies for promoting further reform while reducing the risk of sudden upheaval. Ross, NSC staffer Samantha Power, and Special Assistant to the President Gayle Smith led the review that followed, reaching out to others in the interagency community and looking in particular at four countries identified as particularly high-risk: Egypt, Bahrain, Yemen, and Jordan. The review's conclusion that efforts needed to be stepped up to promote political reform was perhaps inevitable. The study's greatest value, however, was that when protests broke out in Tunisia in December 2010, the working group was better prepared for what was to follow. However, because of the complexities associated with each individual country, devising and implementing tailored policies on a case-by-case basis proved to be a real challenge, especially given the rapidity and the cascading nature with which one set of massive, destabilizing demonstrations led to others both within countries and across borders.

Samantha Power later commented on the thinking behind the study: "we were going to have to deal soon with the political succession in Egypt, and the social drivers of discontent were becoming uncontainable. It was clear that it was just getting harder and harder to keep a lid on these things. We were more and more implicated by our friendships with authoritarian regimes that were using ever more brutal tactics to repress their people." For all the merits of the study and the efforts of prior groups to warn of the storm clouds on the horizon, many still felt the government had no idea how to respond to what followed in the Arab World. Panetta himself testified before Congress in February 2011 that the intelligence community needed better means to identify "triggers" for uprisings like those that were taking place at the time in Tunisia and Egypt.

Sullivan argues that developments on the ground in the region did not dramatically alter his view of foresight mechanisms within the government: "it's my view that a more effective foresight mechanism would not have caught the speed, breadth, scope, or nature of the Arab Spring. It was the sort of event that even a better-designed process would not have been able to capture. It surprised the very people who were carrying it out on the ground in terms of how quickly and in what way it brought about changes and transformations." Sullivan pointed out the irony that the secretary of state had been in the region the day before Tunisian leader Zine el-Abidine Ben Ali actually fell and gave an entire speech laying out the Arab Human Development Report, talking about how the institutions of the region were sinking into the sand, sounding the alarm bells on how creaky the whole thing was. But speeches aren't policy. And whether the turmoil to come was predictable or not, it left the United States and much of the world off balance and unprepared to deal with the unprecedented upheaval to come.

CHAPTER 9

Leading from Behind

Fear those who are afraid of you.

—ARAB PROVERB

It is now common lore that the uprisings that swept the Arab world began in December 2010 when twenty-six-year-old Tunisian fruit vendor Mohamed Bouazizi set himself aflame after a police officer seized his goods. That act in turn sparked ten days of demonstrations in a country where roughly a third of adult males, and even more of the youth population, were unemployed. By the end of December, demonstrations reached the capital city of Tunis, and within two weeks the country's ruler for almost a quarter century, President Ben Ali, would flee the country.

But although the above is true, the crisis did not begin merely with Bouazizi. It had multiple roots. One was that the price of fruit and food generally had gone up, causing stress, especially among the poor and unemployed. Part of the reason for the high prices was that droughts in Russia and the United States affected commodities markets worldwide. Other reasons, of course, had to do with decades of political corruption, inequality, and economic struggle in Tunisia, the lack of democracy, and the growing sense that the leadership cared little about the fate of their people. Because these were slowly developing issues, or "soft" concerns, like economic or social issues, they had trouble showing up as flashing lights on the dashboard of a national security system that gives higher status to issues of urgency and on issues of armed conflict and force.

This is partly because limited resources force decision-makers to prioritize. It is also partially because most top national security decision-makers have little economic or "soft" social science background. More are trained in military or political affairs than in the factors that typically underlie upheavals and wars.

The speed with which protests spread was fueled in part by new information technologies—Internet forums, new television outlets, Twitter, and Facebook—which enabled protestors to communicate, convene, and respond quickly to government actions. It also provided protestors with cameras on their cell phones to bear witness and reach global audiences. Building on the way technology had fueled the unrest during Iran's Green Revolution in 2009, social networking was a sea change in the region's and the world's politics. (China would later ban the use of the word *jasmine* from social networks because it became associated with the idea of a possible "Jasmine Revolution" that might erupt in that country in the same way unrest exploded in the Middle East and North Africa.) During protests in Tunisia one protestor held up a sign that said "thank you, Al Jazeera" and toward the end, one tweet read "today Ben Ali, tomorrow, Hosni Mubarak."

Even as the revolution in Tunisia was literally spreading at the speed of light, it took the White House several weeks to publicly shape a response to what was happening. For an administration extolling its focus on net-driven "21st Century Statecraft," much of its diplomacy was still plodding along as it did when diplomats still wore top hats and striped pants. "We had to walk a fine line," said one senior official, "between respecting our existing relationships and recognizing that the tide of history was on the side of the protestors." Secretary Clinton offered remarks on January 11 expressing her worry about the instability. Two days later at a conference in Doha, Qatar, she challenged leaders in the region again to embrace reform. Forcefully, her words reflecting the headlines from Egypt and the Maghreb, she said, "in too many places, in too many ways, the region's foundations are sinking in the sand."

Behind the scenes, the usual collection of realists, Clinton, Gates, Biden, and Donilon, sought to counteract the impulses of younger staffers who were, in Clinton's words, "swept up in the drama and idealism of the moment."

The spread of the revolution to Egypt, beginning on January 25, 2011, brought the uprisings from the periphery of US national concerns to the center. Few allies were more important to the region or to US interests than Egypt. Indeed, only Israel seemed to rival its critical role over the preceding four decades. January 28 was the first of the "days of rage" that would shake the region's confidence in the sustainability of its old order. The situation was exacerbated by the techniques used by the Mubarak regime to put down the protests, from shutting down communications to the use of tear gas, rubber bullets, harassment, and worse. Those tactics, however, prompted the burning of police stations and attacks on the headquarters of the ruling party, and ultimately the mass occupation of Tahrir Square, the plaza that was to become the symbolic heart of the movement. Mubarak went on television and offered too few reforms too late, which inflamed protestors further. The next day, he ordered the army to help support the police in quashing the protests, but the troops announced they would not fire on Egyptian civilians. The political momentum in the country shifted for the first time in four decades.

In 2009, new president Obama had come to Egypt to make his pitch to the Muslim world, and he stirred the crowd with a vision of reform and the seeming promise of a new era. In contrast now, America's first response, as in Tunisia, was cautious and uninspiring to the protestors. On January 25, Hillary Clinton offered support for the right of people to protest against their government but also asserted that the government "is stable and is looking for ways to respond to the legitimate needs and interests of the Egyptian people." That evening, in Obama's State of the Union address, he offered words of encouragement for the people of Tunisia but was silent on Egypt. Two days later, Jim Lehrer of *PBS NewsHour* asked the vice president whether Mubarak should step aside. Biden said "no." And while he encouraged the Egyptian president to be more responsive to the needs of his people, he also said, "Mubarak's been very responsible . . . relative to geopolitical interests in the region: Middle East peace efforts, the action Egypt has taken relative to normalizing the relationship with Israel. . . . I would not refer to him as a dictator." By January 28, the White House called on both sides to "refrain from violence," saying the administration would review its "assistance posture." Press Secretary Robert Gibbs responded with "absolutely not" to the question of whether Mubarak should resign.

Despite the preparations that had taken place, despite the administration's awareness from the outset that Mubarak was on thin ice, despite the enormous resources available to the Obama NSC, despite the prior experiences during the Green Revolution and in Tunisia, the system choked: there was no clear plan for what the administration should do. Internally, the realists like Clinton pushed to put more pressure on Mubarak to transition power to his successor in a smooth, gradual fashion. Clinton was concerned that the United States should not be seen as abandoning an old ally without a clear vision of where it would lead, especially given the unease she knew that the shift in policy would generate in traditional regional partners like Israel, Jordan, and in the Gulf. The president, however, characteristically hesitated. Paradoxically, because Egypt was such an important ally, there was a fear of making a wrong move, of sending the wrong signal. The result was silence mixed with vagueness that was alienating to all sides in Egypt. Additionally, the White House had to consider the countervailing fact that despite what Biden had said, Mubarak was widely acknowledged not only to be a dictator, but to be long past the time when he should have arranged a transition from power. Obama called Mubarak and urged him to embrace change but did not directly suggest he step aside. Mubarak was intransigent. Later that evening Obama would publicly call upon Mubarak's government to recognize the rights of the Egyptian people.

"In all of these regimes" that were ousted, David Petraeus suggested, "there was a pattern. Each of these autocratic leaders generally had ten pretty good years at the outset, then ten okay years, and then ten years during which there was an accumulation of discontent over corruption, nepotism, hijacking of the rule of law, oppression of the political opposition, you name it. What's ironic about Mubarak was a repetitive theme that he would always use with me. . . . I remember he literally put his hand on my knee, looked me in the eye, and he said, 'General, don't ever forget about the street, listen to the Arab street.' And I've always wanted to go back and say, hey, Mr. President, you know, what about that street?"

On Saturday, January 29, at a meeting in the White House situation room, the Obama team decided that they would announce their support for a transition in Egypt without explicitly calling for Mubarak to quit. They feared a power vacuum and debated which way it might go. One senior White House official was asked whether there was much discussion about the impending role of the Muslim Brotherhood and whether anyone had considered whether they were really the only available and not very appealing alternative to Mubarak, given the radical Islamist views of many of their leaders. The official replied, "people did consider that. But of course, even that is subject to substantial debate, right? Some said at the beginning that there's only one organized political force, it's the

Brotherhood, they're going to take over, that's a huge problem. Others said that problem can be managed and, over time, alleviated. And so you actually do have people looking down the road at what a first election will look like." The official continued, "I think that our response to the Arab Spring has been complicated less by a lack of looking out into the future and being able to analyze the trends in the right way and more by the fact that there are just fundamental contradictions and tensions built into the collection of interests we have in the region and how it impacts on our values."

A discussion of the possible successors to Mubarak found each potential candidate seriously flawed. The national security team decided to send an envoy to meet with Mubarak. Their choice was distinguished retired diplomat Frank Wisner, who had once been ambassador to Egypt and knew Mubarak well. The hope was to have someone close to Mubarak have a heart-to-heart with him, someone Mubarak viewed as senior but out of the public and media eye because almost any photo op would look bad.

Another NSC meeting took place on February 1, at which officials waited for a readout from Wisner's meeting with Mubarak. As next steps were debated, an aide let Donilon know that Mubarak was appearing on the television. Mubarak said he would step down at the end of his term, but he didn't take any concrete steps that would placate the protestors. According to press reports, in the wake of the broadcast there was silence, followed by the president's apt assessment, "that's not going to cut it." Robert Gates and Mike Mullen, the officials who probably dealt most regularly with America's allies in the Gulf, watched this upheaval with real apprehension about what it might mean for the region and, ultimately, for them. They led a group that suggested the president should not call for an immediate transition.

But Obama's mind was made up. "If *now* is not in my remarks, there's no point in my going out there and talking."

When Obama presented the message to Mubarak on the phone that it was time to move on, the Egyptian president bridled. He played for time. He made the standard case that the United States did not understand Egyptian culture. He said the protests would soon be over. But Obama pushed back. He argued the United States had a different view and then asked whether arrangements could be made that would make a caretaker government possible. According to "The Consequentialist,"

an excellent piece by Ryan Lizza in the *New Yorker*, Mubarak's response was "Muslim Brotherhood, Muslim Brotherhood, Muslim
Brotherhood." What could not be known at that moment was that raising the specter of radical Islam as the alternative to a strongman-led
regime would later be used to considerable effect not only by the next
Egyptian military-led government but also by Assad in Syria and other
monarchies throughout the region. It was too late for Mubarak. But the
chaos and missed opportunities that followed his departure from office
actually raised the likelihood that the Arab Awakening would produce
not democracy in the region but a new era of updated, sometimes even
more brutal authoritarianism.

So ended the last call between Obama and Mubarak. Shortly afterward, the US president called for an orderly transition, one that should
begin right away. The next challenge for the United States was to try to
remain influential in a fluid situation in which the old order was dissolv-
ing. The United States had spent decades training Egyptian military officers and the relationship between the American officer corps and that of
the Egyptians was excellent. Senior officers with good Egyptian contacts
were asked to call those contacts and maintain open lines of communication. Diplomats did likewise. The response and the message from the
government was unified, until four days later when Wisner, appearing at
the Munich Security Conference, made off-the-cuff comments in which
he said, "President Mubarak remains utterly critical in the days ahead
as we sort our way towards the future." Given that this was precisely the
opposite of the president's stated view on this issue, that was the end of
Wisner's role with the Obama administration and the latest example of
the pitfalls of the president's overreliance on czars and emissaries who,
because they did not fit into the established bureaucracies, often acted as
though they were in, but not necessarily of, the administration.

Meanwhile, back in the White House, the foreign-policy tradition-
alists like Clinton, Gates, Biden, and Donilon continued to push for a
move to transitional government that was drawn from Mubarak's inner circle and would not exacerbate upheaval with more doubt. On the
other side was the more pro-democratic, pro–human rights group that
included Rhodes, Power, and McFaul—a group that one very senior
Obama official referred to as the "be true to yourself" crowd. Often
abetted by political aides like Valerie Jarrett, these officials would appeal to Obama by directly or indirectly urging him to remain consistent

with the change agent, the community organizer, who first began the run for higher office. They saw this moment as a chance to advance change that might spread throughout the region. In this instance, they had the advantage of the support of Denis McDonough and, most important, of the president himself. As someone who had been uncomfortable working with the old order in the region, Obama felt comfortable telling his team that the way the United States had worked in the region in the past was "out of date." Citing Tunisia as an example, he made the case that he did not want America to be on the wrong side of history at this pivotal moment.

When on February 10 Mubarak again resisted stepping down immediately, Obama more quickly than before sided with the infuriated protestors. "We . . . urge," a White House statement said, "the Egyptian government to move swiftly to explain the changes that have been made and to spell out in clear and unambiguous language the step-by-step process that will lead to democracy and representative government." The next day, Egyptian vice president Omar Suleiman announced that Mubarak had resigned, passing power to a council of military leaders. Among the youth of the Arab world it was a watershed moment of hope and a moment at which Washington at least appeared to be on their side. Among the established leaders of other US-allied regimes from Israel to the Persian Gulf, it was a moment of considerable anxiety, during which they confronted extreme doubts about what being friends with America and an ally of Barack Obama really meant.

To calm the fears of the latter, Obama and Clinton reached out to leaders throughout the region. Mike Mullen and Bill Burns went to see King Abdullah of Jordan, who was concerned that such unrest might come next to Amman. They urged him to get ahead of the problem by embracing reforms, which he did to a degree no other leader in the region contemplated. But even as the United States was working the issue diplomatically, demonstrations were spreading. In Libya, Bahrain, Yemen, and Syria, as well as Jordan, crowds were chanting for change.

Donilon began a process to study the aftereffects on countries that had sought to transition out of authoritarian rule, looking in particular at revolts against US-backed leaders. At this time, the administration also made an effort to rank those who might go next. Yemen and Jordan were at the top. Next came Libya, Bahrain, and Oman. Finally, at the bottom, were Saudi Arabia and Syria, where the governments were thought to be firmly in control. Clearly, in retrospect, the assessment was flawed, but the process was indisputably necessary.

By the time of this study, Derek Chollet was at the NSC doing strategic planning work for Donilon. He recalled, "when I started the job, the Arab Spring was just springing and so that period was defined by the revolution in the Arab world. And so a process started because we knew the president wanted to give a speech about the Arab Spring. And so all through the Spring Ben [Rhodes] and I and others were working on what the president would say. . . . And the focus was on what would we, as a government, say about the Arab Spring and what would our priorities be and what was our theory of the case." Although it is tempting to observe that this is yet another instance in which a speech rather than action was seen as a "deliverable" by the administration at watershed moments like the Arab Awakening, speeches can be vehicles for developing policy or outlining doctrines. They serve as action-forcing events requiring thought to be given to key questions and often therefore provide a useful goad to the policy process.

David Lipton, Larry Summers's deputy, was the point person on vital issues associated with Egypt's economic recovery. "We had then a reasonable process of defining the economic objectives and the economic subjects we need to impact on the run-up to the president's speech in May.* There was a difference of views about what to spend money on because Mrs. Clinton wanted to do something that demonstrated to Egypt that America was with it, and she chose debt relief as an objective. We had a lot of back and forth about that and about how much money the Congress would agree we could use, how to best use it, whether it would be a one-time thing, whether it would be conditional or not. Frankly, I think they're still talking about it."

Hormats agreed with Lipton, recalling, "I went out to Egypt four or five times after the revolution. So did many other officials in State, Treasury USTR, and NSC. And there were endless meetings on what type of assistance program to suggest, how much money would be committed to it, what the conditions would be, etc. And we sent so many different signals to the Egyptians that I am sure they were totally confused. And I think that after so many meetings and changes of course

---

*Again we see the importance of speeches as deliverables.

most US officials involved were confused and frustrated as well. It was an historic moment in the Middle East and the process we employed to respond to it did not rise to the levels this moment in the history of the region required. At a time when clear decisions and clear leadership were required, we got lots of meetings instead. I don't think anyone connected with this was happy with the process. It was hardly our finest hour—or month or year."

Chollet added that the entire process was complicated by the fact that the world was in financial distress when the crisis broke. He observed, "the region picked a lousy time to have a revolution. You know, the Eastern Europeans had theirs—the wall fell at a time when Europe was strong, the United States was strong, and integration was not a burden to the United States and Europe. And these guys had the luck of bad timing and that's a problem. But that needs to be distinguished when assessing our response from whether the best effort was made and reasonable approaches were made, and I really think it's quite clear they were."

Donilon's study group concluded that the current upheavals represented a sea change comparable to the end of the colonial era; that given this historical dimension, all countries were susceptible; that bad governments led to unhappy people and unrest; and that the events really could not have outcomes dictated by outside powers like the United States or Iran. This last point was to some degree untrue, or at least the truth in it was lost on many in the region. In the case of each and every revolution that would follow, outside powers would play a critical role, from Yemen to Libya to Bahrain to Syria to what happened next in Egypt. Another flaw in the White House's first analysis was an impulse to suggest that the government of Turkey might offer a model to be emulated. Obama had established something of a rapport with Turkish leader Recep Tayyip Erdogan—unusual, given that Obama did not have such links to many other world leaders. But as the Arab Awakening progressed, Erdogan increasingly demonstrated himself to be paranoid and more authoritarian than democratic and often aligned with supporting extremist Islamic groups in places like Syria, who were sworn enemies of both the United States and its ideological objectives in the region.

Yemen was next. Again the administration's public response was the rote formulation condemning violence and seeking to promote peaceful dialogue and reform. Behind the scenes, the administration maintained its support again for President Ali Abdullah Saleh, given the help he was affording them in the war on terror, in which Yemen was a key battle-ground, thanks to the presence there of al-Qaeda in the Arabian Penin-sula (AQAP). Again protests did not subside and again the US-backed leader did not help matters with his behavior. In the case of Yemen, how-ever, concerned Gulf Cooperation Council (GCC) governments, worried both about the changes in the region, and about what they perceived as a disloyal, "weak and waffling" US response, stepped up with a plan that called for Saleh to leave power peacefully and elections to be held. By a year later, in February 2012, a new Yemeni government was continuing to work on the GCC plan. The transition was smoother here, and the model of neighboring governments playing a bigger role in resolving the issue would prove to be one of the untold important shifts associated with this period. With foreign powers not stepping up as they once may have, the Saudis, Emiratis, Bahrain, Kuwait, Oman, and Qatar started to dominate.

In Bahrain, when unrest came, the intervention of Saudi and Emirati troops helped put down the problem, which was related to Sunni-Shiite tensions. The means were forceful and the government was criticized by an independent commission of inquiry for its human rights abuses, but the swift intervention was a sign of how seriously neighboring govern-ments took the threat of unrest, and the extent to which they would act to avoid another Egypt or Tunisia. The US Fifth Fleet is based in Bah-rain and US military and political leaders maintain a traditionally close relationship with the Bahrainis. The response of the United States to the unrest and the crackdown was therefore measured and again followed the now-standard pattern of urging a friendly leader to "get out ahead of change," and deploring violence. Clinton and Gates also delivered a sim-ilar message and pushed—within limits—for reform. But beyond that, the United States played this crisis in an anodyne way, with exquisitely parsed language again revealing that we had divided interests: hoping for more democracy while also needing stable relationships with depend-able, if autocratic, allies. The response to Saudi and Emirati intervention reflected this as well with a formulaic and bland call for "restraint and respect for the rights of the people of Bahrain and to act in a way that supports dialogue instead of undermining it." It was seen by the Saudis in particular as a sign of American unreliability as partners. Gates, and later Donilon, went to the Kingdom to explain themselves and repair relations, but the damage lingers to this day. In the words of one Gulf leader, "with Bush you knew where he stood. With Obama you are never sure. With Bush he was on offense, engaged in the region. With Obama, he is on defense, pulling back, risk averse."*

Leading from Behind

The response of the United States to the crises in Tunisia, Egypt, Yemen, and Bahrain all followed a fairly predictable pattern of hesitation, followed by words of encouragement for reform and restraint from authorities, followed by a flurry of diplomatic engagement. Yet there were exceptions. The degree to which the president responded to the situation in Egypt and made the choice to join the protestors in calling for Mubarak's ouster was one. But the case of Libya stands out. There, circumstances came together to result in a limited US intervention that many at the time speculated might be a model for future US engagement worldwide, but that soon proved absolutely idiosyncratic, short-lived, and unique to the circumstances of the desolate North African country that for forty-two years had been the uncontested domain of Muammar Qaddafi.

Three factors made the situation in Libya different from the others. In the first, Qaddafi's reputation as a brutal tyrant made his vows to hunt down and kill his opposition particularly ominous and suggested that a real humanitarian catastrophe was in the cards. Second, America's

---

*It is worth noting that Donilon's trip to the region after the Bahrain crisis was a classically well-executed trip of a national security advisor. It was not secret, but it was low-key. It took place over a weekend. It was followed with an anodyne press release. It was about listening as much as delivering a message. It was a trip for a presidential advisor offering an alternative to the high profile interaction involved with formal diplomacy. It gave the Saudis the chance to speak with someone they knew had the president's ear. This is a valuable role for national security advisors to play, and it is one that was continued effectively by Susan Rice. In fact, one regional leader commented that they noticed that, when President Obama spoke of Rice, it was with a different tone than when he spoke of other cabinet members; there was a clear trust and closeness that gave her enormous credibility when she would undertake these private exchanges. "She was," he said, "clearly an insider, clearly had his confidence."

European and regional allies had strong vested interests in Libya and were willing to take the lead in pressing for action. Third, it was possible for the United States to take military action, but do so in a very low-risk way, in support of others, with essentially no boots on the ground, and to get in and out quickly. In other words, it offered the chance to address a humanitarian crisis with a light-footprint intervention—a jab, not a full-fledged fight—and to do it via a multilateral approach that took much of the burden of responsibility off American shoulders. This in turn led to the accusation that, in the words of *New Yorker* correspondent Ryan Lizza, "Obama may be moving toward something resembling a doctrine. One of his advisers described the president's actions in Libya as 'leading from behind.'" However apposite the phrase, it is certain that its unnamed White House author wishes he or she had kept it to him- or herself.

Unrest began in the city of Benghazi, in eastern Libya, on February 17. Soon thousands had taken to the streets, and Qaddafi was threatening to search for the opposition and root them out. "There will be no mercy," he promised. "Our troops will be coming to Benghazi." The military followed suit, with brutal assaults on the protestors and those thought to be organizing them. Rebels pleaded for help. From the international community they sought a no-fly zone and UN military assistance. Qaddafi called the protestors terrorists, asserting, "the people who don't love me don't deserve to live." By March, the death count was over 6,000.

According to a report by my former colleague Laura Rozen for Yahoo News, "Dennis Ross told a small group of experts that any impending assault by Gaddafi on Benghazi would be "Srebrenica on steroids"—a reference to the massacre in July 1995 of more than 8,000 Bosnian Muslims. His point was that another massacre loomed but was preventable, and that the United States faced a choice and would own a share of responsibility if no action were taken.

Demonstrating yet again that creativity was not a hallmark of this moment in American diplomacy, the administration churned out yet another statement that called for restraint and expressed support for the rights of the Libyan people. (Were they taking recent press releases and just changing the names of the countries?) Behind the scenes, some in the White House hoped that the erratic Qaddafi might behave like Mubarak or Ben Ali and step down. But beyond hoping and issuing the traditional measured statements, little was done publicly, even as it was clear that Qaddafi was choosing a different and more brutal path than his counterparts.

It was French president Nicolas Sarkozy who took the lead in calling for international sanctions against Libya. France, like Italy and other European nations, had significant interests in Libya; they depended on the country for oil. Further, social unrest in Libya would almost certainly lead to a massive immigration problem that would be a political nightmare for all EU nations with a Mediterranean coastline.

Quietly, the United States had been getting American citizens and their dependents out of the country. Once the Tripoli embassy was closed on February 25, the United States changed course and took aggressive action against the Libyan regime in the form of unilateral sanctions and the freezing of billions in Libyan assets. The same day they did this, the White House spokesperson, Jay Carney, asserted that Qaddafi's legitimacy "had been reduced to zero." The next day, the United States supported UN Security Council Resolution 1970, banning international travel by Qaddafi and other officials, imposing an arms embargo, and referring the actions of the regime to the International Criminal Court for review.

By early March, it was clear that the UN's actions were having no deterrent effect on the Libyan leader. His troops were on the move toward Benghazi. In the view of France and the United Kingdom, the only way to level the playing field and give the opposition a chance to succeed would be to establish a no-fly zone to negate Qaddafi's ability to pound his citizens from the air. Behind the scenes, the British and French made the case to the United States that they had been there when the Americans sought support in Afghanistan and elsewhere, and that it was time for a quid pro quo. Although Donilon ordered the Pentagon to study all military options carefully, Obama was extremely hesitant to use force. His rationale, supported by many of his closest White House aides, was that such action would make it look like the United States was starting to play a broader role in the Arab Spring. But of course, part of the reason he was reluctant to intervene was that he had been elected to get America out of wars in the region, not enter into new ones. This point reportedly was made to him by his top political advisors.

The hesitation on this issue was linked to yet another divide within the national security team. Again Biden and Donilon were skeptics. In this instance, so too were McDonough and Gates. Meanwhile, an unlikely alliance had formed between Hillary Clinton, who was typically one of the most dependable voices for strong US action, and two officials who were closely associated with efforts to avoid humanitarian catastrophes:

Samantha Power, author of the landmark book, *A Problem from Hell: America and Genocide*, and Susan Rice, who had been the NSC senior director for Africa during the Rwandan genocide and who was deeply committed to ensuring the United States would do what it could to avoid similar catastrophes in the future. Although relations between Clinton and Rice could often be chilly, in this case, they allied to argue that the sanctions would not be enough. Clinton, usually allied with Gates, ultimately concluded that if Qaddafi were successful, or if the international coalition appeared fractured by US inaction, the consequences would be damaging to the United States.

During a March 15 NSC meeting, the intelligence assessment was that if Qaddafi took Benghazi, a mass atrocity would result. The Pentagon presented two options: a no-fly zone or nothing at all. But Obama demanded a more rigorous analysis, asking whether a no-fly zone would actually work. When the principals failed to provide him with options he felt were adequate, he broke with tradition and polled even the more junior members present, who were lining the room in the backbench chairs. Secretary of Defense Gates and Chairman of the Joint Chiefs of Staff Michael Mullen told Obama they didn't see core US security interests at stake. They were supported by Biden and Chief of Staff Bill Daley. The other side argued the risks of not intervening and having a humanitarian disaster take place on their watch. This group included Clinton, participating from Cairo, Rice, Power, Ben Rhodes, Denis McDonough, and Tony Blinken.

After the Libya intervention was launched, a theme emerged in some of the reporting that the president had been supported by a coalition of the strong women in the national security team. One senior official who was part of the deliberations commented that, "it was way more complicated than that. They were very influential, don't get me wrong but it was the president who was the one who demanded the right plan. It was the president who took the bull by the horns and made the big decisions. And he had a lot of advice from different quarters, but I don't think it was right to suggest he was just this empty vessel who was then pushed around by these advisors. And I am sure they would be the first to say that's not the case. I know Sam wouldn't say that and I'm sure Susan wouldn't either."

Obama was frustrated. Action, it seemed, was called for, but a no-fly zone was not likely to stop Qaddafi's tanks and troops as they made a military assault against Benghazi and the opposition there. He ordered them to come back with new ideas, and in a meeting after dinner that night, they offered another possibility: a UN resolution that would authorize the use of force to protect Libyan civilians, which would in turn allow the United States and allies not just to enforce a no-fly zone but to actually destroy Qaddafi's army. As Obama would later tell *Vanity Fair*'s Michael Lewis, "what I didn't want is a month later a call from our allies saying, 'it's not working—you need to do more.'"

Rice pushed for intervention and said the reputation of the UN was also at stake. Gates continued to push back. He feared that America would end up owning a situation that could easily devolve to a stalemate and a third war in the Muslim world. The back and forth continued with Obama ultimately saying, as reported by Michael Hastings, "the question of who rules Libya is probably not a vital interest to the United States. The atrocities threatened don't compare to atrocities in other parts of the world. I hear that. But, there's a big *but* here. First of all, acting would be the right thing to do, because we have an opportunity to prevent a massacre and we've been asked to do it by the people of Libya, their Arab neighbors, and the United Nations."

He would later add—in a rare and vaguely weird instance of using regional psychological factors as a motivation for military intervention—that he felt failing to intervene would set in motion a "psychological pendulum, in terms of the Arab Spring, in terms of intervention." Strange cocktail party language aside, the rationale would later ring especially hollow given American inaction in Syria, and a much more horrific humanitarian catastrophe at the hands of an even more brutal regime. What, we are left to wonder, did he make of the psychological consequences of the deaths of more than 100,000 Syrians or the seeming impunity with which the Assad regime was able to use chemical weapons? In any event, as far as Libya was concerned, and with his decision made, he sent Rice back to the UN to seek the authorization for use of force.

Obama then began to work the phones with foreign leaders to ensure they would support the UN effort. That same day, Qaddafi was on the radio threatening, "it's over. We are coming tonight. We will find you in your closets." Clinton talked to Lavrov, after Obama had spoken to Medvedev, to ensure Russia would not veto the Security Council vote. Russia was resistant but ultimately agreed to abstain, which in turn meant China would do likewise. The path was clear.

Donilon cites this effort, and the ability to mobilize support among the Europeans—particularly given the challenges the alliance had faced not only in Afghanistan but also financially—as a significant accomplishment: "in 2008 if you had said that the United States will be able to get the Europeans to agree to a missile defense system, a project in Afghanistan through 2014, a new out-of-area project like Libya—I don't think people would have thought that was credible at that point."

Rice made a powerful call to action at the UN. It was so compelling that according to one report, when she finished, "you could hear a pin drop." Within hours, UN Security Council Resolution 1973 called for "all necessary measures" to be used to "protect civilians and civilian populated areas under the threat of attack." The overall vote was ten to zero, with abstentions from Russia, China, India, Brazil, and Germany. Although Indyk, Lieberthal, and O'Hanlon called the action a "milestone for humanitarian intervention," it was nothing of the kind. The United States and the Europeans had significant communication problems during the early phases of its implementation. An initial coalition of ten nations grew to seventeen. But it was a fractious coalition, and efforts to unify the command were met with protests from many of the governments, until ultimately NATO oversaw maintaining the no-fly zone.

Further, as one top US military commander observed, members of the coalition were not always pulling in the same direction, and the divisions reflected tensions that would carry forward beyond Libya. "The Qataris and the Emiratis were literally supporting different groups, the Qataris a slightly more Islamist group, the Emiratis a slightly more secular group. You later saw the same thing in Syria in which the Saudis have been supporting more secular groups, the Qataris more Islamist groups, and then there were wealthy individuals from the Gulf states who are truly supporting extremists."

Even after it had successfully neutralized Qaddafi's army, leading to the dictator's capture and execution by the opposition, the divisions continued. In the wake of the fighting, the successor regime has had a very difficult time restoring order to the country. Widespread reports indicate rebel activity from Qaddafi loyalists and, perhaps more threatening, from Islamist extremist groups reportedly funded by, among others, Qatar, as well as other militias in the region, all of whom see the ongoing turmoil in Libya as an invitation to advance their political views in a country that has the added benefit of substantial petroleum reserves. In fact, in the wake of the "triumph of humanitarian intervention," the country has been thrown into utter chaos, thus revealing that exit strategies, while very important, are not enough. You need an effective post-exit strategy and the commitment to follow through on it. The United States and its allies did not have that in Libya—which played directly into the better defined post-exit plans of extremists and other groups that actively thrive on chaos.

Throughout, administration critics on the right argued that the United States had been goaded into action by the Europeans, and that it had accepted a role as a supporting player in the intervention that was out of keeping with US traditions. Those, including many on the US left, who had long been seeking a more effective form of US multilateralism or an approach to our allies that was less heavy-handed, saw the collaborative approach to addressing this issue as a step forward. Notably, but not exclusively, partisan critics of the president continued to hammer the fresh new refrain that America was "leading from behind," and sought to apply it more broadly to what they suggested was a certain passivity or risk aversion among the Obama team in its responses to other crises in the region. In my view, it is possible that all of the critics and supporters of the approach were actually right. Working with our allies more effectively was certainly a step forward from the ham-fisted unilateralism of the Bush years. "Leading from behind" took on a pejorative connotation. But if the United States was truly leading, while letting others get out in front, take credit, assume greater responsibility, assume more risks—leading in a more collegial, first-among-equals way rather than that of an international bully-boy—that too represented progress. But seeking to do these things does not obviate the need for the United States to actually be more assertive or have a clearer vision or take more risks than the Obama administration has done throughout much of the upheaval in the Middle East.

Wendy Sherman made the case that a positive and deliberate strategy was being followed, saying that "one of the things this president has done and that Secretary Clinton did is understand that we could make things happen and push to get things to happen, even if the person who stood in front of the microphone was the Arab League or the African Union or the European Union. That didn't mean we were not leading and it didn't even mean we weren't leading in front. It just meant that sometimes we weren't in the press conference out front in a way that undermined the importance of our infusing regional organizations or other players with responsibility, burden sharing, and their own leadership."

A former senior military commander concurred, "I've asked myself a great deal about how much of what we did during the Arab Spring was actually the US pulling back. I don't think we could have held back the forces in Tunisia once they were unleashed and I don't think there's anything we could do in Egypt. I know our partners in the region are a bit resentful we didn't stand with Mubarak for a while before he fell, that we were too quick to side with the opposition or at least go neutral. But I think the clear assessment was he was going down and you know, it was probably the wise move at the time not to go down with him. So I don't know how much of this is in a sense actually leading from behind or withdrawing from trying to influence because I think our influence in Egypt was pretty limited for a while anyway. I know our influence in Tunisia was limited. And we had no influence in Libya to speak of."

Some of the limitations on our influence were simply endemic to the problems of the region and America's role as an outsider. Some were linked to the fact that regional political trends were afoot that were beyond the influence of our policy, given the levers we had that we were willing to use. And some had to do with the damage done to America's reputation as consequences of the Iraq War and the excesses and abuses associated with the war on terror.

Hadley offers a different perspective: "there are two views of how you work with allies. One view is you lead, you have a clear sense of where you want to go, you talk to your allies, you listen to them, you bring them on board. That's what I would call leading from the front. That's Bush. That's Tony Blair. An alternative way is if you are an enabler of letting your allies take the lead. That's what Libya was about. That said, President Obama is willing to make hard decisions on covert stuff, the Osama bin Laden raid, the drones. That kind of high-tech stuff he's willing to do. . . . The problem is what you're seeing in the Middle East today. I mean, we toppled Gaddafi but then we didn't get in there and try to stabilize the situation and as a consequence guns and fighters go from Libya to Syria to Mali. Not good."

In the end Libya cannot be considered a significant development in terms of humanitarian intervention. Since the small, not-terribly-well-executed, too-rapidly-exited, UN-backed foray took place, not only has Libya festered but other, much greater, humanitarian crises have taken place, producing little but inaction, lamentations, and staggering human losses. The greatest of these crises is Syria, the crowning catastrophe of the "Arab Awakening" thus far.

People Are Patient in Our Region

As the Arab world entered the turmoil of January 2011, Bashar al Assad did an interview with the *Wall Street Journal* in which he said, "we have more difficult circumstances than most of the Arab countries but in spite of that Syria is stable." He suggested that reform would have to wait another generation, arguing that would be possible because "people are patient in our region."

His people were patient only until March. The first demonstrations took place on March 18 in Syria's south. A number of teenagers sprayed graffiti on local walls, offering Arab Spring–inspired messages challenging the regime. They were arrested and brutalized. When demonstrators came out to protest the harsh treatment of the teens, sixty people were gunned down by the police. Assad sent a message early that he would not be victimized like the slower moving, older leaders in Tunisia, Libya, and Egypt.

Assad announced reforms, including greater press freedom, but they were not enough to stem the tide of resistance. Within weeks, thousands of demonstrators were taking to the streets. On April 22, over eighty were killed by Assad forces. The protests soon spread to larger cities like Homs and Hama. Assad responded with tanks and assertions that the army was there to confront an army of terrorists, criminals, and fundamentalists. In the first seven weeks of the uprising, there were tens of thousands of arrests and approximately 600 deaths.

Refugees started to stream over the border by the thousands into Turkey. Ramshackle refugee camps were filled with hardships but were safer than a growing number of Syrian cities. With increasing violence during the holy month of Ramadan at the end of July, the world began to take note. Assad told the UN that he was winding down military operations and invited in observers. But as soon as the UN inspectors were out of the country, another wave of military crackdowns against opposition forces occurred. By mid-October the death toll was 3,000 and the country seemed to be embroiled in a full-scale civil war. Somehow, without any active intervention from the rest of the world, Syria—the country that both US analysts and its own leader felt was least likely to be rocked by the Arab Awakening—had become the one most devastated by its consequences.

For six months precious little was done by the rest of the world, which was far too patient. Syria was on the list of countries that were least at risk, all evidence to the contrary notwithstanding. When asked in the last week of March why the United States wasn't taking decisive action, Secretary Clinton said "members of Congress of both parties who have gone to Syria in recent months said they believe he's a reformer." She added that the United States would not become involved in the conflict as it had done in Libya because, in the case of Libya, there had been international condemnation and a UN Security Council resolution. The United States sidelined itself.

By April, the president released statements saying that the Syrian regime's use of violence was "outrageous" and must "end now." He also signed Executive Order 13572, which imposed limited sanctions on Syrian officials and government entities. In his May speech on the Arab Spring, the president urged Assad to initiate a transition to democracy or "get out of the way."

But behind the scenes at the State Department, the Pentagon, and the White House, some leading policymakers were starting to worry that the civil war might have broader regional impacts in Lebanon, Jordan, Iraq, Turkey, or Israel. Hillary Clinton was at the forefront of those suggesting that the situation was reaching a critical point and that it was time for the United States to do more. She told reporters on July 11 that "President Assad is not indispensable and we have absolutely nothing invested in him remaining in power." Obama followed with comments suggesting Assad was losing legitimacy. By August the official stance progressed further. The White House issued a statement asserting that "the future of Syria must be determined by its people, but President Bashar al Assad is standing in their way. . . . For the sake of the Syrian people, the time has come for President Assad to step aside."

Slowly, international pressure was building. By November, the Arab League suspended Syria's membership—a striking act, given that Syria, in 1945, was one of the six founding countries of the organization. (The League had since grown to a membership of 22.) But as the United States considered its options, it kept running into the Russians. Russia supplied Assad with arms and saw him as a vital ally, giving the Russians a foothold in the Middle East and providing them with a buffer against extremists. This meant that almost any anti-Assad action in the UN Security Council would be vetoed by Russia. Without the blessing of the UN, the Obama administration had declared itself extremely reluctant to act. It had handed the initiative to Moscow.

President Obama told his staff that he was appalled by the catastrophe in Syria. Top advisors like Clinton urged that action be taken before the crisis spun further out of hand, that more support be provided to the opposition, and that we weigh our options for helping keep the crisis from spiraling out of control. But the president was strongly disinclined to intervene with force, as were his military commanders and his closest White House advisors. He also resisted efforts to actively provide support to the opposition based on the uncertainty surrounding the intentions of some of those opposing Assad. The unique conditions that made it possible to get in and out of Libya quickly, have others play a major role, and to do so with the UN's blessing were simply not available in Syria. Further, Libya had since descended into chaos, costing the life of a US ambassador and several members of the team entrusted with protecting him. As a result, the administration was even more reluctant to put itself at risk on the ground in a conflict that, if anything, was turning into something even worse than the nightmare that had once been envisioned as taking place in Benghazi, had Qaddifi carried out his threats of brutality.

At one press conference in March 2012, Obama said, "the notion that the way to solve every one of these problems is to deploy our military—that hasn't been true in the past and it won't be true now." In an interview with the *New Republic* early in 2013, he said, "how do I weigh tens of thousands who have been killed in Syria versus the tens of thousands who are currently being killed in Congo? These are not simple questions. . . . You hope that at the end of your presidency, you can look back and say, I made more right calls than not and that I saved lives where I could." It was just this kind of ruminative rationalization of inaction that had contributed to a sense that Obama—the master of the compelling call to action in his early speech—was quite something else when it came to taking action, especially in higher-risk situations worldwide, even when such action was the kind of strong humanitarian response he and many in his inner circle of advisors had called for in the past.

Obama would later seek to clarify this approach in an extraordinary reflection on his foreign-policy legacy during an April 2014 trip to Asia in which he similarly lowered expectations. "You hit singles, you hit doubles," he said during remarks in the Philippines. "Every once in a while we may be able to hit a home run. But we steadily advance the interests of the American people and our partnership with folks around the world."

He continued, "there are going to be times where there are disasters and difficulties and challenges all around the world, and not all of those are going to be immediately solvable by us."

On Air Force One after making these comments, the president went back to chat with the press corps on the plane. He was, according to one of those present, clearly angry, apparently upset that he was having to defend himself against accusations that he was not decisive but instead was unwilling to take action—an accusation that turned in large part on his hesitation on the issue of Syria while it became the planet's number one humanitarian disaster and a threat to the entire Middle East. So he went further than his earlier defense of incrementalism, foreign policy "small ball." He described the guiding principle of his foreign policy as "don't do stupid shit." In fact, he repeated it and then, for emphasis, after getting up to leave the gob-smacked reporters, turned to them and like an elementary school teacher asked, "so what's my foreign policy?" And the collected assortment of representatives of major media outlets repeated in unison, "don't do stupid shit."

It was in some ways the crystallization not only of Obama's views on foreign policy and risk but of the post-Iraq, post-Afghanistan mood that swept him into office. You could accuse him of inaction. You could accuse him of ignoring the plight of millions or the ideals he himself es- poused during speeches. But you were not going to find him making the same kind of errors as his predecessors. It was a view embraced by many of his supporters, who celebrated it in tweets and blogs and newspaper columns. But he and those supporters neglected a core fact: inaction can produce calamities as great as those caused by the wrong kind of action. Further, the creation of false choices—such as ruling out "boots on the ground" in Syria when no one was actually calling for that—that pitted one extreme view against another, ignored the fact that the right answer often lay somewhere in the middle, that the opposite of a great wrong choice was not safe inaction but rather well-calibrated, moderate, effec- tive, situation-appropriate action. As an increasing number of situations were revealing, a core problem of the Obama administration, especially in the second term when the realist voices with contrasting views largely departed, was that it had no effective middle game with which to respond to calamities like Crimea or Syria that lay between Iraq-like catastrophes and pinpricks or inaction.

Speculating on emotional factors that came into play in keeping the United States from taking action in Syria, one former top national security official from the Obama team said, "you can't discount the fact that the most visceral recent and personal experiences are those that influence you most in a crisis situation, which is where we were with respect to Syria. And those were Afghanistan and Iraq."

Privately, he and other top White House aides feared that Syria looked much more like the wars from which they were trying to extricate America. Further, Syria was an ally not just of Russia but also of Iran. As a consequence, Assad was receiving considerable support, and an intervention would have had very negative implications for the region and for other important diplomatic initiatives. Ben Rhodes once again channeled his boss's growing sense of the limitations of American power, saying "we have to have humility about our ability to determine what's going to happen in a place where people are dealing with very deep-seated grievances and sectarian divisions."

Contemplating the tough choices confronted by the NSC at this moment, former CIA director and defense secretary Leon Panetta said, "the real issue is not to kind of rub your hands together and go woe is me, but to make some decisions about how in fact do you engage these kind of situations and what's the best way to do that? Do you use the CIA? Do you do it clandestinely? Do you put more into that? Do you use other means? Do you build international coalitions that have a strategy to engage? Do you work with NATO? Do you work with the Gulf states to do this? I mean it requires an awful lot of work to be able to build an approach that can suddenly make a difference in a Syria or a Libya. I think the next three to five years is going to be a period of growing instability in the Middle East and the one thing we have not thought enough about even now is how do we engage in that part of the world to be able to get ahead of events rather than continuously being caught behind them?"

There was one area in which the president was seemingly prepared to act, however. In a throwaway comment that was apparently not pre-planned or a result of internal deliberations, he stated that were Assad to make use of Syria's chemical weapons stockpiles against his people, he would be crossing a "red line." When pressed about the red line, senior officials immediately tried to walk the comment back. They said it didn't refer merely to any use but instead to "a whole bunch" of chemical weapons being employed in a "systemic" way. Although the president said the use of such weapons would be "a game changer," he was unspecific about what that meant. The threat, however, remained hanging in the air.

In 2012 Petraeus and Clinton floated a proposal to supply weapons to the rebels. Obama overruled it. But by April of 2013, the CIA was covertly operating a program to train rebels in Jordan, and the United States had agreed to provide nonlethal aid to them. Even so, the promised aid came painfully slowly. Unprecedented numbers of extremists flocked to Syria because it offered the ideal microclimate for them: it was breaking into ungovernable fragments, places that offered a chance to establish a foothold and train fighters, pockets of anarchy. Reports of battles involving scores of different factions became common. Groups like the al-Nusrah Front and ISIS evolved from being small bands of terrorists into more effective armies through battlefield experience. They swelled with recruits. It was becoming apparent that, with every day of delay, that the costs of resolving this crisis rose along with the risks associated with it. The Jordanians, watching hundreds of thousands of refugees streaming across their border, and their Gulf allies pushed harder to seek more active support from the United States. Their leaders, like King Abdullah of Jordan and Sheikh Mohammed bin Zayed of the United Arab Emirates, came to Washington and shared intelligence that suggested US estimates of the number of foreign extremists on the ground were low at 7,000 and that the number might be three times that. They spoke of the potential threat such groups might pose to the region and, when these foreign fighters returned home to Europe, Africa, and even the United States, to those places as well. They also emphasized that they were not asking for US military intervention but clearer support, more aid to rebels, and more diplomatic pressure. They wanted the United States to, in the words of one, assume the role of "not being a player on the field but of being a coach, offering some leadership." But what they heard were views like that of a senior White House aide who said, "if we're not careful, we'll be cleaning this up for years."

The administration was, however, courting risk by seeking to avoid it. Should the crisis spill out to the rest of the region or become—as hard to imagine as that was—even more ghastly on a humanitarian level, they would be seen as weak or disengaged, fatally leaning away or "leading from behind."

Advocating a more active approach to leadership, Condoleezza Rice asserts, "the one thing the US has that other powers don't is a kind of universalist creed. Of course it is self-interested in the way great powers are who tend to have been competitive with one another. But what you are seeing in Syria by ceding the initiative to regional powers is fragmentation and conflict and no coherence. . . . You know, the Turks back some folks and keep the Kurds at bay. That's their agenda. The Sunni states back the Sunnis. The Qataris don't even care much which Sunnis they back, so they end up backing some really bad guys . . . as they did in Libya. And the Iranians, who would basically like to unite the Shia, go in and try to help the Alawites. I mean it's kind of World War I in microcosm. . . . The United States, of course, could have gone in at one point with an agenda that was nonsectarian but it's now kind of too late for that agenda."

One by one, military options, like a no-fly zone, were ruled out. Because the country was so fragmented, it would be difficult, administration spokespeople argued, to use air power to stop the killing. Military leaders argued the United States had the capability to make a difference but at the same time they also were growing more concerned about just who our allies on the ground might be or who to arm. There were too many groups with motives that were far from clear. At the same time, in the words of one senior State Department official, "we received constant pleas from Beirut and Amman for humanitarian assistance. And concerns grew that these massive inflows of distraught and needy human beings could destabilize these countries that were trying to be generous and helpful to their neighbors. Yet international help was inadequate, which compounded the crisis in ways that wouldn't have happened had more funds been provided sooner by us and by others who were working with us on the Syria issue."

The rise of the al-Nusra Front and ISIS, and the growing strength of similar extremist groups with tens of thousands of fighters, raised the prospect that the defeat of Assad—or even a stand-off with him—might lead to the establishment of an Islamic state in all or part of Syria. In an interview with the *New Yorker*, one senior US official captured the concern when he said, "you could have a situation where the more secular rebel groups could well be fighting the more Islamist-oriented groups. I call it the Sinkhole. I think there is an appreciation, even at the highest levels, of how this is getting steadily worse. This is the discomfort you see with the president, and it's not just the president. It's everybody." Assad used this threat cannily to begin to effectively mount a kind of "devil you know" defense within the international community.

A Long, Hot Summer

In late June 2013, as Tom Donilon was preparing to hand over the reins of the NSC to Susan Rice, the people of Egypt were again becoming restive. Rather than restoring democracy to the country, the government led by the Muslim Brotherhood's Mohamed Morsi adopted the harsh policies of Mubarak.

Throughout the year that the Muslim Brotherhood governed Egypt, alarm grew among Egyptians as well as among US allies from Israel to the Persian Gulf that the country was not only headed in an undemocratic direction, it was headed in a direction that would soon make Egypt a potential contributor to broader unrest throughout the Middle East. The Brotherhood, as critics in the Gulf would point out, based on first-hand experience, was not just a domestic political party. It had a wing that was focused on spreading its message and unrest internationally. It ran training camps on the Syrian border for extremist fighters. It had cells in Jordan, the Emirates, and elsewhere seeking to foment Islamic uprisings to upset the existing governments. Morsi's rise, therefore, was not just an affront to the spirit of Tahrir Square, it was also potentially destabilizing for one of the world's already unstable regions.

The United States government reacted very deliberately with regard to Morsi even as he began to behave in a more autocratic, less tolerant way. Fearing the perception of meddling in the affairs of a government brought to power by a democratic process it had called for, the administration was seen as unresponsive by its allies. In the words of a senior official from a neighboring government, "they didn't put pressure on Morsi when it could have made a difference. They watched and did nothing. But the people of Egypt couldn't watch and do nothing. They were on the verge of going from Mubarak to something rather worse." One Latin American diplomat based in Cairo said, "in the end, the only thing I think that unites all Egyptians now is their anger at the Americans. No one trusts them or knows who or what they support."

By late June 2013 the Egyptian people were back on the streets. By some estimates millions protested against Morsi in massive demonstrations that looked and felt just like those that had so recently brought down his predecessor. Within days the military called for Morsi to meet the protestors' calls for restored freedoms and gave him two days to respond. When he failed to reply, he was ousted by the military, led by Defense Minister Abdel Fattah el-Sisi, and a coalition of other voices from the political opposition and religious groups that had been threatened by Morsi. Morsi was then jailed.

Susan Rice took over the NSC the day after Morsi's ouster. It was a baptism by fire. She sought to minimize upheaval by changing very little in the way of the NSC structure. But her style was very different from that of the studious Donilon. He was more comfortable behind the scenes. He was less confrontational by nature. He embraced the role of honest broker, which has become DC shorthand for the kind of national security advisor who checks his or her ego at the door and is comfortable with refereeing and guiding with a light touch the policy process rather than directing it, serving as its principal spokesperson, or playing an activist or pronouncedly ideological role within it. He often spoke to the press but frequently did so on background. Rice was more accustomed to being out in front of the camera, both from her time at the UN and as a spokesperson for the Obama campaign. She was articulate, poised, and forceful. She had strong opinions, and she did not keep them to herself. She did not shy away from confrontations. She was also used to being a public spokesperson from the campaign and her role in the UN and was an active diplomat from her time at the State Department and then again at the UN. She also had a longstanding relationship with the president that gave her enormous insight into his thinking and enabled her to start with a degree of trust that has been a hallmark of the most successful national security advisors.

Said a longtime associate and admirer of Rice's who worked closely with her both during the campaign and in the administration, and who had known her well since the Clinton years, "I think she can bang heads together in an interagency process. . . . I think she actually has intellectual rigor and discipline that is incredibly thoughtful and deliberate in terms of digging deeper as a scholar and as someone who's not going to buy anything without intellectually putting it through the test."

The ouster of Morsi in Egypt presented Rice with a controversy in her very first hours in office. Morsi had been democratically elected, but he had not behaved in a remotely democratic way. His presidency was the result of a US-supported change, but Morsi was leading the country in a direction even some top Obama cabinet officials found unsettling. One described it as, "frankly, very dangerous." The United States sheltered behind a bland statement from Obama: "an honest, capable, and representative government is what ordinary Egyptians seek and what they deserve. The longstanding partnership between the United States and

Egypt is based on shared interests and values and we will continue to work with the Egyptian people to ensure that Egypt's transition to democracy succeeds." Meanwhile, the president was asking Rice to review aid options and implications of the events that had transpired. This review initially centered around an internal debate about whether or not to call the process by which Morsi had been ousted a *coup*. To do so would mean the United States would automatically have to suspend aid to the Egyptians, some of which was viewed as vital not only to Egyptian but regional security. On CNN, spokespeople close to the Egyptian military went to great pains to say that what had happened was "definitely not a coup" and "not a military coup whatsoever" but rather an expression of the interests of the people and the beginning of a more democratic chapter in Egyptian history. Now the former president, Morsi was reduced to using Twitter to address his erstwhile constituents: *coup* was much used by him.

So the United States hemmed and hawed. The State Department sent Bill Burns to the country on July 15, but he was careful not to take a strong stand. It was not until July 26 that the US government made the official determination that it would not actually make a determination as to what to call the events that had led to Morsi's departure from office. Something had happened, but in the interests of statecraft the United States would not give it a name. By not using the word *coup*, the United States could then continue providing the $1.5 billion a year in aid it offered to Egypt, which was not entirely an act of charity. Much of the money goes to military purchases that benefit big US defense contractors.

A July 29, 2013, article in the UK newspaper *The Guardian* captured the dilemma enveloping the administration:

in January 2011, Barack Obama had stayed true to a George W. Bush pledge of 2006 to invert U.S. foreign policy in the Middle East, which for 60 years had valued stability over democracy. When Hosni Mubarak was wavering, Obama was scorned by the old guard—especially Saudi Arabia for not standing by him. Riyadh took several years to cool down after Obama withdrew support from Mubarak, overtly threatening to reorientate its strategic focus away from Washington, in favor of new world powers such as India and China. . . . This time around, Obama is in the sights of both sides, accused by anti-Morsi followers of backing terrorists and by Morsi supporters of turning his back on democracy. Washington still refuses to call the

armed overthrow of a democratically elected government, the detention of its leaders, shutdown of its media outlets and killing of its
supporters a coup. There is no doubt that the events of the past three
weeks have large popular support, which is arguably just as relevant as
results at the ballot box a year ago. This gives the White House some
political room to not denounce what has taken place.

The White House's indecision produced enormous frustration in
the Gulf where the Saudis, Emiratis, and Kuwaitis felt support for the
new military regime in Egypt was essential if the threat of the Muslim
Brotherhood within and beyond Egypt's borders was to be stopped. They
stepped up and provided the first big tranches of aid to the new government with over $5 billion initially pledged by the Saudis and over $3
billion committed by the UAE. Those numbers would later rise substantially. The Gulf states knew that it was essential that Egypt's new government be able to pay its bills and deliver services to the people of Egypt to
consolidate its power. In many meetings with leaders from these countries
as well as from Jordan, Israel, Bahrain, and Egypt itself, the sense was
that the US government was perhaps too sympathetic to Morsi and the
Brotherhood or alternatively that it was simply indecisive.

Internally, both John Kerry and Chuck Hagel pushed to preserve assistance to Egypt and to soft-pedal criticism of the new government, instead seeking to work behind the scenes for reform. Hagel, in particular,
had extremely close ties to the military leadership, including especially
Field Marshal Abdel Fattah el-Sisi, who assumed the country's interim
leadership and would be elected its next president in mid-2014. Hagel
felt they should be given an opportunity. Kerry was more in touch with
America's other allies in the region and thus regularly heard their arguments that an Egypt led by the interim government was more likely to
contribute to overall peace and stability and that, in any event, it was
brought to power by an extraordinary expression of popular will.

Susan Rice led a group in the White House who felt that the aid
should be suspended until there were real signs of commitment to democratic reform from the interim government. These divisions festered
into the fall of 2013, when they came out into the open during a trip by
Secretary Kerry to Cairo. He chose to focus on the positive steps taken
by the new government and not to mention the legal fate of Morsi, then
awaiting trial. This was in direct contravention to guidance from Rice.
Indeed, in the view of one senior diplomat from the region, "it started

to seem as though the US had two policies toward Egypt. One in the White House. One at the State Department." This public rift was accompanied by other behind-the-scenes battles over issues like whether the new Egyptian government would be invited to a pan-African summit. The White House—that is, Rice—working with the organizers, pushed to exclude Egypt. When presented with this information by an outraged Middle Eastern supporter of the Sisi government, a top State Department advisor expressed shock. He simply had not been consulted. Just as would happen later during the Ukraine crisis, communications between the White House of Susan Rice and the mobile, freewheeling, and fairly independent road team of John Kerry was sometimes spotty and periodically tense. (At least that was the State Department view. White House staff close to Rice downplayed any such failures of coordination and collaboration.)

Throughout the time that the Egypt issue was testing the coherence of the White House foreign-policy apparatus and giving Rice precious little time to adjust to her new job, conditions in Syria worsened and the red line was crossed. On the twenty-first of August 2013, in the Ghoula suburbs of Damascus, rocket fire from the Syrian army released deadly sarin gas in what has subsequently come to be known as the worst chemical weapons attack since the Iran-Iraq war. Over a thousand people were dead, the vast majority civilians. Within hours YouTube videos would show the wounds of the victims and the telltale symptoms of a chemical attack. It was not the first reported instance of the use of chemical weapons since Barack Obama had announced his red line a year earlier; in fact, according to later reports it was perhaps the thirteenth. But the others had been smaller and their details had been contested. This was too big to ignore.

Immediately, there was outrage. The rebels blamed the government and the government and its supporters like the Russians blamed the rebels. The UN was unable to send in inspectors for several days due to the intensity of the fighting. But back in Washington as in capitals across Europe, discussion turned to whether military action against the Assad regime was finally called for. Well over 100,000 Syrians had already died, including an astounding number of civilians; roughly 40 percent of the country's population had been displaced. Syria had become one of the world's greatest humanitarian catastrophes on a scale far beyond Libya or Bosnia. But the United States had done next to nothing.

On August 22, top national security officials deliberated at the White House for hours over possible military responses. One possibility would employ Tomahawk cruise missiles launched from US Navy vessels in the Mediterranean waters off the coast of Syria. Another would involve manned aircraft. The goal in both cases was to take out military and artillery installations involved in the delivery of chemical weapons. Old rifts remained even though Clinton, Gates, and Donilon had moved on. There were those who felt military action was risky and likely to be politically unpopular. There were others who felt it was long overdue. Obama, it seemed, was now resolved. At an NSC meeting on August 24, he left no doubt in the minds of his NSC principals that he intended to act.

Two days later, Kerry stated that the use of chemical weapons in attacks on civilians in Syria was undeniable and that the Obama administration would hold the Syrian government accountable for a moral obscenity that has shocked the world's conscience. On August 30, the administration released intelligence to support the assertion that a chemical attack had taken place. The report said 1,429 people had been killed. A third of them were children.

Kerry became the point person for taking action, laying the groundwork in remarks to justify such a step. "With our own eyes," he said in powerfully delivered remarks at the State Department, "we have seen the thousands of victims with breathing difficulties, people twitching with spasms, coughing, rapid heartbeats, foaming at the mouth, unconsciousness, and death. . . . Some cite the risk of doing things. We need to ask, what is the risk of doing nothing?" He continued, saying: "it matters deeply to the credibility and the future interests of the United States of America and our allies. It matters because a lot of other countries whose policies challenge the international norms are watching. They are watching. They want to see whether the United States and our friends mean what we say. It is directly related to our credibility and whether countries still believe the United States when it says something. They are watching to see if Syria can get away with it because then, maybe, they too can put the world at great risk."

Kerry's was a compelling call to action. It would also be a stinging indictment of inaction should the United States do nothing. According to press reports, the White House's Ben Rhodes said Kerry "had been seized with the importance of making sure that President Bashar al-Assad of Syria was held accountable." Kerry's perspective gained traction within the national security team. Even as Obama let it be known that he was reluctant to act without the blessing of the UN Security Council—a blessing that remained impossible—he approved setting the wheels in motion.

Finally action from the United States seemed imminent. Warships were moved into position off the Syrian coast.

Pushing for at least some international support, Obama, as Bush had done before, turned to the dependable British, and Prime Minister David Cameron quickly sought to assemble the votes to support military intervention. However, the parliament was returning from a holiday and many who might have supported the measure were unavailable. Sufficient time had not been given; groundwork had not been laid. The result was a deeply embarrassing no vote rejecting Cameron's call to action. In Washington, it was a shock to the system, a public political embarrassment from our closest ally. Only the French appeared ready to act with us. Arab states that had condemned the attacks would go no further. Russia forcefully argued that any action without the blessing of the UN would violate international law.

The world refused to line up behind the United States. An NBC news poll said 80 percent of the American people felt the president should seek Congressional approval prior to taking military action, although the War Powers Act gave the president the authority to initiate an attack on his own without seeking such approval. Even as Kerry laid out the *casus belli* with great passion on the afternoon of August 31, the president was wavering. Although the NSC approved action and there was strong support for it, in this case including both Kerry and Rice, the chief executive hit the pause button. He took a walk around the South Lawn of the White House with his chief of staff, Denis McDonough. McDonough had grown to be one of the president's closest confidants, and, given his role as former deputy national security advisor, was especially well-equipped for such a conversation. He was also one of the voices arguing caution when it came to intervention in Syria. (As it happened, he was also the one who liked the walks around the lawn.) During the walk, Obama told McDonough that he wanted to wait, to seek the approval of Congress before taking action. He wanted to share responsibility with them. The president must have known that his decision would paralyze an already motionless response.

After his Rose Garden moment, Obama convened a team of his closest White House and national security advisors, including Rice and McDonough. They filed into the Oval Office assuming that they were on the eve of a major military operation. The president's view was presented and his team was stunned. A two-hour debate ensued. Rice and Hagel led the counterarguments, noting, for example, that seeking Congressional approval invited the kind of humiliation that had just been suffered by Cameron. Others were concerned at the message that the delay and apparent indecision would send. Obama's response was that "seeking legislative backing was the approach most consistent with his philosophy."

Kerry was called and according to close advisors was equally stunned. He had been asked hours earlier to frame a course of action, to put his personal credibility on the line, and now the rug was being pulled out. French president François Hollande was called and was also reportedly surprised and disappointed. For the second time in two years the Americans had proved to be less militarily committed than the French in the Middle East. It was a different world. Obama, back in the Rose Garden, spoke to the American public: "having made my decision as commander-in-chief, based on what I'm convinced is our national security interests, I'm also mindful that I'm president of the world's oldest constitutional democracy. I've long believed that our power is rooted not just in our military might, but in our example as a government of the people, by the people, and for the people. And that's why I've made a second decision: I will seek authorization for the use of force from the American people's representatives in Congress." A president who made his name by taking action independent of the Congress—whether in increasing troops in Afghanistan or launching action in Libya, whether on implementing healthcare legislation or environmental regulations, one who, in fact, would make executive action in the face of congressional intransigence a centerpiece of his second-term action plan—had chosen to punt the decision on taking action against Assad for the use of chemical weapons back to Congress. (His political opponents pointed out this contradiction when, a year later, the same president ignored legal obligations to consult the Congress on the release of prisoners from Guantanamo. His impulse for collaboration was, apparently, selective.)

Another two-hour NSC session followed, at which Joint Chiefs chairman Martin Dempsey assured the president that the military would be ready to take action whenever ordered to do so. But he must have guessed there would be no great hurry. The president then began to lay the groundwork for selling the Syria action to Congress. There were risks, of course, that went beyond the politics. By deferring to Congress, he set a precedent. He made it highly unlikely that at any time during the remainder of his term would he be able to initiate military action without seeking congressional approval. Many who have opposed actions taken by the president under the War Powers Act without congressional approval (see: Libya) might have welcomed Obama's newly consultative approach as being more in keeping with the kind of executive-legislative collaboration envisioned in the Constitution. But Obama had set a precedent—and for a military action that would have been exceptionally limited by any standard (a couple of days, no boots on the ground, perhaps 100 cruise missiles fired against a limited number of military targets). And that would make it very hard to do anything of comparable or greater magnitude without again returning to Congress for support. He had limited himself and perhaps his successors, too.

A very bad message had been sent by hesitating to take action against Assad, who not only had killed over 100,000 of his people but now felt free to employ weapons of mass destruction in his campaign of national self-destruction. Obama's leadership qualities were seriously in doubt. One of his most senior and closest advisors later called it "the low point of the Obama foreign policy record." As a historical checkpoint, in 1939 fewer than a third of Americans had supported intervention in the war in Europe, meaning that 83 percent of the American public misread Hitler and the threat he posed. Making hard choices sometimes means, as Obama has often said himself, taking actions even if they are opposed by the people. The red-line fumble prompted an avalanche of questions from some of Obama's closest allies and supporters about not only his own leadership but on America's future role in the world.

Steve Hadley spoke of the broader message about America's stance in the greater Middle East in this moment: "What are we doing? We are withdrawing. The only thing coming to an end after a decade is our military involvement. And rather than saying well, we're going to withdraw militarily, we need to find non-military, diplomatic means to protect our interests and advance our values in the absence of the military. Instead of trying to do that, we're basically withdrawing diplomatically. And leading from behind is not leading at all. Remember the scene in *Annie Hall* when Woody Allen and Diane Keaton are talking and there are the subtitles and you can see what they're really thinking. The subtitles at the moment just say, 'we want to get out.' Being unwilling to take very modest military action involving no direct risk to American troops in response to the repeated heinous violation of international law and direct warnings that such an action would bring a swift response from the president began sending the message that the United States was on the sidelines and likely to stay there. This made allies who had long counted on US support nervous and, as subsequent events would reveal, emboldened enemies.

Obama did not help his global image when as part of his campaign to "sell" the Syria vote and support his position in remarks in Sweden he argued, "I did not set a red line. The world set a red line." This led the *Washington Post* to quote the president's remarks of almost exactly a year earlier, in which he said, "we have been very clear to the Assad regime, but also to other players on the ground, that a red line for us is we start seeing a whole bunch of chemical weapons moving around or being utilized. That would change my calculus. That would change my equation."

The preceding two months of indecision and missteps had been among the most unsettling of the Obama presidency even for many of his most virulent supporters, and for many within his national security team. But Obama's mistakes were, they argued, sins of omission rather than commission; they did not constitute catastrophes such as those associated with the Iraq War or violating American principles on issues like torture. Instead they spoke not to the abuse of power but to discomfort with American power, perhaps a lack of leadership, a lack of purpose for America in the world.

Fortunately, at the moment things seemed most irrecoverable, Secretary of State Kerry inadvertently created an opening. While at a news conference in London, he said that the way Assad could avoid a military strike was to give up his chemical weapons stockpiles. He added, "he isn't about to do it and it can't be done." But the seed of an idea was planted and later that day Russian foreign minister Sergei Lavrov called to say he had noticed the comment. Lavrov said he would follow up Kerry's chance remark with a proposal that Syria would allow international inspectors in, and that ultimately he expected Syria to give the weapons up. According to press reports, Kerry said, "we are not going to play games. If it was a serious proposal, the Obama administration would consider it but the White House would not slow down efforts to win congressional authorization for a strike."

Rice and Obama in public appearances afterward, following close study of the Russian statements, suggested that the proposal could be "a significant breakthrough." Kerry worked the specifics of the deal with Lavrov and the two agreed to meet in Geneva on a Thursday afternoon, September 12. The United States went in saying the deal had to be very specific and realistic, but they were desperate to claim some progress. They also knew the Russians had leverage with Assad. Further, the Russians saw this as a chance to portray Assad as a more constructive actor, to turn a liability into an asset, and to pivot to the argument they felt would win the day for them, which is that Assad was a bulwark against al-Qaeda and other extremists.

Intensive, detailed negotiations followed. Technical teams hammered out differences. And though Lavrov had threatened to leave after talks got bogged down, by the next day, a framework agreement was announced. The Syrian government shortly afterward publicly announced they would comply and the diplomatic victory was greeted with immense relief in the White House. The Russians had bailed them out by producing a textbook multilateral diplomatic agreement to rid the world of a particularly pernicious weapons stockpile.

In the months that followed, slow progress was made in implementing the agreement. But by April 2014 over 80 percent of Syria's chemical weapons had been destroyed. Meanwhile, the Syrians, Russians, and Iranians also achieved their objective. In the view of President Obama's own director of national intelligence, James Clapper, testifying before Congress in early 2014, Bashar al Assad had actually grown stronger in the wake of the chemical weapons deal. Reflecting this, in March 2014, the *Los Angeles Times* ran a story headlined, "As Syria civil war enters fourth year, rebels are clearly losing."

As a consequence, Assad grew bold again and reportedly began to use chlorine bombs to poison opponents, a form of chemical weapon not covered in the agreement the Russians and the United States had engineered with Syria. Even as the international community called for an investigation, Assad refocused on preparations for early June elections for which the outcome would not be in doubt. He would, of course, win handily in what would be a laughable charade if the consequences were not so odious. He would maintain power. He will have rendered his country a graveyard but for the foreseeable future he and his allies will have delivered a powerful message that will resonate across the Middle East and around the world: brutality can triumph. The international community is leaderless and risk averse. The Assads and the Putins can have their way, violate international law, and pay only a minimal price.

This is not, of course, solely the fault or responsibility of the United States of America or the administration of Barack Obama. The UN is inert more often than it is active, paralyzed by bylaws and practices intended to keep it weak. America's European allies are still the loosest of confederations when it comes to foreign policy, NATO has had bad experiences in Afghanistan and Libya, and economic issues dominate the concerns of EU leaders. Japan is constrained by its constitution. China demurs that it is not ready to play a global leadership role. Other emerging powers keep their focus regional or domestic.

At almost the same time as Assad was celebrating both his sham re-election and his real battlefield gains, another dark consequence of the world's inaction in Syria began manifesting itself in a way that shockingly reinvoked America's unhappy experience in Iraq. ISIS, having used the war in Syria to grow from being little more than a street gang into a real army, strengthened by a government-like organizational structure, commanders drawn from Saddam's disbanded army, and an escalating reputation for fearsome brutality, had sought to fulfill the promise of its name by seizing ground in Iraq itself. Having recaptured Fallujah in January 2014, in June it made a lightning attack across the country, capturing Mosul, the second largest city in the country, seizing massive amounts of military supplies, capturing hundreds of millions of dollars from looted banks, and ending up on Baghdad's doorstep. By the time it did, not only was it the richest and most powerful terrorist organization the world had ever known, it had also raised the prospect that it was redrawing the borders of the Middle East. American ground troops had fought and died to stabilize what was now actively under the control of an al-Qaeda offshoot. The possibility of an Islamic state's encompassing parts of Syria and Iraq was a real one. Alternatively, the possibility of the region becoming a giant failed state, a Somalia dropped down in the middle of the Middle East, with a long border abutting Jordan and poised to threaten greater destabilization to come, was looming as never before. In the very best scenario, some combination of forces that might include the Iraqis, the United States, and others, possibly working in some form of collaboration with the Iranians, faced a protracted battle with a large, brutal, well-armed foe that was vastly more committed to contesting control of Sunni Iraq than they were.

It was a nightmare. It raised questions not only about the inaction of America and its allies in Syria years before when the cost of containing or neutralizing ISIS might have been much more modest, but it reopened debate about whether Obama's decision to pull all US troops out of Iraq without leaving some modest residual force might have precipitated such alarming developments. (Obama argued to the press in mid-June that the decision to withdraw even a residual force was made not by him but by the Iraqis when they refused to sign a new Status of Forces Agreement, or SOFA, early in his presidency. As had been the case with his attempt to argue that it was the world and not he who set the Syria red line, within twenty-four hours the *Washington Post* published an article noting that during the 2008 campaign in a debate with opponent Mitt Romney, Obama had in fact taken credit for making the decision to get all US troops out of Iraq. At a moment during which America's policies in the region were being called into question, the gaffe did not help. It is an example of how attention to small things like the wording of statements can have a big impact on public perceptions and a president's credibility. The fact was that the Iraqis did refuse to sign the SOFA. But it was also true that the president invited the circumstances in which that was the case and did not press the point. "He wanted out," said one of the president's national security advisors since the 2008 campaign.)

It was not until ISIS had claimed not only major cities like Fallujah and Mosul but controlled significant portions of both Syria and northern and central Iraq that Obama took action. The cited cause for his reversal was to rescue thousands of members of the Yazidi minority trapped atop a mountain and to protect American personnel. But the action, air attacks, continued after the Yazidis had for the most part found safe refuge and American personnel were largely taken from harm's way. As of this writing, it is not clear how long the US mission will continue. But it is clear that as much as it was a response to the growing threat of ISIS, Obama's action was also a response to a growing sense that the consequences of American withdrawal from the region had become too dangerous to ignore.

Obama, elected to get America out of Iraq, was back, it seemed, at least in part because he had gotten out too quickly, too completely. The situation was linked as much to Bush's inflammation of the region as it was to Obama's desire to be well done with it. Nothing so well illustrated the extremes of America's era of fear—of overreaction and overreach in the wake of 9/11 and of the ensuing self-doubt and risk aversion that followed. Error begat error and America's interests and those of our allies suffered, as did millions in the region buffeted by the fact that we had gone in twenty years from a bi-polar world to the costs of contending with a bi-polar superpower.

The question is now whether this period of swinging from one extreme to another may be followed by one of greater balance, whether the era of fear through which America has just passed may in fact be drawing to a close. There are some encouraging signs. But there are also serious challenges associated with adapting to the requirements of the new forms of American leadership that will be demanded in the era to come.

CHAPTER 10

The Beginning of the End
of the Age of Fear

You gain strength, courage, and confidence by every
experience in which you really stop to look fear in the
face. You are able to say to yourself, "I lived through
this horror. I can take the next thing that comes along."

—ELEANOR ROOSEVELT

For over a decade, America saw threats everywhere. We accepted the pernicious idea planted in our national psyche by the attacks on the World Trade Center and the Pentagon that if a handful of men, unaffiliated with any nation, could wreak the kind of havoc and destruction that had been beyond the capability of great traditional enemies, then we were in a new, more dangerous era. First the Bush administration and then that of Barack Obama accepted the central premise, fueled by the darkest part of our imaginations, that if a few individuals living in a far corner of desolate Afghanistan could do us great damage, then perhaps anyone, anywhere could as well.

But this new world was one in which, if anyone anywhere could harness anger and new technologies of destruction, then everyone everywhere was a potential threat to the United States. As irrational as this was—since few had the means or the will to pursue attacks against America, our allies, or our interests—it fueled American overreach on an unprecedented scale, not just in Iraq or Afghanistan but also in fighting extremists, employing drone attacks, or creating a state surveillance apparatus that knew few apparent limits.

Then, and in some cases simultaneously, we reacted to our own reactions. When we saw the cost of the foolishly ill-conceived use of force that our national mind-set had fueled in the Middle East, it then led to a seeming desire to withdraw from the international stage, to act as though we believed that the use of force by us anywhere, anytime carried with it unacceptable risks—that when we saw everyone as a potential enemy, we included ourselves on the list.

These spasms seemed to be a national bout with post-traumatic stress disorder, but they also followed an understandable pattern. We came to recognize a new source of danger for which we had been unprepared, and which exacted a terrible toll. Despite the extremes of our national mood swings since 9/11, we also developed new capabilities to identify threats and protect ourselves. We scored some victories against our enemies. And we even began to recover from the economic shocks that rocked our self-confidence perhaps even more than did the cycle of pain and misadventure associated with our national security.

As a result, errors aside, the actions of the Bush and Obama administrations may have planted the seeds for the beginning of the end of the age of fear. Certainly, important steps remain to be taken. America's position in the world is fragile and still at risk. Old threats have metastasized. New threats are emerging. We remain unsure of ourselves and of the right path forward. But despite the political noise and polarization, despite their mistakes and misjudgments, both presidents entrusted with the helm of state during this period have, via a twisting, sometimes halting route, brought us to a point at which a rebound is possible. Given the resilience of the American people, a budding energy revolution that can enhance American self-sufficiency and prosperity, and a new era of technological innovation, a significant American renaissance is not out of the question. It is even possible, if our current leaders and their immediate successors truly learn the lessons of the recent past, that America's strength in the twenty-first century may be greater than it has ever been, its role in the world more constructive.

To achieve that goal, however, will require that we also closely scrutinize how our national security apparatus responded to this unsettling era, where it and those within it made errors, what has been strengthened, and where additional changes are called for. While we have made progress in some areas—having made extensive strides to heighten our counterterrorism defenses at home and abroad, for example—we have also watched as a bloated system, tendencies toward concentrating too much power in the White House, the dysfunction of the US Congress and our politics more generally, and a Washington culture that eschews intellectual creativity and lacks expertise in critical areas that will be needed for the world we are entering has created as many problems for us as it has solved. There are lessons to be learned and applied from this extraordinary period—lessons that can be traced to the raid launched against the man responsible for its triggering event and to one of the great technological transformations that has dominated the period.

Call It Justice or Call It Revenge

About a decade ago, I visited the New York City Police Department's counterterrorism bureau that had been set up in the wake of the September 11 attacks. It was in a backwater of Brooklyn, on a nondescript street featuring industrial lots surrounded by tall wire fences and graffiti-splashed brick walls.

The center was still in its relative infancy but featured banks of computer monitors and a cadre of officers and staff who spoke and read the many languages in which the millions of residents and visitors to the city conducted their daily affairs. One of the cops I met told me a story. He was a low-key guy, an Asian American. He had been among the police who responded to the first radio calls on 9/11. Arriving in the South Tower, he was looking to connect with a partner when the building came down. He ran and, as he described it, "darkness came down all around me."

It was "dumb luck" that, in his view, saved him, landing him in the hospital and then forcing him through months of rehab to recover. He lost many of his friends. But he never for a moment considered not returning to his job. When I met him, his new mission was to prevent another similar catastrophe from occurring. He was matter-of-fact in describing his circumstances, and cool in describing what he was doing to identify potential terrorists and foil budding plots before they happened. Beneath his impassive expression, unmistakably revealed in his eyes, was the resoluteness of a man who had no doubts about his purpose. Whether he felt a desire for revenge or not, I could not tell. But he was absolutely committed to the idea that no one again experience what he and his friends and his comrades had gone through on that late summer morning. Even though he experienced the trauma of the attacks on the World Center in the most direct and horrific ways imaginable, his reaction contrasted distinctly from that of the government in Washington. He sustained the blow and recovered, remained collected, and rededicated himself to protecting his city. He did not lash out. He embraced what he knew would be effective—the cool, methodical, workaday vigilance and heroism of the New York City police department.

His reaction seemed almost miraculous amid the welter of emotions that blew outward from those collapsing towers, like those black clouds of smoke pouring through the grey streets of lower Manhattan, menacing and pursuing the fleeing crowds. There was so much anger and sadness. So much shock and loss. And there was that new, awful sense of vulnerability that had never existed before.

In the days after 9/11, when George W. Bush visited the victims' families and toured the gaping wound full of twisted metal where the twin towers had once stood, his compassion and humanity showed. He was heartbroken and he connected to people. In terms of the cheap metrics of Washington, DC, he achieved approval ratings he would never again approach. But with each turn of the policy process in Washington, with each debate about how to respond to the horror, the natural post-attack reactions were distorted. The theater of politics debased real feeling with rhetoric and self-interest, pandering, and opportunism. Fears that had been purely visceral were translated into formulations designed to maintain support or frame political positions. Soon the differing agendas of individual actors and political factions—all almost certainly emanating from a sincere desire to respond to what had shocked them as well— became the prevailing dramas within the White House meeting rooms. Each meeting was one more layer that separated the actors from their original motivations. What was to come reflected that an inexperienced president sat at the helm of the process by which different views were tempered by debate where a few voices could therefore dominate often via backchannels. Those involved in that process, unprepared due to a lack of appreciation for what foresight mechanism warned, responded reactively to the crisis. The results: a first response to Afghanistan that any president would have had, but then a shift in attention to an unrelated front in Iraq that sapped American resources from the primary mission; the creation of unnecessary bureaucratic superstructures at the NDI and the Department of Homeland Security; and the waiving or violation of rights, laws, and standards in Guantanamo and Abu Ghraib, via the Patriot Act.

It requires discipline not to consider these choices through the lens of political biases. But such discipline is needed. Were these responses appropriate? Were they the best allocation of limited assets? Did they produce the desired results? Did they trigger unintended consequences? In many cases, the answers are unsettling. But lessons were gradually learned and, as we have seen, some important gains were achieved.

Through all this, for all the flaws and twists and victories and defeats in the policy process, it was, however, impossible to forget the moment this new era began. That is why the least disputed mission undertaken by the Bush administration was the search for Osama bin Laden and the mission to destroy al-Qaeda. That is why, when Barack Obama was first briefed by the intelligence community when he took office, one of the areas he most aggressively drilled his briefers about was the progress in finding bin Laden.

John Brennan "was at the CIA on 9/11, and in the days, weeks, and months following it." He saw at firsthand the great uncertainty about the nature of this new threat: "there was such a cascading stream of reporting about the WMD capabilities of al-Qaeda. . . . It was really difficult to discern what was real and what was not. And you know, there were some very active follow-on plots in terms of trying to attack the West Coast of the United States."

But within a couple of years the sense of threat had stabilized, and that, for Brennan, was the moment when the Bush administration was at fault. They never dialed back the rhetoric or regularized the legal framework within which the government responded to the threat: "I think there have been a lot of criticisms of the previous administration in the aftermath of 9/11. But for the first two years we were all really quite uncertain about whether or not we were going to face something that was almost existential. And if I fault the previous administration, it's because once we had a better appreciation of it, then they didn't go back and they didn't take their proper steps as far as Congress and other things are concerned as far as getting the program on a firmer legal footing and a firmer policy footing." In short, they let the mood that prevailed immediately in the aftermath of 9/11, the terrifying uncertainty and unease, continue way too long—not just publicly, but within their own debates. The rationale that took root in the circumstances of 9/11 permitted the rule book to be thrown aside and any means necessary to be used to get America's enemies. It affected every department of government.

The Pointy End of the Spear

Nonetheless, with regard to the essential mission triggered by 9/11, the initial impulse of the Bush team was to pursue terrorists in a way that, in fact, resembled the model later embraced by the Obama team—what has come to be known as the "light footprint." Donald Rumsfeld wrote a justification for "unconventional conflict": "in the twenty-first century . . . the enemy was not the local population but the terrorists and the insurgents living, training and fighting among them." As early as his job interview for defense secretary, Rumsfeld argued that the future of the military lay with a focus on "agility, speed, deployability, precision, and lethality." Even up to the morning of September 11, his team that was preparing the quadrennial plan for military priorities included individuals like Michael Vickers, one of the architects behind the CIA's efforts assisting the Afghan *mujahideen* when they fought the Red Army during the 1980s. One of those *mujahideen*, of course, was Osama bin Laden. The rules of war had been rewritten.

In the wake of the 9/11 attacks, with Bush's national security principals gathered in the shelter beneath the White House and the president at Offutt Air Force Base in Nebraska, an instantaneous and rapid intelligence and defense-community-wide effort began increasing understanding of al-Qaeda and bin Laden. (This was the same kind of effort that Richard Clarke had argued for since Bush assumed office, and that other members of the Clinton national security team had advised should be a priority during the transition in late 2000 and early 2001.) On September 12, CIA director George Tenet and counterterror director Cofer Black briefed the president on their plans to go after their new highest priorities. Their core point was that "this war would be driven by intelligence, not the pure projection of power. The challenge wasn't to defeat the enemy, militarily. The challenge was to find the enemy." It was as clear-eyed an assessment as was made in those first days. It would echo through the succeeding decade and grow louder as intelligence became increasingly critical to address the range of perceived threats the United States would face, from terrorism to cyber-attacks. In a meeting the next day, when asked whether the CIA could handle this new role, Black responded, "by the time the CIA was done with al-Qaeda, bin Laden and his brethren would have flies walking across their eyeballs." On this front, he was only half right. Osama himself would, after a decade-long manhunt, be dispatched, but as we have seen, al-Qaeda would grow and adapt at a speed faster than the US intelligence community could keep up with.

Four short days after the attacks, the president met with his top national security advisors at Camp David to discuss action against al-Qaeda. It was here that Paul Wolfowitz, deputy secretary of defense, tried to broaden the discussion from Afghanistan to include Iraq, but he, like the others in the room, concurred that intel plus special forces was the right recipe for addressing the terror threat in the near term. On September 17, Bush authorized a CIA-led initiative into Afghanistan called "Operation Jawbreaker." That day, the president also issued a still-classified directive that granted the CIA power to imprison and interrogate prisoners without the burdens of heavy oversight that usually constrained the agency. It was designed to open the way to swifter, broader, covert initiatives worldwide that could strike quickly, without bureaucratic impediments that were perceived as unduly burdensome, given the crisis mood.

Rumsfeld, unhappy that the CIA was the designated pointy end of the spear, pushed hard within the Pentagon to ramp up special forces capacity, operating under the aegis of the US Special Operations Command (SOCOM). SOCOM was predictably gung-ho about taking on the challenge. In early October, Rumsfeld offered a clear insight into what was at the forefront of his mind when he sent a memo to his top military commanders and senior political aides, "What Will Be the Military Role in the War on Terrorism?" Battle lines were not just being formed between the United States and its new adversaries. As often happens in Washington, they were quickly shaping up between bureaucracies eager to take the lead with regard to the great national priority of the moment.

By November, Rumsfeld had witnessed a demonstration at Fort Bragg, North Carolina, that clarified for him that perhaps the military outfit with the most apposite capacity to fight this new war was the elite Joint Special Operations Command (JSOC), the most secretive component of SOCOM. JSOC includes special-mission units of the Army's Delta force, the Navy's SEALs, and the Air Force's Special Tactics Squadron. With special research and intelligence capabilities, and the best of the best among America's military under their command, JSOC was ideally suited to the shadow warfare that was the only way to combat the new terrorist enemies. Ultimately, they would justify the faith placed in them by eliminating bin Laden. But their primacy started with Rumsfeld: SOCOM as a whole would grow from a force numbering roughly 33,000 in 2001 to 66,000 in 2014. Part of that growth would be an effort by Rumsfeld to grow the unit's intelligence capacities to make it less dependent on the CIA, a classic illustration of the DC turf-warrior mentality that produces redundant expenditures rather than enhances necessary, even critical, collaboration.

Rumsfeld followed this by creating a position for an under secretary for defense intelligence within the Pentagon and filling this post with one of his most trusted and loyal aides, Steve Cambone. The creation of the directorate of national intelligence was an unmistakable sign of recognition that intelligence was the sine qua non of effective counterterrorism operations. The creation of New York's counterterrorism bureau was another. The rapid expansion of the National Security Agency yet another. The decade that followed would see the greatest expansion of intelligence capacity in history, a renaissance for organizations that had wondered about their role and centrality only a few years earlier in the immediate aftermath of the end of the Cold War. But it has to be acknowledged that at the core of this impulse was a sound recognition that the invisible actions of the intelligence community, often linked to the invisible actions of US special forces and the gradual introduction of drone technology, were the most effective way of actually combating terrorists. As it turned out, massive ground wars had more of a tendency to create new terrorists than to eliminate old ones. In the giant swirling, overwrought, mistake-laden American response to 9/11, some responses were as sound and pragmatic as those of that police officer I met in the counterterrorism center. We shouldn't lose sight of the fact that in some important ways, the system did work as it was intended to, even as it evolved.

"The agency [CIA] was the pointy end of the spear," said former director Mike Hayden, "I can't confirm or deny anything the government hasn't confirmed or denied. But we played many roles. We had certainly done detentions and interrogations. . . . We'd done renditions. . . . And that started within a year of the attack. And then later, after you get [long-term Guantanamo detainee] Abu Zubaydah about a year later, you get enhanced interrogation techniques." And then, he noted, the role grew and grew—from expanding HUMINT (human intelligence) capacity to drones. The unconventional, stealth war-making capacity had taken over wholesale.

Abbottabad

Distracted by a much more conventional, footslogging war in Iraq, the search for bin Laden went more slowly than anyone at the top had hoped. Frustration grew. "Don't think this issue did not surface regularly. It did. And from time to time, tempers flared," said one former Bush NSC official. By late 2003, a Rumsfeld memo leaked to *USA Today* revealed some of that frustration. "We lack the metrics to know if we are winning or losing the war on terror." The memo was optimistic about eventual victory but accurately predicted that "it will be a long hard slog." Rumsfeld in early 2004 gave SOCOM "broad authority to launch operations across an arc of territory from North Africa all the way to the Philippines" via something called the al-Qaeda Executive Order. Missions were to remain classified and the order was backed up by a National Security Presidential Directive (NSPD-38) that laid out SOCOM's mission and further established it as a centerpiece of America's military efforts.

Efforts against al-Qaeda took another important turn later that year when Nek Muhammad, leader of the Pakistani Taliban, was located, and an opportunity to eliminate him arose. The United States approached the Pakistanis for permission to take him out, recognizing he had been a thorn in the side of the Pakistani military for some time. In exchange, the Americans hoped for the okay from the Pakistanis to allow regular drone flights over the country. The Pakistanis imposed conditions: they wanted approval of each mission and they wanted all drones to operate under the CIA to ensure their operations were both covert and deniable. The Hellfire missile that blasted Nek Muhammad on June 18, 2004, indicated that the deal was done. It was the first targeted drone strike in Pakistan. A new era in America's war in terror began—a new and valuable tool was unleashed, as was the potential for a torrent of future disputes.

The following year, a Pakistani tip led the CIA to conclude that a high-level al-Qaeda meeting would take place in Bajaur, in Northwest Pakistan. Senior leaders of the organization like Ayman al-Zawahiri and Abu Faraj al-Libi were rumored attendees. The possibility of a SEAL attack was raised. The CIA and General Stanley McChrystal, the JSOC Commander, argued the mission was worth the risks, but Rumsfeld and Cambone were concerned it was too perilous. They argued for so many more troops that the mission became unwieldy and impractical—"practically an invasion" was the description of the CIA chief in Islamabad. The mission died on the vine, showing that for all the post-9/11 adjustments in our laws and missions and agency procedures, neither the military nor the intelligence community had yet evolved the kind of plans or tactics that would let them take the war on terror to some of the most important places it needed to be fought—like Pakistan.

In fact, Pakistan had emerged as the problem child of the war on terror. The country posed multiple layers of problems: wily enemies, tough terrain, terrorist-coddling sympathizers in high places, and a degree of nationalism and anti-American hostility among the populace that made any operation in that country profoundly complicated from a diplomatic and legal perspective.

Pakistan's borders were absolutely porous, too. Taliban and al-Qaeda fighters could pass one way or another between Pakistan and Afghanistan while US military were often hamstrung by diplomatic challenges. For this reason, when a lead arose late in 2007 that a big meeting of extremists was likely to take place in Afghanistan and Afghan president Karzai reached out to the United States to attack the meeting, it seemed, in relative terms, a special opportunity. Some intelligence suggested that bin Laden might attend the meeting himself, which made the action an even more tantalizing prospect. A massive air and special operations meeting was planned. Last-minute doubts about bin Laden's presence, and concerns about the risks to civilians, led the mission to be dialed back. "We were, to put it mildly, very disappointed," said one military leader close to the operation.

By 2008 the Pakistanis were not making things easier on their side of the border and al-Qaeda was gaining strength. They and their Taliban allies were becoming bolder. The ISI was an impediment to the use of drones. Only twenty-five drone strikes had taken place between the killing of Nek Muhammed and March 2007. In the meantime, the Pakistani government had been working to better relations with the extremists. Matters were made worse in 2008 when, during a battle on the AfPak border between US troops and the Taliban, eleven Pakistani soldiers were killed by an American airstrike. Pakistan howled, asserting the strikes were "unprovoked and cowardly." But the new JSOC commander, Admiral William McRaven, a smart, articulate war-fighter as comfortable on the battlefield as around a Washington, DC, conference table, made the case to Bush that there was no way to achieve US goals without broader latitude to strike in Pakistan.

In the same vein, resulting from deep frustration that the 9/11 attacks were now almost seven years past and the Bush administration's time in office was running out, the president, Hadley, Gates, Rice, and Admiral Mullen heard and accepted a pitch from CIA director Michael Hayden arguing for an escalation in the drone war. Bush was ready for a change in approach. He approved an order significantly increasing the number of CIA Predator and Reaper drone sorties and granted McRaven the latitude he was seeking. According to the assessment of Eric Schmitt and Thom Shanker in their insightful book, *Counterstrike: The Untold Story of America's Secret Campaign Against Al Qaeda,* the measures Bush approved "made the CIA director America's combatant commander in the hottest covert war in the global campaign."

Bush's recommitment started to produce results and, in due course the policy was adopted seamlessly by Obama's security team. "You saw," Hayden described, "beginning in July '08, more direct action against al-Qaeda leadership in terms of taking them off the battlefield. It was remarkably successful." He added, "a lot has been made about the Obama administration and what they did in 2009. But if you normalize the last six months of 2008 when this began, 2009 is precisely the same pace as those six months in terms of unexplained explosions in the tribal regions of Pakistan. And it is not until 2010 that the total numbers double."

Periodically, Americans would be torn between their mission and their respect for the sensibilities of their Pakistani frenemies, even after Bush proclaimed his new resolve and the new order was signed. When a September 2008 Navy SEAL raid in South Waziristan resulted in a protracted gun battle and a number of civilian casualties, the Pakistanis were outraged again. And again, the decision was made to reduce ground attacks in that country. But drone operations expanded.

As all this was happening, Barack Obama was campaigning on a platform that included the assertion that President Bush had neglected the war in Afghanistan and the original mission against al-Qaeda. This played to the lingering appetite for justice among the American people, allowing an antiwar candidate to take on a view associated with an over-appetite for armed conflict, urge the end of his predecessor's big wars, and still not appear anti-military or weak. Obama argued early on that "we did not finish the job against al-Qaeda in Afghanistan. We did not develop new capabilities to defeat a new enemy, or launch a comprehensive strategy to dry up the terrorists' base of support. We did not reaffirm our basic values or secure our homeland." He also said of the Pakistanis, "if we have actionable intelligence about high-value terrorist targets and [Pakistani president] Musharraf won't act, we will."

During Obama's very first briefings as president, he came to see that the challenges of following through on these promises would be more difficult than expected. In a briefing in Chicago from the director of national intelligence, Admiral Mike McConnell, shortly after Obama's election, the scope of America's covert drone program was explained to him, as was the precarious situation in both Afghanistan and Pakistan. Obama also received a briefing from CIA director Hayden in which the conversation focused heavily on drones and covert activities in pursuit of al-Qaeda. "I went to Chicago in mid-December," Hayden recounts, "and briefed President Obama on all the ongoing covert actions of the Central Intelligence Agency. The one area he asked the most questions about was detention and interrogation. He suggested he was prepared to end the programs and wanted to know more about them. But there were other programs where he was very supportive." Hayden confirms that "there was surprising continuity between the forty-third and forty-fourth presidents of the United States despite the great difference in personality between the two men, despite the campaign rhetoric. I can't summarize it any better. He ran against Bush 43.1 and governed like Bush 43.2 in terms of security issues."

Tony Blinken explains Obama's first-term policy priorities thusly: "we were about the defeat of core al-Qaeda and preventing its return to Afghanistan and ideally, Pakistan, and making sure, to the extent that we could, that Pakistan's nuclear weapons didn't fall into the wrong hands. Those have been the North Stars of what we have done." (The point about Pakistan's nuclear weapons is essential to understanding why, despite all the difficulties with the Pakistani government, military, and intelligence communities, it was deemed essential to maintain ties to those in charge and to shore up voices who would be responsible stewards of that deadly program. The notion that one Pakistani nuke might someday go missing and fall into terrorist hands was, in fact, one of the central fright-inducing memes of the whole, jittery period.)

In their meeting immediately before Obama took office, Bush took care to underscore to the president-elect how important he felt the drone program was. He also emphasized another effort, a secret cyber-initiative targeting Iran's nuclear program. The outgoing president had clearly come a long way since being the champion of "shock and awe" in Iraq. Unconventional, high-tech, lower risk, lower-visibility methods were, after eight years, the means he felt would be most effective in winning the war that started in September 2001.

These briefings led Obama to continue these programs and maintain the empowerment of the CIA, a fact that frustrated the incoming DNI, Admiral Dennis Blair, and effectively ended his tenure as the intelligence community's top dog before it even got started. He had the title, but Panetta as CIA director had the responsibility and the authority to get the critical job done. It was yet another indication that the flawed intelligence community reorganization was not going to gain much traction under the new president.

Obama essentially decided to follow Bush's advice. He and his team largely kept in place the elements of the prior administration's covert campaigns in Pakistan and against Iran. He also kept in place a number of the personnel responsible for those campaigns. Indeed, within the first three days of the Obama presidency, outgoing CIA director Hayden (Leon Panetta had yet to be confirmed) briefed the president on the first drone strikes of his administration in Pakistan. Within hours, it became clear that the strikes, in North and South Waziristan, had claimed civilian lives. Brennan told Obama, who was furious. This led to a confrontation with the CIA's leadership in which they explained such incidents were hard to avoid and the president demanded higher standards that included giving the director of central intelligence the final say in approving attacks.

Satisfied with the new approach, the administration began to ramp up the attacks. As described in a May 2012 article by Jo Becker and Scott Shane in the *New York Times*, a methodical process for evaluating intelligence and identifying individuals who might be targeted for "personality strikes" led a weekly debate among "more than 100 members of the government's sprawling national security apparatus," who gathered by teleconference, weighed the evidence, and then determined whether or not targets should be added to "kill lists." The nominations from the group were then sent to John Brennan, the counterterrorism advisor, who sought Obama's approval on each. From the very beginning, the centrality of this issue and the importance Obama placed on restoring the focus of the national security effort to fighting terror led Brennan to assume an ever more important role and gain ever more trust from his boss.

Squeezing al-Qaeda in Afghanistan and Pakistan and regularly attacking its leadership, as well as undertaking the war in Iraq, had unintended consequences. Al-Qaeda began to change its shape. New cells emerged throughout the Middle East and in Africa. Yemen and the East Coast of Africa became sites of drone and special forces attacks.

Al-Qaeda's numbers grew. Threats began to emanate from these groups, including some, such as those from Yemen, targeting the United States. But throughout, the metric that mattered most in the Obama White House, in terms of measuring progress on the war on terror, was the damage inflicted on "core al-Qaeda," the leadership of the original organization that staged the September 11 attacks against the United States. As Obama made clear in his first meetings with the intelligence community leadership, the talisman at the core of "core al-Qaeda" was Osama bin Laden.

Obama would have to wait until the summer of 2010 for the first big break in the world's best known, most closely followed manhunt. As is now widely known, the NSA intercepted a phone call involving an al-Qaeda courier named Abu Ahmed al-Kuwaiti. When he reported that he was "back with the people I was with before," it triggered an effort by intelligence analysts that ultimately led them to him and his white Suzuki, which they followed into the Pakistani town of Abbottabad, home to Pakistan's military academy. There al-Kuwaiti entered a compound surrounded by high stucco walls, barbed wire, and other clear security features that suggested that the resident might indeed be a high-value target. It would take a year of investigation and analysis to conclude that the likelihood it was the residence of bin Laden was sufficient for serious mission planning to begin. It was an operation that began with an intelligence breakthrough, the intercept. It required intelligence legwork and further confirmation from the intelligence community in several forms. The operation used a CIA Sentinel drone that could take high-altitude photos of the compound and its residents while evading Pakistani detection. Ultimately, it would utilize the unique and lethal skills of JSOC to close the deal. Also, as was consistent with the long patterns of this war, the mission was to take place in Pakistan, so close to the Pakistani military elite that it is hard to imagine some among them did not know of bin Laden's presence. It took a long time before the United States was ready to pull the trigger.

The target was a figure in the Abbottabad compound called "the pacer" because of his regular walks within its walls. Even as Leon Panetta called McRaven into CIA headquarters in February 2011 to prepare for the mission, there was a debate going on higher up in the administration about what the purpose of that mission should be. Sensitive to Obama's risk aversion and, in this case, supported by Defense Secretary Gates, Vice President Biden, and the staffers closest to him, Panetta argued that the compound should be taken out with precision munitions. Obama on the other hand wanted proof that bin Laden was there. That would require a riskier mission. But Obama felt, according to a top NSC official, that if there were not clear evidence bin Laden was dead, speculation would linger that he had escaped. He felt the message to al-Qaeda that their leader was gone was an important one, and that the same was true with regard to the world. Getting bin Laden, knowing he was neutralized, was a vital step—*the* vital step—in achieving some degree of true post-9/11 closure. He had to slay the boogie man; it was not enough for bin Laden to just disappear without a trace.

On March 14, 2011, the president and his NSC team met to review the options McRaven and the CIA developed. The tug-of-war over the two approaches drove much of the discussion, and Obama ended the meeting as he had so many others, by postponing a decision and seeking a more refined plan for a special forces operation into Abbottabad. Two weeks later, the plan for flying two helicopters full of Navy SEALs into the compound was revealed and again Gates, Biden, and Hoss Cartwright argued instead for B-2 stealth bombers to flatten the compound. A drone attack was ruled out because it would not produce the kind of additional intelligence from the mission the president sought. The president's view prevailed, and by mid-April two dozen Navy SEALs were training for the mission in a replica of the compound built in North Carolina. It was a clear example in which Obama's deliberative nature and careful judgment were combined with a willingness to undertake a calculated risk given the importance of the mission. This was the process working well.

Nonetheless, efforts to confirm, with as much certainty as possible, that this was really bin Laden's residence continued. Red teams, authorized by Donilon, challenged all the assumptions and evidence on hand. The results reported to the NSC rated the likelihood that bin Laden would be at the compound when they got there at between 40 and 70 percent. Most of those present urged caution.

Two of those present did not think hesitation was the right answer. One was Panetta, who felt that the intelligence was likely to be the best the United States would ever get. The other who leaned toward action was Obama himself. As Petraeus noted, behind the scenes Obama regularly made tough calls on issues like these, often, ultimately okaying actions with real risks involved. "And I don't think it's just because he thought nobody was going to find out about them," the general added, "because ultimately somebody sooner or later figures out what's happened. I thought he was very gutsy on many tough issues. So too was Tom Donilon, who I thought was a superb national security advisor."

The next morning, on April 29, in a meeting with Donilon, Brennan, McDonough, and his chief of staff, Bill Daley—his White House team, it is worth noting, not a larger group from the various national security agencies—Obama coolly let them know that the raid was "a go." He left the option to McRaven to call it off if weather or other changes in conditions made the risk equation worse. The president then went off to conduct business as usual, keeping up appearances that nothing major was underway, even joking his way through the ritual of the White House Correspondents' Dinner. Ironically a room full of the nation's best journalists had no inkling of the story.

Then, an image that later became a symbol of the Obama presidency was released, a photograph of a secret meeting that, like some of the previously classified details of the raid that would follow, was intended to ensure that credit went where credit was due. Obama was depicted with many of his top national security team members in a secure communications facility next to the White House situation room, watching the Abbottabad raid as it transpired in real time. (This pattern of releasing classified information after a security or diplomatic triumph was repeated periodically during the Obama years, as when it was leaked to the press that the foundations for a diplomatic breakthrough with Iran had come through secret White House–led diplomacy. For an administration that was avowedly going to be the toughest ever on leaks, it was a particularly cynical page to have in their playbook.)

The Abbottabad operation, called Neptune Spear, involved the two helicopters full of SEALs and four support Chinook helicopters as well. For fifty minutes, punctuated with images from the ground, bits of radio traffic, and commentary by Leon Panetta, Obama, Donilon, Clinton, and the others watched nervously. The hard landing of one of the helicopters carrying the SEALs evoked the helicopter crash that had foiled the Carter-era rescue attempt of the hostages in Iran and raised the tension level palpably. McRaven managed his team through the twists and turns of the mission coolly. In the end, they received the transmission "for God and country—Geronimo, Geronimo, Geronimo. Geronimo EKIA [enemy killed in action]"—meaning that bin Laden had been cornered, killed, and identified. Obama himself was a picture of calm, saying only, "we got him."

The consequences of those three words, however, were both weighty and easy to misunderstand. In terms of the era of fear, of national insecurity, it was a vital step toward bringing it to an end. The mastermind of 9/11 had grown from a mere terrorist to a living, breathing symbol of a new sort of anti-American, anti-Western hatred made lethal. It is no exaggeration to say that in the minds of Americans bin Laden had evolved into a metaphor for evil itself, much as had Hitler. But bin Laden was no Hitler, al-Qaeda was no existential threat to the United States or the West, and core al-Qaeda, led by bin Laden, was not what it once was. In fact, although the death of bin Laden was emotionally satisfying and a clear triumph for President Obama and his team—not to mention the thousands of CIA and military personnel who participated in the decade-long pursuit that culminated in the attack and the Bush officials who helped establish many of the programs that led to the operation—it was not the watershed the president portrayed it to be during his 2012 presidential campaign. It was actually a moment that ultimately proved that bin Laden was no longer central to the future of an al-Qaeda that had morphed into something more dangerous, more global, and many times larger than the small organization behind the 9/11 attacks.

"This War, Like All Wars, Must End"

In the remaining years of the Obama administration, the transformation of al-Qaeda into a collection of loosely linked franchise-like operations would at first be minimized as somehow being less threatening to the United States than the predecessor structure. This was emphasized in part by the repeated reference to "core al-Qaeda" as the greatest and original threat and target. Later, however, as the shifting situation became clearer, the dangers of the looser terrorist structures became more widely acknowledged, if not always publicly. As Tony Blinken recalls, "we recognized from virtually day one that we were dealing with a metastasizing problem with organizations that were either inspired by or directly affiliated with al-Qaeda. . . . Look back at what John Brennan was saying virtually from day one about Yemen and the intense focus we put on that, Somalia shortly thereafter, North Africa after that. . . . But when it came to the folks that had the capability to hit the United States as on 9/11, that was a 'core' problem."

Brennan said, "al-Qaeda is much different than it was on 9/11. At that time it exerted a fair amount of organizational pull over its membership, wherever they may be. There was communication. There was contact. There was some flow of operatives in and out and there was a hierarchical direction to it. Over the course of the last decade, because of some of the gains we have made, there is less of that. It's much more difficult for al-Qaeda's core to get their messages to AQAP [al-Qaeda in the Arabian Peninsula] or AQIM [al-Qaeda in Mali] or the Muhammad Jamal network inside Egypt."

He went on to add, "as a result, we're seeing a couple of things. One is that there's much more of a localized agenda. . . . In addition, I think the phenomenon we're seeing now more and more is an atomization and the growth of these cells that have the same sort of ideology as al-Qaeda but will have no interaction with it. They will nominally be al-Qaeda, but they won't really be part of the organization in some key respects. . . . And they're basically doing their own thing."

As a direct consequence of these changes, by 2014, when the State Department issued its annual report on terror, it was clear that after thirteen years of a war on terror, major improvements in technology, and vast increases in our intelligence and military resources devoted to fighting terror, the United States and the world were nonetheless actually losing ground against the phenomenon of violent extremism. According to the State Department report, terrorism increased 43 percent from 2012, the year after the raid on the bin Laden compound, to 2013. Attacks increased from 6,700 to 9,700 worldwide. More than 18,000 people were killed, and almost twice that were injured. Tellingly, the report explicitly noted that although the United States had success against the tiny group that had been "core al-Qaeda," the loose network of al-Qaeda "affiliates" from the Persian Gulf to Syria to Iraq to Africa had, as we have seen, grown much more dangerous.

Still, something had changed. It was captured in the Obama reelection campaign mantra: General Motors is alive and Bin Laden is dead. It was everything you might want and expect in a bumper sticker. While simplistic, it cut to the two core emotional traumas borne by the American people since 2011. It suggested that we were healing. It offered evidence even if that evidence was largely symbolic. It spoke, in nine words, as directly as possible to the central questions churning within the American zeitgeist.

Getting bin Laden did not actually reduce the terrorist threat in any material way, yet the American people chose to believe that it did—wanted and needed to believe it did—supporting in poll after poll a pullback from engagement in the regions where the real violent extremists were to be found even as their strength grew. Gradually, the US government, although unable to win something with such sweeping and unrealistic goals as those embodied in "the war on terrorism," had been able to begin to defuse the terror that had so perverted American national security policy. Killing bin Laden was only part of it.

Systematically and over time, by increasing intelligence assets, developing better homeland defenses and awareness, giving counterterror operators new tools, and simply working the brief, progress was made. As Brennan observed, "whenever you do a net assessment, you look at three things. You look at the nature and the seriousness of the threat. You look at the vulnerabilities that exist. And you look at the mitigation steps that are under way. And if we compare ourselves now to 9/11, those vulnerabilities that existed within this country have, I think, really been reduced significantly." He sums up the ability of groups like al-Qaeda "to carry out the attack they did on 9/11 or even other types of attacks has been really whittled down significantly because we have reduced vulnerabilities and we've enhanced mitigation measures." We had, distractions aside, developed a better system for doing what we should have done in the first place and exclusively—making Americans feel safer—because it is there in people's psyches and not on battlefields that terrorists ultimately can be defeated. Look at other places where terror strikes: Although narrow missions to capture or kill the terrorists are sought, the real victory occurs the day after an attack, when life goes on undisturbed. We tried to remake the world when what we really needed to do was seek to heal ourselves. It is an unsettling and unproductive thought experiment to imagine how many people would be alive today and how many resources could have been directed to better purposes if we had set our goals more wisely and narrowly in the wake of the 9/11 attacks. But we know now what has worked and what has not. With some luck that will be of some use to future US policymakers.

In May 2013, Obama spoke at the National Defense University. "We relentlessly targeted al-Qaeda's core leadership"—that phrase again—he said, "and today Osama bin Laden is dead and so are most of his top lieutenants." Although the war set "the core of al-Qaeda in Afghanistan and Pakistan . . . on a path to defeat," he spoke of an evolving threat. "Lethal, yet less capable al-Qaeda affiliates. Threats to diplomatic facilities and businesses abroad. Homegrown extremists. This is the future of terrorism." That said, he declared, "America is at a crossroads" and that "the decisions we are making will define the type of nation . . . that we leave to our children." Obama then called for the refinement and ultimate repeal of the Authorization for the Use of Military Force (AUMF), which had been the initiating tool for much of the war on terror under President Bush, and his intention not to "sign laws that expand this mandate further." Going after terrorists "must continue" he acknowledged, "but this war, like all wars, must end."

Within just over a year, the rise of ISIS would introduce the world to a new kind of terror threat from a group that was far better financed, equipped, organized, and attractive to foreign recruits than had al-Qaeda. Suddenly Obama and his national security team were forced to ask themselves whether the war they sought to end was not only not over but entering a dangerous new phase. Indeed, in retrospect, it was hard not to wonder whether the NDU speech and others like it might have been Obama's own "mission accomplished" moment, the triumph of hope over clear-headed analysis.

Telling Glimpses of the Next War

Drone attacks increased to unprecedented levels in the Obama years. For all the benefits such technologies may have brought, it also must be acknowledged that they, like other new technologies of conflict, raise important questions that future national security policymakers must be ready to better address.

For example, Obama encountered a host of new doctrinal, ethical, and legal challenges with the serial violations of national sovereignty made by America's drone programs and other tools in the light-footprint arsenal employed in pursuit of a better way to conduct the wars he inherited. The cautious lawyer may, in fact, have set new records in violating global norms of national behavior. In one such incident, against a rising al-Qaeda mastermind in Yemen, Anwar al-Awlaki, new questions were raised when it was revealed that al-Awlaki and his son, both killed in drone attacks, were American citizens. Battles with the Pakistanis and others over the US drones program's serial violation of national sovereignty triggered other such debates and more criticism of the United States. The concerns that high-tech powers like the United States will be able to wage white-collar wars, in which their citizens are not at risk while those of poorer nations die, also loom as technologies for fighting "over the horizon" proliferate and grow more sophisticated. It is clear that new issues will emerge because we are at the dawn of a new era in the conduct of conflict.

The average American is now well aware that once-secret drone strikes and technologies have become the centerpiece of a massive new apparatus within the US military. Still, misconceptions about their nature are prevalent. As described by one of the fathers of the program, former Air Force chief of staff Norty Schwartz, "a twenty-four-hour orbit of a Predator or a Reaper requires 160 or more airmen. It's hardly unmanned. It's a few operators, a few maintainers, a few command and controllers, and a whole bevy of intelligence and imagery processing people. This is big business, which is one reason why I don't think you have to fret too much about others becoming immediately proficient in this area."

John Brennan offers a somewhat contradictory view from his perspective as a specialist in counterterrorism. "It's not just going to be the Predators. It's going to be miniaturized drones. . . . You can do a fair amount of damage by loading up several kilos of explosives onto an aerial platform that you can direct into someone's office. And the technology is there." He concludes, somewhat ominously, "you know, looking out over the next five years, technology can be our best friend—but it's also our worst enemy, because the terrorists are taking advantage of it."

The New America Foundation estimated that the United States conducted 370 such strikes in Pakistan between 2005 and 2013, with 122 in 2010 alone. The *Long War Journal* and the Bureau of Investigative Journalism offer roughly similar numbers. Numbers have decreased since the peak years of 2010 and 2011. The Bureau of Investigative Journalism estimates between three and nine such strikes in Somalia since 2007 and between eight and eleven "other covert operations" resulting in between 47 and 188 deaths.

But it was in another area of next-generation, tech-centric warfare, also recommended to Obama by his predecessor, that the most sweeping and unsettling example of American overreach since the invasion of Iraq took place. By 2014, the incoming head of the National Security Agency, Admiral Mike Rogers, would say, "cyber will be an element of almost any crisis we're going to see in the future." If correct, what he was asserting—with the evidence of US encounters with Iran, China, Russia, Syria,and others to back it up—was that we were in the midst of the most important change in military and national security affairs since the dawn of the nuclear age. As we would discover, it was a period in which our technological capabilities would outstrip the ability of our policymakers to understand or manage them properly, and even our underlying laws and philosophies to guide our behavior.

George Bush initially paid little attention to the cyber threat, according to Richard Clarke. Since Clarke was special advisor to the president for cyber security, his perspective is telling. Essentially, in Clarke's view, Bush simply picked up where the Clinton administration had left off, "except that the Republican administration not only continued to eschew regulation, they downright hated the idea of the federal government issuing new regulations on anything at all." The policy framework that guided this was called the National Strategy to Secure Cyberspace. Clarke later wrote: "Bush's personal understanding and interest in cybersecurity early in his administration were best summed up by a question he asked me in 2002. I had gone to him in the Oval Office with news of a discovery of a pervasive flaw in software, a flaw that would allow hackers to run amok unless we could quietly persuade most major networks and corporations to fix the flaw. Bush's only reaction was, "What does John think?" John was the CEO of a large information technology company and a major donor to the Bush election committee." After Clarke left the White House in 2003, he was not replaced. This meant that the most senior person with responsibility for cyber issues was buried in the bureaucracy of the fledgling Department of Homeland Security. Even as major cyber-attacks, including one that grabbed between ten and twenty terabytes of data from the Pentagon, took place, cyber did not capture the attention of top officials as it should have.

This began to change during the second term of the Bush administration when, rather than viewing the threat cyber-attacks posed, the focus shifted to the promise of America's growing offensive capabilities in this area. The target was Iran's nuclear program. The White House wanted to slow it down or stop it and was weighing covert options. General James "Hoss" Cartwright and DNI Mike McConnell offered Bush and Hadley another option. The idea was to infiltrate the software within those facilities with bits of code that would essentially act as a virtual digital spy, sending back to the United States information about how the nuclear enrichment facilities worked.

Early on, because of their own advanced cyber capabilities and understanding of the targeted Iranian facility at Natanz, Israel became a partner in the initiative. The first phase of the effort, gathering information about the facility, took months. The next step was to fashion a cyber worm, called Stuxnet, that would cause Iranian centrifuges to speed up without warning or to stop suddenly. In either case, the result was not only mayhem at Natanz, it was the destruction of the centrifuges.

As awareness of the reach and impact of cyber grew within the administration, so too did new threats. In 2007, again prodded by McConnell, the president and Treasury Secretary Hank Paulson, when briefed about threats to America's financial system, urged that new action be taken. The immediate step was the Comprehensive National Cybersecurity Initiative (CNCI) and NSPD-54, both of which sought enhancements in protections of government networks. They did not address the systemic risk to American finance that McConnell had raised—in part because to address such risks required both technological understanding that did not exist within the White House and the kind of public-private partnership that was almost impossible when it came to issues that involved significant classified information.

At around the same time, the fledgling efforts at the US Strategic Command (STRATCOM) to manage cyber defense were recognized as inadequate to address the scope of the problem. A more comprehensive structure, better integrated with those who best understood the issues at the NSA (and less likely to be duplicative of them), became an objective championed by DNI McConnell and Hayden. Gates, who had also served as director of central intelligence during the Bush 41 administration, agreed that a new approach was necessary. He helped orchestrate an arrangement under which the head of the NSA would also direct Cyber Command even as Cyber Command (CYBERCOM) remained within STRATCOM. Individual service units would continue to have their own cyber operations, but all would be under the guidance of US CYBERCOM.

As a consequence, when Barack Obama took office, he found a much more robust cyber operation, one that, as his pre-inauguration briefing from Bush indicated, was already deeply engaged in the execution of the Olympic Games operation against Iran. He received more in-depth briefings on the Iran operation during his first few weeks in office. As with the drone program, Obama would make the key executive decisions regarding launching attacks and he was insistent that the programs remain secret and "unattributable."

With each success the program had in identifying weaknesses in the Natanz operation and then taking advantage of them, Obama became more involved. As often happens in Washington, as it was clear the cyber program was more important to the president, more officials in the White House sought to be brought up to date on the program. This is one way in which leadership works. Obama, who had promised to "make cyber-security the top priority that it should be in the twenty-first century" on the campaign trail, began to elevate cyber to a much more central role in US national security operations and strategies.

In terms of the evolving structure of the military and intelligence communities in cultivating US cyber capacity, a sixty-day review was undertaken, and again Clarke and others in the cyber community were disappointed with the results. "It was CNCI redux," in Clarke's words, with no true strategy, no plan "to defend the private sector" and no plans to "initiate international dialogue on cyberwar." The last point was particularly thorny. There were no doctrines to go with cyberwar. There was no clear understanding as to whether a cyber-attack, for example, might be used to justify a kinetic response. In Clarke's view, Obama also continued to tolerate the coordination gap at the top by failing to establish a person and an office "in the White House trying to orchestrate a government-wide, integrated cyber-security or cyber-war program."

In 2010, the Stuxnet worm was launched at approximately 1,000 machines central to the Iranian nuclear enrichment effort. All went according to the plan until a special challenge of cyberwarfare presented itself. When a bomb is dropped, it blows up not only the target, but itself. It doesn't leave bits and pieces around that can do more damage. All went according to the plan until the unexpected occurred. The ambitious operation came undone when someone at the Nantz facility unplugged the laptop from Iran's contained network and later reconnected it to the general internet. The worm spread across the World Wide Web where Iranian and other cyber pros could analyze it, pick it apart, and repurpose it to their own needs.

This was precisely what Obama did not want. Top US officials blamed the problem—predictably—on the Israelis.

The Washington Post would later report that, encouraged both by its successes and by the cyber escalation from countries like China, Iran, and Russia in 2011, the Obama administration and US intelligence services carried out 231 offensive cyber operations in 2011. This number is disputed by other experts, including *The New York Times'* Sanger, who argues that the true number of such attacks was a tiny fraction of that. But nonetheless, all agree that this is an area where each year is likely to see more activity and the development of new capabilities.

One of the most aggressive of US programs was code-named GENIE and sought to break into foreign networks and implant "back doors" into them that would allow the United States access into those networks whenever it might be of need. The US government considers these not as "offensive" operations but as "exploitation," a distinction that would no doubt be lost on us were the tables turned. It is estimated that the number of networks worldwide penetrated by GENIE was in excess of 85,000. At least 75 percent of all these intrusions took place on the watch of Barack Obama, constitutional lawyer, critic of Bush invasions, public champion of respect for international rights. The leaking of the nature of these programs and the descriptions of their pervasiveness created not only a massive diplomatic crisis for the United States and precisely the kind of "attributability" that Obama feared when he took office, it also went further, fueling a questioning of the credibility of the president and the US government. Many of those networks we tapped into were in allied nations. Many were owned by the private sector. No one, it seemed, was beyond being "exploited" by the NSA and CYBERCOM.

The effort to expand the reach of the US government into networks and computers worldwide employed dedicated centers like the NSA's Tailored Access Operations (TAO) group and its Remote Operations Center (ROC), which employs approximately 600 hackers working around the clock to break into targeted systems. In May 2012, *The Washington Post* reported that the Defense Advanced Research Projects Agency (DARPA) partnered with the private sector and universities to expand its capabilities and resilience. The goal of this effort, rather uncreatively dubbed Plan X, was to enhance the offensive capabilities of the US government in the cyber realm. The CIA's cyber unit became one of its biggest divisions. Because of the level of sophistication of the programs and how highly classified they were, they received comparatively less oversight— especially those at the NSA, which operated usually with considerable more freedom from view than did even the CIA. This puts policymakers at a remove—actually, a greater remove because so few of those actually involved in oversight actually understand the nature and scope of what is going on. The problem is compounded by the fact that so few lawmakers or senior policymakers want to admit they do not understand what they are being briefed on. In the words of one of the country's leading cyberspecialists, "our government is paying the price for our collective mathphobia. We just do not have the officials to do the oversight we need." The only solution in this one expert's eyes is to create a high-level cyber-czar in the US government to oversee all related activities across agencies who will be able to hold informed discussions among officials about oversight. He dismisses the senior director position responsible for this on the current NSC staff as being too junior to "do the heavy lifting that is involved." While I'm generally against the creation of czars and new departments to address problems among old ones, this is one case where doing so seems the right and only path forward to address the lack of oversight issue.

As former NSA and CIA director Mike Hayden observed about the nature of cyber briefings he has seen, "you've got the guy doing the cyber-briefing and three sentences in everyone in that room sitting at the table thinks he's Rain Man, okay? They have no understanding of what the man is presenting. A cyber event occurred during the Bush administration. It did not go as I expected. I was mad. I did my own after-action. And I could not find any two people who had been in that room who would agree on what it was they had approved. They each had a different version of what it was they thought they were raising their hand to." One very senior Obama NSC official echoed the critique: "if you tallied up the amount of time we've spent on cyber issues it would rank very, very high. It's something Obama's pushed himself. But in a way we're not ideally designed for that, in part because the people who are responsible for it, in the senior leadership positions within the NSC, are not steeped in that stuff. So we have officers and experts who can do it, but for the folks at the top of the process, this is not what comes naturally to them."

The problem is compounded, as Tara O'Toole, under secretary for science and technology at the Department of Homeland Security for the Obama administration, noted, because "Among the most damaging cyber effects in the U.S. are a result of industrial espionage . . . and the companies who know they have been hacked don't want to talk about the problem. So you start with the government only have kind of peripheral vision into the extent of the problem. . . . And then the other thing is the Congress doesn't include many people who understand what's happening or what to do about it."

Few understood the consequences or scope of the programs until Edward Snowden, a twenty-eight-year-old independent contractor without a college degree, absconded to Asia and later Russia with massive amounts of data that he systematically released to the press and, one way or another, to America's adversaries.

Although Snowden certainly violated the laws he agreed to uphold when he accepted his security clearance from the US government, he also shed light on a series of programs breathtaking in their scope and in their disregard for the concepts of individual privacy, information as private property, or national sovereignty. It triggered a backlash that was clearly not considered by the cyber architects in the US government. (I have often noted that one of the biggest problems with the US government is that it does not come with a department of consequences.) Countries worldwide—allies and rivals—began to reconsider Internet governance; some formally ceased working with US tech companies (especially after Snowden documents revealed how many had worked with the US government), and several started to rethink the whole idea of the Internet itself. The global blowback would cost American IT providers over $35 billion, according to one association's estimate; another estimated in excess of $100 billion. Worse, the Internet, widely seen as a driver of globalization, integration, converging values, and economic growth was suddenly a tool of of cyber-nationalism, of balkanization as countries like Russia, China, Brazil, India, and Iran considered how to reduce their vulnerability to US surveillance and information predation. As they did, they considered firewalls, new rules, more internal surveillance, embracing new and more secure Internet backbones, and in each case making it a little less easy for their people to connect with the United States and the rest of the planet.

It was a stunning setback. It was complemented by revelations that the government's cyber overreach via a surveillance program called PRISM had included spying on the leaders of America's closest allies, scooping up records of hundreds of millions of phone calls worldwide, and even warehousing the metadata from phone calls within the United States, thus raising real questions of the constitutionality of the efforts. One document showed that in March 2013 there were 97 billion pieces of data collected from networks worldwide. The rationale for undertaking these efforts was that, because terrorists could be almost anyone anywhere, we needed information on essentially everyone everywhere to help us track them down. Tortured logic was advanced to suggest that capturing all the data and storing it but not actually reading it until it was needed was proof of "compliance" with American principles. But surely, had the United States systematically sought to go door to door in your neighborhood and seize all your papers, the argument that they would not read them until later would certainly not placate you or the family next door.

The stakes rose when it was considered that almost all data was now being created in searchable digital form. According to IBM, 2.5 billion new bytes of data are created daily, a pace so brisk that it would mean approximately 90 percent of all data that exists was created in the past two years. This is just the start of "the Big Data" era, a period in which sensors everywhere and new computing devices implanted in household appliances, factory machines, and clothing will all be grabbing information and pumping it into the Internet all the time. By 2020, it is estimated there will be 50 billion devices on the Internet. All this means that the temptation and costs of cyberwarfare, surveillance, and hacking will only grow.

Director of National Intelligence James Clapper defended the program, insisting that "the government 'does not unilaterally obtain information from the servers' of telephone and Internet providers, saying that information is turned over only under court order, when there is a documented foreign intelligence purpose for acquisition of the data." Clapper did not placate many Americans unsettled by the scope of the government's activities. (According to one report in the *Wall Street Journal*, the Foreign Intelligence Surveillance Court heard over 33,000 cases in thirty-three years and declined to issue surveillance warrants for just 11 of them—or .03 percent of all requests.)

Lisa Monaco, the Justice Department lawyer who replaced John Brennan in the basement West Wing office of the counterterrorism advisor to the president, defends the court's low rejection rate. She argues there is "a lot of misunderstanding about the FISA process." She says, "I think what people don't understand is that with a 99.9 percent success rate in approving affidavits there is actually a very robust back and forth between the government and the court before the approval happens. So, for example, the court will get the draft affidavit and might say: 'that's not good enough; I don't understand why X, Y, and Z. And if you don't bring me back more, I'm not going to approve it.' But what the public is seeing is just the end result of that back and forth discussion between the court and the Executive Branch."

Meanwhile, the rest of the world was not standing still. In China, Unit 63198 was busily beavering into US networks. The US government expressed outrage, and Tom Donilon made it a focus of his high-level meetings with the Chinese. What was not revealed until almost exactly a year after the Mandiant report came out—again thanks to revelations from Snowden published by *The New York Times, The Guardian,* and *Der Spiegel*—was that while America was howling about China spying on its companies, it had penetrated companies like China's tech giant Huawei and installed "backdoors" on Huawei systems worldwide, essentially using the exports of the Chinese company as a way of expanding America's intelligence reach even further. We did not, argued US officials, pass the intelligence we gathered onto US companies to help them compete. Therefore our theft of information was somehow more defensible than that of the Chinese who sought to profit off theirs as well as enhance their national defense. It was a feeble defense, and not redolent of the moral high ground.

US government protestations grew less convincing over time. When news of spying on foreign leaders broke in late 2013, the White House spokesperson responded by saying that the president had no idea about the scope of the programs. He went on to say, "we have made it clear that the president spoke with Chancellor Merkel [of Germany] and assured her that we do not and will not collect intelligence on her communications." This was later demonstrated not to be true. Similarly, James Clapper's claims and those of NSA chief Keith Alexander that the surveillance had been effective in preventing terrorist attacks was also called into question when independent studies showed that it had offered little or no benefit in that critical respect.

A study by the Privacy and Civil Liberties Oversight Board released in draft form in early July 2014 and summarized in *The Guardian* concluded that the NSA's 702 program, which permitted gathering massive amounts of foreign data, had been of value. The draft report stated, "It has played a key role in discovering and disrupting specific terrorist plots aimed at the United States and other countries." The report did recommend placing constraints on the US government's ability to conduct warrantless collection of US data, and it disputed NSA assertions that the 702 searches had been central to the disruption of fifty-four terror plots. Finally, the report noted that it was "impressed with the rigor" of the government's targeting of surveillance efforts.

In other words, not only were the programs not doing what they were supposed to be doing, and not only was the government not doing what it was supposed to be doing, it was making everybody angry and not producing the kind of material benefits such a breathtaking, wide-ranging undertaking should have. Its problems were compounded by the fact that it was, well, the government. Communications and processes weren't very good when they needed to be. One Obama administration senior official with direct responsibility for cyber issues told me that they did not see the presidential report on protecting critical infrastructure until the day the White House released it.

Recognizing the scope of the crisis, Barack Obama created a commission to examine the surveillance programs and to come back with recommendations to establish guidelines that would enhance security outcomes, reduce the potential for violations of personal privacy of innocent citizens worldwide, and improve oversight. The group included Richard Clarke, former deputy CIA director Michael Morrell, and Professor Cass Sunstein, the husband of Samantha Power. They were unsettled by the results of their investigation. They found mass surveillance programs, whose overseers had argued were effective tools against terrorism, offering almost zero measurable benefits. When they presented this finding, they were told that the programs were also useful for screening potential suspects. However, when the individual offering that defense was challenged as to how that could be the case when under 30 percent of all data traffic was tracked by the program, this defense, too, was completely undercut.

The December 2013 report, entitled "Liberty and Security in a Changing World," calls on the president to end some of the intelligence community's most controversial practices such as the collection and storage of personal information. They also cited hoarding bulk meta-data and pressuring tech companies to share its customers' private information. They concluded by "recommending prior judicial review except in emergencies" and then doing so in as narrow and as focused a fashion as possible. Some of the steps it encourages to protect the rights of individuals, both US-citizens and those abroad, include establishing strict guidelines for legitimate use of these tools aboard, supporting research into more refined collection methods that would alleviate the need for metadata, creating increased transparency on the collection of information, and strengthening the Civil Liberties and Privacy Protection Board. It also called for increased structural oversight by means of requiring a high-level internal review process on collections and the process therein, an enhanced oversight role for the DNI, improved communication between the intelligence community and policymakers, and breaking up the joint-leadership role of the civil NSA and military Cyber Command, then held by General Keith Alexander.

In the end, President Obama embraced the report and has begun to implement its policy recommendations selectively. In January 2014, he required NSA analysts to appeal to the Foreign Intelligence Surveillance Court before pulling records from the phone records database and narrowing the number of associated phone numbers, or hops, they can then look at from three to two. Two months later, the administration proposed barring the NSA from accessing data held by private telecommunications companies. Congress, whose efforts to pass surveillance and cybersecurity reform thus far have been predictably disappointing, took a step forward in June when the House of Representatives passed a bill barring the NSA and the CIA from pushing tech companies to install back doors, like those revealed to be used in the intelligence community's international activities, in their commercial products. While the bill passed the House by a large, bipartisan majority, it is unclear at the time of this writing if the Senate will follow suit and send the bill to President Obama's desk to sign.

For all of the questions raised by some of the sweeping programs revealed by Snowden, the surveillance programs of the US government include some targeted efforts that are widely regarded within the intelligence and policy communities as extremely helpful. And new capabilities are emerging daily. Although these will require vigilance to avoid future violations of civil liberties, there is also a sense that on the cyber side, as with drones and the development of light-footprint approaches for combating terror, important steps have been taken that actually enhance the security of the American people and reduce the likelihood of future attacks like those that ushered in this era.

These tools have made such a marked difference in US counterterrorism efforts that intelligence community leaders are becoming comfortable with the idea of relaxing other controversial practices. Mike Hayden noted that one reason he was willing to "empty the prisons" and "scale back on the authorized interrogation techniques" is that he was not "nearly as desperate as [Director of Central Intelligence] George [Tenet] was back in 2002, 2003. I've got agent networks. I've got penetrations. I've built up a strong human intelligence collection efforts. I'm less dependent on capturing and questioning than I was in 2002. More sources. Better electronic intelligence. You're hitting on all cylinders now. And with the requisite intelligence, it enables your orthoscopic stuff" (meaning "surgical" or "light-footprint' activities").

Lisa Monaco asserts, "I think the US government has done a good job of creating a counterterrorism structure and apparatus—operationally and policy-wise—to learn the lessons of 9/11 and have an ability to meet the threats that we face, share information, apply the right kind of military, intelligence, diplomatic, and law enforcement tools today. . . . As an example, say we know a terrorist is transiting Germany. We have an apparatus to reach out: The FBI will talk to its German counterparts, share information, get their assistance within the bounds of the rule of law to try and detain that person. So, we have a process. We share intelligence. We try and disrupt that threat." Although she acknowledges the systems are not quite as evolved on the cybersecurity side, the point is that—despite metastasizing terror threats worldwide, and confusion and ill-conceived programs on the cyber front—the national security apparatus of the US government is in a number of important ways fulfilling its core mission of helping to make America and Americans safer.

CHAPTER 11

A Challenge
for the Next President

To conquer fear is the beginning of wisdom.

—BERTRAND RUSSELL

Being President of the United States is the loneliest job in the world. Or so it is said. If you search for the term in Google images, pictures of Barack Obama appear. It must be true.

No one can fully understand the pressures each president faces at any given moment, or the responsibilities with which she or he must contend, but there should be some consolation for those who someday occupy the White House in the fact that no president can do the job alone.

To successfully fulfill the oath of office that each president must utter, "to preserve, protect and defend," each modern president must successfully manage the biggest and most complex organization on the face of the earth. (By one count the US Department of Defense alone is the world's biggest employer with 3.2 million employees.) She or he must find a way to initiate and manage the collaborations, interactions, and conflicts between that government and America's fifty states, its municipalities, other nations around the world, and multilateral organizations, as well as a wide swath of private sector organizations, non-state actors, and individuals. Complicating matters are the realities of dealing with more than 315 million bosses and an unruly set of 535 often unwilling, downright ornery collaborators at the far end of Pennsylvania Avenue (not to mention their staffs, the media, and an Internet full of critics).

This means that being president is at its lonely heart a fantastically complex collaboration. Good managers and collaborators succeed. Bad ones stumble because they fail to delegate power, to communicate effectively to their team, to offer the leadership that is necessary, to listen to advice with the openness that is necessary, or to pick the right partners with which to work.

When it comes to dealing with the rest of the world, the instrument of that collaboration is the National Security Council. It is the primary mechanism by which the President of the United States receives guidance on the international matters with which he must deal and oversees the implementation of the decisions he makes. Created in 1947, in the wake of war years during which President Franklin Roosevelt succeeded in spite of his shortcomings as a manager, the NSC was a kind of plea by the top-level survivors of that effort to make sure that things worked better in a future they also saw as fraught with danger.

The National Security Act of 1947 describes the members of the NSC, the principal advisors to the president, but it only hints at the idea of the staff to support that group. As a consequence, the size of the NSC staff has ebbed and flowed over the years, most iterations growing larger, but always changing to reflect the desires of the president. No other major institution in the US government is so entirely dependent on each individual president for its shape, size, role, and details of its operation. Each president gets the NSC he wants or, to a great extent, deserves. As we have seen, the president can give and take power from individuals at will and sometimes by whim. If the president chooses to consult a junior staffer or a top political advisor rather than the national security advisor or the secretary of state, or if he favors one advisor over another, he rewrites the org chart of the US government with his attention, with a tilt of the head in one direction, or with a simple walk around the South Lawn of the White House. How the group is structured and how it is used to manage the major agencies of the US government and America's interaction with the world are therefore tasks that deserve priority consideration from any incoming president because they will be shaping and changing it whether they intend to or not, and they will manage it either actively or inadvertently.

During the past ten years, while we have seen triumphs of the process and the workaday provision of services on which affairs of state depend, we have also seen great dysfunction and errors that have shaken the world to its foundations and raised questions about America's international standing. We have watched as the Bush administration grappled to learn the lessons of its first term and we have watched as the Obama administration failed to learn some of those lessons. We have seen senior officials ignore the best lessons of the past and we have seen them and the institutions with which they must work unprepared for surprises that should not have been surprises, for emerging technologies of communication and of conflict, and for the leadership demands of a volatile and unforgiving world.

We know the stakes. That is why when, as a new president takes the oath of office in January 2017 and settles into the White House, it will behoove that person to have a clear plan not just for how to use America's national security apparatus but how they want to reinvent it. With some luck, by listening to the voices and studying the stories covered within the pages of books like this one, the new president will find some clues about the best way forward to meet the challenges of once again remaking an institution that will celebrate its seventieth birthday during the new president's first year in office. As with anything or anyone seventy years old, appreciating the best of what is past and maintaining a revitalizing focus on the future and the resolve needed to adapt to it will be the key to success in this respect.

Timing Is Everything

With some luck, the new occupant of the Oval Office will not face a period defined by crises. Indeed, the declinism that has accompanied each momentary downturn in America's recent fortunes may well be abating, along with the other aspects of the age of fear mentality we have discussed. Whoever wins the next election will almost certainly do so by offering the most optimistic vision of the future proffered by the candidates in the race. That's the way American presidential elections have worked in recent years. That candidate will win because the American people believe that he or she can bring an end to the unease that has prevailed through the Bush and Obama eras. Just as the electorate hoped that Bush would bring an end to the controversies and divisiveness of the late Clinton years and that Obama would bring an end to the polarization and international setbacks associated with Bush, the next president will win by offering the most compelling case that he can do better than his or her predecessors.

With some luck voters will recognize that choosing a candidate who actually has international experience matters in the modern world. It is no accident that those presidents with the most such experience have managed our international affairs most effectively and creatively—notably Eisenhower, George H. W. Bush, and even Richard Nixon. Next best are those with relevant experience of some sort who can learn from their mistakes—Bill Clinton comes to mind as one of the better such examples—because those without an international track record will almost certainly make major errors.

Part of the success or failure of the next president will turn, of course, not on policies but on prevailing trends and events within the United States and associated with America's place in the world.

In this respect, the next president stands a reasonable chance of being dealt a better hand than those laid down before George W. Bush or Barack Obama.

America in 2017 will still be the richest and most powerful nation on earth, and its economy should be growing, continuing to recover from the shocks of the worst economic crisis in three-quarters of a century. What's more, it will still be the richest and most powerful nation on earth not by a little but by a lot.

While China may boast a bigger GDP, in purchasing power parity terms, on a per capita basis, nonetheless, the US has the clear edge in terms of natural resources, in terms of the ability to translate those resources into global power, in terms of the vitality and depth of our capital markets, and in terms of the ability of our private sector, scientists, technologists, and other innovators to fuel American rebirth. So too will our unique network of international alliances, an asset that may be old and in need of refreshing but one that in its scope is unlike that of any power in history. Our system, for all its flaws and inequities, contains the seeds of its own reinvention. This is why we rebounded from the economic crisis faster than other developed powers. You may not have liked TARP, but when the US government got together with the leaders of the US financial community, and hard decisions were made with the resources available, pain was inflicted but the rebound came.

For all these reasons America will also continue to have the intangible benefit associated with the expectation of global leadership. We have seen it even at moments of the greatest doubt in the past two presidencies. Not only can no nation lead as America can, but of all the nations with great power, America is the one most will still look to before they act themselves. The most uncomfortable measure of this is the palpable disappointment expressed by so many in the world when America fails to step up to lead as only it can do at the moment. Who would have predicted during the darkest moments associated with America's invasion of Iraq that a few years later the next president would be assailed by some of our closest friends in the Middle East for doing too little rather than too much? It is painfully hard to get this balance right, impossible perhaps. There will always be critics. But no other nation faces that burden of expectation that has been both a great asset and sometimes a great liability.

New developments are likely to fuel the perception of American renaissance. One of these will simply be the recognition we have finally dodged the bullets and outlived most of the consequences of the upheavals of the past few years. Another is that the United States, given recent energy discoveries, is entering a new period in which it will be the world's leading energy consumer *and* producer. Further, not only will it still be true that no nation has the ability to project force as America does, anywhere on earth—from space, from the air, from the sea, on the land—but America will have cultivated the capacity to project influence by means of new technologies, many of which are homegrown or in which American scientists, companies, and government agencies are undisputed world leaders. So for example we will dominate in the cyber realms where much of the world's commerce, politics, education, and social interchange take place. America has the world's leading system of higher education and leads in many next-generation technologies from 3-D printing and advanced manufacturing to biotech. What is more, America has major geographic advantages. Our two closest neighbors and trading partners, Mexico and Canada, are peaceful, friendly, and prospering. Both have significant energy resources, growing manufacturing capabilities, increasing standards of living, and tight relations with the United States. In fact, demographic trends suggest a rebound of influence for North America as the US population is projected to grow to almost 400 million people by 2050, kept younger than the average in places like Europe, Japan, and China because of our embrace of immigrants. Mexico will grow to be 150 million. Canada will grow to be over 41 million. Meanwhile, if current demographic trends hold, China will actually start to contract and will be home to a population that is, on average, a couple of years older than that of North America. Further, of course, we are still surrounded by what some have called our "liquid assets," the Atlantic and Pacific Oceans, which keep us largely insulated from the troubles that bedevil so many parts of the world.

For all of these reasons and the fact that many of America's potential rivals are struggling economically, socially, and politically, and virtually all face major transitions and challenges, it is not unreasonable to project that America can and likely will play the central role that it had become accustomed to for decades to come. But to do so, our next leader, and those who follow, must address a host of challenges within. It is clear from the events of the past few years that a number of urgent priorities in the area of managing and developing US national security and foreign policy loom ahead.

As was the case a generation ago, the clues as to where America will need to do better are all around us—in the lessons learned from the errors of the past decade and a half and in the clues offered up by the world. Some of the areas of concern are process or institutional "gaps" or short-comings, with lessons to be learned by studying what has and has not worked within the national security apparatus of the Bush and Obama administrations. Other areas of concern center on intellectual, doctrinal, or policy gaps associated with bigger trends and emerging issues. In certain areas of special vulnerability, these two sets of gaps intersect and compound one another. The next stewards of the NSC will need to keep these facts in mind as they reshape yet again this most plastic of institutions and rethink the way America's national security and foreign policy apparatus writ large works.

To Begin: Know What Not to Change

There are few case studies that so compellingly underscore the virtues of the NSC structure as the administration of George W. Bush. Admittedly, this is a statement that will shock many who still think of him primarily in terms of the calamities associated with his first four or five years in office. That was a period in which the system, though filled with dedicated and competent people, broke down and delivered policies and execution as bad or worse than all but a few periods in recent history.

This was due to reasons repeatedly cited in this book and in *Running the World*: being reactive; letting ideology drive decision-making; failing to enforce a coherent policy process; letting the vice president and secretary of defense shut down or shut out dissenting voices such as those in the State Department; letting them work outside the system—backdooring it, ignoring its decisions, and going to the president with their own proposals independently; allowing major policy decisions like disbanding the Iraqi Army to happen without a clear, accountable decision process; an inexperienced president; a national security advisor who spent too much time directly supporting the president and too little managing the process itself; and making some bad major personnel decisions.

But then came the second term. With a few key personnel changes and a reversion to the kind of structures and approaches found in the best-working NSCs, performance improved tremendously. Reinvention was not needed. Simple attentiveness to a few long-established rules was. Steven Hadley had studied those rules as a protégé of General Brent Scowcroft, the man who is viewed as the gold standard among national security advisors. Hadley accepted the fact that being national security advisor was a staff job in which, vital though his role was, he was not there to compete with the secretary of state as a spokesperson, and not to become operational, traveling around the world managing big negotiations. He came with a clear management philosophy that involved working to earn and maintain the support of the cabinet as an honest broker of their views. Vitally, he had not only the deep trust of the president to begin with but he had an exceptionally close and established track record with Secretary of State Condoleezza Rice as her former deputy. Bringing in Bob Gates, an established national security professional who, as a former deputy national security advisor to Brent Scowcroft had deep respect for a disciplined policy process, quickly undid the difficulties of the rogue and uncontrollable Rumsfeld, a creative man of often interesting ideas undone by his self-interested bureaucratic ethos. Having a strong White House chief of staff who respected the process was also vitally important. It is often underestimated in the functioning of the NSC and the government as a whole, but few jobs other than that of president are actually more important to establishing the culture of the administration. Further strengthening the team—because the process is only as good as the people within it—with Hank Paulson and giving him the lead in areas where he knew best, including not only the management of the financial crisis but also the China portfolio, was another plus. The fact that he, Gates, and Rice were all committed to managing their agencies well was another key lesson of past successful administrations.

Central to the changes that were made was that the president was committed to learning on the job, to empowering his team, to being engaged in the hardest problems, and to reaching out to other leaders worldwide—critical jobs that require a president. George W. Bush will never be seen as a great president, but if there were a grade for greatest growth in the office he would score high. He and his team have some very considerable accomplishments to their name that are often overshadowed by the errors they made.

In short, the system works pretty well when basic rules are acknowledged and followed, and it can be fixed fairly rapidly if, as will certainly happen again in the future, the cocktail of people involved becomes toxic, events shock it into bad patterns, politics becomes too influential in its management, or a president is unprepared to lead the group.

During the Obama years, each of these basic lessons was proven again, sometimes in the breach. This took place when junior staffers were allowed by the president to undercut and backdoor General Jones; when a small coterie of political advisors and "true believers" created an exclusionary, parallel process for the innermost circle of advisors and essentially cut out many in the NSC and the cabinet from the roles they were intended to play; and when the president remained aloof from his team and his international counterparts. As the NSC became more operational throughout the Obama years in micromanaging counter-terror operations, for example, or usurping from the State Department roles in interactions with senior international officials, or in conducting high-profile international missions, it faltered and was unable to perform its core functions of strategic planning, coordinating policy development, and overseeing policy implementation. Also, as we have seen, top national security officials failed to understand core economic or technological concerns and failed to seek the advice and collaboration of those in the government who did possess the knowledge they needed. But we have also seen clearly positive outcomes result when the core principles of managing the process were adhered to. This was most clearly the case during the tenure of Tom Donilon; when the president was involved and decisive and a clear leader of the process as during the final days of the mission to get Osama bin Laden; and when cabinet secretaries worked in close tandem with the White House, clearly empowered by it but also on the same page, as with the rebalancing to Asia in the Obama first term, the work that produced the New START Treaty in 2011, or key elements of the management of the Iran negotiations and sanctions process. Conversely, when the lessons of the past are not heeded and there is insufficient growth in the president and his team, second terms can be materially worse than the first.

Susan Rice is every bit as capable a national security advisor in terms of pure talent as her predecessors, but it is unclear as of this writing that she is willing to or capable of being the kind of behind-the-scenes manager a national security advisor must be. She has too often sought the limelight as when she conducted high-profile missions to Afghanistan or Israel where she acted much as if she were a secretary of state rather than a national security advisor. (Donilon also led such missions but did so with a much lighter tread in the media.) Rice has not sought to truly build the trust of her cabinet colleagues and there is regularly tension and daylight between the White House, the State Department, and the Defense Department. She has, according to NSC staffers, upbraided her team in large meetings and alienated some among them. Neither has she sought to reverse the ever-growing concentration of power into the ever-growing shadow cabinet that the NSC has become, nor has her president demanded it of her. Indeed, they do not seem to realize that because they assume roles the White House is not capable of fulfilling, they thereby make it impossible to perform the roles that they could and should be doing, like focusing on strategic planning and overseeing an active and creative policy process.

Importantly, as Bush showed in his second term, as Clinton showed in his second term, and as Reagan's NSC showed late in his second term, it is possible to grow, to learn, to get better. But it's a bit like the old joke about how many psychotherapists it takes to change a lightbulb. It only takes one. But the lightbulb really has got to want to change.

It is important to separate these failures of process that can be fixed through management, vision, discipline, and pulling together the right human beings for the jobs in question from those of bad policy or failed leadership. We have seen those too. Often they come when leaders place their political calculus ahead of the long-term national interests at stake in any issue. But sometimes they come by other means. Bad judgment. Risk aversion. The fear of failure. Too little appreciation for potential risks. A failure to read history. The character of the president and of the members of his team. But there should also be comfort in another lesson of the NSC and what is sound in its approach. Like any other properly designed government structure it is not designed so it only works when it is led by great men and women. Such people come around seldom. In fact, it is a vitally important process precisely for this reason: it is designed to offset the weaknesses of any individual and to supplement them with the strengths of a team. It should also help provide a filter to clear away the noise of the public debate of the moment and issues of emotion and fleeting mood. In the end, therefore, the principal reason that future presidents should embrace what is best about the structure and the principles of managing it that have evolved over these past almost seven decades is because it is a process designed with their limitations in mind. If they are self-aware, they should find some comfort in the process's capacity to bridge the gap between those limitations and the performance and protections the country demands.

Having said all that, and fully appreciating the workings of the system when it is managed properly (which, I hasten to add, probably does not require more but instead fewer people on the NSC staff because it will allow more responsibility to revert to the agencies that are prepared to do the work), there are still areas where revision and change are needed. An illustrative set of descriptions of a few such needs follows.

Closing the Creativity Gap

Washington is inherently reactive. As noted in the Introduction, the think tank community, which is theoretically employed to drive the conversation forward and blaze new intellectual trails, plays the official game of the city—a form of mental peewee soccer, crowding around the ball, the issue of the day, the issue most likely to get picked up in the media, the one most likely to get the big thinker into the next administration. This habit is made worse by several other factors.

First, in order to move from the policy community to a role in government, one often has to go through confirmation by the Senate. Given the political gamesmanship that has made this process more difficult in recent years, the system seeks not necessarily the best and the brightest but, often, the safest and the blandest. Presenting contrarian, unconventional, or controversial opinions might inflame just a single senator, who can nonetheless block a nomination, creating an insurmountable career roadblock. So intellectual caution ends up being rewarded—which is risky at any time but is especially dangerous in times of great change, when adaptability, insight, and the willingness to embrace and understand new ideas is essential.

If such conditions prevail year in and year out, not only do you get incentives misaligned with real needs, you end up with a community in which those who have the great success and longevity are selected for the wrong reasons. At the same time, those selectees gain more and more influence as they rise through the ranks. They in turn promote others like them and foster a culture in which they are comfortable. You therefore get think tanks, academic institutions, and journals that are hotbeds of incrementalism rather than the leaps of creativity the country needs.

Finally, heuristic biases—the inevitable shortcuts that people's minds, and, by extension, the institutions and processes those minds manage—make matters worse. These include using the recent past or familiar examples to drive judgments about the future or what might be needed for the future. Or they too heavily base estimates of future risks or costs on past experiences. Or they let past successes or failures or challenges too greatly influence their sense of where future such successes, failures, or challenges might lie.

Changes are clearly needed in a system of think tanks and policy journals that must break out of this mold. New technologies make such changes much easier. It is much easier today for younger voices to be heard, to reach out to new pockets of insight and talent outside the Beltway, to create virtual conversations, to create global interaction. Some think tanks, like the Carnegie Endowment, with which I have been affiliated, and the Brookings Institution, are doing pioneering work in building global coalitions and discussions. So too are some media organizations. But clearly, given the parochial nature of Washington, its institutions, and the system of rewards and obstacles that exist within it, this has been and will likely remain an uphill struggle for some time to come.

We have seen the toll taken by Washington culture during the past decade and a half. We have seen the cost of groupthink. We have seen hyper-partisanship lead to an inability to act. We have seen the cost of fighting the last war. Most recently, we have seen the cost of letting a political mentality and political advisors drive foreign-policy decisions. Politics necessarily has a short-term focus—the next poll, the next primary, the next general election. Foreign-policy decisions are supposed to involve weighing the long-term national interest. Foreign policy cannot be conducted by opinion poll—the American people historically have wanted to turn away from the world even when it was not in our interest to do so, as in the days right before World War II. Leaders must sometimes lead in directions that are uncomfortable for those who put them in office. To do so requires not only courage but strategy, which in turn requires foresight.

It is not a strategy to simply undo the mistakes of the recent past. It is not a strategy to give a visionary speech. Recent years in which speeches have been treated as deliverables in and of themselves have demonstrated that real strategy requires not only clear long-term goals but day-to-day blocking and tackling, cultivating relationships, weighing priorities, anticipating historical shifts. But even having a strategy is not enough. It also has to be the right strategy. We have seen both wrong strategies and the absence of clear strategy in the last two presidencies.

Some of these changes need to be interpolated into the institutions of government responsible for making policy decisions. Few people understand those needs better than Leon Panetta, whose lifetime of experience has given him a view of Washington from Congress and from the executive branch that is unparalleled among his peers. He observes with regard to the national security apparatus, "the NSC has to operate on two tracks. One is you obviously have to deal with crises. But the second has to be a creative side of the NSC that is looking at bigger issues—looking at cyber, looking at how we are dealing with Latin America, how we deal with Africa. How do we build the alliances that we need for the future? How do we deal with upgrading and managing our nuclear arsenal?" Panetta admits there are a host of major problems we haven't faced up to. He envisions "an almost think tank aspect of the NSC that allows some of these key people to sit in a room, not consumed by the crisis, not consumed by politics, not consumed by what the hell the *New York Times* or the *Washington Post* is going to say, but can spend some time just talking about where the hell are we going in the future in some of these big areas. . . . I'm talking about actually framing policies that ultimately the president can wrap his arms around and say, this is what we're going to do. This has to be action-oriented."

Brent Scowcroft, the acknowledged master of the US national security process, frames it this way: "during the Cold War, we were facing nuclear war if we screwed up. That was an incentive to get it right, to stay ahead of developments. Today, we have no strategy that covers the entire world, the changes that are coming. And there's a lot of change going on. For 500 years, we lived under Westphalian nation-state systems. But globalization has eroded borders. For the first time this world's people are politicized, interconnected by technology. The nature of power is changing. The nature of international cooperation is changing. The nature of conflict is changing. We're not evolving well to adapt. This world is not as dangerous as that during the Cold War but it is *much* more complicated."

"Technology Makes the World Now. It Is the World."

Nowhere are the gaps in the system clearer or more dangerous than in the areas of science and technology. The pace of change is breathtaking. Nothing illustrates that like the story of the national security challenges we have faced, the threats that have emerged, and the solutions, tactics, and strategies that we have embraced in the years since the attacks of 9/11. Today, the cutting edge of American military technology used to combat terror are fleets of unmanned aircraft linked to batteries of operators a world away, depending on networks of aircraft and satellites, and massive processing power. They are guided by intelligence that combs the Internet with new surveillance capacity and they are augmented by cyber-offensive capacities that would enable the United States to effectively shut down entire societies without firing a single shot. And our enemies and rivals, and even some of our friends, are employing similar techniques, not just to fight wars, but to steal ideas from us in times of relative peace.

We know several things about these developments. The trends that led to them will not only continue but accelerate. We also know that new changes driven by these trends as well as by emerging developments in advanced manufacturing, advanced materials, neuroscience, bioscience, and the science of creating and harnessing energy will likely be just as transformational, perhaps more so. We know that the pace of change in these areas will accelerate. And we know, from studying what the policy community focuses on, that we won't have as many informed discussions in think tanks as we need. We won't even have the thinkers we need. And finally, we know that however bad the situation is in the policy community, it is worse in the US government.

One senior Obama administration official said even in some of its most tech-savvy precincts the government suffers from "the horse and helicopter problem. The government keeps asking for a faster horse when what they need is a helicopter. But they don't know about helicopters."

It's not that great scientists don't work for the US government. It's not that the government does not play a central role in developing important technologies. It's that those scientists and technologists seldom penetrate the top ranks of government. When they do—as in the case of Obama secretary of energy and Nobel Prize–winning physicist Dr. Steven Chu—they find themselves speaking a language their colleagues don't understand and, as was the case with Chu, being derided by the Washington establishment for their lack of "political skills." No matter how partisan and dysfunctional Washington becomes, it is always united by a few things. It is fundamentally conservative—with a small *c*. It doesn't like change. It has a terrible case of not-invented-here-ism, rejecting outsiders and outside ideas with a time-tested political immune-system response that gangs up on intruders much like leukocytes swarm on a virus and work hard to kill it. And, soaring rhetoric of the pols aside, it is dominated by a "think small" mentality that focuses on risk and self-interest, often to the detriment of those the system is supposed to be serving.

Finally, and perhaps more important than any other point above, whereas much of the greatest change of the modern era in America was driven by a public-private partnership between Washington and the scientific community, that partnership has broken down. Admittedly, much of that partnership came in times of crisis in order to overcome many of the obstacles the country faced. World War II and the Cold War drove much of it. But throughout those periods, from radar to the Internet, from space science to materials science, to breakthroughs in public health, an essential component of America's greatness was tapping into what can happen when the needs and resources of government meet with the creativity of the private sector to find new solutions and then translate them into benefits for society. Unfortunately, in recent decades, that process has atrophied. Much of what is new in science and technology is now being cultivated in places like Silicon Valley, where with much capital available (largely thanks to a venture capital industry that developed out of government-based financing programs during the Eisenhower administration) and a "let's go out in the garage and make it happen" mentality, there is a sense that the techies don't need government. The political mood in Silicon Valley and along much of Route 128 and in other tech centers across the United States runs somewhere along a spectrum between anarchic and libertarian. Government's role is minimized, and the approach to interacting with government has developed much like that of Wall Street—"don't call us, we'll call you." Recently, that has led Google, Microscoft, Facebook, and Amazon, among others, to establish lobbying offices in Washington to make sure regulators don't screw up their payday. As Tara O'Toole, Homeland Security's science and technology under secretary put it, "I think the center of gravity has changed. People now believe that innovation's center of gravity has shifted to California. Silicon Valley has a mystique and special luster associated with it—along with a long list of products and companies that people admire. But in the minds of its leaders, this success is of its own making and has nothing to do with government—even though all the technologies in the iPhone and iPad (GPS, Siri, touch screen, etc.) was funded by the U.S. government. But a lot of people from the IT world see the government as irrelevant, or worse. One senior official from a big tech company told me 'I would never hire anyone who had worked for state or federal government.' I asked why not and he said, 'Because I'd assume they're either stupid or lazy or both.' This arrogance and disdain for government is uneducated and dangerous, but quite pervasive."

She continued, "During and immediately after WWII, top scientists like Vannevar Bush worked very closely with the President and the Sec-Def and other top officials. Over time, R&D became more disconnected from agency missions—until Sputnik, when Eisenhower created DARPA. Today, Congressional leaders especially think that the private sector can produce most of the innovation the country needs. The essential role of government in funding high risk research—even the role government actually played in funding the IT revolution—is not understood."

But she noted that the gap is a two-way street, that government doesn't want to listen even when the private sector has something valuable to add. Talking to her, I recall a circumstance I had encountered myself when a company I worked with discovered signs on the Internet of a disease outbreak in China. It later turned out to be the first signs of the SARS outbreak. We had used open-source intelligence analysis to spot a major development almost three months before the World Health Organization identified the crisis as such. We went to the Center for Disease Control with the information and they rebuffed us. They wouldn't take information from the private sector. "It's probably no wonder we're so bad at this kind of collaboration," O'Toole said, "when you consider how bad we are at the interagency stuff. During the West Nile outbreak in 1999 in New York City, a veterinarian at the Bronx Zoo knew that the CDC's first call, saying it was Saint Louis encephalitis, was wrong because the emus didn't die of it and they should have. They wouldn't take her call. This is the vet from the Bronx Zoo. She finally gets through to their head neurologist in the Rocky Mountain lab and he basically blew her off and yelled at her. 'We're CDC and we don't talk to you civilians,' was his attitude."

The bigger gap is at the top. Jake Sullivan, clearly a rising star in the US national security firmament, is a former head of State Department's policy planning operation and was subsequently the top national security advisor to Vice President Biden. As he put it, "one of the biggest gaps in policymaking today is that we often don't have good means of marrying up the people who understand politics and foreign policy and people who understand science, technology, and other complicated fields. Cyber is the best example where it is so difficult to take people who know the architecture of a network better than anyone and overlap them with the deputies committee—people who can see the big picture and understand priorities and trade-offs—and produce a reasoned, informed policy at the end of the day." In a world of great technical complexity—and the example Sullivan adds of finance is a good one—the generalist policymaker is simply not really equipped to understand the options on the table. This not only leads to gaps in the decision process, it also can lead to the tyranny of the expert—be it an official at the Treasury Department who is one of three people in the US government who truly understand the complexities of international derivative markets, or a cluster of hackers living within the bowels of the NSA who understand the full implications of releasing a particular worm into another country's critical infrastructure.

Hormats, the veteran of five administrations, has considered these issues and feels one way to help address them might be a modest restructuring in places like the State Department (although his thought process can and should be applied when considering the structure of the NSC and other agencies). He says, "it is all about giving the science, technology, and financial/economic issues sufficient weight and the individuals sufficient voice. In the economics bureau at State after the restructuring we did under Secretary Clinton, we combined economics, energy, and the environment—making energy a new bureau because we thought the importance of that subject and its strategic significance required an assistant secretary level person. The department's science advisor and a technology group were also in the E group, but they were not at assistant secretary level, unfortunately. As an illustration of how to address the problem, I would certainly recommend adding one new assistant secretary for science and technology to the group and giving them the ability to recruit outstanding talent from the private and public sectors and from the very best universities and research centers. That would strengthen the department's capacity to conduct twenty-first century diplomacy."

One example that comes up in discussions of this sort refers to the advent of the nuclear age. It is often noted that to understand deterrence and the core concepts of Cold War foreign policy, you had to understand our nuclear weapons capabilities, and issues like throw weights and the limitations of launch systems. But as Jake Sullivan points out, some of those issues were not quite as technical as some of those that are more important today. "The difference for me between then and now is that to understand concepts of deterrence and mutually assured destruction and parity and the things that came out of the 1950s you didn't have to understand how fissile material was weaponized and mated with a warhead. You didn't need to know those things to make policy decisions. What you needed to know was a certain level of general science." In contrast, Sullivan notes, "to be really smart and forward looking on cyber, you've got to understand things at a level of detail that almost no policymaker in the government knows, because there is so much granularity demanded to know things like how you go about stopping intrusions, or what the consequences of retaliatory actions are, or what capabilities we really have at the end of the day vis-à-vis both symmetric and asymmetric actors." Ellen Tauscher, the former member of Congress who later became under secretary of state for arms control, added that the entire process for managing our nuclear arsenal—also cited as a major area of gaps in understanding and modernization by Panetta and others—was in the hands of a Congress, where comprehension of the issues was deeply challenged. "The Congress," she observed, "has no idea, no idea what the nuclear weapons complex in the United States is, what the complex has done, what's important about it."

One top Obama administration official said, "science and technology is treated as a kind of ancillary 'over there' footnote to how we think about national security. But . . . technology makes the world now. It is the world. We have failed to understand how powerful this is and where it's going." That official pointed out that the government expends almost no effort thinking about the future trajectory of technology and what it means economically or to our national security. For one example, "the president announces with great fanfare we're going to spend $100 million on brain science. And the *New York Times* announces this terrific study . . . that shows the number of cases of Alzheimer's is going to double along with the costs by 2040. But the juxtaposition of the two—you know here's the president announcing this piddling amount of money for this very poorly thought out initiative and at the same time we have this massive freight train bearing down on the economy and society, on the well-being of the generation that is going to have to take care of us, etc., etc."

O'Toole enumerated some of the risks associated with this lack of understanding. "What's happening now is the computer revolution of the twentieth century is driving the biological revolution of the twenty-first. The significance of this is mostly unrecognized by government leaders, partly because there are few biologists or people who understand the implications of recent advances in the life sciences among top government officials in the Congress, administration, or agencies, and partly because the advances are not yet producing a lot of consumer products. The top of government is largely blind to this—we are missing both enormous economic opportunities and potentially profound biothreats. We had a blip in interest and funding for biodefense after the 2001 anthrax attacks, but I would contend that we have gone backwards in our biodefense capabilities." But beyond the traditional aspects of national defense there are also economic implications, which also impinge on security issues:

> We are allowing precious intellectual capital to be shoveled to Asia in search of higher profits. Most of the pharma manufacturing has moved out of the U.S. They are making everything elsewhere. Eighty percent of the prescription drugs used in the U.S. originate in India or China. This is a national security problem. . . . Our budgets in these areas have been largely flat. Chinese R&D spending has gone up about 24 percent per year. Asian governments—exclusive of Japan—are, combined, spending as much on R&D as the U.S. What's up with that? Where do we think this is going to take us? We don't do clinical trials in the U.S. anymore. It's too hard. We do them in India. Who is really spending time and attention thinking about the national security implications of our intellectual property policies?

O'Toole elaborates on how America risks abdicating leadership in innovative science and technology. "Recently, there have been many conversations within the government about how to afford the continued operation of the DOE national laboratories. But the national labs are one of the few places in government capable of sophisticated, long-term research. This is not the time to kill the labs, in my view. But as the recent conversations on cyberthreats show, very few members of

Congress, even those who are interested, have a working vocabulary of the issues so it is very difficult to have a conversation about next generation threats."

Clearly, these gaps require not only new policies but concerted efforts to embrace a new generation of policymakers who understand the issues, threats, and tech-driven opportunities we will be facing tomorrow. One way to spark this process forward is to recognize that at the highest levels, the national security apparatus is not structured to address these issues. Science and technology capacity within the NSC itself needs to be beefed up, and new offices should be created. The Office of Science and Technology Policy in the White House is, in the words of one very senior recent official with whom I spoke, "little more than a speech-writing operation." It should be made more substantive. There is, on a wide range of issues, a need for the kind of interdisciplinary conversation that currently does not take place. As we have seen, Internet surveillance policies and cyber-policies have economic consequences; privacy laws or decisions about Internet governance have national security implications; spending on R&D for education or pharmaceuticals ultimately impact whether the country is strong or weak—so too can new laws and regulations. It may not be long before a regular, high-level interagency coordinating mechanism on science and technology issues, led by an assistant to the president, seeking to "marry" different components of the policy community together, as suggested by Jake Sullivan, may be a necessity rather than just a good, long-overdue idea.

From the War to End All Wars to the War That Never Ends

Although some adjustments in structure may be necessary, one of the most reliable and often ignored rules of government, offered up once in conversation with former secretary of commerce Pete Peterson, is "resist the temptation to reorganize." This is in part because the forces that impede such reorganizations are so well-entrenched that the political official who comes in and tries to do it ends up being consumed by the process. It takes too long, there is little time to address real material issues, and the result is almost always unsatisfying. It is also because, as one experienced official said to me, "a secret to success is knowing the difference between reprioritizing and reorganizing. Always try reprioritzing first; only if that doesn't work should you consider the latter."

Further, as we have seen, add fear, politics, or reactive impulses to any other impulse to change, and the results are inevitably worse. The US national security establishment went through the biggest reorganization in more than half a century when, in the wake of the 9/11 attacks, the Bush administration created the Department of Homeland Security, the Directorate of National Intelligence, the Homeland Security Council in the White House, and the newly beefed up Counter-Terrorism Center. All this does not even account for the vastly increased spending for new defense and intelligence programs. Although some of these moves created important missing capacity to address extant and emerging threats, some just created needless fat in the already bloated national security bureaucracy.

Mike Hayden argued against the creation of the DNI: "the DNI right now is weaker in terms of the glue, the centripetal forces than the last true DCI." These sentiments are echoed by Leon Panetta, who says, "there wasn't a hell of a lot of effective power within the office of DNI other than this mission to coordinate." There is no proof of this better than the retrenchment that has taken place in the years since 9/11. The Homeland Security Council has been absorbed back into the NSC. Successive directors of central intelligence have pushed back on the Directorate of National Intelligence to ensure that the CIA still plays a leading operational role and a first-among-equals role in the octopus-like US intelligence community, which currently comprises seventeen separate and distinct entities. (Although that may change—depending on the nature of proposed reforms to the way Internet surveillance is conducted—as the cyber side of the equation grows increasingly more important.) And the Department of Homeland Security, a hodgepodge of agencies once part of other departments, has never really gotten traction as a first-rank department of the US government.

The NSC today is bloated. Although some of that is the carcass of the Bush-era Homeland Security Council as it is still slowly being digested, much of it, as Tom Donilon suggested, is a product of the president who insists he must be central to so many decisions and outcomes that the capacity to advise him and implement his views must necessarily grow. Soon the NSC duplicates other agencies, a widespread view among those I spoke to in those bodies. One Clinton State Department official said of the NSC, "it is critical not to have the NSC grow to be an operational entity. That's the Scowcroft model, right? It is supposed to be a council, not a staff. And whether you call it the NSS or the NSC, it is still a staff. It has grown in exactly the opposite direction it should. Now, it is a shadow State Department. It's the shadow USAID." But there is a paradox, says the official. "They are overstaffed compared to where they were but they are understaffed and underfunded compared to the agencies they are supplanting or pushing aside. What's more, they're so big they produce so much material and conduct so many meetings that they make it very hard for the agencies which also have . . . statutory responsibilities to actually do important parts of their jobs."

Scowcroft cuts to the chase: "you have to step back from operations. The government is bad at stepping back and thinking. The NSC is the only outfit that can do that. You also have to have the courage to practice triage. You cannot deal with every issue. That takes judgment."

In an era of advanced information technologies, when some of the world's most successful companies have moved toward enhancing their responsiveness, nimbleness, and efficiency that flatter more decentralized structures, it makes no sense for the world's biggest organization to grow continually more top heavy, more weighted to the center, and to add more and more layers of bureaucracy. Certainly, we have seen no corresponding benefits to the effectiveness of US foreign-policy management with bigger NSCs. The Obama and Bush NSCs are the two largest in American history, and as we have seen, their records, not just in terms of policy outcomes but in terms of policy processes, implementing those outcomes, and advising their presidents, have not been notably better than their considerably smaller predecessors.

At the heart of the national security establishment of the United States lies a serious organizational problem. The three communities that the process was designed to link—diplomatic, defense, and intelligence— are at a point where their structures are ill-suited to their missions. Their missions are changing and they have yet to develop the kinds of doctrines and underlying philosophies of future operation necessary to help inform the kind of sound restructuring that is required.

The State Department faces challenges from without and within. Externally, they face the reality that the modality of government-to-government interaction they specialize in is a bit of a relic. Today, most interaction between nations takes place at the private-sector level. There are literally millions of channels of contact between nations, many supplanting in importance those that require or involve the government. It is also easier for foreign public and private officials to communicate directly with other parts of the US government, including the White House, and there is very little effort made to resist the impulse. A key role for the State Department is that of middleman, and the technology revolutions have almost universally undercut and eliminated the role of such intermediaries. That said, State has the unique ability to gather insights on the ground in each of the countries of the world, and a greater mission to help the United States shape its foreign-policy priorities. Further, as we reenter a world in which balance-of-power geopolitics seems likely to supplant the bipolar reality of the Cold War or the simplicity of the illusory unipolar moment through which we recently passed, good old-fashioned diplomacy is going to become more and more important again. If we don't want to do everything, to be the planet's policeman, then we are going to have to make an effort to understand others and coax them into action.

The more diplomacy we can do, the better we are at building coalitions and effective multilateral institutions, the less burden falls solely on America. Effectively collaborating with other nations enables us to advance our interests with less risk. Revitalizing the international system we helped create doesn't weaken us by threatening our sovereignty, it strengthens us by leveraging our strengths and promoting international law and cooperation rather than armed intervention as a way to avoid or resolve disputes. It is not America's job alone to save Syria or Crimea or to intervene to help ensure China does not violate the sovereignty of others in the South China Sea. But we have an interest in containing the use of weapons of mass destruction, in ensuring that despots know there is a price to be paid for the mass slaughter of their citizens or the bullying or invasion of their neighbors. Going it alone is clearly not the right path for America. But doing little or nothing is not a viable alternative. The Obama team fell into a trap of reiterating this false choice between putting "boots on the ground" or doing very little indeed. What is neglected here is the middle ground, and almost always that middle ground requires effective coalition building. It is a job that can only be done with an effective, active, empowered State Department. It cannot be done from the White House no matter how big the NSC staff gets to be—it requires too much day-to-day engagement with too many countries on too many issues. Finally, it is a job that can only be effectively achieved if the United States reawakens to the reality that diplomacy is not sipping tea and serving as a glorified messenger service but is a vital foundation of national strength. It can be one of our most effective, efficient force, influence, and prestige multipliers.

Finally, almost all the multilateral mechanisms we use to deal with global interests are relics of the immediate post–World War II era. So reinventing the international system is going to be increasingly important, especially as issues like managing climate change or regulating cyber-commerce or global issues like privacy become more important. As Scowcroft said, "we've never needed international cooperation like we do now. We should turn the UN into something that can actually do something."

State is also often eclipsed by the NSC. There is too much temptation for national security advisors and their staffs to operationalize themselves by conducting negotiations on behalf of the president. When someone is in the room representing the president, no other official is seen as influential. Such activities effectively make the national security advisor another secretary of state. Not only is one enough, but two are infinitely too many. The result of having two is that counterparties seek to identify the gaps that invariably emerge between them and to play those to their advantage. That has happened recently when differences were evident between State and the White House on Egypt policy (the White House was more distrustful and slow to embrace the Sisi regime), or on the talks between Israel and Palestine (the White House was ready to walk away from the talks sooner than Secretary of State Kerry was). When Brent Scowcroft and James Baker undertook the respective roles of national security advisor and secretary of state in the George H. W. Bush administration, they sat down and forged an explicit understanding. Baker would be the spokesperson. Scowcroft would clear public statements with Baker. Both would interact directly with Bush—with whom both had close, trusting relationships—and would share information openly. Neither would try to secretly undercut the other—in part because they knew, thanks to their relationships, that they could not. Scowcroft would not be operational and would focus on advising the president and managing the policy process and its implementation. Baker would be America's chief diplomat. Their staffs would support these two functions.

The challenges within the department of defense and the intelligence community are even deeper. Both have irrationally large, duplicative structures that the United States cannot afford. As the amount of the federal budget available to anything other than servicing debt and funding entitlements has shrunk from 50 percent in 1974 to 16 percent in 2014, the fact that defense makes up by far the largest chunk of that means that it is nudging aside more and more national priorities in education, research, infrastructure, or health. It is not rational to spend more than every other major country combined (between eight and thirteen countries, depending on how you count and whose numbers you trust). So, if we are actually going to prosper and do the little things we need to do to keep the country growing, like building roads, fixing bridges, and investing in research, then we are going to stop spending like we have been.

The reality is that despite the timidity with which politicians of both parties approach this question (in 2012, Barack Obama and Mitt Romney debated the difference between relatively small increases and de minimis cuts), there are plenty of ways to find savings. Each branch of the service has its own air force. We have two expeditionary forces (the army and the navy). We preserve antiquated systems of warfare like carrier battle groups and massive fighter jet programs, even though we know that they will get little use and in all likelihood will be made obsolete by the next time they are needed. And that is to speak nothing of waste, fraud, and abuse (which get spoken a lot of in Washington even as precious little is done about them.) So cuts can come. With so many different intelligence agencies and an intelligence budget that rivals that of the entire defense budget of China, certainly a similar case can be made for rationalization of spending, structure, and priorities there as well.

But before we can do that, we need to understand emerging threats and how we are going to treat them. But we do not yet have a fully developed sense of new threats. For one thing, we have been overreactive during the past decade and a half to one single, narrow set of those threats—the ones associated with terrorism—while we have devoted less than appropriate attention to emerging powers or emerging means of conducting warfare and their consequences. This is one of the hidden but very real costs of responding to terror attacks with terror. We face the prospect of entering an age of big data, in which the world's economy rises and falls on a sea of bits and bytes. Inevitably, as we enter that world, nations and non-state actors are developing, buying, and stealing the technologies they need to make their way in that world—to make themselves safe, to make themselves prosperous, to attack their enemies. Admiral Rogers probably had it right when he said all future crises would have a cyber component. Yet, the United States has no doctrines to guide us in this new era. Whether we can respond to a cyber-attack with traditional kinetic means is perhaps the easiest of these questions. (International law aside, we will if the pain is great enough.) But other issues are much more challenging. Nuclear weapons made global warfare of the twentieth century variety too costly to conduct. But cyber weapons make far more likely an era of nearly permanent or persistent conflict that seeks to degrade rather than destroy enemies, and to do so at a distance, behind cover of anonymity, with few if any human assets at risk. In a hundred years we may have gone from the war to end all wars to the war that never ends.

The advent of this new era will also blur the distinctions between state and non-state actors, and public and private assets that can be targeted or utilized to project a nation's will. It will also make allies and enemies more difficult to tell apart. It is potentially, therefore, much more destabilizing than nuclear technology for a reason that is ironic in the context of the theme of this book—because it is, on the face, substantially less frightening to those who contemplate it or use it.

Mary DeRosa served as deputy counsel to the president for national security affairs and as legal advisor to the National Security Council. Talking of the Bush years she said, "they strained the existing legal structure and international law in particular. But also, take the cyber area. There are a lot of questions about what is an attack and how does the law of armed conflict work with cyber. And it's also true for drones. It may not be quite as complicated with drones. Basically it's a weapon. But it does raise certain sovereignty issues. So, circumstances push us into new areas and questions."

Worlds Apart

Capacity challenges face the US national security establishment much as focus challenges faced the think tank community from which many senior level officials are drawn. There are some areas that just don't get enough attention. Some are regions that have for so long been economically challenged and of limited political interest to the United States that we simply haven't developed a depth of expertise. These include notably Latin America, Africa, and Central Asia. The latter two of these are, however, very likely to be the focus of much greater attention going forward. Africa is home to seven of the world's ten fastest growing economies. Its great resources have attracted Western oil companies and the Chinese government alike, and in turn extremists groups like Boko Haram or al-Qaeda in Mali have become prominent and highly dynamic. Crises in South Sudan, Somalia, Nigeria, the Central African Republic, and Mali during the past couple of years underscore Africa's growing importance.

The US military has established a new command, AFRICOM, to deal with emerging security threats to American interests in Africa. But in the policy sector the United States needs more and better experts. The same story is true in Latin America. One recent assistant secretary of state for Western Hemisphere Affairs said, "I don't like admitting it, but on occasion we have had to jump up and down and wave our arms to get attention. It's not just within this building [the State Department] but interagency and from the White House as well. Almost every administration I have been in starts out thinking they're going to pay a lot of attention to Latin American and then they turn their attention to whatever is in crisis. The fact that we haven't had that many crises has actually hurt us in terms of the number of people devoting attention to our hemisphere. And while there is an assumption that there is a large Hispanic voting bloc in the US and that will drive more attention to the area, outside of immigration policy, I have so far seen little evidence that is correct." Referring to the second-class status certain emerging regions have, and to the tendency to play domestic politics with the appointments to top jobs in that area, that expert in US-Latin American relations said, "if we truly respect our neighbors and our domestic communities, we have to work hard to avoid ghetto-ization of Latin issues."

Other policies have faced a similar fate, none more so than the treatment of women's issues. Although there is no doubt recent administrations have given women senior roles to play in national security agencies of the government, women's issues are regularly derided as being "soft" and of secondary importance. Despite the really valiant and historic efforts of Secretary of State Clinton to move women's issues front and center in the policy debate, much of the most influential part of the policy community, including that in the White House (especially prior to the arrival of Susan Rice), was a boys' club.

Few situations illustrate the tension between these approaches better than America's involvement in Afghanistan. Women in that country have been treated abominably for centuries. Indeed, they are treated today in many parts of Afghanistan as they have been since the Middle Ages. The life expectancy of Afghan women is third lowest in the world. Only one in six Afghan women can read and write. More die in pregnancy than almost anywhere else in the world. More than half of all Afghan women are married or engaged by the time they are sixteen, and most such marriages—inevitably—are arranged or forced. Women have historically been treated as property of the groom's family once they are married. In Sharia law, a woman's testimony has only half the weight of that of a man.

These appalling statistics are a tragedy for Afghanistan. Uneducated women cannot contribute economically or politically. Lack of education among women is proven to raise healthcare costs in a country. Suppressing women is also a violation of fundamental human rights and creates a skewed and divided political system.

As Hillary Clinton said at the 2010 TED Women Conference: "let women work and they drive economic growth across all sectors. Send a girl to school even just for one year and her income dramatically increases for life and her children are more likely to survive and her family more likely to be healthier for years to come. Give women equal rights and entire nations are more stable and secure. Deny women equal rights and the instability of nations is almost certain. Women's equality is not just a moral issue, it's not just a humanitarian issue, it is not just a fairness issue. . . . It is a security issue, it's a prosperity issue, it's a peace issue." Kim Ghattas, the BBC State Department correspondent, wrote in her book, *The Secretary*, "Clinton particularly wanted to use her new position to advance the rights of women and children everywhere, a project that stemmed from her deep belief that the world would never be a better place until half the population was no longer neglected. No matter how many wars, peace efforts, missile launches or nuclear crises lay ahead, women's rights was part of the agenda."

Despite the sound policy reasoning behind this point of view, senior, otherwise liberal-leaning, pro-human rights policy experts, current and former officials—all men—have said to me, "but what did Hillary Clinton really do? I mean yes, she did talk about women's rights and things but what about the big issues?"

A senior official in the Obama administration discussing the next stages of the US involvement in Afghanistan let the mask slip when he appallingly said: "gender issues are going to have to take a back seat to other priorities. There's no way we can be successful if we maintain every special interest and pet project. All these pet rocks in our rucksack were taking us down."

"Pet rocks"? It's a galling way to describe the fate of the majority of the population of Afghanistan. What kind of success is it if the majority population is excluded?

The presence of women in power is not enough. Attitudes must change about who can have top jobs, and there must be equity in how those jobs are filled. Moreover, issues like the fate of women around the world have to be allowed take their place atop agendas in the Situation Room and as the focus of the most highly funded projects in the research and policy communities, rather than being left in the kitchen or the drawing room while the men sit around the table of power and smoke cigars and plan future conquests.

The same can be said of other historically "secondary" issues like climate change or energy policy or development economics. It was the rising price of food, triggered by droughts in Russia and the Americas, that helped catalyze the Arab Awakening. These are national security issues that are every bit as important as taking out a terrorist cell in Pakistan or Somalia. Yet they almost never take precedence.

On Perspective

The years since 9/11 have not been easy ones for those nationally in power in America. They have been whipsawed by external events whether from far away or as a consequence of complex domestic economic cycles. In every case, the revolution in new information technologies has both assisted them and made their jobs more difficult.

Deputy National Security Advisor Tony Blinken explained it this way: "the single biggest change in doing these jobs is information technology, the flow of information and its abundance or overabundance. It challenges our absorptive capacity and makes it harder to be proactive instead of reactive. When I worked here in the 1990s probably everyone in the White House did the same two things. At 6:30 we stopped what we were doing and turned on our televisions and watched the national evening network news. And then in the morning we all opened our front doors and picked up a hard copy of the *New York Times* and the *Washington Post* and maybe the *Wall Street Journal*. Everyone did that. And you got some clips at the office. Now of course, it is this intravenous feed that doesn't let up and that is constant, constant, constant. One statistic: during the eight years of the Clinton administration, there were 1 million emails in the NSC system. During Bush's two terms, about 5.3 million, and now, six years into Obama, 10 million. The pressure that it exerts—and of course it had already started in the '90s—is enormous. And the difference between the early '90s and the '80s when Reagan was president—three networks, no cable, no Internet, not so much talk radio—a totally different world. Clinton endured that as it mushroomed, and so did Bush."

These forces have enabled and fueled the politicization of virtually every act a president or policymaker undertakes or even publicly contemplates. They have made it harder to keep secrets. They have telescoped time so that reactions must come much more quickly under calls from the media, opposition politicians, and other world leaders. Events like the death of Ambassador Chris Stevens in Benghazi encourage the habit of reacting to events before the whole story is known, and facts have been sifted from rumors. The biggest casualty, as Tony Blinken notes, is perspective. It is perspective that would have produced a different reaction to 9/11. Indeed, with a little more perspective, we might have avoided it in the first place. Emotion was an inevitable by-product of such a great tragedy. But it should not have guided our actions to the degree that it did or for as long as it did. To respond to the acts of terrorists with terror gives them the victory. They know that terror weakens us and sends us reeling into bad decisions.

Without perspective we also lose sight of what we are reacting to and what our real goals are. It is not in America's interests to react to our own past errors in ways that compound those errors, to swing from extreme to extreme, from too great a willingness to use force to too little. Similarly, we should not let fears of potential political retribution in the event of a future crisis drive us more than our long-term interests should.

Perspective requires understanding our circumstances and options, which in turn requires knowledge of our resources, our priorities, and the higher values we seek to serve. This is not just a requirement of leaders or policymakers. In a democracy, it is also one of average citizens. If Americans are ill-informed about the world, our true choices, and long-term interests, it is natural that they will revert to biases, prejudices, and political and ideological reflexes.

Today, we live in a society that has become ever more polarized politically and economically. People seek to live among those who share their beliefs. They watch television news broadcasts or listen to radio shows with clear built-in biases designed to play to their prejudices. Civil exchanges in which political factors are set aside are increasingly more difficult to have. Gerrymandering has created Republican and Democratic congressional districts so one-sided for either party that general elections hardly matter. This makes primaries the place where real choices are made, and those are dominated by the most active voters, the ones who tend to be most extreme in their views. This pushes candidates further to the left and right.

The primaries that matter for presidential candidates are not the voting primary held in states but the money primary held on Wall Street and among the country's rich, which are the only places where prospective nominees can collect the hundreds of millions of dollars they need to compete. That the rich choose our national candidates has created a system in which they have their thumbs on the scale of social justice—inequality has grown to levels not seen since the Gilded Age, tax rates for the rich and for corporations are low and while companies and Wall Street recovered quickly from the last recession, the poorest Americans continue to suffer and benefited least.

These deformities in American democracy have created dysfunction in Washington. In 2013 Congress was able to pass less legislation than at any time in the post–World War II era. President Obama became so frustrated with his inability to work with Congress that he has built his second-term agenda around finding ways to work around it (except in those instances when deferring to it suited his purposes, as in the case of the 2013 debate over whether or not to attack Syria). This dysfunction born of polarization is also a threat to US foreign policymaking. Traveling the world during the time of the government shutdown, Secretary of State Hillary Clinton found herself having to explain what had gone wrong in our system and to allay fears that such bizarre behavior was a symptom of American decline. While this is a book about the national security process within the executive branch, it is impossible to conclude it without noting that one of the really great obstacles to meeting America's international challenges going forward will be to find a way to restore an effective working partnership between the White House and the Congress and between Republicans and Democrats.

In some respects, this may be the most difficult and daunting of the diplomatic conundrums the next president will face, but none will be more important to ensuring American strength and our ability to lead internationally. As we learned in late 2008, and has become more clear with every passing year, one reason that our fears about the threat of terror have abated somewhat is that we have come to realize that the greatest threats America faces are, in fact, here at home. Economic, social, and political, they must be seen as a vital part of the next president's international leadership agenda.

America has been sorely tested during the last decade. We have had to confront new threats and doubts about ourselves, our leaders, our values, and our future. Thousands of Americans have died in distant wars and here at home. Trillions have been spent. But we have made it through nonetheless. Our troops have largely come home or the vast majority of them will be home soon. Our economy is creeping back to something like normalcy. With our personnel coming home and our economy on the mend, we finally have the wherewithal to address the much-needed work we need to do here in America.

We have witnessed a tendency to say, "enough," "never again," "let the world take care of itself" by voters from both parties and even by our leaders in the White House, but this is clearly the wrong message to take away from the past decade. Opportunists and much worse are eager to fill the void left by our absence. Some problems require global or regional action among nations that calls for leadership and if America is not at the table, the consequences may be bitter ones for America's people, for our friends, and for those unable to speak for themselves.

We cannot let the bitter experience of the past few years, our broken politics at home, our fatigue, or our lack of clarity about our goals serve as excuses to keep us from grappling with the hard problems that are being thrown at us by the world daily. It is the equivalent of pulling the sheets over our head when the alarm goes off and hoping the day will pass us by. It never works. Just as we have learned, we should neither allow ourselves to be whipped up into an emotional frenzy to achieve impossible goals in the name of revenge or ideology, nor can we let ourselves be lulled into inaction by a litany of false choices—where the only alternative to total war is passivity, where the only alternative to international risk is withdrawal.

For the next president, one of the most important lessons of 9/11—that there is no such thing as a distant problem in the modern world—must counterbalance the impulses that led our two most recent presidents to go either too far or to do too little. The next commander-in-chief cannot afford to let divisions at home keep us from adapting, engaging the world, and advancing our interests as we must. Of all the tools the president has to help find the right path forward in the world and to ensure we follow it, none is so powerful as the NSC when used properly. Fortunately for the next occupant of the Oval Office, his or her immediate predecessors will have left detailed instructions about precisely what and what not to do, what works, and where vital change is needed.

Acknowledgments

The origins of this book can be traced not simply to its predecessor, *Running the World*, nor to the gratifying reaction that book received. Rather, Clive Priddle, the gifted and supportive publisher at PublicAffairs books, encouraged me to pick up where the prior book left off. Not once but several times. He also offered the latitude to make this not a sequel per se, but a book that looks at how America makes decisions about its changing role in the world in new ways. Beyond all this he offered wise guidance, great patience, and an ever-present and welcome sense of humor throughout this process. In this he was abetted by a great organization from top to bottom at PublicAffairs/Perseus, including especially Susan Weinberg, Peter Osnos, Melissa Raymond, Melissa Veronesi, and Jaime Leifer. The result was a wonderful experience from beginning to end, and to him and his colleagues at Perseus I am deeply grateful.

As in each of my prior books, a great debt is also owed to my agent, the intrepid and wise Esmond Harmsworth of Zachary Schuster Harmsworth. He has become a valued friend and remains an invariably helpful guide to the sometimes curious and rapidly changing ways of the publishing industry.

Another constant between this book and four of those that have preceded it has been the support of the Carnegie Endowment for International Peace, where I have had the privilege of being a Visiting Scholar since—well, it seems like since Carnegie himself was there, but my ties to the institution actually only date back to the second term of the Clinton administration. The program I run there now has been generously endowed by Bernard Schwartz, who is not only a committed philanthropist but one who is genuinely interested in finding policy solutions that will help restore American growth and competitiveness. Jessica Mathews, the president of the Carnegie Endowment, who has overseen the transformation of Carnegie into a truly global think tank, has my deepest respect and admiration, and I feel very fortunate to have her as a colleague

371

and a friend. I also want to thank Paul Balaran, Carnegie's EVP, for his continuing support, as well as offering a special thanks to Carnegie's extraordinarily talented and responsive library staff, notably Kathleen Higgs, Keigh Hammond, and Christopher Lao-Scott, who have a knack for taking even the most daunting requests and turning them into something fruitful.

Tara Chandra has been the lead researcher on this project from beginning to end. She has been tireless, creative, rigorous, and diligent. I have never been better supported by a researcher, but she has been more than that, regularly providing the best of advice. No other single individual deserves more credit for what is good in this book. Tara was, however, assisted by a succession of excellent interns including, most recently, Adam Cohen, but also Molly Pallman, Chester Eng, and Christopher McGuire. In addition, two researchers from my last book project, *Power, Inc.*, helped lay the groundwork for this research. They are Chris Zoia and May Sabah.

Also of direct, great, and continuous aid throughout this project has been my wonderful, often hilarious, also extremely patient and deeply valued assistant, Hilary Kline. I am also very grateful for the support of my colleagues at *Foreign Policy* magazine, including the terrific leadership at Graham Holdings Company, Don Graham, Ann McDaniel, and Gerry Rosberg. In addition, the editors and business team at the magazine, website, and events division at *Foreign Policy* have taught me much about the subjects included in this book and are as stellar a group of colleagues as anyone could hope to have.

That would be true of anyone, that is, who was not as lucky as I have been for the better part of the past decade, to also have the partners and colleagues that I have at Garten Rothkopf, the international advisory firm Jeffrey Garten and I started in 2005. Not only has Jeff continued to be one of my closest friends since even before we worked together in the Clinton administration, he has been the best business partner I am capable of imagining, a great teacher, and even a tolerant and helpful reader of manuscripts and columns and whatever else I have thrown his way. It is fair to say no single individual has more influenced my professional life—although I do not know why I feel compelled to heap the blame on him. Claire Casey, our managing director and partner at the firm has also been an essential friend and advisor, and the backbone of the company. I will always be deeply grateful to them, as well as to our many excellent colleagues there including especially Allison Carlson, Alison Williams, Antoine van Agtmael, David Sandalow, and Yuxin Lin.

Several other friends and valued colleagues gave me invaluable advice and, when needed, uplifting and apposite counsel during the preparation of this book. They deserve special thanks and acknowledgment, and include Tom Friedman and David Sanger of the *New York Times*, Edward Luce of the *Financial Times*, Jeffrey Goldberg of *The Atlantic*, Bob Hormats, late of the State Department and now at Kissinger Associates, and Don Baer, of Burson Marsteller.

The very best part of doing this book has been the ability to spend time with a broad array of really gifted and dedicated public servants, policymakers, experts, and military and business leaders from the United States and around the world. In the course of the past several years while planning and working on this project, I have interviewed well over 100 people, including roughly equivalently-sized contingents from both the Bush and Obama administrations, as well as approximately 30 from Europe, the Middle East, Africa, Asia, and Latin America. Some of these people spoke to me off-the-record or otherwise asked not to be acknowledged, but that does not diminish my gratitude to them.

I also want to express my gratitude to those people who have during the past few years generously granted me time either for interviews, conversations, or background discussions that have contributed to the content included in these pages. (These include exchanges undertaken expressly for this book, for its predecessor, *Running the World*, or in conjunction with my work at *Foreign Policy*.) A partial list of them includes Elliott Abrams, Madeleine Albright, Graham Allison, Yaakov Amidror, Celso Amorim, Uzi Arad, Rich Armitage, Evan Bayh, Aluf Benn, Sandy Berger, Bob Blackwill, Tony Blinken, Josh Bolten, Alia Hatoug Bouran, Lael Brainard, Rosa Brooks, Zbigniew Brzezinski, John Brennan, Bill Burns, Nick Burns, Kurt Campbell, Nathalie Cely, Heng Chee Chan, Derek Chollet, Richard Clarke, Hillary Clinton, Jared Cohen, Tom Daschle, Ron Dermer, Mary Derosa, Tom Donilon, Michèle Flournoy, Anwar Gargash, Robert Gates, Tim Geithner, Carlos Gutierrez, Steve Hadley, Husain Haqqani, Caitlin Hayden, Michael Hayden, Fred Hochberg, the late Richard Holbrooke, Bob Hormats, Roberta Jacobson, Nasser Judeh, Bob Kagan, Sergei Kislyak, John Kerry, Zalmay Khalizad, Bob Kimmitt, Peter Lavoy, Mark Lippert, David Lipton, Doug Lute, Sean McCormack, Denis McDonough, David McKean, Ashok Mirpuri, George Mitchell, Lisa Monaco, Luis Alberto Moreno, Vali Nasr, John Negroponte, Peter Orszag, Michael Oren, Yousef al Otaiba, Tara O'Toole, Leon Panetta, Antonio Patriota, Barry Pavel, Mark Penn,

Shimon Peres, David Petraeus, Colin Powell, Ben Rhodes, Tim Roemer, Condoleezza Rice, Gary Samore, Francisco Sanchez, Miriam Sapiro, Arturo Sarukhan, Eric Schmidt, Norton Schwartz, Brent Scowcroft, K. Shanmugam, Tharman Shanmugarantam, Tom Shannon, Wendy Sherman, Michael Singh, Anne-Marie Slaughter, Tara Sonenshine, Jake Sullivan, Larry Summers, Ellen Tauscher, Arturo Valenzuela, John Veroneau, Mauro Vieira, and Lior Weintraub. I'd also like to offer special thanks to former colleagues with great knowledge of these issues, including the late Steve Solarz, Henry Kissinger, Jerry Bremer, Anthony Lake, John Gannon, Susan Rice, and Admiral Steve Smith for over the years having contributed much to the understanding that filled not only this book but *Running the World*, and much else I have written on these subjects as well.

What is good or interesting in this book is due to the contributions of those cited above. As usual, the errors, tedious bits, and run-on sentences are 100 percent my doing.

Naturally, as in all things, my warmest and profoundest thanks must be reserved for my family. They get credit for teaching me how to read and write, and making me crazy enough to want to sit up all night trying to write a book when I have at least two and a half other perfectly respectable day jobs. My mother, sister, and brother lead this list because I have known them longest. My father was also on this list, but sadly he died during the course of my work on this project. I miss him every day, and hope that some aspect of this might have pleased or interested him. In lieu of that, I hope that at least someone else in my family reads it.

My two daughters Joanna and Laura are the unmitigated, soaring joys of my life. They fill me with pride for their accomplishments, but even more so for who they have become. Once upon a time, I taught them things. Now the tables are turned. They teach me every day, among other things, that it is possible to love even more than you thought was possible just moments earlier.

As those of you who have already flipped through the first few pages of this book must know, it is dedicated to my wife, Adrean. She has been there during the long days of impossible stress that preceded my actually developing the willpower to sit down and write—and during the late nights and early mornings of my writing around the clock to make up for the previous days of procrastination and stressed-out lassitude. She is also a great wife, my best friend, and, perhaps most important, our cats, who are otherwise rather fickle, are very fond of her.

Notes

Material used throughout this book comes from interviews with over one hundred primary sources. Those that were on the record are indicated accordingly. The rest were undertaken on background. I am grateful to all those who participated in these interviews for their time and cooperation. This book would not have been possible without them.

Introduction: The Enemy in the Mirror

6   **Although at the time of:** R. Jeffrey Smith, "Hussein's Prewar Ties to Al-Qaeda Discounted," *The Washington Post*, April 6, 2007; Ehab Zahriyeh, "How ISIL Became a Major Force with Only a Few Thousand Fighters," *Al Jazeera America*, June 19, 2014.

6   **There are estimated to be:** "Transcript: Senate Intelligence Hearing on National Security Threats," *The Washington Post*, January 29, 2014.

6   **(Estimates by Israeli intelligence:** Background interviews with Middle Eastern government officials.

6   **In fact, a Rand Corporation:** Seth G. Jones, "A Persistent Threat: The Evolution of a Qa'ida and Other Salafi Jihadists," *The Rand Corporation*, 2014.

6–7   **Northern Mali is the largest al-Qaeda controlled:** "Divided Mali: Where al-Qaeda Rules the Roost," *The Economist*, September 22, 2012.

7   **In fact, al-Qaeda in North Africa:** John Rollins, "CRS Report to Congress: Al Qaeda and Affiliates: Historical Perspective, Global Presence, and Implications for U.S. Policy," *Congressional Research Service*, January 25, 2011.

7   **Nor could bin Laden have:** Peter Beinart, "Obama's Disastrous Iraq Policy: An Autopsy," *The Atlantic*, June 23, 2014; Ali Khedery, "Why We Stuck with Maliki—and Lost Iraq," *The Washington Post*, July 3, 2014.

7   **In 2005, I wrote a book called *Running the World*:** David Rothkopf, *Running the World: The Inside Story of the National Security Council and the Architects of American Power* (New York: PublicAffairs, July 2006).

9   **By the second term of the Obama era the National:** Background interview with a national security official.

11   **Zbigniew Brzezinski, among the most strategically:** "Address to the New American Strategies Conference," *New American Strategies for Security and*

Peace, October 28, 2003, http://www.newamericanstrategies.org/articles /display.asp?fldArticleID=68.

15   **I once rather uncharitably joked:** David Rothkopf, "Getting Back to Basics Is the Way Out of Afghanistan," *Foreign Policy*, September 8, 2010.

Chapter 1: Iraq: Debacle Accomplished

21   **The country is in chaos:** Suhad Al-Salhy and Timi Arango, "Iraq Militants, Pushing South, Aim at Capital," *The New York Times*, June 11, 2014; Thomas Erdbank, "In the Shadows of Shrines, Shiite Forces Are Preparing to Fight ISIS," *The New York Times*, June 26, 2014; Caroline Alexander, "Maliki Turns to Militias to Halt Militant Onslaught," *Bloomberg*, June 12, 2014.

22   **In my previous history of:** Rothkopf, *Running the World*.

22   **The warnings Bush and his team:** Richard A. Clarke, "Strategy for Eliminating the Threat from the Jihadist Networks of al Qida: Status and Prospects," Declassified by D. Sanborn on April 7, 2004; Peter L. Bergen, *The Longest War: The Enduring Conflict between America and al-Qaeda* (New York: Free Press, January 2011), 42.

22   **Within weeks of the 9/11 attacks:** David Rohde and David E. Sanger, "How a 'Good War' in Afghanistan Went Bad," *The New York Times*, August 12, 2007.

23   **Stephen ("Steve") Hadley, the man:** Mike Allen, "Rice Is Named Secretary of State," *The Washington Post*, November 17, 2004.

24   **It is too often forgotten that:** David Halberstam, *The Best and the Brightest* (New York: Ballantine Books, 1972).

25   **Gerald Ford, in his continuation:** Rothkopf, *Running the World*, 154.

25   **When Ronald Reagan's mismanaged National:** Rothkopf, *Running the World*, 248, 252–259.

25   **Bill Clinton fielded a significantly:** R. W. Apple Jr., "A Domestic Sort With Global Worries," *The New York Times*, August 25, 1999; Michael Dobbs and John M. Goshko, "Albright's Personal Odyssey Shaped Foreign Policy Beliefs," *The Washington Post*, December 6, 1996; Bill Powell, "How George Tenet Brought the CIA Back from the Dead (Fortune, 2003)," *Fortune*, November 18, 2012.

25   **Further Berger introduced key process:** Rothkopf, *Running the World*, 371–372.

26   **One of her top aides:** Background interview with State Department official.

26   **He continues, "when you think:** Background interview with State Department official.

26   **One senior member of the Bush:** Background interview with senior Bush administration official.

26   **This insider made it clear:** Background interview with senior Bush administration official.

26   **One former member of the cabinet:** Background interview with Clinton administration official.

27   **One of Bush's top NSC officials:** Background interview with former senior National Security Council official.

28   **Or as another senior Bush:** Background interview with senior Bush
        administration official.

28   **As early as September 1999:** "A Period of Consequences," *The Citadel*,
        September 23, 1999, http://www3.citadel.edu/pao/addresses/pres_bush.html.

28   **He carefully contrasted his policies:** Ibid.

28   **He condemned the fact that:** Ibid.

28   **With a prescience for which:** Ibid.

29   **Others, including Bush cabinet members:** Background interview with senior
        Bush administration official.

30   **In his perceptive book:** Bergen, *The Longest War,* 50.

30   **From the perspective of the Bush:** Background interview with senior Bush
        administration official.

30   **In Afghanistan, to destroy the threat:** Ibid.

30   **Further, as 9/11 had shown:** Ibid.

30   **Additionally, Saddam had flaunted:** Ibid; "Saddam Hussein's Defiance of
        United Nations Resolutions," *White House Archives*, http://georgewbush-
        whitehouse.archives.gov/infocus/iraq/decade/sect2.html.

30–31   **In any event, while the decision:** "Public Attitudes Toward the War in Iraq:
        2003–2008," *Pew Research Center*, March 19, 2008, http://www.pewresearch.
        org/2008/03/19/public-attitudes-toward-the-war-in-iraq-20032008/; Frank
        Newport, "Seventy-Two Percent of Americans Support War Against Iraq,"
        Gallup, March 14, 2003, http://www.gallup.com/poll/8038/seventytwo-percent-
        americans-support-war-against-iraq.aspx; Alison Mitchell and Carl Hulse,
        "Congress Authorizes Bush to Use Force in Iraq," *The New York Times*,
        October 11, 2002.

31   **As Bob Woodward notes in:** Bob Woodward, *Bush at War* (New York: Simon
        and Schuster, July 2003), 49.

31   **Estimates suggest that the Taliban:** Benjamin S. Lambeth, "Air Power Against
        Terror: America's Conduct of Operation Enduring Freedom," *The RAND
        Corporation*, 2005, 76–77; "Taliban Lose Grip on Mazar-i-Sharif," *The
        Guardian*, November 7, 2001.

31   **The country was one of the world's:** "World DataBank: World Development
        Indicators," *The World Bank*, http://data.worldbank.org/data-catalog/
        world-development-indicators.

31   **According to a 2001 assessment:** Anthony Cordesman, "The Military Balance
        in the Gulf: Iraq," *Center for Strategic and International Studies*, August 3,
        2000.

32   **However, two years before our invasion:** Ibid.

32   **UN inspections and sanctions were also believed:** George A. Lopez and David
        Cortright, "Containing Iraq: Sanctions Worked," *Foreign Affairs*, July/August
        2004.

32   **Furthermore, although the entire Iraqi:** Anthony Cordesman, "Iraqi Armed
        Forces on the Edge of War," *Center for Strategic and International Studies*,
        Washington, DC, 2003.

32   **Most Iraqi soldiers fled:** Sharon Otterman, "IRAQ: Iraq's Prewar Military
        Capabilities," *Council on Foreign Relations*, April 24, 2003.

32   **Perhaps 1,800 of its tanks:** Cordesman, "The Military Balance in the Gulf: Iraq."

32   **Also in the words of the CSIS report:** Ibid.

32   **Its navy had just nine:** Ibid.

32   **On September 20, 2001, during an address:** "Text: President Bush Addresses the Nation," *The Washington Post*, September 20, 2001.

33   **"We watched the twin towers collapse":** "President Bush's Address to the Nation," *The New York Times*, September 11, 2006.

33   **In Peter Baker's *Days of Fire*:** Peter Baker, *Days of Fire: Bush and Cheney in the White House* (New York: Doubleday, 2013), 157.

33   **Even sometimes dissenters within the:** Steven R. Weisman, "Threats and Responses: Security Council; Powell, in U.N. Speech, Presents Case to Show Iraq Has Not Disarmed," *The New York Times*, February 6, 2003.

33   **Bush had an average Gallup poll:** "Presidential Approval Ratings—George W. Bush," *Gallup*, accessed May 9, 2014.

34   **A *Wall Street Journal*/NBC:** Neil King Jr. and David S. Cloud, "Thirty Nations Join U.S. in Coalition Against Iraq," *The Wall Street Journal*, March 19, 2003.

34   **By May 2003, after the initial invasion:** Dana Milbank and Jim VandeHei, "No Political Fallout for Bush on Weapons," *The Washington Post*, May 17, 2003.

34   **It was not until over a year later:** Frank Davies, "Public Support for War Declines; Nearly 70 Percent Say Basis for Invasion Was Faulty," *The Kansas City Star*, August 21, 2004.

34   **By 2005, almost six in ten Americans:** "Iraq," *Gallup*, http://www.gallup.com/poll/116500/presidential-approval-ratings-george-bush.aspx.

34   **And by April 2006, in a CBS News poll:** Richard Benedetto, "Iraq Speeches Have Done Little to Buoy War Support; Americans Tune Out as Casualties, Violence Drown Out Bush's Message," *USA Today*, April 14, 2006.

34   **One top NSC official from:** Background interview with senior National Security Council official.

35   **As Bob Woodward has reported:** Bob Woodward, *State of Denial: Bush at War, Part III* (New York: Simon & Schuster, 2007), 109–110.

35   **What's more, the president brushed off:** Ibid.

35   **In her own memoirs, Rice:** Condoleezza Rice, *No Higher Honor: A Memoir of My Years in Washington* (New York: Crown, 2011), 192.

35   **One high-ranking State Department official:** Background interview with State Department official.

36   **Rice wrote that "the President:** Rice, *No Higher Honor*, 191.

36   **She notes that in one:** Rice, *No Higher Honor*, 187.

36   **Rumsfeld has argued that:** Donald Rumsfeld, *Known and Unknown: A Memoir* (New York: Sentinel HC, 2011), 482.

36   **He then added, "in discussions of postwar Iraq":** Rumsfeld, *Known and Unknown*, 486.

36   **Cheney wrote: "a question that came up early":** Dick Cheney and Liz Cheney, *In My Time: A Personal and Political Memoir* (New York: Threshold Editions, 2011), 387.

36   **Rice recalls: "Don argued we had no":** Rice, *No Higher Honor*, 187.

36   **Rumsfeld's encapsulation of his commander-in-chief's:** Rumsfeld, *Known and Unknown*, 499.

36   **Former members of the Bush NSC:** Woodward, *State of Denial*, 241.

37   **To get a sense of the breadth of:** Michael E. O'Hanlon, "Iraq Without a Plan," *Policy Review*, December 1, 2004.

37   **Disbanding and alienating both the:** Jane Arraf, "U.S. Dissolves Iraqi Army, Defense and Information Ministries," *CNN*, May 23, 2003; Tim Arango, "Uneasy Alliance Gives Insurgents an Edge in Iraq," *The New York Times*, June 18, 2014.

37   **In fact, in the months between June and October:** Woodward, *State of Denial*, 244.

37   **General Stanley McChrystal, a senior Iraq:** Stanley McChrystal, *My Share of the Task: A Memoir* (New York: Portfolio Trade, 2013), 106.

37   **While the team in the White House:** Woodward, *State of Denial*, 266; Background interview with senior Bush administration official.

37   **George Bush may have objected:** David E. Sanger, "New Woodward Book Says Bush Ignored Urgent Warning on Iraq," *The New York Times*, September 29, 2006.

38   **The insurgency was complicated:** Edward Cody, "Foes of U.S. in Iraq Criticize Insurgents," *The Washington Post*, June 26, 2004.

38   **Zarqawi's group was composed of:** Ibid.

38   **The fact that the White House:** George W. Bush, *Decision Points* (New York: Crown, November 9, 2010), 261.

38   **One former senior official in:** Background interview with former senior official.

38   **One senior official who served:** Background interview with senior Bush administration official.

39   **Because the Euphrates River:** E. Yarshater, editor, *The Cambridge History of Iran, Volume 3: The Seleucid, Parthian and Sasanid Periods, Part 1 of 2* (Cambridge, UK: Cambridge University Press, 1983), 70.

39   **Once also known as Pumbeditha:** Michael Grant, *A Guide to the Ancient World: A Dictionary of Classical Place Names* (New York: H. W. Wilson Co., 1986), 391; "Academies in Babylonia," JewishEncyclopedia.com, accessed June 27, 2014.

39   **More recently, it has been known as:** Jackie Spinner, "Fallujah Residents Emerge, Find 'City of Mosques' in Ruins," *The Washington Post*, November 18, 2004.

39   **Sitting in the midst of what came:** "Iraq's 'Sunni Triangle' Scene of New Deadly Attacks," *CNN*, January 22, 2004; Anthony Shadid, "Iraq's Forbidding 'Triangle of Death,'" *The Washington Post*, November 23, 2004.

39   **In the most recent battle:** Liz Sly, "Al-Qaeda Force Captures Fallujah Amid Rise in Violence in Iraq," *The New York Times*, January 3, 2014.

39   **On April 28, 2003, two days before:** Human Rights Watch, "Violent Response," June 17, 2003, www.hrw.org/en/node/12318/section/4.

40   **The nearly ninety Iraqi casualties:** Sarah Left, "US Troops 'Kill 13 Protesters,'" *The Guardian*, April 29, 2003.

40   **Roughly a year after the first:** Jeffrey Gettleman, "Enraged Mob in Falluja Kills 4 American Contractors," *The New York Times*, March 31, 2004.

40   **Four contractors from the Blackwater firm:** Ibid.

40   **This triggered what is today known as:** "Marines, Iraqis Join Forces to Shut Down Fallujah," *CNN*, April 6, 2004.

40   **Ill-will against Americans was high:** McChrystal, *My Share of the Task*, 131.

40   **Anti-American rumors were rampant:** Ibid.

40   **Rumors of American atrocities spread:** Ibid.

40   **Marines surrounded the city, but:** Joel Roberts, "Iraqi Forces Taking Over in Fallujah," *CBS News*, May 1, 2004.

40   **Efforts to arm local Iraqi forces:** Glen Kessler, "Weapons Given to Iraq Are Missing," *The Washington Post*, August 6, 2007.

40   **Behind-the-scenes efforts to:** "Battle for Falluja Under Way," *CNN*, November 9, 2004.

40   **Military accounts detail intensive artillery:** Dexter Filkins, "In Fallujah, Young Marines Saw the Savagery of an Urban War," *The New York Times*, November 21, 2004; Jackie Spinner and Karl Vick, "U.S. and Iraqi Troops Push into Fallujah," *The Washington Post*, November 9, 2004.

40   **The attacks included the use:** Robert Burns, "Pentagon Used White Phosphorous in Iraq," *The Washington Post*, November 16, 2005.

40   **The anger was, of course:** Jackie Spinner, "Fallujah Residents Emerge, Find 'City of Mosques' in Ruins," *The Washington Post*, November 18, 2004.

41   **The leadership transition was from:** Suzanne Goldenberg, "Negroponte to Be Bush Envoy," *The Guardian*, April 19, 2004.

41   **Like Bremer, Negroponte had worked:** Wil Haygood, "Ambassador with Big Portfolio: John Negroponte Goes to Baghdad with a Record of Competence, and Controversy," *The Washington Post*, June 21, 2004.

41   **At the same time, George Casey:** Eric Schmitt, "The Reach of War: Man in the News—George William Casey Jr.; A Commander with 4 Stars to Tame the Iraqi Furies," *The New York Times*, July 5, 2004.

41   **Casey's father was a West Point:** Ibid.

41   **Powell's experience in Vietnam led:** Eric Schmitt, "The Powell Doctrine Is Looking Pretty Good Again," *The New York Times*, April 4, 1999.

41   **The sense that it was vital:** James Mann, *Rise of the Vulcans: The History of Bush's War Cabinet* (New York: Penguin Book, 2004), 63–64.

42   **Many on the NSC staff:** Background interview with NSC official.

42   **He was known for his:** Glenn Kessler, "Bush Adviser on Iraq Policy to Step Down," *The Washington Post*, November 6, 2004.

42   **One person who worked very:** Background interview with State Department official.

43   **To get a better understanding:** Michael Gordon and Bernard Trainor, *The Endgame: The Inside Story of the Struggle for Iraq, from George W. Bush to Barack Obama* (New York: Vintage, 2012), 96.

43   **They reported in September of:** Ibid.

43   **The analysts estimated that insurgents:** Ibid.

43   **The group urged an effort to:** Ibid.

44   **(The full short-sightedness of:** Matt Bradley and Bill Spindle, "Unlikely Allies Aid Militants in Iraq," *The Wall Street Journal*, June 16, 2014.

44   **Casey's perspective was therefore:** Ellen Knickmeyer, "Insurgent Violence Escalates in Iraq," *The Washington Post*, April 24, 2005.

Chapter 2: A Very Different President

45   **Given the deteriorating conditions on the ground:** Dan Balz, "Bush Wins Second Term," *The Washington Post*, November 4, 2004.

45   **General Colin Powell had begun:** Background interview with senior Bush administration official.

45   **According to a source familiar with:** Ibid.

45   **Powell reportedly replied that it:** Ibid.

46   **In the exchange, Powell is said:** Ibid.

46   **Those close to Powell say:** Ibid.

46   **Powell reportedly argued that he had:** Ibid.

46   **Bush was reluctant to accept:** Ibid.

46   **He does not address the issue at all:** Rumsfeld, *Known and Unknown*, 631.

46   **Rumsfeld's former protégé and lifelong friend:** Cheney, *In My Time*, 425.

46   **Continuing, Cheney wrote, "Time and again":** Ibid.

46   **Powell had a discussion with Andrew Card:** Background interview with senior Bush administration official.

46   **Card told Powell that the president:** Ibid.

46   **Powell was told that, subject:** Ibid.

46   **Powell reportedly noted that in:** Ibid.

47   **A little later Rumsfeld's deputy:** Todd S. Purdum, "Wolfowitz Nod Follows Spread of Conservative Philosophy," *The Washington Post*, March 17, 2005; Sheryl Gay Stolberg and Jim Rutenberg, "Rumsfeld Resigns as Defense Secretary After Big Election Gains for Democrats," *The New York Times*, November 8, 2006.

47   **Rice had been exceptionally close:** Glen Kessler, *The Confidante: Condoleezza Rice and the Creation of the Bush Legacy* (New York: St. Martin's Press, 2007), 6–8.

52   **After the elections, interim prime minister:** Gordon and Trainor, *Endgame*, 139.

52   **On April 7, Ibrahim al-Jaafari:** Robert F. Worth, "Iraq's New President Names Shiite Leader as Prime Minister," *The New York Times*, April 7, 2005.

52   **Jaafari was a troubling choice to some:** Gordon and Trainor, *Endgame*, 147.

52   **According to Casey, relations with the:** George Casey, *Strategic Reflections: Operation Iraqi Freedom, July 2004–February 2007* (Washington, DC: National Defense University Press, 2012), 55.

53   **Nonetheless, Casey did not deviate from:** Ibid., 70.

53   **In late June 2005, another personnel shift:** Gordon and Trainor, *Endgame*, 128.

53   **Earlier in the year, Negroponte had been:** Ibid.

53   **The creation of the DNI post:** William Branigin, "Bush Nominates Negroponte to New Intel Post," *The Washington Post*, February 17, 2005.

53   **The new post would ostensibly:** Ibid.

53   **In the words of a senior Bush:** Background interview with senior Bush administration official.

53   **At its inception though, Negroponte:** Ibid.

54   **Negroponte's replacement as ambassador:** Joel Brinkley, "Bush Names Envoy in Kabul to Be Ambassador to Iraq," *The New York Times*, March 11, 2005.

54   **His language skills, knowledge of the:** Ibid.

54   **He arrived in Baghdad on July 24, 2005:** Gordon and Trainor, *Endgame*, 158.

54   **Casey welcomed Khalilzad to Baghdad:** Ibid., *Endgame*, 159.

54   **That said, following in the tradition of the:** Gordon and Trainor, *Endgame*, 161–162.

54   **The approach they suggested involved:** Ibid.

55   **Given Casey's clear predispositions against:** Ibid.

55   **The report contradicted a different red-team:** Gordon and Trainor, *Endgame*, 160.

55   **Casey campaigned in the White House:** Casey, *Strategic Reflections*, 66.

55   **Meanwhile, at the State Department:** Woodward, *State of Denial*, 412.

55   **In contrast to the military's take:** Ibid.

55   **He was concerned that the situation was:** Gordon and Trainor, *Endgame*, 175–176.

55   **He came up with an idea:** Ibid.

55   **This approach, with the added recommendation:** Woodward, *State of Denial*, 418.

55   **Not surprisingly, Rumsfeld was not happy:** Gordon and Trainor, *Endgame*, 175–176.

55   **He was also concerned that such an:** Woodward, *State of Denial*, 418.

55   **Meanwhile, the Iraqis ratified their constitution:** Casey, *Strategic Reflections*, 74.

56   **Rumsfeld defended Casey's viewpoint with:** Ibid., 76.

56   **Rumsfeld's memoirs describe an:** Rumsfeld, *Known and Unknown*, 678.

56   **Bush and others present reportedly asked:** Ibid.

56   **Casey argued that "none of:** Ibid.

56   **Rumsfeld wrote of Casey and his team:** Ibid., 678–679.

56   **Intelligence reports in December 2005:** Bob Woodward, *The War Within: A Secret White House History 2006–2008* (New York: Simon and Schuster, 2009), 34.

56   **Further, the December 15 parliamentary elections:** Gordon and Trainor, *Endgame*, 183.

56   **As Gordon and Trainor wrote:** Ibid.

57   **Concerned about the threat that Iran:** Shane Harris and Matthew M. Aid,
            "CIA Files Prove America Helped Saddam as He Gassed Iran," *Foreign
            Policy*, August 26, 2013.

57   **Chalabi and others argued that:** Jane Mayer, "The Manipulator," *The New
            Yorker*, June 7, 2004; Leslie H. Gelb, "Neoconner," *The New York Times*,
            April 27, 2008; Dexter Filkins, "Regrets Only?" *The New York Times
            Magazine*, October 7, 2007.

57   **As a result, the role:** Ned Parker, "Ten Years After Iraq War Began, Iran
            Reaps the Gains," *The Los Angeles Times*, March 28, 2013; Michael R.
            Gordon, "Iran Supplying Syrian Military via Iraqi Airspace," *The New York
            Times*, September 4, 2012.

57   **The December 15 elections went off without:** Casey, *Strategic Reflections*,
            84–85; Gordon and Trainor, *Endgame*, 184.

57   **Terrorist violence fell to a third of:** Gordon and Trainor, *Endgame*, 183.

57   **The brief quiet was shattered in a momentous:** Ibid., 192.

58   **The site, noted for its golden dome:** Ibid.

58   **It was a totemic symbol, arguably:** Woodward, *The War Within*, 35.

58   **Khalilzad and Casey reached out to:** Casey, *Strategic Reflections*, 89–90.

58   **When US intelligence reported that the attack:** Woodward, *The War Within*, 35.

58   **But bigger forces were at work:** "Sunnis and Shias: Islam's Ancient Schism,"
            BBC News, June 20, 2014.

58   **The criticism is echoed by Gordon and Trainor:** Gordon and Trainor, *Endgame*,
            193.

58   **True or not, their approach was not:** Woodward, *The War Within*, 38.

58   **On March 21, 2006, the CIA:** Ibid.

59   **Paradoxically, despite such reports:** Woodward, *State of Denial*, 453; Casey,
            Strategic Reflections, 87; Gordon and Trainor, *Endgame,* 200.

59   **But just as the Americans saw their:** Gordon and Trainor, *Endgame*, 200.

59   **In April 2006, Iraq got its:** Nelson Hernandez and K. I. Ibrahim, "Top Shiites
            Nominate a Premier for Iraq," *The Washington Post*, April 22, 2006.

59   **Khalilzad had, in fact, encouraged Maliki to:** Tim Arango and Michael R.
            Gordon, "Amid Iraq's Unrest, Maliki Campaigns as Strongman," *The New
            York Times*, April 29, 2014.

59   **Bush was pleased with the selection:** Bush, *Decision Points*, 361–362.

59   **"Congratulations, Mr. Prime Minister:** Ibid.

59   **Both men have subsequently reported that they:** Ibid.

59   **In Bush's words, he wanted not to:** Ibid.

60   **Maliki illustrates this point particularly:** Jay Solomon and Carol E. Lee, "U.S.
            Signals Iraq's Maliki Should Go," *The Wall Street Journal*, June 19, 2014.

60   **Enduring the sectarian turmoil:** Loveday Morris and Karen DeYoung, "Maliki
            Steps Aside, Easing Iraq's Political Crisis," *The Washington Post*, August 14,
            2014.

60   **As the situation in Iraq deteriorated:** Lyndsey Layton, "The Story Behind the
            Iraq Study Group," *The Washington Post*, November 21, 2006.

60   **This was "an uncomfortable moment:** Background interview with senior Bush
            administration official.

60   On May 19, 2006, Colin Powell appeared: Woodward, *The War Within*, 46–47.
60   He criticized the decision to go into: Ibid.
60   He reiterated the familiar State Department: Ibid., 49.
60   He criticized his former colleagues': Gordon and Trainor, *Endgame*, 270.
60   Powell also argued that Bremer and Sanchez: Gordon and Trainor, *Endgame*, 270
60–61   When asked directly by study group member: Ibid.
61   According to one of Condoleezza: Background interview with Bush administration official.
61   Matters were not helped by a joint: Rice, *No Higher Honor*, 459–460.
61   Rice wrote that she "doubted: Ibid.
61   While Rice was "skeptical" of the idea: Ibid.
61   Rice wrote of the trip in her memoir: Ibid.
61   After her return, Rice asked Zelikow: Rice, *No Higher Honor*, 506.
61   She confirms that by that time: Ibid.
61   She encouraged her aides to: Ibid.
62   Their response listed three options: Woodward, *The War Within*, 55.
62   Not surprisingly, given the way: Ibid.
62   Frustrated with what she saw: Rice, *No Higher Honor*, 515.
62   "Mr. President," she said, with the confidence of: Ibid.
62   There was, it should be noted: Bush, *Decision Points*, 365.
62   It is telling that when Casey called: Gordon and Trainor, *Endgame*, 207–208.
63   At Camp David on June 12: Gordon and Trainor, *Endgame*, 208–209.
63   The theme—which Cheney: Cheney, *In My Time*, 435.
63   Bush went straight from the meeting: Gordon and Trainor, *Endgame*, 211.
63   Upon his return, Bush was asked: Woodward, *The War Within*, 57–58.
63   He said, "Troop levels will be": CQ Transcripts Wire, "Bush Press Conference," *The Washington Post*, June 14, 2006.
63   But behind the scenes, the president had: Bush, *Decision Points*, 363.
63   Hadley quietly began the NSC's: Woodward, *The War Within*, 71.
63   He sent a long list of questions to: Ibid., 73.
64   The latter two agreed to respond to: Ibid.
64   On Hadley's staff was Meghan O'Sullivan: Ibid.
64   She felt only the United States: Woodward, *The War Within*, 61.
64   After the review, she advanced: Ibid., 190–192.
64   The choices were to "adjust: Ibid.
64   Earlier, there had been an influential trip: Gordon and Trainor, *Endgame*, 277–278.
64   In late August, another NSC staffer: Ibid., 288–289.
64   He, too, concluded Casey was floundering: Ibid.
64   A "Council of Colonels" at the: Ibid.
64   They concluded that "properly characterizing: Ibid.
64   Hadley himself wrote a memo to Bush: Ibid., 290–291.
64   Bush recalled, "Steve's assessment was that: Bush, *Decision Points*, 373.
64–65   By late November 2006, Bush was communicating: Ibid., 374.

65   **Bush reported in his memoirs that:** Ibid.

65   **Again, it is worth:** Background interview with Bush administration official.

65   **His government institutions that were supposed:** Gordon and Trainor, *Endgame*, 227.

65   **The Iraq National Police conducted:** Ibid.

65   **And earlier in the summer, when Casey:** Ibid., 214.

65   **Khalilzad echoed Casey's reluctance to:** Gordon and Trainor, *Endgame*, 293.

65   **In mid-November, he wrote a memo:** Ibid., 294.

65   **On November 22, Casey outlined:** Ibid.

66   **In September 2006, he went to see:** Rumsfeld, *Known and Unknown*, 701.

67   **Rumsfeld, again with the benefit of:** Ibid.

67   **Woodward offered an alternative view:** Woodward, *The War Within*, 129.

67   **Echoing critiques of Vietnam, Keane argued:** Ibid.

67   **He also attacked the trap created by:** Ibid., 130.

67   **Keane asserted that the answer was to increase:** Ibid., 132.

67   **Keane's final point was directed at Casey:** Ibid., 134.

67   **Woodward reports him as telling:** Ibid.

68   **Those at State tout the influence:** Background interviews with US Department of State officials.

68   **All these views were shaped into:** Background interview with senior Bush administration official.

68   **NSC Deputies, led by Hadley:** Ibid.

68   **A "wide range" of outside views:** Ibid.

68   **In the iterative nature of this process:** Ibid.

68   **In addition, the president was able:** Ibid.

68   **The president and Hadley (working with:** Ibid.

68   **He wrote that by the fall he had:** Bush, *Decision Points*, 371.

68   **In his memoir he then goes on to:** Ibid.

68   **"To be credible to the American people":** Ibid.

68   **Rumsfeld himself records that he had:** Rumsfeld, *Known and Unknown*, 705–706.

69   **Further, in the eyes of senior:** Background interview with senior Bush administration official.

69   **Rather, it was seen as a means:** Ibid.

69   **Bush told Cheney of the move:** Cheney, *In My Time*, 442.

69   **He said he had decided that he would:** Ibid.

69   **Twice before, he had discouraged Bush from:** Ibid.

69   **"He knew I'd be opposed:** Ibid., 443.

69   **On the weekend after the election:** Rumsfeld, *Known and Unknown*, 707.

69   **With Rumsfeld's resignation on November 7:** Ibid.

69   **Three days after Rumsfeld's resignation:** Woodward, *The War Within*, 207.

70   **He asked that they undertake:** Ibid.

70   **Hadley recognized that the president was:** Ibid., 264.

70   **He addressed the concern that:** Ibid.

70   **On December 11, Hadley arranged for:** Ibid., 279.

70   **The group, which included Jack Keane:** Cheney, *In My Time*, 449–450.

70   **During an NSC teleconference the next:** Woodward, *The War Within*, 284.

70   **Rice also opposed the surge option:** Rice, *No Higher Honor*, 545.

70   **On April 14, President Bush:** Michael A. Fletcher, "OMB Head to Replace Card as Top Bush Aid," *The Washington Post*, March 29, 2006.

70   **Bolten had been director of:** Ibid.

70   **For much of the 1990s:** Ibid.

70   **He had once been chief:** Ibid.

71   **After trying and failing three:** Michael A. Fletcher and Paul Blustein, "Financier Chosen to Head Treasury," *The Washington Post*, May 31, 2006.

71   **Bolten confirmed Paulson's prescience:** Edmund L. Andrews and Jim Rutenberg, "Bush Nominates Wall Street Chief for Treasury Job," *The New York Times*, May 31, 2006.

72   **One example of the degree:** Gordon and Trainor, *Endgame*, 305.

72   **On that day, Bush and Cheney went:** Ibid.

72   **The purpose of the visit was:** Ibid.

72   **The chiefs held a position:** Ibid.

72   **They wanted to see more:** Ibid.

74   **Rice, who had resisted the surge:** Rice, *No Higher Honor*, 545.

74   **Bush himself wrote that "the decision had been":** Bush, *Decision Points*, 378.

74   **Despite Keane's descriptions of:** Michael Abramowitz and Robin Wright, "Bush to Add 21,500 Troops in an Effort to Stabilize Iraq," *The Washington Post*, January 11, 2007.

74   **By the end of 2008 it had:** David Petraeus, "How We Won in Iraq," *Foreign Policy*, October 29, 2013.

74   **But violence never completely abated:** Steven Lee Myers and Sam Dagher, "Storm of Violence in Iraq Strains Its Security Forces," *The New York Times*, April 24, 2009.

74   **Further, Bush's successor, Barack Obama:** Max Boot, "Obama's Tragic Iraq Withdrawal," *The Wall Street Journal*, October 31, 2011.

74–75   **Critics, including some administration:** Khedery, "Why We Stuck with Maliki."

75   **Casey says he was notified around Christmas:** Casey, *Strategic Reflections*, 145.

75   **A few days later Marine Corps:** Ibid., 146.

75   **Casey has written that he was disappointed:** Ibid.

75   **In his memoirs, Casey wrote:** Ibid., 144.

76   **Cheney has written that Keane:** Cheney, *In My Time*, 454.

76   **Keane's opinion, in the eyes of:** Ibid.

76   **Bush announced the surge in a:** Bush, *Decision Points*, 382.

76   **One month later, command of the:** Ibid.

76   **Bush wrote "General Petraeus drew my attention:** Ibid., 380–381.

76   **Petraeus is seen by some:** Steven Lee Myers, "Generally Speaking," *The New York Times*, April 6, 2008.

77   **A former ambassador to Lebanon:** Robin Wright, "A Diplomat Who Loves the Really Tough Jobs," *The Washington Post*, January 11, 2007.

77   **He was also known by administration:** Ibid.

77	The memo, cowritten with another: Ibid.
77	It also noted—as some assessments, notably: Ibid.
77	Keane was sent to Iraq to conduct: Woodward, *The War Within*, 331–332.
77–78	He reported back that Petraeus: Ibid.
78	Keane also cautioned patience—a not: Ibid., 332.
78	Petraeus, meanwhile, employed the: Andrew J. Bacevich, "The Petraeus Doctrine," *The Atlantic*, October 1, 2008.
79	Petraeus asked H. R. McMaster, a member of: Gordon and Trainor, *Endgame*, 356.
79	Of the report, Gordon and Trainor say: Ibid.
79	Keane visited again in May, reporting: Woodward, *The War Within*, 356.
79	He again cautioned against hoping for quick: Ibid.
79	But overall, he had praise for his: Ibid.
79	After taking the temperature of Capitol Hill: Ibid., 363–364.
79	He recommended replacing him, and Bush: Bush, *Decision Points*, 386
79	Mike Mullen was nominated instead: White House Office of the Press Secretary, "President Bush Nominated Admiral Michael Mullen and General James Cartwright to Chairman and Vice Chairman of the Joint Chiefs of Staff," *White House Press Release* (June 28, 2007).
79	Clearly reporting frustrations that: Woodward, *The War Within*, 377.
80	Rice reported that the mood: Rice, *No Higher Honor*, 592.
80	The surge "was beginning to have: Ibid., 592–593.
80	Rice wrote, "there was less friction inside: Ibid., 595.
81	Crocker argued that a "secure, stable: Gordon and Trainor, *Endgame*, 433.
81	The two offered up statistics that: Bush, *Decision Points*, 384–385.
81	They also underscored steep declines in: Ibid.
81	Bush called their performance "stoic: Ibid.
81	He announced three days after their: Woodward, *The War Within*, 388.
81	Two days after that, Keane delivered a: Ibid., 389–390.
81	Woodward argues that three factors were key: Ibid.

Chapter 3: The Other George W. Bush

84	In the years since, Bush's standing: Chris Cillizza, "George W. Bush's Approval Rating Just Hit a 7-Year High. Here's How." *The Washington Post*, April 23, 2013.
90	Secretary of Commerce Penny Pritzker: Jackie Calmes, "Obama Picks Nominees for Commerce Dept. and Trade Representative," *The New York Times*, May 2, 2013.
90	National Economic Council economic director: Neil Irwin, "Jeffrey Zients, Obama's Next Top Economic Adviser," *The Washington Post*, September 13, 2013.
90	Michael Froman and Jacob Lew: Calmes, "Obama Picks Nominees for Commerce and Trade"; David A. Graham, "Who is Jack Lew, Obama's Nominee for Treasury Secretary," *The Atlantic*, January 9, 2013.

90   **On the flip side, one former:** Background interview with former State Department official.

90   **He would assert that elements:** Ibid.

90   **Although, as the former ambassador:** Ibid.

91   **George W. Bush did not serve:** John Cochran, "Bush's Big Trip: Why Africa? Why Now?" *ABC News*, July 8, 2003.

91   **Bono, U2's front man and:** Karin Tanabe, "Bono Praises George W. Bush," *Politico*, December 1, 2011.

92   **Bush has written that he had decided:** Bush, *Decision Points*, 334–335.

92   **He recalled, "Condi had strong feelings:** Ibid.

92   **The Millennium Challenge Account (MCA):** "Millennium Challenge Account," The White House, http://georgewbush-whitehouse.archives.gov/infocus /developingnations/millennium.html.

92   **When announcing the program, Bush articulated:** White House Office of the Press Secretary, "Remarks by the President on Global Development," *White House Press Release* (March 14, 2002).

92   **Distinguishing the program from past:** Larry Nowels, "The Millenium Challenge Account: Congressional Consideration of a New Foreign Aid Initiative," *Congressional Research Service*, August 26, 2003.

92   **In her memoir, Rice writes of the program:** Rice, *No Higher Honor*, 226.

92   **The criteria involved included commitments:** Curt Tarnoff, "The Millennium Challenge Corporation," *Congressional Research Service*, April 12, 2012.

92   **From 2002 through 2008:** Bush, *Decision Points*, 350.

92   **Rice wrote that "the MCC used strict:** Rice, *No Higher Honor*, 428.

92   **I was one of the first to speak:** Bush, *Decision Points*, 349–350.

93   **The program gradually gained:** Tarnoff, "Millennium Challenge Corporation"; Celia W. Dugger, "El Salvador: $461 Million U.S. Antipoverty Grant," *The New York Times*, November 30, 2006; Celia W. Dugger, "Tanzania: U.S. Aid Plan Announced," *The New York Times*, September 20, 2007.

93   **Some, like Bono, were:** Nina Easton, "Foreign Aid, Capitalist Style," *Fortune*, November 21, 2011.

93   **Rice observed, "he agreed with:** Rice, *No Higher Honor*, 227.

93   **Bush, for his part, would later salute:** Bush, *Decision Points*, 349.

93   **In a 2006 *Foreign Policy* article:** Colin Powell, "No Country Left Behind," *Foreign Policy*, January/February 2006.

93   **Powell observed that the:** Ibid.

93   **Powell, noting that US foreign assistance:** Ibid.

93   **Powell also argued, correctly, in my:** Ibid.

94   **Nor is it surprising that two:** Susan E. Rice, "We Must Put More on the Plate to Fight Poverty," *Washington Post*, July 5, 2005; Susan E. Rice, "The Threat of Global Poverty," *The National Interest*, Spring 2006; Susan E. Rice and Stewart Patrick, "The 'Weak States' Gap," *The Washington Post*, March 7, 2008; Gene Sperling and Tom Hart, "A Better Way to Fight Global Poverty: Broadening the Millennium Challenge Account," *Foreign Affairs*, March /April 2003.

94   **A year after the MCA was launched:** Sperling and Hart, "A Better Way to Fight Global Poverty."

94   **They argued that it represented:** Ibid.

94   **Susan Rice, then a senior fellow at:** Rice, "We Must Put More on the Plate to Fight Poverty."

94   **She minimized the impact of MCA:** Ibid.

94   **She added that "the president also":** Ibid.

94   **Once in office, the Obama team kept:** "President Obama Requests $1.125 Billion for MCC to Continue Innovative Approach to Development Assistance," Millennium Challenge Corporation, February 15, 2011.

94   **On one key metric, Obama does outshine:** White House Office of the Press Secretary, "Fact Sheet: The Obama Administration's Comprehensive Efforts to Promote Gender Equality and Empower Women and Girls Worldwide," *White House Press Release* (April 19, 2013).

94   **Under Obama's influence, that has:** Ibid.

95   **Early in his presidency, Bush concluded:** Bush, *Decision Points*, 336

95   **He turned to his deputy chief of staff:** Jay P. Lefkowitz, "AIDS and the President—An Inside Account," *Commentary*, January 1, 2009.

95   **Bolten pulled together a team from:** Ibid.

95   **His deputy, Jay Lefkowitz, described:** Ibid.

95   **This idea, later dubbed the Mother and Child:** Ibid.

95   **Bush embraced the idea but felt:** Lefkowitz, "AIDS and the President"; Bush, *Decision Points*, 337–338.

95   **Lefkowitz later recalled Bolten coming:** Lefkowitz, "AIDS and the President."

95–96   **The result was PEPFAR, which originally:** Lefkowitz, "AIDS and the President"; Bush, *Decision Points*, 339.

96   **"The next question," Bush wrote:** Bush, *Decision Points*, 339.

96   **Despite the economic hardships the United States:** "Text of President Bush's 2003 State of the Union Address," *The Washington Post*, January 28, 2003.

96   **Despite facing hurdles on Capitol Hill:** Lefkowitz, "AIDS and the President."

96   **That stood for "abstinence for youth:** Scott H. Evertz, "How Ideology Trumped Science: Why PEPFAR Has Failed to Meet Its Potential," *Center for American Progress*, January 2010.

96   **This approach led to a number of criticisms:** Ibid.

96   **The report argued that under the program:** Ibid.

96   **Although Bush himself was fond of:** Bush, *Decision Points*, 340; Sarah Boseley, "U.S. Defends Abstinence Policy Amid Uproar," *The Guardian*, July 15, 2004.

96   **A 2006 General Accountability Office:** David Brown, "GAO Criticizes Bush's AIDS Plan; Abstinence-and-Fidelity Provision Sowing Confusion," *The Washington Post*, April 5, 2006.

96   **Another criticism was that the:** Raymond W. Copson, "The Global Fund and PEPFAR in U.S. International AIDS Policy," *Congressional Research Service*, November 3, 2005; Evertz, "Why PEPFAR Has Failed to Meet Its Potential."

96   **(The Bush Administration did eventually approve:** "President's Emergency Plan for AIDS Relief," *Government Accountability Office*, March 2013.

97   **By 2008, the program had supported:** Lefkowitz, "AIDS and the President."

97   **Condoleezza Rice drew attention to:** Rice, *No Higher Honor*, 229; "Data:
          Population (Total)," *The World Bank*, http://data.worldbank.org/indicator
          /SP.POP.TOTL?page=1.

97   **In 2007, Bush sought another:** Bush, *Decision Points*, 341.

97   **President Obama has maintained roughly:** Tiaji Salaam-Blyther, "The
          President's Emergency Plan for AIDS Relief (PEPFAR): Funding Issues After
          a Decade of Implementation, FY2014-FY2013," *Congressional Research
          Service*, October 10, 2012.

97   **In a 2010** *New York Times* **editorial:** Desmond Tutu, "Obama's Overdue AIDS
          Bill," *The New York Times*, July 20, 2010.

97   **In 2013, a major study by the independent:** Editorial Board, "PEPFAR's
          Glowing Report Card, 10 Years Later," *The Washington Post*, February 25,
          2013.

97   **Prior to PEPFAR, fewer than 100,000:** Salaam-Blyther, "The President's
          Emergency Plan for AIDS Relief (PEPFAR).

97   **By the end of Bush's time in office:** "The Power of Partnerships: The U.S.
          President's Emergency Plan for AIDS Relief, 2008 Annual Report to
          Congress," The Office of the United States Global AIDS Coordinator, 2008.

97   **Bush's malaria initiative, according to the BBC:** Martin Plaut, "Has Bush Been
          Africa's Best Friend?" *BBC News*, January 16, 2009.

98   **Referring to the fact that the Bush:** Dana Hughes, "George W. Bush's Legacy
          on Africa Wins Praise, Even from Foes," *ABC News*, April 26, 2013.

98   **Bill Clinton said that he had:** Ibid.

98   **Another rocker-activist, Bob Geldof:** Plaut, "Has Bush Been Africa's Best
          Friend?"

98   **Obama himself has acknowledged the impact:** Office of the White House Press
          Secretary, "Press Gaggle by President Obama Aboard Air Force One," *White
          House Press Release* (June 28, 2013.)

98   **Obama entered office with high:** Stephanie Hanson, "Imagining Obama's
          Africa Policy," Council on Foreign Relations, December 22, 2008; Todd Moss,
          "Missing in Africa: How Obama Failed to Engage an Increasingly Important
          Continent," *Foreign Affairs*, October 2, 2012.

98   **In one** *Foreign Policy* **article, a Sudanese-born:** Ty McCormack, "Mo Ibrahim
          Prize for Achievement in African Leadership," *Foreign Policy*, October 17,
          2012.

98   **In 2001, Goldman Sachs economist:** Jim O'Neill, "Building Better Economic
          BRICs," *Goldman Sachs*, Global Economic Paper no. 66. November 30, 2001.

98   **Just the four countries in question:** "Country Comparison: Population,"
          CIA World Factbook, https://www.cia.gov/library/publications/the-world-
          factbook/rankorder/2119rank.html; "Country Comparison: Area," *CIA World
          Factbook*, https://www.cia.gov/library/publications/the-world-factbook
          /rankorder/2147rank.html.

98–99   **China was the world's most populous:** "Country Comparison: Population";
          David Barboza, "China Passes Japan as Second-Largest Economy," *The New
          York Times*, August 15, 2010.

99   **The two countries' economies were:** David Barboza, "China's Treasury Holdings Make U.S. Woes Its Own," *The New York Times*, July 18, 2011; Menzie D. Chinn, "American Debt, Chinese Anxiety," *The New York Times*, October 20, 2013.

99   **And yet we needed to find:** "Dust-up at the Shangri-La," *The Economist*, June 1, 2014; Fred Hiatt, "Rocky Waters Between China and Japan Could Affect America," *The Washington Post*, January 26, 2014.

99   **Russia, although a shadow of:** Jim Nichol, "Russian Political, Economic, and Security Issues and U.S. Interests," *Congressional Research Service*, March 31, 2014.

99   **Brazil was the next most populous country:** "Country Comparison: Population"; "Country Comparison: Area"; "GDP ranking," The World Bank, last updated May 8, 2014.

99   **(India, the fourth of the:** "UN: India to Be World's Most Populous Country by 2028," *BBC News*, June 14, 2013; Krista Mahr, "The World's Largest Democracy Is Heading to the Polling Booth," *Time*, April 7, 2014.

99   **First Lady Hillary Clinton made:** Todd S. Purdum, "Hillary Clinton Finding a New Voice," *The New York Times*, March 30, 1995; Strobe Talbott, *Engaging India: Diplomacy, Democracy, and the Bomb* (Washington, DC: Brookings Institution Press, 2004).

100   **When Bob Blackwill took over:** Kessler, *The Confidante*, 51.

100   **His regular cables back:** Ibid.

100   **India was, in his view:** Ibid.

100   **As the *Washington Post*'s Glenn Kessler noted:** Ibid.

100   **The 2002 National Security Strategy:** "The National Security Strategy of the United States of America," *White House Office of the President,* September 2002, 10, http://www.state.gov/documents/organization/63562.pdf.

100   **Kessler wrote that the section was:** Kessler, *The Confidante*, 51.

100   **The tests elevated tensions between:** John F. Burns, "Nuclear Anxiety: The Overview; Pakistan, Answering India, Carries Out Nuclear Tests; Clinton's Appeal Rejected," *The New York Times*, May 29, 1998.

100   **In addition, the ability to offer civil:** Rama Lakshmi and Steven Mufson, "U.S., India Reach Agreement on Nuclear Fuel Reprocessing," *The Washington Post*, March 30, 2010.

100   **In accordance with the treaty:** Ibid.

100   **The section prepared by Zelikow read:** Kessler, *The Confidante*, 51.

100   **By 2004, a bilateral mechanism called the:** Ibid., 52.

101   **In *No Higher Honor*, she wrote that:** Rice, *No Higher Honor*, 437.

101   **She continued, "and for us, even:** Ibid.

101   **Rice then actively sought to:** Kessler, *The Confidante*, 57.

101   **He also unwittingly accelerated progress:** Ibid.

101   **When Deputy Secretary of State Bob Zoellick:** Ibid., 50.

101   **The strategy would be for Rice:** Ibid.

101   **During these meetings Rice told:** Ibid., 54.

102   **The deal to work together:** Rice, *No Higher Honor*, 438–439.

102   **With the Indians in Washington and the White House:** Ibid.

102   **Prime Minister Singh was losing confidence:** Ibid.

102   **Behind the scenes diplomatic scrambling took place:** Ibid.

102   **Rice dispatched Under Secretary Nick Burns:** Ibid.

102   **After having gone to bed with:** Ibid.

102   **This produced further negotiations and:** Ibid.

102   **During the encounter, Rice recalls saying:** Ibid.

102   **The push worked, and later:** Steven R. Weisman, "U.S. to Broaden India's Access to Nuclear-Power Technology," *The New York Times*, July 19, 2005.

103   **For the deal to be legal under US law:** Rice, *No Higher Honor*, 696–698.

103   **This required extensive negotiations with:** Ibid.

103   **In addition, a "Section 123 Agreement:** Ibid.

103   **And after all that, Congress:** Ibid.

103   **Singh also faced pushback, especially:** Ibid.

103   **Indeed, the Indian PM faced:** Niraj Sheth and Paul Beckett, "Indian Leader Survives Vote; Onus Now on U.S. Congress," *The Wall Street Journal*, July 23, 2008.

103   **Rice recalls that when it came to:** Rice, *No Higher Honor*, 698.

103   **She then credits Josh Bolten in helping to:** Ibid., 698–699.

104   **George W. Bush and Luiz Inácio:** Bush, *Decision Points*, 2; Richard Bourne, *Lula of Brazil: The Story So Far* (Berkeley: University of California Press, 2008), 1.

104   **Lula was raised in humble surroundings:** Bourne, *Lula of Brazil*, 1–7, 12–13.

104   **Bush worked in the oil industry and:** Brooks Jackson, "Bush as a Businessman: How the Texas Governor Made his Millions," *CNN*, May 13, 1999.

104   **Lula worked in factories much of his life:** Bourne, *Lula of Brazil*, 16.

104   **Lula became a union leader:** Ibid., 34, 44.

104   **After Lula was elected president:** Liz Throssell, "Lula's Legacy for Brazil's Next President," *BBC News*, September 30, 2010; Raymond Colitt, "Odd Friends, Bush and Lula Foster Brazil-US Ties," Reuters, March 30, 2007.

105   **A few weeks after he took office:** William M. LeoGrande, "A Poverty of Imagination: George W. Bush's Policy in Latin America," *Journal of Latin American Studies*, vol. 39, no. 2, May 2007.

105   **In this spirit, Bush met with Mexico's president:** Office of the White House Press Secretary, "Remarks by President George Bush and President Vicente Fox of Mexico at Arrival Ceremony," *White House Press Release* (September 5, 2001).

105   **Condoleezza Rice was succinct in her:** Rice, *No Higher Honor*, 257.

105   **At the first meeting however, after an:** Ibid., 257–258.

105   **A chemistry between the two men:** Ibid.

105   **Rice characterized Lula as "authentic,":** Ibid.

105   **"Lula," she wrote, "seemed to be:** Ibid.

105   **The relationship evolved, and a year later:** Luiz Alberto Moniz Bandeira, "Brazil as a Regional Power and Its Relations with the United States," *Latin American Perspectives*, vol. 33, no. 2, May 2006.

106   **Afterward Lula said, "without any:** Office of the White House Press Secretary, "President Bush Welcomes Brazilian President Lula to White House," *White House Press Release* (June 20, 2003).

106   **Over the years that followed, the:** Colitt, "Odd friends."

106   **Throughout this time, Lula was:** Tim Padgett, "Brazil's Lula: A Bridge to Latin America's Left?" *Time*, March 14, 2009.

106   **Indeed, his ability to act:** Background interview with Bush administration official.

107   **A centerpiece of this was Plan Colombia:** LeoGrande, "A Poverty of Imagination."

107   **Begun during the Clinton Administration:** Ibid.

107   **After the American side hammered:** Ibid.

108   **The program's authors felt they needed:** Ibid.

108   **At one dark moment in:** Ibid.

108   **Talking points were prepared:** Ibid.

108   **When Clinton made the call:** Ibid.

108   **Clinton got Pastrana on the line:** Ibid.

108   **After they hung up, Clinton turned to:** Ibid.

108   **He had tears in his:** Ibid.

108   **And then, so frustrated with:** Ibid.

108   **Clinton did that and used all:** Ibid.

108   **Fortunately for this initiative, as good as:** Ibid.

109   **It did not hurt that Colombia's ambassador:** "Luis Alberto Moreno, President," Inter-American Development Bank, October 2013, http://www.iadb.org/en /about-us/departments/biographies,1347.html?bioid=4.

109   **Bush wanted to reevaluate and redirect:** Rice, *No Higher Honor*, 257.

109   **In Rice's words: Uribe "made clear:** Ibid.

109   **Employing an approach that became:** LeoGrande, "A Poverty of Imagination."

109   **Border issues with Mexico became not:** Michael A. Fletcher and Jonathan Weisman, "Bush Signs Bill Authorizing 700-Mile Fence for Border," *The Washington Post*, October 27, 2006.

110   **Health programs grew to ensure:** Sheryl Gay Stolberg, "The President's Budget Proposal: Health Spending; Bucks for Bioterrorism, but Less for Catalog of Ills," *The New York Times*, February 5, 2002.

110   **Police departments got more money:** Radley Balko, "A Decade After 9/11, Police Departments Are Increasingly Militarized," *The Huffington Post*, September 12, 2011.

110   **A 2006 Congressional Research Service report:** Connie Veillette, "Plan Colombia: A Progress Report," *Congressional Research Service*, June 22, 2005.

110   **Critics also note that while Bush:** Ibid.

110   **Only toward the very end of:** June S. Beittel, "Colombia: Background, U.S. Relations, and Congressional Interest," *Congressional Research Service*, November 28, 2012; "US: Colombia Human Rights Improved," *Al Jazeera*, September 12, 2009.

110   **Felipe Calderón made it clear:** Steve Coll, "Whose Drug War?" *The New Yorker*, November 10, 2011; Clare Ribando Seelke, "Mérida Initiative for

Mexico and Central America: Funding and Policy Issues," *Congressional Research Service*, August 21, 2009.

110–111 **Bush's team embraced the idea, framing it:** Rice, *No Higher Honor*, 565–566.

111 **The initiative was different from past:** Seelke, "Mérida Initiative."

111 **The United States would have to work on curbing demand:** Clare Ribando Seelke and Kristin M. Finklea, "U.S.-Mexican Security Cooperation: The Mérida Initiative and Beyond," *Congressional Research Service*, August 15, 2011.

111 **The United States pledged $1.5 billion for:** Ibid.

111 **The Congressional Research Service evaluation of:** Ibid.

111 **A sign of the success of the:** Clare Ribando Seelke and Kristin M. Finklea, "U.S.-Mexican Security Cooperation: The Mérida Initiative and Beyond," *Congressional Research Service*, April 8, 2014.

111 **In the case of the new and improved:** Ibid.

111 **Funding levels for Mérida have gone down:** Ibid.

111 **In April 2001, Bush had made the case for:** Luisa Angrisani, "More Latin, Less America?" *The National Interest*, Fall 2003.

111 **He envisioned a market that would:** Ibid.

112 **These included deals with the countries:** "CAFTA-DR (Dominican Republic-Central America FTA)," Office of the United States Trade Representative, accessed June 25, 2014; J. F. Horneck, "The U.S.-Panama Free Trade Agreement," *Congressional Research Service*, November 8, 2012; "Peru Trade Promotion Agreement," Office of the United States Trade Representative, accessed June 25, 2014; Choe Sang-Hun, "U.S. and South Korea Reach Free Trade Agreement," *The New York Times*, April 2, 2007; William Mauldin and Siobhan Hughes, "Fast-Track Trade Bill's Path in Congress Gets Bumpier," *The Wall Street Journal*, February 5, 2014.

Chapter 4: Elections Select Presidents, Crises Reveal Them

114 **During the last three years:** "U.S. Treasury Secretary Timothy Geithner to Join CFR as Distinguished Fellow," *Council on Foreign Relations*, February 6, 2013.

114 **A former Asian studies major:** Ibid.

114 **His next major stop, in 2003:** Ibid.

116 **Recognizing the limitations on the:** Background interview with senior US economic official.

117 **The Arab Spring would be triggered:** "Let Them Eat Baklava," *The Economist*, March 17, 2012.

118 **Between the late Clinton years:** Marc Labonte, "CRS Report to Congress: Asset Bubbles: Economic Effects and Policy Options for the Federal Reserve," *Congressional Research Service*, September 25, 2007.

118 **This growth was fed by the availability:** Alec Klein and Zachary A. Goldfarb, "The Bubble," *The Washington Post*, June 15, 2008.

118 **The derivatives that Geithner had:** Klein and Goldfarb, "The Bubble."

118 **They were helping bankers repackage:** Ibid.

118   **Bad loans accumulated within big:** Ibid.

118   **The day before the financial crisis:** Chuck Todd and Seldon Gawiser, *How Barack Obama Won: A State-by-State Guide to the Historic 2008 Presidential Election* (New York: Vintage, January 6, 2009), 24.

118   **Within days, due to McCain's:** Ibid.

118   **Barack Obama attended college during:** The Associated Press, "Old Friends Recall Obama's College Years," *Politico*, May 16, 2008.

118   **Obama entered politics when he was:** Margot Mifflin, "Obama at Occidental," *The New Yorker*, October 3, 2008.

118   **He illustrates the speed of:** Barack Obama, *The Audacity of Hope: Thoughts on Reclaiming the American Dream* (New York: Vintage July 2008).

118   **Four years later, Democratic:** David S. Broder, "Democrats Focus on Healing Divisions," *The Washington Post*, June 28, 2004.

119   **Nowhere in his seventeen-minute speech:** "Transcript: Illinois Senate Candidate Barack Obama," *The Washington Post*, July 27, 2004.

119   **His personal story, woven through:** Ibid.

119   **Not only was his father's family:** Ibid.

119   **Barack Obama had attended schools:** Ibid.

119   **His first public speech, at Occidental:** Mifflin, "Obama at Occidental."

119   **At Columbia he focused on:** James Traub, "Is (His) Biography (Our) Destiny?" *The New York Times Magazine*, November 4, 2007.

119   **Obama helped make his name:** "Transcript: Obama's Speech Against the Iraq War," *National Public Radio*, January 20, 2009, http://www.npr.org/templates/story/story.php?storyId=99591469.

119   **He remained active on that issue:** Richard Wolffe, *Renegade: The Making of a President* (New York: Broadway Books, May 4, 2010), 218.

119   **Following a trip they made:** Wolffe, *Renegade*, 43.

119   **He made trips to Europe, the Middle East**: Paul Kane, "Obama Supports FISA Legislation, Angering Left," *The Washington Post*, June 20, 2008.

119   **In actions that would later:** Ibid.

119   **In one account, the issue:** John Heilemann and Mark Halperin, *Game Change: Obama and the Clintons, McCain and Palin, and the Race of a Lifetime* (New York: HarperCollins, February 23, 2010), 26.

120   **And his chief campaign advisors:** Ibid.

120   **Following his 2005 trip to Russia:** Wolffe, *Renegade*, 43.

120   **When television interviews posed the question:** Heilemann and Halperin, *Game Change*, 30–31.

120   **(Daschle himself would be:** Perry Bacon Jr., "Obama Accuses Clinton of Deception," *The Washington Post*, March 10, 2008.

120   **Rouse was a former Daschle:** Sheryl Gay Stolberg, "Filling an Aide's Shoes with Very Different Feet," *The New York Times*, September 30, 2010.

120   **According to accounts like that:** Heilemann and Halperin, *Game Change*, 33–34.

120   **Reid also recounts in his:** Harry Reid and Mark Warren, *The Good Fight: Hard Lessons from Searchlight to Washington* (New York: Penguin Group LLC, 2008), 300.

120 **Her election would make them:** Maria Liasson, "Notion of Political Dynasty a Problem for Clinton," *NPR*, December 4, 2007, http://www.npr.org/templates/story/story.php?storyId=16869068.

121 **Reid and Daschle were joined by:** Heilemann and Halperin, *Game Change*, 37.

121 **Bush was reelected in 2004:** Balz, "Bush Wins Second Term."

121 **George H. W. Bush had defeated:** Josh King, "Dukakis and the Tank," *Politico Magazine*, November 17, 2013.

121 **Reagan promised to restore:** Rothkopf, *Running the World*, 208.

121 **Nixon had a plan to end:** "Address to the Nation on the War in Vietnam," *PBS American Experience*, November 3, 1969.

121 **Ike was the former supreme allied commander:** Rothkopf, *Running the World*, 62–63.

122 **The big democratic victory in:** Heilemann and Halperin, *Game Change*, 62.

122 **The Obama who had spent:** Ibid.

122 **When Obama met with big-time:** Heilemann and Halperin, *Game Change*, 69.

122 **And when he touched base:** Ibid., 69–70.

122 **Obama advisors suggested Powell:** Background interview with Obama campaign advisor.

122 **Although Powell had long since:** Ibid.

122 **Powell would later help Obama:** Rachel Weiner, "Colin Powell Endorses President Obama," *The Washington Post*, October 25, 2012.

122 **In the run up to:** Heilemann and Halperin, *Game Change*, 73.

122 **Senator Hillary Clinton made a trip:** Patrick Healy, "Senator Clinton Heads to Iraq, Afghanistan," *The New York Times*, January 12, 2007.

123 **Obama followed by launching:** Jeff Zeleny, "Obama Takes Big Step Toward 2008 Bid," *The New York Times*, January 16, 2007.

123 **Clinton announced she was running:** Patrick Healy and Jeff Zeleny, "Clinton Enters '08 Field, Fueling Race for Money," *The New York Times*, January 21, 2007.

123 **On February 10, 2007, in Springfield:** Adam Nagourney and Jeff Zeleny, "Obama Formally Enters Presidential Race," *The New York Times*, February 11, 2007.

123 **Obama's announcement began much like:** "Senator Obama's Announcement," *The New York Times*, February 10, 2007.

123 **It ultimately turned to a few:** Ibid.

123 **Several core points touched on:** Ibid.

123 **He decried the idea that:** Ibid.

123 **He spoke of climate change:** Ibid.

123 **And then he made a core:** Ibid.

124 **(Even within Bush's own administration:** Richard N. Haass, *War of Necessity, War of Choice: A Memoir of Two Iraq Wars* (New York: Simon and Schuster, 2010).

124 **Later, this approach would be:** "Obama's Remarks on Iraq and Afghanistan," *The New York Times*, July 15, 2008.

124   **At the center were those who:** James Mann, *The Obamians: The Struggle Inside the White House to Redefine American Power* (New York: Viking, 2012), 82–83.

125   **Others playing significant roles from the earliest days:** Mann, *Obamians*, 81.

125   **(McDonough had also spent some time:** Ibid., 70.

125   **Among the most important of:** Ibid., 78.

125   **Rice, a Stanford-educated Rhodes Scholar:** Ibid., 77; Kate Pickert, "U.N. Ambassador: Susan E. Rice," *Time*, December 3, 2008.

125   **Rice left Brookings to join:** Background interview with 2008 Clinton campaign official.

125   **Known for her tenacity and:** Mann, *Obamians*, 77.

125   **Like many such advisors on:** David E. Sanger and Jodi Kantor, "Rice's Blunt Style Endeared Her to President, but Not All," *The New York Times*, December 13, 2012.

125   **She bonded with the president on:** Ibid.

125   **Obama came to rely on:** Ibid.

125   **Many of those long close to Rice:** Mann, *Obamians*, 79.

127   **In June 2007, two Bear Stearns:** Daniel Burns, "12 Key Dates in the Demise of Bearn Stearns," Reuters, March 17, 2008.

127   **By August, Geithner learned that:** Bethany McLean and Joe Nocera, "How the Roof Fell in on Countrywide," *CNN Money*, December 23, 2010.

127   **By January 2008, the World Bank warned:** "Timeline: The Credit Crunch of 2007/2008," Reuters, August 5, 2008.

127   **President Bush and Paulson responded with:** Michael Grunwald, *The New New Deal: The Hidden Story of Change in the Obama Era* (New York: Simon and Schuster, 2013), 67; Burns, "12 Key Dates."

128   **Assertions that the rumors were:** "Interview: Alan 'Ace' Greenberg," *PBS Frontline*, February 17, 2009, pbs.org/wgbh/pages/frontline/meltdown.

128   **The next day the current CEO:** Andrew Fisher, "Bear Stearns CEO: No Liquidity Crisis for Firm," *CNBC*, March 12, 2008.

128   **By the evening of March 13:** Kate Kelly, "Fear, Rumors Touched Off Fatal Run on Bear Stearns," *The Wall Street Journal*, May 28, 2008.

128   **While seeking new money from:** Ibid.

128   **Schwartz pushed J.P. Morgan CEO:** Ibid.

128   **He sought a $25 billion:** Ibid.

128   **Dimon said he would consider:** Ibid.

128   **At 4:45 the next morning:** Ibid.

128   **If they didn't authorize a loan:** Ibid.

128   **They agreed to put a package:** Ibid.

128   **It took a couple of:** Ibid.

128   **The goal was an announcement:** Ibid.

128   **After a small blip upward:** Ibid.

128   **Paulson initiated a call with:** Hank Paulson, "Hank Paulson: This Is What It Was Like to Face the Financial Crisis," *Bloomberg Businessweek*, September 12, 2013.

128   **The only thing that would save Bear:** Burns, "12 Key Dates."

128   **By Sunday afternoon, March 16:** Andrew Ross Sorkin, "JP Morgan Pays $2 a Share for Bear Stearns," *The New York Times*, March, 17, 2008.

128   **Later that night the Fed:** Kate Kelly, "Inside the Fall of Bear Stearns," *The Wall Street Journal*, May 9, 2009.

129   **Paulson would say in the wake of the crisis:** Edmund L. Andrews, "Senators Seek Details About Bear Stearns Deal," *The New York Times*, March 27, 2008.

129   **He had beaten her handily in:** Adam Nagourney, "Obama Triumphs in Iowa Contest as Clinton Falters; Huckabee Rolls," *The New York Times*, January 3, 2008; Ann E. Kornblut, "N.Y. Senator Defies Polls, Edges Obama," *The Washington Post*, January 9, 2008.

129   **It was at precisely this moment that:** Barack Obama, "Transcript of Obama Speech," *Politico*, March 18, 2008.

130   **By the time the primaries and:** Jeff Zeleny, "Obama Clinches Nomination; First Black Candidate to Lead a Major Party Ticket," *The New York Times*, June 4, 2008; "McCain wins GOP nomination; Huckabee bows out," *CNN Politics*, March 5, 2008.

130   **With over 300 members:** Elisabeth Bumiller, "A Cast of 300 Advises Obama on Foreign Policy," *The New York Times*, July 18, 2008.

130   **The Obama foreign-policy team:** Ibid.

130   **Denis McDonough was quoted in:** Ibid.

130   **Thanks to the efforts of:** Ibid.

130   **McDonough and Lippert handled the:** Ibid.

130   **In addition a "senior working:** Ibid.

130   **They included former secretary of state:** Ibid.

130   **Notably, Albright had been a:** Ibid.

131   **He named as his vice president:** Adam Nagourney and Jeff Zeleny, "Obama's Pick Adds Foreign Expertise to Ticket," *The New York Times*, August 23, 2008.

131   **He said, on ABC's *This Week*:** Jennifer Parker, "3 a.m. Call: Why Obama Picked Biden," *ABC News*, August 23, 2008.

131   **They had a good working relationship:** Heilemann and Halperin, *Game Change*, 341.

131   **He was also well-known:** Background interview with 2008 Obama campaign staffer.

131   **The Iraqi parliament failed to pass:** Campbell Robertson and Richard A. Oppel Jr., "Iraqis Fail to Agree on Provincial Election Law," *The New York Times*, August 6, 2008.

131   **A judgment came down in:** William Glaberson, "Bin Laden Driver Sentenced to a Short Term," *The New York Times*, August 7, 2008.

131   **The Taliban was on the move:** Carlotta Gall and Sangar Rahimi, "Taliban Escalates Fighting with Assault on U.S. Base," *The New York Times*, August 20, 2008.

131   **Perhaps one of the most:** Peter Finn, "Russia Pushes into Georgia," *The Washington Post*, August 12, 2008.

132   **Although the United States and:** Nicholas Kulish and Tom Rachman, "Rice Signs Missile Deal with Poland," *The New York Times*, August 20, 2008.

132   **Condoleezza Rice announced a deal:** Ibid.

132   **Later during the campaign, vice:** Alexander Marquandt, "Biden predicts early crisis will test Obama," *CNN Political Tracker*, October 20, 2008.

132   **("Remember I said it standing:** Ibid.

133   **Jobs bled out of the economy:** David Goldman, "Worst year for jobs since '45," *CNN Money*, January 9, 2009.

133   **The continuing fall in the value:** Ron Suskind, *Confidence Men: Wall Street, Washington, and the Education of a President* (New York: Harper, September 20, 2011), 96.

133   **Big financial institutions on Wall Street:** Larry Elliott, "Three Myths that Sustain the Economic Crisis," *The Guardian*, August 5, 2012.

133   **Regular meetings took place:** Ryan Lizza, "Inside the Crisis: Larry Summers and the White House Economic Team," *The New Yorker*, October 12, 2009.

133   **And in the Bush administration**: Background interview with Bush administration official.

134   **The triumvirate of Paulson, Geithner:** Suskind, *Confidence Men*, 73.

134   **The calls and meetings increased in**: Paulson, "What It Was Like to Face the Financial Crisis."

134   **For the public perhaps and:** Andrew Ross Sorkin, "Lehman Files for Bankruptcy; Merrill Is Sold," *The New York Times*, September 14, 2008.

134   **When Merrill Lynch simultaneously faced**: David Mildenberg and Bradley Keoun, "Bank of America to Acquire Merrill as Crisis Deepens (Update 4)," *Bloomberg*, September 15, 2008.

134   **It went to the US government.:** Matthew Karnitschnig, Deborah Solomon, Liam Plevin, and Jon E. Hilsenrath, "U.S. to Take Over AIG in $85 Billion Bailout; Central Banks Inject Cash as Credit Dries Up," *The Wall Street Journal*, September 16, 2008.

134   **Within days, AIG, the insurance:** Ibid.

134   **Lehman was allowed to go:** Sorkin, "Lehman Files for Bankruptcy."

134   **Just two days later the Fed:** Karnitschnig et al, "U.S. to Take Over AIG."

135   **Simultaneously, with the express support:** Suskind, *Confidence Men*, 114; Jon Hilsenrath, Deborah Solomon, and Daminan Paletta, "Paulson, Bernanke Strained for Consensus," *The Wall Street Journal*, November 10, 2008; James B. Stewart, "Eight Days: The Battle to Save the American Financial System," *The New Yorker*, September 21, 2009.

135   **Two more big financial institutions:** Robin Sidel, David Enrich, and Dan Fitzpatrick, "WaMu Is Seized, Sold Off to J.P. Morgan, in Largest Failure in U.S. Banking History," *The Wall Street Journal*, September 26, 2008; Binyamin Appelbaum, "Wachovia Is Sold as Depositors Flee," *The Washington Post*, September 30, 2008.

135   **The bailout was rejected by:** David M. Herszenhorn, "Bailout Plan Wins Approval; Democrats Vow Tighter Rules," *The New York Times*, October 3, 2008.

135   **By October 3, Bush signed:** Ibid.

135   **The stock market continued to:** Vikas Bajaj, "Whiplash Ends a Roller Coast Week," *The New York Times*, October 10, 2008.

135   **The Fed announced major new:** Edmund L. Andrews and Mark Landler, "U.S. Considers Cash Injects into Banks," *The New York Times*, October 9, 2008.

135   **Tax laws were relaxed to:** Jesse Drucker, "Obscure Tax Breaks Increase Cost of Financial Rescue," *The Wall Street Journal*, October 18, 2008.

135   **The Fed led a coordinated:** Jon Hilsenrath, Joellen Perry, Sudeep Reddy, and Deborah Solomon, "Central Banks Launch Coordinated Attack," *The Wall Street Journal*, October 9, 2008.

135   **The United States convened the G-7:** WSJ Staff, "G-7 Leaders Welcome 'Extraordinary Actions,'" *The Wall Street Journal*, September 22, 2008; Mark Landler, "World Leaders Vow Joint Push to Aid Economy," *The New York Times*, November 15, 2008.

135   **Paulson took another vital step:** Hank Paulson, "Hank Paulson: This Is What It Was Like to Face the Financial Crisis," *Bloomberg*, September 12, 2013.

135   **McCain's slight edge in the polls:** Todd and Gawiser, *How Barack Obama Won*, 24.

135   **He first minimized it with:** Heilemann and Halperin, *Game Change*, 379, 384.

136   **Contributing to that shift was:** Ibid., 380–381.

136   **He was briefed by an:** Jonathan Alter, *The Promise: President Obama, Year One* (New York: Simon and Schuster, 2011), 8.

136   **They helped prepare him for:** Ibid.

136   **Obama offered a generally conciliatory tone:** Ibid., 10; Wolffe, *Renegade*, 275–276.

136   **According to Jonathan Alter's account:** Alter, *The Promise*, 13–14.

136   **He came out of the meeting:** Ibid.

136   **Harry Reid later wrote:** Reid and Warren, *Good Fight*, 299.

136   **I tend to agree with the:** Keith Hennessey and Edward Lazear, "Who really fixed the financial crisis?" *Politico*, September 16, 2013.

136   **Hennessy and Lazear wrote in *Politico*:** Ibid.

138   **One former cabinet secretary called:** Background interview with former Bush administration official.

139   **On November 4, 2008:** Adam Nagourney, "Obama Elected President as Racial Barrier Falls," *The New York Times*, November 4, 2008.

139   **The country was largely divided:** Ibid.

140   **Even before the election, Obama:** Alter, *The Promise*, 16.

140   **To manage the process, Obama:** Peter Baker and Jeff Zeleny, "For Obama, No Time to Bask in Victory as He Starts to Build a Transition Team," *The New York Times*, November 5, 2008.

140   **Podesta knew how a White House should work:** Lois Romano, "John Podesta Leads Obama's Transition Team with His Usual Energy," *The Washington Post*, November 25, 2008.

140   **The effort, dubbed the Obama-Biden transition project:** "Obama-Biden Transition Project," http://change.gov/learn/transitionstaff.

140   **Bush pledged to cooperate completely:** Jon Ward, "Hadley pulls curtain back
          on transition," *The Washington Times*, January 7, 2009; Michelle Munn,
          "Clinton Transition Left $15,000 Damage, GAO Says," *The Los Angeles
          Times*, June 12, 2002.

140   **Obama had been advised to:** Alter, *The Promise*, 16.

140   **Obama had also pledged to:** "Obama's Speech from 2007 Jefferson-Jackson
          Dinner," *The Washington Post*, December 17, 2008.

140   **In retrospect, it can be:** Kenneth P. Vogel and Mike Allen, "Obama Finds
          Room for Lobbyists," *Politico*, January 30, 2009.

140   **The very first appointment made by Obama:** Baker and Zeleny, "No Time to
          Bask in Victory."

141   **Within days, Rouse, Axelrod, and Jarrett:** Peter Baker and Jackie Calmes,
          "Building a White House Before the Election Is Decided," *The New York
          Times*, October 24, 2008.

141   **Obama surprised his inner circle:** Wolffe, *Renegade*, 313.

141   **It was a pick that came as a surprise:** Alter, *The Promise*, 72.

141   **Obama invited her to his:** Ibid.

141   **In his *Renegade: The Making*:** Wolffe, *Renegade*, 180.

141   **It is also revealing, though**: Background interviews with senior 2008 Obama
          campaign officials.

142   **Clinton was, by all accounts:** Alter, *The Promise*, 72.

142   **In her memoir, *Hard Choices*, she:** Hillary Clinton, *Hard Choices* (New York:
          Simon and Schuster, 2014), 15.

142   **When presented with the secretary:** Ibid.

142   **Obama pursued the idea tenaciously:** Clinton, *Hard Choices*, 16–17.

142   **The pressure did not initially work:** Ibid., 18.

142   **Obama pressed on, arguing:** Ibid.

142   **Clinton mulled the issue overnight:** Ibid.,16–17.

142   **The next morning Obama received:** Ibid., 18–19.

142   **Given the swirling economic crisis:** Jeanne Sahadi, "Obama Names His
          Economic Team," *CNN Money*, November 24, 2008.

143   **An initial call among them:** Background interview with senior Obama
          administration official.

143   **Summers reportedly did not have:** Ibid.

143   **During that meeting Summers proposed:** Ibid.

143   **Rubin brought a clout to:** Jackie Calmes, "Obama's Economic Team Shows
          Influence of Robert Rubinwith a Difference," *The New York Times*, November
          24, 2008.

144   **Even when, as during the:** Jonathan Weisman, "Obama Taps Froman for Joint
          Security, Economic Post," *The Wall Street Journal*, January 30, 2009.

144   **Accordingly, Obama asked Robert Gates:** Peter Baker, "Defense Secretary Said
          to Be Staying On," *The New York Times*, November 25, 2008.

144   **For these reasons he settled:** Woodward, *Obama's Wars* (New York: Simon and
          Schuster, 2010), 37–39.

144   **Jones was initially hesitant about:** Ibid.

144   **Ultimately, Thomas Donilon, the head:** David E. Sanger and Helene Cooper, "Civilian Replaces General in Key Foreign Policy Job," *The New York Times*, October 8, 2010.

144   **Obama announced the Clinton, Gates, and Jones:** Peter Baker, "Appointments Begin a New Phase for Obama," *The New York Times*, December 1, 2008.

144   **Joining them alongside Obama were:** Ibid.

144   **At the event, Obama made:** Ibid.

145   **He suggested he would welcome:** Ibid.

145   **Michèle Flournoy and former deputy defense:** "Obama-Biden Transition Team Announces Agency Review Team Leads for Dept of Treasury, State, Defense," *Change.Gov: The Office of the President-Elect*, accessed May 15, 2014.

145   **To round out the national:** Joby Warrick, "Brennan Withdraws from Consideration for Administration Post," *The Washington Post*, November 25, 2008.

145   **However, Brennan had become a:** Ibid.

145   **He therefore withdrew his name:** Ibid.

145   **In his place, also at the suggestion:** Carl Hulse and Mark Mazzetti, "Panetta to Be Named C.I.A. Director," *The New York Times*, January 5, 2009.

145   **Though he had limited prior direct national:** Ibid.

145   **Furthermore, he had recently been immersed:** Ibid.; Woodward, *Obama's Wars*, 58.

146   **He was named deputy national security advisor:** Mann, *Obamians*, 105; Karen DeYoung, "Obama's NSC Will Get New Power," *The Washington Post*, February 8, 2009.

Chapter 5: Hello, I Must Be Going

148   **"Afghanistan has been called the:** Milton Bearden, "Afghanistan: Graveyard of Empires," *Foreign Affairs*, November/December 2001.

148   **As activist fimmaker Michael Moore:** "Most liberals I know were for invading Afghanistan right after 9/11 Michael Moore at BrainyQuote," *BrainyQuote*, http://www.brainyquote.com/quotes/quotes/m/michaelmoo580117.html#7W4rWo5XQTog71J2.99.

148   **Writing in the first post-9/11:** Bearden, "Afghanistan Graveyard."

149   **In the late 1980s Bearden oversaw:** Milton Bearden and James Risen, *The Main Enemy: The Inside Story of the CIA's Final Showdown with the KGB* (New York: Presidio Press, 2003), 283.

149   **He had seen the challenges:** Bearden and Rise, *The Main Enemy*.

149   **The initial US effort in Afghanistan:** Peter Tomsen, *The Wars of Afghanistan: Messianic Terrorism, Tribal Conflicts, and the Failures of Great Powers* (New York: PublicAffairs, 2011), 595–596.

149   **Just about five weeks after:** Kenneth Katzman, "CRS Report to Congress: Afghanistan: Post-Taliban Governance, Security, and U.S. Policy," *Congressional Research* Service, April 9, 2014, 8; Tomsen, *The Wars of Afghanistan*, 604.

149 **It created the International Security Assistance Force:** Katzman, "Post-Taliban Governance, Security, and Policy."

149 **The same month, at an international:** Norimitsu Onishi, "Clan Leader Turned Statesman: Hamid Karzai," *The New York Times*, December 6, 2001.

149 **The new president was Hamid:** Ibid.

149 **Over the next year, according to the Congressional:** Amy Belasco, "Troop Levels in the Afghan and Iraq Wars, FY2001-FY2012: Costs and Other Potential Issues," *Congressional Research Service*, July 2, 2009.

149 **It doubled again by fiscal year:** Ibid.

149 **In that country, the total:** Ibid.

149 **In the words of one:** Background interview with senior Bush administration official.

150 **We knew it because the CIA:** Tomsen, *Wars of Afghanistan*, 246–247.

150 **And whereas Afghanistan was a desperately:** Husain Haqqani, "Breaking Up Is Not Hard to Do," *Foreign Affairs*, March/April 2013.

150 **At the beginning of American:** "Table of Pakistani Nuclear Forces, 2002," *National Resource Defense Council*, November 25, 2002, http://www.nrdc.org/nuclear/nudb/datab21.asp.

150 **The prospect that extremists, who were:** Greg Miller, Craig Whitlock, and Barton Gellman, "Top-secret U.S. intelligence files show new levels of distrust of Pakistan," *The Washington Post*, September 2, 2013.

150 **As a general once told me:** Background interview with U.S. military general.

150 **As Condoleezza Rice noted:** Condoleezza Rice, *No Higher Honor*, 345.

150 **Until then the invasion had:** Kenneth Katzman, "Afghanistan: Post-Taliban Governance, Security, and U.S. Policy," *Congressional Research Service*, May 29, 2014; David Rohde and David E. Sanger, "How a 'Good War' in Afghanistan Went Bad," *The New York Times*, August 12, 2007.

151 **Indeed, it had been May:** David E. Sanger, *The Inheritance: The World Obama Confronts and the Challenges to American Power* (New York: Broadway Books, 2009), 146–147.

151 **But, as Rice also observed with regard:** Rice, *No Higher Honor*, 345.

151 **Further, in the view of senior Bush:** Background interview with senior Bush administration official.

151 **Bush officials sought to be seen:** Ibid.

151 **By 2006, there was rapidly growing unease:** Rumsfeld, *Known and Unknown*, 687; Bush, *Decision Points*, 210–211.

151 **The Taliban were regrouping in Pakistan:** Ahmed Rashid, *Descent into Chaos: The U.S. and the Disaster in Pakistan, Afghanistan, and Central Asia* (New York: Penguin Books, 2009), 364.

151 **Not only had US financial aid:** Rohde and Sanger, "Afghanistan Went Bad"; Curt Tarnoff, "Afghanistan: U.S. Foreign Assistance," *Congressional Research Service*, August 12, 2010; Rashid, *Descent into Chaos*, 355.

151 **The Afghan government could only spend:** Rashid, *Descent into Chaos*, 194.

151 **Meanwhile, throughout 2005 and 2006:** Rumsfeld, *Known and Unknown*, 689; Rashid, *Descent into Chaos*, 353.

151 **Rumsfeld's impulses, combined with the:** Rashid, *Descent into Chaos*, 353.

152   **When Rumsfeld and CENTCOM chief General:** Rashid, *Descent into Chaos*, 334.

152   **Shifting responsibility to NATO, as:** Sanger, *The Inheritance*, 115.

152   **Rumsfeld acknowledged that:** Rumsfeld, *Known and Unknown*, 687.

152   **What he didn't admit was that the United:** Rashid, *Descent into Chaos*, 223.

152   **Worrying about a resurgence:** Rumsfeld, *Known and Unknown*, 687.

152   **Strmecki's report to Rumsfeld was:** Ibid., 687–688.

153   **Rumsfeld characterizes his efforts:** Rumsfeld, *Known and Unknown*, 689, 691.

153   **He recalled in his memoirs receiving:** Bush, *Decision Points*, 210.

153   **It noted that in the past:** Ibid.

153   **Like Rumsfeld, he blamed the:** Ibid.

153   **He also noted what he and his successors:** Ibid., 211.

153   **In keeping with another Washington:** Ibid., 212.

153   **This was accompanied by a very sharp:** Rashid, *Descent into Chaos*, 366.

153   **In the last six months:** Ibid.

153   **The number increased over twentyfold:** Ibid.

153   **In his book, *Descent into Chaos*:** Raymond Bonner, "War in Progress," *The New York Times*, August 10, 2008; Rashid, *Descent into Chaos*, 194–195.

154   **Bush NSC officials note that it was:** Background interview with senior Bush administration official.

154   **Rather, there was a concerted effort:** Ibid.

154   **They provided, in their eyes:** Ibid.

154   **In Afghanistan, throughout the Bush:** Gilles Dorronsoro, "The Taliban's Winning Strategy in Afghanistan," *The Carnegie Endowment for International Peace*, 2009; Katzman, "Afghanistan: Post-Taliban Governance, Security, and U.S. Policy."

155   **Not only did significant portions:** William Dalrymple, "A Deadly Triangle: Afghanistan, Pakistan, and India," *The Brookings Institution*, June 25, 2013.

155   **These are linked in part:** Background interview with U.S. diplomat.

155   **For many in Pakistan, including military leaders:** Dalrymple, "A Deadly Triangle."

155   **The fear that a new government:** Ibid.

155   **Therefore Pakistan saw as:** Ibid.

155   **Few events so dramatically captured:** Bush, *Decision Points*, 214.

155   **According to Bush, "at one:** Ibid., 215.

155   **Rice recounted that Karzai had:** Rice, *No Higher Honor*, 444–445.

155   **After listening for an extended:** Ibid.

156   **Rice, the former competitive figure skater:** Ibid., 445.

156   **Within months, the United States was intently:** Rashid, *Descent into Chaos*, 370.

156   **The new secretary of defense:** Ibid.

156   **Doubts grew about Musharraf:** Bush, *Decision Points*, 213.

156   **The problem was that neither diplomacy:** Rashid, *Descent into Chaos*, 370.

156   **In his memoirs Bush recounted the watershed:** Bush, *Decision Points*, 217.

156   **David Sanger, one of the foremost analysts:** Sanger, *The Inheritance*, 122–123.

156   **Instead, the administration mounted a public:** Ibid.

157   **One top Bush advisor with whom:** Background interview with senior Bush administration official.

157   **In mid-July of that year, in a speech:** "Barack Obama's remarks on Iraq and National Security," *Council on Foreign Relations*, July 15, 2008.

157   **He went on to say that:** Ibid.

158   **The process of preparing the president-elect:** Bob Woodward, *Obama's Wars* (New York: Simon and Schuster, 2010), 40–41.

158   **Bush had wanted a no-holds-barred:** Ibid.

158   **So Lute took an interagency:** Ibid.

158   **Back in Washington, he began:** Bush, *Decision Points*, 218.

158   **They might not be able to follow through:** Ibid., 218.

158   **The report itself was presented at:** Woodward, *Obama's Wars*, 40–41.

158   **Hadley's admonitions aside, the report:** Ibid., 43.

158   **The report flagged three problems:** Ibid., 43–44.

158   **What it did not do was clarify:** Background interview with NSC official.

159   **Said one insider, "this was:** Background interview with Bush administration security official.

159   **Rice, in both her memoirs and in private:** Rice, *No Higher Honor*, 635–636.

159   **Bush wrote, "our rapid success with low:** Bush, *Decision Points*, 207.

159   **Strikingly, Rumsfeld suggested that he:** Rumsfeld, *Known and Unknown*, 691.

159   **One particularly resonant comment came:** Background interview with US government official.

159   **That war began for Obama just two days:** Woodward, *Obama's Wars*, 1.

159   **Bush had ordered that key elements:** Ibid., 1–2.

159   **One key element, according to Bob Woodward's:** Ibid., 3–4.

159   **It highlighted the American perception that:** Ibid.

159   **Important cyber and special ops:** Ibid., 7–8.

159–160   **According to Woodward, Obama left:** Ibid., 11.

160   **A subsequent meeting, about two weeks later:** Ibid., 33–34.

160   **Mullen asserted that Afghanistan had:** Ibid.

160   **Vice President-elect Biden and:** Ibid., 62–63.

160   **Biden was blunt about the need:** Ibid.

160   **Zardari was more conciliatory than Musharraf:** Ibid., 63.

160   **During the meeting with Karzai they also put down:** Robert M. Gates, *Duty: Memoirs of a Secretary at War* (New York: Alfred A. Knopf, 2014), 337–338; Woodward, *Obama's Wars*, 67.

160   **Woodward quotes Biden as saying:** Woodward, *Obama's Wars*, 67.

160   **The intent, according to staffers:** Background interviews with Obama administration officials.

160   **On this trip Biden also indicated to:** Woodward, *Obama's Wars*, 70

161   **Hillary Clinton fought hard for her friend and ally:** Clinton, *Hard Choices*, 28–29; Jonathan Allen and Amie Parnes, *HRC: State Secrets and the Rebirth of Hillary Clinton* (New York: Crown, 2014), 71–73, 76–77; Glenn Kessler, "Mitchell and Holbrooke to Be Named Envoys," *The Washington Post*, January 21, 2009.

161 **Holbrooke, a brilliant diplomat who:** Robert D. McFadden, "Strong American Voice in Diplomacy and Crisis," *The New York Times*, December 10, 2010.

161 **He served with Kissinger during:** Ibid.

161 **Later, in the Carter administration:** Ibid.

161 **During the Clinton years, he:** Ibid.

161 **Holbrooke had also been Hillary Clinton's chief:** Vali Nasr, "The Inside Story of How the White House Let Diplomacy Fail in Afghanistan," *Foreign Policy*, March 4, 2013.

161 **Lake and Holbrooke had once been very close:** George Packer, "The Last Mission: Richard Holbrooke's plan to avoid the mistakes of Vietnam in Afghanistan," *The New York Times*, September 28, 2009.

161 **Rice was defensive and abrasive, and Holbrooke:** Background interview with senior US Department of State official.

161 **The future successor to Holbrooke as America's:** Dana Milibank, "Susan Rice's tarnished resume," *The Washington Post*, November 16, 2012.

161 **He meant that he felt he:** Packer, "The Last Mission."

161 **Clinton embraced the process, and the:** Ibid.

162 **One example, among the many cited by:** Background interviews with State Department officials.

162 **As a senior advisor, Holbrooke appointed:** Nasr, "The Inside Story."

162 **Husain Haqqani was appointed by Zardari:** Husain Haqqani, *Magnificent Delusions: Pakistan, the United States, and an Epic History of Misunderstanding* (New York: PublicAffairs, 2013), 316.

163 **Another footnote to Holbrooke's start:** Tom Wright, "Richard Holbrooke's Controversial Role in South Asia," *The Wall Street Journal*, December 14, 2010.

163 **But as soon as the Indian:** Ibid.

163 **They did not want to be:** Ibid.

163 **The United States took the Indian:** Nasr, "The Inside Story."

163 **Members of Obama's transition team:** Gerald F. Seib, "Old Hands Meld Continuity, Change," *The Wall Street Journal*, November 11, 2008.

163 **Obama, as was typical, read White House:** Philip Rucker, "Obama Inspired by, Compared to Lincoln," *The Washington Post*, November 19, 2008; John M. Broder, "Obama and Bill Clinton to Hold Summit, *The New York Times*, September 7, 2008; Seib, "Old Hands Meld."

163 **Jones at the NSC also:** Office of the White House Press Secretary, "Remarks by National Security Adviser Jones at 45th Munich Conference on Security Policy," *White House Press Release* (February 9, 2009); David Ignatius, "Gen. James Jones's Outlook as Barack Obama's National Security Adviser," *The Washington Post*, April 30, 2009.

163 **Tom Donilon, who started out as Jones's Deputy:** Steve Clemons, "Obama's Donilon Machine," *The Atlantic*, October 27, 2011.

163 **He had developed a close:** Peter Baker, "A Manager of Overseas Crises, as Much as the World Permits," *The New York Times*, September 23, 2012.

163 **Further, Donilon was the closest:** Ibid.

164 **(Donilon's brother Mike was:** Ibid.

164 **Because he helped oversee the:** Huma Khan, "Transition Heads for State Department About to Be Announced," *ABC News*, November 12, 2008.

167 **Donilon asserts that political:** Background interviews with Obama administration officials.

167 **One other senior Obama official said:** Background interview with senior Obama administration official.

168 **Obama's first national security meeting:** Peter Baker and Thom Shanker, "Obama Meets with Officials on Iraq, Signaling His Commitment to Ending War," *The New York Times*, January 21, 2009; Gates, *Duty*, 337–338.

168 **Also, according to one senior insider:** Background interview with Obama administration official.

168 **This began a long, often frustrating:** Ibid.

168 **That effort later manifested itself:** Eric Schmitt and Charlie Savage, "Bowe Bergdahl, American Soldier, Freed by Taliban in Prisoner Trade," *The New York Times*, May 31, 2014.

168 **The President also asked Bruce Riedel, the former:** Mann, *Obamians*, 123.

168 **Obama had reportedly initially wanted Riedel:** Background interview with Obama administration official.

169 **It would be an interagency process co-chaired by:** Woodward, *Obama's Wars*, 90.

169 **He wanted it done prior to his first NATO summit:** Ibid., 123.

169 **Riedel's recommendation would become a:** Ibid., 99–100.

169 **During early discussions with Jones:** Ibid.

169 **"Very early on," however, noted:** Background interview with Obama administration official.

169 **Biden's answer was to narrow the focus:** Woodward, *Obama's Wars*, 101–102.

169 **His idea was that we had:** Ibid.

169 **Clinton and Gates supported the broader:** Peter Baker, "How Obama Came to Plan for 'Surge' in Afghanistan," *The New York Times*, December 5, 2009.

169 **Obama took into consideration the**: David E. Sanger, *Confront and Conceal: Obama's Secret Wars and Surprising Use of American Power* (New York: Broadway Books, April 23, 2013), 20.

170 **His speech, from the White House:** Woodward, *Obama's Wars*, 113.

170 **Yet within just four and a half:** Michael R. Gordon and Mark Landler, "Decisions on Afghan Troop Levels Calculates Political and Military Interests," *The New York Times*, February 12, 2013; Mark Mazetti and Matthew Rosenberg, "U.S. Considers Faster Pullout in Afghanistan," *The New York Times*, July 8, 2013; Peter Baker and Matthew Rosenberg, "Old Tensions Resurface in Debate Over U.S. Role in Post-2014 Afghanistan," *The New York Times*, February 4, 2014.

170 **Further, while the review was:** Woodward, *Obama's Wars*, 108.

170 **That was the sense that Pakistan:** Ibid.

170 **"I personally found the risks:** Background interview with senior Defense Department official.

171 **Another perspective, described by a top:** Ibid.

171 **One immediate casualty of the Riedel process:** Ann Scott Tyson, "Gen. David McKiernan Ousted as Top U.S. Commander in Afghanistan," *The Washington Post*, May 12, 2009.

171 **On May 11, Secretary of Defense Gates:** Woodward, *Obama's Wars*, 119.

171 **In his remarks announcing the McChrystal:** Ibid.

171 **Woodward recounts Riedel listening:** Ibid.

171 **At McChrystal's confirmation hearing in:** Ibid., 123.

171 **McChrystal recounts in his memoirs that:** McChrystal, *My Share of the Task,* 294.

171 **These included undertaking "a:** Ibid.

171 **As Obama had done with Riedel:** Thom Shanker, "A New Afghanistan Commander Rethinks How to Measure Success," *The New York Times*, June 19, 2009.

171 **Two weeks after arriving in the country, Jim Jones:** McChrystal, *My Share of the Task*, 306.

171 **The general concluded that meant:** Ibid.

172 **By the summer of 2009, in fact:** Mann, *Obamians*, 224.

172 **Phone calls from people in:** Background interviews with Obama administration officials.

172 **He was seen as stiff and:** Background interviews with Obama administration officials.

172 **There were emerging tensions between him**: Woodward, *Obama's Wars*, 137–138.

172 **One *New York Times* story:** Helene Cooper, "The Adviser at the Heart of National Security," *The New York Times*, July 9, 2010.

173 **One of these was that Jones was military:** Mann, *Obamians*, 224.

173 **One senior civilian at Defense:** Background interview with Defense Department official.

173 **The long-time Obama supporter:** Background interview with Defense Department official.

173 **Cartwright, his undeniable qualities as:** Gordon Lubold, "Obama's Favorite General Stripped of His Security Clearance," *Foreign Policy*, September 24, 2013.

173 **He told his team to be as objective:** McChrystal, *My Share of the Task*, 316–317.

173 **His draft document was sixty pages long:** Ibid., 330.

173 **While it didn't seek additional:** Ibid.

173 **It specifically stated that "continued:** Ibid.

173 **Gates, sensing the pushback from the White House:** Gates, *Duty*, 356.

173 **Meanwhile, at the White House, the president:** Sanger, *Confront and Conceal*, 29.

173 **As Sanger writes in *Confront and Conceal*:** Ibid.

174 **Matters were complicated by the fact:** Ibid., 24.

174 **There were widespread Taliban attacks:** Ibid.

174 **Turnout was weak:** Ibid.

174 **And Karzai, increasingly difficult for:** Ibid.

174   **"The election fueled the doubters,":** Background interview with State Department official.

174   **On the one hand, McChrystal's:** Stanley McChrystal, "COMISAF's Initial Assessment," *US Department of Defense*, June 26, 2009.

174   **The bureaucratically savvy Gates:** Woodward, *Obama's Wars*, 153.

174   **Biden's reaction was to hammer out:** Ibid., 159.

174   **On Sunday morning September 13:** Ibid., 161–162.

174   **Obama was respectful of McChrystal's:** Ibid.

174   **Peter Lavoy, then a deputy director:** Ibid., 162.

174   **While the number of core al-Qaeda present:** Ibid.

174   **Lavoy was one of those who:** Ibid., 163.

174   **He and his boss, Admiral Dennis Blair:** Ibid.

174   **Clinton recounted the diplomatic:** Ibid., 163–164.

175   **In fact, ironically, after all the campaign:** James Traub, "The Biden Doctrine," *Foreign Policy*, October 10, 2012.

175   **Obama chaired the discussion by:** Woodward, *Obama's Wars*, 164.

175   **He made the case that what:** Ibid.

175   **But he was essentially allowing Biden:** Ibid., 166–167.

175   **Indeed, that was one of the points:** Peter Baker, "Biden No Longer a Lone Voice on Afghanistan," *The New York Times*, October 13, 2009.

176   **A central debate was framed in:** Baker, "How Obama Came to Plan for 'Surge' in Afghanistan."

176   **Another debate turned on the:** Baker, "How Obama Came to Plan for 'Surge' in Afghanistan"; Baker, "Biden No Longer a Lone Voice."

176   **Yet another turned on:** Baker, "How Obama Came to Plan for 'Surge' in Afghanistan."

176   **Other issues focused on how:** Ibid.

176   **Most tellingly, even as the debate over:** Ibid.

176   **He didn't feel he was getting a clear enough:** Ibid.

176–177 **At the core of this was:** Ibid.

177   **Biden, Donilon and others on:** Background interview with Obama administration official.

177   **Obama finally took command of:** Woodward, *Obama's Wars*, 270–271.

177   **After the old debate started again:** Ibid.

177   **Biden supporters, like Donilon, had reached:** Ibid., 272.

177   **That ambassador, former general Karl Eikenberry:** Baker, "How Obama Came to Plan for 'Surge' in Afghanistan."

177   **Needless to say, for some, especially:** Background interview with Defense Department official.

177   **Although the high and low options:** Woodward, *Obama's Wars*, 272–273.

177   **The military insisted that 20,000:** Ibid., 273, 275.

177   **Biden and his allies pushed back:** Ibid., 270, 275; Gate, *Duty*, 342.

177   **Obama tipped his hand by:** Woodward, *Obama's Wars*, 278; Background interview with NSC official.

177   **There was also an open:** Woodward, *Obama's Wars*, 284–285.

177   **Biden was conducting his own:** Background interviews with Obama administration officials.

177   **Woodward wrote, making apparent reference:** Woodward, *Obama's Wars*, 289.

178   **The process also revealed that there:** Ibid., 236, 275; Background interview with senior Defense Department official.

178   **It was also clear that Obama had:** Woodward, *Obama's Wars*, 211.

178   **And finally, as a kind of:** Background interview with Obama administration official.

178   **Finally, there was one more:** Baker, "How Obama Came to Plan for 'Surge' in Afghanistan."

178   **Two days later, a meeting took place**: Woodward, *Obama's Wars*, 301.

178   **They discussed the speech in which:** Ibid., 313.

178   **But even with this kind:** Ibid., 313–314.

178–179 **Donilon said he got the idea:** Baker, "How Obama Came to Plan for 'Surge' in Afghanistan."

179   **Donilon felt that the process:** Woodward, *Obama's Wars*, 314.

179   **Finally it was determined that:** Baker, "How Obama Came to Plan for 'Surge' in Afghanistan."

179   **(Donilon's reading of history was:** Background interview with Obama administration official.

179   **However, yet again reflecting the:** Woodward, *Obama's Wars*, 319.

179   **And when the final speech was delivered:** Sheryl Gay Stolberg and Helene Cooper, "Obama Adds Troops, but Maps Exit Plan," *The New York Times*, December 1, 2009; Background interview with senior Defense Department official.

179   **One senior military officer said:** Background interview with senior Defense Department official.

179   **Said one intimate participant of:** Ibid.

180   **One problem cited was that:** Ibid.

180   **After thirteen paragraphs outlining the history:** Office of the White House Press Secretary, "Remarks by the President in Address to the Nation on the Way Forward in Afghanistan and Pakistan," *White House Press Release* (December 1, 2009).

180   **He then said, in an understatement:** Ibid.

180   **And then he outlined goals, which:** Ibid.

180   **He also soft-peddled the language:** Ibid.

180   **The rest of the speech was an explication:** Ibid.

180   **He concluded by offering a message:** Ibid.

181   **The *New York Times* headline echoed the:** Stolberg and Cooper, "Obama Adds Troops."

181   **And nothing would confirm these:** White House Office of the Press Secretary, "Overview of the Afghanistan and Pakistan Annual Review," *White House Press Release* (December 16, 2010).

181   **Jim Jones would leave his office:** Scott Wilson, "James Jones to step down as national security adviser," *The Washington Post*, October 8, 2010.

181   **In 2014, as unrest in Iraq:** Peter Baker and Matthew Rosenberg, "Old Tensions Resurface in Debate Over U.S. Role in Post-2014 Afghanistan," *The New York Times,* February 4, 2014.

181   **The decision was also colored:** William Dalrymple, "How Is Hamid Karzai Still Standing?" *The New York Times*, November 20, 2013; Mirwais Harooni and Praveen Menon, "Thousands March Across Kabul to Protest Election Fraud," Reuters, June 27, 2014.

181   **After Secretary of State John Kerry:** Matthew Rosenberg, "Kerry Visits Afghan Leader, Seeking an End to an Impasse," *The New York Times* October 11, 2013; Matthew Rosenberg, "Talks Clear Path for U.S.-Afghan Deal on Troops," *The New York Times,* October 12, 2013; Mark Landler, "U.S. Troops to Leave Afghanistan by End of 2016," *The New York Times*, May 27, 2014; Dalrymple, "Karzai Still Standing?"; Anne Gearan and Ernesto Londoño, "U.S. Backing Off Its Deadline for Afghan Security Agreement," *The Washington Post*, December 11, 2013.

181   **Further, given the unrest in Iraq:** Colin H. Kahl, "No, Obama Didn't Lose Iraq," *Politico Magazine*, June 15, 2014.

Chapter 6: The Most Powerful Man in the World

183   **It was as infused with the language of divine:** "President George W. Bush's Inaugural Address, 2005," *Council on Foreign Relations*, January 20, 2005.

183   **The speech goes on to say:** Ibid.

183   **He continued, "we will persistently:** Ibid.

184   **But they were all, in the:** Background interview with State Department official.

184   **On her first trip to Asia:** Robert Marquand, "As China Rises, US Taps Japan as Key Asian Ally," *The Christian Science Monitor*, March 21, 2005.

184   **In an August 2005 interview:** Joel Brinkley, "Rice Warns China to Make Major Economic Changes," *The New York Times*, August 19, 2005.

184   **Among the good parts, she noted:** Ibid.

184–185 **It's a sentiment reiterated by Bush:** Peter Baker, "President Revisits Foreign Policy," *The Washington Post*, September 14, 2005.

185   **Deputy Secretary of State Robert Zoellick:** Robert B. Zoellick, "Wither China: From Membership to Responsibility?" *US Department of State Archive*, September 21, 2005.

185   **At the Defense Department, China's growing:** "Annual Report to Congress: The Military Power of the People's Republic of China 2005," Office of the Secretary of Defense, 13.

185   **The trade deficit continued to grow:** Keith Bradsher, "As Trade Deficit Grows, So Do Tensions with China," *The New York Times*, March 10, 2006.

185   **So were tensions associated with:** Ibid.

185   **The efforts to improve relations:** Sanger, *Inheritance*, 392.

185   **And shortly later, a representative:** Ibid.

185   **For example, the White House:** Joseph Kahn, "Bush and Hu Vow New Cooperation," *The New York Times*, April 21, 2006.

185   **Secretary Rice argued that such:** Rice, *No Higher Honor*, 525.

185   **When he was recruited into the administration:** Paul Blustein, "Treasury Nominee Has Ties to China," *The Washington Post*, June 6, 2006.

185   **However, in conversations with his senior:** Background interviews with Bush administration officials.

186   **Against this background, the US-China:** Peter S. Goodman, "Paulson Gets Promise Only of Dialogue With China," *The Washington Post*, September 21, 2006.

186   **The undertaking would involve multiple:** Ibid.

186   **With the election of a Democratic:** Charles Hutzler, "China Anticipates Bumpy Road with U.S." *The Washington Post*, November 9, 2006.

186   **Any foreboding that the Chinese may have felt:** Steven R. Weisman, "U.S. Rebukes China on Trade Ahead of Paulson Trip," *The New York Times*, December 11, 2006.

186   **As a consequence, the initial meeting of the SED:** Ariana Eunjung Cha, "U.S., China Clash on Currency," *The Washington Post*, December 15, 2006.

186   **As had been the case under Robert Rubin:** David M. Lampton, *Same Bed, Different Dreams: Managing U.S.-China Relations, 1989–2000* (Oakland, CA: University of California Press, May 2002), 34.

186   **Even as relations between the two giant countries:** William J. Broad and David E. Sanger, "Flexing Muscle, China Destroys Satellite in Test," *The New York Times*, January 19, 2007.

187   **During a May 2007 meeting, Vice Premier:** "UPDATE 1-China's Wu urges trade cooperation, not confrontation," Reuters, May 22, 2007.

187   **And again speaking the language of commerce:** Michael M. Phillips and Rick Carew, "U.S. Presses for Results from China Talks," *The Wall Street Journal*, May 23, 2007.

187   **But enough progress was being made via dialogue:** Steven R. Weisman, "Chinese Officials Extol Benefits of U.S. Relations," *The New York Times*, May 25, 2007.

187   **The positive trajectory in the relationship:** Brian Knowlton, "Bush and Congress Honor Dalai Lama," *The New York Times*, October 18, 2007.

187   **They condemned the action but within:** Mark Mazzetti, "Gates Offers to Work with China's Military," *The New York Times*, June 2, 2007.

187   **similar in purpose to the one the United States:** Edward Cody, "China and U.S. to Establish Military Hotline," *The Washington Post*, November 6, 2007.

187   **Further new military exchanges:** Ibid.

187   **For example:** Ibid.

187   **In addition, Bush had won considerable:** Sheryl Gay Stolberg, "Bush to Attend Opening Ceremonies of the Beijing Olympics," *The New York Times*, July 4, 2008; Background interview with senior Bush administration official.

187   **Bush told Hu personally of his:** Background interview with senior Bush administration official.

188 **This was seen by the Chinese:** Ibid; Robert Marquand, "E.U. weighs Olympic Boycott Over Tibet," *The Christian Science Monitor*, March 27, 2008.

188 **In the immediate foreground were games:** Amy Shipley, "China's Show of Power," *The Washington Post*, August 25, 2008.

188 **The games were exceptionally well:** Ibid.

188 **The Chinese had regularly been in touch:** Henry M. Paulson, *On the Brink: Inside the Race to Stop the Collapse of the Global Financial System* (New York: Business Plus, 2010), 82–83, 128.

188 **Particularly striking were revelations in Paulson's:** Ibid., 160–161.

188 **During the opening ceremonies of:** Bush, *Decision Points*, 434; Baker, *Days of Fire*, 602.

188 **Meanwhile, Paulson learned that the Russians:** Paulson, *On the Brink*, 160–161.

188 **"The report," Paulson wrote, "was deeply:** Ibid., 161.

189 **Wikileaks cables showed that throughout:** Emily Flitter, "China Flexed Its Muscles Using U.S. Treasures: The U.S. Did a Lot of Hand Holding with Its Biggest Lender During the Financial Crisis," Reuters, February 17, 2011.

189 **Mid-crisis estimates of CIC losses:** Jamil Anderlini, "China Lost Billions in Diversification Drive," *The Financial Times*, March 15, 2009.

189 **When Fannie Mae and Freddie Mac:** Flitter, "China Flexed Its Muscles."

189 **"Several interlocutors have told us that:** Ibid.

189 **Because of Paulson's relationships with the Chinese:** Paulson, *On the Brink*, 52.

189 **Indeed, as a sign of respect, Under Secretary:** Flitter, "China Flexed Its Muscles."

189 **A Wikileaks cable reported:** Ibid.

189 **The Chinese did say that unless concerns:** Ibid.

189 **McCormick, for his part, delivered a message:** Ibid.

189 **Nonetheless, it was "committing:** Ibid.

189 **In taking this trip and in sending this kind of message:** Ibid.

189–190 **At the same time, Beijing's huge investment exposure:** Ibid.

190 **One final way that the:** Sheryl Gay Stolberg, "As Leaders Wrestle with Economy, Developing Nations Get Ringside Seats," *The New York Times*, November 15, 2008.

191 **That meeting, which took place on November 14:** Ibid.

191 **In a footnote to that meeting:** Mark Landler, "World Leaders Vow Joint Push to Aid Economy," *The New York Times*, November 15, 2008.

191 **In fact, they invited Obama, but he chose:** Ibid.

193 **Of those formative early days:** Jeffrey A. Bader, *Obama and China's Rise: An Insider's Account of America's Asia Strategy* (Washington, DC: Brookings Institution Press, 2013), 3.

193 **He added:** Ibid.

194 **With Clinton's first trip to the region:** Glen Kessler, "Clinton Packs Full Asia Agenda for First Trip as Secretary of State," *The Washington Post*, February 6, 2009; Mann, *Obamians*, 175.

194 **Clinton and her colleagues felt State should:** Mann, *Obamians*, 175–176.

194 **Geithner sought to continue the dominant role:** Ibid.

194   **And there was even a move to keep the central:** Bader, *Obama and China's Rise*,
        22; Ted Osius, "Legacy of the Clinton-Gore Administration's China Policy,"
        Asian Affairs, 28.3, Fall 2001, 125–134; James Mann, *About Face: A History
        of America's Curious Relationship with China from Nixon to Clinton* (New
        York: Alfred A. Knopf, 1999), 351–352; Wolf Blitzer, "Republicans Hammer
        Gore over U.S. Policy Toward China," *CNN.com,* March 10, 1999.

194   **Hillary Clinton asserted that, although economic issues:** Mann, *Obamians*, 176.

194   **She also argued that during the Bush years:** Bader, *Obama and China's Rise*,
        105.

194   **Geithner's response turned on the sensitivity:** Background interview with senior
        Treasury Department official.

194   **In fact, even in the earliest days of the Obama:** Ibid.

194   **Within the NSC, Donilon and Bader also supported:** Bader, *Obama and China's
        Rise*, 22.

194   **There were questions as to whether the Chinese:** Ibid., 22.

194   **However, those would be worked out:** Ibid.

195   **The process was to be rechristened the Strategic:** Mann, *Obamians*, 176.

195   **In her first major address on her first major:** Mark Landler, "Clinton Seeks a
        Shift on China," *The New York Times*, February 13, 2009.

195   **Her message to the media:** Ibid.

195   **This involved not just a focus:** Ibid.

195   **For that strategic reason she:** Jill Dougherty, "Clinton Heads to Asia on First
        State Trip," *CNN Politics*, February 16, 2009.

195   **She characterized the approach:** Landler, "Clinton Seeks a Shift on China."

195   **During her stop in China, Clinton:** Ibid.

195   **Deftly communicating both elements of the:** Ibid.

195   **On the topic of human rights:** Ibid.

195   **Many on the American left and:** Washington Post Editorial Board, "Hillary
        Clinton's Silence on Chinese Human Rights," *The Washington Post*, February
        24, 2009; "US: Clinton Remarks Undermine Rights Reform in China,"
        Human Rights Watch, February 20, 2009; Bret Stephens, "Does Obama
        Believe in Human Rights?" *The Wall Street Journal*, October 19, 2009.

195   **"It was a very mature:** Background interview with senior foreign government
        official.

195   **The G-20 summit took place in London:** Henry J. Pulizzi, "Obama to Visit
        China, Resume Dialogue," *The Wall Street Journal*, April 2, 2009.

195   **Obama underscored the American:** White House Office of the Press Secretary,
        "News Conference by President Obama," *White House Press Release* (April 2,
        2009).

195   **On the other hand, Hu, highlighting:** Office of the White House Press
        Secretary, "Statement on Bilateral Meeting with President Hu of China,"
        White House Press Release (April 1, 2009).

196   **And although both committed to boosting:** Pulizzi, "Obama to Visit China."

196   **Finally, Hu and Obama agreed to proceed:** Ibid.

196   **This was followed again by a bit of back and forth:** Bader, *Obama and China's
        Rise*, 22–23.

196 **Clinton and State argued that:** Ibid.

196 **Geithner followed with his own trip to China:** David Barboza, "Geithner Says China Has Faith in U.S.," *The New York Times*, June 3, 2009.

196 **A week later at the ASEAN summit in Thailand:** Simon Montlake, "Clinton Stresses US Commitment at ASEAN Forum," *The Christian Science Monitor*, July 23, 2009.

196 **Clinton and Geithner kicked it off with:** Hillary Clinton and Timothy Geithner, "A New Strategic and Economic Dialogue with China," *The Wall Street Journal*, July 27, 2009.

196 **Obama himself opened the meetings:** "U.S. and China launch 'new dialogue,'" *CNN*, July 27, 2009.

196 **If there were few concrete deliverables:** Background interview with senior American official.

197 **He added, "you could tell:** Ibid.

197 **Two months later, Deputy Secretary:** Sanger, *Confront and Conceal*, 387–288.

197 **He said it "rests on a core:** Ibid.

197 **He specifically cited several areas:** Ibid.

197 **Although the strategic reassurance:** Al Pessin, "U.S. Calls on China for 'Strategic Reassurance,'" *Voice of America*, September 24, 2009.

197 **Steinberg, frustrated by his near-miss:** Background interviews with Obama administration officials.

197 **Derogatory nicknames for him were bandied:** Ibid.

197 **One of Clinton's closest aides:** Background interview with senior aide to Hillary Clinton.

197 **"But," the aide said, "those:** Ibid.

198 **A "deal" that Clinton struck with Obama:** Allen and Parnes, *HRC,* 59, 102.

198 **Plus, White House aides felt some of Hillary's:** Ibid., 99–101, 141–145; Alter, *The Promise*, 236–237; Jonathan Alter, "Woman of the World," *Vanity Fair*, June 2011.

198 **And so there was also an effort:** Mann, *Obamians*, 211–212; Allen and Parnes, *HRC*, 102–103; Ben Smith, "Hillary Clinton Toils in the Shadows," *Politico*, June 23, 2009.

198 **I had some personal experience with this when:** David Rothkopf, "It's 3 a.m. Do You Know Where Hillary Clinton Is?" *The Washington Post*, August 23, 2009.

198 **Citing some lingering tensions over the definition:** Ibid.

199 **At the November 2009 G-20 summit:** Background interview with Latin American government official.

199 **Even a top US State Department official:** Background interview with US State Department official.

199 **Leaks from the White House—an essential tool:** Josh Rogin, "The end of the concept of 'strategic reassurance'?," *Foreign Policy*, November 6, 2009.

199 **On the trip, Obama began:** Mike Allen, "America's First Pacific President," *Politico*, November 13, 2009.

199 **Obama's trip to Beijing carried forward:** Bader, *Obama and China's Rise*, 54–55.

199 **Although it began with the president:** Ibid.

199   **The Chinese also limited Obama's access:** Mann, *Obamians*, 180–182.

199   **The joint statement at the end:** Bader, *Obama and China's Rise*, 55–56.

199   **An assessment in the *New York Times*:** Michael Wines and Sharon LaFraniere, "During Visit, Obama Skirts Chinese Political Sensitivities," *The New York Times*, November 17, 2009.

200   **Not only was State periodically frustrated:** Mann, *Obamians*, 211–212; Allen and Parnes, *HRC*, 102–103; Smith, "Clinton in the Shadows"; George Packer, "Long Engagements," *The New Yorker*, February 11, 2013; Michael Hirsh, "The Clinton Legacy," *Foreign Affairs*, May/June 2013; Josh Gerstein and Patrick Gavin, "Why Reporters Are Down on President Obama," *Politico*, April 28, 2010; Linda Feldmann, "Obama and the Press: Who Said They Were Cozy?" *The Christian Science Monitor*, June 1, 2010.

200   **In one instance, a senior reporter:** Background interview with news reporter.

200   **The involvement of Jarrett and political aides:** Edward Luce, "America: A Fearsome Foursome," *The Financial Times*, February 3, 2010.

200   **It was there that a plan led by the Atlantic powers:** Mann, *Obamians*, 183.

200   **The Chinese, Indians, and others knew:** Ibid.

200   **At that meeting, thanks to their unity:** Ibid.

200   **Symbolizing the shift, the Chinese repeatedly:** Ibid.

200   **On one occasion, they sent:** Ibid.

200   **Later, at an evening session for emerging powers:** Ibid.

200   **He then crashed the conversation:** Ibid.

200   **Clinton herself, who witnessed this:** Clinton, *Hard Choices*, 491–492, Allen and Parnes, *HRC*, 178–180; Michael Hirsh, "How Hillary Found Her Groove with Obama," *The Daily Beast*, April 22, 2010.

201   **Sandalow of the Energy Department made:** Matthew L. Wald, "Coming and Going at the Energy Department," *The New York Times*, April 10, 2013.

201   **Said one, "the China and Asia:** Background interview with Obama administration official.

201   **In January 2010, the administration:** "China Complains About Arms Sales to Taiwan," *CNN.com*, January 8, 2010.

201   **It announced a week later the test:** Andrew Jacobs and Jonathan Ansfield, "With Defense Test, China Shows Displeasure of U.S." *The New York Times*, January 12, 2010.

201–202 **And it offered the usual boilerplate that:** Ibid.

202   **Clinton responded by making a strong statement:** Chris McGreal and Bobbie Johnson, "Hillary Clinton Criticizes Beijing over Internet Censorship," *The Guardian*, January 21, 2010; Hannah Beech, "Michelle Obama Defends Free Internet in China Speech," *Time*, March 22, 2014.

202   **She also singled out cyber-attacks as an area:** Mark Landler, "Clinton Urges Global Response to Internet Attacks," *The New York Times*, January 22, 2010.

202   **In February, a meeting in the White House:** Bader, *Obama and China's Rise*, 72–73.

202   **In March, Steinberg and Bader were invited:** Ibid., 76.

202   **Steinberg used this occasion to press for:** Ibid., 77.

202   **In April the mood swung positive:** Ibid., 77–78.

202   **By May, the goals for the S&ED:** Mark Landler, "Clinton and Geithner Face Hurdles in China Talks," *The New York Times*, May 24, 2010.

202   **Obama did push China on its focus on propping:** Sewell Chan and Jackie Calmes, "World Leaders Agree on Timetable for Cutting Deficits," *The New York Times*, June 27, 2010.

202   **Donilon and Bader pushed Obama:** Bader, *Obama and China's Rise*, 14, 96.

202   **Behind the scenes, Campbell worked:** Elizabeth Economy, "Missing in Asia: the Pivotal Person in Obama's Pivot," *Forbes*, May 1, 2014; *Principles of U.S. Engagement in the Asia-Pacific, United States Senate*, 111th Congress (2010) (testimony of Kurt M. Campbell, Assistant Secretary of State, Bureau of East Asian and Pacific Affairs, US Department of State).

203   **Clinton put an emphatic punctuation mark:** Mark Landler, "Offering to Aid Talks, U.S. Challenges China on Disputed Islands," *The New York Times*, July 23, 2010.

203   **She insisted that for the United States:** Ibid.

203   **China's foreign minister was livid:** Bader, *Obama and China's Rise*, 105.

203   **He stated forcefully, "China is a big country:** Ibid.

203   **Later that month, China asserted it's "indisputable:** John Pomfret, "Beijing Claims 'Indisputable Sovereignty' over South China Sea," *The Washington Post*, July 31, 2010.

203   **The paradox in this was, of course, that:** Ronald O'Rourke, "China Naval Modernization: Implications for U.S. Navy Capabilities—Background—and Issues for Congress," *Congressional Research Service*, April 10, 2014.

203   **(China has embarked on a program:** Ibid.

203   **Recognizing the importance of deepening:** Bader, *Obama and China's Rise*, 115–116.

203   **This was a very unusual arrangement:** Ibid.

203   **It created interesting questions of protocol:** Ibid.

203   **The Chinese, however, recognizing the way:** Ibid.

203–204 **Donilon made it clear that for the president:** Ibid., 116–117.

204   **Summers made the case that China needed:** Ibid., 117–118.

204   **The tenor of the discussions was positive:** Ibid., 118.

204   **Then, in October 2010 Donilon ascended:** Scott Wilson, "Security Job Goes to Insider," *The Washington Post*, October 9, 2010.

204   **An aspect of this White House–centric:** Luce, "America: A Fearsome Foursome."

204   **Given the retributive mentality of:** Ibid.

204   **It noted that these four were crucially involved:** Ibid.

204   **"Perhaps the biggest losers are:** Ibid.

204   **He cited Kathleen Sebelius, Obama's:** Ibid.

204   **He noted Rahm Emanuel's famed:** Ibid.

204   **Said one big Obama supporter:** Ibid.

204   **Describing the Obama China visit:** Ibid.

204   **On Mr. Obama's November trip:** Ibid.

205   **But its thesis was also confirmed and:** Background interviews with Obama administration officials, American donors, and current and former members of Congress.

205   **Steve Clemons, a thoughtful, well-known:** Steve Clemons, "Core Chicago Team Sinking Obama Presidency," *The Washington Note*, February 7, 2010.

205   **Supporting and adding nuance to:** Background interview with former senior Obama administration official.

205   **This official, a former top:** Ibid.

205   **But underscoring Luce's analysis he added:** Ibid.

206   **Other senior officials in multiple:** Background interviews with Obama administration officials.

206   **"Nobody would do anything unless:** Background interview with US State Department official.

207   **Another deficiency fed by the concentration:** Background interview with Obama administration official.

207   **A senior Obama advisor on national security:** Ibid.

207   **But, "during the Obama years:** Ibid.

207   **The NSC veteran noted that this not:** Ibid.

207   **This was another, albeit inadvertent:** Ibid.

207   **Said a top White House lawyer:** Ibid.

207   **By the end of Jones's tenure, the NSC staff:** Background interview with NSC official.

208   **As one former NSC principal put it:** Background interview with former Bush administration official.

208   **Because Donilon was one of the principal:** Mark Landler, "Rice to Replace Donilon in the Top National Security Post," *The New York Times*, June 5, 2013.

208   **He had won, during the first two years:** Wilson, "Security Job Goes to the Insider."

208   **At the same time, his counterparts:** Ibid.

209   **Clinton further articulated the policy:** Hillary Rodham Clinton, "America's Engagement in the Asia-Pacific," *US Department of State*, October 28, 2010.

209   **At the summit, she sought to defuse:** Mark Landler, "U.S. Works to Ease China-Japan Conflict," *The New York Times*, October 30, 2010.

209   **The dispute over control of the islands:** Ibid.

209   **In private meetings, Clinton offered:** Ibid.

209   **The tensions would grow well into:** Simon Denyer, "Obama's Asia Rebalance Turns into Headache as China, Japan Relations Spiral Down," *The Washington Post,* January 23, 2014.

209   **Consistent with the overall strategy:** Ewan MacAskill and Jason Burke, "Barack Obama Begins 10-Day Asia Tour," *The Guardian*, November 5, 2010.

209   **In India, in a decision that insiders:** Background interviews with senior Obama administration officials; Sheryl Gay Stolberg and Jim Yardley, "Countering

China, Obama Backs India for U.N. Council," *The New York Times*, November 8, 2010.

209   **The offer, even though it came:** Stolberg and Yardley, "Obama Backs India for U.N. Council."

209   **Despite this and tensions over issues in Korea:** Austin Ramzy, "Will Obama and Hu Jintao Find Middle Ground?" *Time*, January 18, 2011.

209   **During Hu's visit, Steinberg's idea:** Bader, *Obama and China's Rise*, 120–127.

210   **Seeking to define the policy, Clinton:** Hillary Clinton, "America's Pacific Century," *Foreign Policy*, October 11, 2011.

210   **She began, "as the war:** Ibid.

210   **It had six lines of action:** Ibid.

210   **She went on: "in the last:** Ibid.

210   **Leon Panetta, who replaced Gates:** Elisabeth Bumiller, "U.S. to Sustain Military Power in the Pacific, Panetta Says," *The New York Times*, October 23, 2011.

210   **Obama then capped the effort:** White House Office of the Press Secretary, "Opening Remarks by President Obama at APEC Session One," *White House Press Release* (November 13, 2011).

210   **He called the Asia-Pacific:** Ibid.

211   **Four days later, he illustrated his:** Jackie Calmes, "A U.S. Marine Base for Australia Irritates China," *The New York Times*, November 16, 2011.

211   **Donilon also followed with a reinforcing:** Tom Donilon, "America Is Back in the Pacific and Will Uphold the Rules," *The Financial Times*, November 27, 2011.

211   **The term *pivot* was attacked by allies:** Chris Carroll, "Hagel: US Pivot to Asia Doesn't Mean Abandoning Middle East," *Stars and Stripes*, December 6, 2013; Vali Nasr, "America Must Assuage Saudi Anxiety," *The New York Times*, February 5, 2014.

211   **The Chinese, of course, were angered:** Kevin Rudd, "Beyond the Pivot: the Future of U.S.-Chinese Relations," *Foreign Affairs*, March/April 2013.

211   **Campbell and Donilon, in particular:** Background interview with senior Obama administration official.

211   **Donilon preferred the term *strategic rebalancing*:** White House Office of the Press Secretary, "Remarks by Tom Donilon, National Security Advisor to the President—as Prepared for Delivery," *White House Press Release* (March 11, 2013).

211   **By announcing the policy as a major change:** Philip Ewing, "Obama's Asia Pivot: A Work in Progress," *Politico*, April 20, 2014.

212   **John Kerry would focus more:** Ely Ratner, "Has Foggy Bottom Forgotten Asia?" *Foreign Policy*, July 2, 2013; Robert D. Kaplan, "Kerry's Middle East Obsession," *Forbes*, September 25, 2013; Julie Pace, "Rice Helping Obama Juggle Foreign Policy Crises," The Associated Press, May 31, 2014.

212   **The year began with the president:** Mark McDonald, "Obama Gives China the Business," *International Herald Tribune*, January 25, 2012.

212   **He boasted of bringing WTO cases:** McDonald, "Obama Gives China the
        Business."

212   **Then, over the next nine months:** Michael Scherer, "Obama Welcomes
        Campaign Season with China Trade Complaint," *Time*, July 5, 2012; Carol
        E. Lee and Damian Paletta, "U.S. to File WTO Charges on China," *The Wall
        Street Journal*, September 17, 2012; Helene Cooper, "Obama Orders Chinese
        Company to End Investment at Sites Near Drone Base," *The New York Times*,
        September 28, 2012.

212   **Then in late April, shortly before a trip:** Kim Ghattas, *The Secretary: A
        Journey with Hillary Clinton from Beirut to the Heart of American Power* (New
        York: Times Books, 2013), 332.

212   **This was done with the White House's:** Ibid., 332; Background interviews with
        US State Department officials.

212   **Donilon was reportedly uneasy about:** Ghattas, *The Secretary*, 332.

212   **Campbell informed the Chinese ambassador:** Steven Lee Myers and Mark
        Landler, "Behind Twists of Diplomacy in the Case of a Chinese Dissident,"
        The New York Times, May 9, 2012.

212   **Campbell undertook negotiations seeking:** Ibid.

212   **China's opening position was that they:** Ibid.

213   **Intense back-and-forth exchanges:** Ibid.

213   **She then personally intervened with:** Ibid.

213   **Chen was freed to seek medical:** Ghattas, *The Secretary*, 333.

213   **What had been a near-fiasco had:** Michael Wines and Annie Lowrey, "China
        Agrees to Measures to Ease Trade," *The New York Times*, May 4, 2012.

213   **In the middle of the year:** William Wan, "Panetta, in speech in Singapore, seeks
        to lend heft to U.S. pivot to Asia," *The Washington Post*, June 1, 2012.

213   **Almost simultaneously, working the:** Patrick Barta, "Southeast Asia Gets a
        Boost from Clinton," *The Wall Street Journal*, July 13, 2012.

213   **Later that year, Obama traveled:** Daniel Ten Kate and Margaret Talev,
        "Obama Courts ASEAN as China-Japan Tensions Rise: Southeast Asia,"
        Bloomberg Businessweek, November 15, 2012.

213   **This was Clinton's last trip with the president:** Peter Baker, "For Obama
        and Clinton, Their Final Tour in Asia as Partners," *The New York Times*,
        November 20, 2012.

213   **China was considered by the US intelligence:** Ellen Nakashima, "U.S. Said to
        Be Target of Massive Cyber-Espionage Campaign," *The Washington Post*,
        February 10, 2013.

213   **In February 2013, a National Intelligence:** Nakashima, "U.S. Said to Be
        Target."

213   **Although Russia, Israel, and France were:** Ibid.

214   **Cyber rose in profile to such:** White House Office of the Press Secretary,
        "Inaugural Address by President Barack Obama," *White House Press Release*
        (January 21, 2013).

214   **A week after that speech, computer:** David E. Sanger, David Barboza, and
        Nicole Perlroth, "Chinese Army Unit Is Seen as Tied to Hacking Against
        U.S.," *The New York Times*, February 18, 2013.

214   **It had apparently targeted 141 organizations:** Ibid.
214   **Almost all of these thefts could be traced:** Ibid.
214   **Working closely with Brennan:** Mark Landler and David E. Sanger, "U.S. Demands China Block Cyberattacks and Agree to Rules," *The New York Times*, June 4, 2013.
214   **He made a speech addressing this:** White House Office of the Press Secretary, "Remarks By Tom Donilon, National Security Advisor to the President: The United States and the Asia-Pacific in 2013," *White House Press Release* (March 11, 2013).
214   **The issue was seen as so important:** Siobhan Gorman, "Obama Raises Cybersecurity in Call to China's Xi," *The Wall Street Journal*, March 14, 2013.
214   **Within the first six weeks of the Xi:** Jane Perlez, "U.S. Treasury Secretary and Chinese President Meet," *The New York Times*, March 19, 2013.
214   **Two months later, a Pentagon report:** "Annual Report to Congress: Military and Security Developments Involving the People's Republic of China 2013," Office of the Secretary of Defense, May 2013.
214   **It was a topic that would dominate:** Jackie Calmes and Steven Lee Myers, "U.S. and China Move Closer on North Korea, but not on Cyberespionage," *The New York Times*, June 8, 2013.
214   **On May 20, 2013, Edward Snowden:** Devlin Bartlett and Te-Ping Chen, "Snowden on the Run," *The Wall Street Journal*, June 24, 2013.
214   **He was, as the world would soon:** Ibid.
214   **He sought Chinese asylum:** Ibid.
214   **Although China did not grant it:** Ibid.
214–215 **Russia ultimately allowed Snowden to take:** Ibid.
215   **Just as happened over the financial:** Ibid.
215   **When traveling to the region after:** Background interview with former Obama administration official.

Chapter 7: Eyeball to Eyeball Again

216   **Russia's economic system after 1991:** Jim Nichol, "Russian Political, Economic, and Security Issues and U.S. Interests," *Congressional Research Service*, March 31, 2014.
216   **Since 1999, the political landscape:** Ibid.
216   **He oversaw a major push to tap:** Ibid.
217   **He granted favors to oligarchs to help:** Andrew S. Weiss, "Russia's Oligarchy, Alive and Well," *The New York Times*, December 30, 2013; Andrew Foxall, "Kicking Putin off the Island," *Foreign Policy*, April 29, 2014; Peter Baker, "Sanctions Revive Search for Secret Putin Fortune," *The New York Times*, April 27, 2014.
217   **One estimate said his:** Leonid Bershidsky, "Vladimir Putin, the Richest Man on Earth," *Bloomberg View*, September 7, 2013.
217   **He also put down potential opponents:** Nichol, "Russian Issues and U.S. Interests."

217   **But he promoted nationalism and Russian:** Kathy Lally and Will Englund, "In Russia, Politics and Nationalist Pride Are Basis of Putin's Anti-American Turn," *The Washington Post*, September 14, 2013.

217   **He could resort to rough techniques:** Alan Taylor, "Vladimir Putin, Action Man," *The Atlantic*, September 13, 2011; Lizzie Crocker, "Meet Putin's Olympic Torch-Lighting Paramore," *The Daily Beast*, February 7, 2014.

217   **One technique for winning that support:** Nichol, "Russian Issues and U.S. Interests."

217   **This ranged from Islamic extremist groups:** Ibid.

218   **Early in his tenure as president:** White House Office of the Press Secretary, "Press Conference by President Bush and Russian Federation President Putin," *White House Press Release* (June 16, 2001).

218   **In her first meeting with her counterpart:** Steven R. Weisman, "Rice Chides Russia on Quieting Dissent but Rejects Penalty," *The New York Times*, February 6, 2005.

218   **It was clear, given Russia's recent:** Ibid.

218   **"Condi and Lavrov could get:** Background interview with former State Department official.

218   **On point during this period in Moscow:** Colby Itkowitz, "Bill Burns, a 'diplomat's diplomat' retires," *The Washington Post*, April 11, 2014.

218   **At a face-to-face meeting in Slovakia:** Elisabeth Bumiller and David E. Sanger, "Bush and Putin Exhibit Tension Over Democracy," *The New York Times*, February 25, 2005.

219   **Bush insisted on democratic reforms:** Ibid.

219   **The two did agree to further dismantling:** Ibid.

219   **Bush touched a very raw nerve:** Elisabeth Bumiller, "Bush Tells Putin Not to Interfere with Democracy in Former Soviet Republics," *The New York Times*, May 8, 2005.

219   **Bush fanned the flames:** Ibid.

219   **Putin took off the gloves:** Elisabeth Bumiller, "In Pointed Message to Putin, Bush Hails Freedom in Georgia," *The New York Times*, May 10, 2005.

219   **Hadley and Rice publicly described:** "Interview with Condoleezza Rice," *CNN Larry King Live*, May 11, 2005; Rice, *No Higher Honor*, 363; "Bush in Moscow to Mark Victory in Europe," *CNN World*, May 8, 2005.

219   **Of greater consequence for the US-Russia:** Bumiller, "Bush Hails Freedom in Georgia."

219   **There the president hailed:** Ibid.

219   **He also portentously stated:** Ibid.

219   **Condoleezza Rice, of course, was in the business:** The Associated Press, "Rice Is Concerned for Russian Democracy," *The Washington Post*, February 13, 2006.

219   **A year into her term as secretary:** Ibid.

220   **Bush, too, even as he prepared:** Elisabeth Bumiller, "Bush Rejects Idea of Boycotting Meeting in Russia," *The New York Times*, March 30, 2006.

220   **Backstage, though, there was still:** Jim Rutenberg and Andrew E. Kramer, "As Tensions Rise, U.S. and Moscow Falter on Trade," *The New York Times*, July 16, 2006.

220   **Over dinner, Bush told Putin:** Ibid.

220   **In the penultimate year of Bush's:** Stuart D. Goldman, "Russian Political, Economic, and Security Issues and Implications for U.S. Policy," *Congressional Research Service*, August 26, 2008, 22–23.

220   **Despite American arguments that the systems:** Michael R. Gordon, "U.S. Is Proposing European Shield for Iran Missiles," *The New York Times*, May 22, 2006.

220   **Putin responded vehemently:** Thom Shanker and Mark Landler, "Putin Says U.S. Is Undermining Global Security," *The New York Times*, February 11, 2007.

220   **He accused the United States of provoking:** Ibid.

220   **He attacked "unilateral" and "illegitimate":** Ibid.

220   **Robert Gates followed the next day:** Thom Shanker, "Gates Counters Putin's Words on U.S. Power," *The New York Times*, February 11, 2007.

220   **But Rice and Hadley, and, behind:** William J. Burns, "Russia's Economy and Prospects for U.S.-Russian Economic Relations," Johnson's Russia List, October 23, 2007, http://www.russialist.org/archives/2007-222-33.php; R. Nicholas Burns, "Challenges and Opportunities Facing the Transatlantic Community," *US Department of State Archive*, March 26, 2007.

220   **Rice pulled Lavrov aside:** Thom Shanker and Helene Cooper, "U.S. Moves to Soothe Growing Russian Resentment," *The New York Times*, March 6, 2007.

220   **Hadley went to Moscow to brief:** Ibid.

220   **Subsequently, the administration offered a proposal:** Thom Shanker, "Pentagon Invites Kremlin to Link Missile Systems," *The New York Times*, April 24, 2007.

220   **Gates flew to Moscow to continue:** Linda D. Kozaryn, "Gates Announces Formation of U.S.-Russia Working Group on Missile Defense," *American Forces Press Service*, April 23, 2007.

221   **But Putin, raw over the missile:** C. J. Chivers and Mark Landler, "Putin to Suspend Pact with NATO," *The New York Times*, April 27, 2007.

221   **Rice sought to offset this move:** Matthew Lee, "Harsh U.S.-Russia Words at NATO Meet," *The Washington Post*, April 26, 2007.

221   **At a NATO conclave she said:** Ibid.

221   **Lavrov responded with another:** Ibid.

221   **Punch followed counterpunch, and by midyear:** Luke Harding, "The New Cold War: Russia's Missiles to Target Europe," *The Guardian*, June 3, 2007.

221   **As for a new Cold War he said:** Ibid.

222   **As relations worsened—despite:** Peter Baker, "Putin Proposes Broader Cooperation on Missile Defense," *The Washington Post*, July 3, 2007.

222   **Again seeking to defuse this:** Thom Shanker and Steven Lee Myers, "Putin Criticizes U.S. Officials on Missile Defense," *The New York Times*, October 13, 2007.

222 **Putin showed up forty minutes late:** Ibid.

222 **Then, on December 17, Russia:** Helene Cooper, "Iran Receives Nuclear Fuel in Blow to U.S.," *The New York Times*, December 18, 2007.

222 **Instead, Dmitri Medvedev was elected:** Nichol, "Russian Issues and U.S. Interests."

222 **However, Putin remained a constant:** Ibid.

222 **He became prime minister and continued:** Ibid.

222 **Although Medvedev presented a more muted:** Ibid.

222 **A pivotal moment came in April 2008:** Peter Baker, "Bush Pressing NATO to Set Membership Path for Ukraine, Georgia," *The Washington Post*, April 2, 2008.

222 **Welcoming applications from Ukraine and Georgia:** Steve Erlanger and Steven Lee Myers, "NATO Endorses Europe Missile Shield," *The New York Times*, April 4, 2008.

222 **One German diplomat who was in attendance:** Background interview with German government official.

222 **US officials admit Bush was:** Background interviews with Bush administration officials.

222 **The effort foundered because:** Steven Erlanger, "Putin, at NATO Meeting, Curbs Combative Rhetoric," *The New York Times*, April 5, 2008.

222 **Putin showed his contempt:** Ibid.

222 **In a portent of things to come:** Peter Baker, "After Recent Discord, Bush to Meet with Putin in Russia," *The Washington Post*, March 27, 2008.

223 **Near both Georgia and Ukraine:** Baker, "Bush to Meet with Putin."

223 **Rice called the meeting, the last:** Rice, *No Higher Honor*, 681.

223 **It featured an apparent:** Peter Baker, "No Pact, but Bush, Putin Leave a Map," *The Washington Post*, April 7, 2008.

223 **In addition, a framework:** Ibid.

223 **However, Bush called the agreement:** Ibid.

223 **In August 2008—as Beijing's:** "Russian Tanks Enter South Ossetia," *BBC News*, August 8, 2008.

223 **The United States decried the violation:** Karen DeYoung, "Bush Question's Moscow's Motives," *The Washington Post*, August 12, 2008.

223 **Just as Vice President Biden would be:** "Cheney: 'Russian Aggression Must Not Go Unanswered,'" Reuters, August 10, 2008; Julie Pace, "Biden at Center of US Diplomacy with Ukraine," The Associated Press, February 25, 2014; Marina Koren, "Joe Biden Lurks Behind Every US Action on Ukraine," *National Journal*, March 13, 2014; Andrew Higgins and Andrew Roth, "Biden Offers Strong Support to Ukraine and Issues a Sharp Rebuke to Russia," *The New York Times*, April 22, 2014.

223 **Bush, who later wrote that he feared:** Bush, *Decision Points*, 434–435.

223 **He called the action:** DeYoung, "Bush Question's Moscow's Motives."

223 **And he then indicated that:** Ibid.

223 **The Bush NSC had actively:** Background interview with former NSC official.

223 **Instead, as under Obama later, the goal:** Tom Parfitt, Helen Womack, and Jonathan Steele, "Russia Brushes Aside Ceasefire Calls After Georgia Withdraws," *The Guardian*, August 10, 2008.

223 **And Putin, just as he would:** Ibid.

224 **He said in a press interview:** Steven Lee Myers and Thom Shanker, "Bush Aides Say Russia Actions in Georgia Jeopardize Ties," *The New York Times*, August 15, 2008.

224 **For while the Bush team did respond:** Daniel Michaels, "U.S.-Poland Deal on Missile Base Riles Russia," *The Wall Street Journal*, August 21, 2008; Peter Baker, "Obama Resets Ties to Russia, but Work Remains," *The New York Times*, July 9, 2009.

224 **A senior Bush advisor explained that:** Background interview with senior Bush administration official.

225 **Characterizing his counterpart:** Bush, *Decision Points*, 433.

225 **Dick Cheney suggested he had:** Cheney, *In My Time*, 514–515.

225 **"I always felt in my dealings:** Ibid.

225 **And Condoleezza Rice signed off:** Rice, *No Higher Honor*, 693.

225 **Russia welcomed Barack Obama:** Ellen Barry and Sophia Kishkovsky, "Russia Warns of Missile Deployment," *The New York Times*, November 5, 2008.

225 **The absurdity of Medvedev's explanation:** Steven Lee Myers, "Russian Hopes Obama's Win Will Warm Relations," *The New York Times*, November 15, 2008.

225 **But the course to "repair:** Background interview with 2008 Obama-Biden transition leader.

225 **In fact, in his first major foreign:** Helene Cooper and Nicholas Kulish, "Biden Signals U.S. Is Open to Russia Missile Deal," *The New York Times*, February 8, 2009.

226 **This included not only undoing:** Peter Baker and David E. Sanger, "U.S. Makes Concessions to Russia for Iran Sanctions," *The New York Times*, May 21, 2010.

226 **The first concrete sign of the reset:** Peter Baker, "Obama Offered Deal to Russia in Secret Letter," *The New York Times*, March 3, 2009.

226 **It said the United States would not:** Ibid.

226 **Perhaps unsurprisingly, Medvedev:** Ellen Barry, "Russia Welcomes Letter from Obama," *The New York Times*, March 3, 2009.

226 **Meeting for the first time on April 1:** Helene Cooper, "Promises of a 'Fresh Start' for U.S.-Russia Relations," *The New York Times*, April 2, 2009.

226 **Furthermore, it was during their discussions:** Background interview with senior Obama administration official.

227 **Obama not only agreed to pursue:** Nichol, "Russian Issues and U.S. Interests."

227 **This second agreement was one:** Steven Pifer, "George W. Bush Was Tough on Russia? Give Me a Break." *Politico*, March 24, 2014.

227 **Then, in the hope of reenergizing:** Baker and Sanger, "U.S. Makes Concessions."

227   **Obama declared the first meeting:** Cooper, "'Fresh Start.'"
227   **During Obama's July 2009 trip:** Clifford J. Levy and Peter Baker, "U.S.-Russia Nuclear Agreement Is First Step in Broad Effort," *The New York Times*, July 7, 2009.
227   **The two sides also agreed to:** Ibid.
227   **Finally, they also established:** Nichol, "Russian Issues and U.S. Interests."
227   **Obama had his first lengthy:** Mann, *Obamians*, 186.
227   **The two tried to paper over:** Ibid.
228   **Later, however, the president:** Baker, "Obama Resets Ties to Russia."
228   **In an address during his Moscow visit:** Ibid.
228   **But he also sent an important message:** Ibid.
228   **On September 17, Obama officially:** Peter Baker, "White House Scraps Bush's Approach to Missile Shield," *The New York Times*, September 18, 2009.
228   **The move placated the Russians:** Ibid.
228   **The distinction was not lost:** Ibid.
229   **Hillary Clinton, who had been relegated:** Luke Harding, "Clinton Hails US-Russia Cooperation on Iran," *The Guardian*, October 13, 2009.
229   **She underscored the themes established:** Ibid.
229   **The trip made further progress:** Ibid.
229   **Mike McFaul, the highly respected:** Mann, *Obamians*, 188.
229   **A group in the White House:** Ibid.
229   **Obama sided with this latter group:** Ibid.
229   **Said one top State Department official:** Background interview with US State Department official.
229   **On the edges of the otherwise:** Helene Cooper, "U.S. and Russia Close on Arms Pact, Leaders Say," *The New York Times*, December 19, 2009.
229–230 **They didn't formally conclude:** Ibid.
230   **The new deal seemed only:** Ellen Barry, "Russia Cool to U.S. Plan for Missiles in Romania," *The New York Times*, February 5, 2010.
230   **They had sensed that they could:** Wolffe, *Renegade,* 259.
230   **Obama personally intervened to say:** Michael D. Shear, "Obama, Medvedev Sign Treaty to Reduce Nuclear Weapons," *The Washington Post*, April 8, 2010.
230   **The impasse was short-lived:** Ibid.
230   **The Prague visit also gave Obama:** White House Office of the Press Secretary, "Remarks by President Barack Obama," *White House Press Release* (April 5, 2009).
230   **But the words in the speech:** Michael D. Shear and David E. Sanger, "Japan to Let U.S. Assume Control of Nuclear Cache," *The New York Times*, March 23, 2014.
230   **The United States pushed efforts:** Ellen Barry, "Russia Declares Deal to Join Trade Group," *The New York Times*, November 3, 2011.
230   **The two sides announced new initiatives:** Jackie Calmes, "Obama and Medvedev Talk Economics," *The New York Times*, June 24, 2010.
230   **By midyear, Obama and Medvedev:** Ibid.

230   **Things started to get rocky:** Thom Shanker and Ellen Barry, "U.S. and Romania Move on Missile Plan," *The New York Times*, May 3, 2011.

230   **Medvedev declared that Russia would:** Alla Eschenko and Maxim Tkachenko, "Russia Threatens Nuclear Build-Up over U.S. Missile Shield," *CNN.com*, May 18, 2011.

230   **This was especially frustrating to:** Background interviews with Obama administration officials; "Ballistic Missile Defense Review Report," US Department of Defense, February 2010.

230   **They argued that the announced installations:** Background interviews with Obama administration officials.

231   **Matters worsened in July:** Andrew E. Kramer, "Russians Linked to Jail Death Are Barred from U.S.," *The New York Times*, July 26, 2011.

231   **(It should be noted in retrospect:** Anne Gearan, "U.S. Applies Sanctions Against 10 More Russians in Magnitsky Case," *The Washington Post*, May 20, 2014.

231   **Relations took a further turn:** Thom Shanker, "U.S. Report Accuses China and Russia of Internet Spying," *The New York Times*, November 3, 2011.

231   **Russia then threatened to withdraw:** David M. Herszenhorn, "Russia Elevates Warning About U.S. Missile-Defense Plan in Europe," *The New York Times*, December 8, 2011.

231   **The US NATO ambassador, Ivo Daalder:** Thom Shanker and David M. Herszenhorn, "U.S. Official Says Missile-Defense Shield Will Move Forward," *The New York Times*, December 2, 2011.

231   **Hillary Clinton's efforts again to push:** David M. Herszenhorn and Ellen Barry, "Putin Contends Clinton Incited Unrest over Vote," *The New York Times*, December 8, 2011.

231   **Effectively reversing the earlier policy:** Ibid.

231–232 **(Later, American political critics on the right:** John Ransom, "Hillary, Obama and the Russian Reset," *Townhall Finance*, March 2, 2014; Clinton, *Hard Choices*, 243–245, 461–463.

232   **The United States and its allies sought:** Henry Meyer, Brad Cook, and Ilya Arkhpov, "Russia Warns U.S., NATO Against Military Aid to Syria Protests After Libya," *Bloomberg*, June 2, 2011.

232   **Lavrov emerged as the principal international:** Ibid.

232   **He said at the UN, "it is:** Ibid.

232   **Russia's client in Damascus:** David Kenner, "How Putin Turned Moscow Back into a Middle East Powerhouse," *Foreign Policy*, September 13, 2013.

232   **One senior Russian diplomat said:** Background interview with senior Russian official.

232   **Mike McFaul was known to share:** Ellen Barry, "Putin Aide Says Foreign Hands Are Behind Protests," *The New York Times*, February 3, 2012.

232   **Assigning him to Moscow in 2012:** Ibid.

232   **McFaul responded, as he would often:** Ellen Barry, "New U.S. Envoy Steps into Glare of a Russia Eager to Find Fault," *The New York Times*, January 23, 2012.

232   **Donilon arrived in Moscow in his:** Peter Baker, "U.S.-Russian Ties Still Fall Short of 'Reset' Goal," *The New York Times*, September 2, 2013.

232   **But newly reelected president Putin:** Baker, "Ties Still Fall Short of 'Reset.'"

232   **He was confrontational and brusque:** Ibid.

232   **Ironically—or perhaps characteristically:** Ibid.

232   **The Russians followed this up by:** Neil MacFarquhar and Anthony Shadid, "Russia and China Block U.N. Action on Crisis in Syria," *The New York Times*, February 4, 2012.

233   **Clinton rejected Russian assertions:** Bradley Klapper and Matthew Lee, "U.S. Pressuring Russia over Syria," *The Christian Science Monitor*, May 31, 2012.

233   **Russia's entry into the WTO:** Patrick Wintour and Ewan MasAskill, "Obama Fails to Secure Support from Putin on Solution to Syria Crisis," *The Guardian*, June 18, 2012.

233   **By July, it had gotten to the point:** Joe Lauria, "Russia, China Veto Syrian Resolution at U.N." *The Wall Street Journal*, July 19, 2012.

233   **One Latin diplomat asked me:** Background interview with Latin American government official.

233   **In late 2012, Russia demanded:** David M. Herszenhorn and Ellen Barry, "Russia Demands U.S. End Support of Democracy Groups," *The New York Times*, September 18, 2012.

233   **Then the US Senate passed legislation:** Samuel Rubenfeld, "Obama Signs Magnitsky Act into Law," *The Wall Street Journal*, December 14, 2012.

233   **Obama signed the bill into law:** Rubenfeld, "Obama Signs Magnitsky Act"; Will Englund and Tara Barhampour, "Russia's Ban on U.S. Adoptions Devastates American Families," *The Washington Post*, December 27, 2012.

234   **John Kerry had his first meeting:** David M. Herszenhorn and Michael R. Gordon, "U.S. Cancels Part of Missile Defense That Russia Opposed," *The New York Times*, March 16, 2013; Nichol, ""Russian Issues and U.S. Interests."

234   **Both sides dutifully reported the discussions:** Ibid.

234   **According to a senior NSC staffer:** Background interview with NSC official.

234   **Donilon continued his own diplomacy:** David M. Herszenhorn, "As U.S. Seeks Security Pact, Obama Is Set to Meet Putin," *The New York Times*, April 15, 2013.

234   **Once again, he sought areas of potential:** Ibid.

234   **He also tried to defuse the:** Ibid.

235   **Lavrov and Putin made Russia:** Kenner, "How Putin Turned Moscow Back into a Middle East Powerhouse."

235   **It could have been, had it not:** Andrew Higgins and Steven Erlanger, "Gunmen Seize Government Buildings in Crimea," *The New York Times* February 27, 2014.

235   **Blindsided by the Russian move:** Peter Baker, "Pressure Rising as Obama Works to Rein in Russia," *The New York Times,* March 2, 2014.

235   **Preceding the invasion had been:** David D. Herszenhorn, "Unrest Deepens in Ukraine as Protests Turn Deadly," *The New York Times,* January 22, 2014.

235   **Pro-EU Ukrainians protested the Ukrainian:** Andrew Higgins and Andrew E. Kramer, "Archrival Is Freed as Ukrainian Leader Flees," *The New York Times*, February 22, 2014.

235   **This inflamed pro-Russian Ukrainians:** Yuras Karmanau, "Pro-Russian Rally in Crimea Decries Kiev 'Bandits,'" The Associated Press, February 25, 2014.

235   **The United States and the West:** Jamie Dettmer, "Euromaidan Protestors: We Want U.S. Protection," *The Daily Beast*, March 3, 2014.

235   **Russia decried it as unconstitutional:** Kathy Lally and Will Englund, "Putin Defends Ukraine Stance, Cites Lawlessness," *The Washington Post*, March 4, 2014.

235   **Much like Bush, Obama quickly:** Michael D. Shear, "Obama Rules Out Military Force over Ukraine," *The New York Times*, March 20, 2014.

235   **Unfortunately, the Obama team had not worked out:** Scott Wilson, "Obama Warns Russia on Ukraine," *The Washington Post*, February 28, 2014; Colum Lynch, "U.S. Increasingly Isolated on Russia Sanctions," *Foreign Policy*, March 3, 2014.

235   **Germany and other European countries:** Lynch, "U.S. Increasingly Isolated on Sanctions."

235   **"We also kept getting blindsided by:** Background interview with US State Department official.

236   **"Susan Rice and her team at the NSC:** Ibid.

236   **Although the rhetoric was heated:** Dmitri Trenin, "Welcome to Cold War II," *Foreign Policy*, March 4, 2014.

236   **In the first wave of those sanctions:** David M. Herszenhorn, Michael R. Gordon, and Alissa J. Rubin, "Crimea Approves a Secession Vote as Tensions Rise," *The New York Times,* March 6, 2014.

236   **Meanwhile, Russia took hold of Crimea:** Gregory L. White, "Russia's Putin Signs Treaty to Annex Crimea," *The Wall Street Journal*, March 18, 2014.

236   **In the immediate aftermath of:** Peter Baker and Michael D. Shear, "U.S. Challenge Now Is to Stop Further Putin Moves," *The New York Times*, March 25, 2014; Background interview with senior Obama administration official.

236   **Russia did not, however, stop there:** Eli Lake, "U.S. Eyes Russia Spies Infiltrating Ukraine," *The Daily Beast*, March 21, 2014.

236   **A second wave of sanctions followed:** Karen DeYoung and Michael Birnbaum, "U.S. Imposes New Sanctions on Russia," *The Washington Post*, April 28, 2014.

236   **Another smattering of financial and trade-related:** Ibid.

236   **But at this writing the sanctions:** Peter Baker and Andrew E. Kramer, "So Far, U.S. Sanctions over Ukraine May Be Inflicting Only Limited Pain on Russia," *The New York Times*, May 2, 2014.

236   **His support among his people at home:** Ibid.

236   **One top Obama national security official:** Background interview with senior Obama administration official.

236   **He went on to say, "the Europeans:** Ibid.

236   **This frustration with America's European allies:** Lynch, "U.S. Increasingly Isolated on Sanctions."

237   **As of late March 2014, the primary concern:** Baker and Shear, "U.S. Challenge Now Is to Stop Further Putin Moves."

237   **The two had a working relationship stronger:** Hanna Kozlowska, "Idaho Potatoes and Furry Pink Hats: This Is What Now Passes for Diplomacy," *Foreign Policy*, January 13, 2014.

237   **International efforts to deescalate:** Michael Birnbaum and Anthony M. Faiola, "Missile Downs Malaysia Airlines Plane Over Ukraine, Killing 298; Kiev Blames Rebels," *The Washington Post*, July 18, 2014.

237   **All 298 passengers aboard:** Birnbaum and Faiola: "Missile Downs Malaysia Airlines Plane"; Karen DeYoung, "Obama Says Malaysian Plane Shot Down by Missile from Rebel-Held Part of Ukraine," *The Washington Post*, July 18, 2014.

237   **President Obama declared the tragedy:** White House Office of the Press Secretary, "Statement by the President on Ukraine," *White House Press Release* (July 19, 2013.)

237   **The action both finally shocked Europeans:** White House Office of the Press Secretary, "Statement by the President on Ukraine," *White House Office Press Release* (July 29, 2014); Peter Baker, Alan Cowell, and James Kantor, "Coordinated Sanctions Aim at Russia's Ability to Tap Its Oil Reserves," *The New York Times*, July 29, 2014.

237   **What it did not do:** Michael R. Gordon, "Russia Moves Artillery Units Into Ukraine, NATO Says," *The New York Times*, August 22, 2014.

Chapter 8: The Place Where Good Intentions Go to Die

240   **"I'm not so sure the role of the United States is to":** "Presidential Debate Excerpts: Gov. George W. Bush vs. Vice President Al Gore," *PBS Newshour*, October 12, 2000.

240   **By the time Bush reached his second inaugural:** "Transcript: Inaugural Address by George W. Bush," *The New York Times*, January 20, 2005.

240   **Rice later wrote that "US policy for:** Rice, *No Higher Honor*, 325.

240   **She went on to assess that they had come:** Ibid., 326.

240   **Rumsfeld offered a stinging critique of Rice:** Rumsfeld, *Known and Unknown*, 632.

240–241 **He cites as a particular example:** Ibid., 635.

241   **"At an NSC meeting," he wrote:** Ibid.

241   **Although this is a view that one:** Background interview with senior Israeli government official.

242   **Part of the reason Bush was so closely:** "Powerful, but Not That Powerful," *The Economist*, September 27, 2007.

242   **The word *neocon* gradually became:** Burgess Everett, "Harry Reid Slams Neocons on Iraq," *Politico*, June 18, 2014; Jacob Heilbrunn, "The Neocons' War Against Obama," Reuters, October 19, 2012.

242   **Used to describe a pro-Israeli:** "Powerful, but Not That Powerful."

242   **The unpopularity of the:** Ibid.

242   **John Mearsheimer and Stephen Walt:** John Mearsheimer and Stephen Walt, "The Israel Lobby," *London Review of Books*, March 2006.

242   **The president most closely:** Rice, *No Higher Honor*, 293.

242   **As for a bias within the administration:** Elliot Abrams, *Tested by Zion: The Bush Administration and the Israeli-Palestinian Conflict* (New York: Cambridge University Press, 2013), 2.

242–243 **Abrams goes on to say:** Abrams, *Tested by Zion*, 3.

243   **He offered another important insight into:** Ibid., 307.

244   **After Sharon, his successor:** Baker, *Days of Fire*, 590–591; Abrams, *Tested By Zion*, 253–256; Carol Migdalovitz, "Israeli-Palestinian Peace Process: The Annapolis Conference," *Congressional Research Service*, December 7, 2007.

244   **But then Olmert got into:** Rice, *No Higher Honor*, 723–724; Baker, *Days of Fire*, 611; Ian Black, "Ehud Olmert resignation throws Israel's politics into turmoil," *The Guardian*, July 30, 2008.

244   **She called it, "one of the:** Interview with the author.

245   **Little did he know that within months:** Richard Boudreaux, "Israel Picks Michael Oren, Historian, as Ambassador to U.S.," *The Los Angeles Times*, May 3, 2009.

245   **Obama had also been closely associated:** Marc Santora and Elissa Gootman, "Political Storm Finds a Columbia Professor," *The New York Times*, October 30, 2008.

245   **When it was asserted during the campaign:** Michael James, "Obama on the Defensive Before Fla. Jewish Voters," *ABC News*, May 22, 2008.

245   **But one senior Democratic insider pointed out:** Background interview with Democratic Party operative.

245   **It is telling that in April:** Neil A. Lewis, "U.S. Jews Create New Lobby to Temper Israel Policy," *The New York Times*, April 25, 2008.

246   **The Mearsheimer-Walt book, *The Israel Lobby*:** John J. Mearsheimer and Stephen M. Walt, *The Israel Lobby and U.S. Foreign Policy* (New York: Farrar, Straus and Giroux, 2007).

246   **Earlier that year, candidate Obama:** Glenn Kessler, "Obama's Signals on Middle East Scrutinized by All Sides," *The Washington Post*, January 24, 2009.

246   **Later at the annual convention of AIPAC:** "Obama's Speech at the AIPAC Conference," *Council on Foreign Relations*, June 4, 2008.

246   **He said Bush's policies caused the United States:** Ibid.

246   **At the same time, Obama actively sought:** Martin S. Indyk, Kenneth G. Lieberthal, and Michael E. O'Hanlon, *Bending History: Barack Obama's Foreign Policy* (Washington, DC: Brookings Institution Press, 2012), 116–117.

246   **He met actively with Jewish leaders:** Ibid.

246   **Once in office, Obama began to make:** Jeffrey Heller, "Israeli envoy Sees 'Historic Crisis' with U.S.: Report," Reuters, March 15, 2010.

246   **On his first day as president he called:** Ori Lewis, "Palestinians Set Out Basis for Talks with Israel," Reuters, January 21, 2009.

246   **He affirmed that the region:** Ibid.; David Ignatius, "The West Bank
       Settlements Dilemma," *The Washington Post*, June 28, 2009.
246   **Obama also urged Israel to finish:** The Associated Press, "Pelosi Welcomes
       Netanyahu: 'We in Congress Stand by Israel,'" *The Huffington Post*, March
       24, 2010.
246   **In his midsummer address in Cairo:** "Remarks by the President on a New
       Beginning," *White House Office of the Press Secretary*, June 4, 2009.
246   **Behind closed doors at a meeting:** Scott Wilson, "Obama Searches for Middle
       East Peace," *The Washington Post*, July 14, 2012.
246   **He also granted his first foreign interview:** Dan Gilgoff, "Barack Obama
       Grants First TV Interview as President to Arabic Network," *U.S. News and
       World Report*, January 27, 2009.
246–247 **During the al-Arabiya interview he said:** Ibid.
247   **Martin Indyk, Ken Lieberthal, and:** Indyk et al, *Bending History*, 117–118.
247   **On his second day in office:** Ed Henry and Elise Labott, "George Mitchell
       Named Special Envoy for the Middle East," *CNN*, January 22, 2009.
247   **Mitchell was a no-nonsense, canny lawyer:** Ibid.
247–248 **The "czars" were top appointments:** David Rothkopf, "It's Official: Obama
       Creates More Czars than the Romanovs," *Foreign Policy*, April 16, 2009.
248   **The overlap in responsibilities and interests:** Glenn Kessler, "A Key Back
       Channel for U.S., Israeli Ties," *The Washington Post*, October 6, 2010.
248   **Mitchell's first trip to the region:** Ewan MacAskill and Rory McCarthy,
       "Mitchell Heads to Middle East to Initiate Dialogue Between Israel and
       Hamas," *The Guardian*, January 27, 2009.
248   **Mitchell then met with the president's staff:** Interview with the author.
249   **During his first months in office:** Mark Landler, "Obama Sends Special Envoy
       to Mideast," *The New York Times*, January 26, 2009.
249   **However, the process was complicated:** Howard Schneider and Samuel Sockol,
       "Labor Votes to Join Netanyahu Coalition," *The Washington Post*, March 25,
       2009.
249   **Netanyahu had served previously:** Scott Wilson, "Where Obama Failed on
       Forging Peace in the Middle East," *The Washington Post*, July 14, 2012.
249   **He made his first official visit:** Ibid.
249   **Standing beside Netanyahu, before reporters:** Ibid.
249   **Privately, Netanyahu was shocked:** Ibid.
249–250 **This was, in fact, a common:** Background interviews with Middle Eastern
       government officials.
250   **At around the same time as the Netanyahu meeting:** Mann, *Obamians*, 144.
250   **He expressed his desire to deliver:** Ibid.
250   **Rhodes and McDonough again assumed:** Ibid., 143.
250   **Rhodes in particular, as both:** Background interview with senior Obama
       administration official.
250   **"A New Beginning" departed from past addresses:** "Remarks by the President
       on a New Beginning."
250   **Its rhetoric about the rule of law:** Ibid.
250   **Nonetheless, there was no mistaking the impact:** Ibid.

250 **Obama described his own extensive:** Ibid.

251 **He said, "there must be:** Ibid.

251 **When he turned to the issue of Israel:** Ibid.

251 **He also argued again for the end:** Ibid.

251 **"For centuries," he said, "black people:** Ibid.

251 **Although justifying the conflict in Afghanistan:** Ibid.

251 **He added, "although I believe":** Ibid.

251 **To underscore his awareness of our history:** Ibid.

251 **Mahmoud Abbas called the speech "clear and frank":** Abraham Rabinovich, "Palestinians Hail Barack Obama's Speech," *The Australian*, June 5, 2009.

252 **More extreme factions in the region:** Michael Slackman, "Message on Obama Attributed to bin Laden," *The New York Times*, June 3, 2009; Jon Leyne, "Iran Marks Ayatollah Khomeini Anniversary," *BBC News*, June 4, 2009; Daniel Nasaw, "American Right Blasts Obama's Cairo Speech," *The Guardian*, June 4, 2009.

252 **Later analysis would suggest it may have helped:** Fouad Ajami, "Five Myths About the Arab Spring," *The Washington Post*, January 12, 2012.

252 **As one former top Obama foreign policy:** Background interview with former senior Obama administration official.

252 **By the end of 2009, Obama had to acknowledge:** Joe Klein, "Q&A: Obama on His First Year in Office," *Time*, January 21, 2010.

252 **The efforts continued, and by March:** Laura Rozen, "As Biden Heads to Israel, Plan for Proximity Talks Advances," *Politico*, March 7, 2010.

252 **Vice President Biden went to Israel:** Ibid.

252 **The planned impact of the Biden trip:** Wilson, "Where Obama Failed."

252 **Although Netanyahu insisted that he was blindsided:** Indyk et al, *Bending History*, 125.

253 **Obama was finding it hard:** Jeffrey Heller, "Israeli Envoy Sees 'Historic Crisis with U.S.'" Reuters, March 15, 2010.

253 **Obama, especially sensitive to appearances:** Fawaz A. Gerges, *Obama and the Middle East: The End of America's Moment?* (New York: Palgrave MacMillan, 2012), 120.

253 **It was also, in fact:** Gerges, *Obama and the Middle East*, 120.

253 **The Palestinians simply suspended involvement:** Rory McCarthy, "Palestinians Snub Peace Talks Because of Israeli Homes Expansion," *The Guardian*, March 10, 2010.

253 **Mitchell and Clinton postponed planned trips:** "Daily Press Briefing," *US Department of State*, March 12, 2010.

253 **Worse, separate emissaries representing the White House:** Background interviews with US State Department officials.

253 **Reports emerged that Mitchell staffers:** Ibid.

253 **Further, the Israelis and the Palestinians:** Scott Wilson, "James Jones to Step Down as National Security Adviser," *The Washington Post*, October 8, 2010; Michael D. Shear and Jeff Zeleny, "Emanual's Departure Set; Rouse to Replace Him," *The New York Times*, September 30, 2010.

253   **In the aftermath of Donilon's appointment:** Indyk et al, *Bending History*, 132.

253   **Secretary Clinton also began a push:** Ibid.

253   **The president agreed in principle:** Ibid.

253   **Donilon and Ross were uncomfortable:** Ibid.

253   **When word got out that the president:** Wilson, "Where Obama Failed."

253   **The White House then determined:** Indyk et al, *Bending History*, 133.

253   **Donilon and Ross argued for a speech:** Ibid.

253–254 **Clinton felt it was important to continue:** Ibid.

254   **For all this debate, when Obama:** White House Office of the Press Secretary, "Remarks by the President on the Middle East and North Africa," *White House Press Release* (May 19, 2011).

254   **In his address to Congress:** "Netanyahu: No Return to 'Indefensible Boundaries of 1967,'" *PBS Newshour*, May 24, 2011.

254   **Netanyahu received enthusiastic support:** Helene Cooper and Ethan Bronner, "Netanyahu Gives No Ground in Congress Speech," *The New York Times*, May 24, 2011.

254   **Days later at the AIPAC event:** Andrea Stone, "Obama AIPAC Speech 2011: President Seeks to Smooth Out U.S.-Israel Tensions," *The Huffington Post*, May 22, 2011; "Netanyahu's Speech at the AIPAC Conference, May 2011," *Council on Foreign Relations*, May 23, 2011.

254   **The response to Obama was especially cool:** Jennifer Rubin, "Reaction to Obama's AIPAC speech," *The Washington Post*, May 23, 3011.

254   **Unsurprisingly, given that stance:** Joby Warrick and Karen DeYoung, "Mideast Envoy George Mitchell to Resign," *The Washington Post*, May 13, 2011.

254   **The battle with Netanyahu also diminished:** Mann, *Obamians*, 325.

254   **As global public opinion shifted:** Neil MacFarquhar and Steven Lee Myers, "Palestinians Request U.N. Status; Powers Press for Talks," *The New York Times*, September 23, 2011.

254   **This gambit gradually gained ground:** Mann, *Obamians*, 325.

254–255 **At the end of the first term:** Indyk et al, *Bending History*, 136.

255   **Thus, "Obama damaged U.S. credibility:** Ibid.

255   **The Arab-Israel initiative was being resumed:** David Rohde, "How John Kerry Could End Up Outdoing Hillary Clinton," *The Atlantic*, November 20, 2013.

255   **As those close to Kerry note:** Anne Gearan and Scott Wilson, "Obama Nominates John Kerry as Secretary of State," *The Washington Post*, December 21, 2012.

255   **They worked together closely in the Senate:** Ibid.

255   **Kerry endorsed Obama for president:** Carrie Budoff Brown, "Kerry Endorses Obama," *Politico*, January 10, 2008.

255–256 **Kerry helped Obama with debate prep:** Gearan and Wilson, "Obama Nominates John Kerry."

256   **As a result, the process:** Rohde, "Kerry Could End Up Outdoing Hillary Clinton."

256   **It was still widely considered:** Mark Landler, "'Framework' for Talk on Mideast in Progress," *The New York Times,* January 30, 2014.

256   **The Israeli defense minister attacked:** Shimon Shiffer, "Ya'alon: Kerry Should Win His Nobel and Leave Us Alone," *Yedioth Ahronoth*, January 14, 2014.

256   **The United States was again furious:** Michael R. Gordon and Jodi Rudoren, "Kerry Brushes Aside Israeli Officials' Reported Criticisms of Peace Effort," *The New York Times,* January 14, 2014.

256   **But weeks later, in early March:** Edward-Isaac Dovere, "Benjamin Netanyahu Sounds Optimistic Note at AIPAC," *Politico*, March 4, 2014.

256   **Speaking again at an AIPAC event:** John Hudson, "Netanyahu Praises Kerry's Peace Efforts," *Foreign Policy*, March 4, 2014.

257   **After months of talks with:** Jodi Rudoren and Isabel Kershner, "Arc of a Failed Deal: How Nine Months of Mideast Talks Ended in Disarray," *The New York Times*, April 28, 2014.

257   **Without a commitment from the Palestinians:** Anne Gearan, "Palestinians Threaten Walkout in Mideast Talks over Israel's Refusal to Free Prisoners," *The Washington Post*, March 29, 2014.

257   **In response, the Palestinian leadership:** Jodi Rudoren, Michael R. Gordon, and Mark Landler, "Abbas Takes Defiant Step, and Mideast Talks Falter," *The New York Times*, April 1, 2014.

257   **Abbas put the nail in the:** Jodi Rudoren and Michael R. Gordon, "Palestinian Rivals Announce Unity Pact, Drawing U.S. and Israeli Rebuke," *The New York Times*, April 23, 2014.

257   **Frustrated, senior officials in the:** Mirjam Donath, "Israel, Palestinians at U.N. accuse each other of sabotaging peace," Reuters, April 29, 2014; David Horovitz, "12 Ways the US Administration Has Failed Its Ally Israel," *The Times of Israel*, June 3, 2014; Danny Danon, "We Will Not Be Threatened: How Secretary Kerry's 'Apartheid' Warning Set Back the Cause of Peace," *Politico Magazine*, April 29, 2014; Yossi Beilin, "Why Kerry Failed at Peace," *Politico Magazine*, May 14, 2014.

257   **Missile fire from Hamas:** Steven Erlanger and Isabel Kershner, "Israel and Hamas Trade Attacks as Tension Rises," *The New York Times*, July 8, 2014; Nidal Al-Mughrabi and Jeffrey Heller, "Israel Launches Ground Offensive in Gaza Strip," Reuters, July 17, 2014.

257   **The Israeli assault not only:** Jodi Rudoren, "Israel Kills 3 Top Hamas Leaders as Latest Fighting Turns Its Way," *The New York Times*, August 21, 2014; David Rothkopf, "On Israel's Strategic Defeat in Gaza," *Foreign Policy*, August 6, 2014; Leon Wieseltier, "Israel and Gaza: A Just and Unjust War," *The New Republic*, August 6, 2014; Chemi Shalev, "The Shaming of John Kerry and the Downturn in the Battle for Israel's Image," *Haaretz*, July 26, 2014; Matthew Lee and Julie Pace, "US Fuming Over Israeli Criticism of Kerry," The Associated Press, July 28, 2014; Adam Entous, "Gaza Crisis: Israel Outflanks the White House on Strategy," *The Wall Street Journal*, August 14, 2014.

257   **As a consequence:** Background interview with US State Department official.

258   **Iran was the first country Obama had mentioned:** Michael R. Gordon and Jeff Zeleny, "Obama Envisions New Iran Approach," *The New York Times*, November 2, 2007.

258   **He reached out to the supreme leader:** Sanger, *Confront and Conceal*, 158.

258   **Meanwhile, Israelis saw the Iranian nuclear program:** Ibid., 159.

258   **They let Dennis Ross know that if:** Ibid.

258   **The president ordered the entire national security team:** David Sanger, "Obama Order Sped Up Wave of Cyberattacks Against Iran," *The New York Times*, June 1, 2012.

258   **Meanwhile, regional allies in the Gulf:** Sanger, *Confront and Conceal*, 159–160.

258   **King Abdullah of Saudi Arabia:** Ibid.

258   **Iranian elections took place in June 2009:** Indyk et al, *Bending History*, 191–192.

258   **Finally, on June 23, the president:** Office of the White House Press Secretary, "Press Conference By The President," *White House Press Release* (June 23, 2009).

258   **The supreme leader subsequently denounced Obama:** Indyk et al, *Bending History*, 192.

259   **During the Green Revolution, Clinton's small team:** Jonathan Allen and Amie Parnes, *HRC: State Secrets and the Rebirth of Hillary Clinton* (New York: Crown, 2014), 154–157, 164; Mark Landler and Brian Stelter, "Washington Taps into a Potent New Force in Diplomacy," *The New York Times*, June 16, 2009.

259   **Later, another initiative of the administration:** Patricia Moloney Figliola, Kennon H. Nakamura, Casey L. Addis, and Thomas Lum, "U.S. Initiatives to Promote Global Internet Freedom: Issues, Policy, and Technology," *Congressional Research Service*, April 5, 2010.

259   **The United States and the Israelis, with European:** Sanger, "Obama Order Sped Up Wave of Cyberattacks Against Iran."

259   **The operation, known within the:** Ibid.

259   **The effort, which targeted the Siemens software:** Ibid.; Barton Gellman and Ellen Nakashima, "U.S. Spy Agencies Mounted 231 Offensive Cyber-Operations in 2011, Documents Show," *The Washington Post*, August 30, 2013.

259   **Continuing what was perhaps the best-coordinated:** Indyk et al, *Bending History*, 194.

259   **And the administration scored its biggest victory:** Ibid., 195.

259   **Donilon, Bader, Steinberg, and Ross:** Ibid., 196.

259–260 **The United States and the EU worked together:** Kenneth Katzman, "Iran Sanctions," *Congressional Research Service*, May 31, 2013.

260   **The US Treasury, for example, put pressure:** Ibid.

260   **One uneasy top general said, "we don't:** Background interview with senior US Defense Department official.

260   **Israeli officials would regularly report:** Rick Gladstone and David E. Sanger, "Nod to Obama by Netanyahu in Warning to Iran on Bomb," *The New York Times*, September 27, 2012.

260   **"What we just don't know:** Background interview with Israeli government
        official.

260   **Michael Oren was always among those:** Michael Oren, "Time Is Short For Iran
        Diplomacy," *The Wall Street Journal*, August 6, 2012.

260   **In an interview with Jeff Goldberg:** Jeffrey Goldberg, "Obama to Iran and
        Israel: 'As President of the United States, I Don't Bluff,'" *The Atlantic*, March
        2, 2012.

260   **Adding an exclamation point to this:** Ibid.

260   **Speaking later to an AIPAC event:** Office of the White House Press Secretary,
        "Remarks by the Vice President to AIPAC Political Conference," *White House
        Press Release* (March 4, 2013).

260   **This was especially relevant because some:** Tucker Reals, "Ex-CIA chief
        Michael Hayden: 'Only the U.S.' Can Strike Iran Nuclear Sites Effectively,"
        CBS News, September 4, 2012.

260   **For example, certain of Iran's:** Ibid.

260   **Delivering the deep-penetrating munitions:** Ibid.

261   **Said one NSC official, "what he:** Background interview with NSC official.

261   **It nonetheless went through a substantial:** Jason Rezaian and Joby Warrick,
        "Moderate Cleric Hassan Rouhani Wins Iran's Presidential Vote," *The
        Washington Post*, June 15, 2013.

261   **Rouhani was by no means a reformer:** Nicole Gaouette, "Iranian Leader's
        Tweets: Healing #Wound with U.S.," *Bloomberg*, August 2, 2013.

261   **Within a very short time of:** Ibid.

261   **A former head of Iran's Supreme National Security Council:** Rezaian and
        Warrick, "Rouhani Wins."

261   **One of Rouhani's campaign pledges:** Ibid.

261   **A more specific objective was to relax:** Ibid.

261   **Speaking to a small group of journalists:** Thomas L. Friedman, "Hassan Does
        Manhattan," *The New York Times*, September 28, 2013.

261   **They even went to the lengths:** Saeed Kamali Dehghan, "Hassan Rouhani
        to Take Iran's Only Jewish Member of Parliament to UN," *The Guardian*,
        September 19, 2013.

261   **(When asked to speak, the allegedly Jewish:** Adiv Sterman and Elhanan Miller,
        "Jewish Iranian MP Lauds Country's Religious Freedom," *The Times of
        Israel*, September 29, 2013.

261   **Also at the UN, there was buzz that:** Mark Landler, "Obama and Iranian Leader
        Miss Each Other, Diplomatically," *The New York Times*, September 24, 2013.

261   **According to the Iranians, that did not:** Ibid.

261   **Just what they wanted became clearer:** Anne Gearan, "Kerry, Iranian Foreign
        Minister Zarif Hold Private Meeting on Sidelines of Nuclear Talks," *The
        Washington Post*, September 26, 2013.

261   **Two days after the photo-op:** Jeff Mason and Louis Charbonneau, "Obama,
        Iran's Rouhani Hold Historic Phone Call," Reuters, September 28, 2013.

262   **Immediately, Netanyahu and leaders:** Tom Watkins, "Netanyahu: Iranian
        President Is 'Wolf in Sheep's Clothing,'" *CNN*, October 2, 2013.

262   **These assertions were unable to stop:** Anne Gearan and Joby Warrick,
           "Iran, World Powers Reach Historic Nuclear Deal," *The Washington Post*,
           November 24, 2013.

262   **As it turned out, the Obama team:** Bradley Klapper, Julie Pace, and Matthew
           Lee, "How the Nuclear Deal Happened," The Associated Press, November 24,
           2013.

262   **According to an Associated Press account:** Ibid.

262   **With the approval of the president:** Ibid.

262   **They met Iranian officials "at least:** Ibid.

262   **The Oman meeting was orchestrated even before:** Ibid.

262   **After the meeting, Kerry went to Oman:** Ibid.

262   **Following Rouhani's election, Obama sent:** Ibid.

262   **More secret talks involving Burns:** Ibid.

262   **Fits and starts marked the move:** Jeffrey Lewis, "Vive la Freeze!" *Foreign
           Policy*, November 20, 2013.

262   **The initial deal was for interim discussions:** Gearan and Warrick, "Historic
           Nuclear Deal."

262   **"We needed," said one senior:** Background interview with senior US State
           Department official.

262–263   **As of this writing, the focus is on:** John Kerry, "Iranian Nuclear Deal Is Still
           Possible, but Time Is Running Out," *The Washington Post*, June 30, 2014;
           George Jahn, "Envoys Report Progress an [*sic*] Iranian Nuclear Talks," The
           Associated Press, June 20, 2014.

263   **Opposition in the US Congress:** Jennifer Rubin, "Congress Nearly Unanimous
           in Its Dismay over Obama's Iran Policy," *The Washington Post*, March 19,
           2014.

263   **Indeed, a top Israeli predicted to me:** Background interview with senior Israeli
           government official.

263   **One senior former Israeli national security:** Background interview with senior
           Israeli government official.

263   **As he observed, many discuss:** Ibid.

263   **They are certainly working hard to:** Ibid.

263   **Gulf allies worried that a possible:** Gideon Lichfield, "Why Israelis, Saudis,
           and Republicans Hate a Deal That Stops Iran Building a Nuclear Bomb,"
           Quartz, November 24, 2013.

263   **Notably, the spreading unrest in Iraq:** Jason Rezaian and Anne Gearan, "Iran,
           U.S. Signal Openness to Cooperate on Iraq," *The Washington Post*, June 16,
           2014; Laurence Norman and Jay Solomon, "U.S., Iran Discuss Crisis in Iraq,"
           The Wall Street Journal, June 17, 2014.

263–264   **This latter concern is common:** Background interviews with Persian Gulf
           government officials.

264   **The intelligence community has forward-looking:** "Global Trends 2030:
           Alternate Worlds," *National Intelligence Council*, December 2012.

264   **The headlines in the "Game-Changers" section:** Ibid.

265   **One of the best small pockets of insight:** Craig Whitlock, "Yoda Still Standing: Office of Pentagon Futurist Andrew Marshall, 92, Survives Budget Ax," *The Washington Post*, December 4, 2013.

265   **Marshall, ninety-three, still runs the operation:** Ibid.

267   **Under Jim Jones, a five-page memo:** Ryan Lizza, "The Consequentialist," *The New Yorker*, May 11, 2011.

267   **Worried that allies like Mubarak:** Ibid.

267   **The objective of the memo:** Ibid.

267   **Ross, NSC staffer Samantha Power, and:** Ibid.; Mark Landler, "Secret Report Ordered by Obama Identified Potential Uprisings," *The New York Times*, February 16, 2011.

267   **The review's conclusion that efforts:** Lizza, "Consequentialist"; Mann, *Obamians*, 258.

267   **Samantha Power later commented on the thinking:** Mann, *Obamians*, 257–258.

268   **Panetta himself testified before Congress:** Landler, "Secret Report Ordered by Obama."

268   **Sullivan pointed out the irony:** Alex Arieff and Carla E. Humud, "Political Transition in Tunisia," *Congressional Research Service*, January 29, 2014.

Chapter 9: Leading from Behind

269   **It is now common lore:** Kareem Fahim, "Slap to a Man's Pride Set Off Tumult in Tunisia," *The New York Times*, January 21, 2011.

269   **That act in turn sparked ten days:** Ibid.

269   **By the end of December, demonstrations reached:** David D. Kirkpatrick, "Tunisia Leader Flees and Prime Minister Claims Power," *The New York Times*, January 14, 2011.

269   **One was that the price:** "Let them eat baklava."

269   **Part of the reason for the high prices:** Brad Plumer, "Drought Helped Cause Syria's War. Will Climate Change Bring More Like It?" *The Washington Post*, September 10, 2013.

269   **Other reasons, of course, had to do with:** Stuart Levey, "Corruption and the Arab Spring," *CNN*, June 20, 2011.

270   **The speed with which protests spread:** Blake Hounshell, "The Revolution Will Be Twittered," *Foreign Policy*, June 20, 2011.

270   **Building on the way technology had fueled:** Jared Keller, "Evaluating Iran's Twitter Revolution," *The Atlantic*, June 18, 2010.

270   **(China would later ban:** Ian Johnson, "Call for a 'Jasmine Revolution' in China Persist," *The New York Times*, February 23, 2011.

270   **During the protests in Tunisia:** Leila Fadel and Liz Sly, "Overthrow Delivers a Jolt to Arab Region," *The Washington Post*, January 16, 2011.

270   **Even as the revolution in Tunisia was literally spreading:** Indyk et al, *Bending History*, 144.

270   **"We had to walk a fine line,":** Background interview with senior Obama administration official.

270   **Secretary Clinton offered remarks on January 11:** Hillary Rodham Clinton
          interview with Taher Barake (of Al Aarabiya), January 11, 2011.
270   **Two days later at a conference in Doha:** Mark Landler, "Clinton Bluntly
          Presses Arab Leaders on Reform," *The New York Times*, January 13, 2011.
270   **Forcefully, her words reflecting the headlines:** Ibid.
270   **Behind the scenes, the usual:** Clinton, *Hard Choices*, 339.
270   **The spread of the revolution to Egypt:** David D. Kirkpatrick, "Mubarak
          Orders Crackdown, with Revolt Sweeping Egypt," *The New York Times*,
          January 28, 2011.
271   **January 28 was the first of the "days of rage":** Ibid.
271   **The situation was exacerbated by:** "Timeline: Egypt's revolution," *Al Jazeera*,
          February 14, 2011.
271   **Those tactics, however, prompted in response**: Ibid.
271   **Mubarak went on television:** Yasmine Saleh and Dina Zayed, "Highlights:
          Egyptian President Hosni Mubarak's Speech," Reuters, January 29, 2011.
271   **The next day, he ordered the army:** David D. Kirkpatrick, "Mubarak Orders
          Crackdown, with Revolt Sweeping Egypt," *The New York Times*, January 28,
          2011.
271   **On January 25, Hillary Clinton offered support:** "US Urges Restraint in Egypt,
          Says Government Stable," Reuters, January 25, 2011.
271   **That evening in Obama's State of the Union:** Office of the White House Press
          Secretary, "Remarks by the President in State of Union Address," *White
          House Press Release* (January 25, 2011).
271   **Two days later, when Jim Lehrer of *PBS NewsHour*:** "Biden: Mubarak Is Not
          a Dictator, but People Have a Right to Protest," *PBS NewsHour*, January 27,
          2011.
271   **Biden said "no":** Ibid.
271   **And while he encouraged the Egyptian president:** Ibid.
271   **By January 28, the White House called:** Office of the White House Press
          Secretary, "Remarks by the President on the Situation in Egypt," *White House
          Press Release* (January 28, 2011).
271   **Press Secretary Robert Gibbs responded:** Office of the White House Press
          Secretary, "Press Briefing by Press Secretary Robert Gibbs, 1/28/2011," *White
          House Press Release* (January 28, 2011).
271–272 **Internally, the realists like Clinton pushed:** Clinton, *Hard Choices*, 340–341.
272   **Clinton was concerned that the United States:** Ibid.
272   **Obama called Mubarak and urged him:** David D. Kirkpatrick and David E.
          Sanger, "A Tunisian-Egyptian Link That Shook Arab History," *The New York
          Times*, February 13, 2011.
272   **Later that evening Obama would publicly call:** Office of the White House Press
          Secretary, "Remarks by the President on the Situation in Egypt," *White House
          Press Release* (January 28, 2011).
272   **On Saturday, January 29:** David E. Sanger and Helene Cooper, "Obama
          Presses for Change but Not a New Face at the Top," *The New York Times*,
          January 29, 2011.

272 **They feared a power vacuum:** Ibid.

272 **The official replied, "people did consider that:** Background interview with senior Obama administration official.

273 **The official continued, "I think:** Ibid.

273 **A discussion of the possible successors:** Sanger and Cooper, "Obama Presses for Change."

273 **The national security team decided to send:** Mark Landler, "U.S. Official with Egypt Ties to Meet with Mubarak," *The New York Times*, January 31, 2011.

273 **Their choice was distinguished retired:** Ibid.

273 **The hope was to have someone close to Mubarak:** Ibid.

273 **Another NSC meeting took place:** Helene Cooper and Robert F. Wolf, "In Arab Spring, Obama Finds a Sharp Test," *The New York Times*, September 24, 2012.

273 **As next steps were debated:** Cooper and Wolf, "Obama Finds a Sharp Test."

273 **Mubarak said he would step down:** "Text—President Mubarak's Speech After Mass Protest," Reuters, February 1, 2011.

273 **According to press reports:** Cooper and Wolf, "Obama Finds a Sharp Test."

273 **Robert Gates and Mike Mullen, the officials:** Ibid.

273 **They led a group who suggested:** Ibid.

273 **"If *now* is not in my remarks:** Ibid.

273 **When Obama presented the message to Mubarak:** Mann, *Obamians*, 263.

273 **He played for time:** Ibid.

273 **He made the standard case:** Ibid.

273 **He said the protests would soon:** Ibid.

273 **He argued the United States had a different view:** Ibid.

273–274 **According to "The Consequentialist":** Lizza, "Consequentialist."

274 **What could not be known:** Stephen Adler, "Exclusive: Egypt's Sisi Asks for U.S. Help in Fighting Terrorism," Reuters, May 15, 2014; Neil MacFarquhar, "Assad Condemns Houla Massacre, Blaming Terrorists," *The New York Times*, June 3, 2012.

274 **Shortly afterward, the US president:** Office of the White House Press Secretary, "Remarks by the President on the Situation in Egypt," *White House Press Release* (February 1, 2011).

274 **The United States had spent decades training:** Scott Wilson, "Mubarak Resignation Creates Political Vacuum for U.S. in Middle East," *The Washington Post*, February 12, 2011.

274 **Senior officers with good Egyptian contacts:** Wilson, "Mubarak Resignation Creates Political Vacuum."

274 **Diplomats did likewise:** Mann, *Obamians*, 264.

274 **The response and the message:** Jake Tapper, David Kerley, and Kirit Radia, "Obama Administration Distances Self from Own Envoy to Mubarak," *ABC News*, February 5, 2011.

274 **Given that this was precisely the opposite:** Ibid.

274 **Meanwhile, back in the White House:** Mann, *Obamians*, 266.

274 **On the other side was the more pro-democratic:** Ibid.

274–275 **Often abetted by political aides:** Ibid.

275   **They saw this moment as a chance:** Ibid.

275   **In this instance, they had the advantage:** Ibid.

275   **As someone who had been uncomfortable:** Ibid., 267.

275   **Citing Tunisia as an example:** Ibid.

275   **When on February 10 Mubarak again resisted:** Office of the White House Press Secretary, "Statement of President Barack Obama on Egypt," *White House Press Release* (February 10, 2011).

275   **The next day, Egyptian vice president Omar Suleiman:** David D. Kirkpatrick, "Egypt Erupts in Jubilation as Mubarak Steps Down," *The New York Times*, February 11, 2011.

275   **Among the established leaders of other US-allied regimes:** Mark Landler and Helene Cooper, "Allies Press U.S. to Go Slow on Egypt," *The New York Times*, February 8, 2011.

275   **To calm the fears of the latter:** Ibid.

275   **Mike Mullen and Bill Burns went to see King Abdullah:** Ibid.

275   **They urged him to get ahead:** Indyk, *Bending History*, 150; Massoud A. Derhally, "Jordan's King Abdullah Seeks Rapid Change from New Government Amid Protest," *Bloomberg*, February 21, 2011.

275   **Donilon began a process:** Scott Wilson, "Obama Administration Studies Recent Revolutions for Lessons Applicable in Egypt," *The Washington Post*, February 13, 2011.

275   **At this time, the administration:** Ibid.

275   **Yemen and Jordan were at the top:** Mann, *Obamians*, 270.

275   **Next came Libya, Bahrain, and Oman:** Ibid.

275   **Finally, at the bottom, were Saudi Arabia:** Ibid.

277   **Donilon's study group concluded:** David Ignatius, "Tom Donilon's Arab Spring Challenge," *The Washington Post*, April 26, 2011.

277   **In the case of each and every revolution:** Laura Kasinof and David E. Sanger, "U.S. Shifts to Seek Removal of Yemen's Leader, an Ally," *The New York Times*, April 3, 2011; Colum Lynch, "Security Council Passes Resolution Authorizing Military Intervention in Libya," *Foreign Policy*, March 17, 2011; Ethan Bronner and Michael Slackman, "Saudi Troops Enter Bahrain to Help Put Down Unrest," *The New York Times*, March 14, 2011; Thomas Grove and Erika Solomon, "Russia Boosts Arms Sales to Syria Despite World Pressure," Reuters, February 21, 2012; Sharp, "Egypt: Background and U.S. Relations."

277   **Another flaw in the White House's first analysis:** Mann, *Obamians*, 271.

277   **Obama had established something of a rapport:** David Ignatius, "U.S. and Turkey Find a Relationship That Works," *The Washington Post*, December 7, 2011.

277   **But as the Arab Awakening progressed:** "Turkish Politics: No Longer a Shining Example," *The Economist*, January 4, 2014.

277   **Again the administration's public response:** Office of the White House Press Secretary, "Statement of President Barack Obama on the Violence in Yemen," *White House Press Release* (March 18, 2011).

277–278 **Behind the scenes, the administration maintained its support:** Laura Kasinof and David E. Sanger, "U.S. Shifts to Seek Removal of Yemen's Leader, an Ally," *The New York Times*, April 3, 2011.

278 **Again protests did not subside:** Kasinof and Sanger, "U.S. Shifts to Seek Removal."

278 **In the case of Yemen, however:** Tom Finn, "The Specter of Civil War Grows in Yemen as Saleh Backs Out of Peace Deal," *Time*, May 23, 2011.

278 **By a year later, in February 2012:** Jeremy M. Sharp, "Yemen: Background and U.S. Relations," *Congressional Research Service*, November 1, 2012, 4–5.

278 **In Bahrain, when unrest came:** Ethan Bronner and Michael Slackman, "Saudi Troops Enter Bahrain to Help Put Down Unrest," *The New York Times*, March 14, 2011.

278 **The means were forceful:** Kenneth Katzman, "Bahrain: Reform, Security, and U.S. Policy," *Congressional Research Service*, March 24, 2014, 11–12.

278 **The US Fifth Fleet is based in Bahrain:** Joby Warrick and Michael Birnbaum, "As Bahrain Stifles Protest Movement, U.S.'s Muted Objections Draw Criticism," *The Washington Post*, April 14, 2011; Office of the White House Press Secretary, "Press Conference by the President," *White House Press Release* (February 15, 2011).

278 **The response of the United States:** Ibid.

278 **Clinton and Gates also delivered a similar message:** Mark Landler, "Unrest in Bahrain Presents Diplomatic Puzzle for Obama," *The New York Times*, February 17, 2011; Elisabeth Bumiller, "Gates Tells Bahrain's King That 'Baby Steps' to Reform Aren't Enough," *The New York Times*, March 12, 2011.

278 **But beyond that, the United States played this crisis:** Landler, "Bahrain Presents Diplomatic Puzzle."

278 **The response to Saudi and Emirati intervention:** Office of the White House Press Secretary, "Statement by the President on Violence in Bahrain, Libya and Yemen," *White House Press Release* (February 18, 2011).

278 **It was seen by the Saudis:** Warrick and Birnbaum, "As Bahrain Stifles Protest Movement."

278 **Gates, and later Donilon, went to the Kingdom:** Elisabeth Bumiller, "Defense Chief Is on Mission to Mend Saudi Relations," *The New York Times*, April 6, 2011; Mark Halperin, "Donilon Returns from Saudi Arabia, *Time*, October 1, 2011.

278–279 **In the words of one Gulf:** Background interview with Persian Gulf government official.

279 **In the first, Qaddafi's reputation as a brutal tyrant:** Neil MacFarquhar, "An Erratic Leader, Brutal and Defiant to the End," *The New York Times*, October 20, 2011.

279–280 **Second, America's European and regional allies:** Michael Elliott, "Viewpoint: How Libya Became a French and British War," *Time*, March 19, 2011.

280 **This in turn led to the accusation:** Lizza, "Consequentialist."

280 **Unrest began in the city of Benghazi:** Ian Black, "Libya's Day of Rage Met by Bullets and Loyalists," *The Guardian*, February 17, 2011.

280 **Soon thousands had taken to the:** "'Day of Rage' Kicks Off in Libya," *Al Jazeera*, February 17, 2011.

280 **"There will be no mercy," he promised:** Marc Lynch, *The Arab Uprising: The Unfinished Revolutions of the New Middle East* (New York: PublicAffairs, 2012), 168.

280 **The military followed suit:** Kareem Fahim and David D. Kirkpatrick, "Qaddafi's Grip on the Capital Tightens as Revolt Grows," *The New York Times*, February 22, 2011.

280 **From the international community they sought:** Leila Fadel and Liz Sly, "Gaddafi Foes Consider Requesting Foreign Airstrikes as Stalemate Continues," *The Washington Post*, March 1, 2011.

280 **Qaddafi called the protestors terrorists:** Chris McGreal, "Gaddafi's Army Will Kill Half a Million, Warn Libyan Rebels," *The Guardian*, March 12, 2011.

280 **By March, the death count was over:** "Rights Group Says 6000 Dead in Libya," *The Australian*, March 3, 2011.

280 **According to a report by my former:** Laura Rozen, "Averting 'Srebrenica on Steroids': White House Defends Libya Operations," *Yahoo! News*, March 23, 2011.

280 **His point was that another massacre loomed:** Ibid.

280 **Demonstrating yet again that creativity:** Office of the White House Press Secretary, "Press Briefing by Press Secretary Jay Carney, 2/23/2011," *White House Press Release* (February 23, 2011).

280 **Behind the scenes, some in:** Background interview with senior Obama administration officials.

280 **But beyond hoping and issuing:** McGreal, "Gaddafi's Army Will Kill Half a Million."

281 **It was French president Nicolas Sarkozy:** Ibid.

281 **France, like Italy and European nations:** "Relying on Libya," *The Economist*, February 25, 2011.

281 **Further social unrest in Libya:** Rachel Donadio, "Fears About Immigrants Deepen Divisions in Europe," *The New York Times*, April 12, 2011.

281 **Quietly the United States had been getting American citizens:** Rachel Donadio, "American Ferry from Libya Arrives in Malta," *The New York Times*, February 25, 2011.

281 **Once the Tripoli embassy was closed:** William Branigin, "U.S. Closes Embassy in Tripoli, Prepares Sanctions," *The Washington Post*, February 25, 2011.

281 **The same day they did this, the White House:** Ibid.

281 **The next day, the United States supported:** McGreal, "Gaddafi's Army Will Kill Half a Million."

281 **By early March, it was clear:** Mann, *Obamians*, 290.

281 **His troops were on the move:** Ibid.

281 **Behind the scenes, the British and French:** Ibid.

281 **Although Donilon ordered the Pentagon:** Ibid.

281 **His rationale, supported by many:** Helene Cooper and Mark Landler, "U.S. Imposes Sanctions on Libya in Wake of Crackdown," *The New York Times*, February 25, 2011.

281   **Again Biden and Donilon were skeptics:** Michael Hastings, "Inside Obama's War Room," *Rolling Stone*, October 13, 2011.

281   **In this instance, so too were:** Ibid.

281   **Meanwhile, an unlikely alliance had formed:** Josh Rogin, "How Obama Turned on a Dime Toward War," *Foreign Policy*, March 18, 2011; Hastings, "Obama's War Room"; Samantha Power, *A Problem from Hell: America and the Age of Genocide* (New York: Basic Books, 2002).

281   **Although relations between Clinton and Rice:** Rogin, "How Obama Turned on a Dime."

282   **Clinton, usually allied with Gates:** Ibid.

282   **During a March 15 NSC meeting:** Michael Lewis, "Obama's Way," *Vanity Fair*, October 5, 2012.

282   **The Pentagon presented two options:** Ibid.

282   **But Obama demanded a more rigorous:** Ibid.

282   **When the principals failed to provide him with options:** Ibid.

282   **Secretary of Defense Gates and Chairman:** Ibid.

282   **They were supported by Biden:** Ibid.

282   **The other side argued the risks:** Ibid.

282   **This group included Clinton, participating from Cairo:** Ibid.

282   **One senior official who was:** Background interview with senior Obama administration official.

282   **Obama was frustrated:** Hastings, "Obama's War Room."

282   **Action, it seemed, was called for:** Ibid.

282–283 **He ordered them to come back:** Lewis, "Obama's Way."

283   **As Obama would later tell *Vanity Fair*'s Michael Lewis:** Ibid.

283   **Rice pushed for intervention:** Hastings, "Obama's War Room."

283   **Gates continued to push back:** Ibid.

283   **He feared that America would end up owning:** Ibid.

283   **The back and forth continued:** Ibid.

283   **He would later add:** Ibid.

283   **In any event, as far as Libya:** Ibid.

283   **Obama then began to work the phones:** Lewis, "Obama's Way."

283   **That same day, Qaddafi was on the radio:** Lynch, *The Arab Uprising*, 170–171.

283   **Clinton talked to Lavrov:** Massimo Calabresi, "Hillary Clinton and the Rise of Smart Power," *Time*, November 7, 2011.

283   **Russia was resistant but ultimately agreed:** Lizza, "Consequentialist."

284   **Rice made a powerful call to action:** Julia Ioffe, "Susan Rice Isn't Going Quietly," *The New Republic*, December 20, 2012.

284   **It was so compelling that:** Ibid.

284   **Within hours, UN Security Council Resolution 1973:** Colum Lynch, "Security Council Passes Resolution Authorizing Military Intervention in Libya," *Foreign Policy*, March 17, 2011.

284   **The overall vote was ten to zero:** Ibid.

284   **Although Indyk, Lieberthal, and O'Hanlon called the action:** Indyk et al, *Bending History*, 163.

284 **The United States and the Europeans had significant:** Jeremiah Gertlet, "Operation Odyssey Dawn (Libya): Background and Issues for Congress," *Congressional Research Service*, March 30, 2011; Mark Landler and Steven Erlanger, "Obama Seeks to Unify Allies as More Airstrikes Rock Tripoli," *The New York Times*, March 22, 2011.

284 **An initial coalition of ten nations:** Ivo H. Daalder and James G. Stavridis, "NATO's Victory in Libya," *Foreign Affairs*, March/April 2012.

284 **But it was a fractious coalition:** Landler and Erlanger, "Obama Seeks to Unify Allies."

284 **Further, as one top US military:** Background interview with senior US Department of Defense official.

284 **Even after it had successfully neutralized:** Lindsay Benstead, Alexander Kjaerum, Ellen Lust, and Jakob Wichmann, "Libya's Security Dilemma," *The Washington Post*, April 7, 2014.

284 **In the wake of the fighting:** Ibid.

284 **Widespread reports indicate rebel activity:** Ibid.

285 **Throughout, administration critics on the right:** "Is There an Obama Doctrine?" *The New York Times*, March 29, 2011.

285 **Those, including many on the US left:** Lizza, "Consequentialist."

285 **Notably, but not exclusively, partisan critics:** David Remnick, "Behind the Curtain," *The New Yorker*, September 5, 2011.

286 **A former senior military commander:** Background interview with former senior US Department of Defense official.

286 **As the Arab World entered the turmoil:** "Interview With Syrian President Bashar al-Assad," *The Wall Street Journal*, January 31, 2011.

287 **He suggested that reform would have to wait:** Ibid.

287 **His people were patient only until March:** Lynch, *The Arab Uprising*, 179–180.

287 **A number of teenagers had sprayed graffiti:** Indyk et al, *Bending History*, 170.

287 **They were arrested and brutalized:** Ibid.

287 **When demonstrators came out to protest:** Ibid.

287 **Assad announced reforms:** Rania Abouzeid, "With Syria on the Brink, Assad Promises Reform," *Time*, March 24, 2011.

287 **Within weeks, thousands of demonstrators:** Anonymous Syrian writer in Homs, "Syria: Fear and Defiance in Homs," *The New Yorker*, June 1, 2011.

287 **On April 22, over eighty:** Khaled Yacoub Oweis, "Almost 90 dead in Syria's bloodiest day of unrest," Reuters, April 22, 2011.

287 **The protests soon spread to larger cities:** Indyk et al, *Bending History*, 170–171.

287 **Assad responded with tanks:** Ibid.

287 **In the first seven weeks of the uprising:** Ibid., 171.

287 **Refugees started to stream:** Ibid.

287 **Ramshackle refugee camps were filled with hardships:** Ibid.

287 **With increasing violence during the holy month:** Khaled Yacoub Oweis, "Syrians Mark Bleak Ramadan After 80 Killed in Hama," Reuters, July 31, 2011.

287 **Assad told the UN that he was winding down:** Indyk et al, *Bending History*, 171–172.

287   **But as soon as the UN inspectors:** Ibid.

287   **By mid-October the death toll was 3,000:** "Syria Uprising: UN Says Protest
        Death Toll Hits 3,000," *BBC News*, October 14, 2011.

287–288 **Syria was on the list:** Wilson, "Obama Administration Studies Recent
        Revolutions for Lessons Applicable in Egypt."

288   **When asked in the last week of March:** Brett Stephens, "Remember Bashar
        Assad, 'Reformer'?" *The Wall Street Journal*, July 23, 2012.

288   **She added that the United States:** Glenn Kessler, "Hillary Clinton's Uncredible
        Statement on Syria," *The Washington Post*, April 4, 2011.

288   **By April, the president had released:** David W. Lesch, *Syria: The Fall of the
        House of Assad* (New Haven, CT: Yale University Press, 2012), 152.

288   **He also signed Executive Order 13572:** Office of the White House Press
        Secretary, "Executive Order 13572—Blocking Property of Certain Persons
        with Respect to Human Rights Abuses in Syria," *White House Press Release*
        (April 29, 2011).

288   **In his May speech on the Arab Spring:** Lesch, *The Fall of the House of Assad*,
        152.

288   **Hillary Clinton was at the forefront:** Mark Landler and David E. Sanger,
        "White House, in Shift, Turns Against Syria Leader," *The New York Times*,
        July 12, 2011.

288   **She told reporters on July 11:** Ibid.

288   **Obama followed with comments:** Ibid.

288   **The White House issued a statement:** Office of the White House Press
        Secretary, "Statement by President Obama on the Situation in Syria," *White
        House Press Release* (August 18, 2011).

288   **By November, the Arab League suspended:** David Ignatius, "By Suspending
        Syria, Arab League Finally Breaks from Its Past," *The Washington Post*,
        November 13, 2011.

288   **Russia supplied Assad with arms:** Thomas Grove and Erika Solomon, "Russia
        Boosts Arms Sales to Syria Despite World Pressure," Reuters, February 21,
        2012.

288   **This meant that almost any anti-Assad action:** Michelle Nichols and Louis
        Charbonneau, "Russia, China Veto U.N. Bid to Refer Syria to International
        Court," Reuters, May 23, 2014.

288   **Without the blessing of the UN:** "Statement of Robert Ford, Ambassador to
        the Syrian Arab Republic Before the Senate Committee on Foreign Relations,
        August 2, 2010, http://www.foreign.senate.gov/imo/media/doc/Ford_
        Testimony2.pdf; Sanger, *Confront and Conceal*, 361; Clinton, *Hard Choices*,
        450–455.

289   **President Obama told his staff:** Dexter Filkins, "The Thin Red Line: Inside the
        White House Debate over Syria," *The New Yorker*, May 13, 2013.

289   **Top advisors like Clinton urged:** Ibid.

289   **He also resisted efforts to actively:** Ibid.

289   **Further, Libya had since descended:** David D. Kirkpatrick and Steven Lee
        Myers, "Libya Attack Brings Challenges for U.S.," *The New York Times*,

September 12, 2012; Anthony Shadid, "Libya Struggles to Curb Militias as Chaos Grows," *The New York Times*, February 8, 2012.

289   **At one press conference in March 2012:** Office of the White House Press Secretary, "Press Conference by the President," *White House Office Press Release* (March 6, 2012).

289   **In an interview with the *New Republic*:** Franklin Foer and Chris Hughes, "Barack Obama Is Not Pleased: The President on His Enemies, the Media, and the Future of Football," *The New Republic*, January 27, 2013.

289   **"You hit singles, you hit:** Office of the White House Press Secretary, "Remarks by President Obama and President Benigno Aquino III of the Philippines in Joint Press Conference," *White House Press Release* (April 28, 2014).

289   **"Every once in a while:** Ibid.

290   **He continued, "there are going to be times where there are disasters:** Ibid.

290   **He was, according to one:** David Rothkopf, "Obama's 'Don't Do Stupid Shit' Foreign Policy," *Foreign Policy*, June 4, 2014.

290   **He described the guiding principle:** Ibid.

290   **In fact, he repeated it and then:** Ibid.

290   **And the collected assortment of representatives:** Ibid.

290–291 **Speculating also on emotional factors:** Background interview with senior Obama administration official.

291   **Privately, he and other top:** Ibid.

291   **Further, Syria was an ally not just of Russia:** Robin Pomeroy, "Analysis: Iran Sees Ally Syria Surrounded by U.S., Arab 'Wolves,'" Reuters, August 15, 2011.

291   **As a consequence, Asad was receiving:** Ibid.

291   **Ben Rhodes once again channeled:** Filkins, "The Thin Red Line."

291   **In a throwaway comment that:** James Ball, "Obama Issues Syria a 'Red Line' Warning on Chemical Weapons," *The Washington Post*, August 20, 2012.

291   **When pressed about the red line:** Peter Baker, Mark Landler, David E. Sanger, and Anne Barnard, "Off-the-Cuff Obama Line Put U.S. in Bind on Syria," *The New York Times*, May 4, 2013.

291   **They said it didn't refer merely to any use:** Ibid.

292   **In 2012 Petraeus and Clinton floated a proposal:** Michael R. Gordon and Mark Landler, "Backstage Glimpses of Clinton as Dogged Diplomat, Win or Lose," *The New York Times*, February 7, 2013; Clinton, *Hard Choices*, 462–464.

292   **Obama overruled it:** Ibid.

292   **But by April 2013, the CIA was covertly operating:** Michael R. Gordon and Mark Landler, "Senate Hearing Draws Out a Rift in U.S. Policy on Syria," *The New York Times*, April 10, 2013; Michael R. Gordon and Mark Landler, "More U.S. Help for Syrian Rebels Would Hinge on Pledges," *The New York Times*, April 19, 2013.

292   **Even so, the promised aid came:** Adam Entous, "Legal Fears Slowed Aid to Syrian Rebels," *The Wall Street Journal*, July 14, 2013.

292   **Unprecedented numbers of extremists flocked:** Filkins, "The Thin Red Line."

292   **Reports of battles involving scores:** Ibid.

292   **Groups like the al-Nusrah Front:** Ibid.

292   **It was becoming apparent that, with every:** Ibid.

292   **The Jordanians, watching hundreds of thousands:** Ibid.
292   **Their leaders, like King Abdullah:** Ibid.
292   **They spoke of the potential threat:** Ibid.
292   **They also emphasized that they were:** Ibid.
292   **They wanted the United States to:** Background interview with senior Persian Gulf government official.
292   **But what they heard were views:** Filkins, "The Thin Red Line."
293   **One by one, military options:** Ibid.
293   **Because the country was so fragmented:** Ibid.
293   **Military leaders argued the United States had the capability:** Filkins, "The Thin Red Line"; Michael R. Gordon, "Top Obama Officials Differ on Syrian Rebels in Testimony to Congress," *The New York Times*, April 17, 2013.
293   **There were too many groups:** Filkins, "The Thin Red Line."
293   **At the same time, in the words:** Background interview with senior US Department of State official.
293   **The rise of the al-Nusra Front:** Filkins, "The Thin Red Line."
293   **In an interview with the *New Yorker*:** Ibid.
294   **In late June 2013, as Tom Donilon:** Mark Landler, "Rice to Replace Donilon in the Top National Security Post," *The New York Times*, June 5, 2013.
294   **Rather than restoring democracy to the country:** Jeremy M. Sharp, "Egypt: Background and U.S. Relations," *Congressional Research Service*, January 10, 2014.
294   **Throughout the year that the Muslim Brotherhood:** Helene Cooper, "Converging Interests May Lead to Cooperation Between Israel and Gulf States," *The New York Times*, March 31, 2014; Marcus Geore and Isabel Coles, "Egypt's Mohamed Morsi Wants to Renew Ties with Iran," *The Christian Science Monitor*, June 25, 2012; Bruce Riedel, "Saudi Arabia Cheers Coup in Egypt," *The Daily Beast*, July 7, 2013.
294   **It had a wing that was focused on spreading:** Jonathan Marcus, "Egypt's Political Unrest Causes Regional Concern," *BBC News*, July 8, 2013.
294   **It ran training camps on the Syrian border:** Hassan Hassan, "How the Muslim Brotherhood Hijacked Syria's Revolution," *Foreign Policy*, March 13, 2013.
294   **It had cells in Jordan:** Ibid.
294   **The United States government reacted very deliberately:** Sharp, "Egypt: Background and U.S. Relations."
294   **In the words of a senior official:** Background interview with senior Persian Gulf government official.
294   **One Latin American diplomat based:** Background interview with Latin American government official.
294   **By late June 2013 the Egyptian people:** Abigail Hauslohner, "Tension Roils Egypt as Protests Grow," *The Washington Post*, June 30, 2013.
294   **By some estimates millions protested:** Patrick Kingsley, "Protesters Across Egypt Call for Mohamed Morsi to Go," *The Guardian*, June 30, 2013.
294–295 **Within days the military called for Morsi:** Anup Kaphle, "Timeline: Egypt's Rocky Revolution," *The Washington Post*, August 19, 2013.

295   **When he failed to reply:** David D. Kirkpatrick, "Army Ousts Egypt's President; Morsi Is Taken into Military Custody," *The New York Times*, July 3, 2013.

295   **Susan Rice took over the NSC:** Mark Landler, "Obama's Choices Reflect Change in Foreign Tone," *The New York Times*, June 5, 2013.

295   **He was more comfortable behind the scenes:** David Rothkopf, "Donilon's Legacy," *Foreign Policy*, June 5, 2013.

295   **He preferred to avoid confrontation:** Ibid.

295   **He embraced the role of honest:** Ibid.

295   **He often spoke to the press:** Ibid.

295   **Rice was more accustomed to being out in front:** Ibid.

295   **She was articulate, poised, and forceful:** Ibid.

295   **She had strong opinions, and she:** Ibid.

295   **She did not shy away:** Ibid.

295   **She was also used to being a public spokesperson:** Ibid.

295   **She also had a longstanding:** Ibid.

295   **Said a longtime associate and admirer:** Background interview with senior Obama administration official.

295   **One described it as, "frankly:** Background interview with senior Obama administration official.

295   **The United States sheltered behind:** Office of the White House Press Secretary, "Statement by President Barack Obama on Egypt," *White House Press Release* (July 3, 2013).

296   **Meanwhile, the president was asking:** Mark Landler, "Rice Offers a More Modest Strategy for Mideast," *The New York Times*, October 26, 2013.

296   **This review initially centered around:** Ibid.

296   **On CNN, spokespeople close to the Egyptian military:** David Rothkopf, "Egypt and the C-Word," *Foreign Policy*, July 3, 2013.

296   **Now the former president, Morsi:** Hamza Hendawi, "Egypt's Army Ousts Morsi, Who Calls It a Coup," The Associated Press, July 4, 2013.

296   **The State Department sent Bill Burns:** Sarah El Deeb, "American Diplomat: US Not Backing a Side in Egypt," The Associated Press, July 15, 2013.

296   **It was not until July 26:** Bradley Klapper, "Obama Administration Won't Use 'Coup' for Egypt," The Associated Press, July 25, 2013.

296   **By not using the word *coup*:** Sharp, "Egypt: Background and U.S. Relations."

296   **Much of the money goes to military purchases:** Ibid.

296   **A July 29, 2013, article in the UK newspaper:** Martin Chulov, "How the Middle East and US Have Reacted to Egypt's Post-Morsi Regime," *The Guardian*, July 29, 2013.

297   **The White House's indecision produced enormous frustration:** Ibid.

297   **They stepped up and provided:** Sharp, "Egypt: Background and U.S. Relations."

297   **In many meetings with leaders from these countries:** Chulov, "How the Middle East and US Have Reacted."

297   **Internally, both John Kerry and Chuck Hagel:** Josh Rogin, "Exclusive: John Kerry Defies the White House on Egypt Policy," *The Daily Beast*, November 18, 2013.

297   **Hagel, in particular, had extremely close ties:** Shadi Hamid, "Hey General, It's Me, Chuck. Again," *Politico*, January 12, 2014.

297   **Kerry was more in touch with America's other allies:** Rogin, "Kerry Defies the White House on Egypt."

297   **Susan Rice led a group:** Ibid.

297   **These divisions festered into the fall:** Ibid.

297   **He chose to focus on the positive:** Ibid.

297   **This was in direct contravention:** Ibid.

297–298 **Indeed, in the view of one:** Background interview with Middle Eastern government official.

298   **This public rift was accompanied by other:** Background interview with senior US Department of State official.

298   **The White House—that is, Rice:** Ibid.

298   **When presented with this information:** Ibid.

298   **He simply had not been consulted:** Ibid.

298   **On the twenty-first of August:** Ben Hubbard and Hwaida Saad, "Images of Death in Syria, but No Proof of Chemical Attack," *The New York Times*, August 22, 2013.

298   **Over a thousand people were dead:** Ibid.

298   **Within hours YouTube videos:** Ibid.

298   **It was not the first:** Masuma Ahuja, "A partial list of Syria's suspected chemical weapons attacks this year," *The Washington Post*, August 21, 2013.

298   **But the others had been smaller and:** Ibid.

298   **The rebels blamed the government:** Hubbard and Saad, "Images of Death in Syria"; Lee Keath and Zeina Karam, "Syrian Official Blames Rebels for Deadly Attack," The Associated Press, August 22, 2013; Holly Yan, "Syria Allies: Why Russia, Iran and China Are Standing by the Regime," *CNN*, August 29, 2013.

298   **The UN was unable to send in inspectors:** Noah Rayman, "U.N. Inspectors in Syria Delay Second Trip," *Time*, August 27, 2013.

298   **But back in Washington:** Mark Landler, Mark Mazzetti, and Alissa J. Rubin, "Obama Officials Weigh Reponses to Syria Assault," *The New York Times*, August 22, 2013.

298   **Well over 100,000 Syrians had already died:** Sarah El Deeb, "Activists Say Death Toll in Syria Now Tops 100,000," The Associated Press, June 26, 2013; Erin Banco, "U.N. Reports Increased Number of Displaced People," *The New York Times*, June 18, 2013.

298   **On August 22, top national security officials:** Landler et al., "Officials Weigh Responses to Syria."

298–299 **One possibility would employ Tomahawk cruise missiles:** Ibid.

299   **Another would involve manned aircraft:** Ibid.

299   **The goal in both cases was:** Ibid.

299   **There were those who felt military action was risky:** Ibid.

299   **There were others who felt it was long overdue:** Ibid.

299   **Obama, it seemed, was now resolved:** Adam Entous and Carol E. Lee, "At the Last Minute, Obama Alone Made Call to Seek Congressional Approval," *The Wall Street Journal*, September 1, 2013.

299   **At an NSC meeting on August 24:** Ibid.

299   **Two days later, Kerry stated that the use:** Michael R. Gordon and Mark Landler, "Kerry Cites Clear Evidence of Chemical Weapon Use in Syria," *The New York Times*, August 26, 2013.

299   **On August 30, the administration released intelligence:** Office of the White House Press Secretary, "Government Assessment of the Syrian Government's Use of Chemical Weapons on August 21, 2013," *White House Press Release* (August 30, 2013).

299   **Kerry became the point person for taking action:** Peter Baker and Michael R. Gordon, "Kerry Becomes Chief Advocate for U.S. Attack," *The New York Times*, August 30, 2014.

299   **"With our own eyes," he said:** Washington Post Staff, "Full Transcript: Secretary of State John Kerry's Remarks on Syria on Aug. 30," *The Washington Post*, August 30, 2013.

299   **He continued, saying: "it matters:** Ibid.

299   **According to press reports:** Baker and Gordon, "Kerry Becomes Chief Advocate."

299   **Kerry's perspective gained traction within:** Ibid.

299   **Even as Obama let it be known:** Entous and Lee, "Obama Alone Made Call."

300   **Warships were moved into position:** Julian Barnes, "Navy Moves Ships as U.S. Preps for 'All Contingencies,'" *The Wall Street Journal*, August 23, 2013.

300   **Pushing for at least some international support:** Mark Mazzetti and Michael R. Gordon, "Support Slipping, U.S. Defends Plan for Syria Attack," *The New York Times*, August 30, 2013.

300   **However, the parliament was returning:** Hugo Dixon, "Cameron, UK Hurt by Syria Vote Fiasco," Reuters, August 30, 2013.

300   **Sufficient time had not been given:** Ibid.

300   **The result was a deeply embarrassing:** Ibid.

300   **In Washington, it was a shock to the system:** David E. Sanger, "After British Vote, Unusual Isolation for U.S. on Syria," *The New York Times*, August 30, 2013.

300   **Only the French appeared ready to act:** Rebekah Metzler, "Britain Out, France in for Looming U.S. Strike in Syria," *U.S. News and World Report*, August 30, 2013.

300   **Arab states that had condemned the attack:** David D. Kirkpatrick and Mark Landler, "Arab League Stance Muddies U.S. Case," *The New York Times*, August 27, 2013.

300   **Russia forcefully argued that any action:** Alexei Anuishchuk, "Russia Warns Against Military Intervention in Syria," Reuters, August 26, 2013.

300   **An NBC news poll said 80 percent:** "The White House Walk-and-Talk That Changed Obama's Mind on Syria," *NBC News*, August 31, 2013.

300   **Even as Kerry laid out the *casus belli*:** Ibid.

300   **Although the NSC had approved action:** Ibid.

300   He took a walk around the South Lawn: Ibid.

300   McDonough had grown to be one of the president's: Ibid.

300   He was also one of the voices arguing caution: Ibid.

300   (As it happened, he was also the one: Ibid.

300   During the walk, Obama told McDonough: Ibid.

300   He wanted to share responsibility: Ibid.

300   After his Rose Garden moment: Scott Wilson, "Syria Debate in Oval
         Office Focused on Whether to Put a Military Strike Before Congress," *The
         Washington Post*, August 31, 2013.

300   They filed into the Oval Office: Ibid.

300   The president's view was presented: Ibid.

300   A two-hour debate ensued: Ibid.

300–301 Rice and Hagel led the counterarguments: "White House Walk-and-Talk."

301   Others were concerned at the message: Entous and Lee, "Obama Alone Made
         Call."

301   Worse, what if the Congress: "White House Walk-and-Talk."

301   Obama's response was that "seeking legislative backing: Ibid.

301   Kerry was called and according: Julie Pace, "In First Major Test, Obama
         Overrules New Team," The Associated Press, September 2, 2013.

301   French president François Holland was called: Entous and Lee, "Obama Alone
         Made Call."

301   Obama, back in the Rose Garden: Office of the White House Press Secretary,
         "Statement by the President on Syria," *White House Press Release* (August 31,
         2013).

301   (His political opponents pointed out: Tim Mak, "Obama Shut Out Congress
         for 2 Years About Bergdahl Deal, Key Senator Says," *The Daily Beast*, June 3,
         2014.

301   Another two-hour NSC session followed: Entous and Lee, "Obama Alone
         Made Call."

302   As a historical checkpoint, in 1939: Ole R. Holsti, *Public Opinion and American
         Foreign Policy* (Ann Arbor, MI: The University of Michigan Press, 1996),
         14–15.

303   Obama did not help his global image: Tom Cohen, "Obama: It's the World's
         'Red Line' on Syria; Senate Panel Backs Military Strike Plan," *CNN*,
         September 4, 2013.

303   This led the *Washington Post* to quote the president: Glenn Kessler, "President
         Obama and the 'Red Line' on Syria's Chemical Weapons," *The Washington
         Post*, September 6, 2013.

303   Fortunately, at the moment things seemed: Peter Baker and Michael R.
         Gordon, "An Unlikely Evolution, from Casual Proposal to Possible
         Resolution," *The New York Times*, September 10, 2013.

303   While at a news conference: Ibid.

303   He added, "he isn't about to do it": Ibid.

303   But the seed of an idea was planted: Ibid.

303   Lavrov said he would follow: Ibid.

303   According to press reports, Kerry said: Ibid.

303   **Rice and Obama in public appearances:** Michael D. Shear, Michael R. Gordon, and Steven Lee Myers, "Obama Backs Idea for Syria to Cede Control of Arms," *The New York Times*, September 9, 2013.

303   **Kerry worked the specifics of the deal:** Baker and Gordon, "From Casual Proposal to Possible Resolution."

303   **The United States went in saying the deal:** Shear et al., "Obama Backs Idea for Syria."

303   **They also knew the Russians had leverage:** Major Garrett, "Why Russia Is Now in Control of the Syria Situation," *The Atlantic*, September 11, 2013; Simon Shuster, "Taking Lead in Syria Talks, Russia Works to Preserve Assad Regime," *Time*, September 12, 2013; Rick Ungar, "Putin Offers Surprise Plan for International Control of Syrian Chemical Weapons—Moves to Steal Obama's Thunder?" *Forbes*, September 9, 2013.

303–304 **Further, the Russians saw this:** Garrett, "Why Russia Is Now in Control"; Dominic Evans, "Chemical weapons deal wins time for Syria's Assad but at a cost," Reuters, September 16, 2013; Shuster, "Taking Lead in Syria Talks, Russia Works to Preserve Assad."

304   **Technical teams hammered out differences:** Karen DeYoung, "How the United States, Russia Arrived at a Deal on Syria's Chemical Weapons," *The Washington Post*, September 16, 2013.

304   **And though Lavrov had threatened to leave:** Ibid.

304   **The Syrian government shortly afterwards:** Anne Gearan and Scott Wilson, "U.S., Russia Reach Agreement on Seizure of Syrian Chemical Weapons Arsenal," *The Washington Post*, September 14, 2013.

304   **In the months that followed:** Naftali Bendavid, "Syria Making Good Progress in Chemical Weapons Removal," *The Wall Street Journal*, April 25, 2014.

304   **In the view of President Obama's own director:** "Transcript: Senate Intelligence Hearing on National Security Threats."

304   **Reflecting this, in March 2014:** Patrick J. McDonnell, "As Syria Civil War Enters Fourth Year, Rebels Are Clearly Losing," *The Los Angeles Times*, March 28, 2014.

304   **As a consequence, Assad grew bold again:** Colum Lynch, "Is Assad Now Using Chlorine to Gas His Own People?" *Foreign Policy*, April 29, 2014.

304   **Even as the international community called for an investigation:** Anne Barnard and Nick Cumming-Bruce, "Pro-Assad Areas Are Attacked in Syria, Pointing to Election Trouble," *The New York Times*, April 29, 2014; Bassem Mroue, "Syria's Bashar Assad Prepares to Run for President Despite Bloody War," The Associated Press, March 29, 2014; Steven Heydemann, "Assad's Hollow Mandate," *Foreign Policy*, June 2, 2014.

304   **He would, of course, win:** Albert Aji, "Syria's Assad Wins Presidential Vote in Landslide," The Associated Press, June 4, 2014.

304   **He will have rendered his country a graveyard:** Liz Sly and Ahmed Ramadan, "Syrian Election Sends Powerful Signal of Assad's Control," *The Washington Post*, June 3, 2014.

304   **The UN is inert more often:** Colum Lynch, "Why Has the U.N. Given Assad a Free Pass on Mass Murder?" *Foreign Policy*, November 17, 2013.

304–305 **America's European allies are still the loosest of confederations:** David
Alexander, "Ukraine Crisis Highlights NATO Defense Spending Problem:
Hagel," Reuters, May 2, 2013.

305 **Japan is constrained by its constitution:** Alexander Martin, "Abe Looks for
Speedy Clearance of Japan Defense Change," *The Wall Street Journal*, June
11, 2014.

305 **China demurs that it is not ready:** Anne-Marie Brady, "Chinese Foreign Policy:
A New Era Dawns," *The Diplomat*, March 17, 2014.

305 **Having recaptured Fallujah in January:** Liz Sly and Ahmed Ramadan,
"Insurgents Seize Iraqi City of Mosul as Security Forces Flee," *The
Washington Post*, June 10, 2014; Chelsea J. Carter, Mohammed Tawfeeq,
and Hamdi Alkhshani, "In Iraq, Militants Press on Toward Baghdad," *CNN
World*, June 23, 2014.

305 **By the time it did, not only was it:** Rod Nordland and Alissa J. Rubin, "Iraq
Insurgents Reaping Wealth as They Advance," *The New York Times*, June 20,
2014; Jeffrey Goldberg, "The New Map of the Middle East," *The Atlantic*,
June 19, 2014.

305 **It raised questions not only about:** Jason Brownlee, "Was Obama Wrong
to Withdraw Troops from Iraq?" *The Washington Post*, June 26, 2014; Bill
Schneider, "Obama's Impossible Choices on Iraq," Reuters, June 16, 2014;
Jeffrey Sparshott, Michael R. Crittenden, and Kristina Peterson, "President
Obama to Consult with Congressional Leaders on Iraq," *The Wall Street
Journal*, June 17, 2014; Michael Tomasky, "GOP Iraq Hypocrisy Hits
Overdrive," *The Daily Beast*, June 16, 2014.

305 **(Obama argued to the press in:** White House Office of the Press Secretary,
"Remarks by the President on the Situation in Iraq," *White House Press
Release* (June 19, 2014).

305–306 **As had been the case:** Scott Wilson, "President Obama Took Credit in 2012 for
Withdrawing All Troops from Iraq. Today He Said Something Different," *The
Washington Post*, June 19, 2014.

306 **But it was also true:** Beinart, "An Autopsy"; Khedery, "Why We Stuck with
Maliki."

306 **"He wanted out," said one:** Background interview with 2008 Obama campaign
advisor.

306 **The cited cause for his reversal:** White House Office of the Press Secretary,
"Statement by the President," *White House Press Release* (August 7, 2014.)

306 **But the action, air attacks:** Dan Lamothe and Karen DeYoung, "Islamic State
Can't Be Beat Without Addressing Syrian Side of Border, Top General Says,"
The Washington Post, August 21, 2014.

Chapter 10: The Beginning of the End of the Age of Fear

310 **In the days after 9/11:** Bush, *Decision Points*, 147–150; Cheney, *In My Time*,
341–344.

310 **He was heartbroken and he connected:** Ibid.

310 **In terms of the cheap metrics:** "Approval Highs and Lows," *The Washington Post*, July 24, 2007.

311 **That is why, when Barack Obama:** Clinton, *Hard Choices*, 191; Gates, *Duty*, 538; David Corn, *Showdown: The Inside Story of How Obama Fought Back Against Boehner, Cantor, and the Tea Party* (New York: HarperCollins, 2012), 257; Sanger, *Confront and Conceal*, 73.

312 **Donald Rumsfeld wrote a justification:** Rumsfeld, *Known and Unknown*, 650.

312 **As early as his job interview:** Ibid., 280.

312 **Even up to the morning of September 11:** Eric Schmitt and Thom Shanker, *Counterstrike: The Untold Story of America's Secret Campaign Against Al Qaeda* (New York: Times Books, 2011), 25.

312 **In the wake of the 9/11 attacks, with Bush's national security principals:** Stephen F. Hayes, *Cheney: The Untold Story of America's Most Powerful and Controversial Vice President* (New York: HarperCollins, 2007), 343.

312 **(This was the same kind of effort:** Scott Shane, "'01 Memo to Rice Warned of Qaeda and Offered Plan," *The New York Times*, February 12, 2005.

312 **On September 12, CIA director:** George Tenet, *At the Center of the Storm: The CIA During America's Time of Crisis* (New York: HarperCollins, 2007), 175–176.

312 **Their core point was that:** Ibid.

312 **In a meeting the next day, when asked:** Mark Mazzetti, *The Way of the Knife: The CIA, a Secret Army, and a War at the Ends of the Earth* (New York: Penguin Press, 2013), 12.

313 **Four short days after the attacks:** Rumsfeld, *Known and Unknown*, 359.

313 **It was here that Paul Wolfowitz:** Ibid.; Cheney, *In My Time*, 334.

313 **On September 17, Bush authorized:** Bergen, *The Longest War*, 56.

313 **That day, the president also issued:** Jeremy Scahill, *Dirty Wars: The World Is a Battlefield* (New York: Nation Books, 2013), 20.

313 **It was designed to open the way:** Ibid.

313 **Rumsfeld, unhappy that the CIA was the designated:** Rumsfeld, *Known and Unknown*, 346.

313 **SOCOM was predictably gung-ho about taking:** Hayes, *Cheney: The Untold Story*, 295.

313 **In early October, Rumsfeld offered:** Bradley Graham, *By His Own Rules: The Ambitions, Successes, and Ultimate Failures of Donald Rumsfeld* (New York: PublicAffairs, 2009), 301.

313 **By November, Rumsfeld had witnessed:** Mazzetti, *Way of the Knife*, 63–64.

314 **But their primacy started with:** Ibid., 129; Andrew Feickert, "U.S. Special Operations Forces (SOF): Background and Issues for Congress," *Congressional Research Service*, May 8, 2014.

314 **Part of that growth would be an effort:** Scahill, *Dirty Wars*, 95–96.

314 **Rumsfeld followed this by creating:** Graham, *By His Own Rules*, 368.

314 **The creation of New York's counterterrorism:** Richard A. Best Jr., "The National Counterterrorism Center (NCTC)—Responsibilities and Potential Congressional Concerns," *Congressional Research Service*, December 19, 2011.

315   **"Don't think this issue did not surface:** Background interview with Bush administration NSC official.

315   **By late 2003, a Rumsfeld memo:** Rumsfeld, *Known and Unknown*, 666–668.

315   **"We lack the metrics to know":** Ibid., 667.

315   **The memo was optimistic about eventual:** Ibid., 668.

315   **Rumsfeld in early 2004 gave SOCOM:** Mazzetti, *Way of the Knife*, 129.

315   **Missions were to remain classified:** Scahill, *Dirty Wars*, 171.

315   **Efforts against al-Qaeda took another important turn:** Mazzetti, *Way of the Knife*, 108.

315   **The United States approached the Pakistanis:** Ibid.

315   **The Pakistanis imposed conditions:** Ibid, 108–109.

315   **The Hellfire missile that blasted Nek Muhammad:** Ibid., 110.

315   **It was the first targeted drone strike in Pakistan:** Ibid.

315   **The following year, a Pakistani tip:** Ibid., 115–116.

315   **Senior leaders of the organization:** Ibid.

315   **The possibility of a SEAL attack was raised:** Ibid.

315   **The CIA and General Stanley McChrystal:** Ibid.

315   **They argued for so many more troops:** Ibid.

315–316 **The mission died on the vine:** Ibid., 117.

316   **In fact, Pakistan had emerged as:** Daniel S. Markey, "Reorienting U.S. Pakistan Strategy: From Af-Pak to Asia," *Council on Foreign Relations*, CSR No. 68, January 2014.

316   **Taliban and al-Qaeda fighters could:** Ibid.

316   **For this reason, when a lead arose:** Schmitt and Shanker, *Counterstrike*, 115.

316   **Some intelligence suggested:** Ibid.

316   **A massive air and special operations meeting:** Ibid., 116.

316   **Last-minute doubts about bin Laden's presence:** Ibid., 118.

316   **"We were, to put it:** Background interview with senior US military official.

316   **The ISI was an impediment:** Mazzetti, *Way of the Knife*, 266.

316   **Only twenty-five drone strikes had taken place:** Ibid.

316   **In the meantime, the Pakistani government:** Sanger, *The Inheritance*, 159–160.

316   **Matters were made worse in 2008:** Scahill, *Dirty Wars*, 217; Jane Perlez; "Pakistani Fury over Airstrikes Imperils Training," *The New York Times*, June 18, 2008; Viola Gienger and Haris Anwar, "Pakistani Troop Deaths at Afghan Border Spur U.S. Military Investigation," *Bloomberg*, November 28, 2011.

316   **Pakistan howled, asserting the strikes:** Perlez, "Pakistani Fury over Airstrikes."

316   **But the new JSOC commander, Admiral William McRaven:** Ibid.

316–317 **In the same vein, resulting from deep frustration:** Schmitt and Shanker, *Counterstrike*, 101–102.

317   **Bush was ready for a change:** Ibid.

317   **He approved an order significantly increasing:** Ibid., 102.

317   **According to the assessment of Eric Schmitt:** Ibid., 102–103.

317   **When a September 2008 Navy SEAL raid:** Ibid., 123–124.

317   **And again, the decision was made to reduce:** Ibid.

317   **But drone operations expanded:** Ibid., 124.

317 **Obama argued early on that:** "Obama's Speech at Woodrow Wilson Center," *Council on Foreign Relations*, August 1, 2007.

317 **He also said of the Pakistanis:** Ibid.

318 **In a briefing in Chicago:** Daniel Klaidman, *Kill or Capture: The War on Terror and the Soul of the Obama Presidency* (New York: Houghton Mifflin Harcourt, 2012), 21.

318 **Obama also received a briefing from CIA director Hayden:** Klaidman, *Kill or Capture*, 28–29.

318 **(The point about Pakistan's nuclear weapons:** David E. Sanger, "Pakistan Strife Raises U.S. Doubt on Nuclear Arms," *The New York Times*, May 3, 2009.

318 **In their meeting immediately before Obama took office:** Sanger, *Confront and Conceal*, 190.

318 **He also emphasized another effort:** Ibid.

319 **These briefings led Obama to continue:** Mazzetti, *Way of the Knife*, 225; Greg Miller, "Dennis C. Blair to Resign as Director of National Intelligence," *The Washington Post*, May 21, 2010.

319 **He had the title, but Panetta as CIA:** Ibid.

319 **He and his team largely kept in place:** Klaidman, *Kill or Capture*, 39.

319 **He also kept in place:** Ibid.

319 **Indeed, within the first three days of the Obama presidency:** Ibid.

319 **Within hours, it became clear that the strikes:** Scahill, *Dirty Wars*, 248.

319 **Brennan told Obama:** Ibid., 249.

319 **This led to a confrontation with the CIA's leadership:** Klaidman, *Kill or Capture*, 41–42.

319 **As described in a May 2012 article:** Jo Becker and Scott Shane, "Secret 'Kill List' Proves a Test of Obama's Principles and Will," *The New York Times*, May 29, 2012.

319 **The nominations from the group were then sent:** Ibid.

319 **From the very beginning, the centrality of this issue:** Ibid.

319 **New cells emerged throughout the Middle East:** Rollins, "Al Qaeda and Affiliates."

320 **Threats began to emanate from these groups:** Mark Mazzetti, Charlie Savage, and Scott Shane, "How a U.S. Citizen Came to Be in America's Cross Hairs," *The New York Times*, March 9, 2013.

320 **But throughout, the metric that mattered most:** "Remarks by the President in Address to the Nation on the Way Forward in Afghanistan and Pakistan"; Evan Harris, "CIA: At most, 50–100 Al Qaeda in Afghanistan," *ABC News*, June 27, 2010; Office of the White House Press Secretary, "Remarks by the President on the Way Forward in Afghanistan," *White House Press Release* (June 22, 2011); White House Office of the Press Secretary, "Remarks by the President at the National Defense University," *White House Press Release* (May 23, 2013).

320 **As Obama made clear in his first:** Clinton, *Hard Choices*, 191; Gates, *Duty*, 538; Corn, *Showdown*, 257; Sanger, *Confront and Conceal*, 73.

320 **As is now widely known, the NSA intercepted:** Sanger, *Confront and Conceal*, 71.

320   **When he reported that he was:** Ibid., 71–72.

320   **There al-Kuwaiti entered a compound:** Ibid., 72.

320   **It would take a year of investigation:** Ibid., 74.

320   **It was an operation that began:** Ibid.

320   **The operation used a CIA Sentinel drone:** Ibid.

320   **The target was a figure:** Ibid.

320   **Even as Leon Panetta called McRaven:** Ibid., 79–80.

320–321 **Sensitive to Obama's risk aversion:** Ibid.

321   **Obama on the other hand wanted:** Ibid.

321   **But Obama felt, according to a top:** Background interview with senior NSC official.

321   **On March 14, 2011, the president and his NSC team:** Sanger, *Confront and Conceal*, 88.

321   **The tug-of-war over the two:** Ibid.

321   **Two weeks later, the plan:** Ibid.

321   **A drone attack was ruled out:** Ibid.

321   **The president's view prevailed:** Ibid., 89.

321   **Nonetheless, efforts to confirm:** Ibid., 91.

321   **The results reported to the NSC:** Ibid., 93.

321   **Most of those present urged caution:** Ibid., 94.

321   **Two of those present did not think hesitation:** Ibid.

321   **One was Panetta, who:** Ibid.

321   **The other who leaned toward action:** Ibid.

322   **The next morning, on April 29:** Klaidman, *Kill or Capture*, 243; Scahill, *Dirty Wars*, 400.

322   **He left the option to McRaven:** Scahill, *Dirty Wars*, 440.

322   **The president then went off to:** Sanger, *Confront and Conceal*, 96–97.

322   **Then, an image that later became a symbol:** Scahill, *Dirty Wars*, 442.

322   **Obama was depicted with many:** "President Obama Monitors the bin Laden Mission, *Time*, http://content.time.com/time/photogallery/0,29307,2069208,00.html.

322   **The Abbottabad operation, called Neptune Spear:** Sanger, *Confront and Conceal*, 97.

322   **For fifty minutes, punctuated with images:** Ibid., 98.

322   **The hard landing of one of the helicopters:** Ibid., 99.

322   **McRaven managed his team through:** Scahill, *Dirty Wars*, 445–446.

322   **In the end, they received the transmission:** Sanger, *Confront and Conceal*, 101.

322   **Obama himself was a:** Ibid.

323   **In the remaining years of the:** Eli Lake, "'Over My Dead Body': Spies Fight Obama to Downsize Terror War," *The Daily Beast*, May 21, 2014.

323   **This was emphasized in part:** Ty McCormick, "Al Qaeda Core: A Short History," *Foreign Policy*, March 17, 2014.

323   **Later however, as the shifting situation:** Lake, "Spies Fight Obama."

324   **As a direct consequence of these changes:** Bureau of Counterterrorism, "Country Reports on Terrorism 2013," *US Department of State*, April 2014.

324   **According to the State Department report:** Ibid.

324 **Attacks increased from 6,700:** Ibid.

324 **More than 18,000 people were killed:** Ibid.

324 **Tellingly, the report explicitly noted:** Ibid.

324 **It was captured in the Obama:** David Horsey, "'GM is Alive, Osama Is Dead' Is Obama's Answer to Republicans," *The Los Angeles Times*, September 5, 2012.

325 **Look at other places where terror strikes:** Dov Waxman, "Living with Terror, Not Living in Terror: The Impact of Chronic Terrorism on Israeli Society," *Perspectives on Terrorism*, vol. 5, no. 5–6, 2011.

325 **In May 2013, Obama spoke:** "Remarks by the President at the National Defense University."

325 **"We relentlessly targeted al-Qaeda's:** Ibid.

325 **Although the war set:** Ibid.

325 **"Lethal, yet less capable:** Ibid.

325 **That said, he declared, "America:** Ibid.

326 **Obama then called for the refinement:** Ibid.

326 **Going after terrorists "must:** Ibid.

326 **For example, Obama encountered a host:** Micah Zenko, "Reforming U.S. Drone Strike Policies," *Council on Foreign Relations*, CSR no. 65, January 2013.

326 **In one such incident, against a rising:** Mazzetti, *Way of the Knife*, 310–311.

326 **Battles with the Pakistanis and others:** Philip J. Victor, "Pakistan PM Uses UN Address to Press US over Drone Strikes," *Al Jazeera*, September 27, 2013.

327 **The New America Foundation estimated:** "Drone Wars in Pakistan: Analysis," *New America Foundation*, http://natsec.newamerica.net/drones/pakistan/ analysis.

327 **The *Long War Journal* and the Bureau:** Bill Roggio, "Charting the Data for US Airstrikes in Pakistan, 2004–2014," *The Long War Journal*, http://www .longwarjournal.org/pakistan-strikes.php#; "Obama 2010 Pakistan Strikes," *The Bureau of Investigative Journalism*, August 10, 2011, http://www.the bureauinvestigates.com/2011/08/10/obama-2010-strikes/.

327 **Numbers have decreased since the peak years:** "Drone Wars in Pakistan: Analysis; "Drone Wars Yemen: Analysis," *New America Foundation*, http://natsec.newamerica.net/drones/yemen/analysis.

327 **The Bureau of Investigative Journalism estimates:** "US covert actions in Somalia," *The Bureau of Investigative Journalism*, http://www. thebureauinvestigates.com/category/projects/drones/drones-somalia/.

327 **By 2014, the incoming head:** David E. Sanger, "N.S.A. Nominee Promotes Cyberwar Units," *The New York Times*, March 11, 2014.

327 **George Bush initially paid little attention:** Richard A. Clarke and Robert K. Knake, *Cyber War: The Next Threat to National Security and What to Do About It* (New York: HarperCollins, 2010).

327 **Essentially, in Clarke's view, Bush simply:** Clarke and Knake, *Cyber War*, 112–113.

328   The policy framework that guided: Ibid.

328   Clarke later wrote: "Bush's personal: Ibid., 113.

328   After Clarke left the Whie House in 2003: Ibid., 113–114.

328   Even as major cyber-attacks—including one: Ibid., 58.

328   The White House wanted to slow it down or stop it: Sanger, *Confront and Conceal*, 191.

328   General James "Hoss" Cartwright and: Sanger, "Obama Order Sped Up Wave of Cyberattacks Against Iran."

328   The idea was to infiltrate the software: Sanger, *Confront and Conceal*, 193.

328   Early on, because of their own advanced cyber capabilities: Sanger, *Confront and Conceal*, 195; Ellen Nakashima and Joby Warrick, "Stuxnet Was Work of U.S. and Israeli Exports, Officials Say," *The Washington Post*, June 2, 2012.

328   The first phase of the effort, gathering information: Sanger, *Confront and Conceal*, 196.

328–329 The next step was to fashion a cyber worm: Ibid.

329   In either case, the result was: Ibid., 200.

329   In 2007, again prodded by McConnell: Clarke and Knake, *Cyber War*, 114.

329   The immediate step was the Comprehensive National: Ibid., 115.

329   They did not address the systematic risk: Ibid.

329   At around the same time: Ibid., 38.

329   A more comprehensive structure, better: Ibid.

329   Gates, who had also served as director: Ibid., 40.

329   He helped orchestrate an arrangement: Ibid.

329   Individual service units would: Ibid.

329   As a consequence, when Barack Obama took office: Sanger, *Confront and Conceal*, 201.

329   He received more in-depth briefings: Ibid.

329   As with the drone program: Ibid., 202.

329   With each success the program had: Ibid., 201.

329–330 As often happens in Washington: Ibid., 330.

330   Obama, who had promised to "make: "Barack Obama's Speech at the University of Purdue," *Council on Foreign Relations*, July 16, 2008.

330   In terms of the evolving structure of the military: Clarke and Knake, *Cyber War*, 118.

330   "It was CNCI redux," in Clarke's words: Ibid.

330   In Clarke's view, Obama also continued to tolerate: Ibid.

330   In 2010, the Stuxnet worm: Sanger, *Confront and Conceal*, 204.

330   The ambitious operation came undone: Ibid.

330   The worm spread across the World Wide Web: Ibid.

330   This was precisely what Obama did not want: Ibid., xii.

330   Top US officials blamed the problem: Ibid.

330   *The Washington Post* would later: Barton Gellman and Ellen Nakashima, "U.S. Spy Agencies Mounted 231 Offensive Cyber-Operations in 2011, Documents Show," *The Washington Post*, August 30, 2013.

330   **This number is disputed by other:** Background interviews with cybersecurity experts.

331   **One of the most aggressive of US programs:** Gellman and Nakashima, "231 Offensive Cyber-Operations in 2011."

331   **The US government considers these:** Ibid.

331   **It is estimated that the number of networks:** Ibid.

331   **At least 75 percent of all these intrusions:** Ibid.

331   **The effort to expand the reach of the US government:** Ibid; Matthew M. Aid, "Inside the NSA's Ultra-Secret China Hacking Group," *Foreign Policy*, June 10, 2013.

331   **But in May 2012, *The Washington Post* reported:** Ellen Nakashima, "With Plan X, Pentagon Seeks to Spread U.S. Military Might to Cyberspace," *The Washington Post*, May 30, 2012.

331   **The goal of this effort, rather uncreatively dubbed Plan X:** Ibid.

331   **The CIA's cyber unit became one of its biggest divisions:** Ibid.

331   **And because of the level of sophistication:** Ibid.

332   **Few understood the consequences or scope:** Glenn Greenwald, "NSA Collecting Phone Records of Millions of Verizon Customers Daily." *The Guardian*, June 5, 2013; "Snowden Got Stuck in Russia After Cuba Blocked Entry: Newspaper," Reuters, August 26, 2013.

333   **Although Snowden certainly violated the laws:** Alexander Petri, "Traitor or Patriot? What a Silly Question, After 'Inside Snowden,'" *The Washington Post*, May 29, 2014.

333   **It triggered a backlash:** Simon Romero, "Obama Tries to Soothe Brazil and Mexico over Spying Reports," *The New York Times*, September 6, 2013; Alyssa J. Rubin, "French Condemn Surveillance by N.S.A.," *The New York Times*, October 21, 2013; Anton Troianovski, Siobhan Gorman, and Harriet Torry, "European Leaders Accuse U.S. of Violating Trust," *The Wall Street Journal*, October 24, 2013.

333   **The global blowback would cost American IT:** Tim Risen, "Study: NSA Spying May Cost U.S. Companies $35 Billion," *U.S. News and World Report*, November 27, 2013; Juergen Baetz, "EU Spying Backlash Threatens Billions in US Trade," The Associated Press, October 30, 2013.

333   **Worse, the Internet, widely seen:** Zachary Keck, "Has Snowden Killed Internet Freedom?" *The Diplomat*, July 13, 2013; Robin Emmott, "EU Lawmakers Seek to Block U.S. Financial Spying," Reuters, October 23, 2013; Andrew E. Kramer, "N.S.A. Leaks Revive Push in Russia to Control Net," *The New York Times*, July 14, 2013; Maddy Fry, "China Looks to Strengthen Internet Security After Spying Reports," *Time*, March 27, 2014; Sandipan Deb, "The Prism Effect," *Livemint*, June 13, 2013.

333   **As they did, they considered:** Ibid.

333   **It was complemented by revelations:** Troianovski, Gorman, and Torry, "European Leaders Accuse U.S. of Violating Trust"; NYT Editorial Board, "N.S.A. Snooping and the Damage Done," *The New York Times*, October 25, 2013.

333   **One document showed that in March 2013:** Jonathan Weisman and David E. Sanger, "White House Plays Down Data Program," *The New York Times*, June 8, 2013.

333   **The rationale for undertaking these:** Charlie Savage, "N.S.A. Chief Says Surveillance Has Stopped Dozens of Plots," *The New York Times*, June 18, 2013.

333   **Tortured logic was advanced to suggest:** Peter Baker and David E. Sanger, "Obama Calls Surveillance Programs Legal and Limited," *The New York Times*, June 7, 2013; Weisman and Sanger, "White House Plays Down Data Program."

334   **According to IBM, 2.5 billion:** James Risen and Eric Lichtblau, "How the U.S. Uses Technology to Mine More Data More Quickly," *The New York Times*, June 8, 2013.

334   **By 2020, it is estimated there:** Ibid.

334   **Director of National Intelligence James Clapper:** Weisman and Sanger, "White House Plays Down Data Program."

334   **Clapper did not placate many Americans:** Ibid.

334   **(According to one report in:** Evan Perez, "Secret Court's Oversight Gets Scrutiny," *The Wall Street Journal*, June 9, 2013.

334   **In China, Unit 63198 was busily:** David E. Sanger and Nicole Perlroth, "Hackers from China Resume Attacks on U.S. Targets," *The New York Times*, May 19, 2013.

335   **What was not revealed until almost:** William Wan, "China Demands U.S. Explanation About Reports of NSA Hacking into Huawei," *The Washington Post*, March 24, 2014.

335   **We did not, argued US officials:** Gellman and Nakashima, "U.S. Spy Agencies Mounted 231 Offensive Cyber-Operations in 2011."

335   **When news of spying on foreign:** Jared A. Favole, "White House Deflects Questions on Journal's NSA Article," *The Wall Street Journal*, October 28, 2014.

335   **He went on to say:** Ibid.

335   **This was later demonstrated not:** NYT Editorial Board, "N.S.A. Snooping and the Damage Done."

335   **Similarly, James Clapper's claims:** Weisman and Sanger, "White House Plays Down Data Program"; Peter Baker, "After Leaks, Obama Leads Damage Control Effort," *The New York Times*, June 28, 2013.

335   **A study by the Privacy and Civil:** Spencer Ackerman, "Some NSA Data Collection Is 'Legal and Effective', Says Independent Board," *The Guardian*, July 2, 2014.

335   **The draft report stated, "It has:** Ibid.

335   **The report did recommend placing:** Ibid.

335   **Finally, the report noted that:** Ibid.

336   **Recognizing the scope of the crisis:** Ellen Nakashima and Ashkan Soltani, "NSA Shouldn't Keep Phone Database, Review Board Recommends," *The Washington Post*, December 18, 2013.

336   **The group included Richard Clarke:** "Liberty and Security in a Changing
       World: Report and Recommendations of The President's Review Group on
       Intelligence and Communications Technologies," *The President's Review
       Group on Intelligence and Communications Technologies*, December 12, 2013.

336   **They were unsettled by the results:** Background interview with member of The
       President's Review Group on Intelligence and Communications Technologies.

336   **They found mass surveillance programs:** "Liberty and Security in a Changing
       World."

336   **When they presented this finding:** Background interview with member of The
       President's Review Group on Intelligence and Communications Technologies.

336   **However, when the individual offering that defense:** Ibid.

336   **The December 2013 report, entitled:** "Liberty and Security in a Changing
       World."

336   **They also cited hoarding bulk meta-data:** Ibid.

336   **They concluded by "recommending:** Ibid.

336   **Some of the steps it encourages:** Ibid.

336   **It also called for increased structural:** Ibid.

337   **In January 2014, he required NSA:** Brian Fung, "Everything Yyou Need to
       Know About Obama's NSA Reforms, in Plain English," *The Washington Post*,
       January 17, 2014.

337   **Two months later, the administration:** Charlie Savage, "Obama to Call for End
       to N.S.A.'s Bulk Data Collection," *The New York Times*, March 24, 2014.

337   **Congress, whose efforts to pass surveillance:** Trevor Timm, "Congress Wants
       NSA Reform After All. Obama and the Senate Need to Pass It," *The
       Guardian*, June 20, 2014.

337   **While the bill passed the House:** Ibid.

Chapter 11: A Challenge for the Next President

339   **(By one count the US Department:** Elizabeth Flock, "Department of Defense
       Employs 1 Percent of Americans," *The Washington Post*, September 12, 2011.

340   **Created in 1947, in the wake:** Rothkopf, *Running the World*, 4–5.

340   **The National Security Act of 1947:** Ibid., 4–8.

340   **As a consequence, the size:** Ibid.

342   **While China may boast a bigger GDP:** "China Set to Overtake U.S. as Biggest
       Economy in PPP Measure," *Bloomberg*, April 30, 2014.

343   **Another is that the United States:** Grant Smith, "U.S. to Be Top Oil Producer
       by 2015 on Shale, IEA Says," *Bloomberg*, November 12, 2013.

343   **America has the world's leading system:** Justin Baeder, "Why U.S. Schools Are
       Simply the Best," *Education Week*, June 30, 2014.

343   **Both have significant energy:** David Luhnow and Santiago Pérez, "Mexico
       Expects Modest Revival Now, Bigger Bang Later On," *The Wall Street
       Journal*, May 6, 2014; Carl Ek and Ian F. Fergusson, "CRS Report to
       Congress: Canada-U.S. Relations," *Congressional Research Service*, January 2,
       2014.

343   **In fact, demographic trends suggest:** "Population Projections," *Population Reference Bureau*, http://www.prb.org/DataFinder/Topic/Rankings. aspx?ind=15.

343   **Meanwhile, if current demographic trends hold:** Ibid.

347   **She has too often sought the limelight:** The Associated Press, "Obama Adviser Susan Rice Visits Afghanistan," *Politico*, November 25, 2013; "Obama Asks Top Aide Susan Rice to Travel to Israel," The Associated Press, March 5, 2014.

347   **Rice has not sought to truly:** Background interview with NSC official.

347   **She has, according to NSC staffers, upbraided her staff:** Ibid.

347   **Neither has she sought to:** Ibid.

351   **One senior Obama administration official:** Background interview with senior Obama administration official.

351–352 **When they do—as in:** Coral Davenport, "The Education of Steven Chu," *The National Journal*, January 13, 2013.

352   **But throughout those periods, from:** Sean Pool and Jennifer Erickson, "The High Public Return on Investment for Publicly Funded Research," *Center for American Progress*, December 10, 2012.

352   **Recently, that has led Google:** Rolfe Winkler, "Facebook Closes in on Google in DC Lobbying Spending," *The Wall Street Journal*, April 23, 2014.

355   **One top Obama administration official:** Background interview with senior Obama administration official.

355   **For one example, "the president:** Ibid.

357   **The Office of Science and Technology Policy:** Background interview with former senior Obama administration official.

357   **It is also because, as one:** Background interview with senior Obama administration official.

358   **The US national security establishment went:** David Stout, "Bush Proposes Restructuring of Homeland Security," *The New York Times*, June 6, 2002; David Stout, "Bush Signs Bill to Revamp U.S. Intelligence Community," *The New York Times*, December 17, 2004; Office of the White House Secretary, "Executive Order Establishing Office of Homeland Security," *White House Press Release* (October 8, 2001).

358   **All this does not even account for:** Brad Plumer, "America's Staggering Defense Budget, in Charts," *The Washington Post*, January 7, 2013; Ewen MacAskill and Jonathan Watts, "US Intelligence Spending Has Doubled Since 9/11, Top Secret Budget Reveals," *The Guardian*, August 29, 2013.

358   **The Homeland Security Council has been absorbed:** Helene Cooper, "In Security Shuffle, White House Merges Staffs," *The New York Times*, May 26, 2009.

358   **One Clinton State Department official:** Background interview with former senior US Department of State official.

359   **But there is a paradox:** Ibid.

359   **"They are overstaffed compared to where:** Ibid.

361   **When Brent Scowcroft and James Baker:** Rothkopf, *Running the World*, 262.

361   **Baker would be the spokesperson:** Ibid.

361   **Scowcroft would clear public statements:** Ibid.

361   **Both would interact directly with Bush:** Ibid.

361   **Neither would try to secretly:** Ibid.

361   **Scowcroft would not be operational:** Ibid.

361   **Baker would be America's chief:** Ibid.

361–362 **As the amount of the federal budget:** David Wessel, "Robbing the Next Generation of Fiscal Freedom," *The Wall Street Journal*, May 2, 2014.

362   **It is not rational to spend more:** Peter W. Singer, "Comparing Defense Budgets, Apples to Apples," *Time*, September 25, 2012.

362   **The reality is that despite:** Michael E. O'Hanlon, "Obama, Romney Playing Same Defense," *The Brookings Institution*, September 19, 2012.

363   **Africa is home to seven:** Howard W. French, "The Next Asia Is Africa: Inside the Continent's Rapid Economic Growth," *The Atlantic*, May 21, 2012.

363   **Its great resources have attracted:** Aaron L. Friedberg, *A Contest for Supremacy: China, America, and the Struggle of Mastery in Asia* (New York: W. W. Norton and Co., 2011), 228; Thomas E. Ricks, "Out of China, into Africa: Tracking the Ways of Private Chinese Investment," *Foreign Policy*, March 4, 2013; Alexis Okeowo, "China in Africa: The New Imperialists?" *The New Yorker*, June 12, 2013; Mark Scott, "As Stability Eludes Region, Western Oil Giants Hesitate," *The New York Times*, October 1, 2013.

363   **Crises in South Sudan, Somalia:** Sudarsan Raghavan, "With Oil at Stake, South Sudan's Crisis Matters to Its Customers," *The Washington Post*, January 20, 2014; Michelle Nichols and Louis Charbonneau, "Western Oil Exploration in Somalia May Spark Conflict—U.N. Report," Reuters, July 17, 2013; Lauren Ploch, "Nigeria: Current Issues and U.S. Policy," *Congressional Research Service*, April 24, 2013; Alexis Arieff, "Crisis in the Central African Republic," *Congressional Research Service*, May 14, 2014; Michael R. Gordon, "North Africa Is a New Test," *The New York Times*, January 20, 2013.

364   **The US military has established:** Walter Pincus, "U.S. Africa Command Bring New Concerns," *The Washington Post*, May 28, 2007.

364   **One recent assistant secretary of state:** Background interview with former senior US Department of State official.

364   **Despite the really valiant and historic efforts:** Mark Landler and Amy Chozick, "Hillary Clinton Struggles to Define a Legacy in Progress," *The New York Times*, April 16, 2014.

364   **The life expectancy of Afghan women:** "Country Comparison: Life Expectance at Birth," *CIA World Factbook*, https://www.cia.gov/library/publications/the-world-factbook/rankorder/2102rank.html.

364   **Only one in six Afghan women:** "Field Listing: Literacy," *CIA World Factbook*, https://www.cia.gov/library/publications/the-world-factbook/fields/2103.html; Lauryn Oats, "The Mother of All Problems: Female Literacy in Afghanistan," *The Guardian*, June 21, 2013.

364   **More die in pregnancy than anywhere:** "Country Comparison: Maternal Mortality Rate," *CIA World Factbook*, https://www.cia.gov/library/publications/the-world-factbook/rankorder/2223rank.

Index

David Rothkopf is the CEO and editor of the FP Group, publisher of *Foreign Policy Magazine, ForeignPolicy.com,* and presenter of FP Events. He is also president and CEO of Garten Rothkopf, an international advisory firm. He is a visiting scholar at the Carnegie Endowment for International Peace, where he chairs the Bernard L. Schwartz Program in Competitiveness and Growth Policies. He is the author of *Power, Inc.: The Epic Rivalry Between Big Business and Government and the Reckoning That Lies Ahead; Superclass: The Global Power Elite and the World They're Making*; and *Running the World: The Inside Story of the National Security Council and the Architects of American Power.*

PublicAffairs is a publishing house founded in 1997. It is a tribute to the standards, values, and flair of three persons who have served as mentors to countless reporters, writers, editors, and book people of all kinds, including me.

I. F. STONE, proprietor of *I. F. Stone's Weekly*, combined a commitment to the First Amendment with entrepreneurial zeal and reporting skill and became one of the great independent journalists in American history. At the age of eighty, Izzy published *The Trial of Socrates*, which was a national bestseller. He wrote the book after he taught himself ancient Greek.

BENJAMIN C. BRADLEE was for nearly thirty years the charismatic editorial leader of *The Washington Post*. It was Ben who gave the *Post* the range and courage to pursue such historic issues as Watergate. He supported his reporters with a tenacity that made them fearless and it is no accident that so many became authors of influential, best-selling books.

ROBERT L. BERNSTEIN, the chief executive of Random House for more than a quarter century, guided one of the nation's premier publishing houses. Bob was personally responsible for many books of political dissent and argument that challenged tyranny around the globe. He is also the founder and longtime chair of Human Rights Watch, one of the most respected human rights organizations in the world.

·   ·   ·

For fifty years, the banner of Public Affairs Press was carried by its owner Morris B. Schnapper, who published Gandhi, Nasser, Toynbee, Truman, and about 1,500 other authors. In 1983, Schnapper was described by *The Washington Post* as "a redoubtable gadfly." His legacy will endure in the books to come.

Peter Osnos, *Founder and Editor-at-Large*